DATE DUE

FEB - 7 1996	MAR 3 0 2001
APR 1 5 1996	Richmond Public
	due Oct 3/02
OCT 3 0 1996	DEC - 9 2004
DEC 1 9 1996	JAN 1 9 2005
Jan 2/97	870181
MAR 3 1 1997	
JUL - 4 1997	
JAN 2 0 1998	
FEB 2 6 1998	
DEC 1 1 1998	
JAN 0 8 1999	
FEB 1 9 1999	
NOV - 4 1999	
NOV 2 4 1999	
DEC - 7 1999	
NOV 2 2 2000	

Handbook of Alcoholism Treatment Approaches

Related Titles of Interest

Handbook of Alcoholism Treatment Approaches
Effective Alternatives

Second Edition

Edited by

REID K. HESTER
Behavior Therapy Associates and
The University of New Mexico

WILLIAM R. MILLER
The University of New Mexico

ALLYN AND BACON
Boston   London   Toronto   Sydney   Tokyo   Singapore

Library of Congress Cataloging-in-Publication Data

Handbook of alcoholism treatment approaches : effective alternatives /
   Reid K. Hester, William R. Miller, editors. — 2nd ed.
      p.   cm.
   Includes bibliographical references and index.
   ISBN 0–205–16376–9
   1. Alcoholism—Treatment.   I. Hester, Reid K.   II. Miller,
William R.
   [DNLM: 1. Alcoholism—therapy.   WM 274 H236 1995]
RC565.H26   1995
616.86'10651—dc20
DNLM/DLC
for Library of Congress   94–35263
                                            CIP

ISBN 0-205-16376-9
H63761

Printed in the United States of America
10 9 8 7 6 5 4 3 2 1   99 98 97 96 95

To the clinical researchers whose efforts through the years
have advanced our understanding of the assessment
and treatment of alcohol problems.
Much of their work forms the bases
for the chapters in this book.
Their many years of hard work are appreciated.

To the counselors and therapists who strive to provide
the most helpful treatments for their clients.
May this work assist you in your efforts.

Contents

Foreword

The editors and authors are to be warmly applauded for their efforts in preparing this handbook. The book meets important needs of both practitioners and researchers in the field of alcoholism treatment by identifying and clearly describing promising treatment interventions. A sophisticated analytic model at the beginning of the book allows readers to contrast effectiveness studies for a wide variety of possible interventions. The remainder of the book elaborates in careful detail those treatment strategies best supported by rigorous, scientific investigation. Researchers will find the introductory critique of the clinical trials quite valuable as well as the highly focused reviews of research in the individual chapters.

The primary audience for *Handbook of Alcoholism Treatment Approaches*, however, is likely to be the alcoholism treatment community. While even under optimal conditions, effective, enduring treatment for alcohol problems is difficult, this book provides a rich source of information on treatments demonstrated to be most helpful. Most of these interventions can be readily incorporated into an existing program. Beyond describing each of these strategies, evidence for effectiveness is reviewed and clear descriptions of how to perform the treatment are given. In all instances, the chapter authors are themselves experts on the intervention and have substantively contributed to its development. They thus bring to their discussions unique, applied experience that the alcoholism treatment practitioner will value. The clinician reading this book is able to clearly grasp the underlying concepts and techniques specific of each of the interventions. It is difficult to imagine information that would be more relevant to the needs of alcoholism treatment professionals.

No book in the rapidly changing field of treatment for alcohol problems will remain fully relevant forever. In fact, this book is a revision of an earlier highly popular handbook by the editors and many of the same chapter authors. Funding for research specifically on alcohol treatment supported by the National Institute on Alcohol Abuse and Alcoholism has rapidly expanded over the past 10 years, increasing more than threefold. Consequently, future handbooks will continue to be necessary to assist in transmitting new knowledge to the ultimate consumers of this research—those who directly treat people with alcohol problems. This second edition of the handbook summarizes very recent research and developments in various treatment strategies and is therefore clearly welcome.

It would be naive to believe that even careful implementation of the interventions described in this book would make alcohol treatment easy or universally effective. However, strengthening the practitioners' armamentarium of skills, made possible by studying this book, should materially improve outcome rates and likely make treatment of alcohol problems a more professionally rewarding experience.

John P. Allen, Ph.D.
National Institute on Alcohol Abuse
and Alcoholism

Preface

It has now been 17 years since our paths first crossed in Albuquerque, New Mexico. In 1978, we began what has been a most enjoyable collaboration in reading, discussing, and reviewing the immense research literature available on how to treat people who have alcohol problems.

When we set out to read everything that had been published in the way of alcohol treatment outcome research, we had little appreciation for what lay in store for us. There had been a virtual explosion of studies in this area during the 1970s, and it took us six months just to read the 600 articles and books that we found. It took another half year to write what became a 110-page review chapter summarizing this literature.

Several facts stood out for us as we completed this initial review in 1980. First, we were impressed with the sheer number of treatment methods that had been tried. This is a field with many alternative approaches. Second, we were nearly overwhelmed with the amount of information available, often with immediate practical implications. The intimidating size and scope of the literature suggested to us why so little of this knowledge has found its way into clinical practice. Third, the literature illustrated the value of systematic, cumulative, and programmatic research. A number of treatments had a characteristic history: A few initial, uncontrolled studies yielded glowing reports of success, but later and more controlled studies found little or no specific benefit from the same technique. In other cases, a technique seemed to hold up well over a range of studies conducted by different teams in various locations. Improved methodology, in fact, seemed to show the treatment's power more clearly.

This led us, in 1986, to update our original review. This time, we focused our attention only on studies with proper control or comparison groups. We excluded uncontrolled studies because the results of such research are confounded and often unreliable, making it difficult to draw firm inferences about the value of the treatment under study. Using this methodological filter, we were led to two surprising and unavoidable conclusions. First, we were pleased to see that a number of treatment methods were consistently supported by controlled scientific research. On the other hand, we were dismayed to realize that virtually none of these treatment methods was in common use within alcohol treatment programs in the United States.

Another conclusion of our review was that there is no single treatment approach for alcohol problems that is superior to all others. Rather, there are a number of promising alternative approaches. This led us to a third collaboration to review the literature on matching clients to treatments. Here, we found evidence that different people respond best to different approaches. This makes sense, of course. Why should any one approach be best for everybody? Yet in our observations, relatively few treatment programs were, in reality, putting this common-sense fact into practice. Instead, most programs offered a relatively consistent program to all clients. Worse, clients who failed to respond to the offered approach were often blamed for the failure because of being "unmotivated" or "in denial." Would it not be more effective to offer a range of alternative approaches, from which each individual could be offered an optimal strategy for his or her particular personality and situation?

Our fourth review focused on the question of whether more "intensive" treatment programs would be superior in effectiveness to less intensive alternatives. Again, we focused only on controlled studies using random assignment or matching designs. We found two dozen studies comparing longer with shorter treatment, residential with nonresidential programs, or more versus less intensive interventions. The results were startling. Without a single exception, the studies failed to show any advantage for the more intensive, longer, or residential approaches over less intensive and less expensive alternatives.

We then faced a vexing question: Why has all of this knowledge not been put into practice? Why are so many alcohol treatment programs still offering homogeneous programs that include neither scientifically validated options nor individualized treatment based on the available literature? One possibility is that the alternatives and the literature have not really been *available* to the average program or practitioner providing alcohol treatment. Indeed, it took us a decade to unearth this knowledge from the literature!

This led us to our fifth collaboration—the first edition of this book. We decided to assemble a handbook describing a variety of alternative treatment methods available for helping those with alcohol problems. We included every treatment approach for which we found promising scientific evidence. Our strategy was to identify some of the best clinical researchers in the English-speaking world, asking each to write a practically focused chapter in the area of his or her expertise. Our goal was to provide practitioners with enough working knowledge of each particular strategy to get started.

Following the publication of this first edition in 1989, we began work on a new review of the literature. Instead of a strictly qualitative analysis of controlled studies, we developed a quantitative model for assessing both the methodological soundness of the studies and the relative effectiveness of the interventions. The development of the quantitative model, the

review itself, and its data analysis have taken five years. The results of this review are presented in Chapter 2, representing an important addition to this second edition. Happily (for us), the results of this latest analysis of the literature are consistent with our prior qualitative reviews.

The authors of clinical chapters in this volume have also provided a state-of-the-art description of particular treatment strategies, and the evidence for their efficacy. Each of these clinical chapters includes several sections. It begins with an overview of the technique, to give you a general idea of how it works. Special clinical considerations are provided next, with particular focus on factors that may help you to match these treatment methods to the clients most likely to benefit from them. Cautions are also inserted regarding types of clients for whom the method may be inappropriate. The bulk of each chapter provides specific guidelines for the clinical application of the methods being described. A final section briefly outlines the scientific evidence currently available, to document the effectiveness of the methods discussed.

At the end of each clinical chapter are two reference lists. The first offers clinical resources you can turn to for further detail about how to administer each treatment approach. The second is a bibliography of research regarding the treatment strategy. These sections are meant to help you go beyond this handbook, to explore in greater depth the treatment alternatives that you find most helpful and feasible for your own clinical setting.

A book such as this is never finished. As we write this Preface, important new research is being published monthly. The years ahead will doubtless reveal still more alcohol treatment methods than we have included here, and further research will clarify the effectiveness of these alternatives for different clients. We have done our best to give you up-to-date descriptions of what we believe are the best treatment alternatives available, each written by outstanding researchers with extensive firsthand experience in treating alcohol problems. The ultimate value of this for you will be found in your own attempts to apply these methods in your day-to-day efforts with those who seek your help. We commend you for working in such a challenging area, and for the open-minded seeking that brought you to this book. May you find here some new alternatives to help you help others.

ACKNOWLEDGMENTS

Many people have made this book possible. First, we would like to thank the contributing authors. We appreciate the time they took from their evenings and weekends to complete their manuscripts. Second, we would like to thank Mylan Jaixen, our editor at Allyn and Bacon. His encouragement and suggestions enhanced our motivation to meet our publication deadlines. Third, we would like to thank our respective staffs: Joann Leitka, Jeanne Schnapp, Dee Ann Quintana, Delilah Yao, and Brenda Carreon. They helped us to pull together the innumerable bits and pieces necessary to produce this book. Finally, we would like to thank the reviewers of our first edition for their constructive criticism: Judith Lewis of Governors State University, Connie Schick of Bloomsburg University, and Bradford DeNoce of Alternative Counseling Services, Bloomsburg, Pennsylvania.

About the Editors

Reid K. Hester is in private practice with Behavior Therapy Associates in Albuquerque, New Mexico, where he directs the Alcohol Self-Control Program. He is also a research associate professor in the Department of Psychology at the University of New Mexico. His professional career balances clinical work with research, writing, and training. Dr. Hester received his Ph.D. in clinical psychology from Washington State University in 1979. He has been involved in treatment of alcohol problems since 1978 and research in alcohol abuse since 1974. He has also published a number of literature reviews, articles, and book chapters on the treatment of alcohol problems. He has directed clinical research projects investigating various behavioral treatments for alcohol problems. He was also a co-principal investigator on the NIAAA-sponsored multisite study of matching, Project MATCH. Currently, he is evaluating the effectiveness of an interactive computer software program of Behavioral Self-Control Training. He has been a technical advisor and consultant to the World Health Organization (WHO), the National Institute on Alcohol Abuse and Alcoholism (NIAAA), and the National Institute on Drug Abuse (NIDA). When not working professionally, he enjoys sailing, skiing, and running.

William R. Miller is professor of psychology and psychiatry at the University of New Mexico and director of the Research Division of UNM's Center on Alcoholism, Substance Abuse, and Addictions. He is a Fellow of the American Psychological Association and the American Psychological Society, and has also served as director of UNM's Ph.D. training program in clinical psychology. He has published 20 books and more than 100 articles and chapters, focusing especially on the treatment of alcohol problems and other addictive behaviors. He has developed and evaluated a variety of innovative clinical strategies, including Motivational Interviewing, the Drinker's Check-Up, Behavioral Self-Control Training, and Azrin's Community Reinforcement Approach. With Alan Marlatt, he designed the Drinker Profile system, a comprehensive set of structured clinical interviews for pretreatment and follow-up assessment of alcohol problems. He has held numerous research grants, founded a private practice group, and served as a consultant to many organizations, including the United States Senate, the World Health Organization (WHO), the National Academy of Sciences, the National Institute on Alcohol Abuse and Alcoholism (NIAAA), and the National Institute on Drug Abuse (NIDA). He maintains an active interest in pastoral counseling and the integration of religion and psychology. Currently, he holds a senior career Research Scientist Award from NIAAA. He received his Ph.D. in clinical psychology from the University of Oregon in 1976.

About the Contributors

David B. Abrams is the director of the Division of Behavioral Medicine and the Center for Health Promotion at the Miriam Hospital/Brown University, and is professor of psychiatry and human behavior at Brown University. His focus of research has been health promotion/behavioral medicine, especially smoking, alcohol abuse, and obesity.

John P. Allen is chief of the Treatment Research Branch of the National Institute on Alcohol Abuse and Alcoholism. As such, he awards and monitors over $20,000,000 per year in grants and contracts dealing with behavioral, pharmacologic, and psychometric investigations related to treatment of alcoholism. His personal areas of research expertise are assessment, measurement of treatment outcome, and effective assignment of patients to alternative treatments.

Thomas H. Bien holds a B.A. from Rutgers College; an M.Div. from Princeton Theological Seminary; and an M.S. and a Ph.D. in clinical psychology from the University of New Mexico. Interests include brief interventions for addictive and other health behaviors and psychology and spirituality. He is a licensed clinical psychologist at the Samaritan Counseling Center of Albuquerque, New Mexico.

Janice M. Brown is a clinical psychology intern at the Medical University of South Carolina. Her coursework for the doctoral degree was completed at the University of New Mexico. While fulfilling the requirements for graduate training, she worked on several research and writing efforts that focused on alcohol abuse and prevention.

Suzanne M. Colby is a research associate and project director of two grants at the Center for Alcohol and Addiction Studies at Brown University. Her work focuses on methodological issues in addictions research.

Ned L. Cooney is associate professor of psychiatry at Yale University School of Medicine and director of the Substance Abuse Treatment Program at the West Haven Veterans Affairs Medical Center. He received his Ph.D. in clinical psychology from Rutgers University in 1981.

Sadi Irvine Delaney received her Master of Science degree from Rutgers University in 1989. She has worked in the field of alcoholism treatment for a number of years. Her research has focused on psychological and behavioral change models.

Linda A. Dimeff is currently a graduate student in clinical psychology at the University of Washington and is associate faculty at Shoreline Community College in the Chemical Dependency Program. She has recently coauthored a manual (Guilford, in press) describing a brief intervention for high-risk college drinkers based on relapse prevention.

Michael F. Fleming is an associate professor of family medicine and director of the Office of Alcohol and Addiction Studies. He received his advanced training from Wayne State University, Medical College of Wisconsin, and the University of North Carolina at Chapel Hill.

Richard J. Frances is director of the Department of Psychiatry at Hackensack Medical Center, Hackensack, New Jersey, and professor of clinical psychiatry at the University of Medicine and Dentistry of New Jersey, Newark. Frances has published over 100 articles, books, and reports, including co-editing the *Clinical Textbook of Addictive Disorders.* He is the founding president of the American Academy of Psychiatrists in Alcoholism and Addiction and is currently chairman of the Council on Addiction Psychiatry of the American Psychiatric Association.

Richard K. Fuller is director of the Division of Clinical and Prevention Research at the National Institute of Alcohol Abuse and Alcoholism (NIAAA). Before coming to NIAAA, Fuller was on the faculty of Case Western Reserve University and employed by the Veterans Administration. He has done research evaluating pharmacological treatments for alcoholism, treatments for alcohol-related diseases such as cirrhosis and pancreatitis, studied energy metabolism of cirrhosis, and the pharmacokinetic/pharmacodynamic properties of medications to treat consequences of cirrhosis. At the Case Western Reserve University School of Medicine, he taught gastroenterology/hepatology, alcoholism, and biostatistics.

Nancy S. Handmaker completed B.S. and Ph.D. degrees in psychology at the University of New Mexico, and an M.A. at New Mexico State University. While a student, she received national awards for training in alcohol and drug treatment and in mental health services evaluation, minority fellowships, and grants for her research on the prevention of fetal alcohol syndrome. Following an internship at the University of California in San Diego, she has been a consultant in brief interventions.

Nick Heather, after working as a clinical psychologist in the British National Health Service, developed the Addictive Behaviours Research Group at the University of Dundee, Scotland (1979–87) before becoming founding director of the Australian National Drug and Alcohol Research Centre (1987–94). He is now consultant clinical psychologist with the Newcastle City Health NHS Trust in England.

Marian L. Hilfrink received her B.A. in 1978 and her certification in chemical dependency counseling in 1992. She is currently an addictions therapist on the Inpatient Unit of the Seattle Veterans Affairs Addictions Treatment Center. She also is a counselor at a local women's health center.

Matthew O. Howard received his Ph.D. in social welfare in 1990. He is currently director of the Drug Abuse Treatment Services Evaluation Project, a national investigation of Department of Veterans Affairs drug dependence treatment, and research assistant professor in the University of Washington Department of Psychiatry and Behavioral Sciences.

Ronald M. Kadden is professor of psychology in the Department of Psychiatry at the University of Connecticut School of Medicine. He is an attending doctor in the ambulatory programs of the Alcohol and Drug Abuse Treatment Center. His research interest is in alcoholism treatment effectiveness, especially patient-treatment matching.

Lorenzo F. Luckie received his doctorate in psychology at the University of New Mexico. His research interests center on issues of brief screening measures and minimal interventions for alcohol problems. Currently, he serves as a psychologist for the United States Army Medical Department.

G. Alan Marlatt is currently professor of psychology and director of the Addictive Behaviors Research Center at the University of Washington. In addition to his pioneering in relapse prevention, he has researched many areas within the field of addictions, including alcohol expectancies, prevention approaches for high-risk college drinkers, and harm-reduction approaches.

Barbara S. McCrady is professor of psychology and clinical director of the Rutgers University Center of Alcohol Studies. Her primary research is on alcoholism treatment models, and the interactions between alcoholics and their families. She is author of more than 100 scientific articles, chapters, and essays.

Robert J. Meyers has extensive research and clinical experience in substance abuse. He was a therapist and coauthor on the original Community Reinforcement Approach (CRA) outpatient studies, and served as co-principal investigator for the National Institute on Alcohol Abuse and Alcoholism-funded CRA trial. He is a research program coordinator at the University of New Mexico's Center on Alcohol, Substance Abuse, and Addictions.

Sheldon I. Miller is the Lizzie Gilman Professor and chairman of the Department of Psychiatry and Behavioral Sciences of Northwestern University Medical School. He is also the director of the Stone Institute of Psychiatry of Northwestern Memorial Hospital. Prior to his arrival at Northwestern, Miller was chairman of the Department of Psychiatry at the University of Medicine and Dentistry of New Jersey/New Jersey Medical School. Miller is a graduate of Oberlin College and received his medical training at Tufts University School of Medicine. He is a graduate of the psychiatry residency program of Case Western Reserve University, where he also served on the faculty for eleven years. His principal area of interest is alcoholism and other chemical dependencies. He is also the editor of the *American Journal on Addictions*. Miller was appointed a director of the American Board of Psychiatry and Neurology. He is a Fellow of the American Psychiatric Association and the American College of Psychiatrists, and is chairman of the American Hospital Association Governing Council on Psychiatry and Substance Abuse. He is past-president of the American Academy of Psychiatrists in Alcoholism and Addictions, and serves on a number of committees of the American Psychiatric Association and other national organizations.

Henry A. Montgomery has an M.S. in counseling psychology from Lewis & Clark College (Portland, OR) and a Ph.D. in clinical psychology from the University of New Mexico. He is a substance abuse specialist at Heights Psychiatric Hospital in Albuquerque and is a therapist on a grant researching the efficacy of spouse intervention to engage clients in substance abuse treatment.

Peter M. Monti is professor of psychiatry and human behavior and director of the Clinical Psychology Training Program at Brown Univeristy, career research scientist at the Provi-

dence VA Medical Center, and associate director of the Center for Alcohol and Addiction Studies at Brown University. His work focuses on social learning theory approaches to addictive behaviors.

Timothy J. O'Farrell is associate professor of psychology in the Department of Psychiatry at Harvard Medical School. He also is associate chief of the psychology service at the Veterans Affairs Medical Center in Brockton and West Roxbury, Massachusetts, where he directs the Counseling for Alcoholics' Marriages (CALM) Project.

Carl T. Rimmele received his Ph.D. in clinical psychology in 1988. He is currently assistant chief of the inpatient unit, Seattle Veterans Affairs Addictions Treatment Center, and acting instructor in the University of Washington Department of Psychiatry and Behavioral Sciences.

Damaris J. Rohsenow is a research director at the Center for Alcohol and Addiction Studies and associate professor of community health at Brown University, research clinical psychologist at the Providence VA Medical Center, and principal investigator or co-principal investigator of four grants. Her research focuses on social learning approaches to the addictions.

Lisa A. Rone is incoming chief resident in psychiatry at Northwestern Memorial Hospital in Chicago. She is a 1991 graduate of the University of Tennessee Medical School and has a wide variety of research interests, including treatment of affective disorders. Most recently, she participated in the Collegium Internationale Neuropsychopharmacologicum in Paris, presenting work on rapid treatment of depression. She is currently working on treatment strategies for dysthymic disorder.

Tracy L. Simpson is a doctoral candidate in experimental psychology (clinical emphasis) at the University of New Mexico in Albuquerque. Her primary research focuses on the relationship between various childhood factors and the development of substance abuse and dependence.

Jane Ellen Smith is an associate professor and the director of clinical training at the University of New Mexico's Psychology Department. She recently received the University's Regents

Lectureship Award for excellence in teaching, research, and service. Her primary research areas are eating disorders and substance abuse.

Tim Stockwell is an associate professor and deputy director of the National Centre for Research into the Prevention of Drug Abuse, based in Perth, where his main research interests concern the prevention of alcohol- and tobacco-related harm. He studied psychology and philosophy at Oxford University, obtained a Ph.D. at the Institute of Psychiatry, University of London, and is also a qualified clinical psychologist. Before migrating to Australia in 1988, he was principal clinical psychologist with the Exeter Health Authority in England, where he worked closely with general practitioners to set up one of the first home detoxification programs in the UK. He is regional editor for Australasia of the journal *Addiction* and has published over 75 articles and one book. His current interests include liquor licensing legislation, the evaluation of drunk-driving countermeasures, host responsibility, and the measurement of alcohol consumption and related problems.

J. Scott Tonigan received his doctorate at the University of New Mexico and is deputy director of the Research Division at Center on Alcoholism, Substance Abuse, and Addictions (CASAA) and assistant research professor in psychology. Primary areas of research are Alcoholics Anonymous, meta-analytic techniques, and outcome evaluation of substance abuse treatment programs.

Holly B. Waldron received her doctorate at the University of Utah and is an associate professor of psychology at the University of New Mexico. Her research focuses on family interaction and adolescent psychopathology, with an emphasis on adolescent substance abuse and family therapy process and outcome.

Verner S. Westerberg received his Ph.D. in neuropsychology at the University of Victoria. He is currently research assistant professor in psychology at the University of New Mexico and heads Program Evaluation Services at the Center on Alcoholism, Substance Abuse, and Addictions (CASAA). His research interests include drug craving, alcohol relapse, and pharmacotherapies for alcohol problems.

Allen Zweben is associate professor in the School of Social Welfare at the University of Wisconsin-Milwaukee. He also serves as director of the Center for Addiction and Behavioral Health Research, a consortium of academic and professional organizations conducting research in mental health and substance abuse.

Handbook of Alcoholism Treatment Approaches

CHAPTER 1

Treatment for Alcohol Problems: Toward an Informed Eclecticism

William R. Miller
Reid K. Hester

Until recently, most therapists were trained to treat clients with alcohol problems from a "one true light" perspective. A student of the field would be trained in one of several rival "schools" of treatment and thoroughly indoctrinated into that perspective. Trainers expounded the subtleties of praxis in that mode and gave an impelling rationale for its superiority over all others. Students learned by heart the faults and failures of all other approaches to treatment, and were taught that their own approach was the one true avenue toward the lasting alleviation of human problems.

Eclecticism is a more recent rival to this narrow view. It acknowledges the potential value of a wide range of alternatives. Indeed, in some circles and professions, "eclectic" has become the predominant self-proclaimed orientation of helpers. On the surface, this sounds enlightened, but an uncritical eclecticism can easily result in unfocused therapy. It can lead to the naive position that all approaches have equal merit, or the related cynical stance that it makes little differ-

ence what one does in treatment. An uninformed and undisciplined eclectic therapist roams from one trend or fad to another, reaching into a bulging bag of tricks to draw out whatever is convenient, interesting, familiar, or seemingly appropriate to the immediate case. Trial and error reigns supreme (Goldstein & Stein, 1976).

We have argued elsewhere (Miller & Hester, 1980, 1986a) against the view that all treatments for people with alcohol problems are equally (in)effective, or (in contrast) that there is a single superior approach. There is instead persuasive evidence in the treatment research literature that there are a number of different approaches that are significantly better than no intervention or alternative treatments (cf. Holder, Longabaugh, Miller & Rubonis, 1991; also see Chapter 2 in this volume). No one approach stands out as superior to all others, but neither are all treatments equally effective (or ineffective). The reason for hope and optimism in this field of alcohol treatment lies not in the presence of a single outstandingly effective approach. Rather, hope is to be found in the array of promising and effective alternatives, each of which may be most effective for different types of individuals. For most people, the chances are good for finding an acceptable and effective intervention among these choices.

CONCEPTUAL MODELS AND THEIR IMPLICATIONS FOR INTERVENTION

Unfortunately, the alcohol treatment field in the United States remains largely mired in a competitive spirit, with each program or approach asserting its supremacy. This may result partly from factors inherent in a for-profit health care economy. However, it also reflects disagreements and uncertainty regarding the nature and etiology of alcohol problems. Contemporary books confidently ascribe alcoholism to inherent biochemical abnormalities (Milam & Ketcham, 1981), social learning processes (Peele, 1985), family pathology (Steiner, 1971), sociocultural influences (Cahalan, 1987), and personal choice (Fingarette, 1988). Given such disagreement about their essence and causes, it is little wonder that there has been such confusion about how best to treat clients with alcohol problems.

As a context for the chapters that follow, we will provide a brief developmental history of the ways in which people have thought about and addressed alcohol problems. How you think about the nature of alcohol problems guides how you go about treating them. As we describe the various models of alcohol problems and alcoholism, we invite you to consider which of them is most consistent with your own current thinking.

Moral Models

There haven't always been alcoholics. Indeed, there were no "alcoholics" prior to 1849, when the Swedish physician Magnus Huss introduced the term to describe the adverse consequences of excessive drinking. Of course, the dangers of alcohol abuse have been recognized from the beginning of recorded history, but until very recently these were understood as the natural consequences of unfortunate personal decisions to drink excessively. Moral models emphasize personal choice as a primary causal factor.

From this perspective, alcohol problems are viewed, either explicitly or implicitly, as willful violations of societal rules and norms. In modern society, we clearly understand drunk driving in this way, whether or not the driver is diagnosed as "alcoholic." Indeed, U.S. courts and juries have rarely excused criminal behavior because it was committed under the influence of alcohol or other drugs. This issue of personal responsibility for alcohol problems remains very much alive and unresolved (Fingarette, 1988). For example, a classic Supreme Court case dealt with the question of whether alcoholism is a "disease" beyond the person's control and responsibility or "willful misconduct" for which the individual is accountable (Connors & Rychtarik, 1989). At various points in history, public intoxication has itself been a punishable crime. In some societies, the mere possession or consumption of alcohol is a serious offense.

Whether understood as a moral or a criminal issue, these views point to the person as the primary causal factor in problem drinking. The individual is seen as making choices and decisions to use alcohol in a problematic fashion and as capable of making other choices. In a moral model, emphasizing choice and willful violations of social codes, social sanctions seem the appropriate intervention, and agents of change would include legislators, law enforcement personnel, and the courts.

The Temperance Model

Often confused with moral models, the temperance model arose from a very different understanding of the causes of alcohol problems. In the United States, this view predominated from the late nineteenth century through the repeal of Prohibition in 1933. In its early years, the temperance movement emphasized just that: the moderate and cautious use of alcohol. In the temperance model, alcohol is viewed (quite appropriately) as a hazardous substance, a drug with great potential for inflicting harm. Indeed, if alcohol were only now being introduced to society, it is doubtful whether it would ever be legalized, given current knowledge about its devastating health and social consequences (National Institute on Alcohol Abuse and Alcoholism, 1994).

As the temperance view gained political momentum, it evolved into a Prohibition movement. Temperance advocates saw alcohol as an extraordinarily dangerous drug that no one could use safely or in moderation. Writings from the early twentieth century asserted that it was impossible for anyone to be a moderate drinker; everyone must either return to the social norm of abstinence or inevitably progress to alcoholism and death. A Prohibition party emerged and exerted enormous political pressure on the Congress to ban the manufacture, sale, transportation, and importation of alcoholic beverages. In 1919, the 18th Amendment to the U.S. Constitution, to make these acts criminal, was proposed. In 1920, it was ratified into law. Alcohol use and related health problems dropped to the lowest levels in U.S. history, but the law was highly unpopular and difficult to enforce. In 1933, the 21st Amendment repealed Prohibition, again legalizing alcohol and making it the only subject of two contradictory amendments to the U.S. Constitution.

The core assumption of the temperance model is that the cause of alcohol problems is alcohol itself. The drug is considered so dangerous as to warrant great caution in use, if it is to be used at all. This is similar to current popular views of drugs such as heroin and cocaine. The drug is understood to contain such addictive and destructive power that the emergence of problems can be explained simply by the pharmacologic properties of the drug itself. In first describing a syndrome of alcoholism, Magnus Huss construed it as the effects of excessive use of alcohol, a view akin to the temperance model.

How would one intervene to reduce and prevent alcohol problems from a temperance perspective? One approach is exhortation of others to practice temperance or abstinence. This would presumably be done by those who are themselves either currently temperate or abstinent. A second approach is to control the cost, availability, and promotion of alcohol to the general public.

Spiritual Models

In 1933, the United States was in a conceptual quandary. The dominant view of alcohol problems had been that they were caused by the pernicious nature of alcohol itself. Yet the nation had just voted to make alcohol freely available again. We needed a new model.

It was just two years later that Alcoholics Anonymous (AA) came into being. Beginning with the meeting of two alcoholics struggling to resist drinking, it has grown into a worldwide social movement emphasizing a new approach for understanding and recovering from alcoholism. Its original writings and current practices center around 12 steps that provide guidelines for sober living.

Although its individual members espouse many different personal views, AA itself endorses no particular theory regarding the causes of alcoholism. Its source writings reflect an openness to biological, psychological, and social influences, but the central focus is unambiguously on a spiritual approach to recovery (Miller & Kurtz, 1994). Alcoholism is understood as a condition that people are powerless to overcome on their own. The hope for this hopeless condition lies in appeal for help from and turning over one's life to a higher power, and in following a spiritual path to recovery.

AA is not, of course, the only spiritual model for understanding alcohol problems. Historically, this view has taken various forms. Major religions have long considered drunkenness to be sinful behavior, reflecting a state of alienation from one's intended spiritual path. A public policy statement of the Presbyterian Church (1986) set forth a more complex theological conception of alcohol abuse (but not use) as a sin, by virtue of the harm caused to oneself or others (cf. Miller, 1994). The view, implicit in AA writings, that alcoholism arises, at least in part, from a more general spiritual deficit can be found in many forms. More rarely, alcohol problems have been attributed to demonic possession. Overtones of these views echo in our language, describing alcoholic beverages as "spirits" or denouncing liquor as "demon rum."

Dispositional Disease Models

A very different understanding of alcoholism, often confused with an AA approach (Miller & Kurtz, 1994), is the view that it is a dispositional disease, a condition rooted in constitutional differences between alcoholics and others. A central assertion of this model is that alcoholism is a unique and progressive condition that is qualitatively (not just quantitatively) different from normality. Alcoholics are regarded as substantially different from nonalcoholics, possessing a distinct condition that renders them incapable of drinking in moderation. The disease is sometimes likened to an allergy to alcohol. The central symptom of alcoholism, in this view, is loss of control over alcohol, the inability to restrain oneself from further drinking once started ("One drink, one drunk"). The disease is understood as irreversible, incapable of being cured, but possible to arrest through total abstinence from alcohol. A dominant American view since the 1960s, this model is much less prevalent outside the United States (Miller, 1986).

The dispositional disease model further served as a useful transition from the period of Prohibition. Moderate drinking was reconstrued as impossible not for all people, but only for certain people—namely, alcoholics. This model was benevolent for alcoholics, in that it absolved them of responsibility for their condition and justified humane treatment instead of punishment. It likewise proved to be a view attractive to other drinkers, in its implication that only alcoholics are at risk and that nonalcoholics may drink with relative impunity. Use of the term *disease* to describe alcoholism was appealing to and endorsed by the medical profession, with the implication that the proper course of action is medical treatment. Lastly, a dispositional disease model has often been promoted by the manufacturers of alcoholic beverages, in that it removes the blame from alcohol itself and shifts the emphasis to an abnormality found only within certain individuals. It is sometimes said that there are alcoholics in the world who have never had a drink, and so haven't discovered that they are alcoholic. The implication is that alcoholism is inherent in the physical or psychological makeup of the individual. Within the context of a dispositional disease model, it makes sense to assert that "alcoholism is not caused by alcohol"—a statement that sounds absurd from other perspectives.

Although a biological/dispositional model can be held in its pure form, to the exclusion of other causal factors (Milam & Ketcham, 1981), in practice this view has become blended in the United States with other models. Professionals who endorse the central tenets of a dispositional disease model also tend to espouse a characterological model (see below) and to agree with moralistic assertions such as "Alcoholics are liars and can't be trusted" (Moyers & Miller, 1993).

The intervention implications of a dispositional disease model are relatively straightforward. Persons with the disease of alcoholism must be identified, informed of their condition, brought to accept their diagnosis, and persuaded to abstain from alcohol for the remainder of their lives. Prevention efforts would focus on the early identification of persons with this unique condition, an endeavor termed by one group "the quest for the test." Because of their personal experience with the condition, recovering alcoholics may be seen as the optimal intervention agents to help others recognize, accept, and adjust to their disease. Peer support groups provide an ongoing resource for recovery.

Educational Models

Other approaches have relied on education as a tool for prevention and treatment. U.S. alcohol treatment often includes a series of lectures and films, as do programs dealing with drunk-driving offenders. Efforts designed to prevent alcohol and drug abuse have long relied on educational approaches.

Implicit in such strategies is the assumption that alcohol problems evolve from deficient knowledge—from a lack of accurate information. When armed with correct and up-to-date knowledge, individuals presumably will be less likely to use alcohol (and other drugs) in a hazardous fashion and to suffer the consequences. Some educational approaches have included an "affective" component as well, seeking to instill motivation to change or avoid alcohol abuse. The appropriate intervention agents within this model would be educators.

Characterological Models

Characterological models emphasize that the roots of alcohol problems lie in abnormalities of personality. In the mid-twentieth century, psychoanalysts proposed a variety of hypotheses regarding the causes of alcohol problems. Some asserted that alcohol abuse represents an early fixation of normal psychological development, involving severe unresolved conflicts regarding dependence. Arrested at the oral stage of development, the person acts out his or her dependence conflict by literally continuing to suck on a bottle. Other psychodynamic hypotheses asserted that alcohol problems arise from latent homosexuality, low self-esteem, sex-role conflicts, or a drive for power and control by persons who feel particularly impotent or powerless. Until 1980, the American Psychiatric Association (1968) classified alcoholism and drug addiction as subtypes of sociopathic personality disturbance.

The central assumption here is that alcoholics are people with particular personality types or problems, and that the resolution of symptomatic drinking requires a restructuring of the personality. This spawned the search for an "alcoholic personality" or "addictive personality." A related belief is that alcoholics display unusually high levels of certain character defense mechanisms, particularly the primitive defenses (such as denial) associated with disturbances early in development. The logical intervention within characterological models is psychotherapy to resolve the basic underlying conflicts and to bring the person to more mature levels of functioning. Preventive interventions would focus on fostering normal psychological development.

Conditioning Models

As basic principles of learning and conditioning were clarified during the first half of the twentieth century, psychologists began to speculate that such processes may explain how alcohol problems develop. Proponents of classical or Pavlovian conditioning (S-R theory) emphasized the role of such learning in shaping drinking behavior and craving for alcohol. Other research documented a significant role of classical conditioning in drug tolerance. Skinner's operant conditioning principles likewise showed a logical fit: If drinking leads to rewarding consequences, it is likely to continue or increase. Researchers have studied a variety of potential incentives for drinking, including tension reduction, time out from social rules, and positive social reinforcement from companions. The popular concept of "enabling" suggests that those close to an alcoholic may inadvertently reinforce (or at least remove the negative consequences of) excessive drinking.

The premise of conditioning models is that excessive drinking is a learned habit, responding to ordinary principles of behavior. It follows that the same principles could be employed to help an individual relearn behavior patterns. A variety of treatment strategies rely on classical (e.g., aversion therapies, see Chapter 8) or operant learning principles (e.g., community reinforcement approach, see Chapter 15). Prevention efforts from a learning perspective might focus on factors that create positive associations with alcohol (e.g., advertising) and contingencies that encourage or discourage drinking.

Social Learning Models

During the latter half of the twentieth century, principles of behavior expanded well beyond basic conditioning processes to yield more complex learning models. Like the conditioning models, these focus on interactions between the individual and the environment in shaping patterns of alcohol use. Researchers have examined more closely the influence of peers and others, emphasizing the importance of modeling of drinking behaviors and of peer pressure. Studies have found that heavy-drinking companions evoke increased consumption among those around them.

Social learning perspectives also emphasize the importance of coping skills. Alcohol can be used as a strategy for coping with problem situations or for altering one's psychological state. Reliance on a drug for such a purpose defines the process of psychological dependence. In the absence of alternative and competing skills, the individual may continue to rely on alcohol as a coping strategy.

Interventions from a social learning perspective focus on altering the client's relationship to his or her environment. Therapists may recommend that clients make changes in their circle of friends to avoid further reinforcement for problematic drinking and exposure to negative models. They may also teach new skills so that the person need not rely on a drug for coping purposes. Preventive interventions within this model are concerned with conditions of the social environment that foster problematic alcohol use, provide heavy-drinking role models, or encourage the use of alcohol and other drugs to cope with problems.

Cognitive Models

Learning theory in the last decades of the twentieth century also went decidedly cognitive, emphasizing the importance of covert mental processes in guiding behavior. Increased attention has been devoted to cognitive processes in addictions, such as expectations about the effects of alcohol. Positive expectancies—beliefs that a drug causes beneficial and desirable effects—may promote more frequent and heavy use (Brown, 1993). Recent models of "relapse prevention" (see Chapter 11) stress the importance of cognitive processes in evoking or averting relapse.

Cognitive restructuring may be used to alter positive expectancies, either within treatment or as part of prevention approaches designed to diminish harmful use. Cognitive therapies more generally are being applied to cope with craving and urges, manage concomitant mood problems, and modify beliefs that promote problematic use (e.g., Beck, Wright, Newman, & Liese, 1993).

Sociocultural Models

A still larger view points to the role of society and subculture in shaping an individual's drinking patterns and related problems. The level of per-capita alcohol consumption in a society, for example, is powerfully influenced by the availability of alcoholic beverages: their cost, convenience of access, legal regulation, and so forth. The more readily available, the more alcoholic beverages are consumed. A further key assumption is that the more alcohol a society consumes, the higher the levels of alcohol problems it will experience. The social control of alcohol availability, then, becomes an important consideration. The nature of drinking environments is also of interest from a sociocultural perspective. Certain characteristics of a drinking establishment favor heavier drinking. Recent legal trends have increased the liability of those who serve alcohol for any harm inflicted by the drinker who was served (e.g., in a vehicular crash). This development acknowledges the responsibility of the larger environment for the actions of the individual. Other cultural factors may also be important determinants of the level of alcohol problems in a society. Among those often discussed are the level of societal stress or alienation, encouragement or punishment for drunkenness, attitudes about alcohol, and the symbolic or functional importance of alcohol within the society.

Interventions that follow from a sociocultural model are those that would impact all or a large part of the society. The availability of alcohol might be restricted by increasing taxation on (and thereby the price of) alcoholic beverages or tightly regulating the number, location, and hours of shops through which they are sold. Advertising that encourages unrealistic positive expectancies about alcohol may be prohibited. Establishments serving alcohol may be encouraged or required to follow "server intervention" guidelines to discourage intoxication and drunk driving. The means for enacting such social policy are often legislative, through the creation of appropriate laws or the actions of the courts. In this way, a sociocultural approach overlaps with a temperance model in emphasizing the causal role of the drug itself, but the goal is social control rather than removal of the drug from society.

General Systems Model

A general systems approach views individual behavior as an interactive part of a larger social system. Actions of the individual (such as problematic drinking) cannot be understood without considering their relationship to other members and levels of the systems to which the individual belongs. The person's actions are an inherent part of a bigger system, interlocking with this larger pattern of relationships. A general systems model asserts that a system (such as a family) tends to maintain an overall homeostasis and will resist change. Working only with the individual, then, is a very limited endeavor because it overlooks the extent to which that person's behavior has functional importance within the system. What appears to be an individual's alcohol problem is, in fact, the malfunctioning or "dysfunction" of a larger system.

The system most often considered is the family. Several theorists have argued that alcoholism is a family disorder, requiring that the whole family system be treated. Transactional analysts (e.g., Steiner, 1971) have described alcoholism as the product of interactional "games" in which there are payoffs not only for the drinker but also for other family members. Family systems approaches argue similarly that the individual's alcoholism represents a coping strategy within the family structure. If the individual is treated alone, the family system may resist change, and if the individual does change, the family system may deteriorate or another family member may become dysfunctional to compensate. From this perspective, only family therapy is likely to be effective in untangling the complex interactions that underlie alcohol problems.

Another systems model asserts that the children of alcoholics (COAs) have a unique kind of pathology as a result of the dysfunctional family atmosphere in which they were raised. Writers have hypothesized lists of "characteristics" of COAs, or the various pathological roles that they may adopt within the alcoholic family (e.g., Wegscheider, 1981). This model asserts that it is the dysfunctional family that gives rise to the abnormal set of needs and traits in the COA. This in turn renders the COA uniquely vulnerable to addictive behaviors or pathological relationships. Some have asserted that this pattern of personality pathology is passed even to the second generation, the grandchildren of alcoholics (Thanepohn, 1986). The usually recommended path to recovery is to recognize the COA pattern, accept it as the cause of one's difficulties, and work through one's dysfunctional history toward a more adaptive style.

Biological Models

Sometimes blended with a dispositional disease model, true biological models emerged in the 1970s, placing strong emphasis on genetic and physiological processes as determinants of alcoholism. Some have stressed the importance of hereditary risk factors, drawing on strong evidence that the offspring of alcoholics have a higher risk of alcohol problems themselves. Others have posited the existence of unique biological conditions (e.g., abnormal alcohol metabolism, unique brain sensitivity) that predispose some individuals to alcoholism—a version resembling a dispositional disease model. Still others have looked to the pharmacology of alcohol itself to explain how drinking can escalate into alcoholism. A popular hypothesis of the late 1970s was of this kind, focusing on natural opiate-like chemicals (THQs) produced as a by-product of alcohol metabolism. Pharmacologic addiction itself represents a biological model, when used to explain continued and escalating alcohol (or other drug) abuse.

The intervention implications of biological models vary. Where risk factors are emphasized, special caution in the use of alcohol may be advised for those at risk, and genetic counseling may be considered. Proponents of models that focus on the pharmacologic impact of alcohol on the body may counsel drinkers to avoid levels of consumption likely to cause bodily harm or activate the accelerating spiral of tolerance and dependence. Those who advocate a unique suscep-

tibility might counsel those at risk to abstain from alcohol altogether.

Public Health Model

The history of alcohol problems is largely a history of contention among the previously described models. Each has had its champions who have defended it as the most (if not only) correct understanding of the nature of alcohol problems. Emotion-laden debates have often centered around a clash between two rival models of the nature of alcohol problems.

Indeed, the practical implications of these models do differ greatly (see Table 1.1). Consider, for example, the kinds of prevention measures that would be promoted by proponents of a dispositional disease model and by those holding to a sociocultural model. For the former, efforts to regulate the price and availability of alcohol appear futile, because the cause of alcoholism is seen as residing within the alcoholic and unrelated to alcohol. From a sociocultural perspective, on the other hand, the attempt to identify and intervene individually with a relatively small number of diagnosed alcoholics appears hopelessly narrow in focus.

It is far beyond the scope of this chapter to review the evidence regarding the validity of each of the models described here. Suffice it to

Table 1.1 Thirteen Conceptual Models of Alcohol Problems

MODEL	EMPHASIZED CAUSAL FACTORS	EXAMPLES OF INTERVENTIONS
Moral	Personal responsibility, self-control	Moral suasion, social and legal sanctions
Temperance	Alcohol	Exhortation, "just say no," control of supply
Spiritual	Spiritual deficit	Spiritual growth, prayer, AA
Dispositional Disease	Irreversible constitutional abnormality of individual	Identification of alcoholics, confrontation, lifelong abstention
Educational	Lack of knowledge and motivation	Education
Characterological	Personality traits, defense mechanisms	Psychotherapy
Conditioning	Classical and operant conditioning	Counterconditioning, extinction, altered contingencies
Social Learning	Modeling, skill deficits	Skill training, appropriate behavioral models
Cognitive	Expectancies, beliefs	Cognitive therapy, rational restructuring
Sociocultural	Environmental, cultural norms	Social policy, price and distribution controls
General Systems	Boundaries and rules, family dysfunction	Family therapy, transactional analysis
Biological	Heredity, brain physiology	Risk identification, genetic counseling, medical treatment
Public Health	Agent, host, and environment	Interdisciplinary, multiple levels of simultaneous intervention

say that some evidence supports each of these models. Each can likewise be shown to be limited in its ability to account for alcohol problems. No one of these models appears to be the whole truth, though each contains truth. No one of them is likely to be adequate in guiding efforts to intervene with and prevent alcohol problems.

A public health model, the last to be considered here, does offer some hope for integration. Public health professionals have espoused an approach that considers three types of causal factors in understanding and intervening with any disease. One important factor is the *agent*, often a germ but in this case ethyl alcohol. The agent itself contains a certain destructive potential. Some agents (e.g., the HIV virus) take their toll on most or all individuals exposed to them. Others can be found in many or most human bodies, of whom only a few manifest the disease. This points to the importance of *host* factors as well, individual differences that influence susceptibility to the condition. Think of them as personal risk factors (e.g., family history) that increase or decrease one's susceptibility to the disease. A third important factor is the *environment*. With infectious diseases, attention might be directed to the water supply, insect populations, or other means by which the agent spreads to new hosts. In alcoholism, emphasis is on aspects of the environment that promote alcohol use and abuse. Within a public health perspective, then, the presence or absence of a disease or illness is a result of the interactions of the agent, host, and environment.

All of the preceding models can be understood as emphasizing one of these factors, usually to the exclusion of the other two. A temperance model points to the destructive power of the agent itself, alcohol. Moral, dispositional disease, spiritual, educational, characterological, and biological models all place strong emphasis on host factors. Emphasis on the environment can be found in conditioning, social learning, general systems, and sociocultural perspectives.

A hallmark of the public health approach is its emphasis on the importance of considering and addressing all three components of the model. An approach that focuses on only one component is likely to be limited in its ability to eradicate the problem. A comprehensive effort acknowledges the importance of agent, host, and environment. Within the alcohol field, a public health approach acknowledges that alcohol is a hazardous drug, which places anyone at risk who consumes it unwisely or beyond mod-

eration. It also recognizes that there are significant individual differences in susceptibility to alcohol problems, mediated by factors such as heredity, tolerance, brain sensitivity, and metabolic rates. Finally, it stresses the importance of environmental factors in determining rates of alcohol use and related problems, attending to influences such as the availability and promotion of alcohol products.

A public health model offers hope for integrating what have previously been rival and seemingly incompatible perspectives. It adopts from each perspective the factors that have been found to influence the occurrence of alcohol problems, integrating them into a complex and interactive model. The interventions that follow from a public health approach are necessarily diverse, addressing all three types of factors: agent, host, and environment. This perspective moves one away from the search for a single "correct" way to intervene, and toward a larger strategy that incorporates a variety of alternative tactics (Moore & Gerstein, 1981).

There is a clear relationship between models and treatment strategies. Treatment approaches have too often been guided by a single model, operating as if it were the only complete and accurate understanding of alcohol problems and their etiology. Yet alcohol problems and the individuals who have them are diverse. Effective treatment is likely to require not one but a range of effective alternatives. It is in this spirit that we have prepared this handbook. The chapters present you with alternatives, a variety of promising tools to use in working with different types of alcohol problems and individuals. No one chapter holds "the answer." Each offers a piece of the larger solution.

AN INFORMED ECLECTICISM

We began this chapter by describing three myths of alcoholism treatment. One of these asserts that there is a single, outstandingly effective approach that is better than all others. The other two (nothing works; everything works) reduce to the assertion that all approaches are equally valid. What lies beyond these too-simplistic orientations—one devoted to the exclusive truth of a single position, the others ascribing equal merit to all alternatives? We propose that future progress and practice should be directed to an *informed eclecticism,* an openness to a variety of approaches that is guided by scientific evidence.

The guidelines for a more informed eclecticism are already beginning to emerge. Proposed systems have been variously described as prescriptive eclecticism (Dimond, Havens, & Jones, 1978), technical eclecticism (Lazarus, 1971), prescriptive psychotherapy (Goldstein & Stein, 1976), client-treatment matching (Miller & Hester, 1986b), and a cafeteria plan (Ewing, 1977). The central assumptions of an informed eclecticism center around the following general assertions:

1. *There is no single superior approach to treatment for all individuals.* This is abundantly clear from a review of the treatment outcome literature (see Chapter 2). Instead, there is an encouraging array of promising alternative interventions. There is no tried and true, "state-of-the-art" treatment of choice for alcohol problems. Rather, the state of the art is an array of empirically supported treatment options.

2. *Treatment programs and systems should be constructed with a variety of approaches that have been shown to be effective.* If treatment is to serve individuals with different characteristics and needs, then it is important to offer a variety of approaches. Such a "menu" of options can address varying needs and provide back-up options when an initial approach is ineffective. In choosing treatment strategies to include in the menu, it is sensible to rely on scientific evidence, selecting approaches shown to be more effective than no treatment or alternative treatments—at least for defined subpopulations.

3. *Different types of individuals respond best to different treatment approaches.* It is not the case that the same type of individual responds best to all forms of alcohol treatment. Although one could describe a generic "good prognosis" profile (e.g., socially stable, employed, married), there are also indications of differential response to alternative treatments (see Chapter 17). For each treatment mode it is at least conceptually possible to describe the profile of the optimal responder. A person who responds very well to Treatment A might do poorly in Treatment B, whereas for another person, B may be a superior treatment to A. Even when treatments appear to be equivalent in their overall effects within a heterogeneous population, they may be very different in their appropriateness and effectiveness for a given subpopulation or individual. The appropriate question, then, is not, Which treatments are best? but rather, Which types of individuals are most appropriate for a given program? or

For this individual, which approach is most likely to succeed?

4. *It is possible to match individuals to optimal treatments, thereby increasing treatment effectiveness and efficiency.* From the preceding assumptions, it follows that matching schemes could be developed to place individuals in different treatment approaches that are most likely to be effective for them. It is inappropriate to offer the same treatment for all individuals. Likewise, as the empirical knowledge on matching improves, it is inappropriate to choose treatment arbitrarily or intuitively. Getting individuals into the right treatment the first time around increases treatment efficacy, avoids unnecessary or ineffective treatment, and can even improve staff morale.

This does not sound like something profoundly new. "Tailoring treatment to individual needs" has long been endorsed, and most professionals and programs recognize the value and importance of matching. Yet the fact is that very few programs even offer a range of alternative approaches, let alone match individuals to them. Though the value of matching is widely recognized, putting it into practice turns out to be much more difficult.

One obstacle to the implementation of an informed eclecticism is the unavailability of true alternatives. Professionals in remote or rural areas may be frustrated by a lack of treatment options. Even in a large metropolitan area, the actual alternatives may be few. Our own community contains more than 50 different programs offering treatment for alcohol and drug abuse. Yet a close examination of these programs reveals that most are strikingly similar in content—virtual carbon copies of one another. A "standard formula" often pervades what appear on the surface to be different programs. When there is only one treatment available, there is no opportunity for matching.

A second obstacle is the absence of clear criteria for matching individuals to treatments. Writers have variously proposed matching based on clients' preferences (Miller, 1987), personality patterns and the path of least client resistance (Dimond et al., 1978), empirical criteria (Goldstein & Stein, 1976; Miller & Hester, 1986b), or clinical judgment (Lazarus, 1971). The literature on matching clients to treatments is relatively young at this point. Though it does offer some helpful guidelines for client-treatment matching (see Chapter 17), much more knowledge is needed to provide comprehensive criteria for triage. Many studies currently underway should greatly improve practical knowledge in this area. Among these is Project MATCH (1993), a multisite collaborative trial with 1,728 cases, the primary purpose of which is to yield research-based practice guidelines for matching clients to different treatment approaches.

A third substantial obstacle to effective matching persists even when treatment alternatives and plausible assignment criteria are available. This has to do with the health-care economy. Factors of limited resources, economic competition, professional loyalties, third-party reimbursement, program linkages, and referral bias serve to constrain the range of options available or recommended to a given individual. Persons referred to Program X for screening are likely to be judged as needing the services that Program X has to offer (Hansen & Emrick, 1983). The pressure to fill beds or appointment slots may override attention to the individual's best interests. Health maintenance organizations (HMOs) and preferred provider organizations (PPOs) limit the range of professionals and programs from which a subscriber may seek treatment. Insurers reimburse treatment alternatives differentially. Finally, the counselor conducting screening may be strongly committed to a particular treatment program or approach, and uninformed about or even hostile toward alternatives.

Factors such as these have led some to propose that pretreatment assessment should be conducted by an independent evaluation agent with no affiliation or commitment to particular treatment programs or approaches (Glaser et al., 1984). The evaluator, then, is free to assess each individual and make referrals within the full range of available options varying in content, setting, and intensity. Though relatively rare in past practice, such a scheme is becoming increasingly feasible. In employee assistance programs (EAPs) and some court screening programs for alcohol-related offenders, individuals are evaluated by a professional who typically will not be the treatment agent. Rather, the evaluator's task is to assess the need for treatment and to recommend optimal intervention levels and options. Given adequate information, primary care physicians, clergy, or attorneys could serve a similar function.

One of the primary goals of this book is to help practicing clinicians move toward a more informed eclecticism. The range of chapters is intended to help overcome the first obstacle by providing knowledge of treatment alternatives. Each chapter is a self-contained treatment manual that details the practicalities of one approach. The final chapter attempts a step toward overcoming the second obstacle by offering some tentative criteria for client-treatment matching.

In passing, we offer the further observation that the staff member who sits "at the front door," the one who is responsible for steering individuals to treatments, ought to be the most knowledgeable and highly trained professional in the system. Matching is one of the most challenging and important professional tasks. Inappropriate matching can result in wasted money, treatment and staff time, and even lost families and lives. We believe that appropriate matching can substantially improve the effectiveness and efficiency of treatment within a system in general, as well as in the individual case. The more common practice, however, has been to assign intake interviewing to staff with relatively less training and experience.

The third obstacle may be the most formidable of all but is not insurmountable. Even in a competitive health-care market, matching is possible if alternatives and assignment criteria are available. Referral of appropriate clients to a competitor, for example, can go a long way toward establishing cooperative working relationships. To the extent that evaluation services can be separated from treatment providers, the opportunities for matching improve. Of course the "independent and objective" evaluator is corruptible too, particularly if not accountable to peer or public review.

The most important reason to persist in pursuing true matching, however, is the welfare of one's clients. It is odd that consumer awareness has been so slow in coming to the field of mental health services in general and alcohol treatment in particular. It is clear that inappropriately matched clients can be harmed, faring worse than if they had received no treatment at all. Individuals matched to the right treatment the first time can be spared years of needless suffering and impairment. A common concern for those who suffer from alcohol problems should, in the end, be the most persuasive ground for agreement and cooperation toward a comprehensive system of informed eclecticism.

REFERENCES

Alcoholics Anonymous. (1976). *Alcoholics Anonymous: The story of how many thousands of men and women have recovered from alcoholism* (3rd ed.). New York: Alcoholics Anonymous World Services.

American Psychiatric Association. (1968). *Diagnostic and statistical manual of mental disorders* (2nd ed.). Washington, DC: Author.

Beck, A. T., Wright, F. D., Newman, C. F., & Liese, B. S. (1993). *Cognitive therapy of substance abuse*. New York: Guilford Press.

Brown, S. A. (1993). Drug effect expectancies and addictive behavior change. *Experimental and Clinical Psychopharmacology, 1*, 1–13.

Cahalan, D. (1987). *Understanding America's drinking problem*. San Francisco: Jossey-Bass.

Connors, G. J., & Rychtarik, R. G. (1989). The Supreme Court VA/disease model case: Background and implications. *Psychology of Addictive Behavior, 2*, 101–107.

Dimond, R. E., Havens, R. A., & Jones, A. C. (1978). A conceptual framework for the practice of prescriptive eclecticism in psychotherapy. *American Psychologist, 33*, 239–248.

Ewing, J. A. (1977). Matching therapy and patients: The cafeteria plan. *British Journal of Addiction, 72*, 13–18.

Fingarette, H. (1988). *Heavy drinking: The myth of alcoholism as a disease*. Berkeley: University of California Press.

Glaser, F. B., Annis, H. M., Skinner, H. A., Pearlman, S., Segal, R. L., Sisson, B., Ogborne, A. C., Bohnen, E., Gazda , P., & Zimmerman , T. (1984). *A system of health care delivery*. Toronto: Addiction Research Foundation.

Goldstein, A. P., & Stein, N. (1976). *Prescriptive psychotherapies*. New York: Pergamon.

Hansen, J., & Emrick, C. D. (1983). Whom are we calling "alcoholic"? *Bulletin of Society of Psychologists in Addictive Behaviors, 2*, 164–178.

Holder, H., Longabaugh, R., Miller, W. R. & Rubonis, A. V. (1991). The cost-effectiveness of treatment for alcoholism: A first approximation. *Journal of Studies on Alcohol, 52*, 517–540.

Lazarus, A. A. (1971). *Behavior therapy and beyond*. New York: McGraw-Hill.

Milam, J. R., & Ketcham, K. (1981). *Under the influence: A guide to the myths and realities of alcoholism*. Seattle, WA: Madrona Publications.

Miller, W. R. (1986). Haunted by the Zeitgeist: Reflections on contrasting treatment goals and conceptions of alcoholism in Europe and the United States. *Annals of the New York Academy of Sciences, 472*, 110–129.

Miller, W. R. (1987). Motivation and treatment goals. *Drugs & Society, 1*, 133–151.

Miller, W. R. (in press). Towards a biblical view of drug use. *Journal of Ministry in Addiction and Recovery*.

Miller, W. R., & Hester, R. K. (1980). Treating the problem drinker: Modern approaches. In W. R. Miller (Ed.), *The addictive behaviors: Treatment of alcoholism, drug abuse, smoking, and obesity* (pp. 11–141). Oxford: Pergamon.

Miller, W. R., & Hester, R. K. (1986a). The effectiveness of alcoholism research: What research reveals. In W. R. Miller & N. Heather (Eds.), *Treating addictive behaviors: Processes of change* (pp. 121–174). New York: Plenum.

Miller W. R., & Hester, R. K. (1986b). Matching problem drinkers with optimal treatments. In W. R. Miller & N. Heather (Eds.), *Treating adictive behaviors: Processes of change* (pp. 175–204). New York: Plenum.

Miller, W. R., & Kurtz, E. (1994). Models of alcoholism used in treatment: Contrasting A.A. and other perspectives with which it is often confused. *Journal of Studies on Alcohol, 55*, 159–166.

Moore, M. H., & Gerstein, D. R. (1981). *Alcohol and public policy: Beyond the shadow of prohibition*. Washington, DC: National Academy Press.

Moyers, T. B., & Miller, W. R. (1993). Therapists' conceptualizations of alcoholism: Measurement and implications for treatment. *Psychology of Addictive Behaviors, 7*, 238–245.

National Institute on Alcohol Abuse and Alcoholism. (1994). *Alcohol and health: Eighth special report to Congress*. Rockville, MD: Author.

Peele, S. (1985). *The meaning of addiction*. Lexington, MA: Lexington Books.

Presbyterian Church U.S.A. (1986). *Alcohol use and abuse: The social and health effects*. New York: Program Agency, The Presbyterian Church (U.S.A.).

Project MATCH Research Group. (1993). Project MATCH: Rationale and methods for a multisite clinical trial matching patients to alcoholism treatment. *Alcoholism: Clinical and Experimental Research, 17*, 1130–1145.

Steiner, C. (1971). *Games alcoholics play*. New York: Grove Press.

Thanepohn, S. G. (1986). Grandchildren of alcoholics at risk. *Changes, 5*, 6–7.

Wegscheider, S. (1981). *Another chance: Hope and health for the alcoholic family*. Palo Alto, CA: Science and Behavior Books.

What Works?
A Methodological Analysis
of the Alcohol Treatment
Outcome Literature

William R. Miller
Janice M. Brown
Tracy L. Simpson
Nancy S. Handmaker
Thomas H. Bien
Lorenzo F. Luckie
Henry A. Montgomery
Reid K. Hester
J. Scott Tonigan

The field of addictions treatment is rapidly moving toward accountability for outcomes. Just two decades ago, virtually anyone could claim to be an alcohol/drug specialist and provide whatever form of counseling he or she thought to be appropriate. The ensuing years have seen increasing professionalization of this field, specialized training programs, certifica- tion and licensure, and a growing emphasis by accrediting and funding bodies on accountability for treatment outcomes. Efforts to contain health-care cost have led to the closing of more expensive treatment programs and greater demand for proof of the efficacy of services. Moves toward "outcome funding" (e.g., Williams & Webb, 1991) place increasing emphasis on the extent to which providers are achieving their stated aims.

During these same two decades, there has been a rapid expansion of new knowledge on the relative efficacy of different alcohol treatment approaches. The methodology of treatment research has grown in sophistication and rigor, and many new and talented clinical researchers have entered what was once regarded to be a scientific Siberia. The result is a large and complex treatment outcome literature that compares favorably with those for the most-studied psychological and medical disorders.

REVIEWING TREATMENT OUTCOME RESEARCH

Since the late 1970s, our research group has been reviewing alcohol treatment outcome studies. The first of these reviews was a narrative summary of the available literature, already with 579 references (Miller & Hester, 1980). A subsequent summary focused only on controlled trials, in which treatments had been compared with control groups or alternative modalities (Miller & Hester, 1986a). Other specialized narrative reviews have considered the evidence on inpatient versus outpatient settings (Miller & Hester, 1986b, 1989) and on the matching of individuals to optimal treatment strategies (Miller & Hester, 1986c). General conclusions of these reviews were that (1) there are a number of promising treatment approaches supported by efficacy research and (2) current practice reflects little of this knowledge, and instead relies largely on various strategies for which scientific evidence is lacking.

The next step in refining our outcome literature analysis was to examine the *cost* effectiveness of various approaches (Holder, Longabaugh, Miller, & Rubonis, 1991). Following on the above reviews, a weighted evidence index was derived for each of 33 treatment modalities, based on the number of positive and negative controlled trials. Then, by surveying experts in each modality and compiling data on health-care delivery costs, estimates of the cost of delivering each kind of treatment were derived. A significant negative correlation ($r = -.385$) was found between the strength of efficacy evidence for modalities and their cost; that is, the more expensive the treatment method, the less the scientific evidence documenting its efficacy. In other specialized reviews we have summarized the evidence on brief interventions (Bien, Miller, & Tonigan, 1993) and Alcoholics Anonymous (Emrick, Tonigan, Montgomery, & Little, 1993).

A noteworthy shortcoming of these reviews has been a failure to give differential weight to studies of better quality (Howard, 1993). Prior reviews have given equal weight to controlled trials with better or poorer methodology. The present review grew out of a public discussion on this point between the senior author and Professor Griffith Edwards during a meeting at the Royal Society of Medicine in London (Miller, 1988). Edwards asserted a negative relationship between methodological quality and findings: The better the study, the less likely a finding of a significant treatment effect. Miller opined the opposite: The better-designed studies would be more likely to detect treatment differences. Neither had evidence to support his belief.

THE METHODOLOGY OF THIS REVIEW

Consequently, we started afresh with a meta-analytic approach that would take into account the methodological quality of outcome studies. A first step was to define the criteria by which studies would be included in the review. Studies were reviewed if they met all of the following criteria: (1) the study included at least one treatment intended to impact problematic alcohol consumption; (2) the study compared the treatment(s) with a control condition or with any alternative treatment(s); (3) a proper procedure (e.g., randomization, case control matching) was used to equate groups prior to treatment; and (4) the study included at least one outcome measure of drinking and/or of alcohol-related problems.

We then sought to clarify the logic of outcome inference. Many studied treatments have included multiple components, so we devised a classification system for coding the content of each treatment or control condition described within an outcome study. This permitted a clearer specification of logical inferences that can be drawn from each design. It became apparent that there are various types of comparisons that occur in controlled designs. A treatment may be compared with no treatment, with minimal treatment, with a clearly different treatment, or with a condition adding or subtracting certain components. This led to a logical system for determining the specific treatment modalities for which effects could be imputed within each design. Further, we reasoned that certain types of comparisons (e.g., additive designs and contrasts with no treatment) provide stronger evidence for the specific efficacy of a treatment than do others (e.g., comparison of two treatments without a control). We therefore devised an index of the strength of support for treatment efficacy, ranging from +2 (positive effect) to –2 (lack of positive effect), based on the logic of the outcome design. This index is shown in Table 2.1. For each study, an outcome logic score was assigned to each scorable treatment modality at each follow-up point.

Next, we devised a set of rating scales representing important aspects of the methodology of treatment outcome research. These scales were circulated to a number of clinical research colleagues for comment and were subsequently revised to yield a final set of 12 methodology rating scales. All were judgments of the presence (1) or absence (0) of a methodological attribute except that greater weight was given to three scales. Follow-up rate and follow-up length range from 0 to 2, giving an extra point for a high

(> 85%) follow-up completion rate and for assessment duration of 12 months or more. Strongest weight was given to the method of group allocation, with randomization yielding 4 points. The resulting rating scales are shown in Table 2.2. A total methodological quality score (maximum = 17) was calculated for each study using these scales.

Criteria were also devised for classifying treatment settings (e.g., inpatient, outpatient), formats (individual, group), agents (e.g., Ph.D., M.A.), and goals (e.g., abstinence, harm reduction). Study *N*s were calculated in several ways, including the number entered, starting treatment, "treated" according to study criteria, and completing treatment. For each follow-up interval, we determined the number of cases assessed and calculated a percentage of completed follow-ups using the number of subjects *initiated* into the study treatments as the denominator. (Note that our percentages may therefore differ from those of authors who used other denominators, such as the number completing treatment.) Each study population was classified for severity of alcohol problems, with further

Table 2.1 Outcome Logic Scores for Specific Treatment "A"

+2   STRONG EVIDENCE FOR SPECIFIC POSITIVE EFFECT

| A > 0 | A > no treatment, sham, placebo (also A=B>0; A >B=0) |
| AB > B | Additive effect > treatment without A |

+1   EVIDENCE FOR SPECIFIC POSITIVE EFFECT

A > B	A > alternative treatment B without control
A > b	A > brief, dissimilar treatment without control
A > a	A > briefer form of same treatment without control
a = B	Brief treatment "a" equal to more intensive alternative

---

–1   NO EVIDENCE FOR SPECIFIC POSITIVE EFFECT

A = B	A = alternative treatment of comparable or greater intensity without control
A = a	A = briefer form of same treatment without control
a < B	a (minimal A) less effective than more extensive B without control
C > A > B	Mixed differences among treatments without control
AB = B	No additive effect above alternative treatment without control
ABC = B	No additive effect of combination of modalities above alternative treatment without control
A < AB	A worse than alternative treatment B with A, without control

---

–2   NO EVIDENCE FOR SPECIFIC POSITIVE EFFECT—STRONGER DESIGNS

A ≤ 0	A ≤ no treatment, sham, placebo, assessment only
A ≤ b	A nsd from brief, dissimilar treatment without control
A < B	A worse than alternative treatment B of comparable intensity, without control
AB < B	Outcome with B is worse when A is added

Notes: "Control" (0) above refers to a group not receiving treatment A or any alternative active treatment: no treatment, sham, or placebo. When a control group is present, the comparison of A with controls takes precedence over any other comparison in determination of the treatment effect classification.

In a dismantling design (e.g., AB vs. B vs. control), the specific component test (AB vs. B) takes precedence over the combined effect (AB vs. control) in judging the effect of an additive component (A). Thus, if AB = B >0, A would be scored –1 and B would be scored +2.

Table 2.2   Methodological Quality Rating Scales

A.	Group Allocation	4 = Randomization 3 = Within-subjects counterbalanced design 2 = Case control, matching, alternating cohorts 1 = Quasi-experimental design 0 = Violated randomization or nonequivalent groups
B.	Quality Control	1 = Treatment standardized by manual, procedures, specific training, etc. 0 = No standardization specified
C.	Follow-Up Rate (at any follow-up point ≥ 3 mos.)	2 = 85–100% follow-ups completed 1 = 70–84.9% follow-ups completed 0 = <70% follow-ups completed
D.	Follow-Up Length	2 = 12 months or longer 1 = 6–11 months 0 = < 6 mo
E.	Contact	1 = Personal or telephone contact for >70% of completed follow-ups 0 = Questionnaire, unspecified, or <70%
F.	Collaterals	1 = Collaterals interviewed 0 = No collateral verification
G.	Objective	1 = Objective verification (records, serum, breath) 0 = No objective verification
H.	Dropouts	1 = Treatment dropouts are enumerated 0 = Dropouts neither discussed nor accounted for (e.g., excluded all noncompleters)
I.	Attrition	1 = Cases lost to follow-up are enumerated and considered in outcome reporting 0 = Lost cases not enumerated or considered in outcome reporting
J.	Independent	1 = Follow-up done by treatment-blind interviewer 0 = Follow-up nonblind; not specified; questionnaire
K.	Analyses	1 = Appropriate statistical analyses of group differences are reported 0 = No statistical analyses; clearly inappropriate analyses
L.	Multisite	1 = Parallel replications at two or more sites, with separate research teams 0 = Single site or comparisons of sites offering different programs

determination of the percentage of male versus female cases and the mean age.

Rating Procedures

The ratings of each study were conducted in six waves. First, the study was read by one of the authors of this review, acting as the *primary reviewer*, who completed all ratings. Second, the study was independently read by another author, acting as *secondary reviewer*, who likewise completed all ratings. These two authors then met to compare their ratings and to resolve any discrepancies by reference to the original article(s) and the coding manual (a copy of which is available on request from the first author). The result was the third step: a set of *consensus ratings*. Fourth, the senior author (or when necessary a coauthor) of the original study was sent a copy of the coding criteria and was asked to complete an independent set of *author ratings* on the same dimensions. We received written responses from 122 authors (56%), ranging from helpful and detailed commentaries to outright hostility. If no ratings were received, the author was subsequently sent our consensus ratings and was asked for comments or corrections. After this process, 96 had provided enough detail to construct an author's methodological quality score for his or her own study. Specific queries were often included in mailings to authors, requesting additional information not reported in the original article that was necessary to complete methodological ratings.

Fifth, the author's own ratings, when provided, were compared with our consensus ratings, and the reasons for discrepancies were determined with reference to the original article(s), coding manual, and new information from the author. We revised our consensus ratings in cases where new information from the author warranted a change. This fifth pass (done only for cases in which the author provided input) yielded the final *resolution ratings* that were used in our primary analyses. When no information was received from the study author, our consensus rating served as the final rating. At this point, the two senior authors also conducted a final review of all outcome logic codes to ensure procedural consistency in this crucial step across studies. Sixth, as a final check, a draft of this review was circulated for comment to the authors of cited studies, and a last set of corrections was made in response to comments received.

RESULTS: THE EFFICACY OF TREATMENT MODALITIES

Using our prior databases, computer searches, and new manual searches of two dozen major journals in the field (through 1991), we identified 219 studies that met our inclusion criteria. Over an 18-month period of correspondence, we received at least some response from 56% of authors (with nonresponse due in some cases to our inability to locate or contact authors).

The result of this four-year process is shown in the Appendix at the end of this chapter. It contains the resolution methodology ratings for each of the 219 controlled studies that met our inclusion criteria, along with the summary scores of methodological quality. Several sample characteristics are also provided for each study: the total N initiated into the study, the percentage of males in the study sample, and the mean age (when reported). For readers' convenience, studies are identified, in this and subsequent tables, by first author and year of publication.

Methodological Ratings

A total of seven readers completed methodological ratings of the studies. Preliminary analyses of interrater agreement during the first (independent coding) phase revealed one coder whose ratings converged poorly with those of other coders, whereas correlations for all other pairs were high and reasonably uniform. Consequently, all studies rated by this outlying coder were independently reread and rated by a new coder, and new consensus ratings were generated.

The convergence of coders' ratings on the 12 methodological dimensions is shown in Table 2.3. Mean agreement during the first (independent) pass exceeded 80%. After these coders' ratings were reconciled, their consensus ratings were compared with those of the authors of the outcome studies, reflecting an 87% mean agreement

Table 2.3 Psychometric Characteristics of Methodological Rating Categories

RATING CATEGORY	RANGE*	PERCENT AGREEMENT Coder 1 & 2	PERCENT AGREEMENT Consensus & Author	MEAN (SD) AFTER RECONCILIATION
A. Allocation	0–4	82.3%	85.0%	3.37 (1.19)
B. Quality Control	0–1	71.2%	84.8%	0.65 (0.48)
C. Follow-Up Rate	0–2	76.6%	79.6%	1.37 (0.79)
D. Follow-Up Length	0–2	89.4%	89.9%	1.32 (0.82)
E. Contact	0–1	73.0%	90.9%	0.78 (0.42)
F. Collaterals	0–1	93.5%	90.9%	0.37 (0.49)
G. Objective	0–1	78.9%	86.9%	0.41 (0.49)
H. Dropouts	0–1	69.3%	82.8%	0.85 (0.36)
I. Attrition	0–1	63.8%	84.8%	0.68 (0.47)
J. Independent	0–1	86.2%	83.0%	0.42 (0.50)
K. Analyses	0–1	86.3%	94.9%	0.83 (0.38)
L. Multisite	0–1	97.3%	91.9%	0.04 (0.19)
Mean Agreement		80.7%	87.1%	

*Higher value represents more favorable rating.

rate. Overall, agreement was poorest for the two scales indicating whether the study had adequately accounted for subjects who dropped out of treatment or were lost to follow-up. For each study, resolution ratings were summarized to calculate a Methodological Quality Score (MQS).

For binary (0–1) coding dimensions, the means in Table 2.3 can be read as the percentage of studies judged to show the methodological characteristic in question. As examples, only 37% of the rated treatment outcome studies had included interviews with collaterals as a means of verifying self-report of drinking, and in only 42% had follow-up data been collected by independent interviewers unaware of treatment condition. On the brighter side, 78% had collected follow-up data by personal contact with subjects, 65% had used some quality control method (treatment manual, specialized training) to standardize the delivery of treatment, 85% had accounted for treatment dropouts, and 83% were judged to have based their conclusions on acceptable if not exemplary statistical analyses. The vast majority (75%) of studies employed unviolated randomization to assign cases to groups. In 54% of studies, follow-up continued for 12 months or longer, whereas only 22% had follow-up periods of less than 6 months. Over half (57%) of the studies accounted for 85% or more of cases at one or more follow-up points, and only 20% accounted for fewer than 70% of cases.

Cumulative Evidence Score

The principal intended end product of this review process was a listing of specific treatment methods for alcohol problems with their Cumulative Evidence Scores (CES). The CES for each treatment modality was calculated in the following manner. First, we determined the list of studies from which a specific outcome could be inferred for the modality in question. Next, for each of these studies we computed a cross-product of the MQS (resolution rating, Appendix) with the outcome logic score derived from the study for this specific modality. For example, if a study's MQS rating was 14, and the design yielded strong evidence of a modality's positive effect (+2), the contribution of the study to that particular modality's overall score would be +28. When, as often occurred, a treatment had been found to exert a significant specific effect at one (usually earlier) follow-up point but not at another, the stronger observed effect was used as the modality's outcome logic score for that study. Thus, a

treatment effect observed at *any* follow-up point was counted as a specific effect, even if it was not maintained across all assessment points. Finally, we summed these cross-products to yield the CES for a treatment modality.

Because the outcome logic score for a modality within a study can be positive (beneficial effect observed) or negative in sign (no beneficial effect observed), each study can increase or decrease the CES for a modality. The extent to which it does so is influenced both by the inferential strength of the design (Table 2.1) and by the methodological quality of the study (Table 2.2). The stronger the methodology of a study, the more it contributes to the CES. Further, designs that permit stronger inference of the presence or absence of specific effects (e.g., additive design or comparison with no treatment) contribute more heavily to the CES because of their higher (+2 or –2) outcome logic scores.

THE CENTRAL FINDINGS OF THIS REVIEW

Treatment Effects

Of the 219 studies reviewed, 8 were designed in such a manner that no clear outcome inference could be drawn for a definable treatment modality. For example, Miller and Dougher (1989) reported a randomized trial of three alternative forms of covert sensitization, employing different unconditional stimuli. The findings of this study, therefore, contribute no knowledge regarding the absolute or relative efficacy of covert sensitization itself, because the modality is present in all treatment groups, and therefore no outcome logic code could be derived from the design.

Of the 211 remaining studies, 146 (69%) reported a significant treatment effect (–2, +1, or +2; see Table 2.1) on at least one alcohol measure for at least one follow-up point. Looked at another way, the 211 studies generated a total of 610 treatment contrasts to which outcome logic codes could be assigned. Of these, 309 (51%) reflected a significant treatment effect as defined above. Thus, a majority of published studies evaluating treatments for alcohol problems have reported some significant outcome difference among the conditions being compared, with about half of all conducted contrasts reflecting reliable differences.

Table 2.4 summarizes the "bottom line" findings of our review for 43 treatment modalities. For 13 of these modalities, only 1 or 2 outcome studies were available, providing too little basis for a conclusion regarding efficacy

Table 2.4 Summary of Cumulative Evidence Scores

TREATMENT MODALITY	Np	Nn	WEIn	MQS	SEV	CES	COST
Brief Intervention	17	6	+26	13.0	2.5	+239	46
Social Skills Training	11	5	+15	11.1	3.8	+128	270
Motivational Enhancement	5	2	+6	13.6	3.0	+87	46
Community Reinforcement Approach	4	0	+6	13.3	3.0	+80	492
Behavior Contracting	4	0	+6	10.8	3.8	+73	164
Aversion Therapy, Nausea	3	3	+1	10.3	3.8	+34	1380
Client-Centered Therapy	3	1	+3	9.8	3.3	+34	738*
Relapse Prevention	3	4	0	12.6	3.0	+34	433
Self-Help Manual	2	1	+1	12.7	3.0	+33	20*
Cognitive Therapy	3	4	0	10.3	3.6	+22	433
Covert Sensitization	3	5	−1	10.9	3.5	+18	328
Marital/Family Therapy, Behavioral	3	2	+2	13.4	3.6	+15	513
Disulfiram	10	11	+7	10.8	3.8	+09	637
Behavioral Self-Control Training	14	16	+10	13.0	2.9	−07	105
Systematic Desensitization	1	2	−1	11.0	3.0	−07	120
Lithium	3	3	+1	11.3	3.8	−08	441
Marital/Family, Nonbehavioral	3	4	0	12.4	3.7	−22	513
Aversion Therapy, Electrical	6	9	+1	11.1	3.8	−25	410
Hypnosis	0	4	−4	10.8	3.8	−41	738
Milieu Therapy	3	7	−3	11.7	3.6	−41	1960
Psychedelic Medication	2	6	−4	9.9	3.6	−45	637
Unspecified "Standard" Treatment	0	3	−3	10.7	3.0	−53	738*
Videotape Self-Confrontation	0	6	−6	10.8	3.8	−77	548
Antianxiety Medication	1	7	−6	7.4	3.3	−79	637
Metronidazole	1	10	−9	9.6	3.7	−102	637
Relaxation Training	3	11	−7	11.1	2.8	−109	120
Confrontational Counseling	0	7	−7	12.4	2.9	−125	375
Psychotherapy	1	9	−8	11.3	3.1	−127	4050
General Alcoholism Counseling	1	15	−14	11.3	3.4	−214	738
Educational Lectures/Films	3	18	−14	9.9	2.2	−239	135

MODALITIES WITH TWO OR FEWER STUDIES

TREATMENT MODALITY	Np	Nn	WEIn	MQS	SEV	CES	COST
Sensory Deprivation	2	0	+2	10.0	1.0	+40	92*
Developmental Counseling	1	0	+1	9.0	2.0	+28	738*
Acupuncture	1	0	+1	10.0	4.0	+20	923
Exercise	1	1	0	10.5	2.5	+9	270*
Aversion Therapy, Apneic	1	1	0	10.0	3.5	0	570
Problem-Solving Training	0	1	−1	12.0	4.0	−12	164*
Functional Analysis	0	2	−2	11.0	2.5	−22	164*
Self-Monitoring	1	1	0	12.5	3.5	−23	20*
Antidepressant Medication	0	2	−2	6.0	3.0	−24	457
BAC Discrimination	0	2	−2	12.0	3.5	−24	500*
Calcium Carbimide	0	2	−2	10.0	4.0	−32	637
Antipsychotic Medication	0	2	−2	9.0	3.5	−36	637
Alcoholics Anonymous	0	2	−2	13.0	3.5	−52	0

Notes:

Np = Number of positive (+1 or +2) studies
Nn = Number of negative (−1 or −2) studies
MQS = Methodological Quality Score (mean for modality)
Sev = Population severity score (mean for modality)
CES = Cumulative Evidence Score

Cost = Estimated cost to deliver treatment modality, in 1990 U.S. dollars. Figures are derived from Holder and colleagues (1991), except for starred (*) items not included in their list, which were estimated by the authors from the costs of similar treatments in the list. The *price* charged for a treatment may, of course, dramatically exceed this estimated base cost of delivery.

(see bottom section of Table 2.4). For all modalities, we have reported seven values:

1. Np: The number of positive studies (+1 or +2, see Table 2.1) supporting beneficial specific effect of the treatment modality

2. Nn: The number of negative studies (−1 or −2) showing no beneficial effect for the modality

3. WEIn: The Weighted Evidence Index calculated by the method of Holder and colleagues (1991), being Np minus Nn plus 1 extra point for each positive study (Np) over 2

4. The mean Methodological Quality Score (MQS) for studies of the modality
5. The mean severity rating for populations treated in studies of the modality (0–4 scale)
6. The Cumulative Evidence Score (CES) for the modality
7. The approximate cost of delivering the treatment modality, in 1990 dollars, by the estimation methods of Holder and colleagues (1991)

The final CES values for treatment modalities range from +239 to –239. A complexity of this rating system is that two treatment modalities could receive identical intermediate (and mediocre) scores for different reasons. In one case, a relatively low score could result from the relative absence of studies. In another case, the same score could result from an approximately equal balance of many positive and negative studies. Thus, for example, similar scores (–7) were obtained for systematic desensitization (from 1 positive and 2 negative studies) and for behavioral self-control training (from 14 positive and 16 negative studies). Reasoning that a larger number of positive studies indicates the presence of some specific effect (stronger evidence than the *absence* of studies), Holder and colleagues (1991) gave double credit for positive trials beyond the first two, when calculating their Weighted Evidence Index (WEIn). We chose not to do so in the present review, but in the following discussion of

specific modalities, we will note points where this seems a significant consideration.

In any event, modality values on our Cumulative Evidence Score (CES) are highly correlated ($r = .93$) with the WEIn scores set by Holder and colleagues (1991) (see Table 2.4), and with the simple difference of Np – Nn ($r = .98$) for the same modalities. (The corresponding Spearman rank-order correlations were .89 and .95, respectively.) This further indicates that, despite our extensive efforts to quantify and weight study methodology, the simple Np – Nn index is an excellent proxy of the strength of scientific evidence for a treatment modality, at least within the alcohol field.

Correlates of MQS and CES

The discussion that served as a catalyst for this review involved a disagreement over the probable relationship between methodological quality of studies and the presence or absence of a significant treatment effect. Using our outcome logic codes (Table 2.1) as a measure of the latter, and MQS to assess the former, we found no significant relationship ($r = .06$). That is, the methodological quality of a study appears to be unpredictive of whether a treatment effect will be observed. The mean MQS for modalities ($n = 30$; see top portion of Table 2.4) was also found to be unrelated to the mean problem severity in the study populations ($r = -.27$), and to the estimated

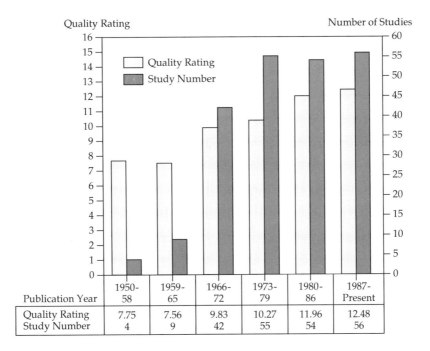

Publication Year	1950–58	1959–65	1966–72	1973–79	1980–86	1987–Present
Quality Rating	7.75	7.56	9.83	10.27	11.96	12.48
Study Number	4	9	42	55	54	56

Figure 2.1 Number of Studies Reviewed and Methodologic Quality by Year of Publication

cost of delivering the treatment ($r = -.14$). With individual studies (rather than modalities) as the level of analysis, MQS ($n = 219$) was found to be unrelated to study population severity ($r = -.02$), sample size ($r = -.13$), mean age of subjects ($r = -.01$), and the percentage of male subjects ($r = -.16$). Thus, the quality of study methodology does not appear to have been influenced by these sample characteristics, nor have better-designed studies been differentially associated with more or less expensive treatment modalities.

To what extent is the amount of scientific evidence for a treatment modality (CES) related to other factors? Within Table 2.4 ($n = 30$), CES for modalities is unrelated to problem severity ($r = .08$) and cost of treatment ($r = -.28$), though the latter trend is consistent with the report of Holder and associates (1991) that more expensive treatments tend to have less scientific support. With studies as the level of analysis, CES was unrelated to sample severity ($r = .00$), sample size ($r = -.08$), mean age ($r = -.06$), and percentage of males in the study sample ($r = -.05$).

Finally, we examined temporal trends in alcohol treatment outcome studies from 1950 through 1991. Figure 2.1 shows the growth in the number of clinical trials conducted over this period, with a relatively steady rate of studies appearing during the past 25 years. The mean quality of study methodology (MQS) shows a similar pattern of growth.

SPECIFIC TREATMENT MODALITIES

This section will provide more detailed information on the evidence for 11 groups of specific alcohol treatment approaches. They are presented roughly in the order of strength of evidence for efficacy (CES), starting with the most strongly supported modalities. A table is also provided for each

Table 2.5 Studies of Brief Intervention and Motivational Enhancement

BRIEF INTERVENTION

Author	Year	Severity	MQS	OLS	Product
Harris	1990	3	16	2	32
Wallace	1988	2	16	2	32
Babor	1992	2	14	2	28
Anderson	1992	2	13	2	26
Chick	1985	2	12	2	24
Elvy	1988	2	11	2	22
Kristenson	1983	2	11	2	22
Maheswaran	1992	2	11	2	22
Persson	1988	2	10	2	20
Chick	1988	3	16	1	16
Sanchez-Craig	1991	3	15	1	15
Edwards	1977	3	15	1	15
Chapman	1988	4	14	1	14
Sannibale	1988	3	14	1	14
Sanchez-Craig	1989	3	14	1	14
Zweben	1988	3	14	1	14
Obolensky	1984	2	13	1	13
Daniels	1992	2	5	-2	-10
Hayashida	1969	3	12	-1	-12
Romelsjö	1989	3	12	-1	-12
Robertson	1986	3	14	-1	-14
Scott	1990	2	13	-2	-26
Heather	1987	3	15	-2	-30

CES = +239

MOTIVATIONAL ENHANCEMENT

Author	Year	Severity	MQS	OLS	Product
Miller	1988	2	15	2	30
Miller	1993	2	15	2	30
Bien	1992	4	13	2	26
Brown	1993	4	13	2	26
Mallams	1982	3	10	2	20
Kuchipudi	1990	3	13	-1	-13
Chick	1988	3	16	-2	-32

CES = +87

Table 2.6   Studies of Broad Spectrum Skill Training Strategies

SOCIAL SKILLS TRAINING

Author	Year	Severity	MQS	OLS	Product
Azrin	1982	4	14	2	28
Chaney	1978	4	14	2	28
Eriksen	1986	4	13	2	26
West	1979	4	12	2	24
Jones	1982	4	10	2	20
Roshenow	1985	2	10	2	20
Freedberg	1978	4	8	2	16
Oei	1980	4	7	2	14
Oei	1982	4	12	1	12
Ferrell	1981	4	11	1	11
Monti	1990	4	11	1	11
Jackson	1978	4	6	−2	−12
Cooney	1991	4	14	−1	−14
Miller	1980	2	16	−1	−16
Ends	1957	4	9	−2	−18
Ferrell	1981	4	11	−2	−22

CES = +128

COMMUNITY REINFORCEMENT APPROACH

Author	Year	Severity	MQS	OLS	Product
Azrin	1982	4	14	2	28
Hunt	1973	4	13	2	26
Azrin	1976	3	14	1	14
Sisson	1986	1	12	1	12

CES = +80

SYSTEMATIC DESENSITIZATION

Author	Year	Severity	MQS	OLS	Product
Lanyon	1972	4	12	2	24
Hedberg	1974	4	11	−1	−11
Cooper	1988	1	10	−2	−20

CES = −7

RELAXATION TRAINING

Author	Year	Severity	MQS	OLS	Product
Steffen	1975	3	12	2	24
Rohsenow	1985	2	10	2	20
Rosenberg	1979	4	9	1	9
Blake	1967	3	9	−1	−9
Sisson	1981	4	9	−1	−9
Freedberg	1978a	4	10	−1	−10
Marlatt	1975	1	5	−2	−10
Connors	1986	2	12	−1	−12
Skutle	1987	3	14	−1	−14
Miller	1980	2	16	−1	−16
Miller	1980	3	16	−1	−16
Murphy	1986	1	10	−2	−20
Monti	1990	4	11	−2	−22
Telch	1984	3	12	−2	−24

CES = −109

PROBLEM SOLVING

Author	Year	Severity	MQS	OLS	Product
Sanchez-Craig	1982	4	12	−1	−12

CES = −12

group, listing the individual studies contributing to each modality's CES, specifying for each the problem severity rating ranging from 1 (nonclinical population recruited for research only) through 4 (severely impaired clinical population with alcohol dependence), MQS, outcome logic score (OLS; Table 2.1), and cross-product of MQS × OLS, which forms the basis for the modality's final CES.

Brief Intervention

Among modalities that have been tested as treatments for alcohol problems, brief intervention has one of the largest literature bases and currently the most positive. Table 2.5 summarizes 30 controlled trials for brief interventions, distinguishing between those explicitly based on a *motivational enhancement* approach (see Chapter 5) and other strategies. It is noteworthy that the latter studies in particular have generally been conducted with somewhat less severe populations, often identified by screening procedures and not presenting for treatment of alcohol problems. Interventions guided by a motivational enhancement strategy have often followed the format of a "drinker's check-up" (Miller & Sovereign, 1989). The content of other brief treatment approaches has been varied, although several elements are commonly present (Bien, Miller, & Tonigan, 1993). Brief interventions are more fully described in Chapter 3.

Broad Spectrum Skill Training

"Broad spectrum" treatment approaches place primary focus not on alcohol consumption per se but on other life problem areas often func-tionally related to drinking and relapse (Miller & Hester, 1980). The underlying assumption has often been that drinking problems arise or continue because the individual lacks important coping skills for sober living. Broad spectrum therapies therefore seek to teach such coping skills to problem drinkers. Most thoroughly tested of these is *social skills training* (Chapter 13), with a current base of 16 controlled trials (see Table 2.6). Azrin's *community reinforcement approach* (Chapter 15) also fares well, with 4 positive trials. Less consistent support has been found to date for stress-management strategies (Chapter 15) such as *systematic desensitization*, and a large body of studies has shown little additive benefit from *relaxation training* alone. Still other strategies such as *problem-solving training* are too little studied to form conclusions at present.

Marital/Family Therapy

Relationship therapies seek to promote sobriety by improving the quality of family and/or marital relationships (see Chapter 13). *Behavioral* marital/family therapies currently finish with a positive CES and tend to focus on teaching communication skills and increasing the level of positive reinforcement within relationships. Somewhat weaker support has been found for other approaches to marital/family therapies with problem drinkers (see Table 2.7). The quality of outcome studies on this modality has been relatively high.

Table 2.7   Studies of Marital/Family Therapies

COGNITIVE BEHAVIORAL MARITAL/FAMILY THERAPY

Author	Year	Severity	MQS	OLS	Product
Bowers	1990	3	15	1	15
O'Farrell	1985	4	15	1	15
Hedberg	1974	4	11	1	11
Monti	1990	4	11	−1	−11
McCrady	1986	3	15	−1	−15
CES = +15					

OTHER MARITAL/FAMILY THERAPY

Author	Year	Severity	MQS	OLS	Product
Cadogan	1973	4	13	2	26
Corder	1972	4	9	2	18
Dahlgren	1989	3	13	1	13
McCrady	1979	4	10	−1	−10
McCrady	1986	3	15	−1	−15
Keso	1990	4	12	−2	−24
O'Farrell	1985	4	15	−2	−30
CES = −22					

Cognitive-Behavioral Approaches

A larger set of strategies is summarized in Table 2.8 under the general heading of cognitive-behavioral counseling. *Behavior contracting*, setting specific goals and reinforcing approximations, has received reasonable support. Few studies have examined the specific impact of behavioral *self-help manuals* in additive or untreated-control designs, but consistent with the literature on brief intervention there is indication that they can be helpful. Seven studies have evaluated the impact of *cognitive therapies* designed to alter beliefs and thinking patterns presumed to underlie

Table 2.8   Studies of Cognitive-Behavioral Counseling Approaches

BEHAVIOR CONTRACTING

Author	Year	Severity	MQS	OLS	Product
Ahles	1983	3	13	2	26
Miller	1975	4	11	2	22
Keane	1984	4	13	1	13
Gerrein	1973	4	6	2	12
CES = +73					

SELF-HELP MANUAL

Author	Year	Severity	MQS	OLS	Product
Miller	1978	3	15	2	30
Miller	1981	3	13	1	13
Guydish	1987	3	10	−1	−10
CES = +33					

COGNITIVE THERAPY

Author	Year	Severity	MQS	OLS	Product
Brandsma	1980	4	14	2	28
Oei	1982	4	12	2	24
Oei	1984	3	11	2	22
Rosenberg	1986	2	7	−1	−7
Ito	1988	4	11	−1	−11
Jackson	1978	4	6	−2	−12
Monti	1990	4	11	−2	−22
CES = +22					

BEHAVIORAL SELF-CONTROL TRAINING

Author	Year	Severity	MQS	OLS	Product
Harris	1990	3	16	2	32
Brown	1980	2	15	2	30
Alden	1988	2	14	2	28
Baker	1975	4	14	2	28
Sobell	1973	4	14	2	28
Caddy	1976	4	12	2	24
Lovibond	1975	2	10	2	20
Miller	1980	2	16	1	16
Sandahl	1990	4	7	2	14
Robertson	1986	3	14	1	14
Heather	1990	3	13	1	13
Baldwin	1991	4	13	1	13
Coghlan	1979	3	10	1	10
Heather	1986	3	10	1	10
Guydish	1987	3	10	−1	−10
Carpenter	1985	2	11	−1	−11
Vogler	1977	3	12	−1	−12
Miller	1981	3	13	−1	−13
Pomerleau	1978	3	14	−1	−14
Sanchez-Craig	1989	3	14	−1	−14

(continued)

Table 2.8   (continued)

BEHAVIORAL SELF-CONTROL TRAINING (continued)

Author	Year	Severity	MQS	OLS	Product
Skutle	1987	3	14	−1	−14
Miller	1978	3	15	−1	−15
Sanchez-Craig	1984	3	15	−1	−15
Sanchez-Craig	1991	3	15	−1	−15
Miller	1980	3	16	−1	−16
Kivlahan	1990	1	10	−2	−20
Connors	1992	2	14	−2	−28
Sannibale	1988	3	14	−2	−28
Heather	1987	2	15	−2	−30
Foy	1984	4	16	−2	−32
CES = −7					

RELAPSE PREVENTION

Author	Year	Severity	MQS	OLS	Product
O'Farrell	1993	4	15	2	30
Chaney	1978	4	14	2	28
Caddy	1984	3	13	2	26
Rosenberg	1986	2	7	−1	−7
Annis	1992	3	12	−1	−12
Skutle	1987	3	14	−1	−14
Obolensky	1984	2	13	−2	−17
CES = +34					

FUNCTIONAL ANALYSIS

Author	Year	Severity	MQS	OLS	Product
Coghlan	1979	3	10	−1	−10
Connors	1986	2	12	−1	−12
CES = −22					

SELF-MONITORING

Author	Year	Severity	MQS	OLS	Product
Eriksen	1986	4	9	1	9
Harris	1990	3	16	−2	−32
CES = −23					

BAC DISCRIMINATION TRAINING

Author	Year	Severity	MQS	OLS	Product
Vogler	1977	3	12	−1	−12
Vogler	1977	4	12	−1	−12
CES = −24					

problem drinking, with mixed but encouraging results.

The largest literature focuses on *behavioral self-control training* (BSCT), an approach designed to teach clients how to modify their own drinking behavior (see Chapter 9) and often applied with less severely impaired populations (mean severity rating = 2.9). Here, there is a large number of positive (14) as well as nega-tive studies (16). Trials indicated as negative were primarily reports of similar benefits from therapist-directed BSCT and alternative (often briefer) approaches, rather than unfavorable comparisons with groups receiving no treatment or alternative modalities. Such variety in findings further suggests that this treatment approach may be more effective with certain populations than others, and that it may be

Table 2.9   Studies of Aversion Therapy

APNEIC

Author	Year	Severity	MQS	OLS	Product
Laverty	1966	3	10	2	20
Clancy	1967	4	10	−2	−20
CES = 0					

COVERT SENSITIZATION

Author	Year	Severity	MQS	OLS	Product
Maletsky	1974	3	13	2	26
Olson	1981	4	11	2	22
Ashem	1968	4	11	2	22
Fleiger	1973	3	6	−1	−6
Hedberg	1974	4	11	−1	−11
Richard	1983	3	11	−1	−11
Sanchez-Craig	1982	4	12	−1	−12
Telch	1970	3	12	−1	−12
CES = +18					

ELECTRICAL

Author	Year	Severity	MQS	OLS	Product
Marlatt	1973	4	15	2	30
Caddy	1976	4	12	2	24
Glover	1977	4	11	2	22
Schaeffer	1972	3	10	2	20
Vogler	1975	4	10	2	20
Vogler	1970	4	5	2	10
Jackson	1978	4	6	−1	−6
McCance	1969	4	12	−1	−12
Vogler	1977	4	12	−1	−12
Vogler	1977	3	12	−1	−12
Miller	1978	3	15	−1	−15
Miller	1973	4	10	−2	−20
Hedberg	1974	4	11	−2	−22
Regester	1971	3	12	−2	−24
Cannon	1981	4	14	−2	−28
CES = −25					

NAUSEA AVERSION

Author	Year	Severity	MQS	OLS	Product
Cannon	1981	4	14	2	28
Smith	1991	4	10	2	20
Boland	1978	4	12	1	12
Jackson	1978	4	6	−1	−6
Wallerstein	1957	4	9	−1	−9
Richard	1983	3	11	−1	−11
CES = +34					

fruitful to identify individual predictors of responsiveness (see Chapter 17). Specific components of BSCT have typically shown little impact when isolated from a larger program of self-control skills. *Functional analysis, self-monitoring,* and training in *discrimination of blood alcohol concentration (BAC)* have been subjected to only two studies each, which reflect little additive benefit of these single components.

Relapse prevention is in one sense a general goal rather than an approach to treatment (see Chapter 11). The studies summarized under this heading in Table 2.8, however, have evaluated specific cognitive-behavioral strategies as outlined by Annis and Davis (1989) and Marlatt and Gordon (1985) for helping people to anticipate and cope with high-risk situations. It is noteworthy that the findings reported in Table 2.8 cannot be regarded as supportive of the "CENAPS" model popularized by Gorski under the same name of relapse prevention. To our knowledge, the Gorski model has never been subjected to a single controlled trial. The studies listed in Table 2.8 focus on cognitive-behavioral coping skill training, drawn primarily from the work of Marlatt and Annis.

Aversion Therapies

Aversion therapies (see Table 2.9) seek to develop in the client, via classical Pavlovian conditioning strategies, a conditioned negative response to the sight, smell, taste, and even

Table 2.10 Studies of Antidipsotropic Medications

DISULFIRAM Author	Year	Severity	MQS	OLS	Product
Fuller	1986	4	17	2	34
Azrin	1982	4	14	2	28
Chick	1992	4	14	2	28
Wilson	1978	4	13	2	26
Wilson	1980	4	12	2	24
Wallerstein	1957	4	9	2	18
Whyte	1974	4	8	2	16
Hoff	1953	4	5	2	10
Reinert	1958	4	8	1	8
Hussain	1972	3	6	1	6
Gerrein	1973	4	6	−1	−6
Aharan	1967	3	8	−1	−8
Levy	1967	4	8	−1	−8
Ludwig	1969	4	13	−1	−13
Fuller	1979	3	16	−1	−16
Gallant	1968	4	9	−2	−18
Ling	1983	4	11	−2	−22
Powell	1985	3	11	−2	−22
Johnsen	1987	4	12	−2	−24
Dahlgren	1989	3	13	−2	−26
Johnsen	1991	4	13	−2	−26
CES = +9					

CALCIUM CARBIMIDE Author	Year	Severity	MQS	OLS	Product
Levy	1967	4	8	−1	−8
Boland	1978	4	12	−2	−24
CES = −32					

METRONIDAZOLE Author	Year	Severity	MQS	OLS	Product
Swinson	1971	4	13	2	26
Merry	1968	4	6	−1	−6
Merry	1968	4	6	−1	−6
Tyndel	1969	3	7	−1	−7
Gallant	1968	4	9	−1	−9
Lal	1969	4	9	−1	−9
Linton	1967	4	10	−1	−10
Penick	1969	3	11	−1	−11
Platz	1970	3	10	−2	−20
Lowenstam	1969	4	12	−2	−24
Egan	1968	4	13	−2	−26
CES = −102					

thought of alcohol (see Chapter 8). Among controlled trials, the oldest of these strategies is *nausea aversion,* in which alcohol is paired with physically induced nausea, usually by the administration of emetic medications. A small literature currently yields a positive CES for nausea aversion. Unconditional responses other than nausea have also been tried, including *apneic paralysis* and painful *electrical shock,* with less encouraging results. The induction of conditioned aversion solely by imaginal processes has been called *covert sensitization,* which has generated a mixture of positive and negative findings.

Antidipsotropic Medications

The antidipsotropic agents (see Table 2.10) sometimes confused with aversion therapies, are medications that induce illness only if one drinks alcohol (see Chapter 8). Under ideal conditions, at least, the client never drinks in the presence of the medication and thus never experiences conditioning. Most familiar and studied of these medications is *disulfiram,* which, with a large and nearly balanced slate of positive (10) and negative studies (11), garners a mildly positive CES. As with aversion therapies, the variability of outcomes again suggests the possibility of differential efficacy based on client or treatment characteristics. Medication compliance is a common obstacle in disulfiram treatment, which when controlled appears to yield clearer treatment effects (e.g., Fuller et al., 1986). *Calcium carbimide,* an alternative and less potent antidipsotropic agent, has been less evaluated. *Metronidazole,* once believed to be an antidipsotropic and used in alcoholism treatment for two decades, was rather uniformly found in controlled trials to be of no benefit.

Psychotropic Medications

Psychotropic medications (see Chapter 16), like broad spectrum skill training methods, are often intended to diminish drinking by alleviating related symptomatology (e.g., *antidepressant* and *antianxiety* agents). Other medications, such as *antipsychotic* and *psychedelic* agents, were thought to facilitate treatment. Still others, such as *lithium* and certain antidepressants, were thought to diminish drinking directly. Such medications may beneficially impact concomitant problems, and except in the case of addictive drugs (such as benzodiazepines) there is no reason to withhold them in treating dually diag-

nosed individuals. CES scores to date, however, reflect no clear specific effects of psychotropic medications on drinking outcomes. The efficacy of newer psychotropic agents, such as selective serotonin reuptake inhibitors, is currently being investigated in a number of studies (see Table 2.11). Positive findings with naltrexone also emerged while this review was being prepared (O'Malley, Jaffe, Chang, Schottenfeld, Meyer, & Rounsaville, 1992; Volpicelli, Alterman, Hayashida, & O'Brien, 1992).

Psychotherapies

Controlled studies of group or individual psychotherapy for alcohol problems have yielded negative findings with remarkable consistency, often despite the predictions of investigators (see Table 2.12). Exploratory psychotherapies have accumulated one of the lowest CES totals of any treatment modality. An apparent exception to this general trend is *client-centered* therapy, based on the writings of Rogers (1951), which has compared favorably with alternative approaches in three of four studies. This is consistent with the literature on effective brief intervention styles (Bien et al., 1993). Other specific types of psychotherapy, such as *developmental counseling,* require more careful study before conclusions can be drawn.

Confrontational Approaches

Confrontational counseling styles have enjoyed particular popularity in U.S. alcoholism treatment. Yet confrontational approaches have failed to yield a single positive outcome study (see Table 2.13). It is noteworthy that in practice, confrontational counseling in many ways represents the conceptual opposite of client-centered therapy, for which findings have been more positive (cf. Miller & Rollnick, 1991).

One particular form of confrontational intervention, practiced and tested in the 1970s, involved videotaping alcoholics while intoxicated, then showing them the recording when sober. Again, studies reflected consistently negative findings.

"Standard" Treatment Components

Several other treatment components are summarized in Table 2.14 as "standard" approaches. Two aspects are reasonably characteristic of these modalities: Their content is often relatively

Table 2.11 Studies of Psychotropic Medications

LITHIUM Author	Year	Severity	MQS	OLS	Product
Fawcett	1987	4	15	2	30
Kline	1974	4	9	2	18
Merry	1976	4	8	2	16
Pond	1981	3	10	−2	−20
Powell	1986	4	10	−2	−20
Dorus	1989	4	16	−2	−32
CES = −8					

ANTIDEPRESSANT Author	Year	Severity	MQS	OLS	Product
Kissin	1968	3	2	−2	−4
Shaffer	1964	3	10	−2	−20
CES = −24					

ANTIPSYCHOTIC Author	Year	Severity	MQS	OLS	Product
Reinert	1958	4	8	−2	−16
Charnoff	1963	3	10	−2	−20
CES = −36					

PSYCHEDELIC Author	Year	Severity	MQS	OLS	Product
Hollister	1969	4	11	1	11
Jensen	1963	4	4	2	8
Tomsovic	1970	3	7	−1	−7
Bowen	1970	3	9	−1	−9
Rhead	1977	4	11	−1	−11
Bowen	1970	3	12	−1	−12
Smart	1966	4	12	−1	−12
Ludwig	1969	4	13	−1	−13
CES = −45					

ANTI-ANXIETY Author	Year	Severity	MQS	OLS	Product
Hoff	1961	3	5	2	10
Kissin	1968	3	2	−2	−4
Gallant	1968	4	9	−1	−9
Shaffer	1963	4	10	−1	−10
Bartholomew	1961	3	6	−2	−12
Mooney	1961	3	6	−2	−12
Powell	1985	3	11	−2	−22
Charnoff	1963	3	10	−2	−20
CES = −79					

poorly defined in evaluation studies, and they are frequent components of treatment as currently practiced.

Milieu therapy suggests that recovery is aided by taking the client to a special place where healing occurs. Implicit is the notion that time spent in such a therapeutic atmosphere is itself beneficial. This ancient idea is now commonly associated with residential or inpatient programs, although the "California social

Table 2.12 Studies of Psychotherapies

CLIENT-CENTERED THERAPY

Author	Year	Severity	MQS	OLS	Product
Ends	1957	4	9	2	18
Telch	1984	3	12	1	12
Valle	1981	4	11	1	11
Rosenberg	1986	2	7	−1	−7
CES = +34					

PSYCHOTHERAPY

Author	Year	Severity	MQS	OLS	Product
Rhead	1977	4	11	2	22
Johnson	1970	3	9	−1	−9
Bruun	1963	3	11	−1	−11
Jacobson	1973	3	11	−1	−11
Zimberg	1974	3	11	−1	−11
Ludwig	1969	4	13	−1	−13
Swenson	1981	2	9	−2	−18
Olson	1981	4	11	−2	−22
Wells-Parker	1988	2	12	−2	−24
Bowers	1990	3	15	−2	−30
CES = −127					

DEVELOPMENTAL COUNSELING

Author	Year	Severity	MQS	OLS	Product
Alden	1988	2	14	2	28
CES = +28					

Table 2.13 Studies of Confrontational Approaches

CONFRONTATIONAL COUNSELING

Author	Year	Severity	MQS	OLS	Product
Swenson	1980	2	9	−1	−9
Bjørnevoll	1972	4	11	−1	−11
Pomerleau	1978	3	14	−1	−14
Miller	1990	2	15	−1	−15
Miller	1973	4	10	−2	−20
Annis	1983	2	14	−2	−28
Sannibale	1988	3	14	−2	−28
CES = −125					

VIDEOTAPE SELF-CONFRONTATION

Author	Year	Severity	MQS	OLS	Product
Faia	1976	4	4	−1	−4
Schaefer	1971	4	11	−1	−11
Vogler	1977	3	12	−1	−12
Vogler	1977	4	12	−1	−12
Baker	1975	4	14	−1	−14
Lanyon	1972	4	12	−2	−24
CES = −77					

Table 2.14   Studies of "Standard Treatment" Components

MILIEU THERAPY

Author	Year	Severity	MQS	OLS	Product
Walsh	1991	2	14	2	28
Wanberg	1974	3	10	2	20
Lal	1969	4	9	2	18
Annis	1979	4	8	−1	−8
Stein	1975	4	11	−1	−11
McLachlan	1982	4	12	−1	−12
Longabaugh	1983	3	14	−1	−14
Edwards	1967	4	16	−1	−16
Eriksen	1986	4	9	−2	−18
Chapman	1988	4	14	−2	−28
CES = −41					

UNSPECIFIED "STANDARD" TREATMENT

Author	Year	Severity	MQS	OLS	Product
Mosher	1975	4	11	−1	−11
Salzberg	1983	2	7	−2	−14
Azrin	1976	3	14	−2	−28
CES = −53					

GENERAL ALCOHOLISM COUNSELING

Author	Year	Severity	MQS	OLS	Product
Chick	1988	3	16	2	32
McLatchie	1988	3	6	−1	−6
Mindlin	1965	3	6	−1	−6
Braunstein	1983	4	10	−1	−10
Powell	1985	3	11	−1	−11
Annis	1992	3	12	−1	−12
Ogborne	1979	4	6	−2	−12
Pittman	1972	4	12	−1	−12
Caddy	1984	3	13	−1	−13
Fitzgerald	1985	4	14	−1	−14
Gallant	1968	4	9	−2	−18
Ditman	1967	3	12	−2	−24
Oei	1982	4	12	−2	−24
Baldwin	1991	2	13	−2	−26
Chapman	1988	4	14	−2	−28
Edwards	1977	3	15	−2	−30
CES = −214					

EDUCATIONAL LECTURES/FILMS

Author	Year	Severity	MQS	OLS	Product
Malfetti	1975	2	9	2	18
McGuire	1978	2	7	2	14
Salzberg	1983	2	7	1	7
Mindlin	1965	3	6	−1	−6
Rosenberg	1979	4	9	−1	−9
Swenson	1980	2	9	−1	−9
Swenson	1981	2	9	−1	−9
Cooper	1988	1	10	−1	−10
Scoles	1977	2	5	−2	−10
Carpenter	1985	2	11	−1	−11
Connors	1986	2	12	−1	−12
Hagen	1978	2	6	−2	−12

(continued)

Table 2.14   (continued)

| EDUCATIONAL LECTURES/FILMS (continued) | | | | | |
Author	Year	Severity	MQS	OLS	Product
West	1979	4	12	−1	−12
Baker	1975	4	14	−1	−14
Cooper	1988	1	10	−2	−20
Heather	1986	3	10	−2	−20
Kivlahan	1990	1	10	−2	−20
Wells–Parker	1988	2	12	−2	−24
Sisson	1986	1	12	−2	−24
Heather	1990	3	13	−2	−26
Brown	1980	2	15	−2	−30
CES= −239					

| ALCOHOLICS ANONYMOUS | | | | | |
Author	Year	Severity	MQS	OLS	Product
Ditman	1967	3	12	−2	−24
Brandsma	1980	4	14	−2	−28
CES = −52					

model" suggests a similar rationale for drop-in centers. Consistent with the conclusions of prior reviews (e.g., Annis, 1985; Miller & Hester, 1986b; U.S. Congress, 1983), studies comparing residential/milieu environments with alternative (e.g., outpatient) settings have reflected few differences. No controlled trial of a California social model program was found.

Studies have sometimes employed unspecified standard treatment or general alcoholism counseling as a treatment modality. Such studies have almost universally found no advantage over untreated or alternatively treated groups. Similarly, studies of *educational lectures and films* have typically found no beneficial effect with populations of problem drinkers.

Although *Alcoholics Anonymous (AA)* is widely recommended by U.S. treatment programs, its efficacy has rarely been studied (McCrady & Miller, 1993). Only two controlled trials were found in which AA was studied as a distinct alternative, both with offender populations required to attend AA or other conditions, and both finding no beneficial effect. Although these findings argue against mandating clients to AA, they shed no light on the efficacy of this approach when used as intended: as a voluntary process of affiliation (Miller & Kurtz, 1994). The larger literature on AA is considerably more complex (see Chapter 10 and Emrick et al., 1993), but has yielded no other controlled trials qualifying for this review (cf. McCrady & Miller, 1993).

Other Approaches

Table 2.15 illustrates the findings for four other less-used methods. Positive but isolated studies have been reported for acupuncture, exercise, and sensory deprivation. The four studies to date on hypnosis as a treatment for alcohol problems, however, have all found no effect on drinking behavior.

DISCUSSION

Like an earlier review of cost effectiveness (Holder et al., 1991), this should be regarded a "first approximation" to summarizing the treatment outcome literature while taking into account the methodological quality of studies. Some would differ with the outcome logic system described in Table 2.1. Others would add to or substract from the methodological rating system in Table 2.2 or give different relative weights to its elements. Despite our six-step review process to minimize errors, it is likely that in any project of this size there are overlooked details, and surely judgment calls for specific studies on which reasonable colleagues would disagree. The outcome logic scores shown in modality tables were based primarily on significance tests reported in the individual articles, which in turn are influenced by variable factors such as the number of tests run and the power to detect treatment effects. We have emphasized

Table 2.15   Studies of Other Approaches

ACUPUNCTURE Author	Year	Severity	MQS	OLS	Product
Bullock **CES = +20**	1987	4	10	2	20

EXERCISE Author	Year	Severity	MQS	OLS	Product
Murphy	1986	1	10	2	20
Levinson **CES = +9**	1969	4	11	–1	–11

HYPNOSIS Author	Year	Severity	MQS	OLS	Product
Edwards	1966	4	8	–1	–8
Wallerstein	1957	4	9	–1	–9
Jacobson	1973	3	11	–1	–11
Ludwig **CES = –41**	1969	4	13	–1	–13

SENSORY DEPRIVATION Author	Year	Severity	MQS	OLS	Product
Cooper	1978	1	10	2	20
Cooper **CES = +40**	1988	1	10	2	20

cumulative evidence, rather than the results of single studies, precisely in hopes that such variance is of less importance when the big picture is examined.

There are situations, however, in which the cumulation of evidence will compound rather than average out the effects of confounding variables. The modality termed "general alcoholism counseling," for example, was often a poorly defined basic treatment against which additive components were contrasted. To the extent that the effectiveness of treatment is promoted by adhering to a clearly defined strategy, well-articulated additive or alternative components are likely to fare well in comparison with "general" counseling.

Given such limitations inherent in a review of this kind, what conclusions seem warranted from the cumulative evidence of these 211 controlled trials? In an earlier review, Miller and Hester (1986a) observed that although the scientific literature points to a list of treatment approaches with reasonable evidence of positive benefit, this list overlaps little, if at all, with those components commonly employed in U.S. alcoholism treatment programs. The same pattern is clearly evident in this review. Indeed, one must read halfway down Table 2.4 before encountering the first modality (disulfiram) with anything like common usage as a component of standard practice, at least in the United States. Instead, a relatively predictable combination of elements has characterized the generic "Minnesota model" program that continues to dominate American addictions treatment: a milieu advocating a spiritual twelve-step (AA) philosophy, typically augmented with group psychotherapy, educational lectures and films, and relatively unspecified general alcoholism counseling, often of a confrontational nature (Cook, 1988).

Some programs have added components such as relaxation training, CENAPS-model relapse counseling, and family therapy (typically nonbehavioral in style). To fill in the complete set of treatment methods with the least evidence of effectiveness (Table 2.4), one need add only metronidazole, antianxiety medication, videotape self-confrontation, psychedelic medication, hypnosis, and electrical aversion therapy. The negative correlation between scientific evidence and application in standard practice remains striking, and could hardly be larger if one intentionally constructed treatment programs from those approaches with the *least* evidence of efficacy.

Such a gap between science and practice will not be reduced without some disciplined and demanding changes. Clinicians, like scientists, must be willing to test their cherished assumptions against hard data and to relinquish views and practices that do not stand up to the test of evidence. Consider the following commentary from a very different context in which the word *clinician* might be substituted for *scholar*:

> To be a critical *scholar means to make empirical, factual evidence—evidence open to confirmation by independent neutral observers—the controlling factor in [professional] judgments. Noncritical scholars are those who put dogmatic considerations first and insist that the factual evidence confirm [their] premises. Critical scholars adopt the principle of methodological skepticism: accept only what passes the rigorous tests of the rules of evidence (Funk, Hoover, & the Jesus Seminar, 1993, p. 34)*

This book is designed to provide clinicians with effective alternatives. Treatment modalities were selected for inclusion largely on the basis of positive studies supporting beneficial impact. There does not seem to be any one treatment approach adequate to the task of treating all individuals with alcohol problems. We believe that the best hope lies in assembling a menu of effective alternatives, and then seeking a system for finding the right combination of elements for each individual (Institute of Medicine, 1990). Such a menu might also include elements for which controlled trials are currently lacking, particularly if they are low in cost and show promise from other types of studies. Nevertheless, it is sensible to constitute treatment programs primarily from modalities with known scientific evidence of efficacy and to seek rational rather than convenience criteria for helping people find the most promising approach. In both research and practice, there is a long way to go in order to achieve such a flexible and person-oriented system of service delivery.

REFERENCES

Aharan, C. H., Ogilvie, R. D., & Partington, J. T. (1967). Clinical indications of motivation in alcoholic patients. *Quarterly Journal of Studies on Alcohol, 28,* 486–492.

Ahles, T. A., Schlundt, D. G., Prue, D. M., & Rychtarik, R. G. (1983). Impact of aftercare arrangements on the maintenance of treatment success in abusive drinkers. *Addictive Behaviors, 8,* 53–58.

Alden, L. (1978). Evaluation of a preventive self-management programme for problem drinkers. *Canadian Journal of Behavioural Science, 10,* 258–263.

Alden, L. E. (1988). Behavioral self-management controlled-drinking strategies in a context of secondary prevention. *Journal of Consulting and Clinical Psychology, 56,* 280–286.

Anderson, P., & Scott, E. (1992). The effect of general practitioners' advice to heavy drinking men. *British Journal of Addiction, 87,* 891–900.

Annis, H. M. (1985). Is inpatient rehabilitation of the alcoholic cost effective? Con position. *Advances in Alcohol and Substance Abuse, 5,* 175–190.

Annis, H. M., & Chan, D. (1983). The differential treatment model: Empirical evidence from a personality typology of adult offenders. *Criminal Justice and Behavior, 10,* 159–173.

Annis, H. M., & Davis, C. S. (1989). Relapse prevention. In R. K. Hester & W. R. Miller (Eds.), *Handbook of alcoholism treatment approaches: Effective alternatives* (pp. 170–182). New York: Pergamon Press.

Annis, H. M., & Liban, C. B. (1979). A follow-up study of male halfway-house residents and matched nonresident controls. *Journal of Studies on Alcohol, 40,* 63–69.

Annis, H. M., & Peachey, J. E. (1992). The use of calcium carbimide in relapse prevention counseling: Results of a randomized control trial. *British Journal of Addiction, 87,* 63–72.

Ashem, B., & Donner, L. (1968). Covert sensitization with alcoholics: A controlled replication. *Behavior Research and Therapy, 6,* 7–12.

Azrin, N. H. (1976). Improvements in the community-reinforcement approach to alcoholism. *Behaviour Research and Therapy, 14,* 339–348.

Azrin, N. H., Sisson, R. W., Meyers, R., & Godley, M. (1982). Alcoholism treatment by disulfiram and community reinforcement therapy. *Journal of Behavior Therapy and Experimental Psychiatry, 13,* 105–112.

Babor, T. F., & Grant, M. (1992). *Project on identification and management of alcohol-related problems. Report on phase II: A randomized clinical trial of brief interventions in primary health care.* Geneva, Switzerland: World Health Organization.

Baker, T. B., Udin, H., & Vogler, R. E. (1975). The effects of videotaped modeling and confrontation on the drinking behavior of alcoholics. *International Journal of the Addictions, 10,* 779–793.

Baldwin, S., Heather, N., Lawson, A., Robertson, I., Mooney, J., & Graggins, F. (1991). Comparison of effectiveness: Behavioral and talk-based alcohol education courses for court-referred young offenders. *Behavioural Psychotherapy, 19,* 157–172.

Bartholomew, A. A., & Guile, L. A. (1961). A controlled evaluation of "Librium" in the treatment of alcoholics. *The Medical Journal of Australia, 2,* 578–581.

Bien, T. H., Miller, W. R., & Boroughs, J. M. (1993). Motivational interviewing with alcohol outpatients. *Behavioural Psychotherapy, 21,* 347–356.

Bien, T. H., Miller, W. R., & Tonigan, J. S. (1993). Brief interventions for alcohol problems: A review. *Addiction, 88,* 315–336.

Bjørnevoll, K. J. (1972). *Alkoholikere i encountergruppe: Encountergruppe som tillegsbehandling for en gruppe pasienter ved Victoria A-sentrum, A-klinikken for Vestlandet.* Unpublished psychology thesis, University of Bergen.

Blake, B. G. (1967). A follow-up of alcoholics treated by behaviour therapy. *Behaviour Research and Theory, 5,* 89–94.

Boland, F. J., Mellor, C. S., & Revusky, S. (1978). Chemical aversion treatment of alcoholism: Lithium as the aversive agent. *Behavior Research and Therapy, 16,* 401–409.

Bowen, W. T., Soskin, R. A., & Chotlos, J. W. (1970). Lysergic acid diethylamide as a variable in the hospital treatment of alcoholism: A follow-up study. *Journal of Nervous and Mental Disease, 150,* 111–118.

Bowers, T. G., & Al-Redha, M. R. (1990). A comparison of outcome with group/marital and standard/individual therapies with alcoholics. *Journal of Studies on Alcohol, 51,* 301–309.

Brandsma, J. M., Maultsby, M. C., & Welsh, R. J. (1980). *The outpatient treatment of alcoholism: A review and comparative study.* Baltimore, MD: University Park Press.

Braunstein, W. B., Powell, B. J., McGowan, J. F., & Thoresen, R. W. (1983). Employment factors in outpatient recovery of alcoholics: A mutivariate study. *Addictive Behaviors, 8,* 345–351.

Brown, J. M., & Miller, W. R. (1993). Impact of motivational interviewing on participation and outcome in residential alcoholism treatment. *Addictive Behaviors, 7,* 211–218.

Brown, R. A. (1980). Conventional education and controlled drinking education courses with convicted drunken drivers. *Behavior Therapy, 11,* 632–642.

Bruun, K. (1963). Outcome of different types of treatment of alcoholics. *Quarterly Journal of Studies on Alcohol, 24,* 280–288.

Bullock, M. L., Umen, A. J., Culliton, P. D., & Olander, R. T. (1987). Acupuncture treatment of alcoholic recidivism: A pilot study. *Alcoholism: Clinical and Experimental Research, 11,* 292–295.

Caddy, G. R., Addington, H. J., & Trenschel, W. R. (1984). *A comparative evaluation of aftercare technologies in the management of alcohol dependence.* Unpublished manuscript.

Caddy, G. R., & Lovibond, S. H. (1976). Self-regulation and discriminated aversive conditioning in the modification of alcoholics' drinking behavior. *Behavior Therapy, 7,* 223–230.

Cadogan, D. A. (1973). Marital group therapy in the treatment of alcoholism. *Quarterly Journal of Studies on Alcohol, 34,* 1187–1194.

Cannon, D. S., & Baker, T. B. (1981). Emetic and electric shock alcohol aversion therapy: Assessment of conditioning. *Journal of Consulting and Clinical Psychology, 49,* 20–33.

Carpenter, R. A., Lyons, C. A., & Miller, W. R. (1985). Peer-managed self-control program for prevention of alcohol abuse in American Indian high school students: A pilot evaluation study. *International Journal of the Addictions, 20,* 299–310.

Chaney, E. R., O'Leary, M. R., & Marlatt, G. A. (1978). Skill training with alcoholics. *Journal of Consulting and Clinical Psychology, 46,* 1092–1104.

Chapman, P. L. H., & Huygens, I. (1988). An evaluation of three treatment programmes for alcoholism: An experimental study with 6-and 18-month follows-ups. *British Journal of Addiction, 83,* 67–81.

Charnoff, S. M., Kissin, B., & Reed, J. I. (1963). An evaluation of various psychotherapeutic agents in the long-term treatment of chronic alcoholism. *American Journal of Medical Sciences, 246,* 172–179.

Chick, J., Gough, K., Wojeciech, F., Kershaw, P., Hore, B., Mehta, B., Ritson, B., Ropner, R., & Torley, D. (1992). Disulfiram treatment of alcoholism. *British Journal of Psychiatry, 161,* 84–89.

Chick, J., Lloyd, G., & Crombie, E. (1985). Counselling problem drinkers in medical wards: A controlled study. *British Medical Journal, 290,* 965–967.

Chick, J., Ritson, B., Connaughton, J., Stewart, A., & Chick, J. (1988). Advice versus treatment for alcoholism: A controlled trial. *British Journal of Addiction, 83,* 159–170.

Clancy, J., Vanderhoof, E., & Campbell, P. (1967). Evaluation of an aversive technique as a treatment for alcoholism. *Quarterly Journal of Studies on Alcohol, 28,* 476–485.

Coghlan, G. R. (1979). *The investigation of behavioral self-control theory and techniques in a short-term treatment of male alcohol abusers.* Unpublished doctoral dissertation, State University of New York at Albany. (University Microfilms No. 7918818.)

Connors, G. J., Maisto, S. A., & Ersner-Hershfield, S. M. (1986). Behavioral treatment of drunk-driving recidivists: Short-term and long-term effects. *Behavioural Psychotherapy, 14,* 34–45.

Connors, G. J., Tarbox, A. R., & Faillace, L. A. (1992). Achieving and maintaining gains among problem drinkers: Process and outcome results. *Behavior Therapy, 23,* 449–474.

Cook, C. C. H. (1988). The Minnesota model in the management of drug and alcohol dependence: Miracle, method or myth? Part II. Evidence and conclusions. *British Journal of Addiction, 83,* 735–748.

Cooney, N. L., Kadden, R. M., Litt, M. D., & Gerter, H. (1991). Matching alcoholics to coping skills or interactional therapies: Two-year follow-up results. *Journal of Consulting and Clinical Psychology, 59,* 598–601.

Cooper, G. O., Adams, H. B., & Scott, J. C. (1988). Studies in REST: I. Reduced environmental stimulation therapy and reduced alcohol consumption. *Journal of Substance Abuse Treatment, 5,* 61–68.

Corder, B. F., Corder, R. F., & Laidlaw, N. D. (1972). An intensive treatment program for alcoholics and their wives. *Quarterly Journal of Studies on Alcohol, 33,* 1144–1146.

Dahlgren, L., & Willander, A. (1989). Are special treatment facilities for female alcoholics needed? A controlled 2-year follow-up study from a specialized female unit (EWA) versus a mixed male/female facility. *Alcoholism: Clinical and Experimental Research, 13*(4), 499–504.

Daniels, V., Somers, M., & Orford, J. (1992). How can risk drinking amongst medical patients be modified? The effects of computer screening and advice and a self-help manual. *Behavioural Psychotherapy, 20,* 47–60.

Ditman, K. S., Crawford, G. G., Forgy, E. W., Moskowitz, H., & MacAndrew, C. (1967). A controlled experiment on the use of court probation for drunk arrests. *American Journal of Psychiatry, 124,* 160–163.

Dorus, W., Ostrow, D. G., Anton, R., Cushman, P., Collins, J. F., Schaefer, M., Charles, H. L., Desai, P., Hayashida, M., Malkerneker, U., Wallenbraing, M., & Sather, M. R. (1989). Lithium carbonate treatment of depressed and nondepressed alcoholics in a double blind, placebo controlled study. *Journal of the American Medical Association, 262,* 1646–1652.

Drummond, D. C., Thom, B., Brown, C., Edwards, G., & Mullan, M. J. (1990). Specialist versus general practitioner treatment of problem drinkers. *The Lancet, 336,* 915–918.

Edwards, G. (1966). Hypnosis in treatment of alcohol addiction. *Quarterly Journal of Studies on Alcohol, 27,* 221–241.

Edwards, G., & Guthrie, S. (1967). A controlled trial of inpatient and outpatient treatment of alcohol dependency. *Lancet, 1,* 555–559.

Edwards, G., Orford, J., Egert, S., Guthrie, S., Hawker, A., Hensman, C., Mitcheson, M., Oppenheimer, E., & Taylor, C. (1977). Alcoholism: A controlled trial of "treatment" and "advice." *Journal of Studies on Alcohol, 38,* 1004–1031.

Egan, W. P., & Goetz, R. (1968). Effect of metronidazole on drinking by alcoholics. *Quarterly Journal of Studies on Alcohol, 29,* 899–902.

Elvy, G. A., Wells, J. E., & Baird, K. A. (1988). Attempted referral as intervention for problem drinking in the general hospital. *British Journal of Addiction, 83,* 83–89.

Emrick, C. D., Tonigan, J. S., Montgomery, H., & Little, L. (1993). Alcoholics Anonymous: What is currently known? In B. S. McCrady & W. R. Miller (Eds.), *Research on Alcoholics Anonymous: Opportunities and alternatives* (pp. 41–76). New Brunswick, NJ: Rutgers Center of Alcohol Studies.

Ends, E. J., & Page, C. W. (1957). A study of three types of group psychotherapy with hospitalized inebriates. *Quarterly Journal of Studies on Alcohol, 18,* 263–277.

Eriksen, L. (1986). The effect of waiting for inpatient treatment after detoxification: An experimental comparison between inpatient treatment and advice only. *Addictive Behaviors, 11,* 389–398.

Eriksen, L., Björnstad, S., & Götestam, K. G. (1986). Social skills training in groups for alcoholics: One-year treatment outcome for groups and individuals. *Addictive Behaviors, 11,* 309–330.

Faia, C., & Shean, G. (1976). Using videotapes and group discussion in the treatment of male chronic alcoholics. *Hospital and Community Psychiatry, 27,* 847–851.

Fawcett, J., Clark, D. C., Aagesen, C. A., Pisani, V. D., Tilkin, J. M., Sellers, D., McGuire, M., & Gibbons, R. D. (1987). A double-blind, placebo-controlled trial of lithium carbonate therapy for alcoholism. *Archives of General Psychiatry, 44,* 248–256.

Ferrell, W. L., & Galassi, J. P. (1981). Assertion training and human relations training in the treatment of chronic alcoholics. *International Journal of the Addictions, 16,* 959–968.

Fitzgerald, J. L., & Mulford, H. A. (1985). An experimental test of telephone aftercare contacts with alcoholics. *Journal of Studies on Alcohol, 46,* 418–424.

Fleiger, D. L., & Zingle, H. W. (1973). Covert sensitization treatment with alcoholics. *Canadian Counselor, 7,* 269–277.

Foy, D. W., Nunn, B. L., & Rychtarik, R. G. (1984). Broad-spectrum behavioral treatment for chronic alcoholics: Effects of training controlled drinking skills. *Journal of Consulting and Clinical Psychology, 52,* 213–230.

Freedberg, E. J., & Johnston, W. E. (1978a). *The effects of relaxation training within the context of a multi-modal alcoholism treatment program for employed alcoholics.* Substudy No. 988 (a). Toronto: Addiction Research Foundation.

Freedberg, E. J., & Johnston, W. E. (1978b). *The effects of assertion training within the context of a multi-modal alcoholism treatment program for employed alcoholics.* Substudy No. 796. Toronto: Addiction Research Foundation, Substudy.

Fuller, R. K., Branchey, L., Brightwell, D. R., Derman, R. M., Emrick, C. D., Iber, F. L., James, K. E., Lacoursiere, R. B., Lee, K. K., Lowenstam, I., Maany, I., Neiderheiser, D., Nocks, J. J., & Shaw, S. (1986). Disulfiram treatment of alcoholism: A Veterans Administration cooperative study. *Journal of the American Medical Association, 256,* 1449–1455.

Fuller, R. K., & Roth, H. P. (1979). Disulfiram for the treatment of alcoholism: An evaluation in 128 men. *Annals of Internal Medicine, 90,* 901–904.

Funk, R. W., Hoover, R. W., & the Jesus Seminar. (1993). *The five gospels: The search for the authentic words of Jesus.* New York: Macmillan.

Gallant, D. M., Bishop, M. P., Camp, E., & Tisdale, C. (1968). A six-month controlled evaluation of metronidazole (Flagyl) in chronic alcoholic patients. *Current Therapeutic Research, 10,* 82–87.

Gallant, D. M., Bishop, M. P., Faulkner, M. A., Simpson, L., Cooper, A., Lathrop, D., Brisolara, A. M., & Bossetta, J. R. (1968). A comparative evaluation of compulsory (group therapy and/or Antabuse) and voluntary treatment of the chronic alcoholic municipal court offender. *Psychosomatics, 9,* 306–310.

Gerrein, J. R., Rosenberg, C. M., & Manohar, V. (1973). Disulfiram maintenance in outpatient treatment of alcoholism. *Archives of General Psychiatry, 28,* 798–802.

Gilbert, F. S. (1988). The effect of type of aftercare follow-up on treatment outcome among alcoholics. *Journal of Studies on Alcohol, 49,* 149–159.

Glover, J. H., & McCue, P. A. (1977). Electrical aversion therapy with alcoholics: A comparative follow-up study. *British Journal of Psychiatry, 130,* 279–286.

Graber, R. A., & Miller, W. R. (1988). Abstinence or controlled drinking goals for problem drinkers: A randomized clinical trial. *Psychology of Addictive Behaviors, 2,* 20–33.

Guydish, J. R. (1987). *Self control bibliotherapy as a secondary prevention strategy with heavy-drinking college students.* Unpublished doctoral dissertation, Washington State University.

Hagen, R. E., Williams, R. L., McConnell, E. J., & Fleming, C. W. (1978). *An evaluation of alcohol abuse treatment as an alternative to drivers license suspension or revocation.* Final report to the legislature of the state of California. Sacramento: Health & Welfare Agency, Department of Alcohol & Drug Abuse, Report No. CAL-DMV-RSS-7868.

Harris, K. B., & Miller, W. R. (1990). Behavioral self-control training for problem drinkers: Components of efficacy. *Psychology of Addictive Behaviors, 4*, 82–90.

Hayashida, M., Alterman, A. I., McLellan, A. T., O'Brien, C. P., Purtill, J. J., Volpicelli, J. R., Raphaelson, A. H., & Hall, C. P. (1989). Comparative effectiveness and costs of inpatient and outpatient detoxification of patients with mild-to-moderate alcohol withdrawal syndrome. *New England Journal of Medicine, 320*, 358–365.

Heather, N., Campion, P. D., Neville, R. G., & Maccabe, D. (1987). Evaluation of a controlled drinking minimal intervention for problem drinkers in general practice (the DRAMS scheme). *Journal of the Royal College of General Practitioners, 37*, 358–363.

Heather, N., Kissoon-Singh, J., & Fenton, G. W. (1990). Assisted natural recovery from alcohol problems: Effects of a self-help manual with and without supplementary telephone contact. *British Journal of Addiction, 85*, 1177–1185.

Heather, N., Whitton, B., & Robertson, I. (1986). Evaluation of a self-help manual for media-recruited problem drinkers: Six month follow-up results. *British Journal of Clinical Psychology, 25*, 19–34.

Hedberg, A. G., & Campbell, L. M. (1974). A comparison of four behavioral treatment approaches to alcoholism. *Journal of Behavior Therapy and Experimental Psychiatry, 5*, 251–256.

Hoff, E. C. (1961). The use of pharmacological adjuncts in the psychotherapy of alcoholics. *Quarterly Journal of Studies on Alcohol, 1*, 138–150.

Hoff, E. C., & McKeown, C. E. (1953). An evaluation of the use of tetraethylthiuram disulfide in the treatment of 560 cases of alcohol addiction. *American Journal of Psychiatry, 109*, 670–673.

Holder, H., Longabaugh, R., Miller, W. R., & Rubonis, A. V. (1991). The cost-effectiveness of treatment for alcoholism: A first approximation. *Journal of Studies on Alcohol, 52*, 517–540.

Hollister, L. E., Shelton, J., & Krieger, G. (1969). A controlled comparison of lysergic acid diethylamide (LSD) and dextroamphetamine in alcoholics. *American Journal of Psychiatry, 125*, 1352–1357.

Howard, M. O. (1993). Assessing the comparative cost-effectiveness of alcoholism treatments: A comment on Holder, Longabaugh, Miller and Rubonis. *Journal of Studies on Alcohol, 54*, 667–675.

Hunt, G. M., & Azrin, N. H. (1973). A community-reinforcement approach to alcoholism. *Behaviour Research and Therapy, 11*, 91–104.

Hussain, M. Z., & Harinath, M. (1972). Helping alcoholics abstain: An implantable substance. *American Journal of Psychiatry, 129*, 363.

Institute of Medicine, National Academy of Sciences. (1990). *Broadening the base of treatment for alcohol problems.* Washington, DC: National Academy Press.

Ito, J. R., Donovan, D. M., & Hall, J. J. (1988) . Relapse prevention in alcohol aftercare: Effects on drinking outcome, change process, and aftercare attendance. *British Journal of Addiction, 83*, 171–181.

Jackson, P., & Oei, T. P. S. (1978). Social skills training and cognitive restructuring with alcoholic. *Drug and Alcohol Dependence, 3*, 369–374.

Jackson, T. R., & Smith, J. W. (1978). A comparison of two aversion treatment methods for alcoholism. *Journal of Studies on Alcohol, 39*, 187–191.

Jacobson, N. O., & Silfverskiold, N. P. (1973). A controlled study of a hypnotic method in the treatment of alcoholism with evaluation by objective criteria. *British Journal of Addiction, 68*, 25–31.

Jensen, S. E., & Ramsay, R. (1963). Treatment of chronic alcoholism with lysergic acid diethylamide. *Canadian Psychiatric Association Journal, 8*, 182–188.

Johnsen, J., & Mørland, J. (1991). Disulfiram implant: A double-blind placebo controlled follow-up on treatment outcome. *Alcoholism: Clinical and Experimental Research, 15*, 532–536.

Johnsen, J., Stowell, A., Bache-Wiig, J. E., Stensrud, T., Ripel, A., & Mørland, J. (1987). A double-blind placebo controlled study of male alcoholics given a subcutaneous disulfiram implantation. *British Journal of Addiction, 82*, 607–613.

Johnson, F. G. (1970). A comparison of short-term treatment effects of intravenous sodium amytal-methedrine and LSD in the alcoholic. *Canadian Psychiatric Association Journal, 15*, 493–497.

Jones, S. L., Kanfer, R., & Lanyon, R. I. (1982). Skill training with alcoholics: A clinical extension. *Addictive Behaviors, 7*, 285–290.

Keane, T. M., Foy, D. W., Nunn, B., & Rychtarik, R. G. (1984). Spouse contracting to increase antabuse compliance in alcoholic veterans. *Journal of Clinical Psychology, 40*, 340–344.

Keso, L., & Salaspuro, M. 1990. Inpatient treatment of employed alcoholics: A randomized clinical trial on Hazelden-type and traditional treatment. *Alcoholism: Clinical and Experimental Research, 14*, 584–589.

Kissin, B., & Gross, M. M. (1968). Drug therapy in alcoholism. *American Journal of Psychiatry, 125*, 31–41.

Kivlahan, D. R., Marlatt, G. A., Fromme, K., Coppel, D. B., & Williams, E. (1990). Secondary prevention with college drinkers: Evaluation of an alcohol skills training program. *Journal of Consulting and Clinical Psychology, 58*, 805–810.

Kline, N. S., Wren, J. C., Cooper, T. B., Varga, E., & Canal, O. (1974). Evaluation of lithium therapy in chronic and periodic alcoholism. *American Journal of Medical Science, 268*, 15–22.

Krasner, N., Moore, M. R., Goldberg, A., Booth, J. C. D., Frame, A. H., & McLaren, A. D. (1976). *British Journal of Psychiatry, 128*, 346–353.

Kristenson, H., Öhlin, H., Hultén-Nosslin, M. B., Trell, E., & Hood, B. (1983). Identification and intervention of heavy drinking in middle-aged men: Results and follow-up of 24–60 months of long-term study with randomized controls. *Alcoholism: Clinical and Experimental Research, 7*, 203–209.

Kuchipudi, V., Hobein, K., Flickinger, A., & Iber, F. L. (1988). Failure of a 2-hour motivational intervention to alter recurrent drinking behavior in alcoholics with gastrointestinal disease. *Journal of Studies on Alcohol, 51*, 356–360.

Lal, S. (1969). Metronidazole in the treatment of alcoholism: A clinical trial and review of the literature. *Quarterly Journal of Studies on Alcohol, 30,* 140–151.

Lanyon, R. I., Primo, R. V., Terrell, F., & Wener, A. (1972). An aversion-desensitization treatment for alcoholism. *Journal of Consulting and Clinical Psychology, 38,* 394–398.

Laverty, S. G. (1966). Aversion therapies in the treatment of alcoholism. *Psychosomatic Medicine, 28,* 651–666.

Levinson, T., & Sereny, G. (1969). An experimental evaluation of "insight therapy" for the chronic alcoholic. *Canadian Psychiatric Association Journal, 14,* 143–146.

Levy, M. S., Livingstone, B. L., & Collins, D. M. (1967). A clinical comparison of disulfiram and calcium carbimide. *American Journal of Psychiatry, 123,* 1018–1022.

Ling, W., Weiss, D. G., Charuvastra, V. C., O'Brien, C. P., Blakis, M., Wang, R., Savage, C., Roszell, D., Way, E. L., & McIntyre, J. (1983). Use of disulfiram for alcoholics in methadone maintenance programs: A Veterans Administration cooperative study. *Archives of General Psychiatry, 40,* 851–861.

Linton, P. H., & Hain, J. D. (1967). Metronidazole in the treatment of alcoholism. *Quarterly Journal of Studies on Alcohol, 28,* 544–546.

Longabaugh, R., McCrady, B., Fink, E., Stout, R., McAuley, T., Doyle, C., & McNeill, D. (1983). Cost-effectiveness of alcoholism treatment in partial vs. inpatient settings: Six-month outcomes. *Journal of Studies on Alcohol, 44,* 1049–1071.

Lovibond, S. H. (1975). Use of behavior modification in the reduction of alcohol-related road accidents. In K. G. Gîtestam, G. L. Melin, & W. S. Dockens (Eds.), *Applications of behavior modification* (pp. 399–406). New York: Academic Press.

Lowenstam, I. (1969). Metronidazole and placebo in the treatment of chronic alcoholism: A comparative study. *Psychosomatics, 10*(3, Sect. II), 43–45.

Ludwig, A., Levine, J., Stark, L., & Lazar, R. (1969). A clinical study of LSD treatment in alcoholism. *American Journal of Psychiatry, 126,* 59–69.

Lysloff, G. O. (1972). Anti-addictive chemotherapy— Metronidazole and alcohol aversion. *British Journal of Addiction, 67,* 239–244.

Maheswaran, R., Beevers, M., & Beevers, D. G. (1992). Effectiveness of advice to reduce alcohol consumption in hypertensive patients. *Hypertension, 19,* 79–84.

Maisto, S. A., Sobell, L. C., Sobell, M. B., & Sanders, B. (1985). Effects of outpatient treatment for problem drinkers. *American Journal of Drug and Alcohol Abuse, 11,* 131–149.

Maletzky, B. M. (1974). Assisted covert sensitization for drug abuse. *International Journal of Addiction, 9,* 411–429.

Malfetti, J. L. (1975). Reeducation and rehabilitation of the drunken driver. *Journal of Drug Issues, 5,* 255–269.

Mallams, J. H., Godley, M. D., Hall, G. M., & Meyers, R. J. (1982). A social-systems approach to resocializing alcoholics in the community. *Journal of Studies on Alcohol, 43,* 1115–1123.

Marlatt, G. A. (1973). *A comparison of aversive conditioning procedures in the treatment of alcoholism.* Paper presented at the annual meeting of the Western Psychological Association, Anaheim, CA.

Marlatt, G. A., & Gordon, J. R. (1985). *Relapse prevention.* New York: Guilford Press.

Marlatt, G. A., & Marques, J. K. (1977). Meditation, self-control and alcohol use. In R. B. Stuart (Ed.), *Behavioral self-management: Strategies, techniques and outcome* (pp. 117–153). New York: Brunner/Mazel.

McCance, C., & McCance, P. F. (1969). Alcoholism in North-East Scotland: Its treatment and outcome. *British Journal of Psychiatry, 115,* 189–198.

McCrady, B. S., & Miller, W. R. (Eds.). (1993). *Research on Alcoholics Anonymous: Opportunities and alternatives.* New Brunswick, NJ: Rutgers Center of Alohol Studies.

McCrady, B. S., Noel, N. E., Abrams, D. H., Stout, R. L., Nelson, H. F., & Hay, W. M. (1986). Comparative effectiveness of three types of spouse involvement in outpatient behavioral alcoholism treatment. *Journal of Studies on Alcohol, 47,* 459–467.

McCrady, B. S., Paolino, T. J. Jr., Longabaugh, R., & Rossi, J. (1979). Effects of joint hospital admission and couples treatment for hospitalized alcoholics: A pilot study. *Addictive Behaviors, 4,* 155–165.

McGuire, F. L. (1978). The effectiveness of a treatment program for alcohol-involved drivers in America. *American Journal of Drug and Alcohol Abuse, 5,* 517–525.

McLachlan, J. F. C., & Stein, R. L. (1982). Evaluation of a day clinic for alcoholics. *Journal of Studies on Alcohol, 43,* 261–272.

McLatchie, B. H., & Lomp, K. G. E. (1988). An experimental investigation of the influence of aftercare on alcoholic relapse. *British Journal of Addiction, 83,* 1045–1054.

Merry, J., Reynolds, C. M., Bailey, J., & Coppen, A. (1976). Prophylactic treatment of alcoholism by lithium carbonate: A controlled study. *Lancet, 2,* 481–482.

Merry, J., & Whitehead, A. (1968). Metronidazole and alcoholism. *British Journal of Psychiatry, 114,* 859–861.

Miller, P. M. (1975). A behavioral intervention program for chronic public drunkeness offenders. *Archives of General Psychiatry, 32,* 915–918.

Miller, P. M., Hersen, M., Eisler, R. M., & Hemphill, D. P. (1973). Electrical aversion therapy with alcoholics: An analogue study. *Behaviour Research and Therapy, 11,* 491–497.

Miller, W. R. (1978). Behavioral treatment of problem drinkers: A comparative outcome study of three controlled drinking therapies. *Journal of Consulting and Clinical Psychology, 46,* 74–86.

Miller, W. R. (1988, May). *The effectiveness of treatment for alcohol problems: Reasons for optimism.* Invited address to the Royal Society of Medicine, London.

Miller, W. R., Benefield, R. G., & Tonigan, J. S. (1993). Enhancing motivation for change in problem drinking: A controlled comparison of two therapist styles. *Journal of Consulting and Clinical Psychology, 61,* 455–461.

Miller, W. R., & Dougher, M. J. (1989). Covert sensitization: Alternative treatment approaches for alcoholics. *Behavioural Psychotherapy, 17,* 203–220.

Miller, W. R., Gribskov, C. J., & Mortell, R. L. (1981). Effectiveness of a self-control manual for problem drinkers with and without therapist contact. *International Journal of the Addictions, 16,* 1247–1254.

Miller, W. R., & Hester, R. K. (1980). Treating problem drinkers: Modern approaches. In W. R. Miller (Ed.), *The addictive behaviors: Treatment of alcoholism, drug abuse, smoking and obesity* (pp. 11–141). Oxford: Pergamon Press.

Miller, W. R., & Hester, R. K. (1986a). The effectiveness of alcoholism treatment methods: What research reveals. In W. R. Miller & N. Heather (Eds.), *Treating addictive behaviors: Processes of change* (pp. 121–174). New York: Plenum Press.

Miller, W. R., & Hester, R. K. (1986b). Inpatient alcoholism treatment: Who benefits? *American Psychologist, 41,* 794–805.

Miller, W. R., & Hester, R. K. (1986c). Matching problem drinkers with optimal treatments. In W. R. Miller & N. Heather (Eds.), *Treating addictive behaviors: Processes of change* (pp. 175–203). New York: Plenum Press.

Miller, W. R., & Hester, R. K. (1989). Inpatient alcoholism treatment: Rules of evidence and burden of proof. *American Psychologist, 44,* 1245–1246.

Miller, W. R., & Kurtz, E. (1994). Models of alcoholism used in treatment: Contrasting A.A. and other perspectives with which it is often confused. *Journal of Studies on Alcohol, 55,* 159–166.

Miller, W. R., & Rollnick, S. (1991). *Motivational interviewing: Preparing people to change addictive behavior.* New York: Guilford Press.

Miller, W. R. & Sovereign, R. G. (1989). The check-up: A model for early intervention in addictive behaviors. In T. Løberg, W. R. Miller, P. E. Nathan & G. A. Marlatt (Eds.), *Addictive behaviors: Prevention and early intervention* (pp. 219–231). Amsterdam: Swets & Zeitlinger.

Miller, W. R., Sovereign, R. G., & Krege, B. (1988). Motivational interviewing with problem drinkers: II. The drinker's check-up as a preventive intervention. *Behavioural Psychotherapy, 16,* 251–268.

Miller, W. R., & Taylor, C. A. (1980). Relative effectiveness of bibliotherapy, individual and group self-control training in the treatment of problem drinkers. *Addictive Behaviors, 5,* 13–24.

Miller, W. R., Taylor, C. A., & West, J. C. (1980). Focused versus broad-spectrum behavior therapy for problem drinkers. *Journal of Consulting and Clinical Psychology, 48,* 590–601.

Mindlin, D. F. (1965). Group therapy for alcoholics: A study of the attitude and behavior changes in relation to perceived group norms. *Dissertation Abstracts, 26,* 2323–2324.

Monti, P. M., Abrams, D. B., Binkoff, J. A., Zwick, W. R., Liepman, M. R., Nirenberg, T. D., & Rohsenow, D. J. (1990). Communication skills training, communication skills training with family and cognitive behavioral mood management training for alcoholics. *Journal of Studies on Alcohol, 51,* 263–270.

Mooney, H. B., Ditman, K. S., & Cohen, S. (1961). Chlordiazepoxide in the treatment of alcoholics. *Diseases of the Nervous System, 22* (supplement), 44–51.

Mosher, V., Davis, J., Mulligan, D., & Iber, F. L. (1975). Comparison of outcome in a 9-day and 30-day alcoholism treatment program. *Journal of Studies on Alcohol, 36,* 1277–1281.

Murphy, T. J., Pagano, R. R., & Marlatt, G. A. (1986). Lifestyle modification with heavy alcohol drinkers: Effects of aerobic exercise and meditation. *Addictive Behaviors, 11,* 175–186.

Obolensky, M. R. (1984). *Recidivism among male DWI first offenders and intervention.* Unpublished doctoral dissertation, University of Rhode Island.

Oei, T. P. S., & Jackson, P. R. (1980). Long-term effects of group and individual social skills training with alcoholics. *Addictive Behaviors, 5,* 129–136.

Oei, T. P. S., & Jackson, P. R. (1982). Social skills and cognitive behavioral approaches to the treatment of problem drinking. *Journal of Studies on Alcohol, 43,* 532–547.

Oei, T. P. S., & Jackson, P. R. (1984). Some effective therapeutic factors in group cognitive-behavioral therapy with problem drinkers. *Journal of Studies on Alcohol, 45,* 119–123.

O'Farrell, T. J., Choquette, K. A., Cutter, H. S. G., Brown, E. D., & McCourt, W. F. (1993). Behavioral marital therapy with and without additional relapse prevention sessions for alcoholics and their wives. *Journal of Studies on Alcohol, 54,* 652–666.

O'Farrell, T. J., Cutter, H. S. G., & Floyd, F. J. (1985). Evaluating behavioral marital therapy for male alcoholics: Effects on marital adjustment and communication before to after treatment. *Behavior Therapy, 15,* 147–168.

Ogborne, A. C., & Wilmot, R. (1979). Evaluation of an experimental counseling service for male Skid Row alcoholics. *Journal of Studies on Alcohol, 40,* 129–132.

Olson, R. P., Ganley, R., Devine, V. T., & Dorsey, G. C., Jr. (1981). Long-term effects of behavioral verses insight-oriented therapy with inpatient alcoholics. *Journal of Consulting and Clinical Psychology, 49,* 866–877.

O'Malley, S. S., Jaffe, A. J., Chang, G., Schottenfeld, R. S., Meyer, R. E., & Rounsaville, B. (1992). Naltrexone and coping skills therapy for alcohol dependence. *Archives of General Psychiatry, 49,* 881–887.

Penick, S. B., Carrier, R. N., & Sheldon, J. B. (1969). Metronidazole in the treatment of alcoholism. *American Journal of Psychiatry, 125,* 1063–1066.

Persson, J., & Magnusson, P. H. (1989). Early intervention in patients with excessive consumption of alcohol: A controlled study. *Alcohol, 6,* 403–408.

Pittman, D. J., & Tate, R. L. (1972). A comparison of two treatment programs for alcoholics. *International Journal of Social Psychiatry, 18,* 183–193.

Platz, A., Panepinto, W. C., Kissin, B., & Charnoff, S. M. (1970). Metronidazole and alcoholism: An evaluation of specific and non specific factors in drug treatment. *Diseases of the Nervous System, 31,* 631–636.

Pomerleau, O., Pertschuk, M., Adkins, D., & d'Aquili, E. (1978). A comparison of behavioral and traditional treatment for middle income problem drinkers. *Journal of Behavioral Medicine, 1,* 187–200.

Pond, S. M., Becker, C. E., Vandervoort, R., Phillips, M., Bowler, R., & Peck, C. C. (1981). An evaluation of the effects of lithium in the treatment of chronic alcoholism I. Clinical results. *Alcoholism: Clinical and Experimental Research, 5,* 247–254.

Powell, B. J., Penick, E. C., Liskow, B. I., Rice, A. S., & McKnelly, W. (1986). Lithium compliance in alcoholic males: A six-month followup study. *Addictive Behaviors, 11,* 135–140.

Powell, B. J., Penick, E. C., Read, M. R., & Ludwig, A. M. (1985). Comparison of three outpatient treatment interventions: A twelve-month follow-up of men alcoholics. *Journal of Studies on Alcohol, 46,* 309–312.

Regester, D. C. (1971). Changes in autonomic responsivity and drinking behavior of alcoholics as a function of aversion therapy. *Dissertation Abstracts International, 32,* 1225-B.

Reinert, R. E. (1958). A comparison of reserpine and disulfiram in the treatment of alcoholism. *Quarterly Journal of Studies on Alcohol, 19,* 617–622.

Rhead, J. C., Soskin, R. A., Turek, I., Richards, W. A., Yensen, R., Kurland, A. A., & Ota, K. Y. (1977). Psychedelic drug (DPT)-assisted psychotheapy with alcoholics: A controlled study. *Journal of Psychedelic Drugs, 9,* 287–300.

Richard, G. P. (1983). *Behavioural treatment of excessive drinking.* Unpublished doctoral dissertation, University of New South Wales.

Robertson, I., Heather, N., Dzialdowski, A., Crawford, J., & Winton, M. (1986). A comparison of minimal versus intensive controlled drinking treatment for problem drinkers. *British Journal of Clinical Psychology, 25,* 185–194.

Rogers, C. R. (1951). *Client-centered therapy: Its practice, implications and theory.* Boston: Houghton Mifflin.

Rohsenow, D. J., Monti, P. M., Binkoff, J. A., Liepman, M. R., Nirenberg, T. D., & Abrams, D. B. (1991). Patient-treatment matching for alcoholic men in communication versus cognitive-behavioral mood management training. *Addictive Behaviors, 16,* 63–69.

Rohsenow, D. J., Smith, R. E., & Johnson, S. (1985). Stress management training as a prevention program for heavy social drinkers: Cognitive, affect, drinking, and individual differences. *Addictive Behaviors, 10,* 45–54.

Romelsjö, A., Andersson, L., Barrner, H., Borg, S., Granstrand, C., Hultman, O., Hässler, A., Källqvist, A., Magnusson, P., Morgell, R., Nyman, K., Olofsson, A., Olsson, E., Rhedin, A., & Wikblad, O. (1989). A randomized study of secondary prevention of early stage problem drinkers in primary health care. *British Journal of Addiction, 84,* 1319–1327.

Rosenberg, C. M. (1974). Drug maintenance in the outpatient treatment of chronic alcoholism. *Archives of General Psychiatry, 30,* 373–377.

Rosenberg, H., & Brian, T. (1986). Cognitive-behavioral group therapy for multiple-DUI offenders. *Alcoholism Treatment Quarterly, 3*(2), 47–65.

Rosenberg, S. D. (1979). *Relaxation training and a differential assessment of alcoholism.* Unpublished dissertation. California School of Professional Psychology, San Diego. (University Microfilms No. 8004362).

Salzberg, P. M., & Klingberg, C. L. (1983). The effectiveness of deferred prosecution for driving while intoxicated. *Journal of Studies on Alcohol, 44,* 299–306.

Sanchez-Craig, M., Annis, H. M., Bornet, A. R., & MacDonald, K. R. (1984). Random assignment to abstinence and controlled drinking: Evaluation of a cognitive-behavioural program for problem drinkers. *Journal of Consulting and Clinical Psychology, 52,* 390–403.

Sanchez-Craig, M., Leigh, G., Spivak, K., & Lei, H. (1989). Superior outcome of females over males after brief treatment for the reduction of heavy drinking. *British Journal of Addiction, 84,* 395–404.

Sanchez-Craig, M, Spivak, K., & Davila, R. (1991). Superior outcome of females over males after brief treatment for the reduction of heavy drinking: Replication and report of therapist effects. *British Journal of Addiction, 86,* 867–876.

Sanchez-Craig, M., & Walker, K. (1982). Teaching coping skills to chronic alcoholics in a coeducational halfway house: I. Assessment of programme effects. *British Journal of Addiction, 77,* 35–50.

Sandahl, C., & Rönnberg, S. (1990). Brief group psychotherapy relapse prevention for alcohol dependent patients. *International Journal of Group Psychotherapy, 40,* 453–476.

Sannibale, C. (1988). The differential effect of a set of brief interventions on the functioning of a group of "early stage" problem drinkers. *Australian Drug and Alcohol Review, 7,* 147–155.

Schaefer, H. H. (1972). Twelve-month follow-up of behaviorally trained ex-alcoholic social drinkers. *Behavior Therapy, 3,* 286–289.

Schaefer, H. H., Sobell, M. B., & Mills, K. C. (1971). Some sobering data on the use of self-confrontation with alcoholics. *Behavior Therapy, 2,* 28–39.

Scoles, P., & Fine, E. W. (1977). Short-term effects of an educational program for drinking drivers. *Journal of Studies on Alcohol, 38,* 633–637.

Scott, E., & Anderson, P. (1990). Randomized controlled trial of general practitioner intervention in women with excessive alcohol consumption. *Drug and Alcohol Review, 10,* 313–321.

Shaffer, J. W., Freinek, W. R., Wolf, S., Foxwell, N. H., & Kurland, A. A. (1963). A controlled evaluation of chlordiazepoxide (Librium) in the treatment of alcoholics. *Journal of Nervous and Mental Disease, 137,* 494–507.

Shaffer, J. W., Freinek, W. R., Wolf, S., Foxwell, N. H., & Kurland, A. A. (1964). Replication of a study of nialamide in the treatment of convalescing alcoholics with emphasis on prediction of response. *Current Therapeutic Research, 6,* 521–531.

Sisson, R. W. (1981). *The effect of three relaxation procedures on tension reduction and subsequent drinking of inpatient alcoholics.* Unpublished dissertation, Southern Illinois University at Carbondale, (University Microfilms No. 8122668).

Sisson, R. W., & Azrin, N. H. (1986). Family-member involvment to initiate and promote treatment of problem drinkers. *Journal of Behavior Therapy and Experimental Psychiatry, 17,* 15–21.

Skutle, A., & Berg, G. (1987). Training in controlled drinking for early-stage problem drinkers. *British Journal of Addiction, 82,* 493–501.

Smart, R. G., Storm, T., Baker, E. F. W., & Solursh, L. (1966). A controlled study of lysergide in the treatment of alcoholism: I. The effects on drinking behavior. *Quarterly Journal of Studies on Alcohol, 27,* 469–482.

Smith, J. W., Frawley, P. J., & Polissar, L. (1991). Six and twelve month abstinence rates in inpatient alcoholics treated with aversion therapy compared with matched inpatients from a treatment registry. *Alcoholism: Clinical and Experimental Research, 15,* 862–870.

Sobell, M. B., & Sobell, L. C. (1973). Individualized behavior therapy for alcoholics. *Behavior Therapy, 4,* 49–72.

Steffen, J. J. (1975). Electromyographically induced relaxation in the treatment of chronic alcohol abuse. *Journal of Consulting and Clinical Psychology, 43,* 275.

Stein, L. I., Newton, J. R., & Bowman, R. S. (1975). Duration of hospitalization for alcoholism. *Archives of General Psychiatry, 32,* 247–252.

Swenson, P. R., & Clay, T. R. (1980). Effects of short-term rehabilitation on alcohol consumption and drinking-related behaviours: An eight month follow-up study of drunken drivers. *International Journal of the Addictions, 15,* 821–838.

Swenson, P. R., Struckman-Johnson, D. L., Ellingstad, V. S., Clay, T. R., & Nichols, J. L. (1981). Results of a longitudinal evaluation of court-mandated DWI treatment programs in Phoenix, Arizona. *Journal of Studies on Alcohol, 42,* 642–653.

Swinson, R. P. (1971). Long term trial of metronidazole in male alcoholics. *British Journal of Psychiatry, 119,* 85–89.

Telch, M. J., Hannon, R., & Telch, C. F. (1984). A comparison of cessation strategies for the outpatient alcoholism. *Addictive Behaviors, 9,* 103–109.

Tomsovic, M., & Edwards, R. V. (1970). Lysergide treatment of schizophrenic and non-schizophrenic alcoholics: A controlled evaluation. *Quarterly Journal of Studies on Alcohol, 31,* 932–949.

Tyndel, M., Fraser, J. G., & Hartleib, C. J. (1969). Metronidazole as an adjuvant in the treatment of alcoholism. *British Journal of Addiction, 64,* 57–61.

U.S. Congress, Office of Technology Assessment. (1983). *The effectiveness and costs of alcoholism treatment.* Washington, DC: Author.

Valle, S. K. (1981). Interpersonal functioning of alcoholism counselors and treatment outcome. *Journal of Studies on Alcohol, 42,* 783–790.

Vogler, R. E., Compton, J. V., & Weissbach, T. A. (1975). Integrated behavior change techniques for alcoholics. *Journal of Consulting and Clinical Psychology, 43,* 233–243.

Vogler, R. E., Ferstl, R., Kraemer, S., & Brengelmann, J. C. (1975). Electrical aversive conditioning of alcoholics: One year follow-up. *Journal of Behavior Therapy and Experimental Psychiatry, 6,* 171–173.

Vogler, R. E., Lunde, S. E., Johnson, G. R., & Martin, P. L. (1970). Electrical aversion conditioning with chronic alcoholics. *Journal of Consulting and Clinical Psychology, 34,* 302–307.

Vogler, R. E., Weissbach, T. A., & Compton, J. V. (1977). Learning techniques for alcohol abuse. *Behaviour Research and Therapy, 15,* 31–38.

Volpicelli, J. S., Alterman, A. I., Hayashida, M., & O'Brien, C. P. (1992). Naltrexone in the treatment of alcohol dependence. *Archives of General Psychiatry, 49,* 876–880.

Wallace, P., Cutler, S., & Haines, A. (1988). Randomised controlled trial of general practitioner intervention in patients with excessive alcohol consumption. *British Medical Journal, 297,* 663–668.

Wallerstein, R. S., Chotlos, J. W., Friend, M. B., Hammersley, D. W., Perlswig, E. A., & Winship, G. M. (1957). *Hospital treatment of alcoholism: A comparative experimental study.* New York: Basic Books.

Walsh, D. C., Hingson, R. W., Merrigan, D. M., Morelock Levenson, S., Cupples, A., Heeren, T., Coffman, G. A., Becker, C. A., Barker, T. A., Hamilton, S. K., McGuire, T. G., & Kelly, C. A. (1991). A randomized trial of treatment options for alcohol-abusing workers. *The New England Journal of Medicine, 325,* 775–782.

Wanberg, K. W., Horn, J. L., & Fairchild, D. (1974). Hospital versus community treatment of alcoholism problems. *International Journal of Mental Health, 3,* 160–176.

Watson, C. G., Herder, J., & Passini, F. T. (1978). Alpha biofeedback in alcoholics: An 18 month follow-up. *Journal of Clinical Psychology, 34,* 765–769.

Wells-Parker, E., Anderson, B. J., Landrum, J. W., & Snow, R. W. (1988). Effectiveness of probation, short-term intervention and LAI administration for reducing DUI recidivism. *British Journal of Addiction, 83,* 415–422.

West, P. T. (1979). *Three modes of training alcoholics in interpersonal communications skills: A comparative study.* Unpublished doctoral dissertation, University of Western Ontario.

Whyte, C. R., & O'Brien, P. M. (1974). Disulfiram implant: A controlled trial. *British Journal of Psychiatry, 124,* 42–44.

Williams, H. S., & Webb, A. Y. (1991). *Outcome funding: A new approach to public sector grantmaking.* Rensselaerville, NY: The Rensselaerville Institute.

Wilson, A., Davidson, W. J., & Blanchard, R. (1980). Disulfiram implantation: A trial using placebo implants and two types of controls. *Journal of Studies on Alcohol, 41,* 429–436.

Wilson, A., Davidson, W. J., Blanchard, R., & White, J. (1978). Disulfiram implantation: A placebo-controlled trial with two-year follow-up. *Journal of Studies on Alcohol, 39,* 809–819.

Zimberg, S. (1974). Evaluation of alcoholism treatment in Harlem. *Quarterly Journal of Studies on Alcohol, 35,* 550–557.

Zweben, A., Pearlman, S., & Li, S. (1988). A comparison of brief advice and conjoint therapy in the treatment of alcohol abuse: The results of the marital systems study. *British Journal of Addiction, 83,* 899–916.

Appendix: Methodologic Quality Ratings of 219 Studies

AUTHOR	YEAR	% MALE	MEAN AGE	N	A	B	C	D	E	F	G	H	I	J	K	L	Σ
Aharan	1967	79.0	38.5	116	4	1	0	1	0	0	0	1	1	0	0	0	8
Ahles	1983	100.0	44.2	50	4	1	1	2	1	1	0	1	0	1	1	0	13
Alden	1978	52.0	39.0	36	4	1	2	0	1	1	0	1	0	0	1	0	11
Alden	1988	53.0	38.8	144	4	1	2	2	1	0	0	1	1	1	1	0	14
Anderson	1992	100.0	44.0	154	4	1	0	2	1	0	1	1	1	1	1	0	13
Annis	1979	100.0		70	2	0	2	0	0	0	1	1	1	0	1	0	8
Annis	1983	100.0	24.5	150	4	0	2	2	1	0	1	1	1	1	1	0	14
Annis	1992	81.0	43.5	56	4	1	0	2	1	0	1	1	0	1	1	0	12
Ashem	1968	100.0	37.0	27	4	1	1	1	0	1	0	1	1	0	1	0	11
Azrin	1976	100.0		18	4	1	2	1	1	1	0	1	1	1	1	0	14
Azrin	1982	83.0	33.9	43	4	1	2	1	1	1	1	1	1	0	1	0	14
Babor	1992	82.0	37.0	1490	4	1	1	1	1	0	1	1	1	1	1	1	14
Baker	1975	100.0	40.5	40	4	1	2	1	1	1	0	1	1	1	1	0	14
Baldwin	1991	100.0	20.0	78	4	1	0	1	1	1	1	1	1	1	1	0	13
Bartholomew	1961	85.0	43.2	40	2	1	1	0	0	0	0	1	1	0	0	0	6
Bien	1993	94.0	44.5	32	4	1	1	1	1	1	0	1	1	1	1	0	13
Bjørnevoll	1972	88.0	40.9	35	4	1	2	1	1	0	0	1	0	0	1	0	11
Blake	1967	76.0		62	1	0	2	2	0	1	0	1	1	0	1	0	9
Boland	1978	100.0	37.5	50	2	0	2	1	1	1	1	1	1	1	1	0	12
Bowen	1970	100.0	44.9	87	1	0	2	2	1	0	0	1	1	1	1	0	10
Bowen	1970	100.0		59	4	0	2	2	1	0	1	0	1	1	0	0	12
Bowers	1990	87.5	39.0	16	4	1	2	2	1	1	0	1	1	1	1	0	15
Brandsma	1980	100.0	39.0	116	4	1	2	2	1	1	1	1	0	0	1	0	14
Braunstein	1983	100.0	45.0	174	4	0	1	2	1	0	1	0	0	0	1	0	10
Brown	1980	100.0	32.0	60	4	1	2	2	1	1	1	1	1	0	1	0	15
Brown	1993	75.0	37.0	28	4	1	2	0	1	0	1	1	1	1	1	0	13
Bruun	1963	100.0		303	4	0	2	2	1	0	1	0	1	0	0	0	11
Bullock	1987	100.0	42.0	54	4	0	2	0	1	0	0	1	1	0	1	0	10
Caddy	1976	82.0	43.8	63	4	0	2	2	1	0	0	1	0	1	1	0	12
Caddy	1984	78.0	47.7	60	4	0	2	2	1	1	1	0	0	1	1	0	13
Cadogan	1973	87.5	43.7	40	4	1	2	1	1	1	0	1	1	0	1	0	13
Cannon	1981	100.0	42.3	21	4	1	2	2	1	1	0	1	1	0	1	0	14
Carpenter	1985	50.0	16.2	30	4	1	1	2	1	0	1	0	0	0	1	0	11
Chaney	1978	100.0	45.6	50	4	1	1	2	1	1	0	1	1	1	1	0	14
Chapman	1988	79.6	42.4	105	4	1	2	2	1	0	1	0	1	1	1	0	14
Charnoff	1963	77.9		835	4	1	0	2	0	0	0	1	1	1	0	0	10
Chick	1985	100.0		156	2	0	2	2	1	0	1	1	1	1	1	0	12
Chick	1988	78.0	40.2	152	4	1	2	2	1	1	1	1	1	1	1	0	16
Chick	1992	84.0	43.0	126	4	1	1	1	1	1	1	1	1	1	1	0	14
Clancy	1967			42	1	1	2	2	0	1	0	1	1	0	1	0	10
Coghlan	1979	100.0	33.0	60	4	1	2	0	0	0	0	1	1	0	1	0	10
Connors	1986	93.0	32.0	67	4	1	2	2	0	1	1	0	0	1	0	0	12
Connors	1992	69.0	36.9	63	4	1	2	2	1	1	0	1	1	0	1	0	14
Cooney	1991	66.0	39.1	113	4	1	1	2	1	1	1	1	1	0	1	0	14
Cooper	1988	49.0	22.7	59	4	1	2	0	1	0	0	1	1	0	0	0	10
Cooper	1988	43.0	26.5	51	4	1	2	1	0	0	0	1	0	0	1	0	10
Corder	1972	100.0	43.0	40	1	0	2	1	1	1	1	1	0	0	1	0	9
Dahlgren	1989	0.0	40.0	200	4	0	1	2	1	0	1	1	1	1	1	0	13
Daniels	1992	61.0	57.0	233	1	1	0	1	0	0	0	1	0	0	1	0	5
Ditman	1967	90.0	40.0	301	4	0	2	2	0	1	1	1	0	1	0	0	12
Dorus	1989	90.0	37.0	426	4	1	2	2	1	0	1	1	1	1	1	1	16
Drummond	1990	75.0	38.9	40	4	0	2	1	1	0	0	1	1	0	1	0	11
Edwards	1966	100.0	43.8	40	2	0	2	2	1	0	0	0	0	0	1	0	8
Edwards	1967	100.0	43.0	40	4	1	2	2	1	1	1	1	1	1	1	0	16
Edwards	1977	100.0	41.0	100	4	1	2	2	1	1	1	1	0	1	1	0	15
Egan	1968	100.0		34	4	1	2	1	1	0	1	1	1	1	0	0	13
Elvy	1988	84.0	29.5	226	4	0	0	2	1	0	1	1	1	0	1	0	11
Ends	1957	100.0	37.0	96	1	1	0	2	1	1	1	1	0	1	0	0	10
Eriksen	1986	79.0	38.5	24	4	1	2	2	0	1	0	1	1	0	1	0	13
Eriksen	1986	88.0	34.5	21	4	0	1	0	1	0	0	1	1	0	1	0	9

(continued)

Appendix   (continued)

AUTHOR	YEAR	% MALE	MEAN AGE	N	A	B	C	D	E	F	G	H	I	J	K	L	Σ
Faia	1976	100.0	38.7	46	2	0	0	2	0	0	0	0	0	0	0	0	4
Fawcett	1987	87.5	39.3	104	4	1	2	2	1	1	1	1	1	0	1	0	15
Ferrell	1981	73.0	42.0	22	2	1	1	2	1	1	0	1	1	0	1	0	11
Fitzgerald	1985	72.0	34.0	332	4	0	2	2	1	0	0	1	1	1	1	1	14
Fleiger	1973	100.0	43.0	32	1	1	2	0	0	0	0	1	1	0	0	0	6
Foy	1984	100.0	46.0	62	4	1	2	2	1	1	1	1	1	1	1	0	16
Freedberg	1978	95.0	46.4	101	1	0	2	2	1	1	0	0	1	0	0	0	8
Freedberg	1978	95.0	46.0	80	0	1	2	2	1	1	0	1	1	0	1	0	10
Fuller	1979	100.0	42.6	128	4	1	2	2	1	1	1	1	1	1	1	0	16
Fuller	1986	100.0	42.0	605	4	1	2	2	1	1	1	1	1	1	1	1	17
Gallant	1968	89.0	44.0	78	2	0	1	1	1	0	0	1	1	1	1	0	9
Gallant	1968	100.0	46.6	84	4	0	2	1	0	0	1	0	1	0	0	0	9
Gerrein	1973	88.0	42.6	121	4	0	0	0	0	0	0	1	1	0	0	0	6
Gilbert	1988	100.0	43.0	96	4	1	1	2	1	0	0	1	1	1	1	0	13
Glover	1977	68.2	44.2	48	2	1	2	1	1	1	0	1	1	0	1	0	11
Graber	1988	71.0	42.8	24	4	1	2	2	1	1	1	1	1	1	1	0	16
Guydish	1987	100.0		46	4	1	2	0	0	0	0	1	1	0	1	0	10
Hagen	1978	80.0	35.0	8275	1	0	0	2	0	0	1	1	0	0	0	1	6
Harris	1990	50.0	37.7	34	4	1	2	2	1	1	1	1	1	1	1	0	16
Hayashida	1969	100.0	41.0	164	4	1	2	1	1	0	0	1	1	0	1	0	12
Heather	1986	81.0	42.3	247	4	1	0	2	0	0	0	1	1	0	1	0	10
Heather	1987	75.0	36.4	104	4	1	2	1	1	1	1	1	1	1	1	0	15
Heather	1990	65.0	45.4	107	4	1	1	1	1	1	0	1	1	1	1	0	13
Hedberg	1974	92.0	38.4	57	4	1	2	1	1	0	0	1	1	0	0	0	11
Hoff	1953	85.0	38.0	792	0	0	2	0	0	0	0	1	1	0	1	0	5
Hoff	1961	80.0		100	2	1	0	0	0	0	0	0	1	0	1	0	5
Hollister	1969	100.0	45.0	72	4	0	1	1	1	0	0	1	1	1	1	0	11
Hunt	1973	100.0	38.0	16	4	1	2	1	1	0	1	1	1	1	1	0	13
Hussain	1972			43	0	1	2	1	0	0	0	1	1	0	0	0	6
Ito	1988	100.0	36.5	47	3	1	1	1	1	1	0	1	1	0	1	0	11
Jackson	1978	75.0	31.5	24	2	0	2	0	0	0	0	1	0	0	1	0	6
Jackson	1978	70.0	50.0	344	0	1	0	2	0	0	0	1	1	0	1	0	6
Jacobson	1973	100.0	37.6	80	4	1	2	1	1	0	1	1	0	0	0	0	11
Jensen	1963		39.3	125	1	0	1	1	0	0	0	1	0	0	1	0	5
Johnsen	1987	100.0	39.0	21	4	1	2	0	1	0	1	1	1	0	1	0	12
Johnsen	1991	88.0	42.1	76	4	1	1	1	1	0	1	1	1	1	1	0	13
Johnson	1970			95	4	0	2	2	0	0	0	1	0	0	0	0	9
Jones	1982	70.6	46.0	74	4	1	0	2	1	0	0	0	0	1	1	0	10
Keane	1984	100.0	43.9	25	4	1	2	0	1	1	1	1	1	0	1	0	13
Keso	1990	83.0	41.3	117	4	0	2	1	1	0	1	1	1	0	1	0	12
Kissin	1968			288	0	1	0	1	0	0	0	0	0	0	0	0	2
Kivlahan	1990	58.1	23.1	50	4	1	1	2	0	0	0	1	0	0	1	0	10
Kline	1974	100.0	45.5	73	4	0	0	2	0	0	1	0	0	1	1	0	9
Krasner	1976	100.0		50	4	0	0	2	1	1	1	1	1	0	0	0	11
Kristenson	1983	100.0	47.0	473	4	1	1	2	1	0	1	0	0	0	1	0	11
Kuchipudi	1990	100.0	52.0	114	4	1	2	0	1	1	1	1	1	0	1	0	13
Lal	1969	100.0		71	0	1	2	1	1	1	1	1	0	0	0	0	9
Lanyon	1972	100.0	40.0	21	4	1	2	1	1	0	0	1	0	1	1	0	12
Laverty	1966			45	4	0	2	2	1	0	0	0	0	0	1	0	10
Levinson	1969	100.0	43.0	60	2	1	2	2	1	0	0	1	1	1	0	0	11
Levy	1967	93.3	43.0	30	4	1	1	0	0	0	1	1	0	0	0	0	8
Ling	1983	100.0	39.0	82	4	1	0	0	1	0	1	1	1	1	1	0	11
Linton	1967	100.0		32	4	1	1	0	1	0	0	1	1	1	0	0	10
Longabaugh	1983	67.0	41.7	174	4	1	2	2	1	1	0	1	1	0	1	0	14
Lovibond	1975	100.0	42.0	58	2	1	1	1	1	0	1	1	1	1	1	0	10
Lowenstam	1969	100.0	47.0	100	4	1	2	1	1	0	1	1	0	0	0	0	12
Ludwig	1969	100.0	40.0	176	4	1	2	2	1	1	1	0	0	1	0	0	13
Lysloff	1972			100	4	0	0	1	1	0	1	1	0	0	0	0	8
Maheswaran	1992	100.0	44.6	44	4	0	2	0	1	0	1	1	1	0	1	0	11
Maisto	1985	100.0	37.8	48	4	0	2	2	1	1	1	1	0	1	1	0	14

Appendix   (continued)

AUTHOR	YEAR	% MALE	MEAN AGE	N	A	B	C	D	E	F	G	H	I	J	K	L	Σ
Maletsky	1974	65.0	29.6	20	4	1	2	1	0	1	1	1	1	0	1	0	13
Malfetti	1975			1000	2	1	2	2	0	0	1	0	0	0	1	0	9
Mallams	1982	71.0	41.0	40	4	0	2	0	1	1	0	1	0	0	1	0	10
Marlatt	1973	100.0	42.5	65	4	1	2	2	1	1	0	1	1	1	1	0	15
Marlatt	1977	100.0	23.5	44	2	1	1	0	0	0	0	1	0	0	0	0	5
McCance	1969	100.0		76	4	0	2	2	1	0	0	1	1	0	1	0	12
McCrady	1979	61.0	42.0	33	4	0	2	2	0	1	0	0	0	0	1	0	10
McCrady	1986	73.0	43.0	53	4	1	2	2	1	1	1	0	1	1	1	0	15
McGuire	1978	85.0		1000	0	1	2	2	0	0	1	0	0	0	1	0	7
McLachlan	1982	82.0	44.0	100	4	0	2	2	1	1	0	1	0	0	1	0	12
McLatchie	1988	85.8	38.0	177	1	0	2	0	0	1	0	1	0	0	1	0	6
Merry	1968	100.0		24	2	0	2	0	0	0	0	1	1	0	0	0	6
Merry	1968	100.0		40	2	0	2	0	0	0	0	1	1	0	0	0	6
Merry	1976	71.1	45.1	71	4	1	0	0	1	0	0	0	0	1	1	0	8
Miller	1973	100.0	45.0	30	2	1	2	0	1	0	1	1	1	0	1	0	10
Miller	1975	100.0	49.0	20	4	0	2	0	1	0	1	1	1	0	1	0	11
Miller	1978	70.0	37.1	65	4	1	1	2	1	1	1	1	1	1	1	0	15
Miller	1980	61.0	45.4	48	4	1	2	2	1	1	1	1	1	1	1	0	16
Miller	1980	51.0	41.6	45	4	1	2	2	1	1	1	1	1	1	1	0	16
Miller	1981	71.0	39.0	35	4	1	2	0	1	1	0	1	1	1	1	0	13
Miller	1988	71.0	40.0	42	4	1	2	2	1	1	0	1	1	1	1	0	15
Miller	1989	83.0	42.0	30	4	1	2	2	1	1	0	1	1	1	1	0	15
Miller	1993	57.1	40.0	42	4	1	2	2	1	1	0	1	1	1	1	0	15
Mindlin	1965			232	1	0	0	1	1	1	1	1	0	0	1	0	7
Monti	1990	100.0	42.9	69	4	1	1	1	1	0	1	0	1	0	1	0	11
Mooney	1961			214	4	0	0	0	1	0	0	0	0	1	0	0	6
Mosher	1975	80.0	40.5	200	4	0	2	1	1	0	0	0	1	1	1	0	11
Murphy	1986	100.0	25.0	46	4	0	2	0	1	0	0	1	1	0	1	0	10
O'Farrell	1993	100.0	43.9	59	4	1	2	2	1	1	1	1	1	0	1	0	15
O'Farrell	1985	100.0	42.0	36	4	1	2	2	1	1	0	1	1	1	1	0	15
Obolensky	1984	90.0	32.0	96	4	1	1	1	1	0	1	1	1	0	1	1	13
Oei	1980	75.0	33.5	32	2	0	0	2	1	0	0	1	0	0	1	0	7
Oei	1982	75.0	31.5	32	2	1	1	2	1	0	1	1	1	1	1	0	12
Oei	1984	78.0	32.0	18	2	0	0	2	1	1	0	1	1	1	1	0	11
Ogborne	1979	100.0	44.0	38	4	0	0	0	1	0	1	0	0	0	0	0	6
Olson	1981	69.0	44.0	137	4	0	1	2	1	1	0	1	1	0	0	0	11
Penick	1969	64.0	49.0	50	4	1	2	1	1	0	0	1	1	0	0	0	11
Persson	1989	78.0	40.0	71	4	0	1	2	1	0	1	0	0	0	1	0	10
Pittman	1972	88.4	41.2	250	4	0	2	2	1	0	0	1	1	0	1	0	12
Platz	1970	83.0	41.0	169	4	1	2	0	1	0	0	1	0	0	1	0	10
Pomerleau	1978	69.0	44.0	32	4	1	1	2	1	1	1	1	1	0	1	0	14
Pond	1981	100.0	43.1	47	4	1	0	1	1	0	0	1	0	1	1	0	10
Powell	1985	100.0	45.0	174	4	0	1	2	1	0	0	1	0	1	1	0	11
Powell	1986	100.0	41.4	100	4	1	0	1	1	0	0	1	0	1	1	0	10
Regester	1971	100.0	46.7	62	4	1	1	1	1	0	0	1	1	1	1	0	12
Reinert	1958	100.0	40.0	48	4	1	0	0	1	0	0	1	1	0	0	0	8
Rhead	1977	100.0	40.0	103	4	0	0	2	1	0	0	1	1	1	1	0	11
Richard	1983	100.0	32.7	112	4	0	0	2	1	0	0	1	1	1	1	0	11
Robertson	1986	81.0	36.1	37	4	1	2	2	1	1	0	1	0	1	1	0	14
Rohsenow	1985	100.0	21.3	40	4	1	2	1	0	0	0	1	0	0	1	0	10
Romelsjö	1989	84.0	46.0	83	4	1	2	2	1	0	1	1	0	0	0	0	12
Rosenberg	1974	90.0	41.6	123	0	1	0	0	1	0	0	0	0	0	1	0	3
Rosenberg	1979	100.0	28.7	75	4	1	1	0	1	0	0	1	0	0	1	0	9
Rosenberg	1986	100.0	29.7	22	1	1	2	1	0	0	0	1	1	0	1	0	8
Salzberg	1983	91.0	37.4	2194	0	0	2	2	0	0	1	1	1	0	0	0	7
Sanchez-Craig	1982	62.2	43.0	90	2	1	1	2	1	0	1	1	1	1	1	0	12
Sanchez-Craig	1984	74.0	34.8	70	4	1	1	2	1	1	1	1	1	1	0	0	15
Sanchez-Craig	1989	58.0	43.0	90	4	1	1	2	1	0	1	1	1	1	0	0	14
Sanchez-Craig	1991	64.0	40.0	96	4	1	1	2	1	0	1	1	1	1	1	1	15
Sandahl	1990	79.0	44.0	53	1	0	0	2	1	0	0	1	1	0	1	0	7

(continued)

Appendix   (continued)

AUTHOR	YEAR	% MALE	MEAN AGE	N	A	B	C	D	E	F	G	H	I	J	K	L	Σ
Sannibale	1988	100.0	31.9	96	4	1	1	2	1	1	1	1	1	0	1	0	14
Schaefer	1971	100.0	39.0	52	2	1	2	2	1	1	0	1	0	0	1	0	11
Schaeffer	1972	100.0		26	2	0	1	2	1	1	0	1	1	0	1	0	10
Scoles	1977	93.0		122	4	0	0	0	0	0	0	0	0	0	1	0	5
Scott	1990	0.0	45.8	72	4	1	0	2	1	0	1	1	1	1	1	0	13
Shaffer	1963	100.0	45.6	199	4	0	0	0	1	0	1	1	1	1	1	0	10
Shaffer	1964	100.0	45.6	145	4	1	1	0	1	0	0	1	0	1	1	0	10
Sisson	1981	100.0	36.0	30	4	1	1	0	0	0	0	1	1	0	1	0	9
Sisson	1986	0.0		12	4	1	2	0	1	1	0	1	1	0	1	0	12
Skutle	1987	79.0	43.0	48	4	1	2	2	1	1	0	1	1	0	1	0	14
Smart	1966	93.0	40.0	30	4	1	2	1	1	0	0	0	1	1	1	0	12
Smith	1991	86.0	38.0	498	2	0	2	2	1	0	0	1	0	1	1	0	10
Sobell	1973	100.0	41.2	70	4	1	2	2	1	1	1	1	0	0	1	0	14
Steffen	1975	100.0	39.0	4	4	1	2	0	1	0	1	1	1	0	1	0	12
Stein	1975	100.0	42.7	58	4	0	2	2	1	0	0	1	0	0	1	0	11
Swenson	1980	85.0	27.0	436	4	1	1	1	1	0	0	0	0	0	1	0	9
Swenson	1981	100.0	30.4	351	4	0	1	2	1	0	0	0	0	0	1	0	9
Swinson	1971	100.0		60	4	1	0	2	1	1	0	1	1	1	1	0	13
Telch	1984	92.8	33.8	29	4	0	2	0	1	0	1	1	1	1	1	0	12
Tomsovic	1970	100.0	44.0	333	2	0	1	2	0	1	0	0	0	0	1	0	7
Tyndel	1969	93.0		46	4	1	0	0	1	0	1	0	0	0	0	0	7
Valle	1981	95.0	44.0	247	4	0	2	2	0	0	1	1	0	0	1	0	11
Vogler	1970	100.0	44.0	73	2	0	0	0	1	0	0	1	0	0	1	0	5
Vogler	1975			67	4	0	0	2	1	1	0	0	1	0	1	0	10
Vogler	1975	88.0	41.2	55	4	1	1	2	1	0	0	1	0	1	1	0	12
Vogler	1977	84.0	37.5	119	4	1	0	2	1	0	1	1	0	1	1	0	12
Vogler	1977	100.0	37.8	39	4	1	0	2	1	0	1	1	0	1	1	0	12
Wallace	1988	71.0	42.4	909	4	1	2	2	1	0	1	1	1	1	1	1	16
Wallerstein	1957	100.0	38.0	178	4	0	0	2	1	0	0	1	1	0	0	0	9
Walsh	1991	95.0	32.6	227	4	0	2	2	1	1	1	0	1	1	1	0	14
Wanberg	1974	81.0	42.8	180	4	0	1	0	1	0	0	1	1	1	1	0	10
Watson	1978	100.0	43.9	50	0	1	2	2	1	0	0	1	1	0	1	0	9
Wells-Parker	1988	92.0	30.0	3431	4	0	2	2	0	0	1	1	1	0	1	0	12
West	1979	95.0	41.9	84	4	1	2	0	1	0	0	1	1	1	1	0	12
Whyte	1974	100.0	43.0	45	2	1	2	0	1	0	0	1	0	0	1	0	8
Wilson	1978	80.0	34.0	20	4	1	2	2	1	0	0	1	1	0	1	0	13
Wilson	1980	89.0	36.0	100	4	1	1	2	1	0	0	1	1	0	1	0	12
Zimberg	1974	100.0		113	4	1	1	2	0	0	0	1	1	1	0	0	11
Zweben	1988	83.0	42.6	218	4	1	0	2	1	1	1	1	1	1	1	0	14

CHAPTER 3

Screening for Alcohol Problems and At-Risk Drinking in Health-Care Settings

Ned L. Cooney
Allen Zweben
Michael F. Fleming

This chapter focuses on theoretical concepts and practical procedures in developing and implementing alcohol screening programs. Screening programs are justified because (1) alcohol problems are common, (2) they are associated with serious health and social consequences, (3) effective treatment is available, and (4) there are valid, cost-effective procedures for screening (Institute of Medicine, 1990; U.S. Department of Health and Human Services, 1994). The Institute of Medicine report strongly recommended

that community and health-care agencies identify individuals with alcohol problems and provide brief intervention or referral to specialized treatment.

It is important to understand the differences between *assessment* and *screening*. The goal of assessment is to establish a diagnosis and develop a specific treatment plan. Assessments are usually conducted over multiple visits by an alcohol and drug abuse specialist in a treatment center. In contrast, the goal of screening is to detect persons with possible alcohol problems or those at risk of developing such problems. Screening procedures are usually brief and can be conducted by persons with limited clinical experience. Screening can occur in any health-care setting or as part of a community-based health program.

This chapter was written with partial support for Ned Cooney from the National Institute on Alcohol Abuse and Alcoholism Center Grant 2P50 AA03510 and Cooperative Agreement 5U10 AA08438.

We wish to thank Tom Babor and Priscilla Morse who provided comments on an earlier draft of this chapter.

You may direct a screening program at either asymptomatic individuals or at individuals who are likely to be experiencing alcohol-related problems. Examples of the former are persons who seek a routine physical exam or those in the health-care system for nonalcohol-related health problems. A higher base rate of alcohol problems is likely to be found in patients with traumatic injuries, hypertension, depression, panic disorders, pancreatitis, or liver disease. The screening methods described in this chapter can be used for screening either asymptomatic individuals or those who are seeking treatment for a disorder that is a likely consequence of drinking.

CONCEPTUAL MODELS OF SCREENING

There are two conceptual models for screening (Safer, 1986). The traditional approach, known as *case finding* or *screening for disease detection,* is to test apparently healthy individuals to identify those who have clear evidence of a disease. A variant of this model is to identify individuals who are only beginning to experience symptoms of a disorder in order to provide treatment before they reach a more serious and destructive phase of the disorder. An alternative model is to test apparently healthy individuals to identify those who are not experiencing symptoms but who have behavioral risk factors that can be modified with counseling. This is known as *screening for risk reduction.* Both screening models offer clinical benefit.

These screening models can be applied to a variety of disorders. When applied to alcohol problems, screening for disease detection seeks to identify individuals with early or advanced symptoms of alcohol dependence. This type of screening is of value because there are an estimated 18 million Americans with alcohol use problems, and less than 15% receive treatment (United States General Accounting Office, 1991). Screening for risk reduction tries to identify individuals who do not have current alcohol-related problems but drink in a way that increases their susceptibility to alcohol problems. The evidence suggests that most individuals who drink in a harmful or hazardous way are not seriously dependent on alcohol. Kreitman (1986) called this epidemiological phenomenon the "preventive paradox" because it implies that more health problems, and possibly more health costs, result from nondependent drinkers.

The risk-reduction model assumes that one can reduce alcohol consumption-related risks by changing drinking behavior. Chapter 2 provides ample evidence to support this assumption. For example, brief interventions are among the most effective treatment methods for problem drinkers who are not severely dependent on alcohol.

The alcohol screening literature focuses predominantly on disease detection and usually does not address the issue of screening for risk reduction. We believe that screening can serve both as an occasion to detect present alcohol problems and as an opportunity to screen for at-risk drinking in individuals who are presently without problems. There are, however, some caveats associated with screening for at-risk drinkers. A positive screening result could have detrimental effects on insurability or employment. Also, some treatments recommended for alcohol-dependent individuals might be inappropriate or even contraindicated for a nonproblem drinker with heavy alcohol consumption. For example, inpatient treatment can lead to worse outcomes than outpatient counseling for persons who are not alcohol dependent (Orford, Oppenheimer, & Edwards, 1976). If you combine disease detection and risk-reduction screening, refer those who screen positive to a standardized assessment that is linked to objective guidelines for matching patients to appropriate types and levels of care.

This chapter will explain how to select screening procedures designed for both disease detection and risk reduction. First, we will discuss the validity of self-reported alcohol consumption. Then we will provide a selective review of recommended alcohol screening methods. Most of this chapter deals with how to implement an alcohol screening program. We discuss (1) setting goals for the screening program, (2) assessing the needs and resources in the screening setting, and (3) gaining acceptance among the providers in the setting. In addition to screening, we discuss in detail methods to enhance compliance with referrals after screening. In this chapter, screening procedures are described in the context of health-care settings, but many of these procedures could also be applied in other settings such as employee assistance, social service, and drunk-driving programs.

VALIDITY OF SELF-REPORTS

To decide whether individuals have developed or are at risk for developing drinking problems, you need to obtain information about their quantity and frequency of alcohol consumption, the negative consequences of their drinking, their behaviors under the influence of alcohol, and alcohol-dependence symptoms. Much of this information can be obtained only by asking individuals to describe their own behavior after the fact. However, many clinicians are skeptical about the validity of self-reported drinking data.

To better understand the validity of self-reported addictive behaviors, Babor, Brown, and Del Boca (1990) outlined a social-psychological model of the question-answering process. They suggested that response accuracy depends on a variety of factors, including:

- Cultural norms
- The institutional or organizational setting
- The presence or absence of other people
- The demand characteristics of the interview situation
- The perceived attitude of the interviewer
- The subject's state of sobriety
- The subject's motivation
- The presence or absence of cognitive impairment

Babor and colleagues (1990) recommended procedures to minimize response bias and enhance validity. The following procedures are applicable to alcohol screening programs.

1. The reliability of self-report in an intoxicated individual is greatly reduced. Defer the screening interview when an individual is seen with alcohol on his or her breath, with a positive breathalyzer, or with a positive alcohol dipstick test. You may refer the intoxicated individual for alcohol-related assessment as if he or she screened positive in an interview.

2. Provide specific instructions about the purpose of the screening interview. If you are using a risk-reduction model, tell clients that screening is being done to examine whether their drinking has any potential impact on their health. It is useful to incorporate alcohol screening into a broader interview of health habits. The purpose of this broader interview would be to learn about various behavioral risk factors that might impact health. This approach is much less offensive than saying that the purpose of the interview is to detect alcoholism.

3. Before conducting a screening interview, obtain samples for biochemical tests that are sensitive to alcohol consumption. Explain to clients

that the tests provide objective information about the impact of alcohol on their health. The implication is that there is no use in minimizing their self-report of drinking because the tests will reveal how much they are drinking.

4. It is important to determine the alcohol content and serving size of the clients' usual beverages when you ask about their level of alcohol consumption.

5. Load sensitive questions by assuming the presence of undesirable behavior (*How often* do you have six or more drinks on one occasion? rather than Do you *ever* have six or more drinks on one occasion?) or by suggesting that heavy drinking is common.

6. Provide clients with nonjudgmental feedback about discrepancies between their self-report data and other sources of information (see Chapter 5).

7. Paper-and-pencil or computer-based questionnaires may be less threatening than face-to-face interviews.

ALCOHOL SCREENING METHODS

Most of the research on alcohol screening tests has used alcohol-dependent White males in treatment programs. However, there is growing evidence of the validity of these clinical tools in primary care settings. The paucity of data on the effectiveness of alcohol screening instruments with women, adolescents, the elderly, the mentally ill, and different cultural settings is a major limitation. The selected sample of tests we review here are screening tools only and were not developed as comprehensive assessment instruments. Table 3.1 at the end of this section provides a summary of our recommendations for screening tests. Because screening tests are set up to be as sensitive as possible, false positive results are common. This is a particular concern in the general population. To minimize any potential adverse effects (e.g., insurability, employment), positive tests should be followed up with a diagnostic assessment.

The most common alcohol screening questions used by health-care professionals focus on the quantity and frequency (Q/F) of drinking. Although there is limited research on the most effective quantity/frequency questions, a number of questions have been recommended (Babor, Korner, Wilber, & Good, 1987; Brown, 1992; Skinner, 1990). Examples include: How many days per week did you drink over the last month? On a day when you drink alcohol, how many drinks do you have? In addition to determining frequency and quantity, it is important to assess the frequency of binge drinking. Periodic heavy use can be associated with motor vehicle accidents, trauma, fights, and other consequences (How many times in the last month did you drink more than five drinks?).

You determine a positive screen, using Q/F questions, by examining health risks at different levels of use (see, e.g., Anderson, Cremona, Paton, Turner, & Wallace, 1993). If a standard drink is equal to 12 grams of ethanol (approximately 12 ounces of beer, 5 ounces of wine, or 1 ounces of distilled spirits), men who drink 15+ drinks per week and women who drink 12+ are at higher risk for alcohol-related health problems. We consider clients who report drinking above these levels to be at-risk drinkers. The health risks associated with a given frequency of binge drinking are not known. In its physician guide, the National Institute on Alcoholism and Alcohol Abuse has selected one or more episodes of binge drinking per month as the cutoff for a positive test if this is a consistent pattern.

The instrument most widely promoted as the standard screening test for clinical practice is the CAGE (Ewing, 1984; King, 1986; Bush, Shaw, Cleary, Delbanco, & Aronson, 1987). The test assesses four areas related to lifetime alcohol use. Two positive responses is the cutoff for a positive test.

C   Have you ever felt the need to **C**ut down on your drinking?

A   Have you ever felt **A**nnoyed by someone criticizing your drinking?

G   Have you ever felt bad or **G**uilty about your drinking?

E   Have you ever had a drink first thing in the morning to steady your nerves and get rid of a hangover? (**E**ye-opener)

Like most of the screening instruments reviewed, the sensitivity and specificity of the CAGE reported in different studies varies from 60 to 95% and 40 to 95% respectively (Bush et al., 1987; Beresford, Blow, Hill, Singer, & Lucey, 1990). The variability of these reports may be related to (1) Different criterion measures used as the "gold standard" for alcoholism, (2) assessment of lifetime use as compared to current use, (3) varying the cutoff score from one to four positive responses, and (4) differences in population

samples. Its major deficiencies are that it does not assess current problems, levels of alcohol consumption, or binge drinking. Consequently, we recommend that you only use the CAGE along with questions on quantity, frequency, and binge drinking.

A working group of the World Health Organization created the Alcohol Use Disorders Identification Test (AUDIT; Babor, de la Fuente, Saunders, & Grant, 1992) as a brief multicultural screening tool for the early identification of problem drinkers (rather than persons who would meet criteria for alcohol dependence). They chose questions that discriminated high-risk drinkers in a six-nation study (Saunders, Aasland, Babor, de la Fuenta, & Grant, 1993). Figure 3.1 shows the core part of the AUDIT. It contains a series of 10 questions that include 3 questions on alcohol consumption, 4 questions on dependence symptoms, and 3 questions about alcohol-related problems. You may ask the 10 questions in interview or in a paper-and-pencil questionnaire. A cutoff score of eight is recommended (Babor & Grant, 1989; Fleming, Barry, & MacDonald, 1991; Barry & Fleming, 1993). The second part of the AUDIT records alcohol-related physical measures and laboratory findings.

Clinical researchers developed the Health Screening Questionnaire (HSQ; Wallace & Haines, 1985; Cutler, Wallace, & Haines, 1988) and its modification, the Health Screening Survey (HSS; Fleming & Barry, 1991), as imbedded lifestyle questionnaires. These screening tests contain parallel questions on smoking, exercise, weight, and alcohol use. The alcohol portion of the HSQ and HSS contains questions on frequency and use of alcohol with three types of beverages in the previous three months, the four CAGE questions, and two questions on problem drinking. Harvey Skinner and colleagues developed the Computerized Lifestyle Assessment questionnaires (Skinner, Allen, McIntosh, & Palmer, 1985) and Graham (1991) developed the Life Style Test. They are two other examples of screening questionnaires that combine alcohol questions with other health issues.

There are also a number of new screening instruments. The POSIT (Problem Oriented Screening Instrument for Teenagers) is a promising new screening instrument developed by Ralph Tartar and an expert panel sponsored by the National Institute on Drug Abuse (1990). Developed as part of the Adolescent Assessment Referral System, the POSIT discriminates

Figure 3.1   Alcohol Use Disorders Identification Test

AUDIT is a brief structured interview, developed by the World Health Organization, that can be incorporated into a medical history. It contains questions about recent alcohol consumption, dependence symptoms, and alcohol-related problems.

Begin the AUDIT by saying: "Now I am going to ask you some questions about your use of alcoholic beverages *during the past year.*" Explain what is meant by alcoholic beverages (i.e., beer, wine, liquor [vodka, whiskey, brandy, etc.]). Record the score for each question in the box on the right side of the question.

1. How often do you have a drink containing alcohol?

Never	(0)
Monthly or less	(1)
2 to 4 times a month	(2)
2 to 3 times a week	(3)
4 or more times a week	(4)

2. How many drinks containing alcohol do you have on a typical day when you are drinking?

None	(0)
1 or 2	(1)
3 or 4	(2)
5 or 6	(3)
7 or 9	(4)
10 or more	(5)

3. How often do you have six or more drinks on one occasion?

Never	(0)
Less than monthly	(1)
Monthly	(2)
Weekly	(3)
Daily or almost daily	(4)

4. How often during the last year have you found that you were unable to stop drinking once you had started?

Never	(0)
Less than monthly	(1)
Monthly	(2)
Weekly	(3)
Daily or almost daily	(4)

5. How often during the last year have you failed to do what was normally expected from you because of drinking?

Never	(0)
Less than monthly	(1)
Monthly	(2)
Weekly	(3)
Daily or almost daily	(4)

6. How often during the last year have you needed a first drink in the morning to get yourself going after a heavy drinking session?

Never	(0)
Less than monthly	(1)
Monthly	(2)
Weekly	(3)
Daily or almost daily	(4)

7. How often during the last year have you had a feeling of guilt or remorse after drinking?

Never	(0)
Less than monthly	(1)
Monthly	(2)
Weekly	(3)
Daily or almost daily	(4)

(continued)

Figure 3.1   (continued)

8. How often during the last year have you been unable to remember what happened the night before because you had been drinking?
   Never   (0)
   Less than monthly   (1)
   Monthly   (2)
   Weekly   (3)
   Daily or almost daily   (4)

9. Have you or someone else been injured as the result of your drinking?
   Never   (0)
   Less than monthly   (1)
   Monthly   (2)
   Weekly   (3)
   Daily or almost daily   (4)

10. Has a relative, friend, or a doctor or other health worker been concerned about your drinking or suggested you cut down?
   Never   (0)
   Less than monthly   (1)
   Monthly   (2)
   Weekly   (3)
   Daily or almost daily   (4)

Record the total specific items.

A score of 8 or greater may indicate the need for a more in-depth assessment.

Source: Developed by the World Health Organization, AMETHYST Project, 1987.

between adolescents in treatment and adolescents drawn from a school population (Klitzner & Rahdert, 1991). It covers 10 problem areas, one of which is substance use/abuse. The substance use/abuse subscale contains 14 questions. One or more positive responses is a positive screen. Several studies are underway assessing the validity of the POSIT in general population samples.

The G-MAST (Blow, Young, Hill, Singer, & Beresford, 1991) is a modification of the Michigan Alcoholism Screening Test (MAST) for older adults. Limitations of this test include absence of Q/F questions, focus on dependence symptoms, and length (25 questions).

Russell (1994) developed the TWEAK as a screen for alcohol problems in women. The TWEAK is a modification of the CAGE. It substituted a question on tolerance for the question on guilt, modified the question on annoyed, and added a question about amnesia.

T   How many drinks can you hold? (3+ drinks suggests **T**olerance)

W   Have close friends or relatives **W**orried or complained about your drinking in the past year?

E   Do you sometimes take a drink in the morning when you first get up? (**E**ye-opener)

A   Has a friend or family member ever told you about things you said or did while you were drinking that you could not remember? (**A**mnesia or blackouts)

K   Do you sometimes feel the need to **K**/cut down on your drinking?

Using a criteria standard based on a seven-day drinking report of two or more drinks per day around the time of conception, these five items proved more sensitive than the CAGE or the MAST in a population of 4,000 primarily inner-city African-American women (Russell et al., 1991).

The four Ps is another instrument developed for women. The major advantages of this screening test are (1) it includes questions on both alcohol and drugs, (2) there is an orientation toward family issues, and (3) the questionnaire is brief. A positive response to one or more questions indicates the need for a more in-depth assessment. The instrument is widely used in a number of women's clinics in California and is currently being validated (Ewing, 1992). The four questions are as follows:

• Do your **P**arents have an alcohol or drug problem?

- Does your **P**artner use alcohol or drugs?
- Have you had an alcohol or drug **P**roblem in the past?
- Have you used any drugs, alcohol, or cigarettes during your **P**regnancy?

The MAST is not included in this review because it is too long to qualify as a screening test in clinical settings. It is more appropriate as an assessment tool than as a rapid screening test. It also focuses on identifying alcohol-dependent persons rather than individuals at risk for alcohol-related problems.

Methods to Administer Screening Tests

You can give screening tests four different ways: (1) in a face-to-face interview by a nonclinical interviewer, (2) in a face-to-face interview by a clinician, (3) with a paper-and-pencil questionnaire, and (4) via a self-guided computer interview. Studies have established the comparability of these methods. Robins (1985) found a high degree of agreement between the interview conducted by nonclinical researchers and expert findings using the Diagnostic Interview Schedule. Barry and Fleming (1990) compared a pencil-and-paper questionnaire with computer administration of the CAGE and the Short-MAST (S-MAST) in a primary care sample and found no significant differences in sensitivity and specificity in the two methods. Bernadt, Daniels, Blizard, and Murray (1989) compared administration of the CAGE, S-MAST, and an alcohol consumption test by a computer, a nurse, and a psychiatrist. The Kappa values varied from .79 to .86, with the CAGE and S-MAST having the highest levels of agreement. Their findings agreed with the work of Skinner and colleagues (1985) and Erdman, Klein, and Griest (1985).

The validity of any of the four methods is enhanced by establishing an environment of trust, safety, and confidentiality. The validity of the responses obtained by these four methods is similar, but pencil-and-paper and computer methods are the least expensive. Patients also seem to prefer the computer method due to its novelty and ability to give immediate feedback (Skinner et al., 1985).

Screening Based on Laboratory Tests

There are three types of laboratory tests currently available. The first type includes breathalyzer testing, blood alcohol levels, and saliva or urine testing. Emergency departments have successfully used alcohol levels for screening (Chang & Astrachan, 1988; Cherpitel, 1989) and to corroborate self-report (Fuller et al., 1986). Health-care professionals have not widely used technology to assess alcohol levels (e.g., hand-held breathalyzers and saliva or urine dipstick testing). These techniques are inexpensive and the results correlate well with blood alcohol levels (see Shepherd, Hargarten & Westlake, 1993).

The second type of screening test measures cellular injury to the liver and hematopoetic cell lines. The plasma gamma glutamyl transferace (GGT) and mean corpuscular volume (MCV) are the primary measures used to screen for alcohol problems. The sensitivity of these tests varies from 20 to 60%, depending on the chronicity and severity of alcohol use. Specificity is higher, but the false-positive rate is 20 to 30% of persons screened (Bernadt, Mumford, & Smith, 1982; Cushman, Jacobson, Barboriak, & Anderson, 1984; Gjerde, Amundsen, Skog, Morland, & Aasland, 1987; Beresford, Blow et al., 1990; Persson, Magnusson, & Borg, 1990).

The third type of laboratory screening test does not measure organ toxicity but measures nonspecific alcohol-related changes. Two relatively new biological measures proposed as screening tests are the plasma carbohydrate deficient transferrin (CDT; Stibler & Hultcranta, 1987; Behrens, Werner, Braly, Schaffner, & Lieber, 1988; Poupon, Schellenberg, Nalpas, & Weill, 1989; Kapur, Wild, Milford-Ward, & Triger, 1989; Schellenberg, Benard, LeGoff, Bourdin, & Weill, 1989) and the ratio of plasma mitochondria aspartate aminotransferase (m-AspAT) to the total AspAT (Nalpas et al., 1984; Nalpas, Vassault, Charpin, Lacour, & Berthelot, 1986; Chan et al., 1989). Investigators have reported sensitivities and specificities as high as .76 and .90, respectively. The CDT test is now being marketed in the United States.

IMPLEMENTING SCREENING PROCEDURES

A screening program should strive to achieve a high rate of participation, a high degree of validity in detecting clients who are at risk or already have alcohol problems, and a high rate of client follow-up with referrals for assessment or intervention. Although these goals are straightforward, implementing a successful screening program is not. Even well-intentioned programs have fallen short of reaching these goals (see, e.g., Schmidt & Cooney, 1992; Stephan, Swindle,

Table 3.1   Recommended Screening Tests

TEST NAME	TEST FORMAT	CLIENT POPULATION
AUDIT	Interview or self-administered	Adults
CAGE plus Q/F and binge questions	Interview	Adults
HSS	Self-administered, imbedded health questions	Adults
TWEAK	Interview	Pregnant women
POSIT (alcohol & drug subscales)	Self-administered	Adolescents
Computerized Lifestyle Assessment	Computerized, imbedded health questions	Adults
Blood, breath, saliva or urine alcohol levels	Biological tests	Emergency department
GGT and MCV	Biological tests	Health-care settings

& Moos, 1992). Achieving each of these goals requires careful attention to how you design and implement the screening program.

Assessing the Setting

Begin by assessing the needs, interests, and resources in the setting where you hope to do the screening. What are the priorities of the administrators and providers in the setting? Is there already a risk reduction or preventive medicine approach in the clinic? If so, you can build on screening procedures that are already in place.

Do the providers view themselves as responsible for a broad range of health problems or are they limited to dealing with specific disorders? Many specialty clinics do not routinely look beyond specific organ systems. How does the clinic staff think about alcohol problems? What does the staff do when they detect an individual with alcohol problems? Some clinicians have little faith in any type of alcohol treatment, others believe that one approach is best for everyone (e.g., Alcoholics Anonymous). You may need to educate the staff about alcohol treatment options and their effectiveness.

Are there adequate resources within the clinic to conduct alcohol screening? The practitioners in some clinics are struggling just to meet the minimal demands of their work and would consider any additional task an undue burden. As discussed below, screening tests may be administered by existing clinic staff or by outside personnel.

Is there continuity from visit to visit regarding treatment providers? It is not uncommon for an acute crisis to preempt an alcohol screening procedure, but when there is a consistent provider, he or she could defer screening until the next visit. Continuity also allows the development of trust that can enhance the validity of self-reported information. Family practice or HMO settings are likely to provide consistent providers, whereas emergency departments are not.

If the screening is in part a research effort, are there any possibilities for collaboration with clinic staff on the screening research? Some clinicians see research as irrelevant or self-serving, yet others are open to the idea of conducting research in the context of clinical practice.

Are there appropriate diagnostic, educational, intervention, and referral procedures available to deal with positive cases? If not, a screening program might not be warranted.

Who Asks the Screening Questions?

We have conducted screening in different ways. In some settings, it works well to train staff physicians or other providers to ask the screening questions. This method may be more efficient, may help integrate screening into an overall assessment of health, and may provide the opportunity for repeated follow-up assessments. On the other hand, the best option in some settings is to bring in personnel from outside the clinic to ask the screening questions. This method may provide more consistency in the implementation of screening and may be the only option if the primary clinicians do not have the time or interest to do screening.

Getting Started and Gaining Acceptance

Before starting, get approval and support at the institutional level from the department or service chief. Approach the clinic chief from the common ground that your aim is to enhance service to the clinic clients. The following questions are frequently raised by administrators:

- Will the alcohol screening be offensive or confusing to the patients?
- What are the benefits of the alcohol screening? Will the findings be useful to healthcare providers?
- What will we do with the information? How will referrals be managed? (Some institutions are afraid of losing potential candidates for their own alcohol treatment programs.)
- Do we have the necessary resources for incorporating alcohol screening into the current assessment procedures used with patients?

Some clinic staffers will claim that they already screen patients for alcohol problems. Focus on the advantages of using a systematic approach with every patient receiving the same screening test. Although you should definitely recommend a specific systematic screening test and referral method, we recommend using a flexible approach to carrying out screening procedures.

Get to know everyone in that system who might be affected by the screening program. Be sensitive about turf issues. Medical practitioners often feel very possessive about their patients and may perceive screening as interference from an outsider. When screening is done by someone outside the regular clinic staff, any referral that results from screening should be coordinated with the medical practitioner who has responsibility for the care of the patient.

Getting a Foot in the Door

If you bring in outside staff to do screening, they need an appropriate introduction to the clinic staff and to the patients. Be seen as part of the medical establishment; wear a local identification badge and dress in clothing customary to the setting. At first, do not ask for much from the clinic staff. It may take time to gain acceptance and for the screening program to prove its

worth. Remember that people are reluctant to have extra demands put on their time.

It is important to find an appropriate place to do the screening. Privacy and proximity to the patients are essential. However, space is at a premium in some settings. You may need to begin the program with less than optimal space and work toward improving the work space over time.

Training the Screener

Physicians often have knowledge deficits and beliefs about their patients that interfere with screening. Many believe that patients will be offended if asked about drinking. The physicians feel that they do not have the time to do screening and they do not know how to assess and refer patients with alcohol problems. Medical schools and residency training programs provide minimal training in alcohol screening and assessment procedures (Fleming et al., 1994).

Effective educational programs for physicians use skills-based training techniques. Several educational programs have been developed for physicians (Fleming et al., 1992; Dube, Goldstein, & Lewis, 1991) that focus on experiential activities such as role-plays and learner-centered strategies. These programs have demonstrated increased screening activities and knowledge of screening tests.

Training is also important if nonphysicians are to serve as screeners. When possible, it is best to select an individual to do screening who has a nonabrasive style and interpersonal skills to fit into what is usually a complex health-care system. Some screening programs have run into problems when using screeners who have been trained in conventional alcohol treatment programs. They may have difficulty adhering to the screening protocol, preferring to rely on their clinical experiences (and biases) obtained in these traditional alcohol treatment settings. When a goal of the program is screening for risk reduction rather than disease detection, you must take care to ensure that the screeners understand and accept this approach.

MOVING FROM SCREENING TO INTERVENTION

Low Rate of Compliance with Referrals for Alcoholism Treatment

The low rate of compliance with referrals has been a major problem in conducting alcohol screening programs (Stephan et al., 1992). A substantial proportion of persons identified as having alcohol-related problems or at-risk drinking do not accept or follow through on a referral for further assessment and possible treatment in specialized alcohol treatment programs. For example, despite the damage incurred to themselves and others, less than 30% of victims of alcohol-related trauma actually follow up on a referral to an alcohol treatment program (Soderstrom & Cowley, 1987). Within the Veterans Administration (VA) medical system, approximately 10% of individuals detected as having alcohol problems eventually enroll in a comprehensive treatment program (Stephan et al., 1992). Similar findings are found in non-VA facilities. A community intervention project conducted by the Addiction Research Foundation in Canada found that only 14% of at-risk drinkers accepted a referral for alcoholism treatment (noted in Babor, Ritson, & Hodgson, 1986). Moreover, even when individuals are successfully referred, most of these identified persons do not remain in treatment past the initial session (Thom, Brown, Drummond, Edwards, & Mullan, 1992b). For example, Rees, Beech, and Hore (1984) reported an immediate dropout rate of 44% in alcoholism treatment programs in the United Kingdom.

Failure to link a client with alcohol treatment can be particularly frustrating to practitioners conducting these screening programs. Such pro-viders sometimes encounter negative attitudes when they confront individuals about their drinking. This is not surprising considering the fact that these at-risk drinkers have come to the health-care setting for medical concerns that may be only indirectly associated with drinking. Unlike individuals seeking treatment in specialized alcohol programs, many of those seen in primary care settings are not experiencing external pressure from family members, friends, or employers to modify their drinking patterns (Pearlman, Zweben, & Li, 1989). Consequently, these clients are usually unaware of having problems related to drinking (Heather, 1989). In short, a different approach is needed when you begin to address drinking with those individuals who are not seeking help.

Improving Referral Compliance: A Brief Review of the Relevant Research

The low compliance rates and resulting frustrations experienced by primary care staff in dealing with at-risk drinkers have led some researchers to conduct studies evaluating methods to enhance compliance with referrals made by health-care professionals in alcohol screening programs. It has been suggested that combining screening with a brief intervention such as a referral compliance approach could result in a 10 to 30% reduction in alcohol use among at-risk drinkers (NIAAA Working Group on Alcohol Screening and Brief Interventions, 1994). A brief review of recent research on this topic is presented below.

Goldberg, Mullen, Richard, Psaty, and Ruch (1991) found that clients were more likely to accept a referral after screening when nurses asked clients about their interest in scheduling an appointment with an alcoholism counselor than when they did not. About 11% of the identified clients in the intervention group, in contrast to 2% of their counterparts in the control group, agreed to see an alcoholism counselor. We advise caution in interpreting these findings because some of the referred clients did not have a current alcohol problem when they were admitted into the study.

Elvy, Wells, and Baird (1988) evaluated a referral compliance intervention with a sample of 263 patients drawn from a surgical unit of a New Zealand hospital. To be eligible for inclusion in the study, individuals had to score three or above on the Canterbury Alcoholism Screening Test (Elvy, 1984). Individuals were excluded from the study if they were categorized as alcohol dependent or were currently in treatment for alcohol problems. Subjects were randomly assigned to either a referral group or a control group. Those assigned to a referral group received feedback on the severity of their alcohol problems, were told they would need professional help to deal with the problems, and were asked whether they would accept a referral for further assessment and perhaps treatment. The control group received no further help following the screening interview. Of the individuals assigned to the referral group, 62% accepted a referral and were subsequently seen by an alcoholism counselor, and 37% of these patients were seen by an alcoholism counselor for two appointments after discharge from the hospital.

Findings revealed that the referral group fared better than the control group in the first 12-month follow-up interview in terms of drinking behavior and social functioning. However, in the 18-month follow-up, there were fewer differences between referral and control groups with regard to the drinking and social adjustment variables. The authors speculated that the 12-month follow-up interview may have had a beneficial impact on the control group, causing them to reexamine and eventually change their drinking behavior.

Anderson and Scott (1992) compared the relative effectiveness of screening combined with a brief intervention versus screening alone with at-risk drinkers seen by their general practitioners (GPs). The GPs in the intervention group were given assessment results and details about an intervention strategy for each respondent. In addition, they were given a package of self-help leaflets to distribute to the clients. In contrast, the GPs in the control group were given neither the screening data nor the self-help pamphlets. At a one-year follow-up, 14% of the respondents in the intervention group became low-risk drinkers, whereas only 4% of participants in the control group made a similar transition.

In summary, the findings emerging from these few limited studies provide support for using brief intervention approaches in dealing with alcohol problems in primary care settings. However, although significant differences were found between the intervention and control groups, only a minority of clients appeared to benefit from the intervention. Only 11% of the intervention group in the Goldberg and colleagues study (1991) accepted a referral for alcohol treatment and only 14% of the intervention group in the Anderson and Scott study (1992) achieved the status of low-risk drinker. It seems that the strategies employed in these studies (i.e., feedback and advice) might be *necessary but not sufficient* to address the needs of at-risk drinkers seen in primary care settings.

There is a need, therefore, to improve methods of referral after screening. What strategies might be used to enhance motivational levels of at-risk clients in order to increase referral compliance rates of alcohol screening programs? This subject is discussed in the next section. It begins with an overview of a referral compliance intervention model and its application with at-risk drinkers.

Overview of the Referral Compliance Intervention Model

This intervention model has been drawn from the work on brief intervention techniques by Orford (1985), Prochaska and DiClemente (1984), Heather (1989), and Miller and Rollnick (1991). A major difference between the present model and the approaches employed in previous research on alcohol screening programs is the emphasis placed on motivational counseling techniques in the screening and referral of at-risk clients. The present model attends to discrepancies between the client and the practitioner concerning such matters as the client's beliefs about the drinking behavior (e.g., health problem versus lifestyle issue, disease versus bad habit, and so on), the level of harm associated with the drinking, and, in certain cases, the role of the family members in resolving the alcohol problem. The extent to which these differences are successfully negotiated may significantly affect the outcome of the referral. A successful referral often requires that disparities between client and practitioner concerning the preceding issues be resolved to the satisfaction of both parties (Thom et al., 1992).

An underlying assumption of the model is that the motivation for change can be enhanced by encouraging client participation in all decision-making activities pertaining to alcohol consumption. For example, before making a referral, the practitioner may ask the client to comment on the following: (1) the client's own understanding of the alcohol problems, (2) the potential consequences of continuing the current level of drinking, (3) his or her willingness to participate in assessment and possible treatment for alcohol problems, (4) various options related to dealing with the drinking behavior (e.g., self-directed change vs. formal intervention), and (5) how family members and/or friends might react to his or her undertaking a comprehensive alcohol assessment.

We recommend incorporating alcohol screening procedures into a standardized health habits interview. This allows questions or concerns about alcohol use to be discussed in the language of health promotion rather than disease detection. Avoid reference to disease labels such as "alcoholism" and "alcoholic." You want to convey to the client that there are potential health risks associated with drinking, and that, based on the information gathered in the screening test, you need to determine whether the client is at risk for such problems. Consequently, when referring a client for assessment, it might be useful to describe such an assessment as a "Drinker's Check-Up" (Miller & Sovereign, 1989) rather than an alcoholism or substance abuse evaluation. You might add that this assessment is designed not for alcoholics but for people who are interested in learning more about alcohol and health.

The overall goal of the referral compliance intervention is to initiate or facilitate clients' help-seeking behavior. This approach is employed either to motivate the client to participate in a detailed alcohol assessment or to facilitate self-directed change (i.e., to help a client abstain or cut down on the drinking without receiving formal intervention). How the intervention is used in a particular setting is often dependent on the availability and accessibility of suitable treatments in the community and the level of knowledge and skill of practitioners in motivational counseling techniques. For example, in circumstances where suitable treatment alternatives are *not* available (e.g., Drinker's Check-Up program), it may be necessary to use brief intervention as a stand-alone treatment approach with at-risk drinkers rather than as a method to motivate these clients to seek further assessment and treatment for their alcohol problems. For those readers interested in using brief intervention to initiate self-directed change, we refer you to Chapters 5 and 6. The primary focus of the present chapter is on how to motivate clients to seek assessment and perhaps treatment for their alcohol problems.

Description of the Referral Compliance Intervention Process

Immediately following a brief screening, the practitioner shares the test results with the client in a supportive and nonconfrontational manner; he or she informs the client systematically about the harmful effects of the drinking behavior. The practitioner then advises the individual about what resources might be contacted for obtaining an assessment of the alcohol problems. Alcohol assessment services may be available within the primary care setting or may only be available outside the setting in which the screening was conducted (e.g., specialized alcohol treatment programs). In most cases, the practitioner will need to help the client arrange an assessment appointment with the appropriate program or treatment facility.

When making any kind of referral, try to remove obstacles that may prevent easy compliance with the recommended action. It is important to establish formal linkages with services that are accessible and available to the kind of individuals seen in your treatment setting. Be sure to inform clients that agencies specializing

in alcohol-related problems usually require a detailed assessment before a decision can be made about what kind of treatment might be most relevant to their needs and capacities.

A practitioner can use a self-help pamphlet for purposes of increasing clients' understanding of the negative consequence of their drinking pattern and enhancing their knowledge about various treatment approaches that might be helpful in changing the drinking pattern (e.g., self-help versus professional treatment, group versus individual therapy, etc.). The self-help pamphlet can also provide clients with information on how to gain access to needed services (e.g., contact person, fees, insurance coverage, and waiting period for initial appointment).

The style of the practitioner is similar to the manner employed by persons conducting motivational counseling sessions (Miller & Rollnick, 1991; Chick, 1992). The practitioner takes a neutral stance in discussing the data and avoids arguments by using techniques such as summarizing, clarifying, and reflective listening. He or she promotes interaction with the client in discussing issues related to the current pattern of consumption. This approach is expected to make it more likely that the client will make a commitment to deal with the alcohol problems (Zweben, Bonner, Chaim, & Santon, 1988).

Giving Feedback to the Client

Present the information in a neutral or consultative manner, summarizing the data in an objective fashion, clarifying complex material (e.g., medical information), and checking repeatedly for understanding and agreement (Miller & Rollnick, 1991; Miller, Zweben, DiClemente, & Rychtarik, 1992; see also Chapter 5). Preface your remarks by saying, "The data seem to indicate . . . ," instead of saying, "In my opinion . . . " Ask the client, "Are you clear about the information? Do you agree? What concerns do you have about the findings?" Getting clients' reactions to the screening data can be helpful in promoting their investment in the change process (Zweben & Barrett, 1993).

With clients who are defensive about their drinking practices, strategies such as reflective listening and normalizing are useful (Miller & Rollnick, 1991). For example, with clients who continually express disbelief and frustration about the drinking data, it can be useful to state the following, "It is not unusual for you to be concerned about the findings, since the information presented is quite different from your own thinking about your drinking." Such an approach can help to achieve a mutuality between you and the client about the drinking behavior.

Offering Advice to the Client

Before offering advice, find out whether agreement has been reached with the client about the primary presenting problems (e.g., at-risk drinking). At the same time, determine the extent to which the client is committed to undergoing assessment for alcohol problems. If consensus has been reached and the client appears committed to examining the drinking behavior, the process of advice giving should be relatively straightforward. Examine the pros and cons of different ways of dealing with the drinking behavior. One alternative of the client's is to do nothing at all. However, before the client responds, remind him or her about the consequences of such inaction. Data derived from the screening can be used to resolve any lingering doubts the client may have about attending an alcohol assessment interview.

Practical motivational strategies can be effective in referring a client for a detailed assessment and possible treatment. Reinforce client statements about changing the drinking behavior. ("I am impressed with your willingness (or desire) to examine your drinking.") Normalize the ambivalence and uncertainty the client expresses about attending an assessment interview. ("Many people investigating their drinking have their doubts about such an exercise.") Emphasize the individual's choices in deciding what action needs to be taken. ("It's up to you to decide whether you will attend an assessment session.")

Despite your efforts to initiate help-seeking behavior, clients may remain uncooperative or defensive about addressing the alcohol problems. Attempts to refer a client for assessment and treatment may be met with strong resistance. If this happens, do not negotiate a referral at this juncture. There is a danger here of the client prematurely agreeing to attend an assessment interview to appease the practitioner. The client then may not return for future appointments in order to avoid embarrassment about his or her inability or unwillingness to follow your recommendations. Instead of negotiating a referral, underscore the client's current misgivings about the need to further examine the drinking behavior by saying, "Perhaps we missed something. You may want to obtain a second opinion."

Before ending the session, offer the client a follow-up appointment where you could do a more detailed assessment. In the meantime, a personal feedback report and a self-help pamphlet can be offered to the client (Miller et al., 1992). The handbook should include a list of community resources in case the individual decides to seek professional help at some future time.

In postponing decision making about alcohol assessment and treatment, you give the client an opportunity to consider, on his or her own, the negative aspects of drinking. It also enables the client to share the information with family members and friends and thereby gain support for pursuing help with the alcohol problems (Longabaugh, Beattie, Noel, Stout, & Malloy, 1993). You might say to the client, "It may be better not to make a decision about undertaking an alcohol assessment at this time. You may need to think more about this, and perhaps explore the matter with some important people in your life before you decide what to do." The rationale underlying such an approach stems from the belief that individuals faced with decisions that may place them in conflict about their current alcohol use may be better prepared to act favorably on them over time (Miller et al., 1992).

SUMMARY

In this chapter, we have attempted to describe some of the key concepts underlying alcohol screening and to provide practical guidance for those wishing to implement such programs. Conceptually, it is important to consider that screening can be done not only for disease detection but also for risk reduction. When using a risk-reduction approach, it is important to follow up screening with detailed assessment and referrals to levels of treatment matched to clients' needs. A number of screening approaches were described. Currently, there is no single best screening test, so the selection of a screening test depends on your client population and clinical situation. Screening programs often fail because few clients follow up with referrals. Attention to motivational issues is essential for obtaining compliance with referrals in an alcohol screening program.

REFERENCES

Clinical Guidelines

Anderson, P., Cremona, A., Paton, A., Turner, C., & Wallace, P. (1993). The risk of alcohol. *Addiction*, *88*, 1493–1508. Reviews 156 studies relating alcohol consumption to risk for physical damage. This article provides a solid scientific basis for defining at-risk drinking.

NIAAA Working Group on Alcohol Screening and Brief Interventions. (1994). *A physicians guide: How to help your patients with alcohol problems.* Unpublished manuscript. Developed by an expert working group on alcohol screening and brief intervention. Loaded with practical suggestions.

Safer, M. A. (1986). A comparison of screening for disease detection and screening for risk factors. *Health Education Research: Theory and Practice, 1,* 131–138. Describes conceptual and practical differences between the traditional model of screening for disease detection and an alternative model of screening for risk factors.

U.S. Department of Health and Human Services. (1994). Screening and brief intervention. In *Special report to the U.S. Congress on alcohol and health* (Chapter 13). Reviews and recommends alcohol screening methods.

Literature Cited

Anderson, P., Cremona, A., Paton, A., Turner, C., & Wallace, P. (1993). The risk of alcohol. *Addiction, 88,* 1493–1508.

Anderson, P., & Scott, E. (1992). The effect of general practitioners' advice to heavy drinking men. *British Journal of Addiction, 87,* 891–900.

Babor, T. F., Brown, J., & Del Boca, F. K. (1990). Validity of self-reports in applied research on addictive behaviors: Fact or fiction? *Behavioral Assessment, 12,* 1–27.

Babor, T. F., de la Fuente, J. R., Saunders, J., & Grant, M. (1992). *The Alcohol Use Disorders Identification Test: Guidelines for use in primary health care.* Geneva: World Health Organization.

Babor, T., & Grant, M. (1989). From clinical research to secondary prevention: International collaboration in the development of the Alcohol Use Disorders Identification Test (AUDIT). *Alcohol Health and Research World, 13,* 371–374.

Babor, T., Korner, P., Wilber, C., & Good, S. (1987). Screening and early intervention strategies for harmful drinkers: Initial lessons from the AMETHYST project. *Australian Drug and Alcohol Review, 6,* 325–339.

Babor, T. F., Ritson, E. B., & Hodgson, R. J. (1986). Alcohol-related problems in the primary health care setting: A review of early intervention strategies. *British Journal of Addiction, 81,* 23–46.

Barry, K., & Fleming, M. (1990). Computerized administration of alcoholism screening tests in a primary care setting. *Journal of the American Board of Family Practice, 3*(2), 93–98.

Barry, K., & Fleming, M. (1993). The alcohol use disorders identification test (AUDIT) and the SMAST–13: Predictive validity in a primary care setting. *Alcohol and Alcoholism, 28,* 33–42.

Behrens, U., Werner, T., Braly, L., Schaffner, F., & Lieber, C. (1988). Carbohydrate-deficient transferrin, a marker for chronic alcohol consumption in different ethnic populations. *Alcoholism: Clinical Experimental Research, 12,* 427–432.

Bernadt, M., Daniels, O., Blizard, R., & Murray, R. (1989). Can a computer reliably elicit an alcohol history? *British Journal of Addiction, 84,* 405–411.

Bernadt, M., Mumford, V., & Smith, T. (1982). Comparison of questionnaire and laboratory tests in the detection of excessive drinking and alcoholism. *Lancet, 1*(8267), 325–328.

Beresford, T. P., Blow, F. C., Hill, E., Singer, K., & Lucey, M. (1990). Comparison of CAGE questionnaire and computer-assisted laboratory profiles in screening for covert alcoholism. *Lancet, 336,* 482–485.

Blow, F., Young, J., Hill, E., Singer, K., & Beresford, T. (1991). *Predictive value of brief alcoholism screening tests in a sample of hospitalized adults.* Fifth annual NIMH international research conference proceedings. Washington, DC: U.S. Government Printing Office.

Brown, R. (1992). Identification and office management of alcohol and drug disorders. In M. Fleming (Ed.), *Addiction disorders: A practical guide to treatment* (pp. 25–43). Chicago: Yearbook Medical Publishers.

Bush, B., Shaw, S., Cleary, P., Delbanco, T., & Aronson, M. (1987). Screening for alcohol abuse using the CAGE questionnaire. *The American Journal of Medicine, 82,* 231–234.

Chan, A. W., Leong, F. W., Schanley, D. L., Welte, J. W., Wieczorek, W., Rej, R., & Whitney, R. B. (1989). Transferrin and mitochondrial aspartate aminotransferase in young adult alcoholics. *Drug and Alcohol Dependency, 23,* 13–18.

Chang, G., Astrachan, B. (1988). The emergency department surveillance of alcohol intoxication after motor vehicle accidents. *Journal of the American Medical Association, 260,* 2533–2536.

Cherpitel, C. (1989). Breath analysis and self reports as measures of alcohol-related emergency room admissions. *Journal of the Studies on Alcohol, 50,* 155–161.

Chick, J. (1992). Emergent treatment concepts. *Annual Review of Addictions Research and Treatment,* 297–312.

Cushman, P., Jacobson, G., Barboriak, J., & Anderson, A. (1984). Biochemical markers for alcoholism: Sensitivity problems. *Alcoholism: Clinical and Experimental Research, 8,* 253–257.

Cutler, S., Wallace, P., & Haines, A. (1988). Assessing alcohol consumption in general practice patients—A comparison between questionnaire and interview (findings of the medical research council's general practice research framework study on lifestyle and health). *Alcohol and Alcoholism, 23,* 441–450.

Dube, C., Goldstein, M., & Lewis, D. (1991, November). *A learner centered faculty development program in alcohol and drug abuse.* Paper presented at the annual meeting of the Association for Medical Education and Research in Substance Abuse, Washington, DC.

Elvy, G. A. (1984). The Canterbury Alcoholism Screening Test (CAST): A detection instrument for use with hospitalized patients. *New England Journal of Medicine, 97,* 111–115.

Elvy, G. A., Wells, J. E., & Baird, K. A. (1988). Attempted referral as intervention for problem drinking in the general hospital. *British Journal of Addiction, 83,* 83–89.

Erdman, H., Klein, R., & Griest, J. (1985). Direct patient computer interviewing. *Journal of Consulting and Clinical Psychology, 53,* 760–763.

Ewing, J. (1984). Detecting alcoholism: The CAGE questionnaire. *Journal of the American Medical Association, 252*, 1905–1907.

Ewing, H. (1992). Care of women and children in the perinatal period. In M. F. Fleming (Ed.), *Addiction disorders: A practical guide to treatment* (pp. 232–248). Chicago: Yearbook Medical Publishers.

Fleming, M., & Barry, K. (1991). A three-sample test of a masked alcohol screening questionnaire. *Alcohol and Alcoholism, 26*, 81–91.

Fleming, M. F., Barry, K. L., Davis, R., Kropp, S., Kahn, R., & Rivo, M. (1994). Medical education about substance abuse: Changes in curriculum and faculty between 1976 and 1992. *Academic Medicine, 69*, 362–369.

Fleming, M., Barry, K., & MacDonald, R. (1991). The alcohol use disorders identification test (AUDIT) in a college sample. *International Journal of the Addictions, 26*, 1173–1185.

Fleming, M., Clark, K., Davis, A., Borwn, R., Finch, J., Henry, R., Sherwood, R., & Politzer, R. (1992). A national model of faculty development in addiction medicine. *Academic Medicine, 67*, 691–693.

Fuller, R., Branchey, L., Brightwell, D, Derman, R. M., Emrick, C. D., Iber, F. L., James, K. E., Lacoursiere, R. B., Lee, K. K., Lowenstam, I., Maany, I., Neiderhiser, D., Nocks, J. J., & Shaw, S. (1986). Disulfiram treatment of alcoholism: A veterans administration cooperative study. *Journal of the American Medical Association, 256*, 1449–1455.

Gjerde, H., Amundsen, A., Skog, O., Mørland, J., & Aasland, O. (1987). Serum gammaglutamyltransferase: Am epidemiological indicator of alcohol consumption? *British Journal of the Addictions, 82*, 1027–1031.

Goldberg, H. I., Mullen, M., Richard, K. R., Psaty, B. M., & Ruch, B. P. (1991). Alcohol counseling in a general medicine clinic. *Medicine Care, 7*, JS49–JS56.

Graham, A. (1991). Screening for alcoholism by lifestyle risk assessment in a community hospital. *Archives of Internal Medicine, 51*, 448–456.

Heather, N. (1989). Psychology and brief intervention. *British Journal of Addiction, 84*, 357–370.

Institute of Medicine. (1990). *Broadening the base of treatment for alcohol problems.* Washington, DC: National Academy Press.

Kapur, A., Wild, G., Milford-Ward, A., & Triger, D. (1989). Carbohydrate deficient transferrin: A marker for alcohol abuse. *British Journal of Medicine, 299*, 427–431.

King, M. (1986). At risk drinking among general practice attenders: Validation of the CAGE questionnaire. *Psychological Medicine, 16*, 213–217.

Klitzner, M., & Rahdert, E. (1991, September). *Screening and assessing adolescent substance abusers in primary care: the adolescent assessment/referral system.* Paper presented at the Fifth Annual Intervention NIMH Conference in Classification, Recognition, and Treatment of Mental Health Disorders, Bethesda, MD.

Kreitman, N. (1986). Alcohol consumption and the preventive paradox. *British Journal of Addiction, 81*, 353–363.

Longabaugh, R., Beattie, M., Noel, N., Stout, R., & Malloy, P. (1993). The effect of social investment on treatment outcome. *Journal of Studies on Alcohol, 54*, 465–478.

Miller, W. R., & Rollnick, S. (1991). *Motivational interviewing: Preparing people to change addictive behavior.* New York: Guilford Press.

Miller, W. R., & Sovereign, G. (1989). The check-up: A model for early intervention in addictive behaviors. In T. Loberg, W. R. Miller, P. E. Nathan, & G. A. Marlatt (Eds.), *Addictive behaviors: Prevention and early intervention* (pp. 219–231). Amsterdam: Swets and Zeitlinger.

Miller, W. R., Zweben, A. DiClemente, C. C., & Rychtarik, R. G. (1992). *Motivational enhancement therapy (MET): A clinical research guide for therapists treating individuals with alcohol abuse and dependence* (DHHS Publication No. ADM 92–1894). Washington, DC: U.S. Government Printing Office.

Nalpas, B., Vassault, A., Charpin, S., Lacour, B., & Berthelot, P. (1986). Serum mitochondrial aspartate aminotransferase as a marker of chronic alcoholism: Diagnostic value and interpretation in a liver unit. *Hepatology, 6*, 608–614.

Nalpas, B., Vassault, A., LeGuillou, A., Lesgourgues, B., Ferry, N., Lacour, B., & Berthelot, P. (1984). Serum mitochondrial aspartate aminotransferase: A sensitive markers of alcoholism with or without alcoholic hepatitis. *Hepatology, 4*, 893–896.

National Institute on Alcohol Abuse and Alcoholism. (1990). Screening for alcoholism. *Alcohol Alert* (PH285). Rockville, MD: U.S. Government Printing Office.

National Institute on Drug Abuse. (1990). Problem oriented screening instruments for teenagers. In E. Rahdert (Ed), *The adolescent assessment/referral system manual*, Rockville, MD: U.S. Government Printing Office.

NIAAA Working Group on Alcohol Screening and Brief Intervention. (1994). *A physicians guide: How to help your patients with alcohol problems.* Unpublished manuscript.

Orford, J. (1985). *Excessive appetites: A psychological view of addictions.* New York: John Wiley & Sons.

Orford, J., Oppenheimer, E., & Edwards, G. (1976). Abstinence or control: The outcome for excessive drinkers two years after consultation. *Behaviour Research and Therapy, 14*, 409–418.

Pearlman, S., Zweben, A., & Li, S. (1989). The comparability of solicited versus non-solicited clients in alcoholism treatment research. *British Journal of Addiction, 84*, 523–532.

Persson, J., Magnusson, P., & Borg, S. (1990). Serum gamma-glutamyl transferase (GGT) in a group of organized teetotalers. *Alcohol, 7*, 87–79.

Poupon, R., Schellenberg, F., Nalpas, B., & Weill, J. (1989). Assessment of the transferrin index in screening heavy drinkers from a general practice. *Alcoholism: Clinical and Experimental Research, 13*, 549–553.

Prochaska, J. O., & DiClemente, C. C. (1984). *The transtheoretical approach: Crossing traditional boundaries of therapy.* Homewood, IL: Dow Jones-Irwin.

Rees, D. W., Beech, H. R., & Hore, B. D. (1984). Some factors associated with compliance in treatment of alcoholism. *Alcohol and Alcoholism, 19*, 303–307.

Robins, L. (1985). Epidemiology: Reflections on testing the validity of psychiatric interviews. *Archives of General Psychiatry, 42*, 918–924.

Russell, M. (1994). New assessment tools for drinking in pregnancy: T-ACE, TWEAK, and others. *Alcohol Health and Research World*.

Russell, M., Martier, S. S., Sokol, R. J., Jacobson, S., Jacobson, J., & Bottoms, S. (1991, June). *Screening for pregnancy risk-drinking: TWEAKING the tests*. Paper presented at the annual meeting of the Research Society on Alcoholism, Marco Island, FL.

Safer, M. A. (1986). A comparison of screening for disease detection and screening for risk factors. *Health Education Research: Theory and Practice, 1*, 131–138.

Saunders, J., Aasland, O., Babor, T., de la Fuenta, J., & Grant, M. (1993). Development of the Alcohol Use Disorders Identification Test (AUDIT): WHO collaborative project on early detection of persons with harmful alcohol consumption II. *Addiction, 86*, 791–804.

Schellenberg, F., Benard, J., LeGoff, A., Bourdin, C., & Weill, J. (1989). Evaluation of carbohydrate-deficient transferrin compared with QF index and other markers of alcohol abuse. *Alcoholism: Clinical and Experimental Research, 13*, 615–610.

Schmidt, P. M., & Cooney, N. L. (1992). Implementing an alcohol screening program. *the Behavior Therapist, 15*, 192–195.

Shepherd, D., Hargarten, S., & Westlake, T. (1993, May). *Alcohol screening in the ED: Blood vs. spit*. Paper presented at the annual meeting of the Society for Academic Emergency Medicine, San Francisco, CA.

Skinner, H. (1990). Spectrum of drinkers and intervention opportunities. *Canadian Medical Association Journal, 143*, 1054–1059.

Skinner, H., Allen, B., McIntosh, M., & Palmer, W. (1985). Lifestyle assessment: Just asking makes a difference. *British Medical Journal, 290*, 214–215.

Soderstrom, C. A., & Cowley, R. A. (1987). A national alcohol and trauma center survey. *Archives of Surgery, 122*, 1067–1071.

Stephan, M., Swindle, R. W., & Moos, R. H. (1992). Alcohol screening in the Department of Veterans Affairs medical centers. In R. E. Parry (Ed.), *Screening for alcoholism in the Department of Veterans Affairs* Washington, DC: Department of Veterans Affairs.

Stibler, H., & Hultcranta, R. (1987). Carbohydrate-deficient transferrin (CDT) in serum in patients with liver diseases. *Alcoholism: Clinical Experimental Research, 11*, 468–473.

Thom, B., Brown, C., Drummond, C., Edwards, G., Mullan, M., & Taylor, C. (1992a). Engaging patients with alcohol problems in treatment: The first consultation. *British Journal of Addiction, 87*, 601–611.

Thom, B., Brown, C., Drummond, C., Edwards, G., & Mullan, M. (1992b). The use of services for alcohol problems: General practitioner and specialist alcohol clinic. *British Journal of Addiction, 87*, 613–624.

United States Department of Health and Human Services. (1994). Screening and brief intervention. In *Eighth Special Report to the U. S. Congress on Alcohol and Health* (Chapter 13). Washington, DC: National Institute on Alcohol Abuse and Alcoholism.

United States General Accounting Office. (1991). *VA health care. Alcoholism screening procedures should be improved* (HRD Publication 91–71). Gaithersburg, MD: United States General Accounting Office.

Wallace, P., & Haines, A. (1985). The use of a questionnaire in general practice to increase the recognition of patients with excessive alcohol consumption. *British Medical Journal, 290*, 1949–1953.

Zweben, A., & Barrett, D. (1993). Assessment and brief advice as a treatment for alcoholic and spouse. In T. J. O'Farrell (Ed.), *Marital and family therapy in alcoholism treatment* (pp. 421–455). New York: Guiford Publications.

Zweben, A., Bonner, M., Chaim, G., & Santon, P. (1988). Facilitative strategies for retaining alcohol-dependent clients in outpatient treatment. *Alcoholism Treatment Quarterly, 5*(1/2), 3–24.

CHAPTER 4

Evaluating Alcohol Problems in Adults and Adolescents

William R. Miller
Verner S. Westerberg
Holly B. Waldron

PURPOSES OF EVALUATION IN CLINICAL PRACTICE

Why spend time on evaluation? To some, "filling out forms" is something that should be kept to a minimum because it is done merely to satisfy bureaucratic requirements and it delays the beginning of treatment. The need for careful evaluation in treatment research is fairly obvious, but how useful is it in clinical practice?

Several important purposes can be served by evaluation of clients who are seeking help for alcohol problems. These different but complementary functions can all contribute to improved treatment services. In this chapter we will describe six different functions of evaluation: (1) screening, (2) diagnosis, (3) assessment, (4) motivation, (5) treatment planning, and (6) follow-up. Specific instruments are available for each of these purposes, and some comprehensive instruments can fulfill several of these functions.

This chapter is a practical guide for selecting and designing evaluation approaches to use

in clinical settings. Given the focus of this volume, we will emphasize alcohol-focused instruments, with the clear recognition that other drugs are often involved as well and thus require consideration. Many of the specific instruments considered here include or have parallel forms for drug use other than alcohol. We will provide an overview of the six purposes of evaluation first, and then discuss the general characteristics of sound evaluation instruments, before offering recommendations on the menu of instruments available for each purpose.

SCREENING

The purpose of *screening* is detection or case identification. Screening instruments typically are designed to provide binary (yes or no) data to indicate the existence of a particular problem or disorder—in this case, alcohol problems. The task in screening is to identify *potential* cases in need of further evaluation.

The importance of screening depends partly on context. If a client is already walking through the doors of an alcohol treatment clinic, screening may be of less importance, and more comprehensive assessment is needed. In a primary health-care clinic, on the other hand, screening may be the most important evaluation function, and the only task for which there is sufficient time in a busy practice. Such screening can be important not only in initiating referrals but also as part of proper health care. Recurrent physical or psychological problems may be secondary to a primary alcohol use disorder. Gastric ulcers or hypertension, for example, may be caused by a variety of factors, but if these conditions are related to or exacerbated by drinking, they may not respond well to conventional therapies without attention to alcohol use. In such cases, screening for excessive drinking can be important in addressing medical concerns, and treatment of the putative alcohol disorder would make good medical sense.

Issues and procedures used in screening are described in detail in Chapter 3. For present purposes, then, we will simply note that screening is often confused with other functions of evaluation, and that screening instruments are sometimes misused as assessment or diagnostic devices.

Popular "laundry list" questionnaires such as the Michigan Alcoholism Screening Test (Selzer, 1971) or the Johns Hopkins 20 Questions (Seliger, 1940) contain a broad mixture of items asking about problems, drinking styles, dependence symptoms, perceptions, and help seeking. Such lists may serve as a crude general screen, indicating a need for more careful assessment. A common misuse, however, is reflected in interpretive guidelines sometimes appended to such lists (e.g., that answering one "yes" gives a warning that one *may be* an alcoholic, two "yes" responses indicate *probable* alcoholism, and three "yes" responses show *definite* alcoholism). This confuses screening with diagnoses, a very different purpose that is described below. Such use oversteps the validity and intended purpose of screening devices, and represents a violation of professional ethical standards (AERA, APA, & NCME, 1985). When properly used, however, screening instruments can be a valuable asset in health care. A relatively small investment of time and resources can indicate the need for further evaluation of a potentially important risk factor, which in turn may trigger intervention with long-term health benefits (e.g., Kristenson, Ohlin, Hulten-Nosslin, Trell, & Hood, 1983).

DIAGNOSIS

This term *diagnosis* (to know the difference, to discern) has had many meanings. In the broad view described by Jacobson (1989), diagnosis "should lead to a clearer understanding of the etiology, development, expression, and purpose of the alcoholism; the formulation of adequate and appropriate treatment plans and programs; some notion of prognosis; and full appraisal of the efficacy and outcome of the treatments" (p. 21). Such a broad view of diagnosis encompasses the purposes of assessment, treatment planning, and follow-up described below.

These broad goals are not fulfilled by diagnostic tools currently in use, which more closely resemble screening instruments. The difference is that the list of symptoms contained in common diagnostic instruments is specifically delimited to those that define a disorder within a particular diagnostic taxonomy. In the United States, the taxonomic systems commonly used for diagnosis are the *Diagnostic and Statistical Manual* (DSM) of the American Psychiatric Association, and the International Classification of Diseases (ICD). Several interview instruments, described later, have been designed specifically to determine whether an individual meets such diagnostic criteria for defined disorders such as alcohol abuse and alcohol dependence. These procedures are used when formal diagnosis is required for purposes such as medical records, triage, or determination of eligibility for health care and other benefits.

The determination of an alcohol disorder diagnosis, however, provides no understanding of the client's unique situation (assessment), and very little help with motivation and treatment planning. Part of the confusion here arises from the fact that there have been dramatic changes in professional understanding of alcohol problems and how to treat them. Alcoholism was once viewed as a unitary condition with a single predictable course (see Chapter 1) for which a one-size-fits-all treatment was sufficient. Within this view, a diagnosis of alcoholism may seem to be all that one needs to know in order to proceed with treatment. A more complex contemporary understanding has evolved with a multidimensional perspective of alcohol use and associated problems as continuous rather than binary variables, with many gradations (Maisto & Conners, 1990). From this perspective, a binary "signal detection" process is a woefully inadequate evaluation. Specific instruments, described below as "assessment" procedures, have been developed to evaluate the range of clinically relevant dimensions.

For the purposes of this chapter, then, we will define *diagnosis* as the process of determining whether an individual meets currently established criteria for a particular diagnostic label according to a specific taxonomic system such as DSM. We readily acknowledge, however, that there are broader conceptions of diagnosis that encompass some of the additional purposes of evaluation described in this chapter.

ASSESSMENT

When there is an indication, from screening or referral, of possible concerns related to alcohol, evaluation procedures are needed to address the more complex questions of *assessment*. As contrasted with screening and diagnosis, assessment is meant to aid in the understanding of a person's unique situation. Comprehensive assessment involves evaluation of several important domains, which are modestly correlated at best. Knowing a client's status on any one of these dimensions tells you little or nothing about the others, and each may be important in understanding and addressing the client's situation. Assessment thus gives breadth to one's understanding, revealing the size and nature of the client's problem. Unlike screening and diagnosis, which are binary detection (yes/no) tasks, assessment tells you where a client stands along a number of important dimensions.

In discussing specific assessment procedures later in this chapter, we will focus on six general dimensions: (1) alcohol use, (2) negative consequences of use, (3) alcohol dependence, (4) family history, (5) neuropsychological functioning, and (6) physical sequelae. These domains can be sampled separately through the use of individual tests. In this way, specific evaluation packages can be constructed to meet the needs of particular individuals, referral situations, or programs. Most of these domains can also be sampled through comprehensive interviews that will be discussed at the end of our section on assessment methods.

Before moving on to other purposes of assessment, note that our discussion here is limited to dimensions specifically related to alcohol disorders. Frequently, it is also important to broaden one's evaluation to include psychological functioning more generally. Research on co-morbidity or "dual diagnoses" clearly indicates that people with substance use disorders show higher rates of many other problems, including depression, anxiety disorders, psychoses, relationship and sexual difficulties, and personality disorders (Gold & Slaby, 1991). Obviously, a comprehensive review of psychological assessment is well beyond the scope of a single chapter such as this. The same levels of evaluation reviewed here can be applied to other disorders. It is important, for example, to screen for depression and anxiety disorders among people in treatment for alcohol problems. An indication (from screening) of possible problems in these areas can lead to further diagnosis and assessment, motivation and treatment planning, and follow-up evaluation. Like the alcohol-specific methods described in this chapter, more general psychological evaluation requires specific training and expertise.

MOTIVATION

A fourth purpose of evaluation is to determine or enhance the individual's *motivation for change*. Although there are differences of opinion about how best to understand substance abuse, an apparent point of agreement is that (lack of) motivation for change is a significant obstacle in addressing alcohol problems. At any given time, the vast majority of individuals with substance abuse problems are in a "precontemplation" stage, not ready to consider or pursue change (e.g., Snow, Prochaska, & Rossi, 1992). Within treatment settings a common complaint of therapists and other health-care workers is of client denial, resistance, and the lack of motivation (Miller, 1985; Miller & Rollnick, 1991).

It can be helpful, therefore, to evaluate a client's current level of motivation for change, and specific instruments are available for this purpose. Other information obtained during assessment may also be used as feedback for the client in order to enhance motivation for change, an application that is discussed in more detail in Chapter 5. In this chapter, we will focus on methods for evaluating the nature and degree of client motivation for change.

TREATMENT PLANNING

The development of clear goals and plans is an important part of treatment and is a requirement of routine practice in accredited treatment programs. As a fifth purpose in evaluation, *treatment planning* may draw from any of the areas described in this chapter. Knowledge of client motivation and of status on a variety of assessment dimensions, for example, can be helpful in choosing optimal treatment strategies. If the same treatment is offered to all clients regardless of their personal characteristics and individual needs, of course, then an individualized treatment plan is superfluous. To the extent that treatment is selected and individualized to address clients' differing needs and problems, comprehensive evaluation provides an informational foundation upon which to plan treatment. The particular treatment strategy that is chosen may also require specific kinds of assessment. Issues and approaches in client-treatment matching are more fully discussed in Chapter 17.

FOLLOW-UP

Within the framework described above, the process of evaluation flows naturally into treatment. The need for treatment may be detected via screening and diagnosis. A clearer picture of the client's situation is obtained by comprehensive assessment, which in turn can be used to enhance motivation and plan treatment strategies. In this understanding, evaluation is not something that is done only before treatment begins. Rather, evaluation is an integral part of the therapeutic process, and continues during and after the delivery of treatment. Therapeutic intervention begins and ends with evaluation.

There are good reasons to extend the evaluation process past the end of formal treatment. All of these have to do with the quality of treatment services. Follow-up interviewing is most often considered as a part of program evaluation and outcome research, for determining the effectiveness of treatment. We argue, however, that systematic follow-up is an integral aspect of commitment to quality care, and a *vital part* of sound treatment.

By *follow-up*, we mean the continuation of assessment during and after treatment. We do not mean an aftercare program that is available to clients on an ad-lib basis, but rather planned, systematic evaluation of progress. One important reason for such follow-up evaluation is that it provides you, as a therapist, with personal feedback. Too often, clinicians work in an information vacuum, offering services with little or no feedback about the ultimate impact of their work. The feedback that does occur is often negative, by selectively encountering clients who have relapsed and need additional services. Any learning requires reliable feedback, and without such knowledge there is no improvement in skills. Conducting treatment without follow-up has therefore been likened to playing golf in the fog. The shot may feel good, and one can see the ball for a short distance, but there is no knowledge of where it finally lands. Systematic follow-up provides feedback that allows clinicians to improve their skills. It also provides the encouragement of seeing positive outcomes from one's own work—a link often missing in practice.

Continuing assessment also allows you to discover unintentionally detrimental aspects of current practice. Though not pleasant to contemplate, treatment practices can yield harmful results, producing outcomes worse than those from no treatment at all. No therapist sets out intending to do harm, so what is the importance of the ancient and traditional oath of healers: "First, do no harm"? Because any therapist can unintentionally and unknowingly inflict harm, feedback is important. Without follow-up, one may never discover whether procedures and changes that are implemented in practice lead to beneficial or detrimental outcomes. If the latter, practices should change, but this cannot occur without feedback.

Beyond these important issues, there are persuasive clinical benefits in follow-up as well. Clients often perceive follow-up visits as continuing treatment and as an indication of caring for their welfare. In several ways, they are right. Follow-up evaluations can serve as booster sessions, raising the client's awareness of his or her current situation and communicating that you, the therapist, are still interested and accessible. Regular follow-up can function as relapse prevention through early identification of emerging client concerns, and allows course correction in treatment plans. Good follow-up also enhances communication between clients and professionals. Such continued care fosters positive relationships with clients and the community, and yields both formal and informal inputs that can be useful in continuing program and practice improvement.

Last, good follow-up provides for good documentation. Funding and accrediting bodies are already requiring increased monitoring of outcomes. In an era of managed care and rapidly evolving health-care policy, such accountability for outcomes is likely to continue to grow.

Table 4.1 Six Purposes of Evaluation

PURPOSE	RESULT	CENTRAL QUESTION
Screening	Categorical	Is there reason for further evaluation?
Diagnosis	Categorical	Are diagnostic criteria met?
Assessment	Continuous	To what extent and in what ways are there problems?
Motivation	Continuous	To what extent and in what ways is the person ready for change?
Treatment Planning	Categorical	What is needed? What type(s) of intervention(s) is(are) most likely to be effective?
Follow-Up	Continuous	What has changed? What is still needed?

Payers are less willing to assume that treatment is effective without hard data to substantiate such claims. Systematic follow-up assessment may therefore serve important program development and survival functions as well. We will return to a discussion of program evaluation issues at the end of this chapter.

In summary, these six purposes of evaluation are outlined in Table 4.1. For each of these six reasons, we have specified the overall question addressed and indicated whether the result of the evaluation is typically categorical (e.g., yes/no) or continuous (e.g., severity).

SPECIAL CONSIDERATIONS IN EVALUATING ADOLESCENTS

The preceding discussion has focused on the evaluation of alcohol problems in adults. When one is working with adolescents, special considerations arise. Compared to adult instruments, for example, most adolescent instruments are still in the developmental stages and their effectiveness for problem identification, diagnosis, and treatment planning is largely unknown. A lack of standardized use of assessment tools across treatment facilities is a problem that limits the degree to which treatment efficacy comparisons can be made. Also, adult measures adapted for use with adolescents often have not been tested for their reliability and validity with adolescent populations.

Another difference between adult and adolescent alcohol use is the ambiguity that exists regarding what constitutes problem use in adolescents (Bailey, 1989; Hawkins, Catalano, & Miller, 1992; Hughes, Power, & Francis, 1992). Some would argue that experimentation with alcohol and other drugs is statistically normal; in fact, it is the case that by late adolescence more youth have tried these substances than have not (Johnston, Bachman, & O'Malley, 1991). In the case of alcohol, 90% of all high school seniors have had some drinking experience. The majority of adolescents (and adults) who experiment with drugs do not become addicted (Shedler & Block, 1990), and many adolescents appear to "mature out" of problem use with a sharp drop in drug use after age 21 (Kouzis & Labouvie, 1992; Raveis & Kandel, 1987). Labouvie (1986) and Shedler and Block (1990) have argued that, to a degree, drug use has developmental and adaptive utility for adolescents. For example, substance use could be used to assert independence from parents, identify with peers, or oppose societal norms and values, all potentially normal exploration of identity issues.

On the other hand, substance use may also serve as an attempt to cope with stress associated with adolescence or may signal a lack of self-regulation (Miller & Brown, 1991), reflecting less psychological health. Similarly, adolescent substance use could be a concomitant of family pathology if used as a method for gaining autonomy, as a method of negative attention seeking or gaining contact with parents, or as a way of influencing family structure (Stanton & Todd, 1982; Szapocznik, Kurtines, Foote, Perez-Vidal, & Hervis, 1983). Research findings do suggest that use of substances during the teen years can interfere with crucial developmental tasks, such as prosocial identity formation, interpersonal and educational skill acquisition, and family and work responsibility assumption (Bentler, 1992). Moreover, alcohol use can increase adolescents' exposure to risky situations such as driving while intoxicated, engaging in unprotected sex, and confronting violent exchanges (Farrell,

Danish, & Howard, 1992; FeCaces, Stinson, & Hartford, 1991). All of this indicates that, particularly in adolescents, substance use cannot be evaluated in isolation from the larger picture of life adjustment. It is important to evaluate across multiple problem domains.

An assessment instrument designed for use with adolescents should reflect the characteristics of substance use in adolescents that have been found to differ from those in adults. Research regarding differences between adult and adolescent substance use has focused primarily on alcohol. Adolescents have been found to differ from adults in that they exhibit less physical dependence and fewer physical problems related to alcohol; consume less overall, but larger amounts at one time; and have a higher likelihood of certain negative social consequences, given their position of dependence and lower status in family and social systems (Barnes, 1984; White & Labouvie, 1989). Also, given a generally smaller body size and weaker tolerance, adolescents can experience dangerous effects and alcohol-related problems at a lower level of consumption than adults.

However, researchers have also noted similarities between adolescents and adults with respect to patterns of alcohol consumption, reasons for drinking, and settings in which drinking occurs (Barnes, 1981). In addition, similarities have been found with respect to patterns of problem drinking, including psychological dependence, binge drinking, and social consequences of drinking (Hughes et al., 1992).

Given some overlap between the signs or symptoms of problematic substance use in adolescents and adults, an adolescent could present with many of the classic symptoms of adult substance abuse, making diagnosis a straightforward process. However, it appears just as likely that an adolescent could be using substances problematically, yet bear little or no resemblance to an adult with a substance use problem. In this respect, the need for adolescent-specific assessment is apparent. In each of the sections describing assessment approaches later in this chapter, we will include, as available, specific instruments that are particularly appropriate in evaluating adolescents.

QUALITIES OF A SOUND MEASUREMENT APPROACH

Before beginning a review of specific measurement instruments and strategies to address these six evaluation tasks, we will discuss briefly the

properties of a properly developed measurement instrument: reliability, validity and interpretability. *Reliability* is concerned with whether a test gives consistent results. *Validity* is more complex, and is generally concerned with whether a test measures what it says it is going to measure. A test can be reliable (consistent) without being valid (accurate), but cannot be valid without being reliable. *Interpretability* refers to how much information is provided to help in understanding the meaning of an individual's results. We have used these as criteria in selecting the menu of instruments offered in the next section of this chapter.

Reliability

Reliability is the most basic prerequisite for an evaluation instrument. If a test gives substantially different results each time it is given to the same person, then one cannot have much confidence in its results. A ruler is a useful tool for measuring length, in part, because every time it is used to measure the same object, it gives the same result. A ruler that gives different lengths each time it is used would be of little value as a measuring device.

One form of test reliability is *internal consistency*, the extent to which the items of an instrument (or scale within the instrument) are interrelated and seem to measure the same thing. This is a desirable quality for most but not all instruments. Internal consistency is important for scales designed to measure a single construct such as alcohol dependence. On the other hand, an instrument that surveys a list of possible options (e.g., what things a client would like to get from treatment) would not be expected or required to have items all of which measure the same idea. Furthermore, depending on the purpose of the measure, it is not necessarily desirable for every item on a scale to be highly correlated with the total score. An item may be clinically important (e.g., suicidal thoughts) without being strongly related to other types of problems.

Another type of reliability is the extent to which an instrument gives the same results when repeated. This can reflect the degree to which two (or more) administrations of the instrument, spaced closely in time, give similar results (*test-retest* reliability), or the degree to which two (or more) different raters get the same results (*interrater* reliability). Such reliability is always expected, except when the state being measured would itself change during the retesting interval. For example, intelligence tests purport to measure a construct about people that should not change significantly across even long periods of time, barring important changes in the brain. On the other hand, a measure of mood might yield different results over a period of hours, if only because what it measures—mood—can change rapidly. The testing of reliability is basic to the confidence that can be placed in a test. It is somewhat surprising, therefore, that many commonly used instruments in the addiction field have never been subjected to even this degree of psychometric evaluation.

Validity

Validity refers to the extent that an instrument measures what it purports to measure. The fact that an instrument is *called* a test of X does not mean that it accurately measures X, any more than calling something a "prevention" program guarantees that it actually prevents anything. As stated earlier, it is possible for a measure to be reliable but not valid. For example, the distance that a person can jump from a stand-still position can be measured reliably, but it is a poor index of intelligence or alcohol dependence. In some cases, there is a clear "gold standard" against which to check the validity of a measurement device. The accuracy of a clock can be checked against Greenwich mean time, and screening tests for pregnancy can be checked against the evidence of time or dependable examination procedures. The instrument's validity in this case is determined by the extent to which its results correctly match the true standard. A screening or diagnostic test's *sensitivity*, for example, is the extent to which it correctly detects positive cases (e.g., says "pregnant" when the woman is, in fact, pregnant). The extent to which the test correctly identifies others as not having the condition (e.g., says "not pregnant" when the woman is, in fact, not pregnant) is known as the instrument's *specificity*.

The question of validity is particularly tricky when there is no "gold standard" against which to evaluate test results, as is often the case in the addictions field. The accuracy of a metric ruler can be checked against standard measures, but if one develops a test of "denial," what is the true standard against which its accuracy is measured? In such cases, an instrument is expected to produce results that agree fairly well with other recognized measures of the same construct (*convergent* or *concurrent* validity), remembering that even the "recognized" technique will be an imperfect tool containing measurement error. When multiple measures converge to give the same results, there is greater confidence in the validity of measures.

Furthermore, an instrument's results should not reflect constructs other than that which it purports to measure (*divergent* validity). The results of a "self-esteem" scale should not be strongly correlated with measures of intelligence or language proficiency; otherwise, it measures something other than self-esteem.

If an instrument purports to foretell future events (e.g., to measure the likelihood that a teenager will have alcohol or other drug problems as an adult, or that a person in treatment will relapse), there is the special concern of *predictive* validity. To demonstrate predictive validity, longitudinal studies are required to determine whether test scores accurately predict the actual occurrence of this future event. For example, a purported predictor of treatment success would be tested by administering it before or during treatment, then following the same clients to study their actual outcomes.

Interpretability

In order to be interpretable, a test must yield results that are both reliable and valid. In addition, certain kinds of information are needed to help users of the instrument to understand what its results mean. The most common type of such information is found in *normative standards* that allow comparison of an individual's results with a larger reference group. It is not very informative, for example, to know that a client's score on an alcohol dependence measure is 25, unless you can compare this score with some standard. It is much more helpful to know that this score is at the 90th percentile for similar people—that is, higher than 89% of those in groups who have been given the same test. Well-developed test manuals include such normative data, distributions or tables of scores that provide a percentile, z, or similar score for the individual.

Norms are, of course, specific to the population on which they are based. The interpretation of an alcohol consumption score may be quite different when compared against general population norms, college student norms, or data from a population of people in treatment for alcohol problems. In comparing individual scores with norms, it is usually important to consider comparability of the person to the reference group on other factors such as age, education, and ethnic background. Some tests have breakdowns of norms according to such factors. Test manuals may provide other information useful in interpretation, such as convergent and divergent validity data showing how test results compare with those of other well-known measures.

Tests can also be constructed in ways that facilitate interpretation. An example is subscaling. Some tests provide not only a total score but also meaningful subscores that aid in understanding an individual's results. An example here is the Alcohol Use Inventory, discussed later in this chapter, which yields a total severity score as well as numerous interpretable subscales that measure various types of alcohol-related problems. The total score gives an index of the overall extent of a person's alcohol problems, whereas the subscores reveal facets of a person's life where these problems arise, suggesting areas of focus for treatment planning. The previously discussed questions of reliability and validity can be applied to a whole test, as well as to its subscales or even items. Most often, subscales are constructed rationally—test authors make them up according to their own sense of which items should go together. For other instruments (e.g., the Alcohol Use Inventory), statistical procedures such as factor analysis are used to group items not by the author's beliefs, but by empirical observation of which items actually occur together.

RECOMMENDED INSTRUMENTS

There are literally hundreds of published instruments for use in assessing alcohol problems. For most of these, even basic psychometric information is lacking, and many have fallen into disuse. Ironically, many of the most useful and carefully developed instruments of the field are virtually unknown and rarely used in general practice. In this section, we will provide specific recommendations regarding instruments that can be used for the six

purposes outlined earlier when evaluating adults and adolescents. We have based our choices both on our group's experience in conducting thousands of alcohol problem assessments and on psychometric research supporting the reliability, validity, and interpretability of measures.

Screening Instruments

As discussed previously and in Chapter 3, screening instruments seek to identify the presence of an alcohol disorder. As such, they are designed to be inclusive (sensitive) rather than exclusive (specific), and a positive result should always be confirmed by more careful diagnosis and assessment. Screening instruments comprise most of the better-known instruments of the alcohol field. Specific recommendations for adult screening measures and procedures are provided in Chapter 3, a few of which are highlighted in Table 4.2. Like each of the instrument tables that follow, it contains several elements:

1. Recommended instruments are listed by title. Citations for locating these instruments are provided with the references at the end of this chapter.

2. We have offered our own assessment of the status of psychometric evidence (Psy) regarding each instrument. Where basic psychometric information is available and supports the instrument's reliability, we have indicated a single plus sign (+). No instruments have been recommended without at least basic reliability information. Instruments with known reliability and either validity or normative data in the literature have been designated as double-plus (++). Those with all three types of information currently available, usually in the form of a well-developed test manual, have been designated as triple-plus (+++).

3. For cost considerations, we have indicated the status (Sta) of each instrument as copyrighted (C), published in generally accessible sources (P), or unpublished and available from the instrument's author (A). Copyrighted (C) instruments are those which may not be photocopied but must

Table 4.2   Recommended Adult Screening Instruments

INSTRUMENT	PSY	STA	MIN	SCALES
CAGE	++	P	1	One screening score
AUDIT	+++	P	2	One screening score
MAST	++	P	5	One severity score
GGT (Blood test)	+++	P	5	One liver function value

be purchased from the publisher or author at a per-use fee. Published (P) instruments are those available (all items) from a publicly accessible source such as a journal, and for which at most reproduction permission must be obtained from the publisher of the original article. Author-available instruments (A) are those provided free of charge or at minimal cost from the author. Specific permission regarding their use and reproduction must be negotiated with their authors.

4. Approximate administration time is indicated in minutes (Min). When an instrument covers a variety of areas including alcohol, the time given is for the alcohol section only.

5. A brief summary is given of the scores and other information provided by the instrument.

It is useful to note here the difference between direct and indirect scales (Miller, 1976), a distinction that is most often used in relation to screening instruments. *Direct scales,* such as those listed in Table 4.2, have high face validity and are quite straightforward in what they are attempting to measure. The items of such scales inquire directly about the person's alcohol use and its consequences. Indirect scales are those that seek to measure problems by asking questions that do not appear to be directly related to the area of concern. Usually these are subtle questions that have been found to be correlated with the target problem but for which the "fake good" answer is not obvious. An example is the MacAndrew Scale (MacAndrew, 1965), comprised of such indirect items that were found to discriminate alcoholics from nonalcoholics.

The obvious nature of direct scales has led some to question their validity in detecting alcohol problems, particularly with populations motivated to deceive (e.g., arrested alcohol-impaired drivers). There is little evidence, however, that indirect or subtle questions are more sensitive or specific than direct scales (Miller, 1976). Selzer (1971), for example, reported that even when hospitalized alcoholics were instructed to lie, 92% still answered enough screening questions in the affirmative to be classified as alcoholics. In MacAndrew's original description of his scale, the two items that discriminated best between alcoholics and psychiatric nonalcoholic clients were those that asked directly about alcohol use (which were subsequently dropped from the scale). Clearly direct self-report measures have high sensitivity in detecting alcohol problems, even relative to biomedical measures such as blood and urine tests (National Institute on Alcohol Abuse and Alcoholism, 1990). Whether indirect self-report tests can increase the accuracy of screening remains to be seen.

Like blood tests, some reasonably simple physical examination procedures can also be used as an alternative to self-report in screening for signs of alcohol problems. The red and bulbous "W. C. Fields nose" is a familiar marker. Another is "spider nevi," blood-filled moles with fine appendages extending like spider legs from the center. Collections of such physical signs have been used in the early detection of alcohol misuse (Babor, Treffardier, Weill, Feguer, & Ferrant, 1983). Such markers, however, have problems of both sensitivity and specificity if used alone. (Most heavy drinkers do not have bulbous noses, and not everyone with a bulbous nose is a problem drinker.) With adolescents, physical signs have particularly poor sensitivity. For this reason, screening often involves a combination of measures (see Chapter 3).

Adolescent Alcohol Screening Instruments

As for adults, several adolescent screening instruments have been developed for use in settings where large numbers of adolescents must be screened in a short period of time, such as within the juvenile justice system, pediatric medical settings, or general mental health agencies serving adolescents who present with a variety of problems. Specific recommendations of two alcohol use screening instruments (ADI, AAIS) and three drug and alcohol use instruments (PESQ, POSIT, DUSI) for adolescents are highlighted in Table 4.3. We will also describe

Table 4.3 Recommended Adolescent Screening Instruments

INSTRUMENT	PSY	STA	MIN	SCALES
ADI	+++	C	5	One alcohol screening score
AAIS	++	P	5	One alcohol severity score
PESQ	++	C	5	One substance severity score
POSIT	+	P	25	One substance subscale score
DUSI	++	P	25	Three substance severity scores

briefly the nature of each of these instruments, along with information on scoring and psychometric properties.

The Adolescent Drinking Index (ADI; Harrell & Wirtz, 1989b) is a 24-item screening instrument whose items represent four domains of problem drinking: loss of control, social indicators, psychological indicators, and physical indicators. These domains have been shown to account for more than half of the variance in assessment of problem drinking severity (Harrell & Wirtz, 1989a). The range of possible ADI total scores is 0 to 62. The cutoff score of 15 indicates that adolescents scoring 16 or higher should be considered for further evaluation. The ADI also includes two subscales. The first subscale, self-medicated drinking, identifies a pattern of alcohol use for mood alteration. The second subscale, rebellious behavior, characterizes adolescents who are aggressive or exhibit delinquent behavior while drinking. Normative data and support for the reliability, convergent, and discriminant validity of the instrument are reported in the manual (Harrell & Wirtz, 1989b).

The Adolescent Alcohol Involvement Scale (AAIS; Mayer & Filstead, 1979) is a 14-item screening questionnaire. Scores range from 0 to 84, and elevated scores (42 and higher) alert the screener to the need for further assessment. The scale categorizes respondents into one of four categories: abstainers or infrequent drinkers (0–19), nonproblem drinkers (20–41), alcohol misusers (42–57), and "alcoholic-like" drinkers (58 and up). Test-retest reliability has generally been found to be high (Filstead & Mayer, 1984; Mayer & Filstead, 1979; Moberg, 1983; Putnins, 1992; Riley & Klockars, 1984).

The Personal Experience Screening Questionnaire (PESQ; Winters, 1992) consists of 18 items addressing problem severity, frequency and onset of use, defensiveness (faking good), and psychosocial functioning, which can be answered "never," "once or twice," "sometimes," or "often." PESQ scores range from 18 to 72. No definitive cutoff score is provided as indicative of problematic use. Winters (1992) reported that the problem severity portion of the PESQ has a high internal reliability estimate (.92), that the PESQ as a whole demonstrated satisfactory discriminant validity, and that overall scores were related to assessment referral recommendations. Also, PESQ scores were found to be highly predictive of scores on a more comprehensive assessment instrument, the Personal Experience Inventory (PEI; Winters & Henly, 1989).

The Drug Use Screening Inventory (DUSI; Tarter, 1990; Tarter & Hegedus, 1991) was de-signed to identify problems in substance use, physical and mental health, and psychosocial adjustment of both adolescents and adults. This questionnaire has 149 yes/no items, and is written at a fifth-grade reading level. It yields indices of functioning in 10 domains: substance use, behavior patterns, health status, psychiatric disorder, social competency, family system, school performance and adjustment, work performance and adjustment, peer relationships, and leisure/recreation. Three scores can be computed: (1) absolute problem density, which is the percentage of items endorsed in each of the 10 domains; (2) overall problem index, which is the average of the number of yes responses over the 10 domains; and (3) relative problem density score, which compares the number of items endorsed in each domain to the overall number of problems endorsed. The authors provide no cutoff score to identify respondents as "at risk," leaving the decision to the individual assessor. One published article reports a psychometric evaluation of the content validity of this measure (Tarter, Laird, Bukstein, & Kaminer, 1992). In this study, DUSI indices were found to be correlated with the Kiddie Schedule for Affective Disorders and Schizophrenia (K-SADS) and DSM-III-R substance abuse criteria in a sample of adolescent substance abusers.

Finally, the Problem Oriented Screening Instrument for Teenagers (POSIT) is one part of the Adolescent Assessment Referral System recently developed by the National Institute on Drug Abuse (Rahdert, 1991). It is a 139-item yes/no questionnaire that measures functioning in 10 areas: substance use, physical health, mental health, family relationships, peer relationships, educational status, vocational status, social skills, leisure and recreation, and aggressive behavior/delinquency. Certain items on the POSIT are designated "red flag" items, meaning that if a child answers "yes" to any one of these items, further assessment is indicated. All of the 16 items that comprise the substance use section of the POSIT are designated "red flag" items, therefore endorsement of any one of these items would exceed the cutoff for that area.

Diagnostic Instruments

Formal diagnosis is not required in all clinical contexts. When the determination of a diagnosis is needed, however, the usual procedure is a structured interview to determine whether criteria are met for particular diagnostic categories (see Table 4.4). The instruments reviewed here conform to the *Diagnostic and Statistical Manual of Mental Disorders* (DSM; American Psychiatric Association, 1994), now its fourth edition (see Grant, 1992). We will discuss three instruments for diagnosis of alcohol and other substance use disorders within the DSM system.

The Structured Clinical Interview for DSM, Patient Edition (SCID-P, Spitzer, Williams, Gibbon, & First, 1990) is probably the most popular of the DSM interviews. Because of copyrights, the entire SCID-P booklet must be purchased in order to use the alcohol questions, which themselves require about 10 to 15 minutes to complete. A diagnosis of "alcohol abuse" or "alcohol dependence" can be determined, with the latter classified as mild, moderate, or severe, or as being in partial or full remission.

The Diagnostic Interview Schedule (DIS; Robbins, Cottler, & Keating, 1989) was developed at the request of the National Institute of Mental Health in response to the need to use lay personnel to administer the test in a large epidemiologic study. The result was a structured, easily scorable test that can be administered (given adequate training) by interviewers with little clinical training. The alcohol section of the DIS (III-R version) consists of 30 questions, most of which have one or more subsections. The questions are asked exactly as written and, in our experience, are readily understood by clients. A further advantage of the DIS is the availability of a version for use with children and adolescents. A computer-administered format is also available for the DIS.

A third option, to be discussed in more detail later, is the Substance Use Disorder Diagnosis Schedule (SUDDS; Harrison & Hoffman, 1989). Focusing only on substance use, this is a more comprehensive interview that requires 45 to 60 minutes to complete.

Diagnostic systems such as the DSM make no distinction between adolescent and adult diagnosis in the area of alcohol abuse or alcohol dependence, although some investigators have proposed separate criteria for an adolescent-specific diagnosis of alcohol abuse (Halikas, Lyttle, Morse, & Hoffmann, 1984). Others have questioned the usefulness of the alcohol dependence diagnosis for adolescents, given that the symptoms of dependence are less common in adolescence and that reasons for drinking and consequences of drinking are more useful criteria for classifying adolescent problem drinkers (Hughes, Power, & Francis, 1992; White & Labouvie, 1989). Given the current reliance on DSM criteria, however, the SCID and the DIS (Child Version) can both be used for diagnosis of adolescent alcohol abuse and dependence.

In addition, the Adolescent Diagnostic Interview (ADI; Winters & Henly, 1993) provides a DSM-criteria-based interview for the symptoms of psychoactive substance use disorders. This highly structured interview was nominated by the National Institute on Drug Abuse as a preferred tool for evaluating diagnostic criteria for substance use in adolescents (Rahdert, 1991). It explores the adolescent's drug use history and signs of abuse or dependence for several drug categories, and also covers level of functioning and psychosocial stressors. The interview takes approximately 45 to 60 minutes to administer. Support has been found for its test-retest and interrater reliability, as well as convergent and discriminant validity (Winters & Henly, 1993; Winters, Stinchfield, Fulkerson, & Henly, in press).

Assessment Instruments

The purpose of assessment is to provide an understanding of a person's unique situation. Assessment can range from fairly simple to

Table 4.4 Recommended Diagnostic Instruments

INSTRUMENT	PSY	STA	MIN	SCALES
DIS (Alcohol section)	+++	P	15–0	Diagnoses corresponding to the DSM
SCID (Alcohol section)	+++	C	15–20	Diagnoses corresponding to the DSM
ADI	++	C	45–60	Diagnoses corresponding to the DSM (for adolescents)
SUDDS	+	C	45–60	Diagnoses corresponding to the DSM, stress, depression

quite complex, and should be designed to measure those dimensions of alcohol problems that are important to the tasks at hand. We will describe here six dimensions of common concern, which, as indicated above, are only modestly interrelated.

Alcohol Use

In the most simplistic conception of alcoholism, one needs to know only one thing about alcohol use: Is the person drinking or not? More recent models, such as that proposed by the Institute of Medicine of the National Academy of Sciences (1990), include a range of problem levels and types of interventions. A better understanding of an individual's drinking history and current consumption patterns can serve several useful functions. It may be helpful in determining an optimal treatment approach (see Chapter 17) and in providing a baseline against which to evaluate change. Knowledge of consumption patterns can also provide clues to other dimensions in need of more careful assessment. A pattern of prolonged heavy consumption without periods of abstinence, for example, increases the urgency of assessing dependence and alcohol withdrawal potential (see below).

Almost all evaluations of consumption determine at least the frequency and the intensity of drinking. For the *frequency* dimension, one asks on how many days (per week, month, etc.) the person consumes at least some alcohol. An obvious goal in the treatment of alcohol problems is to reduce this number, if not to zero, then to a less harmful or risky level, and to increase the proportion of abstinent days. *Intensity* measures usually focus on the amount of alcohol that is consumed on days when the person does drink. Questions of this kind may focus on the number of drinks consumed or the proportion of days on which consumption exceeds a defined level of "heavy" drinking. Tables and computer software are also available to estimate a person's blood alcohol concentration level, enabling additional intensity measures such as peak or average intoxication level during a defined period or the number of hours of intoxication above a specified limit (e.g., Markham, Miller, & Arciniega, 1993; Sobell & Sobell, 1992).

The simplest measure of consumption is found in *quantity/frequency* (QF) questionnaires with items assessing these two dimensions. The frequency question is usually some form of the following: "During the past ____ days, on how

many days did you drink any alcohol?" A common intensity (quantity) question would be: "On days when you did drink, how many drinks did you usually have?" It can be helpful, in asking such questions, to define a standard drink unit (see Miller, Heather, & Hall, 1991). These questions may be asked informally but are also included in a number of screening and diagnostic instruments. One of the formalized and better-known QF scales was developed by Cahalan, Cisin, and Crossley (1969), which consists of three questions that are repeated for each of the major alcohol beverages (beer, wine, distilled spirits).

A second method uses a *grid* to help quantify alcohol use (Miller & Marlatt, 1984). The idea behind the grid is to divide some given time period (often a week) into smaller periods of time (days; morning, afternoon, evening). The amount consumed is then queried for these smaller time periods as a way of quantifying drinking behavior. Thus, rather than the "typical occasion" measure afforded by a Q/F questionnaire, this approach asks in more detail the amount consumed in a typical week, on a day-by-day basis.

A third method is the *timeline followback* (TLFB) procedure (Sobell & Sobell, 1992) a structured interview technique that samples a specific time period, using a monthly calendar and memory anchor points to reconstruct daily consumption during the period of interest. A hybrid of the grid and timeline methods has also been developed, seeking to combine the strengths of these two approaches (Miller & DelBoca, in press).

A fourth method for measuring alcohol consumption is the self-monitoring or *diary* method, in which the person keeps ongoing records of alcohol use. In this approach, people record their drinking on a day-by-day basis, making diary entries at the time of each drink. This avoids reliance on memory or reports of "typical" drinking. A number of studies have compared the results of QF, timeline, and diary methods, with the finding that reasonably similar results are generally obtained.

In terms of adolescent alcohol consumption, research has offered little by way of comparing the various assessment methods. In principle, the timeline followback may offer a sensitive assessment, having the advantage of assessing the widely variable drinking patterns that often characterize teen drinking and that might not be modeled adequately by averaging approaches.

For example, adolescents may drink in association with specific events that occur sporadically—such as homecoming weekends, finding someone to buy alcohol for them, or having money—such that their drinking is driven by irregular external factors more so than for adults. More studies are needed to address questions regarding optimal methods for assessing adolescent consumption.

All of the instruments listed in Table 4.5 are *self-report* instruments. That is, the information is gained by direct report from the client. In cases where the truthfulness of self-report is in doubt, *biomedical markers* are sometimes used as a check on reported alcohol use. While alcohol is still in the body, it can be detected by a variety of breath, urine, saliva, and blood tests for the presence of ethyl alcohol (Litten & Allen, 1992). Alcohol is usually cleared from the body, however, within the first day of abstinence.

Even after alcohol is gone from the body, however, some blood tests can provide clues to recent drinking. This approach does, of course, involve the invasive procedure of drawing a blood sample. A commonly used morphological marker is mean corpuscular volume (MCV), which is simply an index of blood cell size. Two biochemical markers are uric acid and bilirubin, but neither has a high degree of specificity. The most frequently used biochemical markers are enzymes that are found in the liver and many other places in the body. These enzymes perform a variety of functions, but they all have in common that they tend to increase their activity as a result of heavy drinking. The most popular marker, on which the most work has been carried out, and the most specific and sensitive to date is gamma glutamyl transferase (GGT), mentioned above as a screening tool.

Other well-known markers are aspartate amino transaminase, glutamic oxaloacetic tran-saminase (SGOT), and alkaline phosphatase. Although these markers are useful to corroborate self-report, clearly none is accurate enough to replace self-report (O'Farrell & Maisto, 1987; Bush, Shaw, Cleary, DelBanco, & Aronson, 1987). A fairly new marker, also described in Chapter 3, is carbohydrate deficient transferrin (CDT), an isoform of a protein that transports iron. CDT abnormality appears after regular intake of about 5 to 7 standard drinks per day for at least one week. Sensitivity and specificity seem to be very good (Borg, Beck, Helander, Voltaire, & Stibler, 1992; Stibler, 1991). With abstinence, CDT returns to normal values over 20 days or so. This assay is available in kit form with the current warning that it is for use only in research, with FDA approval pending (Kabi Pharmacia Inc).

As with screening, a combination of techniques is best when it is vital to have accurate information about alcohol consumption. Client self-report is still the most sensitive measure and may be checked by interviewing significant others. A further useful aspect of biomedical tests is that they create a "bogus pipeline" effect, giving the impression that there is an accurate check on self-report. This may increase honesty in descriptions of one's own drinking.

Alcohol-Related Problems

Although the measurement of alcohol consumption is important, it by no means gives a complete clinical picture. Even much-reduced use, for example, can still be producing problems in many other aspects of the person's life (cf. Miller, Leckman, Delaney, & Tinkcom, 1992). Certain physical problems, such as sleep disturbances (Mendelson, 1979), may persist for years even with total abstinence. The postwithdrawal syndrome, which posits long-lasting physical sequelae, has been postulated as a determinant of relapse (Roelofs, 1985). Both intra- and

Table 4.5 Procedures for Assessing Alcohol Consumption

INSTRUMENT	PSY	STA	MIN	SCALES
Quantity-Frequency	++	P	2–5	Quantity and frequency of drinking
Grid Method	++	P	20	Total consumption, peak intoxication, BAC
Timeline (TLFB)	+++	P	20	Days of use, total consumption, BAC
Diary	++	P	Daily	Days of use, total consumption, BAC

interpersonal problems and conflicts can be antecedents of relapse (Marlatt & Gordon, 1985). Patterns of alcohol problems, then, can provide important clues in understanding and addressing individual cases.

Many scales and questionnaires consist of checklists of problems related to pathological drinking. Some commonly used screening instruments such as the MAST (mentioned earlier) include lists of problems blended with symptoms of dependence, help-seeking, and self-perception. Such instruments often ask whether these problems have *ever* occurred, which means that the total score could never decrease. Problems are also addressed to a small degree in the diagnostic (DSM) interviews described earlier.

There are several reasons, however, for having a more thorough and focused evaluation of alcohol problems. First, clinicians may be interested in a broader range of potential problems than that covered in screening or diagnostic instruments. Second, problems are not the same as consumption or dependence, and should be measured separately. Third, levels and changes of alcohol-related problems are of interest, both before and after treatment, and may reflect significant effects of treatment. Short measures to sample common problems have been used in survey research (Cahalan, 1970; Polich, Armor, & Braiker, 1981).

More recently, specific instruments have been developed to assess alcohol problems, as distinct from dependence symptoms. Several of these have been developed for special populations. The Rutgers Alcohol Problems Index (RAPI; White & Labouvie, 1989) is a 23-item scale developed for use with adolescents, but apparently also applicable with adults. A principal component analysis, performed on a larger pool of items, yielded three factors for the RAPI. Items for the instrument were chosen that loaded strongly (> .50) on the first factor and weakly (< .35) on the second factor in order to

maximize the internal consistency of the resulting scale. Using a general population sample of 1,308 adolescents, analyses revealed high internal consistency and a moderate range of correlations between RAPI scores and alcohol use intensity, which the authors suggest is comparable to other problem alcohol use measures. However, the authors also note that, due to this moderate relationship, a measure of alcohol-use intensity should be used in conjunction with the RAPI to maximize accurate identification of problem drinkers.

The Drinking Problems Index is a 17-item questionnaire designed specifically to measure alcohol problems in older adults (Finney, Moos, & Brennan, 1991). Similarly, a 27-item instrument has been developed to assess negative consequences among college students (Hurlbut & Sher, 1990). The Drinker Inventory of Consequences (DrInC; Miller, Tonigan, & Longabaugh, 1994) was developed for clinical and research applications with adults. It queries 50 problems for occurrence ever (lifetime) and during the past three months. It has five scales (physical, social responsibility, intrapersonal, impulse control and interpersonal) comprising 7 to 12 items each. Though the instrument was unpublished as this chapter was prepared, three psychometric studies have been completed with college students, outpatients, and aftercare patients, supporting its internal consistency and test-retest reliability. Problem scores from the DrInC have also been found to be only moderately correlated with measures of consumption and dependence, supporting the usefulness of a separate measure of problems.

Dependence

From the classic writings of Jellinek (1960) to the more recent documents of the Institute of Medicine (1990), it has been recognized that an individual may have significant alcohol problems without being addicted. Diagnosis in the

Table 4.6 Recommended Alcohol Problem Measures

INSTRUMENT	PSY	STA	MIN	SCALES
Rutgers Alcohol Problem Inventory	+	P	5	Overall score, three factor scales normed for adolescents
Drinker Inventory of Consequences	+++	A	15	Physical, social responsibility, intrapersonal, interpersonal, impulse control, and total

DSM system has distinguished between alcohol abuse (problematic use) and alcohol dependence, a syndrome originally described by Edwards and Gross (1976).

Although no instruments have been developed specifically to assess dependence in adolescents, several excellent scales have been developed for adults. The best known of these in North America is the Alcohol Dependence Scale (ADS; Skinner & Horn, 1984), a set of 25 questions adapted from the larger Alcohol Use Inventory (Horn, Wanberg, & Foster, 1987). The ADS is psychometrically sound and is well accepted by clients in assessment. It is self-administered, taking under 10 minutes to complete. Its standard form queries the last 12 months, a point worth emphasizing to clients who are taking the scale. Scoring is simple with questions being scored from 0 to 1, 2, or 3. Normative data are given in the excellent test manual (Skinner & Horn, 1984).

A second well-tested instrument is the Severity of Alcohol Dependence Questionnaire (SADQ; Stockwell, Hodgson, Edwards, Taylor, & Rankin, 1979). It was specifically designed to focus on the elements of the alcohol dependence syndrome and to ignore alcohol-related problems (Stockwell, Murphy, & Hodgson, 1983). The SADQ is a 20-item self-administered questionnaire that focuses on a 30-day period of heavy drinking. It takes about five minutes to complete. Clients are asked to rate each of the statements for frequency of occurrence. The SADQ appears to have good test-retest reliability and internal consistency, and its scores converge with clinical signs of withdrawal severity (Stockwell et al., 1983).

A third option to measure the alcohol dependence syndrome is the 39-item Alcohol Dependence Data (ADD) questionnaire, and its shorter form, the Short-form Alcohol Dependence Data Questionnaire (SADD; Raistrick, Dunbar, & Davidson, 1983). As originally written, the SADD is a 15-item self-report format where the questions are rated "never," "sometimes," "often," and "nearly always." Like the ADS, the SADD was designed to measure the full syndrome of alcohol dependence rather than focusing exclusively on withdrawal signs.

An instrument of practical utility for treatment programs is the Clinical Institute Withdrawal Assessment for Alcohol (CIWA-A), developed by the Addiction Research Foundation (Shaw, Kolesar, Sellers, Kaplan, & Sandor, 1981). This 15-item scale can be used to assess the need for monitored or medication-assisted withdrawal, and to follow the progress of patients during the detoxification process. Training videotapes are available from the Addiction Research Foundation to prepare nursing and other personnel in use of the CIWA-A.

Neuropsychological Assessment

It is clear that heavy use of alcohol can lead to severe neurological and neuropsychological dysfunction. Whereas the most obvious forms of severe damage, such as Wernicke's encephalopathy and Korsakoff's psychosis, are relatively easy to identify, most neuropsychological deficits are much more subtle. There does seem to be a clear pattern of brain damage and neuropsychological impairment associated with alcoholism (for a review, see Miller & Saucedo, 1983). The particular importance of neuropsychological assessment is that it appears to be one of the earliest and most sensitive indicators of alcohol-related impairment, thus detecting deleterious effects before more widespread damage is

Table 4.7 Recommended Alcohol Dependence Measures

INSTRUMENT	PSY	STA	MIN	SCALES
Alcohol Dependence Scale (ADS)	+++	C	5	One alcohol dependence score
Severity of Alcohol Dependence Questionnaire (SADQ)	++	P	5	One alcohol dependence score
Clinical Institute Withdrawal Assessment for Alcohol	+++	P	3	Severity of alcohol withdrawal
Alcohol Dependence Data (ADD/SADD)	+	P	5	One alcohol dependence score, short form available

done. For adolescents, problems in sustaining attention and in learning tend to be overrepresented among substance abusers. Moreover, factors associated with cognitive functioning and impulsivity may play a role in treatment effectiveness, arguing for an assessment of neuropsychological variables.

Neuropsychological assessment is a specialty of its own. For present purposes, we will indicate some of the instruments that have been shown to be sensitive to alcohol-related impairment. Several subscales on the Wechsler Adult Intelligence Scale-Revised (WAIS-R) and Wechsler Intelligence Scale for Children (WISC-III) seem to be sensitive in this regard. Generally speaking, clinical alcoholics show relatively normal behavior on the Verbal subtests, but impairment frequently is present on several of the Performance subtests such as Block Design, Digit Symbol or Coding, Picture Arrangement, and Object Assembly. Most of these subtests take no more than 15 minutes or so to administer, but they do require a fairly high level of practice before proficiency is attained, permitting valid comparison of results with normative data.

Some of the subscales of the Halstead-Reitan Neuropsychological Test Battery are also highly sensitive to alcohol-related brain impairment in adults and adolescents. Among the most sensitive measures are the Categories Test, the Tactual Performance Test (total time and location scores), the Trail-making Test (particularly section B), and the Finger-tapping Test. A problem with performance and motor tasks, however, is that although they may exhibit high sensitivity, they are not correspondingly specific.

Other measures of visuospatial performance and information processing that reflect alcohol-related impairment are the Wisconsin Card Sorting Test, the Benton Visual Retention Test, and Raven's Progressive Matrices. Measures of field dependence such as the Embedded Figures Test also appear to be sensitive to alcohol's effects.

Biomedical Sequelae

The chronic effects of heavy drinking can be observed not only in the central nervous system but also in nearly every system of the body. Negative effects are well documented in the liver, endocrine and immune systems, gastrointestinal tract, and cardiovascular system (National Institute on Alcohol Abuse and Alcoholism, 1994). Such problems, more likely to be seen in adults than in adolescents, are obviously of medical concern, and can also have marked effects on a client's behavior and psychological functioning. These may range from mood effects such as depression to social consequences such as being unable to get or hold a job.

Again, the degree of health impairment from drinking cannot be known from the types of assessment described above. It is advisable, therefore, to use at least a general health screen such as the Health Questionnaire (HQ; Brodman, Erdman, Lorge, & Wolff, 1949). The HQ is a 195-question self-administered test that asks health-related questions with "yes" or "no" answers. Eleven questions are gender specific. The HQ takes about 15 or 20 minutes to complete, and the questions are written at an easily comprehended level. Studies with addictive populations support the utility of the HQ in clinical practice (for a review, see Addiction Research Foundation, 1993). A blood test and serum chemistry profile (see Alcohol Consumption section above) is also often used as a screen for common alcohol-related health problems. Potential problems detected during screening should be followed up with proper medical consultation.

Comprehensive Instruments and Interviews

A comprehensive understanding of your client's situation is useful in treatment planning and helps you avoid overlooking important aspects that need to be addressed. In the view represented here (cf. Institute of Medicine, 1990; Maisto & Connors, 1990), alcohol disorders occur not in binary fashion, but in degree along multiple loosely related continua. This understanding is reflected in most recently developed assessment instruments.

An alternative to multiple instruments for measuring separate domains is to use a comprehensive instrument that covers several domains in a single format. Far and away the strongest comprehensive paper-and-pencil instrument is the Alcohol Use Inventory, refined through three decades of research by Horn and colleagues (1987). It requires less than an hour for a client to complete, and can be scored by a clerical worker within a few minutes. Computer scoring is also available. Its 228 items yield an individual profile with 24 scales developed by factor analysis with large clinical samples. The 17 primary scales provide continuous scores on clinically meaningful dimensions, including motivations for and styles of drinking, physical dependence, loss of behavioral control, relationship of drinking to marital problems, and readiness for change. Second-order scales combine the primary scales into six more general factors, and a third-order factor provides a convenient single scale of overall severity of alcohol involvement. The well-developed test manual provides clear guidelines for interpretation and normative data.

Other comprehensive instruments are completed by the clinician on the basis of a structured interview. Although test manuals are available to guide administration of these interviews, specific training and practice are typically needed in order to yield reliable results.

The Addiction Severity Index (ASI) is a well-known and widely used instrument applicable to both primary alcohol and other drug areas. The ASI (McLellan et al., 1980, 1985, 1990) is a structured interview requiring about 40 minutes to complete. It is divided into eight subscales in addition to a general information scale. The eight subscales focus on life problems, medical, legal, employment/support, alcohol, other drugs, family/social, and psychiatric functioning. In addition interviewers are asked to rate the severity of each area for each client and their own confidence in (1) the client's truthfulness and (2) the client's ability to understand. There is an administration manual with instructions for each of the areas. In a number of studies, the ASI has consistently been shown to be psychometrically sound (McLellan, Luborsky, O'Brien, & Woody, 1980; Kosten, Rounsaville, & Kleber, 1983), with good test-retest and interrater reliability and concurrent validity.

The Comprehensive Drinker Profile (CDP; Miller & Marlatt, 1984) is a structured interview requiring about two hours for completion. The drinking history section includes a grid method for assessing alcohol consumption, alcohol-related life problems, drinking settings, beverage preferences, medical history, and associated behaviors, which includes the use of other drugs. The CDP uses a set of card sorts to help clients specify these areas. Demographic data and information on motivations for use and for change are also covered. A shorter version (Brief Drinker Profile; BDP) is also available, as are parallel forms for follow-up assessment and for interviewing significant others (Miller & Marlatt, 1987).

The Substance Use Disorder Diagnosis Schedule (SUDDS; Harrison & Hoffman, 1989) is a structured 20- to 30-minute interview. Its focus is on establishing a DSM-III-R diagnosis, but it also covers areas that are only lightly, if at all, touched on in a DSM-III inquiry. The SUDDS is divided into several large topic areas: general (demographics), stress, depression, coffee, smoking, alcohol, and drugs. The alcohol and drug sections are by far the most inclusive and parallel the DSM criteria. The other sections give a larger picture of the individual's associated behaviors and mental states.

A Structured Addictions Assessment Interview for Selecting Treatment (ASIST; Addiction Research Foundation, 1984) was, as the name implies, constructed to gather information relevant in choosing an optimal treatment approach. The ASIST consists of questions that cover patterns of drug and alcohol use, physical and psychological problems, family, employment and mental health problems, previous treatment experiences, and treatment preferences.

Several comprehensive assessment instruments are also available specifically for use with adolescents. The Adolescent Drug Abuse Diagnosis (ADAD; Friedman & Utada, 1989) is a 150-item structured interview modeled after the adult measure, the Addiction Severity Index (ASI; McLellan et al., 1980). The ADAD is designed for use in diagnosis, treatment planning, and research. The interview addresses nine areas: medical, school, employment, social, family, psychological, legal, alcohol, and drugs. Severity ratings (on a 10-point scale) can be computed for each of these nine areas, and indicate the client's "need for treatment" in each area. Friedman and Utada (1989) reported sound psychometric characteristics of the ADAD, including interrater reliability, test-retest reliability, and concurrent, convergent, and discriminant validity.

The Adolescent Self-Assessment Profile (ASAP; Wanberg, 1991) is a 203-item multiple-choice format questionnaire designed to assess a broad range of variables potentially associated with substance use problems in adolescents referred for assessment and treatment. The ASAP contains 20 basic scales that cover six general areas of assessment: family, mental health, peer influence, school problems, deviant behavior, and drug use. Raw scores on each of the 20 scales can be converted to decile ranks to determine degree of severity of problem. Wanberg (1991) reported reliability (internal consistency) of the scales, but no reports have yet been published regarding the validity of this instrument.

The Personal Experience Inventory (PEI; Winters & Henly, 1989) is a 276-item self-administered (by hand or computer) questionnaire written at a fifth-grade reading level. It covers drug problem severity, drug use frequency and onset, personal risk factors, environmental risk factors, select problem screens (e.g., physical and sexual abuse), and faking tendencies, and as such is designed to be of use in treatment planning. The five PEI basic problem severity scales are personal involvement, effects from drug use, social benefits of drug use, personal consequences of drug use, and polydrug use. Formal training is not required to administer this instrument but is available from the developers. Percentile and t-score norms are available by age and sex, and are based on a sample of approximately 2,000 adolescents. The psychometric properties of the PEI have previously been supported by two preliminary studies (Henly & Winters, 1988; Winters & Henly, 1989). Recently, in a more thorough investigation of concurrent validity, the PEI basic problem severity scales were found to be significantly related to groupings made on the basis of DSM-III-R substance use criteria and by recommendations for treatment referral (Winters, Stinchfield, & Henly, 1993).

Motivation

The direct assessment of motivational factors in problem drinkers is a more recent emphasis. One approach is to ask clients about their rea-

sons for drinking and reasons to change, approximating a *decisional balance* assessment (Janis & Mann, 1977). Open-ended questions of this type are included in the Comprehensive Drinker Profile (Miller & Marlatt, 1984). Information regarding the attractions of drinking and readiness for change is also provided by the Alcohol Use Inventory (Horn et al., 1987). Other structured survey schedules for this purpose include the Inventory of Drinking Situations (Annis, Graham, & Davis, 1987) and the Reasons for Drinking Questionnaire (Heather, Stallard, & Tebbutt, 1991).

The Alcohol Expectancy Questionnaire (AEQ; Brown, Goldman, Inn, & Anderson, 1980) was designed to measure expectations of positive reinforcement from drinking. Positive outcome expectancies as measured by this instrument have been found to predict relapse among alcoholics at one-year follow-up (Brown, 1985). Two adaptations of this scale are also available. The Alcohol Effects Questionnaire (Rohsenow, 1983) contains eight subscales, tapping both positive and negative effects of alcohol. Rohsenow's instrument in turn has been modified by Collins, Lapp, Emmons, and Issac (1990) to assess the strength of beliefs. This 40-item Alcohol Beliefs Questionnaire (ABQ) assesses degree of agree-

Table 4.8 Recommended Comprehensive Assessment Instruments

INSTRUMENT	PSY	STA	MIN	SCALES
ADAD	++	A	60	Adolescent problem severity scores and need for treatment across nine domains
ASAP	+	A	60	Profile of adolescent adjustment, functioning, and substance use across six domains
ASI	+++	A	40	Eight adult subscales of substance use and more general functioning
ASIST	+	C	60	Substance use, problems, general adjustment, treatment planning
AUI	+++	C	60	Twenty-four factor scales
CDP	++	C	90	Alcohol/drug use patterns
BDP	++	C	60	Problems, motivation, treatment planning
PEI	++	C	60	Adolescent problem severity scores, personal and environmental risk factors
SUDDS	+	P	30	Alcohol/drug use, stress, depression, diagnosis

ment or disagreement with various statements about alcohol.

Modeled after the AEQ, the Alcohol Expectancy Questionnaire-Adolescent Version (AEQ-A; Brown, Christiansen, & Goldman, 1987) is a 100-item self-report questionnaire that measures the effects an individual expects from drinking. Scores are obtained on seven different expectancies: global positive effects, social behavior change, improvement of cognitive/motor abilities, sexual enhancement, deteriorated cognitive/behavioral functioning, increased arousal, and relaxation/tension reduction. Psychometric investigations have indicated adequate reliability and validity (Brown et al., 1987). Expectancy scores have also been found to predict the onset and severity of drinking in adolescents (Christiansen, Smith, Roehling, & Goldman, 1989).

The Alcohol Attitude Scale for Teenagers (AAST; Torabi & Veenker, 1986) is a 54-item paper-and-pencil questionnaire that measures three components of attitudes: feelings, beliefs, and intentions to act. It was developed primarily for research and evaluation of health education programs. Reliability and validity information is available for the whole instrument (Torabi & Veenker, 1986; Veenker & Torabi, 1984) and for its short form (Torabi, 1989).

A different motivational model influential in the addictions field is the transtheoretical approach described by Prochaska and DiClemente (1986), which posits a series of progressive stages of change readiness. Three instruments have been constructed to measure these stages. The authors of the model have used extensively their University of Rhode Island Change Assessment (URICA), a 32-item self-administered questionnaire. The instructions refer generically to "your problem," but can be directed toward substance abuse problems in particular. The URICA has a robust factor structure.

A Stages of Change Readiness and Treatment Eagerness Scale (SOCRATES; Miller, 1993) was specifically designed to tap stages of change readiness with regard to alcohol use. The full SOCRATES comprises 40 items; a shorter 20-item version is also available, as are parallel forms for other drug use and for assessing the motivation of significant others. Initial psychometric evaluations indicate sound internal consistency of scales, a stable factor structure, and test-retest reliability. Finally, a 12-item scale has been developed as an efficient measure of three stages (4 items each) from the model: precontemplation, contemplation, and action (Rollnick, Heather, Gold, & Hall, 1992).

Treatment Planning

Optimal client treatment is dependent on knowing some information about the client. As an extreme example, one would not provide family therapy to a client who has no family. In the same way, it would be helpful to know about a client's alcohol problem in some depth before attempting a therapeutic regimen. Obviously, the possibilities for what to measure pose a nearly infinite variety of choices.

Most of the instruments that we have discussed thus far can be useful in treatment planning. Only a few, however, were developed specifically for this purpose. Among these are three discussed earlier as comprehensive instruments: the Alcohol Use Inventory (Horn et al., 1987) the Drinker Profile instruments (Miller & Marlatt, 1984, 1987), and the ASIST (Addiction Research Foundation, 1984). For adolescents, the DUSI (Tarter, 1990) is one component of a decision-tree method of evaluation and treatment of substance use.

One specific strategy in planning treatment is to anticipate the most likely causes of relapse and to target these with specific therapeutic

Table 4.9   Recommended Measures of Motivation

INSTRUMENT	PSY	STA	MIN	SCALES
AEQ (or variants) AEQ-A	++	P	10	Seven positive alcohol expectancy scales
AAST	++	A	15	Three adolescent attitude scores
URICA	++	P	10	Five stages of change
SOCRATES	++	A	10	Five stages of change
Readiness to Change	++	A	5	Three stages of change

components (Marlatt & Gordon, 1985). This is the strategy underlying the Inventory of Drinking Situations (Annis et al., 1987). This 100-item questionnaire divides potential drinking situations into intrapersonal and interpersonal categories, each of which has subcategories. The client reports the frequency of drinking in each type of situation. A complete user's manual gives guidelines for administration, psychometric properties, normative data, and other useful interpretive information. A shorter (42-item) version is also available. A companion Situational Confidence Questionnaire assesses the client's confidence (self-efficacy) to resist future drinking in each situation.

Follow-Up

The "when" and "how" practicalities of follow-up will be discussed in more detail in the final section of this chapter, focusing on program evaluation. Here, we will address the issue of *what* to measure.

The most obvious answer is to measure that which you hope to change. Because most alcohol treatment programs hope, among other things, to change the client's problematic use of alcohol, each of the assessment dimensions previously discussed might be evaluated at follow-up. The question, Are you drinking or not? was once thought to be sufficient to judge outcome. As conceptions of alcohol problems and their treatment have broadened (Institute of Medicine, 1990), however, so have outcome measures. As before treatment, the knowledge of one assessment dimension gives you a very limited picture of a client's status after treatment. At a minimum, evaluate the client's current use of alcohol (and, if applicable, other drugs) and any current problems or negative consequences related to such use. If program goals include hopes for change on other dimensions (such as self-esteem, spirituality, employment, relationship stability), these can be assessed as well.

Many of the instruments can be readministered at follow-up. An important issue here is the period of time about which an instrument asks. Some, for example, ask about problems during the past three months. Others focus on the past year. It may be necessary to modify instructions to adjust for the length of time being evaluated. The pretreatment versions of some instruments ask about lifetime occurrence of symptoms, whereas at follow-up the interest is

usually in the period of time since treatment. Some instruments have parallel forms specifically designed to be used at follow-up (e.g., Miller & Marlatt, 1987).

It is often of interest, too, to know what additional treatment, self-help, or health services a client has received. The Treatment Services Review (McLellan, Alterman, Cacciola, Metzger, & O'Brien, 1992) is a 41-item, five-minute structured interview that provides data on the types of services received by clients. A Twelve-Step Participation Questionnaire (Tonigan, Miller, & Montgomery, 1990) has been newly developed to determine the extent to which clients have participated in AA before and after treatment. The Follow-up Drinker Profile (Miller & Marlatt, 1987) also includes questions on additional services received.

PROGRAM EVALUATION

The preceding discussion has emphasized evaluation of the *individual* with alcohol problems. This final section will focus on evaluation of alcohol treatment *programs*. There is considerable overlap in these topics, of course, because the effectiveness of a program is judged by the extent to which it meets its goals, which presumably include favorable outcomes for the individuals it serves.

Purposes of Evaluation

Just as we outlined six purposes in evaluating individuals, so there are different reasons for evaluating programs. One classic distinction is between formative and summative evaluation (Edwards, Guttentag, & Snapper, 1975).

What often comes to mind first in hearing the word *evaluation* is some judgment about "the bottom line." How well, in the end, did the program accomplish its goals? This kind of looking-back determination of what happened in a program is usually called *summative evaluation*, because it seeks to sum up the outcome, the results. This approach to evaluation is most characteristic of those who fund programs, as part of the decision-making process in how future funding should be allocated (e.g., "To what extent should we continue to invest in these services?"). Needless to say, this can be the most threatening purpose of evaluation from the viewpoint of program personnel.

A rather different, though not incompatible, approach is *formative evaluation*. Programs, like individual professionals, need feedback in order to grow and improve (e.g., "Where are we doing well, and where should we consider making some changes?"). The motivation behind such evaluation is to provide better services for your clients.

In truth, these two purposes are not so very different when it comes down to how you actually conduct the evaluation. In both cases, the goal is to gain accurate feedback in order to make adjustments in how services are provided, but the motivations may be different. A summative perspective is usually that of someone outside the program, or seeking to reach a verdict after a program has ended. A formative perspective is characteristic of those inside an ongoing program, seeking to improve and strengthen it. The difference, then, comes down to this: What is going to be *done* with the information gained through this evaluation? How will the data be used?

Another helpful distinction is among levels of evaluation (e.g., James, 1969). Four levels are often distinguished that provide different kinds of information. The simplest level of evaluation, most often found in program reports, is of program *effort* expended. How many hours of services were provided, by whom and to whom? A report of this kind documents service delivery. To assess program *performance*, the effort is judged against need. How adequate are the efforts to the community's needs for services? A report of this kind might, for example, compare service delivery efforts with the number of people estimated to need such services within the program's catchment area. It might also compare demographics of served and community populations, to determine whether there are underserved groups in need of special outreach.

Neither of these two levels of evaluation address the question of the effectiveness of services that were delivered. An evaluation of program *outcome* examines the actual impact of services on those who received them. It is only at this step that evaluation begins to yield feedback useful in improving the quality (rather than quantity) of services. One's own professional hunches about what works and what doesn't are well known to be fallible. One outcome evaluation, for example, showed that a "prevention" program, about which both teachers and students were highly enthusiastic, actually *increased* students' use of drugs (Stuart, 1974). Though we would like to believe that it isn't so, "therapeutic" interventions similarly can be ineffective or even detrimental. Without outcome evaluation,

it is very difficult to separate these from effective and helpful program services, precisely because program staff (like the teachers in the prevention program) *believe* in what they offer but are relatively poor predictors of actual outcome. Without reliable outcome feedback, the quality of program services is unlikely to improve.

Finally, evaluation can focus on program *efficiency*. This requires assessment of program outcomes as well as cost. How much benefit is being derived in relation to the amount being spent for services? Such considerations of cost effectiveness have had a major impact on how services are provided. The consistent finding, for example, that inpatient and outpatient alcohol treatment programs yield similar overall outcomes has led to a marked shift away from reliance on more expensive residential programs (Institute of Medicine, 1990). Low-cost treatments capable of reaching a large number of problem drinkers are weighed against higher-cost services which, for the same total budget, serve a smaller number of people (Holder, Longabaugh, Miller, & Rubonis, 1991).

Thus, to evaluate effort, one needs to monitor the provision of services. To advance evaluation to the level of performance, a needs assessment is added. To study program outcome, one adds a system for monitoring the impact of services (which will be our main focus in the rest of this chapter). To study efficiency, one needs information about the cost of services.

Defining Program Goals

In order to have feedback about how a program is doing, one needs to know the *goals* that the program is meant to achieve. This immediately raises the question, Who is the client/customer? Goals may vary quite a bit across groups. For a program treating drunk-driving offenders, the principal "customer" may be the court system, which is interested primarily in reducing future offenses. Those presenting for treatment may have very different concerns: to satisfy court requirements or to deal with other life problems such as poverty, unemployment, or domestic violence. Therapists are concerned about their clients' welfare and about practical considerations such as time demands and paperwork. Program managers want quality services and are also concerned to have continued support for the program. Each may give different answers when asked to define the goals of the program.

A first step, then, is to come to some agreement regarding the goals to be achieved through program services. A treatment program's general priority list might look, in part, like this:

1. To reduce clients' use of alcohol, tobacco, and illicit drugs
2. To reduce clients' life problems related to alcohol/drug use
3. To improve clients' self-esteem
4. To reduce clients' frequency of driving while impaired

Of course, there will be additional goals in individual cases. The list of program priorities is meant to describe goals that are more generally applicable across those who are served by the program.

Assembling an Evaluation Package

Once a list of priority goals has been developed, it is time to put them in specific, observable terms. How would you know if this goal is being achieved? How can it be measured? It is this consideration that should guide your selection of measures to include in program evaluation. What measures could you use to define these goals?

We have discussed quite a few instruments in this chapter, and many more are currently in development. We strongly advise *against* constructing your own home-grown measures. It is quite difficult to develop a reliable, valid measure, and it is generally better to stay with instruments that already have been tested. We offer the same caution against making changes in established instruments. Beyond concerns about possible copyright violations, an instrument may no longer be reliable or valid if its content and format are altered. Decades of work have gone into psychometric development of instruments in the alcohol field, so take advantage of it!

With this caution in mind, the next step is to choose instruments (questionnaires, interviews, etc.) that will meet the needs of your program and clients. Very often, instruments can serve several purposes. A careful pretreatment evaluation of clients' drinking, for example, can be helpful in: (1) describing the severity of the population you treat; (2) comparing your population with those served elsewhere or those in need of services; (3) determining the individual client's need for detoxification; (4) planning treatment, matching the client to appropriate services; and (5) establishing a baseline against which goal attainment can be evaluated. The art in choosing an evaluation package is to combine it with measures that you need for other purposes. This reduces the amount of additional work involved, and makes it clearer to clients and staff how the assessment is relevant.

For each program goal, then, decide what reliable measures you will use to determine whether the goal is being achieved in each individual case. Once these measures have been chosen, use them consistently with all cases, first before treatment begins (which also helps in treatment planning), and then at one or more points after treatment.

Conducting Follow-Up

Follow-up is the piece most often missing in program evaluation. It is sometimes seen as a desirable but disposable element. That's a bit like saying that drug companies should not waste time testing how well their drugs work; most important is just to get the medications out there for people to use. Again, without feedback, services do not improve.

The simplest form of follow-up is to conduct a brief interview with clients on an anniversary of their completion of treatment. But which anniversary? This is not an easy question. One consideration is that the longer the follow-up, the lower the "success rate." Typically, high rates of success (e.g., abstinence from tobacco, decreased drinking and problems) are found within the first 3 months after treatment for addictive behaviors. By 12-month follow-up, it is common for these rates to decline substantially. The reason for this, of course, is that people relapse. Thus, the longer you wait before your follow-up, the more likely you are to find relapses or unfavorable outcomes.

If your goal in follow-up is not only to evaluate program outcomes but also to improve your clients' long-term success, it makes sense to schedule your follow-up interviews at a point where risk of relapse is high, but not too much time has passed. Given relapse curves, we suggest that the 6-month anniversary is a good compromise if only one follow-up is to be conducted. Better still would be follow-ups at both 6 and 12 months. The latter gives you a picture of longer-term outcomes (which stabilize reasonably well after one year). Each follow-up also provides you with an opportunity to contact your client again and to reassess the need for additional services before recovery is seriously compromised. This is a good reason to attempt follow-up with all clients, if possible. If time and resources do not permit follow-up with all clients, then a representative (such as random) sample should be followed, rather than relying on the highly biased information from clients who choose to resume or stay in touch with the program.

What to Evaluate?
A Practical Example

The formative uses of evaluation data are many. Evaluation can give an overall picture of success, but it can also yield much more useful information for shaping a program toward still better services.

Consider a practical example. A private substance abuse treatment program was considering whether to add a motivational feedback component (see Chapter 5) for clients at intake. To do so would mean more staff time (two to three hours per person) devoted to assessment and motivational interviewing. Would it really make a difference? Of course, the new component could be implemented to see how it "feels" to staff and patients, but this is not really a good indication of its impact. Instead, the program chose, for a period of a few months, to assign new clients randomly to receive or not receive this additional component at intake. Therapists in the program did not know who had or had not received the special assessment and interview.

To evaluate this new component, it was necessary first to define the goals it was meant to achieve. First, staff thought the intervention might increase clients' motivation for and involvement in treatment during the program. Second, if this were true, clients' outcomes after treatment should also be improved. The first goal was measured by asking both clients and therapists to rate the clients' motivation and participation in treatment on several dimensions. The second goal was evaluated by following up all these clients (both those who received and who did not receive the motivational interview before treatment) at three months after discharge.

The results were surprisingly good (Brown & Miller, 1993). Therapists saw a significant difference between the groups in their motivation for and involvement in treatment (although no difference was found in what clients said about themselves). Three months after discharge, abstinence rates were twice as high in the group that had received the additional interview, who also showed substantially less alcohol use and intoxication when they did drink. The extra two to three hours of individual time proved to be an excellent investment for this program, by increasing their clients' chances for recovery.

This is an example of how evaluation can be used in a formative manner. Does it make a difference for our clients if we . . . ? A new method can be tried, just for a month or two, to see whether it has good results. If it does, the change can be kept. If not, it can be dropped. Another example of this is found in research showing that a single telephone call or handwritten note can double the rate of clients returning for treatment after a single counseling contact (for a review, see Miller, 1985).

An important point here is to be *consistent* about the method being tested. If many different therapists offer many different approaches, it is difficult to know what is being evaluated. The more you can be consistent about what is being tested, the clearer your findings are likely to be.

Understanding Your Findings

Many a program evaluation has ended with a filing cabinet full of unexamined data. This is what happens if there is no plan (or no staff time allocated) for making use of what is learned. Particularly for formative evaluation, it is important for program staff to have timely feedback. When results do not appear until years later, their relevance to the program is often lost.

One approach is to make program evaluation a priority. We have argued that proper evaluation is an essential component of quality care. Some federal, state, and other funding sources now require that a certain proportion of treatment and prevention dollars be used for program evaluation. If evaluation is a regular part of a staff member's job, it is more likely to be done and done well. An alternative that can work well, if available, is to establish a cooperative research relationship with a local university. Faculty or graduate students may be happy to help with research that has practical importance, and can offer assistance in tabulating, analyzing, or even collecting data. Such collaboration is helpful if the needed expertise is not available among program staff.

An important point is that *evaluation does not need to be complicated*. Important information can be gained within the time and financial resources of most programs. Even relatively simple approaches can be useful. Pick just one or two key measures and compare your results before and after treatment. Try a new method for just a month or two, offering the new approach carefully and consistently, then find out whether it makes a difference on one or two simple measures where you ought to be able to see its effect. Even this level of evaluation is far more than is currently done by most programs. Such questions can be answered in a relatively short period of time, providing encouraging and helpful formative information for program staff. Evaluation data of this kind may also provide a competitive edge in funding considerations.

PUTTING IT ALL TOGETHER

We have tried, in this chapter, to summarize a large and complex topic, with special emphasis on practical applications. If we have succeeded, you are further along toward being able to design an evaluation approach that fits your own program needs.

Consider first which of the six purposes apply to your own setting. *Screening*, for example, may be less relevant in treatment settings where people come through the door asking for help with alcohol problems. It is most important in contexts where large numbers of people are seen, some of whom have alcohol problems, and most of whom are not asking for help in regard to their drinking. *Diagnosis*, in the limited sense we have used, is important in settings where determination of a formal diagnosis is required for institutional or reimbursement purposes. *Assessment* is the broad task of understanding the individual's unique situation, likely an important task in most clinical settings. *Motivation* for change is a more significant problem in some settings than in others. *Treatment planning* is important unless the same services are offered to all individuals regardless of their characteristics. Finally, *follow-up* is a key part of program evaluation, and can also promote long-term quality care.

A well-chosen set of measures will serve these purposes, as appropriate to your setting, without adding needless time and detail. Many measures can fulfill multiple purposes. The real art here is to refine an evaluation program that meets your own needs and those of your clients, and that can be conducted within the practical time and staffing limitations of your setting. The alcohol field is blessed with a wide array of well-developed measures, from which we have recommended those that currently seem both psychometrically sound and well suited to program needs. A consistent, well-chosen evaluation pro-

gram can both help to improve the quality of care for your clients and strengthen your own professional or program development.

REFERENCES

Addiction Research Foundation. (1984). *A structured addictions assessment interview for selecting treatment.* Toronto, Ontario: Author.

Addiction Research Foundation. (1993). *Directory of client outcome measures for addictions treatment programs.* Toronto, Ontario: Author.

American Educational Research Association, American Psychological Association, and National Council on Measurement in Education. (1985). *Standards for educational and psychological testing.* Washington, DC: American Psychological Association.

American Psychiatric Association. (1994). *Diagnostic and statistical manual of mental disorders* (4th ed., rev.). Washington, DC: American Psychiatric Association.

Annis, H. M., Graham, J. M. & Davis, C. S. (1987). *Inventory of Drinking Situations (IDS): User's guide.* Toronto, Ontario: Addiction Research Foundation.

Babor, T. F., Treffardier, M., Weill, J., Feguer, L., & Ferrant, J-P (1983). Early detection and the secondary prevention of alcoholism in France. *Journal of Studies on Alcohol 44*, 600–616.

Bailey, G. W. (1989). Current perspectives on substance use in youth. *Journal of the American Academy of Child and Adolescent Psychiatry, 28*, 151–162.

Barnes, G. M. (1981). Drinking among adolescents: A subcultural phenomenon or a model of adult behaviors? *Adolescence, 16*(61), 211–229.

Barnes, G. M. (1984). Adolescent alcohol abuse and other problem behaviors: Their relationships and common parental influences. *Journal of Youth and Adolescence, 13*, 329–348.

Bentler, P. M. (1992). Etiologies and consequences of adolescent drug use: Implications for prevention. *Journal of Addictive Diseases, 11*, 47–61.

Borg, S., Beck, O., Helander, A., Voltaire, A., & Stibler, H. (1992). Carbohydrate-deficient transferrin and 5-hydroxytryptophol: Two new markers of high alcohol consumption. In R. Z. Litten & J. P. Allen (Eds.), *Measuring alcohol consumption: Psychosocial and biochemical methods* (pp. 149–159). Totowa, NJ: Humana Press.

Brodman, K., Erdman, A. J., Lorge, I., & Wolff, H. G. (1949). The Cornell Medical Index: An adjunct to medical interview. *Journal of the American Medical Association, 140*, 530–534.

Brown, J. M., & Miller, W. R. (1993). Impact of motivational interviewing on participation and outcome in residential alcoholism treatment. *Psychology of Addictive Behaviors, 7*, 211–218.

Brown, S. A. (1985). Reinforcement expectancies and alcoholism treatment outcome after a one-year follow-up. *Journal of Studies on Alcohol, 46*, 304–308.

Brown, S. A., Christiansen, B. A., & Goldman, M. S. (1978). The Alcohol Expectancy Questionnaire: An instrument for the assessment of adolescent and adult alcohol expectancies. *Journal of Studies on Alcohol, 48*, 483–491.

Brown, S. A., Goldman, M. S., Inn, A., & Anderson, L. R. (1980). Expectations of reinforcement from alcohol: Their domain and relation to drinking patterns. *Journal of Consulting and Clinical Psychology, 48*, 419–426.

Bush, S., Shaw, S., Cleary, P., DelBanco, T. L., & Aronson, M. D. (1987). Screening for alcohol use using the CAGE questionnaire. *American Journal of Medicine, 82*, 231–235.

Cahalan, D. (1970). *Problem drinkers: A national survey.* San Francisco: Jossey-Bass.

Cahalan, D., Cisin, I., & Crossley, H. (1969). *American drinking practices: A national study of drinking behavior and attitudes.* Rutgers Center of Alcohol Studies, Monograph no. 6, New Brunswick, NJ.

Christiansen, B. A., Smith, G. T., Roehling, P. V., & Goldman, M. S. (1989). Using alcohol expectancies to predict adolescent drinking behavior after one year. *Journal of Consulting and Clinical Psychology, 57*, 93–99.

Collins, R. L., Lapp, W. M., Emmons, K. M., & Issac, L. M. (1990). Endorsement and strength of alcohol expectancies. *Journal of Studies on Alcohol, 51*, 336–342.

Donovan, J. E., & Jessor, R. (1983). Problem drinking and the dimension of involvement with drugs: A Guttman scalogram analysis of adolescent drug use. *American Journal of Public Health, 73*, 543–552.

Edwards, G., & Gross, M. M. (1976). Alcohol dependence: Provisional description of a clinical syndrome. *British Medical Journal, 1*, 1058–1061.

Edwards, W., Guttentag, M., & Snapper, K. (1975). A decision-theoretic approach to evaluation research. In E. L. Struening & M. Guttentag (Eds.), *Handbook of evaluation research* (pp. 139–181). Beverly Hills, CA: Sage Publications.

Farrell, A. D., Danish, S. J., & Howard, C. W. (1992). Relationship between drug use and other problem behaviors in urban adolescents. *Journal of Consulting and Clinical Psychology, 60*, 705–712.

FeCaces, M., Stinson, F. S., & Hartford, T. C. (1991). Alcohol use and physically risky behavior among adolescents. *Alcohol Health and Research World, 15*, 228–233.

Filstead, W. J., & Mayer, J. E. (1984). Validity of the Adolescent Alcohol Involvement Scale: A reply to Riley and Klockars. *Journal of Studies on Alcohol, 45*, 188–189.

Finney, J. W., Moos, R. H., & Brennan, P. L. (1991). The Drinking Problems Index: A measure to assess alcohol-related problems among older adults. *Journal of Substance Abuse, 3*, 395–404.

Friedman, A. S., Tomko, L. A., & Utada, A. (1991). Client and family characteristics that predict better family therapy outcome for adolescent drug abusers. *Family Dynamics of Addiction Quarterly, 1*, 77–93.

Friedman, A. S., & Utada, A. (1989). A method for diagnosing and planning the treatment of adolescent drug abusers: The Adolescent Drug Abuse Diagnosis (ADAD) instrument. *Journal of Drug Education, 19*, 285–312.

Gold, M. S., & Slaby, A. E. (Eds.). (1991). *Dual diagnosis in substance abuse.* New York: Marcel Dekker.

Grant, B. (1992). Pevalence of the proposed DSM-IV alcohol use disorders: United States, 1988. *British Journal of Addiction, 87*, 309–316.

Halikas, J. A., Lyttle, M. D., Morse, C. L., & Hoffmann, R. G. (1984). Proposed criteria for the diagnosis of alcohol abuse in adolescents. *Comprehensive Psychiatry, 25*, 581–585.

Harrell, A. V., & Wirtz, P. W. (1989a). Screening for adolescent problem drinking: Validation of a multidimensional instrument for case identification. *Psychological Assessment, 1*, 61–63.

Harrell, A. V., & Wirtz, P. W. (1989b). *Adolescent Drinking Index test and manual.* Odessa, FL: Psychological Assessment Resources.

Harrison, P. A., & Hoffman, N. G. (1989). *SUDDS, Substance Use Disorder Diagnosis Schedule manual.* Ramsey Clinic, St. Paul, MN.

Hawkins, J. D., Catalano, R. F., & Miller, J. Y. (1992). Risk and protective factors for alcohol and other drug problems in adolescence and early adulthood: Implications for substance abuse prevention. *Psychological Bulletin, 112*, 64–105.

Heather, N., Stallard, A., & Tebbut, J. (1991). Importance of substance cues in relapse among heroin users: Comparison of two methods of investigation. *Addictive Behaviors, 16*, 4 1–49.

Henly, G. A., & Winters, K. C. (1988). Development of problem severity scales for the assessment of adolescent alcohol and drug use. *The International Journal of the Addictions, 23*, 65–85.

Holder, H., Longabaugh, R., Miller, W. R., & Rubonis, A. V. (1991). The cost effectiveness of treatment for alcoholism: A first approximation. *Journal of Studies on Alcohol, 52*, 517–540.

Horn, J. L., Wanberg, K. W., & Foster, F. M. (1987). *Guide to the Alcohol Use Inventory.* National Computer Systems, Minneapolis, MN.

Hughes, S. O., Power, T. G., & Francis, D. J. (1992). Defining patterns of drinking in adolescence: A cluster analytic approach. *Journal of Studies on Alcohol, 53*, 40–47.

Hurlbut, S. C., & Sher, K. J. (1990, November). *Assessing alcohol problems in college students.* Paper presented at the annual meeting of the Association for Advancement of Behavior Therapy, San Francisco.

Institute of Medicine, National Academy of Sciences. (1990). *Broadening the base of treatment for alcohol problems.* Washington, DC: Author.

Jacobson, G. R. (1989). A comprehensive approach to pretreatment evaluation: I. Detection, assessment, and diagnosis of alcoholism. In R. K. Hester & W. R. Miller (Eds.), *Handbook of alcoholism treatment approaches: Effective alternatives* (pp. 17–53). New York: Pergamon Press.

James, G. (1969). Evaluation in public health practice. In H. C. Schulberg & F. Baker (Eds.), *Program evaluation in the health field.* New York: Behavioral Publications.

Janis, I. L., & Mann, L. (1977). *Decision-making: A psychological analysis of conflict , choice, and commitment.* New York: Free Press.

Jellinek, E. M. (1960). *The disease concept of alcoholism.* New Brunswick, NJ: Hillhouse Press.

Johnston, L. D., Bachman, J. G., & O'Malley, P. M. (1991). *Monitoring the future: Questionnaire responses from the nation's high school seniors 1990.*

Ann Arbor, MI: Institute for Social Research, University of Michigan.

Kabi Pharmacia Diagnostics Inc. Carbohydrate Deficient Transferrin kit. Piscataway, NJ 08855.

Kaminer, Y., Bukstein, O., & Tarter, R. E. (1991). The Teen-Addiction Severity Index: Rationale and reliability. *International Journal of the Addictions, 26,* 219–226.

Kandel, D. B., Yamaguchi, K., & Chen, K. (1992). Stages of progression in drug involvement from adolescence to adulthood: Further evidence for the gateway theory. *Journal of Studies on Alcohol, 53,* 447–457.

Kline, R. B., Canter, W. A., & Robin, A. (1987). Parameters of teenage alcohol use: A path analytic conceptual model. *Journal of Consulting and Clinical Psychology, 55,* 521–528.

Kosten, T. R., Rounsaville, B., & Kleber, H. D. (1983). Concurrent validity of the Addiction Severity Index. *Journal of Nervous and Mental Disease, 171,* 606–610.

Kouzis, A. C., & Labouvie, E. W. (1992). Use intensity, functional elaboration, and contextual constraint as facets of adolescent alcohol and marijuana use. *Psychology of Addictive Behaviors, 6,* 188–195.

Kristenson, H., Öhlin, H., Hulten-Nosslin, M. B., Trell, E., & Hood, B. (1983). Identification and intervention of heavy drinking in middle-aged men: Results and follow-up of 24–60 months of long-term study with randomized controls. *Alcoholism: Clinical and Experimental Research, 7,* 203–209.

Labouvie, E. W. (1986). The coping function of adolescent alcohol and drug use. In R. K. Silbereisen, K. Eyferth, & G. Rudinger (Eds.), *Development as action in context: Problem behavior and normal youth development.* New York: Springer-Verlag.

Litten, R. Z., & Allen, J. P. (Eds.). (1992). *Measuring alcohol consumption: Psychosocial and biochemical methods.* Totowa, NJ: Humana Press.

MacAndrew, C. (1965) The differentiation of male alcoholic outpatients from nonalcoholic psychiatric outpatients by means of the MMPI. *Quarterly Journa l of Studies on Alcohol, 26,* 238–246.

Maisto, S. A., & Connors, G. J. (1990). Clinical diagnostic techniques and assessment tools in alcohol research. *Alcohol Health & Research World, 14,* 232–238.

Markham, M. R., Miller, W. R., & Arciniega, L. (1993). BACCuS 2.01: Computer software for quantifying alcohol consumption. *Behavior Research Methods, Instruments, and Computers, 25,* 420–421.

Marlatt, G. A., & Gordon, J. R. (Eds.). (1985). *Relapse prevention.* New York: Guilford Press.

Marlatt, G. A., & Miller, W. R. (1984). *Manual for the Comprehensive Drinker Profile.* Odessa, FL: Psychological Assessment Resources.

Mayer, J., & Filstead, W. J. (1979). The Adolescent Alcohol Involvement Scale: An instrument for measuring adolescents' use and misuse of alcohol. *Journal of Studies on Alcohol, 40,* 291–300.

McLellan, A. T., Alterman, A. I., Cacciola, J., Metzger, D., & O'Brien, C. (1992). A new measure of substance abuse treatment. *The Journal of Nervous and Mental Disease, 180,* 101–110.

McLellan, A. T., Luborsky, L., Cacciola, J., Griffith, J., Evans, F., Barr, H. L., & O'Brien, C. P. (1985). New data from the Addiction Severity Index: Reliability and validity in three centers. *Journal of Mental and Nervous Disease, 173,* 412–423.

McLellan, A. T., Luborsky, L., O'Brien, C. P., & Woody, G. E. (1980). An improved evaluation instrument for substance abuse patients: The Addiction Severity Index. *Journal of Nervous and Mental Disease, 168:* 26–33.

McLellan, A. T., Parikh, G., Bragg, A., Cacciola, J., Fureman, B., & Incmikofki, R. (1990). *Addiction Severity Index administration manual* (5th ed.). Philadelphia: Penn-VA Center for Studies of Addiction.

Mendelson, W. B. (1979). Pharmacologic and electrophysical effects of ethanol in relation to sleep. In E. Majchrowitz & E. P. Noble (Eds.), *Biochemistry and Pharmacology of Ethanol, 2,* 467–484.

Metzger, D. S., Kushner, H., & McLellan, A. T. (1991). *Adolescent Problem Severity Index administration manual.* Philadelphia, PA: Biomedical Computer Research Institute.

Miller, W. R. (1976). Alcoholism scales and objective assessment methods: A review. *Psychological Bulletin, 83,* 649–674.

Miller, W. R. (1985). Motivation for treatment: A review with special emphasis on alcoholism. *Psychological Bulletin, 98,* 84–107.

Miller, W. R. (1993). *The Stages of Change Readiness and Treatment Eagerness Scale (SOCRATES, Version 6.0).* Unpublished instrument, University of New Mexico, Center on Alcoholism, Substance Abuse, and Addictions (CASAA).

Miller, W. R., & Brown, J. M. (1991). Self-regulation as a conceptual basis for the prevention and treatment of addictive behaviours. In N. Heather, W. R. Miller, & J. Greeley (Eds.), *Self-control and the addictive behaviours* (pp. 3–79). Sydney: Maxwell MacMillan Publishing Australia.

Miller, W. R., & DelBoca, F. K. (in press). Measurement of drinking behavior using the Form–90 family of instruments. *Journal of Studies on Alcohol.*

Miller, W. R., Heather, N., & Hall, W. (1991). Calculating standard drink units: International comparisons. *British Journal of Addiction, 86,* 43–47.

Miller, W. R., Leckman, A. L., Delaney, H. D., & Tinkcom, M. (1992). Long-term follow-up of behavioral self-control training. *Journal of Studies on Alcohol, 53,* 249–261.

Miller, W. R., & Marlatt, G. A. (1984). *Manual for the Comprehensive Drinker Profile.* Odessa, FL: Psychological Assessment Resources.

Miller, W. R., & Marlatt, G. A. (1987). *Manual supplement for the Brief Drinker Profile, Follow-up Drinker Profile, and Collateral Interview Form.* Odessa, FL: Psychological Assessment Resources.

Miller, W. R., & Rollinick S. A. (1991). *Motivational interviewing: Preparing people to change addictive behavior.* New York: Guilford Press.

Miller, W. R., & Saucedo, C. F. (1983). Assessment of neuropsychological impairment and brain damage in problem drinkers. In C. J. Golden, J. A. Moses, Jr., J. A. Coffman, W. R. Miller, & F. D. Strider (Eds.), *Clinical neuropsychology: Interface with neurologic and psychiatric disorders* (pp. 141–195). New York: Grune and Stratton.

Miller, W. R., Tonigan, J. S., & Longabaugh, R. (1994). *DrInC: An instrument for assessing adverse conse-*

quences of alcohol abuse. Rockville, MD: National Institute on Alcohol Abuse and Alcoholism, manuscript in preparation.

Moberg, D. P. (1983). Identifying adolescents with alcohol problems: A field test of the Adolescent Alcohol Involvement Scale. *Journal of Studies on Alcohol, 44*, 701–721.

Moss, H. B., Kirisci, L., Gordon, H. W., & Tarter, R. E. (1994). A neuropsychologic profile of adolescent alcoholics. *Alcoholism: Clinical and Experimental Research, 18*, 159–163.

National Institute on Alcohol Abuse and Alcoholism. (1994). *Alcohol and health: Eighth special report to the U.S. Congress.* Rockville, MD: NIAAA.

O'Farrell, T. J., & Maisto, S. A. (1987). The utility of self report and biological measures of alcohol consumption in alcoholism treatment outcome studies. *Advances in Behavior Research and Therapy, 9*, 91–125.

Owen, P. L., & Nyberg, L. R. (1983). Assessing alcohol and drug problems among adolescents: Current practices. *Journal of Drug Education, 13*, 249–254.

Polich, J. M., Armor, D. J., & Braiker, H. B. (1981). *The course of alcoholism: Four years after treatment.* New York: Wiley.

Prochaska, J. O., & DiClemente, C. C. (1986). Toward a comprehensive model of change. In W. R. Miller & N. Heather (Eds.), *Treating addictive behaviors: Processes of change* (pp. 3–27). New York: Plenum Press.

Putnins, A. L. (1992). The Adolescent Alcohol Involvement Scale: Some findings with young offenders. *Drug and Alcohol Review, 11*, 253–258.

Rahdert, E. R. (Ed.). (1991). *The Adolescent Assessment/Referral System manual.* Rockville, MD: U.S. Department of Health and Human Services.

Raistrick, D., Dunbar, G., & Davidson, R. (1983). Development of a questionnaire to measure alcohol dependence. *British Journal of Addiction, 78*, 89–95.

Raveis, V. H., & Kandel, D. B. (1987). Changes in drug behavior from middle to late twenties: Initiation, persistence, and cessation of use. *American Journal of Public Health, 77*, 607–611.

Riley, K., & Klockars, A. J. (1984). A critical reexamination of the Adolescent Alcohol Involvement Scale. *Journal of Studies on Alcohol, 45*, 184–187.

Robbins, L., Cottler, L., & Keating, S. (1989) *The NIMH diagnostic interview schedule. Version III, revised (DIS-III-R).* Rockville, MD: National Institute on Mental Health.

Roelofs, S. M. (1985). Hyperventilation, anxiety, craving for alcohol: A subacute alcohol withdrawal syndrome. *Alcohol, 2*, 501–505.

Rohsenow, D. J. (1983). Drinking habits and expectancies about alcohol's effect for self versus others. *Journal of Consulting and Clinical Psychology, 51*, 752–756.

Rollnick, S., Heather, N., Gold, R., & Hall, W. (1992). Development of a short "readiness to change" questionnaire for use in brief, opportunistic interventions among excessive drinkers. *British Journal of Addictions, 87*, 743–754.

Seliger, R. (1940). *Johns Hopkins 20 Questions: Are you an alcoholic?* Unpublished instrument. Baltimore, MD: Johns Hopkins Hospital.

Selzer, M. L. (1971) The Michigan Alcoholism Screening Test: The quest for a new diagnostic instru-

ment. *American Journal of Psychiatry, 127*, 1653–1658.

Shaw, J. M., Kolesar, G. S., Sellers, E. M., Kaplan, H. L., & Sandor, P. (1981). Development of optimal treatment tactics for alcohol withdrawal. I. Assessment and effectiveness of supportive care. *Journal of Clinical Psychopharmacology, 1*, 382–388.

Shedler, J., & Block, J. (1990). Adolescent drug use and psychological health: A longitudinal inquiry. *American Psychologist, 45*, 612–630.

Skinner, H. A., & Horn, J. L. (1984). *Alcohol Dependence Scale (ADS) user's guide.* Addiction Research Foundation, Toronto.

Snow, M. G., Prochaska, J. O., & Rossi, J. S. (1992). Stages of change for smoking cessation among former problem drinkers: A cross-sectional analysis. *Journal of Substance Abuse, 4*, 107–116.

Sobell, L. C., & Sobell, M. B. (1992). Timeline followback: A technique for assessing self-reported alcohol consumption. In R. Z. Litten & J. P. Allen (Eds.), *Measuring alcohol consumption: Psychosocial and biochemical methods* (pp. 41–72). Totowa, NJ: Humana Press.

Spitzer, R. L., Williams, J. B. W., Gibbon, M., & First, M. B. (1990). *Stuctured Clinical Interview for DSM-III-R—Patient edition (SCID-P, Version 1.0).* Washington, DC: American Psychiatric Press.

Stanton, M. D., & Todd, T. C. (1982). *The family therapy of drug abuse and addiction.* New York: Guilford Press.

Stibler, H. (1991). Carbohydrate-deficient transferrin in serum: A new marker of potentially harmful alcohol consumption reviewed. *Clinical Chemistry, 37* , 2029–2037.

Stockwell, T. R., Hodgson, R. J., Edwards, G., Taylor, C., & Rankin, H. (1979). The development of a questionnaire to measure severity of alcohol dependence. *British Journal of Addiction 74*, 79–87.

Stockwell, T., Murphy, D., & Hodgson, R. (1983). The Severity of Alcohol Dependence Questionnaire: Its use, reliability and validity. *British Journal of Addiction 78*, 145–155.

Stuart, R. B. (1974). Teaching facts about drugs: Pushing or preventing? *Journal of Educational Psychology, 66*, 189–201.

Szapocznik, J., Kurtines, W. M., Foote, F. H., Perez-Vidal, A., & Hervis, O. (1983). Conjoint versus one-person family therapy: Some evidence for the effectiveness of conducting family therapy through one person with drug-abusing adolescents. *Journal of Consulting and Clinical Psychology, 51*, 889–899.

Tarter, R. E. (1990). Evaluation and treatment of adolescent substance abuse: A decision tree method. *American Journal of Drug and Alcohol Abuse, 16*, 1–46.

Tarter, R. E., & Hegedus, A. M. (1991). The Drug Use Screening Inventory: Its application in the evaluation and treatment of alcohol and other drug abuse. *Alcohol Health and Research World, 15*, 65–75.

Tarter, R. E., Laird, S. B., Bukstein, O., & Kaminer, Y. (1992). Validation of the Adolescent Drug Use Screening Inventory: Preliminary findings. *Psychology of Addictive Behaviors, 6*, 233–236.

Tonigan, J. S., Miller W. R., & Montgomery, H. A. (1990). *The Twelve-Step Participation Questionnaire.*

Unpublished instrument, University of New Mexico, Center on Alcoholism, Substance Abuse, and Addictions (CASAA).

Torabi, M. R. (1989). An alcohol attitude scale for teenagers: A short form. *Journal of School Health, 59*, 385–388.

Torabi, M. R., & Veenker, C. H. (1986). An alcohol attitude scale for teenagers. *Journal of School Health, 56*, 96–100.

Veenker, C. H., & Torabi, M. R. (1984). A three component alcohol attitude scale. *Journal of School Health, 54*, 204–207.

Wanberg, K. W. (1991). *Adolescent Self Assessment Profile*. Arvada, CO: Center for Alcohol/Drug Abuse Research and Evaluation.

White, H. R., & Labouvie, E. W. (1989). Towards the assessment of adolescent problem drinking. *Journal of Studies on Alcohol, 50*, 30–37.

Winters, K. C. (1990). The need for improved assessment of adolescent substance involvement. *Journal of Drug Issues, 20*, 487–502.

Winters, K. C. (1992). Development of an adolescent alcohol and other drug abuse screening scale: Personal Experience Screening Questionnaire. *Addictive Behaviors, 17*, 479–490.

Winters, K. C., & Henly, G. A. (1989). *Personal Experience Inventory test and manual*. Los Angeles, CA: Western Psychological Services.

Winters, K. C., & Henly, G. A. (1993). *Adolescent Diagnostic Interview Schedule and manual*. Los Angeles, CA: Western Psychological Services.

Winters, K. C., Stinchfield, R. D., Fulkerson, J., & Henly, G. A. (in press). Measuring DSM-III-R criteria for alcohol and cannabis use disorders with the Adolescent Diagnostic Interview. *Psychology of Addictive Behaviors*.

Winters, K. C., Stinchfield, R. D., & Henly, G. A. (1993). Further validation of new scales measuring adolescent alcohol and other drug abuse. *Journal of Studies on Alcohol, 54*, 534–541.

CHAPTER 5

Increasing Motivation for Change

William R. Miller

WHAT IS MOTIVATION?

The treatment of alcohol problems now involves a wide range of professionals: psychologists, physicians, nurses, social workers, clergy, and counselors. Between and within these professional groups, there are wide differences in how alcohol problems are viewed and in approaches to treatment and rehabilitation. If there is one point on which all seem to agree, however, it is that client motivation is a key issue in recovery.

A common conception of motivation within the alcohol treatment field is that it is a characteristic of the client—a personal trait or state. The client comes into treatment with a certain level of motivation. Those who refuse, do not comply with, or fail in treatment are often said not to have been "motivated enough." The notion of "hitting bottom" refers to reaching a point where the person is sufficiently motivated to admit having a problem and to accept help.

Along this same line of thinking, lack of motivation has sometimes been explained as the result of strong defense mechanisms inherent in the alcoholic, which are themselves a part of the disease. Most familiar of these is denial—refusing to accept reality that is plain to others. In early writings influenced by psychoanalytic thinking, alcoholics were described as overusing the defense mechanisms of projection, rationalization, and regression (e.g., Fox, 1967). These defense mechanisms were believed to be inherent in the character structure of alcoholics, posing a substantial obstacle to recovery (Clancy, 1961; Moore & Murphy, 1961).

SHIFTS IN THINKING

Over the past 30 years, there has been a gradual but dramatic change in thinking about motivation for change. There are several reasons for these shifts in thinking.

High Bottoms

One early recognition was that most people with alcohol problems do not have to deteriorate all the way to a disastrous "bottoming out"; rather, they can and do turn around earlier. Such individuals came to be called "high bottom" alcoholics. At first, there was interest in what natural life circumstances led to high-bottom turn-arounds. Life crises were recognized as often corresponding to such changes. Then professionals began to ask whether it might be possible to intervene in a way to "raise the bottom," to help a person before he or she reached a traumatic low.

Influence of the Environment

Gradually, it was recognized that factors external to the alcoholic contribute to his or her motivation for change. The term *enabling* came to describe the behaviors of those close to an alcoholic that serve to reinforce the continuation of his or her alcohol abuse. Interlocking behavior patterns of alcoholics and "codependents" were described as a source of continued denial and low motivation for change. Alcoholism came to be seen not just as the pathology of one individual but as a complex pattern involving interactions between the individual and those around him or her. By the 1980s, it was clearly accepted that external factors have a great deal to do with an alcoholic's motivation for change.

Motivational Interventions

This emerging recognition led naturally to the exploration of a variety of strategies for precipitating the kind of life crises that could lead a person to seek and accept help. If external factors can prolong alcohol problems, increase denial, and diminish motivation for change, then surely the opposite can be true as well. Employee assistance programs appeared in industry, making use of contingent pressure from employers to increase motivation for change in employees with drinking problems. Alcohol information and treatment centers began dispensing advice to family members on how to increase a drinker's motivation to seek help. A method that came to be known in the United States as "the intervention" evolved as a specific approach to precipitate a motivational life crisis (Johnson, 1980; Liepman, 1993). Other strategies evolved for motivating change (Miller & Rollnick, 1991) and teaching skills to help a loved one with a drinking problem (Sisson & Azrin, 1993; Thomas & Ager, 1993).

Research on the "Alcoholic Personality"

Another factor that contributed to the shift away from a character-trait view of motivation was the consistent finding that alcoholics do not manifest a characteristic type of personality. Fifty years of both psychological (Miller, 1976) and

longitudinal studies (Jones, 1968; Vaillant, 1983) have failed to reveal a consistent "alcoholic personality." Attempts to derive a set of alcoholic psychometric personality subtypes have yielded profiles similar to those found when subtyping a general population (e.g., Løberg & Miller, 1986). That is, alcoholics appear to be as variable in personality as are nonalcoholics. Studies of character defense mechanisms among alcoholics have yielded a similar picture. Denial and other defense mechanisms have been found to be no more or less frequent among alcoholics than among people in general (Chess, Neuringer, & Goldstein, 1971; Donovan, Rohsenow, Schau, & O'Leary, 1977; Skinner & Allen, 1983). There was simply no support for the view that alcoholics in general come into treatment with a consistent set of personality traits and defenses.

Research on Therapist Effects

Yet another piece of the puzzle questioning a client-trait view of motivation emerged from studies of the effects of therapist characteristics in alcohol treatment. An early observation was that the degree of clients' "motivation" for treatment varied widely among the caseloads of therapists. One common index of motivation, for example, is dropout from treatment. Early studies showed that treatment staff differed greatly in the number of their patients who dropped out. Some lost very few patients; for others, nearly half their patients failed to return. Within a given treatment center, a majority of dropouts were accounted for by the caseloads of a relatively small number of staff (Greenwald & Bartmeier, 1963; Raynes & Patch, 1971; Rosenberg, Gerrein, Manohar, & Liftik, 1976; Rosenberg & Raynes, 1973). As will be discussed later in this chapter, staff who have more "motivated" clients have predictable characteristics and styles themselves. The implication was that whereas "motivated" versus "unmotivated" clients cannot be readily differentiated on personal characteristics, their therapists can!

A NEW PERSPECTIVE

All of these factors led to an important shift in thinking about client motivation. No longer do therapists need to feel helpless if a client seems "unmotivated." No longer is it appropriate to blame clients for lacking in motivation or to attribute treatment failure to character defense mechanisms. No longer is it necessary to wait for drinkers to hit bottom. Motivation is now understood to be the result of an *interaction* between the drinker and those around him or her. This means that there are things a therapist can do to increase motivation for change. This chapter is written from that perspective—to help you enhance motivation for change in your clients.

Before turning to a description of effective methods for increasing client motivation, however, I should clarify what I mean by "motivation." If, as is increasingly recognized, motivation is not a client trait, a personality characteristic, a set of overused defense mechanisms, then what is it?

For clues, one can look to the experience of alcohol treatment professionals, who express common frustrations related to motivation. In listening to these frustrations and complaints, I find that therapists are not, in fact, describing generalized defense mechanisms in the sense that I would understand them as a psychologist. Rather, they are describing particular practical problems. "How can I get my client to recognize the seriousness of her problem?" "Why does this client continue to insist that he is not an alcoholic and that he can drink without losing control?" "How can I get my clients to do what they need to do to recover and to stop procrastinating?"

These motivational concerns are problems of perception and compliance. They are not at all unique to alcoholism. Physicians express the same frustrations in trying to get overweight patients to lose weight, heart patients to quit smoking, hypertensives and diabetics to take their medications and maintain a proper diet, and so on. Dentists and dental assistants complain that their patients won't floss and brush properly. World religions have long recognized the difficulty of faithfully following a set of precepts and teachings, and the human tendency to ignore rather than see and confess one's shortcomings. Inertia seems to be part of human nature.

In this broader view, motivation can be understood not as something that one *has* but rather as something one *does*. It involves recognizing a problem, searching for a way to change, and then beginning and sticking with that change strategy. There are, it turns out, many ways to help people move toward such recognition and action.

Stages of Change

One helpful model for change has been described by Prochaska and DiClemente (1982, 1986). They developed their model by studying how change occurs naturally, outside of treatment. They studied people who were self-changers, who accomplished significant change (e.g., stopped smoking) on their own, without formal outside help. When comparing self-change to what occurs in therapy, they noticed many similarities. This led the authors to describe change as occurring in *stages*, or steps. Change is rarely a sudden event, occurring in a moment of transformation, although such change does happen, as it did for Bill Wilson, the cofounder of Alcoholics Anonymous (1976; Miller & C'de Baca, 1994). Usually, though, change happens gradually, in stages or cycles.

Figure 5.1 shows a wheel of change reflecting the stages originally described by Prochaska and DiClemente. In *precontemplation*, the person is not even considering change. Told that he or she has a problem, the precontemplator may be more surprised than defensive. The person is just not considering (contemplating) that there might be a problem, or that change is possible. To hear that there is a problem or a way to change is news. (To call someone a precontemplator, by the way, implies that there really is a problem, and that someone else perceives it while the person does not.) Precontemplators would not ordinarily be seen in treatment settings (unless coerced), precisely because they do not perceive that they have a problem or need help.

Figure 5.1 A Stage Model of the Process of Change

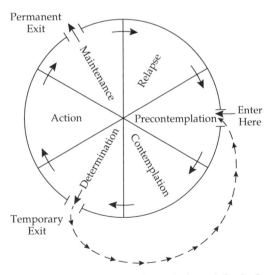

Source: Adapted from James O. Prochaska and Carolo C. DiClemente (1982), "Transtheoretical therapy: Toward a more integrative model of change." *Psychotherapy: Theory, Research, and Practice, 19:* 276–288. Reprinted with permission from W. R. Miller & K. A. Jackson (1985), *Practical Psychology for Pastors.* Englewood Cliffs, NJ: Prentice Hall, page 130.

As awareness dawns, a person begins to see some causes for concern—reasons to change. Again, this does not usually occur in a flash of insight, but emerges over time. It is a normal part of the change process (not just in addictions) for a person simultaneously to "want it and not want it," to see reasons to change and reasons to stay the same. In this second stage, *contemplation*, the person is ambivalent. Allowed to talk and explore freely, a contemplator might say something like this:

> Sometimes I wonder if I drink too much, though I don't really drink more than most of my friends do. It's just that when I wake up with a hangover, I feel like maybe I'm hurting myself. I don't think I'm an alcoholic, because I can stop drinking when I want to. But it worries me that sometimes I can't remember what happened the night before, and that's not normal. I like drinking, though, and I'd hate to give it up.

The normal and characteristic style of the contemplator is "yes, but . . . ." It reflects the fact that part of the person wants to change and part does not. It's as if there were an internal balance or seesaw that rocks back and forth between motivations to change on one side and to stay the same on the other.

Determination is a hypothetical point where the seesaw or balance tips in favor of change. Enough weights are placed on the "change" side (or taken off the status quo side) that there is an imbalance in favor of change. Sometimes this occurs suddenly, as when one's partner jumps off the other end of a seesaw. Sometimes it is a gradual process of slowly tipping further and further in the direction of change, a process that Prochaska now calls "preparation" for change (Prochaska, DiClemente, & Norcross, 1992). At some point, a decision or determination is reached that it is time to change. Unlike contemplators, those in determination say things like, "Something's got to change! I can't go on like this! What can I do?"

My own experience has been that this stage is like a window or a door that opens up for a period of time. If the person gets through to the next stage, the process of change continues. If not, the door closes and he or she is back to contemplation or (if completely discouraged that change is impossible) even to precontemplation.

Action is the process of doing something. The person chooses a strategy for change and pursues it. What is ordinarily thought of as treatment would come at this point.

Maintenance is the real challenge in all of the addictive behaviors (Marlatt & Gordon, 1985). It is not that difficult to stop drinking; it's hard to *stay* sober. It is not hard to quit smoking or using drugs, but it is challenging to stay away. It is easy to go on a diet and lose weight, but harder to keep it off. During the maintenance stage, the person's challenge is to maintain the gains that he or she has made, to keep from relapsing.

Finally, *relapse,* as every alcohol professional knows, is a common phenomenon in addictive behaviors. Long-term follow-up data suggest that more than 90% of clients will drink again at some time after treatment (e.g., Helzer et al., 1985; Polich, Armor, & Braiker, 1981). A slip, however, need not turn into a disastrous relapse (see Chapter 11). The challenge in this stage is to recover from the slip or relapse as quickly as possible and to resume the change process. In this sense, relapse is just another step in the process of change that leads to stable recovery. It is typical in problem drinking (as well as in smoking, weight control, drug abuse, and so forth) to go around the wheel of change several times before finally escaping through the permanent exit of maintenance.

The important point to recognize here is that clients need different kinds of help, depending on where they are in this cycle. The precontemplator needs to have his or her awareness raised, starting the change balance moving. In the contemplation stage, the client needs to resolve ambivalence, to place weights on the change side of the balance and lift them from the side of the balance favoring status quo. At the point of determination, however, the key help needed is in sorting out the alternative change strategies that are available and choosing the one most likely to be effective for this individual (see Chapter 17). In action, the client may need help in carrying out and complying with strategies for change. In maintenance, the client may need to develop new skills to maintain a sober lifestyle. If relapse occurs, the therapist's job is to help the person recover from it as quickly as possible rather than prolonging it, and to resume the process of change. Therapists have usually focused on the action stage, but in fact effective treatment encompasses the entire process of change.

Later chapters of this book provide a wide array of strategies appropriate to use with clients in the action, maintenance, and relapse stages. This chapter is devoted to strategies to increase motivation, helping clients to move from the point of precontemplation or contemplation into determination and action. The effectiveness of a motivation strategy is judged by whether the client undertakes and sticks with a change strategy. The client's ultimate success with regard to recovery, of course, will also be influenced by the effectiveness of the change strategy chosen. Helping clients to comply with an ineffective change strategy is of little use.

FRAMES: SIX KEYS TO MOTIVATION FOR CHANGE

What can a therapist do to help precontemplators or contemplators strengthen motivation for change? A reasonable place to start is with research on what works. Literally hundreds of studies have examined influences on motivation to change alcohol problems (Miller, 1985). A particularly interesting literature focuses on brief motivational interventions, which have been found to be surprisingly effective in changing drinking behavior (see Chapters 2 and 6; for a specific review, see Bien, Miller, & Tonigan, 1993). These studies, conducted in 14 different nations, have tested a variety of counseling strategies lasting for one to several sessions. In examining the content of interventions found to be effective, we noticed that there seemed to be at least six common elements (Bien et al., 1993; Miller & Sanchez, 1994). These can be remembered via the acronym FRAMES: Feedback, Responsibility, Advice, Menu, Empathy, and Self-Efficacy.

F: Feedback

One general finding in the motivation literature is the persuasiveness of personal, individual feedback. Lectures and films about the detrimental effects of alcohol on people, *in general,* seem to have little or no impact on drinking behavior, either in treatment or in prevention settings. *Personal* feedback of ways in which alcohol is harming the individual, however, does seem to have a strong motivational effect. Kristenson and colleagues (1983), for example, identified from a health screening those individuals who had an elevated liver enzyme (GGT) indicative of excessive and health-damaging drinking. He briefly intervened with half of these individuals by giving them personal feedback of this finding and advising them to change their drinking. Five years later, those receiving this intervention (as compared to the other half of the group not given brief intervention) showed lower rates of disease, death, hospitalization, sick days, and work absences. Personal feedback of impairment has been an element in most effective minimal interventions (see Bien et al., 1993).

One feasible way to implement this in practice is to use information from a structured and objective intake evaluation as a basis for individual feedback of results (Miller, Sovereign, & Krege, 1988). The client's individual scores can be compared with normative data from a general population or from groups of clients already in treatment. Measures of alcohol consumption, dependence, family history, and problem severity are useful in this regard. Serum chemistry profiles and neuropsychological testing have also been used to examine the physical effects of excessive drinking. When follow-up evaluations are completed, clients can be given feedback of their improvement as a reinforcement of their progress.

R: Responsibility

A second common element in effective motivational interventions is an emphasis on the client's personal responsibility and freedom of choice. Rather than giving restrictive messages (You have to, can't, must, etc.), the counselor acknowledges that ultimately it is up to the client whether or not to change: "No one can change your drinking for you, or make you change. It's really up to you. You can choose to keep on drinking as you have been. You can choose to make a change. Even if I wanted to, I can't decide this for you." In addition to being therapeutic, this message is quite simply the truth. A therapist cannot alter the client's ultimate personal responsibility and choice.

Why is this message helpful in triggering change? A strong and consistent finding in research on motivation is that people are most likely to undertake and persist in an action when they perceive that they have personally chosen to do so. One study, for example, found that a particular alcohol treatment approach was more effective when a client chose it from among alternatives than when it was assigned to the client as his or her only option (Kissin, Platz, & Su, 1971). Perceived freedom of choice also appears to reduce client resistance and dropout (Costello, 1975; Parker, Winstead, & Willi, 1979). When clients are told they have no choice, they tend to resist change. When their freedom of choice is acknowledged, they are freed to choose change.

A: Advice

A relatively simple strategy to increase motivation for change is to give the client clear and direct advice as to the need for change and how it might be accomplished. It has long been recognized, for example, that smokers are significantly more likely to quit if a physician clearly advises them to do so for health reasons, and provides sound recommendations for how to do so (e.g., Russell, Wilson, Taylor, & Baker, 1979). Many studies have similarly demonstrated that brief advice interventions can trigger change in drinking problems (Bien et al., 1993).

Does this seem inconsistent with an emphasis on personal responsibility? Not at all! There is no inconsistency in advising change while also acknowledging that the client makes the ultimate choice. Advice is different from ordering, directing, or coercing. The key element is a clear recommendation for change, given in an empathic manner.

M: Menu

In order to perceive that one has a choice, there must first be *alternatives* from among which one can choose. It is sensible, therefore, that counseling methods that effectively get people moving on a course of action have frequently offered a variety of alternative strategies for change. There is a predictable outcome in telling an ambivalent (contemplator) person that there is only one thing to do: "Yes, but . . . ." Better to say something like this: "There are several different ways that people have successfully changed their drinking. Let me tell you about some of them, and you can tell me which of these might make the most sense for you." Again, the client is actively involved in choosing his or her own approach.

E: Empathy

One of the strongest predictors of therapist success in motivating and treating alcoholic clients is *empathy*, as defined by Carl Rogers and his students (Truax & Carkhuff, 1967). An empathic therapist, in this definition, is one who maintains a more client-centered approach, listening to and reflecting the client's statements and feelings. Empathic counselors in this sense are characterized as warm, supportive, sympathetic, and at-

tentive. The opposite of this type of empathy is a directive, confrontational, aggressive, suspicious style of dealing with clients. Empathy should not be confused with the tendency to *identify* with one's clients, or whether one has been through similar experiences. The effectiveness of counselors has been found to be unrelated to whether or not they are themselves "in recovery." Being in the early stages of one's own recovery may, in fact, be associated with lower levels of this kind of therapeutic empathy as a counselor (Manohar, 1973).

An empathic counseling style is a common thread in a variety of interventions that have been shown to yield favorable long-term outcomes with problem drinkers (Bien et al., 1993; Chafetz, 1961; Edwards & Orford, 1977). A comparison of alternative styles of group therapy favored a client-centered approach over three others (Ends & Page, 1957). Two research teams have found a strong positive relationship between therapist empathy and favorable client outcomes (Miller & Baca, 1983; Miller, Taylor, & West, 1980; Valle, 1981). A hostile-confrontational style of counseling, by contrast, has been found in general to be associated with poor long-term results (Lieberman, Yalom, & Miles, 1973). One study identified hostility of the therapist's vocal *tone* as a predictor of dropout among alcoholics (Milmoe, Rosenthal, Blane, Chafetz, & Wolf, 1967).

S: Self-Efficacy

A sixth common element in effective brief motivational counseling is an emphasis on client self-efficacy (Bandura, 1982). Without some degree of optimism that change can be achieved, there is no motivation. Fear of negative consequences in itself is not enough; the person must also believe that he or she *can* change (Rogers & Mewborn, 1976). Effective motivational interventions have included the message: "You *can* change." Optimism can also be found in the menu of different approaches available.

Relatedly, a therapist's own optimism may also powerfully influence client motivation and outcome. Leake and King (1977) demonstrated experimentally that therapist expectations of good prognosis are predictive of favorable outcomes among alcoholic clients. More generally, clients who perceive their therapist as wanting and expecting to help are more likely to stay in treatment and be receptive to change (Thomas, Polansky, & Kounin, 1955).

MOTIVATIONAL INTERVIEWING

Rationale

Attempting to devise a clinical approach that combines these therapeutic elements, I described a counseling style called "motivational interviewing" (Miller, 1983). My initial attempt was much enriched by a subsequent collaboration with Stephen Rollnick, in which the principles and procedures of motivational interviewing were clarified (Miller & Rollnick, 1991).

In many ways, motivational interviewing seems the opposite of a confrontational approach. Instead of telling clients that they have a problem, they are asked to talk about their own perceptions of the situation, and the counselor responds largely in a reflective manner. Instead of telling clients what to do, they are asked what, if anything, they want to do. Diagnostic labeling is avoided. The therapist rolls with client "resistance" or "denial" instead of challenging it head-on. To a therapist accustomed to a hard-hitting, denial-busting style, a motivational interviewing session can appear impossibly slow and ineffectual.

Yet motivational interviewing *is* a confrontational process. The meaning of the word *confront* is, literally, "to bring face to face." This approach is intended precisely to bring a client to greater awareness of and personal responsibility for his or her problem with alcohol, and to instill a commitment to change. In the language of Prochaska and DiClemente's model, it is intended to move the individual from precontemplation or contemplation to determination and action. Viewed in this way, confrontation is not a style but a goal.

What, then, are the best methods for accomplishing this goal? What is the most effective way to help people see and accept a difficult and threatening reality, and let it change them? Although direct and forceful persuasion is effective with some, motivational interviewing relies on a somewhat different strategy. The guiding principle is to create a salient dissonance or discrepancy between the person's current behavior and important personal goals (e.g., self-esteem, self-protection, health). One method for accomplishing this is to have the *client* express verbally his or her own concerns about drinking and its effects, to state perceptions that drinking is a problem, and to express a need for willingness to change. The therapist specifically avoids taking responsibility for these statements, for persuading the client that he or she has a serious problem and needs to change. Instead, the therapist seeks to evoke these perceptions from the client.

There are several reasons for this approach. One already stated is the fact that clients tend to be more committed to a plan that they perceive as their own, addressing personal concerns. A related social psychological principle is that "as I hear myself talk, I learn what I believe." It is in the client's interest, then, to have the *client* rather than the therapist express perceptions of the problems and the need for change. A second reason is the paradoxical effect of therapist arguments. A therapist statement, "You have a serious problem and you need treatment," is likely to evoke from an ambivalent client the opposite, countering argument: "No, I don't." These are exactly the *wrong* words to evoke from the client. Although client statements of this kind are often understood as the product of alcoholic systems of denial, there is persuasive evidence that they are powerfully evoked by the way in which the therapist approaches the client (Miller, Benefield, & Tonigan, 1993; Patterson & Forgatch, 1985). Remember, also, that current research points to no particular personality or defensive character structure that is unique or universal to alcoholics. The resistant behavior that is labeled "denial" does not just walk through the door with the client, but is strongly influenced by the way in which the therapist approaches the client. Said provocatively, denial is not a client problem. It is a therapist problem.

As an example, consider the issue of the client "admitting the problem." Many counselors place great importance on the client accepting the label "alcoholic." Power struggles emerge in which the client and therapist clash on whether the label is appropriate. Unfortunately, research suggests no strong relationship between self-labeling and outcome. Many treatment failures are quite willing to accept the label "alcoholic," and many people respond favorably to treatment without ever calling themselves alcoholic (e.g., Miller & Joyce, 1979; Polich et al., 1981). In our clinic, where we have deemphasized labeling, we have experienced very little of this kind of client resistance. It is common for our clients to say, "I don't think I'm an alcoholic, but . . . ," and proceed to talk about their concerns. The recognition of a serious problem in need of change does not require the acceptance of a particular diagnostic label. To fight against a client's reluctance to accept a label is one way to evoke unnecessary resistance.

There is one aspect of truth to common concerns about denial. The more resistance a client shows during initial counseling, the less likely it is that the client will change (Miller et al., 1993). It *is* desirable, therefore, to minimize initial client resistance. What many therapists fail to understand, however, is that they are substantially in control of their clients' level of resistance. Resistance behavior is the result of an interpersonal interaction. One study demonstrated that therapists can dramatically increase and decrease client resistance within the same session simply by shifting their own style (Patterson & Forgatch, 1985). Directive, confrontational counseling tends to increase resistance. Reflective, supportive counseling tends to minimize resistance.

Miller and Rollnick (1991) described five general principles underlying motivational interviewing. The first is *express empathy*. The Rogerian skill of reflective listening is used extensively to help clarify ambivalence without eliciting resistance. This principle is a bit paradoxical: By communicating acceptance of clients as they are, they are freed to change.

Second, the therapist seeks to *develop discrepancy*. The key here is to help clients to see and feel how their current behavior threatens important personal goals or is inconsistent with more central personal values. This principle, too, can seem puzzling. By the time a drinker reaches treatment, the negative consequences of drinking are usually quite apparent, yet they continue to drink. Why don't the consequences themselves cause a change? That is exactly the problem of ambivalence. The negatives are refuted by counterarguments, and the person remains stuck in the status quo. The key is for the client to "let in" the awareness of harm, and that process seems to be facilitated by a safe environment in which to explore the pros and cons openly, without criticism or coercion.

Remember that the primary goal here is to increase the individual's personal, salient awareness of his or her problems and risk. One way of eliciting such statements from clients is to *ask* for them: "Tell me what things you have noticed about your drinking that concern you, or that you think might become problems." Similarly, with regard to the need for change, a therapist can ask, "What makes you think that maybe you should do something about your drinking?" Though some clients stonewall in response to such questions, many will volunteer at least a few tentative concerns, often qualifying them with "buts," representing the other side of their ambivalence (typical of contemplators).

How you respond to these initial offerings will determine whether the client risks exploring and exposing further concerns. If the initial revelations are immediately seized upon as evidence of alcoholism and thrown back to the client as such, additional disclosures may not be forthcoming. If, on the other hand, you meet the client's concern statements with empathic reflection, the client will be more likely to continue exploring these and other concerns. The skillful therapist will reflect *both* sides of the client's ambivalence, but place greater stress on the perceived problems. ("So, on the one hand, you don't think of yourself as an alcoholic, but on the other hand, you can see that your drinking is having some scary effects on you, and you worry that you may be doing serious damage to yourself.") A simple "What else?" can also help the client to continue expressing worrisome aspects of his or her drinking.

With some clients, I find it useful to employ a mildly paradoxical strategy by taking a devil's advocate role and asking the client to persuade me that there really is a problem here in need of attention. I may say, "Surely there must be more than this for you to be concerned enough to come here." In screening a client for treatment, I may also pose a paradoxical challenge: "This program requires a great deal of motivation, and the person must really want to change. Frankly, I wonder whether you are clear enough about your problem, and whether you're motivated enough to stick with a program like this." Such paradoxical statements must be handled carefully, but often they have an effect of eliciting additional client statements of concern and commitment.

The third principle, *avoid argumentation*, has already been mentioned. It is counterproductive for the therapist to take the "good" role with an ambivalent client. This leaves clients with the role of defending drinking, and so they talk themselves into not changing. Instead, the therapist uses a variety of strategies to elicit the client's own perceptions of problems and concerns. Arguing just breeds resistance.

Relatedly, in this style therapists *roll with resistance*. Instead of opposing client "denial," the therapist uses the client's own momentum to shift perceptions. Various forms of reflection can serve this function, as can reframing, paradox, or (as above) simply acknowledging the client's personal responsibility and freedom of choice.

Opposing resistance tends to entrench it. Rolling with and exploring resistance, on the other hand, helps the client to move through it and to resolve ambivalence.

Finally, the therapist seeks to *support self-efficacy*. The reasons for this were discussed earlier. Clients will not consider change unless they think it possible. It can be helpful here to explore how clients have succeeded in the past, perhaps in other problem areas, and apply these same skills to the current situation (Berg & Miller, 1992).

THE DRINKER'S CHECK-UP

Feedback of objective assessment findings can be integrated nicely into a motivational interviewing approach. When doing so, the therapist presents the findings to the client in a low key, objective fashion. Instead of employing the findings as proof and attempting to persuade the client (a strategy likely to evoke resistance), the therapist presents the data and asks the client what he or she makes of them. Again, client statements of concern are likely to be evoked, and can be reflected empathically.

For our initial work with motivational interviewing, we developed an assessment-feedback intervention approach called the Drinker's Check-Up (DCU; Miller, Sovereign, & Krege, 1988). This method can be used as a motivational prelude to treatment, or as a stand-alone minimal intervention in settings where one has only relatively brief contact with problem drinkers (e.g., family practice, employee assistance programs, screening programs, health maintenance systems; see Miller, Jackson, & Karr, 1994).

As we have offered it, the DCU consists of a two-hour evaluation that yields several dozen objective indicators of alcohol-related problems. We have combined the Brief Drinker Profile (Miller & Marlatt, 1987), the Alcohol Use Inventory (Horn, Wanberg, & Foster, 1987), a serum chemistry panel of tests sensitive to alcohol's impact on physical systems, and a neuropsychological screening comprised of measures sensitive to alcohol's chronic effects on the brain (Miller & Saucedo, 1983). The precise content of the assessment package is not definitive, however, and one could use any valid measures of alcohol use and its consequences. The assessment is done in a single session, and the client returns a week later for a feedback visit.

We have advertised this check-up through local news media, describing it in a fashion we believed likely to evoke minimal resistance and threat. The DCU is described as being for drinkers (not for alcoholics) who would like to find out whether alcohol is harming them in any way. The check-up is free, confidential, and not part of any treatment program. Objective results are given, and it is up to the drinker to decide what, if anything, to do with the findings. This recruitment strategy worked, in that we received a substantial number of calls. Those who referred themselves for the DCU proved to be alcohol impaired in almost every case, yet few had ever consulted anyone to seek help. Most said they had never been treated for alcohol problems and were not eager to enter treatment. Fewer than one in three considered themselves even to be "problem drinkers."

A check-up can also be offered as the first phase of treatment, to provide a motivational head start. We have tested the DCU in this context as well, in research that will be summarized at the end of this chapter. In this case, it may be possible to use, as the assessment base for feedback, measures that are completed as part of routine intake evaluation.

OTHER STRATEGIES FOR ENHANCING MOTIVATION

Removing Barriers

Sometimes motivation for change is impeded by simple but significant practical barriers. The need for child care may prevent a parent from seeking treatment. Attendance at aftercare meetings has been found to be most strongly predictable not from client characteristics but rather from the distance a client has to travel to reach the meeting (Prue, Keane, Cornell, & Foy, 1979). The cost of treatment is an obvious obstacle for many. Accessibility to people who are disabled, women, minorities, and economically disadvantaged populations is an important consideration for a treatment center. The more practical obstacles one can remove, the more likely it is that a client will participate. It can be important, therefore, to explore, "What would stand in the way of your taking a first step?" Removal of practical barriers can open the door for change.

External Contingencies

What about using external contingencies—leverage or pressure from the outside—to persuade or coerce a client to change or seek help?

This is, in a way, the opposite of approaches emphasized in this chapter thus far, which seek to create *internal* motivation for change. External contingencies can and do work. Faced with the options of seeking treatment versus losing one's job or going to jail, most people will choose the former. Spouses of alcoholics are sometimes counseled to pose an alcoholic with the ultimatum of staying sober or losing the marriage. Abstinence or taking disulfiram may be assigned by judges during sentencing as a condition of probation. Participation in treatment may be placed as a condition for restoration of a driver's license.

There is evidence that problem drinkers brought into treatment by such external contingencies respond with about the same rate of success as those who are self-referred. A caution here, however, is that if an external contingency is to be used, one should ensure that it will be enforced, or at least that the client believes it will be. Further, brief contingencies are likely to yield a rebound effect. It is a common phenomenon, for example, that a 90-day mandate to monitored disulfiram will be followed by a discontinuation of medication on day 91. When external contingencies are used rather than personal choice, the contingency should be a firm and enduring one.

External contingencies and personal choice are not necessarily mutually exclusive. Even within a population required to seek treatment (e.g., drunk-driving offenders), it is feasible to use an empathic counseling style and to offer a choice among a variety of alternative treatments, fostering the perception of personal responsibility and control over the change process.

There is also clear evidence that positive reinforcement can influence substance abuse. Studies have shown the effectiveness of even the simplistic approach of paying drug addicts to stay clean (Stitzer & Kirby, 1991). Even apparently addictive drinking can be altered by social reinforcement (for a review, see Heather & Robertson, 1981).

Unilateral Family Approaches

These findings suggest that it might be possible to train the family and friends of alcoholics in skills for motivating change. Sisson and Azrin (1986, 1993) worked with the wives of alcoholics using a community reinforcement approach (see Chapter 15). The wives were taught to reinforce sobriety by not drinking and to allow natural negative consequences to occur. Most succeeded

in getting their spouse into treatment within two months, during which time the alcoholic's drinking had already been cut in half. Thomas and Ager (1993) have studied similar strategies for increasing motivation for change through family members, when a problem drinker is initially unwilling to seek help.

More Coercive Strategies

Motivational strategies with a more directive and coercive flavor have enjoyed popularity in the United States. Employee assistance programs have sometimes practiced "constructive coercion" to get employees into treatment. The impact of such intervention may depend, of course, on the effectiveness of the treatment method chosen and its appropriateness for the client.

One particularly coercive motivational approach, associated with the Johnson Institute and its training efforts, emphasizes a dramatic intervention in which multiple members of the alcoholic's family and larger social circle simultaneously confront the person with his or her problems. Greenberger (1983), in a front-page story for *The Wall Street Journal*, offered the following description of such an intervention arranged through an employee assistance program:

> They called a surprise meeting, surrounded him with colleagues critical of his work and threatened to fire him if he didn't seek help quickly. When the executive tried to deny that he had a drinking problem, the medical director . . . came down hard. "Shut up and listen," he said. "Alcoholics are liars, so we don't want to hear what you have to say." (p. 1)

Many interventions of this kind would have a less hostile tone and would place greater emphasis on compassionate concern. Indeed, there seems to be a trend away from highly confrontational approaches, even within the "Minnesota model" programs with which they are often associated (Hazelden Foundation, 1985). The widespread popularity of this intervention method, particularly in residential treatment centers, suggests that it is at least effective in transporting the alcoholic into treatment. To my knowledge, however, there have been no properly controlled studies of the effectiveness of the Johnson Institute approach.

Certainly, there may be a place for more directive approaches, particularly when alternatives have failed. It seems sensible to begin with less intrusive strategies for motivating change and then move to the use of more directive interventions and external contingencies if the former are insufficient. Informed judgment about which motivational strategies are optimal for which types of problem drinkers must await the emergence of new research.

Practical Persistence

Finally, there are also some specific therapist behaviors that can powerfully influence a client's persistence and compliance. Consider the following situation. An alcohol clinic decides to experiment with a simple procedure. Following a first visit for evaluation, clients are (without their knowledge) assigned at random to one of two conditions. Those in one group are sent a handwritten letter the next day, in which the intake staff member says, in essence, "I'm glad you came in. I think you do have a problem to work on, and I am concerned about you. I hope you will come back, and we'll be glad to work with you if you do." Those in the other group are sent no letter. This was actually done, with the finding that 50% of those receiving the single letter returned, as compared with 31% of those getting no letter (Koumans & Muller, 1965). A similar letter, sent when a client missed an appointment, decreased dropout from 51 to 28% (Panepinto & Higgins, 1969). Similarly, a group receiving a single personal telephone call during the week after initial consultation returned for treatment 44% of the time, as compared with 8% of those receiving no call (Koumans, Muller, & Miller, 1967). Personal calls have also been shown to increase aftercare attendance (Intagliata, 1976). These small investments of time may yield a substantial increase in outpatient treatment retention.

Consider another issue relevant to referral. An alcoholic has been evaluated, and it is recommended that the person go for treatment. Is it better to place the referral call and make an appointment *for* the person or to give him or her the number of the treatment program and the responsibility for placing the call? Some believe that personal responsibility is so vital that the latter procedure should be used. An experimental comparison of these two referral procedures yielded an enormous difference: the referral was completed in 82% of cases where the counselor made the call, as compared with 37% of cases where the client was told to call (Kogan, 1957).

The message here is to be persistent in your efforts on behalf of clients. For one thing, this communicates an active caring. It can also overcome mild surmountable obstacles of shyness, reticence, or procrastination that stand in the way of the client's taking the next step. Oddly enough, such therapist actions are sometimes denigrated as "enabling" or "codependent"— terms applied to behaviors that tend to promote or prolong addiction. Clearly, the opposite is true. Any minor concern that the client must be "responsible" for initiating treatment should be weighed against the fact that you cannot help much unless the client first comes back. Make that extra call. Send the caring note. Such simple acts can make all the difference.

NEGOTIATING A CHANGE PLAN

If the initial counseling process goes well, sufficient motivation is generated for the client to begin considering change and wondering what alternatives may be available. The client's speech begins to shift from "Is there a problem?" to "What can I do?" The work of Prochaska and DiClemente (1986) suggests that these two questions (and indeed the contemplation and action stages) overlap considerably. In fact, the client's willingness to admit that there is a problem may, in part, be determined by the perceived availability of acceptable alternatives for resolving it. Why go through the pain of admitting that there is a serious problem if there is nothing to be done about it, or if the change strategies are unacceptable?

This raises another important point from motivational research. Once a perceived discrepancy has been created, once the person perceives a risk, several things happen. One of them is emotional. Openly confronting personal risk and problems is upsetting. The client may become more anxious, depressed, agitated, sad, or angry. This is an *uncomfortable* state, which is one reason why it is motivating. From here, the process can go in one of two ways. The client may resolve the discrepancy either by *risk reduction* or by *fear reduction*. The risk-reduction route involves changing behavior, doing something to reduce the risk (e.g., stopping drinking). That is, the person moves on to the action stage of change. The fear-reduction route, by contrast, involves *cognitive* changes to decrease the perceived discrepancy: denial, rationalization, projection, and other defensive strategies. That is, the person copes by reducing the perceived problem, thus returning to the contemplation stage. Because a state of discrepancy arouses aversive emotions, the person will use one or the other route to escape from it. The therapist, obviously, is interested in promoting risk reduction rather than fear reduction.

What makes the difference in which approach a client will choose? As mentioned earlier, the work of Rogers suggests that self-efficacy is a key (Rogers, Deckner, & Mewborn, 1978; Rogers & Mewborn, 1976). *Self-efficacy* refers to the client's perception that there is an effective and realistic change strategy available and that he or she is capable of carrying it out. If the client perceives that such a change method is available, he or she is likely to pursue it as a risk-reduction strategy. If not, then the client is likely to use defense mechanisms to reduce the discomfort of perceiving the discrepancy.

The key at the determination stage, then, is to encourage self-efficacy in the client, to assure him or her that there are available, effective, acceptable, and realistic avenues for change. A good strategy for doing this is to provide the client with a set of *alternatives* (the "Menu" that is part of FRAMES). The chapters later in this book present a range of such strategies. Describe to a client the variety of options available and discuss together which of these alternatives might be the best place to start. The options, of course, include not only treatment alternatives but also self-directed efforts, self-help groups (see Chapter 10), and doing nothing at all. The point here is to *negotiate* a workable change strategy with the client.

This approach has a number of advantages. First, you are not in the position of "selling" a single particular approach, thus running the risk of evoking client resistance. Any one approach may be unacceptable (or ineffective) for a client for various reasons. The menu approach defuses the resistance related to accepting versus refusing a particular treatment. Second, research suggests that treatments chosen by a client from among alternatives are more likely to be adhered to and effective. The choice process increases the client's perception of personal control and enhances motivation for compliance. Third, research on matching clients to treatments similarly suggests that individualized strategies lead to increased positive outcomes (Miller & Hester, 1986). Finally, clients can be valuable resources in choosing optimal change strategies, in that they have direct knowledge of the acceptability of different approaches. Although the client's preferences are not the only consideration in choosing a change strategy, to ignore or violate these preferences is to sacrifice motivational potential and to increase the likelihood of resis-

tance. There is also reason to believe that clients have wisdom about what is most likely to work for them.

Goal Setting

A first step in negotiating a change plan is to help the client clarify his or her goals for change. Research clearly points to the importance of goal setting in motivation for change. Feedback of present personal state, for example, will have little impact if the client does not recognize it as being discrepant from where he or she would *like* to be. It is a perceived discrepancy between one's goal and one's present state that strongly motivates change.

Clients come with a wide variety of personal goals. Some choose to pursue total abstinence. Some want to try cutting down on their drinking before or instead of committing to life-long abstinence. Some are aware of their excessive drinking but are more concerned with other life problems they are having. It is more likely to be effective, from a motivational perspective, to acknowledge the client's own goals and negotiate change objectives than to insist *a priori* that the client accept your own particular goals (Miller, 1987). Change goals, like the methods to be used to pursue those goals, are better negotiated than prescribed.

Even when your personal hope for the client is total abstinence, the question still remains as to what may be the most effective means for helping the *client*. There is little sense in losing a client by a standoff on this issue. There appears to be no strong relationship between a client's prognosis and his or her beliefs about the necessity of abstinence (Watson, Jacobs, Pucel, Tilleskjor, & Hoodecheck-Schow, 1984). Effective strategies for teaching moderation are available (see Chapter 9), at least for a subset of problem drinkers.

It has been my clinical experience that an unsuccessful trial at "controlled drinking" may be a more persuasive confrontation of the need for abstinence than any amount of direct argumentation between therapist and client. Our long-term follow-up research with clients treated with a moderation goal found that more wound up abstaining than moderating their drinking without problems (Miller, Leckman, Delaney, & Tinkcom, 1992). Other "warm-turkey" alternatives to cold-turkey abstinence include sobriety sampling—a trial period without drinking (see Chapter 15), or a gradual tapering of drinking toward abstinence (Miller & Page, 1991). The point here is that within a motivational counseling approach, goals are *negotiated* with the client, and head-to-head opposition of a client's desires can be detrimental (Sanchez-Craig & Lei, 1986). In another study, we found that successful outcomes from a residential substance abuse program were related to the extent to which clients received the treatment elements they had requested at intake. Providing other treatment elements that were not requested, however, yielded no apparent benefits in outcome (Brown & Miller, 1993).

EFFECTIVENESS

The FRAMES elements have been applied in a large number of brief intervention studies. The efficacy of such brief intervention has been well established (see Chapter 2 and Bien et al., 1993). It is less clear, however, what the "active ingredients" are in effective brief intervention. Usually, little or no skill training is provided, nor are treatment prescriptions typically offered. If change follows from such brief intervention, then it seems likely that the impact is exerted through motivational channels.

Several studies have evaluated approaches explicitly designed to enhance motivation for change. Motivational interviewing, offered within the context of a Drinker's Check-Up (DCU), has been evaluated in a series of four controlled trials at the University of New Mexico. In the first of these (Miller, Sovereign, & Krege, 1988), problem drinkers were randomized to receive an immediate or delayed DCU. The immediate DCU group showed significantly greater reduction in drinking compared with the waiting list group, who were subsequently offered a DCU after which they showed comparable changes. The finding was replicated in a second study (Miller, Benefield, & Tonigan, 1993), showing reductions of more than 50% in drinking by six weeks after DCU, which were maintained a year later. An analysis of therapist style during these single-session interviews revealed that the more confrontational the therapist was, the more the client resisted. Furthermore, the more the therapist confronted, the more the client drank a year later.

Two other studies were conducted in treatment settings. Clients being admitted to a residential substance abuse program were randomly assigned to receive or not receive a DCU prior to treatment (Brown & Miller, 1993). Program therapists, who were unaware of this assignment, perceived DCU clients to be more motivated and involved during treatment. These same clients, who had received the DCU, showed substantially better outcomes three months after discharge. Similar findings were reported by Bien, Miller, and Boroughs (1993) using the same design with outpatient alcoholics in a Veterans Affairs Medical Center.

In a novel application of motivational interviewing, Handmaker (1993) screened for drinking among patients in a prenatal care clinic. Pregnant drinkers were then randomly assigned to receive or not receive motivational counseling in an empathic style, focusing on fetal risks as well as maternal health. Although both groups showed reduced alcohol use during the remainder of pregnancy, a significant effect of motivational interviewing was observed among heavier drinkers, who showed larger reductions in consumption when compared to controls who were informed by letter of the risks of drinking during pregnancy.

Other motivational enhancement strategies have been tested with mixed results. One study focused on patients with drinking-related gastrointestinal disease, who had previously failed to respond to advice to change their drinking. A motivational counseling approach relying on the "authority" of the physician failed to yield better results than an uncounseled control condition. Mallams, Godley, Hall, and Myers (1982) were successful in using a "systematic encouragement" procedure urging clients to become involved in nondrinking social activities, which in turn was associated with greater changes in drinking. Finally, Chick, Ritson, Connaughton, Stewart, and Chick (1988) tested a motivational enhancement session "encouraging the patient and informant to reflect on the reasons why a radical change in drinking was necessary and discuss how that might be achieved" (p. 160). At two-year follow-up, compared with a five-minute advice control group, those receiving the motivational counseling showed a somewhat higher rate (38 vs. 27%) of abstinence or problem-free drinking for a year or more. A group receiving extended treatment (including the motivational counseling) fared significantly better than the other two groups combined.

In sum, although it is clear that behavior change can be triggered by brief intervention, the optimal counseling procedures for doing so remain to be defined. Motivational interviewing has been specifically tested in several controlled trials, with encouraging results.

REFERENCES

Clinical Guidelines

Berg, I. K., & Miller, S. D. (1992). *Working with the problem drinker: A solution-focused approach*. New York: W. W. Norton.

Miller, W. R., & Rollnick, S. (1991). *Motivational interviewing: Preparing people to change addictive behavior*. New York: Guilford Press.

Miller, W. R., Zweben, A., DiClemente, C. C., & Rychtarik, R. G. (1992). *Motivational Enhancement Therapy manual: A clinical research guide for therapists treating individuals with alcohol abuse and dependence*. Rockville, MD: National Institute on Alcohol Abuse and Alcoholism. (Single copies available free of charge from the National Clearinghouse for Alcohol and Drug Information, P.O. Box 2345, Rockville, MD, 20847-2345)

Literature Cited

Alcoholics Anonymous. (1976). *Alcoholics Anonymous: The story of how many thousands of men and women have recovered from alcoholism* (3rd ed.). New York: Alcoholics Anonymous World Services.

Bandura, A. (1982). Self-efficacy mechanism in human agency. *American Psychologist, 37*, 122–147.

Berg, I. K., & Miller, S. D. (1992). *Working with the problem drinker: A solution-focused approach*. New York: W. W. Norton.

Bien, T. H., Miller, W. R., & Boroughs, J. M. (1993). Motivational interviewing with alcohol outpatients. *Behavioural and Cognitive Psychotherapy, 21*, 347–356.

Bien, T. H., Miller, W. R., & Tonigan, J. S. (1993). Brief interventions for alcohol problems: A review. *Addiction, 88* , 315–336.

Botvin, G. J., Baker, E., Renick, N. L., Fillazola, A. D., & Botvin, E. M. (1984). A cognitive-behavioral approach to substance abuse prevention. *Addictive Behaviors, 9*, 137–147.

Brown, J. M., & Miller, W. R. (1993). Impact of motivational interviewing on participation and outcome in residential alcoholism treatment. *Psychology of Addictive Behaviors, 7*, 211–218.

Chafetz, M. E. (1961). A procedure for establishing therapeutic contact with the alcoholic. *Quarterly Journal of Studies on Alcohol, 22*, 325–328.

Chess, S. B., Neuringer, C., & Goldstein, G. (1971). Arousal and field dependence in alcoholics. *Journal of General Psychology, 85*, 93–102.

Chick, J., Ritson, B., Connaughton, J., Stewart, A., & Chick, J. (1988). Advice versus extended treatment for alcoholism: A controlled study. *British Journal of Addiction, 83* , 159–170.

Clancy, J. (1961). Procrastination: A defense against sobriety. *Quarterly Journal of Studies on Alcohol, 22*, 269–276.

Costello, R. M. (1975). Alcoholism treatment and evaluation: In search of methods. *International Journal of Addictions, 10*, 251–275.

Donovan, D. M., Rohsenow, D. J., Schau, E. J., & O'Leary, M. R. (1977). Defensive style in alcoholics and nonalcoholics. *Journal of Studies on Alcohol, 38*, 465–470.

Edwards, G., & Orford, J. (1977). A plain treatment for alcoholism. *Proceedings of the Royal Society of Medicine, 70* , 344–348.

Ends, E. J., & Page, C. W. (1957). A study of three types of group psychotherapy with hospitalized make inebriates. *Quarterly Journal of Studies on Alcohol, 18*, 263–177.

Fox, R. (1967). A multidisciplinary approach to the treatment of alcoholism. *American Journal of Psychotherapy, 123*, 769–778.

Greenberger, R. S. (1983). Sobering methods: Firms are confronting alcoholic executives with threat of firing. *The Wall Street Journal, 201*(9), 1, 26.

Greenwald, A. F., & Bartmeier, L. H. (1963). Psychiatric discharges against medical advice. *Archives of General Psychiatry, 8*, 117–119.

Handmaker, N. S. (1993). *Motivating pregnant drinkers to abstain: Prevention in prenatal care clinics*. Unpublished doctoral dissertation, University of New Mexico.

Hazelden Foundation. (1985). You don't have to tear 'em down to build 'em up. *Hazelden Professional Update, 4*(2), 2.

Heather, H., & Robertson, I. (1981). *Controlled drinking* (rev. ed.). London: Methuen.

Helzer, J. E., Robins, L. N., Taylor, J. R., Carey, K., Miller, R. H., Combs-Orme, T., & Farmer, A. (1985). The extent of long-term moderate drinking among alcoholics discharged from medical and psychiatric treatment facilities. *New England Journal of Medicine, 312*, 1678–1682.

Horn, J. L., Wanberg, K. W., & Foster, F. M. (1987). *Guide to the Alcohol Use Inventory*. Minneapolis, MN: National Computer Systems.

Intagliata, J. (1976). A telephone follow-up procedure for increasing the effectiveness of a treatment program for alcoholics. *Journal of Studies on Alcohol, 37*, 1330–1335.

Johnson, V. (1980). *I'll quit tomorrow* (rev. ed.). New York: Harper & Row.

Jones, M. C. (1968). Personality correlates and antecedents of drinking patterns in adult males. *Journal of Consulting and Clinical Psychology, 32*, 2–12.

Kissin, B., Platz, A., & Su, W. H. (1971). Selective factors in treatment choice and outcome in alcoholics. In N. K. Mello & J. H. Mendelson (Eds.), *Recent advances in studies of alcoholism* (pp. 781–802). Washington, DC: U.S. Government Printing Office.

Kogan, L. S. (1957). The short-term case in a family agency: Part II. Results of study. *Social Casework, 38*, 296–302.

Koumans, A. J. R., & Muller, J. J. (1965). Use of letters to increase motivation in alcoholics. *Psychological Reports, 16*, 1152.

Koumans, A. J. R., Muller, J. J., & Miller, C. F. (1967). Use of telephone calls to increase motivation for treatment in alcoholics. *Psychological Reports, 21*, 327–328.

Kristenson, H., Öhlin, H., Hultén-Nosslin, M. B., Trell, E., & Hood, B. (1983). Identification and intervention of heavy drinking in middle-aged men:

Results and follow-up of 24–60 months of long-term study with randomized controls. *Alcoholism: Clinical and Experimental Research, 7*, 203–209.

Leake, G. J., & King, A. S. (1977). Effect of counselor expectations on alcoholic recovery. *Alcohol Health and Research World 1*(3), 16–22.

Lieberman, M. A., Yalom, I. D., & Miles, M. B. (1973). *Encounter groups: First facts.* New York: Basic Books.

Liepman, M. R. (1993). Using family influence to motivate alcoholics to enter treatment: The Johnson Institute intervention approach. In T. J. O'Farrell (Ed.), *Treating alcohol problems: Marital and family interventions* (pp. 54–77). New York: Guilford Press.

Løberg, T., & Miller, W. R. (1986). Personality, cognitive and neuropsychological dimensions of harmful alcohol consumption: A cross-national comparison of clinical samples. *Annals of the New York Academy of Sciences, 472,* 75–97.

Mallams, J. H., Godley, M. D., Hall, G. M., & Meyers, R. A. (1982). A social-systems approach to resocializing alcoholics in the community. *Journal of Studies on Alcohol, 43* , 1115–1123.

Manohar, V. (1973). Training volunteers as alcoholism treatment counselors. *Quarterly Journal of Studies on Alcohol, 34,* 869–877.

Marlatt, G. A., & Gordon, J. R. (1985). *Relapse prevention: Maintenance strategies in the treatment of addictive behaviors.* New York: Guilford Press.

Miller, W. R. (1976). Alcoholism scales and objective assessment methods: A review. *Psychological Bulletin, 83,* 649–674.

Miller, W. R. (1983). Motivational interviewing with problem drinkers. *Behavioral Psychotherapy, 11,* 147–172.

Miller, W. R. (1985). Motivation for treatment: A review with special emphasis on alcoholism. *Psychological Bulletin, 98,* 84–107.

Miller, W. R. (1987). Motivation and treatment goals. *Drugs and Society, 1,* 133–151.

Miller, W. R., & Baca, L. M. (1983). Two-year follow-up of bibliotherapy and therapist-directed controlled drinking training for problem drinkers. *Behavior Therapy, 14,* 441–448.

Miller, W. R., Benefield, R. G., & Tonigan, J. S. (1993). Enhancing motivation for change in problem drinking: A controlled comparison of two therapist styles. *Journal of Consulting and Clinical Psychology, 61* , 455–461.

Miller, W. R., & C'de Baca, J. (1994). Quantum change: Toward a psychology of transformation. In T. Heatherton & J. Weinberger (Eds.), *Can personality change?* (pp. 253–280). Washington, DC: American Psychological Association.

Miller, W. R., Gribskov, C. J., & Mortell, R. L. (1981). Effectiveness of a self-control manual for problem drinkers with and without therapist contact. *International Journal of the Addictions, 16,* 1247–1254.

Miller, W. R., & Hester, R. K. (1986). Matching problem drinkers with optimal treatment methods. In W. R. Miller & N. Heather (Eds.), *Treating addictive behaviors: Process of change* (pp. 175–204). New York: Plenum.

Miller, W. R., Jackson, K. A., & Karr, K. W. (1994). Alcohol problems: There's a lot you can do in two or three sessions. *EAP Digest, 14* , 18–21, 35–36.

Miller, W. R., & Joyce, M. A. (1979). Prediction of abstinence, controlled drinking, and heavy drinking outcomes following behavioral self-control training. *Journal of Consulting and Clinical Psychology, 47,* 773–775.

Miller, W. R., Leckman, A. L., Delaney, H. D. & Tinkcom, M. (1992). Long-term follow-up of behavioral self-control training. *Journal of Studies on Alcohol, 53,* 249–261.

Miller, W. R., & Marlatt, G. A. (1984). *Manual for the Comprehensive Drinker Profile.* Odessa, FL: Psychological Assessment Resources.

Miller, W. R., & Marlatt, G. A. (1987). *Manual supplement for the Brief Drinker Profile, Follow-up Drinker Profile, and Collateral Interview Form.* Odessa, FL: Psychological Assessment Resources.

Miller, W. R., & Muñoz, R. F. (1982). *How to control your drinking* (rev. ed.). Albuquerque, NM: University of New Mexico.

Miller, W. R., & Page, A. (1991). Warm turkey: Other routes to abstinence. *Journal of Substance Abuse Treatment, 8,* 227–232.

Miller, W. R., & Rollnick, S. (1991). *Motivational interviewing: Preparing people to change addictive behavior.* New York: Guilford Press.

Miller, W. R., & Sanchez, V. C. (1994). Motivating young adults for treatment and lifestyle change. In G. Howard (Ed.), *Issues in alcohol use and misuse by young adults* (pp. 55–82). Notre Dame, IN: University of Notre Dame Press.

Miller, W. R., & Saucedo, C. F. (1983). Assessment of neuropsychological impairment and brain damage in problem drinkers. In C. J. Golden, J. A. Moses, Jr., J. A. Coffman, W. R. Miller, & F. D. Strider (Eds.), *Clinical neuropsychology: Interface with neurologic and psychiatric disorders* (pp. 141–195). New York: Grune & Stratton.

Miller, W. R., Sovereign, R. G., & Krege, B. (1988). Motivational interviewing with problem drinkers: II. The Drinker's Check-up as a preventive intervention. *Behavioral Psychotherapy, 16,* 251–268.

Miller, W. R., Taylor, C. A., & West, J. C. (1980). Focused versus broad-spectrum behavior therapy for problem drinkers. *Journal of Consulting and Clinical Psychology, 48,* 590–601.

Milmoe, S., Rosenthal, R., Blane, H. T., Chafetz, M. E., & Wolf, I. (1967). The doctor's voice: Postdictor of successful referral of alcoholic patients. *Journal of Abnormal Psychology, 72,* 78–84.

Moore, R. C., & Murphy, T. C. (1961). Denial of alcoholism as an obstacle to recovery. *Quarterly Journal of Studies on Alcohol, 22,* 597–609.

Panepinto, W. C., & Higgins, M. J. (1969). Keeping alcoholics in treatment: Effective follow-through procedures. *Quarterly Journal of Studies on Alcohol, 30,* 414–419.

Parker, M. W., Winstead, D. K., & Willi, F. J. P. (1979). Patient autonomy in alcohol rehabilitation: I. Literature review. *International Journal of the Addictions, 14,* 1015–1022.

Patterson, G. A., & Forgatch, M. S. (1985). Therapist behavior as a determinant for client noncompliance: A paradox for the behavior modifier. *Journal of Consulting and Clinical Psychology, 53,* 846–851.

Polich, J. M., Armor, D., & Braiker, H. B. (1981). *The course of alcoholism: Four years after treatment.* New York: Wiley.

Prochaska, J. O., & DiClemente, C. C. (1982). Transtheoretical therapy: Toward a more integrative model of change. *Psychotherapy: Theory, Research, and Practice, 19*, 276–288.

Prochaska, J. O., & DiClemente, C. C. (1986). Toward a comprehensive model of change. In W. R. Miller & N. Heather (Eds.), *Treating addictive behaviors: Process of change* (pp. 3–27). New York: Plenum.

Prochaska, J. O., DiClemente, C. C., & Norcross, J. C. (1992). In search of how people change: Applications to addictive behaviors. *American Psychologist, 47*, 1102–1114.

Prue, D. M., Keane, T. M., Cornell, J. E., & Foy, D. W. (1979). An analysis of distance variables that affect aftercare attendance. *Community Mental Health Journal, 15*, 149–154.

Raynes, A. E., & Patch, V. D. (1971). Distinguishing features of patients who discharge themselves from psychiatric ward. *Comprehensive Psychiatry, 12*, 473–479.

Rogers, R. W., Deckner, C. W., & Mewborn, C. R. (1978). An expectancy-valve theory approach to the long-term modification of smoking behavior. *Journal of Clinical Psychology, 34*, 562–566.

Rogers, R. W., & Mewborn, C. R. (1976). Fear appeals and attitude change: Effects of a threat's noxiousness, probability of occurrence, and the efficacy of coping responses. *Journal of Personality and Social Psychology, 34*, 54–61.

Rosenberg, C. M., Gerrein, J. R., Manohar, V., & Liftik, J. (1976). Evaluation of training of alcoholism counselors. *Journal of Studies on Alcohol, 37*, 1236–1246.

Rosenberg, C. M., & Raynes, A. W. (1973). Dropouts from treatment. *Canadian Psychiatric Association Journal, 18*, 229–233.

Russell, M. A. H., Wilson, C., Taylor, C., & Baker, C. D. (1979). Effects of general practitioners' advice against smoking. *British Medical Journal, 2*, 231–235.

Sanchez-Craig, M., & Lei, H. (1986). Disadvantages to imposing the goal of abstinence on problem drinkers: An empirical study. *British Journal of Addiction, 81*, 505–512.

Sisson, R. W., & Azrin, N. H. (1986). Family-member involvement to initiate and promote treatment of problem drinkers. *Journal of Behavior Therapy and Experimental Psychiatry, 17*, 15–21.

Sisson, R. W., & Azrin, N. H. (1993). Community reinforcement training for families: A method to get alcoholics into treatment. In T. J. O'Farrell (Ed.), *Treating alcohol problems: Marital and family interventions* (pp. 34–53). New York: Guilford Press.

Skinner, H. A., & Allen, B. A. (1983). Differential assessment of alcoholism. *Journal of Studies on Alcohol, 44*, 852–862.

Stitzer, M. L., & Kirby, K. C. (1991). Reducing illicit drug use among methadone patients. In R. W. Pickens, C. G. Leukefeld, & C. R. Schuster (Eds.), *Improving drug abuse treatment* (pp. 178–203). Rockville, MD: National Institute on Drug Abuse.

Thomas, E., Polansky, N., & Kounin, J. (1955). The expected behavior of a potentially helpful person. *Human Relations, 8*, 165–174.

Thomas E. J., & Ager, R. D. (1993). Unilateral family therapy with spouses of uncooperative alcohol abusers. In T. J. O'Farrell (Ed.), *Treating alcohol problems: Marital and 'amily interventions* (pp. 3–33). New York: Guilford Press.

Truax, C. B., & Carkhuff, R. R. (1967). *Toward effective counseling and psychotherapy.* Chicago: Aldine.

Vaillant, G. M. (1983). *The natural history of alcoholism: Causes, patterns, and paths to recovery.* Cambridge, MA: Harvard University Press.

Valle, S. K. (1981). Interpersonal functioning of alcoholism counselors and treatment outcome. *Journal of Studies on Alcohol, 42*, 783–790.

Watson, C. G., Jacobs, L., Pucel, J., Tilleskjor, C., & Hoodecheck-Schow, E. A. (1984). The relationship of beliefs about controlled drinking to recidivism in alcoholic men. *Journal of Studies on Alcohol, 45*, 172–175.

CHAPTER 6

Brief Intervention Strategies

Nick Heather

OVERVIEW

Unlike other contributions to this book, this chapter is not concerned with a specific treatment method but with a range of interventions called "brief" interventions. Brief interventions are not merely a type of treatment for alcohol problems, like aversion therapy, self-control training, or the community reinforcement approach. Rather, they represent a category of interventions, separate from but not necessarily in conflict with conventional treatment approaches. Therefore, it is difficult to provide an inflexible definition of brief interventions. Indeed, to attempt such a preemptive definition might unnecessarily restrict the range of interventions that could be developed.

The main reason brief interventions are important is that they offer the promise of making therapists' attempts to alter drinking behavior much more cost effective. The evidence strongly suggests that many clients simply do not need a protracted and relatively expensive course of individual or group therapy to benefit. By identifying these clients and offering them a brief intervention appropriate to their needs, therapists can devote more time and energy to those with more severe problems who do probably need a more intensive approach. In this way, therapists can more efficiently use valuable treatment re-

sources. Brief interventions also present the opportunity to help clients at an early point in the history of their drinking problem—before alcohol dependence has developed to a level that makes conventional treatment difficult and before excessive drinking has produced permanent damage. Brief interventions are not intended for people whose problems are sufficiently serious to deserve the label of "alcoholism" but for those with earlier or less severe problems. Such clients are typically unwilling to attend regular treatment programs, and the evidence shows that it is often unnecessary for them to do so. Many other clients of brief interventions will not have sought help for their alcohol problems but have to be identified and persuaded that they are drinking too much for their own good.

The recent boom in interest in brief interventions is a result of several influences. First, there is evidence that they are often no less effective in modifying drinking behavior than traditional forms of therapy. Second, there has been a growing recognition that the damage caused by excessive drinking (e.g., problems due to acute intoxication or adverse physical health consequences) often do not entail a high degree of alcohol dependence. Many people who would not be considered "alcoholics" drink excessively and their lives are adversely affected

(Moore & Gerstein, 1981). This evidence and growing awareness have shifted the focus away from an exclusive preoccupation with problems involving high alcohol dependence. It has also started a trend to move interventions out into community settings and away from the specialized alcohol problems clinic (Department of Health & Social Security, 1978; Institute of Medicine, 1990). Finally, the ever-increasing costs of specialist treatment and the shrinking health budgets of many countries have prompted a search for less expensive interventions that are empirically supported. These influences have conspired to focus attention on the use of brief, low-cost interventions as an alternative to intensive treatment for problem drinkers.

SPECIAL CONSIDERATIONS

Although a concise definition is not possible, brief interventions have certain general characteristics that give them some conceptual coherence. If delivered by personnel with expertise in the alcohol problems area, they involve less specialist time than would normally be devoted to intensive treatment—say, two or three sessions of assessment, advice, or counseling at the most. On the other hand, specialists in the area of alcohol problems often develop brief interventions for delivery by other professional groups. Professionals such as general medical practitioners, hospital physicians, ward and community nurses, health visitors, social workers, probation officers, employee counselors, and others use brief interventions along with their other duties. Paraprofessional workers, voluntary counselors, and clients' relatives and friends may also be important elements in these strategies. Self-help manuals and other forms of "bibliotherapy" are main modes of brief intervention. Even where there is some form of personal contact with clients, it is often supported by written materials for home study. There is a distinction between *brief* and *minimal* interventions. These terms were previously used synonymously but there is a recent trend to reserve the term *minimal* for very brief interventions—say, five minutes of succinct advice and exhortation from a general medical practitioner.

Although there are exceptions, brief interventions thus far have strived for a goal of moderate or harm-free drinking rather than total abstinence. The corollary of this is that they are normally directed at problem drinkers with only low or moderate levels of alcohol dependence or alcohol-related problems.

In the area of brief interventions, the conventional distinction between treatment and education for problem drinkers breaks down. With many brief interventions, it is better to describe them to the public as education rather than treatment. In this context, education means much more than merely providing general alcohol information. It includes methods of behavioral change drawn from the same set of social learning principles that form some of the intensive treatment methods described in this book. However, by emphasizing the educational aspect of brief interventions, one avoids the labeling process inherent in the diagnosis of problem drinking. This reduces the stigma attached to the admission of an alcohol problem that often deters potential clients from tackling their problems. The most promising mode of delivery for many brief interventions is as part of health education and general health promotion initiatives.

The most suitable clients for the majority of brief interventions are those with low levels of alcohol dependence. (This will be operationally defined in the next section.) This is because brief interventions are usually directed at a reduced drinking goal and also because there is often a limited degree of control over progress. Brief interventions by nonspecialists may also be suitable for clients with moderate levels of dependence, but specialized personnel are usually more involved. It is recommended that clients with high levels of dependence and/or high degrees of alcohol-related harm be excluded from brief interventions and instead be referred for intensive treatment. The degree of alcohol dependence is a more important criterion than the extent of alcohol-related problems. It is more relevant to the possibility of change and how much effort is needed to bring this change about.

People who drink above guidelines for safe drinking but who do not yet show signs of alcohol-related problems are also candidates for brief interventions. Their consumption levels put them at increased risk of developing alcohol-related tissue damage or other problems. These are the "hazardous" drinkers described in World Health Organization (WHO) reports (Edwards, Arif, & Hodgson, 1982).

Clients with more serious problems may be appropriate candidates for brief interventions when access to intensive treatment is limited or where there are psychological barriers to seeking help from specialist services. It is likely that only a minority of people with alcohol problems ever come into contact with specialist services (e.g., Hingson, Scotch, Day, & Culbert, 1980). Reasons for this include feelings of shame and guilt at the admission of a problem, difficulty in conceding that their drinking behavior is out of control and they need outside help, and a fear of hospitals and treatment, especially if associated with psychiatric diagnosis (Thom, 1986). The geographical inaccessibility of treatment centers may simply be a barrier sometimes. The effects of all these factors may be mitigated by using nonspecialist, brief interventions. Since one may reasonably assume that many clients would otherwise receive no help at all, the use of brief interventions can be ethically justified. Moreover, most brief interventions contain advice on the conditions where clients should seek more intensive help and procedures for channeling more serious problem drinkers into specialist services if necessary.

To summarize, there are three target groups for brief interventions:

- Hazardous drinkers
- Low- or moderate-dependence problem drinkers
- High-dependence problem drinkers who are not reached by conventional treatment services

DESCRIPTION

Before the main types of brief intervention strategies and recommendations for their application are described, allow me to note two important caveats. First, clinical researchers have developed brief interventions in different parts of the world. You may have to make adjustments when considering these applications in countries other than the country of origin (e.g., taking into account how primary health care is delivered). Second, although there is evidence for the effectiveness of brief interventions, research on optimal practical applications is still in its early stages. For example, there is little evidence regarding optimal cutoff scores for severity of dependence and problems as contraindications for brief interventions. Also, it is not known how minimal brief interventions can become and still be effective. Many of the recommendations in this section are therefore based on a combination of research and clinical experience. In this situation, err, if anything, on the side of caution.

There are two main categories of brief interventions: agency-based interventions and community-based interventions. In each section, issues relating to recruitment and screening of clients, exclusion criteria, the best ways to implement brief interventions, and specific content will be discussed.

AGENCY-BASED INTERVENTIONS

Agency-based refers to specialist alcohol problems agencies—either hospital-based clinics, private for-profit agencies, or voluntary counseling services. Compared with other types of brief intervention that do not involve direct therapist contact, there is an opportunity here for more personal involvement by staff. You can more accurately assess clients and have better control over the effects of the intervention. It is particularly important, as we shall see, to assess the client's level of alcohol dependence.

A Basic Treatment Scheme

Orford and Edwards (1977) provided an outline for a "basic treatment scheme," consisting of assessment and one session of counseling. Although now 18 years old, Orford and Edwards's suggestions are still highly pertinent. The scheme has the following elements:

Comprehensive assessment. Assessment serves three purposes. First, it establishes a sufficient basis of information to help clients and their families formulate a plan of action. Second, it helps the client (and partner) broadly review the situation, which may in itself have some therapeutic value. Third, it helps the advisory team to establish their credibility and hence their persuasiveness.

A single, detailed counseling session for the client and, when the client is in a close relationship, the partner. This is the basic treatment, replacing more intensive forms of care. However, it "in no way contradicts the notion that each person requires an individually formulated approach, and there will be circumstances in which clinical judgement leads to the conclusion that more (or very much more) than the basic intervention is needed" (Orford & Edwards, 1977, p. 110). The counseling session involves a discussion between counselor, client, and partner to define a set of goals. The client and partner should see these goals as logically related to their perception of their problems based on the assessment. They should cover drinking, marital cohesiveness, work, leisure, finances, and housing. Counseling should also strongly emphasize both the client's responsibilities and the shared engagement of the partner. Discuss them rather than merely present them. You should also aim for a definite commitment towards the agreed goals.

Some follow-up system to check on progress. Apart from the therapeutic value such regular contact has, it also serves as a "safety net" for clients who may develop more serious or life-threatening problems. Whatever type of follow-up method you choose, however, it should fall well short of the traditional system of active community care.

Common reasons for going beyond the basic approach. The decision to increase the intensity of care for a client who has received basic treatment must be a matter of clinical judgment. Here are a few situations where it is wise to increase the intensity of care: (1) brief admission for detoxification where, for example, there is evidence of reinstatement of severe dependence, concomitant sedative misuse, or poor social support; (2) underlying or concomitant psychological illness or distress, such as depressive illness or phobic disorder; (3) physical illness requiring referral or admission; (4) life-threatening situations or acute dangers to the family requiring immediate admission; and (5) homelessness, which may require extensive social services and/or halfway house placement.

Orford and Edwards proposed this basic treatment as suitable for the broad range of clients who attend specialized alcohol clinics, bearing in mind the exceptions and qualifications just given. However, it is prudent to assume that clients with high levels of dependence are more likely to benefit from a more intensive approach. This will be discussed in more detail below. Moreover, the basic treatment scheme was evaluated with married, male clients of relatively high social stability. Thus, a conservative choice of client group for this basic treatment would be men with intact sexual relationships, relatively secure employment, and low or moderate levels of alcohol dependence. If the client has a partner, include him or her in the counseling and advice.

Assessment of Level of Dependence

Fortunately, there are now many instruments for measuring dependence. Consider the following:

- *Severity of Alcohol Dependence Questionnaire (SADQ)* (Stockwell, Hodgson, Edwards, Taylor, & Rankin, 1979). This is a 20-item self-administered scale referring to the last month of heavy drinking. It is easy to give and score, and is widely used. However, it is relatively insensitive to lower degrees of dependence and does not tell you the duration of dependent drinking. Stockwell and his colleagues recently released a revised version of the SADQ—the SADQ-C—together with an accompanying Impaired Control Questionnaire (Stockwell, Sitharthan, McGrath, & Lang, 1994). The SADQ-C addresses several deficiencies of the earlier version.
- *Alcohol Dependence Scale (ADS)* (Skinner & Allen, 1982). This is a 34-item scale that can be either self- or therapist-administered. It is more complex to administer and score than the SADQ. On the other hand, more information is obtained about the psychological, in addition to physical, aspects of the client's dependence.
- *Short-Form Alcohol Dependence Data Questionnaire (SADD)* (Raistrick, Dunbar, & Davidson, 1983). This is a 15-item self-administered scale. It is the quickest and most convenient of the scales listed here and was constructed to be sensitive to early signs of dependence. Its main disadvantage is that it is less frequently used than other scales, and comparative data are therefore less available.
- *Ph Score from the Comprehensive Drinker Profile (CDP)* (Miller & Marlatt, 1984). This is an 11-item scale included in a section on the Alcohol-Related Life Problems scale. The Ph score can be assessed at the same time as alcohol-related problems in general. Use of the full CDP will produce a thorough assessment of alcohol-related problems. However, its major limitation is that it is confined to physical aspects of dependence.
- *Edinburgh Alcohol Dependence Scale (EADS)* (Chick, 1980). This is a 34-item interviewer-administered scale. Its main advantage is that it makes use of clinical skill and sensitivity in the measurement of dependence. The EADS also comes in a brief 7-item form, allowing a dichotomous classification into "early" and "late" dependence.

Your choice of instrument(s) will depend on your particular situation. If time and convenience are pressing considerations, you may prefer one of the shorter scales (SADQ-C, SADD). On the other hand, if you have trained staff available to administer it, the EADS offers a more accurate and refined assessment. If you want to assess dependence within the context of a self-contained, thorough assessment of the client's problem, use the Ph score. If your client population generally has low to moderate levels of dependence, the ADS, SADD, or EADS are the best instruments.

Treatment Goals and Levels

Measuring dependence helps you make two major and linked treatment decisions: the goal and the intensity of treatment. Table 6.1 presents cutoff scores for treatment goals and intensity of treatment. These recommendations are based on comments of the authors of the scales (in their manuals or publications) and on my practical experience with them. Moreover, there is no evidence that the corresponding ranges on the various scales shown in Table 6.1 are empirically equivalent. Their correspondence is simply as rules of thumb with a similar purpose in each case.

It cannot be emphasized too strongly that the choice of moderate drinking or abstinence goals and the intensity of interventions are clinical decisions that depend on the unique circumstances and characteristics of the client. Nevertheless, Table 6.1 gives broad guidelines for making these decisions with respect to level of dependence. If measured dependence is below a certain level, a brief intervention with a goal of moderation is recommended. The major exceptions to this would be the presence of medical conditions that precluded further drinking or perhaps the strenuous objections of spouse or relatives to any drinking whatsoever. There may also be certain occupations that make abstinence a preferred option. Above all, if the client expresses a preference for abstinence, accept it irrespective of the level of dependence or any other factor.

For those above a defined level of dependence, intensive treatment aimed at abstinence is advisable. Again, however, there may be a few exceptions. If the client insists on continuing to drink despite strong advice to the contrary, then every effort should be made to help him or her to drink at safer levels (see Heather, 1993, and Chapter 9). If the client has failed with many abstinence-oriented treatments in the past, a moderation training program may be well worth trying, provided there are no contraindications such as alcohol-related organic damage. If you negotiate a goal of moderation with a high-dependence client, you should treat him or her intensively.

In the middle range of dependence, the two key treatment decisions are more difficult to make. This is not the place to discuss the many issues bearing on the choice between the goals of abstinence versus moderation (see Heather & Robertson, 1983, and Chapter 9). Suffice it to say that as the dependence score increases within the moderate range, a goal of abstinence is more likely to be effective.

COMMUNITY-BASED INTERVENTIONS

Included in this category are some of the most innovative and potentially important types of brief intervention. However, intervening in community settings has its own set of challenges. Interventions will often be "opportunistic" (i.e., trying to modify drinking behavior in clients who have not come to the setting to discuss their drinking). Many potential clients will not be

Table 6.1 Suggested Ranges of Scores on Four Measures of Alcohol Dependence for Determining Goal and Intensity of Intervention

INSTRUMENT	LOW DEPENDENCE/BRIEF, MODERATE DRINKING INTERVENTION	MODERATE DEPENDENCE/BRIEF OR INTENSIVE INTERVENTION; MODERATE DRINKING OR ABSTINENCE	HIGH DEPENDENCE/INTENSIVE ABSTINENCE INTERVENTION
SADQ	0–20	21–40	41–60
ADS	0–13	14–30	31–51
SADD	0–9	10–19	20–45
Ph score	0–4	5–14	15–20

seeking help for an alcohol problem and may not recognize the existence of such a problem. Indeed, they may resent the suggestion and underestimate drinking quantities or deny the existence of any problems that may exist.

Identification

Most of the work to date has been in medical settings. Fortunately, Ned Cooney and his colleagues have described in detail how to set up protocols to screen and detect in medical settings; see Chapter 3 for their practical advice. Consequently, I will only briefly discuss identification in nonmedical settings before moving on to the brief intervention itself.

Screening in Nonmedical Situations

In nonmedical situations, you can adjust screening in an *ad hoc* fashion to particular requirements. For example, we (Robertson & Heather, 1982) recruited candidates for an "alcohol education course" for young offenders. We asked court personnel to identify young men who either (1) agreed they had a drinking problem (2) said they were worried about their drinking (3) thought they would get into less trouble if they drank less or (4) had committed more than half of their previous offenses under the influence of alcohol. We then gave referrals a more thorough assessment.

In similar fashion, you could screen in an industrial context by examining decline in work performance, number of days of sick absenteeism, or failure to show up for work on Monday mornings. These are all indicators of a possible alcohol problem. Some potential clients for brief interventions will self-select, such as those arrested for drink-driving offenses. Finally, when other methods are not feasible, the CAGE questionnaire (see Chapter 3) can form a quick, rough-and-ready first step in the identification process.

Interventions at Primary-Care Level

Babor and colleagues (Babor, Ritson, & Hodgson, 1986) have reviewed early intervention strategies in primary health-care settings. The most basic intervention at this level is about five minutes of simple advice from a physician following an assessment of drinking and related problems (Babor & Grant, 1992). Physicians tell identified excessive drinkers they seem to be drinking too much. They also mention any problems the client described during the assessment that may be related to drinking. An illustrated pamphlet helps to structure the advice-giving procedure. You can show

heavy drinkers where their consumption places them in relation to both "sensible drinkers" and "alcoholics." You can also use the leaflet to introduce the idea of a "standard drink" and provide information about the alcohol content of local drinks.

The most important part of the procedure is the clear communication of "sensible drinking limits" for those who choose a nonabstinent drinking goal, including the advisability of two or three days of abstinence per week. Precise drinking limits will depend on the recommendations of medical authorities in the country in question but will usually be around three or four drinks per occasion for men and two or three drinks per occasion for women. Where possible, arrange a six-month follow-up interview. Babor found this type of minimal intervention to be effective in the WHO project (Babor & Grant, 1992). It is recommend as a basic intervention in primary health care.

Several projects have used a more extensive type of brief intervention in primary care that consists of up to four or five consultations with a primary-care physician (Heather, Campion, Neville, & MacCabe, 1987; Wallace, Cutler, & Haines, 1988; Persson & Magnusson, 1989; Anderson & Scott, 1992; Babor & Grant, 1992; Richmond, Heather, Wodak, Kehoe, & Webster, 1994). First, you assess the pattern and amount of alcohol consumption, the number and type of alcohol-related problems, and the degree of alcohol dependence. Then, you tell clients how their drinking compares with the rest of the population and about the harmful or potentially harmful effects of their current level of drinking on their health. Again, you can back up this advice with an information booklet. Next, give clients a drinking diary to monitor their alcohol consumption and take a blood sample to measure gamma glutamyl transferase (GGT). Strongly encourage clients to return for a follow-up visit in one or two weeks. Then give them feedback on their GGT and review the results of their self-monitoring.

You can use a more personal approach to client education at this second visit. Use a flip-over display unit with colorfully illustrated material for the clients on one side and prompts for yourself on the reverse (Richmond et al., 1994). Use a motivational interviewing style of counseling (Miller & Rollnick, 1991, see also Chapter 5). You can also give advice on ways to reduce clients' rate of drinking, how to identify and cope with high-risk situations, discuss alternate activities associated with a changed lifestyle, and provide other advice on relapse prevention. In short, you could provide a condensed form of cognitive-behavioral therapy for problem drinking (Sanchez-Craig, Wilkinson, & Walker, 1987).

Finally, agree on dates for follow-ups. Consider doing up to five visits during a six-month period.

A more sophisticated intervention is the Drinking Reasonably and Moderately with Self-Control (DRAMS) scheme (Scottish Health Education Group, undated). DRAMS is based on Prochaska and DiClemente's (1986) stages of change model and takes into account clients' differing levels of readiness to change drinking behavior. It offers clients interventions appropriate to their current needs, thus encouraging them to remain in contact with you and not abandon the change process. Figure 6.1 shows the process of the intervention.

Figure 6.1 DRAMS: Intervention Process

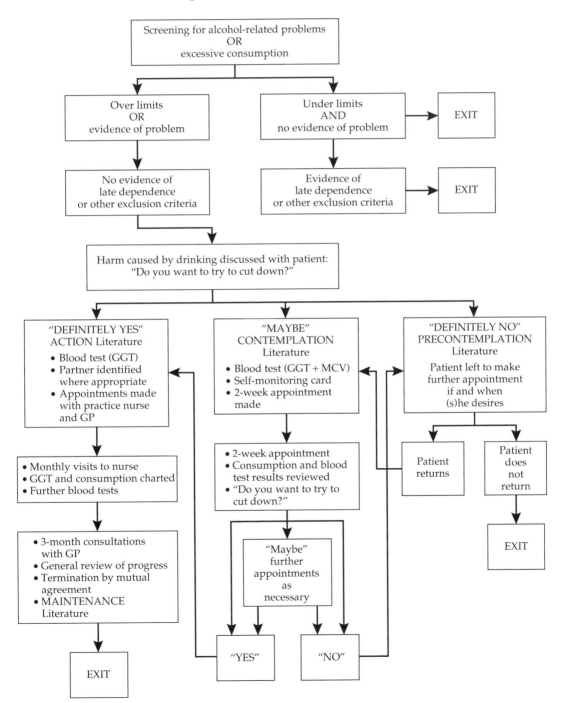

The complete DRAMS kit contains five separate booklets. The first is a guide to the scheme for the general practitioner. It introduces the stages of change model and has a comprehensive guide to the skills needed to manage the excessive drinker. There are also notes for course organizers on how to use two training videotapes and other material in short training sessions. The self-help booklets begin with *How Much Do You Drink?* This contains information about alcohol and its harmful effects, a self-monitoring diary, and structured motivational exercises. It is for clients in the *contemplation* stage of change. For those ready to take action, there is *Cutting Down* or *Coming Off*, depending on whether the goal is responsible drinking or abstinence. Finally, *Keeping Going* is a relapse-prevention booklet for those who have reached the *maintenance* stage.

You can use your clinical judgment to assess the patient's stage of change. Alternatively, you can use the Readiness to Change Questionnaire (Rollnick, Heather, Gold, & Hall, 1992; Heather & Rollnick, 1993; Heather, Rollnick, & Bell, 1993). This is a one-page instrument for use in brief interventions in medical settings. It allocates patients to either the *precontemplation, contemplation,* or *action* stage of change.

Compared with other types of brief intervention, the DRAMS scheme has the advantage of greater flexibility in meeting the particular needs of individual clients. It also makes more use of the skills of medical and nursing staff in the change process. However, DRAMS is only one example among many intervention strategies that you could use at the primary-care level. For additional reading, see Royal College of General Practitioners (1986), Skinner and Holt (1983), and Anderson (1987).

Interventions in General Hospitals

Hospital wards are a fertile source of candidates for brief interventions. Research suggests that between 10 and 30% of general inpatients are excessive drinkers (Jarman & Kellett, 1979; Quinn & Johnston, 1976). Chick, Lloyd, and Crombie (1985) have studied the effects of a single session of counseling given by an experienced nurse and lasting up to 60 minutes. The nurse gives the patient a specially prepared booklet and discusses lifestyle and health. This helps the patient to weigh the drawbacks of the current pattern of drinking and come to a decision about future consumption. The objective is problem-free drinking, although abstinence may be agreed upon in some cases.

The best target for this type of intervention is male patients with good social support. It is this group on which the effectiveness of the method was established, but you may include other patients provided you do follow-up. The relative contributions of counseling, self-help materials, home visits following discharge, or regular feedback of GGT results are unknown, but trying these variations if you have suffcient staff is recommended. Murray (1993) found that home visits by a community nurse after discharge add to the effectiveness of a bedside brief intervention. The roles played by medical staff, ward nurses, community nurses, and health visitors will depend on the type of approach you use.

Antti-Poika (1988) has described another alternative brief intervention that is used in hospital emergency departments. She also noted encouraging results in her evaluation.

Community Health Screening Programs

Scandinavian researchers have developed an important approach to early intervention for alcohol problems. The original, influential study was of a general health screening project in Malmö, Sweden (Kristenson, Trell, & Hood, 1982; Kristenson, Ohlin, Hulten-Nosslin, Trell, & Hood, 1983). They detected problem drinkers by an elevated GGT on two occasions three weeks apart. The intervention included a detailed physical examination and an interview regarding drinking history, alcohol-related problems, and symptoms of dependence. They offered clients appointments with the same physician every three months and monthly visits to a nurse who gave feedback of GGT results. Once the client's drinking reached moderate levels, the frequency of clinical contacts was reduced.

The Drinker's Check-Up

Miller, Sovereign, and Krege (1988) described a procedure known as the Drinker's Check-Up (DCU). They offered it to drinkers as a health check-up focused on drinking. It includes a comprehensive assessment and a session of objective feedback given in a motivational interviewing style. The intent is to increase the client's awareness of risk and to motivate him or her to change.

The DCU is promoted in local news media through advertisements. The following points are stressed: (1) it is free and confidential; (2) it is not part of a treatment program; (3) it is intended for drinkers in general, not alcoholics; (4) participants are not labeled or diagnosed; and (5) it gives clear and objective feedback that drinkers may use as they please. The complete DCU requires two visits—a two-hour assessment and a return visit a week later when clients receive feedback. The battery of tests used include (1) the Brief Drinker Profile (Miller & Marlatt, 1987); (2) a blood test for the measurement of indicators of alcohol-related physical impairment; (3) five neuropsychological tests sensitive to the effects of alcohol on the brain (Miller & Saucedo, 1983); (4) collateral interviews to confirm the client's self-report; and (5) the Alcohol Use Inventory (Horn, Wanberg, & Foster, 1987). The authors emphasize that this list of tests and procedures is not definitive for the DCU and that other types of measure are potentially useful.

Many of the principles of the DCU have been incorporated in a highly structured four-session intervention known as Motivational Enhancement Therapy (MET; Miller, Zweben, DiClemente, & Rychtarik, 1992). MET also relies heavily on the FRAMES model of common ingredients of successful brief interventions (Miller & Sanchez, 1993; see also Bien, Miller, & Tonigan, 1993). FRAMES is an acronym for (1) **F**eedback of personal risk or impairment, (2) emphasis on personal **R**esponsibility, (3) clear **A**dvice to change, (4) a **M**enu of alternative change options, (5) therapist **E**mpathy, and, (6) facilitation of client **S**elf-efficacy or optimism. Project MATCH is evaluating MET. Project MATCH is a large multisite trial of treatments for alcohol abuse and dependence (see Chapter 17). When the results are available, they should provide a useful indication of which clients are best suited to brief interventions rather than more intensive treatments.

Interventions in Nonmedical Settings

We described a model of an "alcohol education course" for young offenders with alcohol-related problems referred from the courts (Robertson & Heather, 1982). This group-based education course included many of the procedures in typical self-help manuals (see Robertson & Heather, 1985). However, group members can discuss various aspects of the change process and can give mutual feedback on progress to each other. The optimum number in a group is probably between six and eight. Baldwin and colleagues have re-ported on the effects of this type of intervention among young offenders (Baldwin et al., 1991a, 1991b). The Scottish Council on Alcohol (1988) has developed an *Ending Offending* pack for use in such interventions.

Another source of clients for this type of alcohol education course is drunk-driving offenders. The use of education as an alternative to legal sanctions has become increasingly popular, particularly in the United States. Unfortunately, the education is typically didactic and ignores performance-based procedures. Brief, behaviorally-based training programs need to be applied with this population and their effectiveness evaluated. In addition to behavioral programs in group settings, home study programs might also be considered (see Swenson & Clay, 1980).

Apart from court referrals, the other major nonmedical source of candidates for brief interventions is the industrial setting. There has been a rapid increase in the number of employee assistance programs in the United States aimed at problem drinkers identified in the workplace. Unfortunately, the great majority of these programs are based on the disease view of alcoholism and are aimed at total abstinence. Rather than being conducive to early intervention, this orientation and goal can be a discouragement to early identification and behavior change. As in the case of drunk-driver programs, what is needed is the systematic application of moderate drinking training courses and other types of brief intervention aimed at reduced drinking for employees with lower levels of dependence and less severe problems (see Walker & Shain, 1983). Such a structured workplace brief intervention (the Workscreen Program) is currently being evaluated at the National Drug and Alcohol Research Centre in Sydney, Australia.

Self-Help Manuals

Apart from making self-help manuals available in your local bookstore, the most direct form of brief intervention is to advertise help and advice for excessive drinking in the media and send a self-help manual aimed at reduced consumption to those who reply. There are obvious restrictions on the ability to screen suitable clients and exclude those who are not suited to a brief intervention or a goal of moderate drinking. However, advertisements and the manuals themselves should stress that the advice offered "is not for alcoholics." You can further explain what you mean by *alcoholism* in this context (i.e., the presence of marked withdrawal symptoms and relief drinking) in the opening pages of the self-help manual. All self-help manuals should contain addresses of specialist agencies to which clients may turn if they are not successful.

Self-help methods need not be limited to the written word. Especially if clients have poor reading skills or habits, audiotapes are an interesting alternative. In view of the increase in home video equipment, you could also produce self-help videotapes. Interactive computer programs for use in the home should also be explored (see Chapter 9).

EFFECTIVENESS

In Bill Miller and his colleagues' latest review of the treatment outcome literature (see Chapter 2), brief intervention scores higher than any other treatment modality. In that chapter, the authors note that among the modalities that have been tested as treatment for alcohol problems, brief intervention has one of the largest literature bases, and currently the most positive. Based on such a thorough and sophisticated analysis of the treatment outcome literature, this conclusion represents a most encouraging justification for application of brief interventions in practice.

Agency-Based Interventions

Interventions with a Primary Goal of Abstinence

The first research study to raise the status of brief intervention was Orford and Edwards's (1977) controlled comparison of treatment and advice among 100 married male problem drinkers seen at the Maudsley Hospital in London. Clients received a comprehensive three-hour assessment and were then randomly assigned to either a single counseling session (described above) or to a group that received a mixture of outpatient and inpatient, psychiatric, and social work care representing the standard package of help available at any well-supported treatment center.

At follow-up 12 months after initial assessment, there was no evidence of any significant differences between these groups on any outcome measure. A long-term follow-up (Taylor et al., 1985) also found no differences between groups after 10 years. Edwards and Taylor (1994) have rejected an interpretation of these results that those with more severe dependence did bet-

ter if they had received treatment than if they had received advice. Others, however, have pointed out that the married and socially stable problem drinkers without significant psychiatric disturbance in this study had a generally good prognosis. Therefore, they may have been more likely to benefit from the brief intervention than the unmarried or less socially stable individuals frequently seen in treatment (e.g., Kissin, 1977).

Chick, Ritson, Connaughton, Stewart, and Chick (1988) used Orford and Edwards's design but made a few important modifications. Following a comprehensive client and informant assessment, they randomly assigned 152 of those attending an alcohol problems clinic to receive either extended inpatient or outpatient treatment, typical of that offered in British treatment centers, or one session of advice. They divided the advice group into two subgroups. The first group received brief standardized advice lasting about five minutes, while the second group's advice session lasted an hour. Unlike Orford and Edwards's sample, they included women and unmarried clients. At two-year follow-up, there was no difference between extended treatment and advice groups in abstinence rates, employment, or marital status. However, the extended treatment group showed evidence of less alcohol-related damage in the year since intake.

This study supported Emrick's (1975) conclusion that, compared with brief intervention, extended treatment does not affect the likelihood of successful abstinence but may reduce the amount of harm caused by drinking. Chick also found no differences in outcome between the very brief and comprehensive advice groups. This finding is difficult to interpret, however, because both groups received numerous research visits in the follow-up period from social work personnel. This may have obscured any potential difference between the two groups.

Interventions with a Goal of Moderation

Although the earlier work on brief interventions was concerned with the abstinence treatment goal, subsequent research has focused on a goal of moderate, nonproblematic drinking with low-dependence problem drinkers. Martha Sanchez-Craig and colleagues demonstrated that, among early or low-dependence problem drinkers, moderate drinking is preferable to abstinence as a treatment goal. Sanchez-Craig (1980) randomly assigned problem drinkers to two similar behavioral conditions that differed mainly in terms of treatment goal—abstinence, or moderate drinking. All clients were asked to abstain during the period of treatment itself, which consisted of six individual 90-minute sessions. At the end of the treatment period, she found that the clients with a moderate drinking goal had drunk only one-third the amount of alcohol that the abstinence groups had consumed, and also had drunk on significantly fewer days and less often to excess.

Although at two-year follow-up there were no significant differences between groups, Sanchez-Craig concluded that moderate drinking was the more appropriate goal since it was more acceptable to the majority of clients and most of those assigned to abstinence had developed moderate drinking patterns on their own (Sanchez-Craig, Annis, Bornet, & McDonald, 1984). On the basis of further analyses, Sanchez-Craig and Lei (1986) concluded that among the heavier drinkers taking part in the study, imposing a goal of abstinence was ineffective in promoting abstinence and counterproductive in encouraging moderate drinking. Other studies have found that brief interventions and bibliotherapy, which teach clients self-control skills, are effective in producing moderate drinking outcomes in clients (see Chapter 9 for a review).

Self-Help Manuals

Bill Miller and his colleagues have pioneered research on the use of self-help manuals in this area. In 1978, Miller designed a study to compare the effectiveness of three behavioral treatment modalities. As an afterthought, he randomly gave half the clients at the end of treatment a self-help manual (Miller & Muñoz, 1982) with the other half receiving it three months later. He found that the manual group continued to show therapeutic gains during the follow-up period and were significantly more improved at the three-month follow-up. The nonmanual group remained at the level reached at termination of treatment. This finding showed that a self-help manual was an effective supplement to treatment. In 1981, Miller and colleagues tested the effectiveness of a manual by itself, with minimal therapist involvement (Miller, Gribskov, & Mortell, 1981). They randomly assigned 31 clients to receive either (1) an interview and then a manual plus self-monitoring cards to mail in to the clinic or (2) 10 group therapy sessions using the same behavioral self-control training (BSCT) methods covered by the manual. There were no significant differences in outcome between these

two groups at three-month follow-up. Trends favored the manual-only group.

There have been several other studies of self-help manuals by this research group. Miller and Taylor (1980) compared a manual-only group with three types of behavioral treatment. At one-year follow-up, all four groups showed significant reductions in consumption but there were no significant differences between groups on any outcome measure. Miller, Taylor, and West (1980) got similar results. In a two-year follow-up of the accumulated cohort from these studies, improvement rates for bibliotherapy clients were equivalent to or better than those in the various treatment conditions, except for those given BSCT in groups (Miller & Baca, 1983). Stability of outcome among these clients was good, with more than 80% showing equal or greater improvement at two years compared with earlier follow-up points. There was no greater risk of relapse from a moderate drinking outcome than from abstinence.

Although the work of Miller and colleagues demonstrates the viability of a self-help approach for low-dependence problem drinkers, it has certain limitations because they evaluated the self-help materials within the context of a conventional service delivery system. This provided the rationale for a study by Heather, Whitton, and Robertson (1986). We placed ads in Scottish newspapers offering free help to cut down drinking. A total of 785 individuals responded to the ads. They were sent either a self-help manual based on behavioral principles (Robertson & Heather, 1985) or a general advice and information booklet that included addresses of helping agencies. At six-month follow-up, we found that the manual group showed a significantly greater reduction in mean alcohol consumption and greater improvement on variables measuring physical health and extent of alcohol-related problems. Within the ranges of the consumption and dependence levels shown in the sample, there was no evidence that improvement was confined to only those showing relatively lower consumption or early as opposed to late dependence. At one-year follow-up (Heather, Robertson, McPherson, Allsop, & Fulton, 1987), the gains we observed at the earlier follow-up had been maintained. There was further evidence of the superiority of manual over control groups when respondents who had received other forms of help were excluded.

To replicate and increase the internal validity of these findings, Heather, Kissoon-Singh, and Fenton (1990) selected individuals who would be available for personal follow-up interviews. We also added other design features to increase our confidence in the findings. A significantly higher proportion of subjects who received a manual was drinking below medically recommended levels at six-month follow-up than in controls. However, there was no evidence from this study that supplementary telephone contact added to the effectiveness of a self-help manual. We speculate that this is probably because clients who favor the self-help approach are especially sensitive to stigma and wish to avoid contact with helping agencies. The effort to reach such clients provides an additional justification for the use of self-administered, self-help manuals.

Community-Based Interventions

The defining characteristic of the research discussed in this section is that the client population has not requested help for a drinking problem. These clients therefore have to be identified by screening and persuaded that they should reduce or give up drinking. This is clearly the domain of public health policy rather than clinical intervention as such.

Health Screening Programs

Kristenson and colleagues conducted the most successful demonstration of the potential of brief interventions of this type in Malmö, Sweden (Kristenson et al., 1982, 1983; Trell, Kristenson, & Fex, 1984). They invited all male residents of Malmî between 45 and 50 years of age to a health screening interview arranged by the local Department of Preventive Medicine. Of these, they selected 585 individuals who were in the top decile of the distribution of GGT readings on two successive occasions for study. They found excessive drinking to be implicated in the raised GGT of 72% of this sample. They then randomly assigned half to an intervention group given the brief intervention procedure described earlier. They informed control group subjects by letter that they showed evidence of impaired liver function and were advised to cut down drinking.

At follow-up two and four years after initial screening, both groups showed significant decreases in GGT levels. However, the control group showed a significantly greater increase in the mean number of sick days per individual, more days of hospitalization in the follow-up pe-

riod, and a strikingly greater number of days in hospital for alcohol-related conditions. At a five-year follow-up, the control group had twice as many deaths, both those probably alcohol related and not so, as the intervention group. Apart from an unfortunate reluctance to report alcohol consumption data, Kristenson and colleagues undoubtedly produced the most impressive and well-substantiated results to date in the field of brief interventions. The implications for the long-term cost effectiveness of attempts to prevent alcohol-related harm are significant.

Other Scandinavian researchers have continued research on brief interventions as part of health screening programs. Romelsjö (Romelsjö et al., 1989) recruited subjects from participants in a health examination of random samples of the adult population in Stockholm County. The authors imply that their results are an exception to the general run of findings showing no advantage for more extended intervention. However, a safer conclusion is that this is another study to show no clear, added benefit of more extended intervention (involving return visits) over short and simple advice. On this occasion, however, there was not much benefit from either intervention.

In a health survey of more than 21,000 men and women aged 12 to 62 years in Tromsø, Norway, Nilssen (1991) randomized "early-stage risk drinkers" to a control group and two (a major and minor) intervention groups. He noted significant decreases in mean GGT and self-reported alcohol intake in the intervention groups compared with the control group. There were no significant differences between the two intervention groups. This study indicates that modest and simple interventions may yield important changes in drinking habits in early-stage risk drinkers.

As part of a general health survey of middle-aged men, Suokas (1992) randomly allocated 247 male excessive drinkers either to a brief advice group or to an intervention group. This latter group received brief advice, follow-up consultations with a nurse, feedback of the GGT results three times during the follow-up year, and a self-help booklet on how to cut down drinking. Soukas concluded that objective signs of alcohol-induced organ damage, combined with brief advice about health hazards of heavy drinking given by a physician, can favorably affect drinking. More intensive (but still low intensity) intervention did not add much to this effect.

General Hospitals

Chick and colleagues (1985) reported the first study of brief intervention in a general hospital setting. They screened 731 male inpatients in general hospital wards for problem drinking. They excluded those who had previous treatment for alcoholism and/or little social support. Some 156 who agreed to a follow-up interview were randomly allocated to a group that received one session of counseling about their drinking habits (see my earlier description) or a control group receiving only routine medical care. At one-year follow-up, both groups showed significant decreases in consumption. However, the intervention group had significantly fewer alcohol-related problems and had a higher proportion of patients who were "definitely improved" in terms of GGT and mean corpuscular volume (MCV) levels.

Elvy, Wells, and Baird (1988) randomly allocated 263 problem drinkers they had recruited by screening from general hospital wards to one of two groups. In one group, they tried to refer patients for treatment, but made no such attempt in the other group. A psychologist approached those in the referral group, confronted them with their self-reported drinking problems, and asked if they would accept referral to an alcohol counselor. At 12-month follow-up, the referred group had improved significantly more than the controls on self-reported alcohol problems and other variables. These effects had diminished at the 18-month follow-up, largely because of improvements in the control group. This was a study of the referral process and not of brief intervention as such, since only 62% of the referral group accepted counseling. It is therefore not possible to determine what was responsible for the favorable results obtained—counseling or the act of referral itself.

In a recent, and as yet unpublished, study at the National Drug and Alcohol Research Centre, University of New South Wales, we evaluated brief counseling to reduce alcohol consumption among male heavy drinkers identified on general hospital wards and investigated the type of brief counseling of most benefit. We screened male inpatients on the wards of four teaching hospitals in Sydney, Australia. We identified 174 heavy drinkers showing predominantly low levels of alcohol dependence and allocated them to one of two forms of brief counseling (skills-based counseling or motivational interviewing) or to a non-intervention control group. At six-month follow-up, the clients who had received either form of counseling showed a significantly greater mean reduction in weekly drinking compared to controls. When we selected patients "not ready to change," as measured by the Readiness to Change Questionnaire, brief motivational interviewing resulted in a greater mean reduction in drinking than skills-based counseling. These findings suggest that one should assess male heavy drinkers identified on hospital wards for their "stage of change" in respect of drinking behavior. Brief motivational interviews should be offered to those who are not ready to change. We anticipate publishing our findings from this study shortly.

General Medical Practice

In the first study of brief intervention in general practice in the United Kingdom, we (Heather et al., 1987) evaluated an earlier version of the Scottish Health Education Group's DRAMS scheme. We found no evidence of superior outcome at six-month follow-up in a group given the DRAMS package compared with one given simple advice by their doctors or a nonintervention control. However, the sample sizes obtained in this study were too small to allow us to draw firm conclusions.

Since then, two studies of general practice brief intervention in the United Kingdom have provided good evidence of effectiveness. In a randomized controlled trial using 47 group practices, Wallace, Cutler, and Haines (1988) showed that intervention by a general practitioner was effective in reducing drinking among clients with excessive alcohol consumption. At one-year follow-up, the proportion of men with excessive consumption at interview had fallen by 44% in the treatment group, compared with 26% in controls, with corresponding proportions among women of 48% and 29%. The mean value for GGT liver enzyme dropped significantly more in treated men than in controls but there were no significant group differences among women. Anderson and Scott (1992) randomly allocated heavy-drinking men to receive brief advice from their general practitioners. At one-year follow-up, the brief intervention group had reduced their drinking in excess of 65 grams of alcohol per week compared with controls. Among women, there were no significant differences in reduced consumption between treated and control groups (Scott & Anderson, 1991).

Now allow me to qualify the results of the studies presented in this section. First, we need to find out whether brief interventions by general practitioners are effective in other socio-cultural settings, especially those countries where the primary health-care system operates on a fee-for-service basis. Second, both successful British studies cited used an "artificial" method of recruiting clients for the intervention. This is in contrast to opportunistic screening of patients in practice waiting-rooms and immediate intervention by the doctor as a routine part of general practice. We need to determine whether brief interventions would be equally effective under naturalistic conditions of routine general practice. Third, we do not yet know how much intervention is necessary to produce benefits. In the two U.K. studies cited and in other studies of brief intervention (Babor & Grant, 1992; Chick, Lloyd, & Crombie, 1985; Elvy, Wells, & Baird, 1988; Heather, Campion, Neville, & Maccabe, 1987; Kristenson, Öhlin, Hultén-Nosslin, Trell, & Hood, 1983; Suokas, 1992), significant reductions in drinking were found in assessment-only control groups. It may be that a relatively intensive assessment focused on the client's drinking behavior can lead to reduced consumption.

We addressed these issues in a recent study in Australia (Richmond, Heather, Wodak, Kehoe, & Webster, 1994). We found a nonsignificant trend for clients who had received the Alcoholscreen program (a five-session intervention over five months similar to Wallace et al.'s, 1988 protocol) to drink less at six-month and one-year follow-ups than clients in other groups. However, clients given Alcoholscreen had significantly fewer alcohol-related problems at both follow-up points. Although less than half of those in the Alcoholscreen group returned for the crucial second consultation with the doctor, those who did drank significantly less at follow-up than other clients. There was no evidence that either a minimal intervention of five minutes advice by the general practitioner or an alcohol assessment only led to reductions in drinking compared with a nonassessment control group. The study is important because it provided evidence of an effect of brief intervention under naturalistic conditions. However, this effect appeared to be weaker than previously reported in the two British studies. We think this is because clients recruited opportunistically are generally less motivated to cut down than those recruited by special procedures.

Other Community Settings

Miller and colleagues (Miller et al., 1987) reported an evaluation of the Drinker's Check-Up (DCU). After screening, they randomly assigned

42 problem drinkers to three groups: (1) the DCU within one week of the screening session; (2) the DCU plus a comprehensive list of sources of help and treatment, given after the feedback session; and (3) a waiting list control who received the DCU six weeks after the initial session. At a follow-up six weeks after the DCU, all groups showed modest but significant reductions in drinking. These were retained at an 18-month follow-up. There were no differences between groups. They concluded that the DCU may prompt less motivated drinkers to seek help and modestly suppress drinking, but that the DCU by itself may be insufficient to alleviate all alcohol-related problems.

From a population of 2,114 patients attending somatic outpatient clinics in Lund, Sweden, Persson and Magnussen (1989) selected 78 individuals who either drank excessively according to questionnaires or had a raised GGT due to alcohol. They randomly assigned subjects to intervention and control groups and found superior outcomes for subjects receiving the brief intervention. They concluded that an early and relatively simple intervention program for problem drinkers may be effective. It can be carried out at a low cost and with a positive response from patients.

The last study to be described is perhaps the most important. This is Phase II of the WHO Project on *Identification and Management of Alcohol-Related Problems: A Randomized Clinical Trial of Brief Intervention in Primary Health Care* (Babor & Grant, 1992). This was a multisite, international collaboration involving 10 countries (Australia, Bulgaria, Costa Rica, Kenya, Mexico, Norway, the former U.S.S.R., U.K., U.S.A., and Zimbabwe) and 1,655 heavy drinkers recruited from a combination of hospital settings, primary care clinics, work sites, and educational institutions. Clients were randomly assigned to a control group, a Simple Advice group, and a Brief Counseling group. They gave all clients a 20-minute assessment, followed in the case of the Simple Advice group by 5 minutes' advice from a "health adviser" (a range of professionals). The Brief Counseling group received the same 5 minutes' advice plus an additional 15 minutes of counseling based on a "habit-breaking plan" and a self-help manual. Some participating centers added an Extended Counseling condition consisting of the initial Brief Counseling session followed by three more sessions with the health worker to monitor progress over six months. They followed all clients for six months after the initial contact.

Among males, there was a significant effect of *any* intervention on average alcohol consumption and "intensity" of drinking (i.e., the typical amount drank on those days when the client consumed alcohol). Males in the intervention groups reported roughly 25% less daily drinking than those in the control group. Among females, both intervention and control groups showed significant reductions in consumption at follow-up. The most surprising finding was that, for men, five minutes of advice was as effective as brief and extended counseling.

This last finding could be interpreted as meaning that all that is needed in brief interventions is a few minutes' plain advice and encouragement. However, the majority of clients given counseling may not have recognized a problem with their drinking and may not have been ready to cut down. In terms of Prochaska and DiClemente's (1987) stages of change model, they were in *precontemplation* or *contemplation* stages. Although it included some motivational components, counseling was largely oriented toward a problem-solving model. It is reasonable to suppose that, in order for this to be effective, clients need to recognize that they have a problem that needs to be solved. The "habit-breaking plan" clients were encouraged to develop may have appeared irrelevant to the majority of them. This would have considerably diminished the chances of finding an effect of counseling over simple advice. What data were recorded indicated that only a small minority of patients said they had read the problem-solving self-help manual. The lesson here is that one needs to sort out those clients who are ready to change drinking behavior from those who are not and tailor the type of brief intervention offered to the client's readiness to change.

The WHO Project has added considerably to our knowledge of the effects of brief interventions. It has also underlined some important issues for further research (e.g., why women appear to benefit less). It has raised the profile of brief intervention strategies among the international alcohol treatment and research community. It has also increased an appreciation of the great potential of this form of intervention in the effort to reduce the harm done by alcohol.

Finally, you should be aware that the National Institute on Alcohol Abuse and Alcoholism in the United States has developed a brief intervention for at-risk drinkers for use by primary care physicians (NIAAA, 1994).

REFERENCES

Clinical Guidelines

Anderson, P. (1987). A strategy for helping people who are drinking excessively. *The Practitioner, 231*, 297–306. Oriented to general practice intervention.

Babor, T. F. & Grant, M. (Eds.). (1992). *Project on identification and management of alcohol-related problems. Report on Phase II: A randomized clinical trial of brief interventions in primary health care*. Geneva: World Health Organization. Although primarily a research report, this contains material essential for anyone wishing to implement a brief intervention in a primary care setting. Write to Programme on Substance Abuse, World Health Organization, Geneva, Switzerland.

Chick, J. (1980). Alcohol dependence: methodological issues in its measurement; reliability of the criteria. *British Journal of Addiction, 75*, 175–186. Description of the EADS. Instrument available from Dr. Jonathon Chick, Alcohol Research Group, Royal Edinburgh Hospital, Morningside Terrace, Edinburgh EH10 5HF, UK.

Heather, N., & Robertson, R. (1983). *Controlled drinking* (revised edition). New York: Methuen. As well as describing the background to the use of controlled drinking treatment, this gives guidance for differential allocation to moderate drinking or abstinence goals (Chapter 9).

Heather, N., & Rollnick, S. (1993). *Readiness to Change Questionnaire: User's manual* (revised version). Technical Report No. 19. Sydney: National Drug & Alcohol Research Centre, University of New South Wales. Background and instructions on how to use this questionnaire in brief intervention work. Write to National Drug & Alcohol Research Centre, University of New South Wales, P.O. Box 1, Kensington, NSW 2033, Australia.

Mayfield, D., McLeod, G., & Hall, P. (1974). The CAGE questionnaire: Validation of a new alcoholism screening instrument. *American Journal of Psychiatry, 131*, 1121–1123. First description of the CAGE. See also: Ewing, J. A. (1984). Detecting alcoholism—The CAGE questionnaire. *Journal of the American Medical Association, 252*, 1905–1907.

Miller, W. R., & Marlatt, G. A. (1984). *Manual for the Comprehensive Drinker Profile*. Odessa, FL: Psychological Assessment Resources Inc. Source for Ph score. Full CDP available from PAR, P.O. Box 98, Odessa, FL 33556.

Miller, W. R., & Marlatt, G. A. (1987). *The brief drinker profile*. Odessa, FL: Psychological Assessment Resources.

Miller, W. R., & Muñoz, R. F. (1982). *How to control your drinking* (revised edition). Albuquerque, NM: University of New Mexico Press. The original controlled drinking self-help manual. It can be criticized only for being somewhat long for some purposes.

Miller, W. R., & Rollnick, S. (1991). *Motivational interviewing: Preparing people to change addictive behavior*. New York: Guilford. An excellent introduction to motivational interviewing. It is highly recommend reading for anyone planning to do brief interventions.

Miller, W. R., Sovereign, R. G., & Krege, B. V. (1988). Motivational interviewing with problem drinkers: II. The Drinker's Check-Up as a preventive intervention. *Behavioural Psychotherapy, 16,* 251–268. First description of the Drinker's Check-Up. For further information, write to Professor W. R. Miller, Department of Psychology, University of New Mexico, Albuquerque, NM 87131.

Miller, W. R., Zweben, A., DiClemente, C. C., & Rychtarik, R. G. (1992). *Motivational enhancement therapy manual: A clinical research guide for therapists treating individuals with alcohol abuse and dependence.* Project MATCH Monograph Series, Volume 2. Rockville, MD: National Institute on Alcohol Abuse & Alcoholism. As used in Project MATCH. Write to NIAAA, 5600 Fishers Lane, Rockville, MD 20857.

National Institute of Alcohol Abuse and Alcoholism. (1994). *Brief intervention for primary healthcare providers (working title).* This is a self-contained brief intervention package that will be released in 1994. Contact Fran Cotter at NIAAA, 301–433–1207, for more information.

Orford, J., & Edwards, G. (1977). *Alcoholism: A comparison of treatment and advice, with a study of the influence of marriage.* Maudsley Monographs no. 26. Oxford: Oxford University Press. Comprehensive account of the authors' influential research study. Chapter 8 contains a description of the basic treatment method and a wider discussion of the implication of the findings. See also: Edwards, G., & Orford, J. (1977). A plain treatment for alcoholism. *Proceedings of the Royal Society of Medicine, 70,* 344–348.

Raistrick, D., Dunbar, G., & Davidson, R. (1983). Development of a questionnaire to measure alcohol dependence. *British Journal of Addiction, 78,* 89–95. Description of the SADD. Available from Leeds Addiction Unit, 40 Clarendon Road, Leeds LS2 9PJ, UK.

Richmond, R., Heather, N., Wodak, A., Kehoe, L. & Webster, I. (1994). *A controlled evaluation of a general practice-based brief intervention for excessive alcohol consumption: The Alcoholscreen Project.* NDARC Monograph Series. Sydney: National Drug & Alcohol Research Centre, University of New South Wales. Report of Alcoholscreen evaluation. For Alcoholscreen and other brief intervention materials (flip-charts, self-help manuals, audio-cassettes etc.), write to Associate Professor Robyn Richmond, Life Style Unit, National Drug & Alcohol Research Centre, Royal South Sydney Hospital, Zetland, NSW 2017, Australia.

Robertson, I., & Heather, N. (1985). *So you want to cut down your drinking?* (revised edition). Edinburgh: Scottish Health Education Group. An example of a self-help manual specifically adapted to local culture and conditions. Attractively produced by SHEG. Distributed free in Scotland only, but sample copies obtainable from Scottish Health Education Group, Woodburn House, Canaan Lane, Edinburgh EH10 4SG, UK.

Robertson, I., & Heather, N. (1986). *Let's drink to your health!* Leicester: British Psychological Society Publications. A slightly expanded and up-market version of the preceding manual.

Rollnick, S., & Bell, A. (1991). Brief motivational interviewing for use by the nonspecialist. In W. R. Miller and S. Rollnick (Eds.), *Motivational interviewing: Preparing people to change addictive behavior* (pp. 203–213). New York: Guilford. An introduction to brief, one-session motivational interviewing. See also: Rollnick, S., Heather, N. & Bell, A. (1992). Negotiating behavior change in medical settings: The development of brief motivational interviewing. *Journal of Mental Health, 1,* 25–37.

Sanchez-Craig, M. (1982). Teaching controlled drinking and abstinence to early-stage problem drinkers: Self-control strategies for secondary prevention. Unpublished manuscript. Toronto: Addiction Research Foundation. One of the best therapist manuals in this area. Write to Dr. Martha Sanchez-Craig, ARF, 33 Russell Street, Toronto, Canada M5S 2S1.

Sanchez-Craig, M., Wilkinson, D. A., & Walker, K. (1987). Theory and methods for secondary prevention of alcohol problems: a cognitively-based approach. In W. M. Cox (Ed.), *Treatment and prevention of alcohol problems: A resource manual.* New York: Academic Press. A comprehensive review of this topic.

Scottish Council on Alcohol. (1988). *Ending offending: An alcohol training resource pack for people working with young offenders.* Glasgow: Scottish Council on Alcohol. Write to Mr. Douglas Allsop, Scottish Council on Alcohol, 147 Blytheswood Street, Glasgow, G2 4EN, Scotland, UK.

Scottish Health Education Group. (undated). *DRAMS scheme. Helping problem drinkers: Skills for the general practitioner.* Edinburgh: Scottish Health Education Group. Write to SHEG, Woodburn House, Canaan Lane, Edinburgh, EH10 4SG, Scotland, UK.

Skinner, H. A., & Allen, B. A. (1982). Alcohol dependence syndrome: Measurement and validation. *Journal of Abnormal Psychology, 91,* 199–209. Description of the ADS. Scale and guidelines for use are available from Dr. Harvey Skinner, Dept. of Behavioural Science, University of Toronto, Toronto, Ontario, M5S 1A8, Canada.

Skinner, H. A., & Holt, S. (1983). Early intervention for alcohol problems. *Journal of the Royal College of General Practitioners, 33,* 787–791. Describes a basic strategy for dealing with patients with alcohol problems in general practice.

Skinner, H. A., Holt, S., & Israel, Y. (1981). Early identification of alcohol abuse: 1, Critical issues and psychosocial indicators for a composite index. *The Canadian Medical Association Journal, 124,* 1141–1152. A comprehensive review of its chosen subject. See also: Holt, L., Skinner, H. A., & Israel, Y. (1981). Early identification of alcohol abuse: 2. Clinical and laboratory indicators. *The Canadian Medical Association Journal, 124,* 1279–1295. An essential companion to the preceding paper.

Skinner, H. A., Holt, S., Sheu, W. J., & Israel, Y. (1986). Clinical versus laboratory detection of alcohol abuse: The alcohol clinical index. *British Medical Journal, 292,* 1703–1708. The index is obtainable from Dr. Harvey A. Skinner, Dept. of Behavioural Science, University of Toronto, Toronto, Ontario, M5S 1A8, Canada.

Stockwell, T. R., Hodgson, R. J., Edwards, G., Taylor, C., & Rankin, H. (1979). The development of a questionnaire to measure severity of alcohol dependence. *British Journal of Addiction, 74*, 79–87. Original description of the SADQ.

Stockwell, T., Sitharthan, T., McGrath, D., & Lang, E. (1994). The measurement of alcohol dependence and impaired control in community samples. *Addiction 89* 167–174. Description of the SADQ-C. For copies of the instrument, write to Associate Professor Tim Stockwell, National Centre for Research Into the Prevention of Drug Abuse, Curtin University of Technology, G.P.O. Box 1987, Perth, Western Australia, 6001, Australia.

Research

Anderson, P., & Scott, E. (1992). The effect of general practitioners' advice to heavy drinking men. *British Journal of Addiction, 87*, 891–900.

Antti-Poika, I. (1988). *Alcohol intoxication and abuse in injured patients*. Dissertationes No. 19, Commentationes Physico-Mathematicae. Helsinki, Finland: The Finish Society of Sciences & Letters.

Babor, T. F., Ritson, E. B., & Hodgson, R. J. (1986). Alcohol-related problems in the primary health care setting: A review of early intervention strategies. *British Journal of Addiction, 81*, 23–46.

Baldwin, S., Heather, N., Lawson, A., Robertson, I., Mooney, J., & Braggins, F. (1991a). Comparison of effectiveness: Behavioural and talk-based alcohol education courses for court-referred young offenders. *Behavioural Psychotherapy, 19*, 157–172.

Baldwin, S., Heather, N., Lawson, A., Ward, M., Robb, E., Williams, A., Greer, C., Gamba, S., & Robertson, I. (1991b). Effectiveness of pre-release alcohol education courses for young offenders in a penal institution. *Behavioural Psychotherapy, 19*, 321–331.

Barrison, I. G., Viola, L., Mumford, J., Murray, R. M., Gordon, M., & Murray-Lyon, A. (1982). Detecting excessive drinking among admissions to a general hospital. *Health Trends, 14*.

Bien, T. H., Miller, W. R. & Tonigan, J. S. (1993). Brief interventions for alcohol problems: A review. *Addiction, 88*, 315–336.

Chick, J., Lloyd, G., & Crombie, E. (1985). Counselling problem drinkers in medical wards: A controlled study. *British Medical Journal, 290*, 965–967.

Chick, J., Ritson, B., Connaughton, J., Stewart, A., & Chick, J. (1988). Advice versus extended treatment for alcoholism: A controlled study. *British Journal of Addiction, 83*, 159–170.

Department of Health and Social Security. (1978). *The pattern and range of services for problem drinkers*. Report of Advisory Committee on Alcoholism. London: Her Majesty's Stationery Office.

Edwards, G., Arif, A., & Hodgson, R. (1982). Nomenclature and classification of drug-and alcohol-related problems: A shortened version of a WHO Memorandum. *British Journal of Addiction, 77*, 3–20.

Edwards, G., & Taylor, C. (1994). A test of the matching hypothesis: alcohol dependence, intensity of treatment and 12 month outcome. *Addiction, 89*, 553–561.

Elvy, G. A., Wells, J. E., & Baird, K. A. (1988). Attempted referral as intervention for problem drinking in the general hospital. *British Journal of Addiction, 83*, 83–89.

Emrick, C. D. (1975). A review of psychologically oriented treatment of alcoholism: II. The relative effectiveness of different treatment approaches and the effectiveness of treatment versus no treatment. *Quarterly Journal of Studies on Alcohol, 36*, 88–108.

Ewing, J. A. (1984). Detecting alcoholism: The CAGE Questionnaire. *Journal of the American Medical Association, 252*, 1905–1907.

Heather, N. (1993). The application of harm-reduction principles to the treatment of alcohol problems. In N. Heather, A. Wodak, E. Nadelmann, & P. O'Hare (Eds.), *Psychoactive drugs and harm reduction: From faith to science* (pp. 168–183). London: Whurr Publishers.

Heather, N., Campion, P. D., Neville, R. G., & MacCabe, D. (1987). Evaluation of a controlled drinking minimal intervention for problem drinkers in general practice (the DRAMS scheme). *Journal of the Royal College of General Practitioners, 37*, 358–363.

Heather, N., Kissoon-Singh, J., & Fenton, G. (1990). Assisted natural recovery from alcohol problems: Effects of a self-help manual with and without supplementary telephone contact. *British Journal of Addiction, 85*, 1177–1185.

Heather, N., Robertson, I., MacPherson, B., Allsop, S., & Fulton, A. (1987). Effectiveness of a controlled drinking self-help manual: One year follow-up results. *British Journal of Clinical Psychology, 26*, 279–287.

Heather, N., Rollnick, S., & Bell, A. (1993). Predictive validity of the Readiness to Change Questionnaire. *Addiction, 88*, 1667–1677.

Heather, N., Whitton, B., & Robertson, I. (1986). Evaluation of a self-help manual for media-recruited problem drinkers: Six month follow-up results. *British Journal of Clinical Psychology, 25*, 19–34.

Hingson, R., Scotch, N., Day, N., & Culbert, A. (1980). Recognizing and seeking help for drinking problems: A study in the Boston metropolitan area. *Journal of Studies on Alcohol, 41*, 1102–1117.

Horn, J. L., Wanberg, K. W., & Foster, F. M. (1987). *The Alcohol Use Inventory*. Minneapolis, MN: National Computer Systems.

Institute of Medicine. (1990). *Broadening the base of treatment for alcohol problems*. Washington, DC: National Academy Press.

Jarman, C. M. B., & Kellett, J. M. (1979). Alcoholism in the general hospital. *British Medical Journal, 285*, 469–472.

Kissin, B. (1977). Comments on "Alcoholism: A controlled trial of treatment and advice." *Journal of Studies on Alcohol, 38*, 1804–1808.

Kristenson, H., Öhlin, H., Hultén-Nosslin, M., Trell, E., & Hood, B. (1983). Identification and intervention of heavy drinking in middle-aged men: Results and follow-up of 24–60 months of long-term study with randomized controls. *Journal of Alcoholism: Clinical and Experimental Research, 20*, 203–209.

Kristenson, H., Trell, E., & Hood, B. (1982). Serum of glutamyl-transferase in screening and continuous control of heavy drinking in middle-aged men. *American Journal of Epidemiology, 114,* 862–872.

Miller, W. R. (1978). Behavioral treatment of problem drinkers: A comparative outcome study of three controlled drinking therapies. *Journal of Consulting and Clinical Psychology, 46,* 74–86.

Miller, W. R. (1983). Motivational interviewing with problem drinkers. *Behavioral Psychotherapy, 11,* 147–172.

Miller, W. R., & Baca, L. M. (1983). Two-year follow-up of bibliotherapy and therapist-directed controlled drinking training for problem drinkers. *Behavior Therapy, 14,* 441–448.

Miller, W. R., Gribskov, C., & Mortell, R. (1981). The effectiveness of a self-control manual for problem drinkers with and without therapist contact. *International Journal of the Addictions, 16,* 829–839.

Miller, W. R. & Sanchez, V. C. (1993). Motivating young adults for treatment and lifestyle change. In G. Howard (Ed.), *Issues in alcohol use and misuse by young adults.* (pp. 55–79). Notre Dame, IN: University of Notre Dame Press.

Miller, W. R., & Saucedo, C. F. (1983). Assessment of neuropsychological impairment and brain damage in problem drinkers. In C. J. Golden, J. A. Moses, Jr., J. A. Coffman, W. R. Miller & F. D. Strider (Eds.), *Clinical neuropsychology: Interface with neurologic and psychiatric disorders* (pp. 141–195). New York: Grune & Stratton.

Miller, W. R., & Taylor, C. A. (1980). Relative effectiveness of bibliotherapy, individual and group self-control training in the treatment of problem drinkers. *Addictive Behaviors, 5,* 13–14.

Miller, W. R., Taylor, C. A., & West, J. C. (1980). Focused versus broad spectrum behavior therapy for problem drinkers. *Journal of Consulting and Clinical Psychology, 48,* 590–601.

Moore, M. H. & Gerstein, D. R. (Eds.). (1981). *Alcohol and public policy: Beyond the shadow of prohibition.* Washington, DC: National Academy Press.

Murray, A. (1993). *The management of problem drinking in general hospital: Problems and possibilities.* Ph.D. thesis, University of Dundee.

Nilssen, O. (1991). The Tromsø Study: Identification of and a controlled intervention on a population of early-stage risk drinkers. *Preventive Medicine, 20,* 518–528.

Persson, J., & Magnusson, P-H. (1989). Early intervention in patients with excessive consumption of alcohol: a copntrolled study. *Alcohol, 6,* 403–408.

Prochaska, J. O., & DiClemente, C. O. (1986). Toward a comprehensive model of change. In W. R. Miller & N. Heather (Eds.), *Treating addictive behaviors: Processes of change* (pp. 3–27). New York: Plenum.

Quinn, M. A., & Johnston, R. V. (1976). Alcohol problems in acute male medical admissions. *Health Bulletin, 34,* 253–256.

Robertson, I., & Heather, N. (1982). An alcohol education course for young offenders. *British Journal on Alcohol and Alcoholism, 17,* 32–38.

Rollnick, S., Heather, N., Gold, R., & Hall, W. (1992). Development of a short Readiness to Change Questionnaire for use in brief, opportunistic interventions among excessive drinkers. *British Journal of Addiction, 87,* 743–754.

Romelsjö, A., Andersson, L., Barrner, H., Borg, S., Granstrand, C., Hultman, O., Hässler, A., Källqvist, A.,

Olsson, E., Rhedin, A., & Wikblad, O. (1989). A randomized study of secondary prevention of early stage problem drinkers in primary health care. *British Journal of Addiction, 84,* 1319–1327.

Royal College of General Practitioners. (1986). *Alcohol: A balanced view.* London: Author.

Royal College of Physicians. (1987). *A great and growing evil: The medical consequences of alcohol abuse.* London: Tavistock.

Sanchez-Craig, M. (1980). Random assignment to abstinence or controlled drinking in a cognitive-behavioral program: Short-term effects on drinking behavior. *Addictive Behaviors, 5,* 35–39.

Sanchez-Craig, M., Annis, H. M., Bornet, A. R., & MacDonald, K. R. (1984). Random assignment to abstinence and controlled drinking: Evaluation of a cognitive-behavioral program for problem drinkers. *Journal of Consulting and Clinical Psychology, 52,* 390–403.

Sanchez-Craig, M., & Lei, H. (1986). Disadvantages of imposing the goal of abstinence on problem drinkers: An empirical study. *British Journal of Addiction, 81,* 505–512.

Saunders, J. B., Aasland, O. G., Babor, T. F., de al Fuente, J. R., & Grant, M. (1993). Development of the Alcohol Use Disorders Identification Test (AUDIT). WHO collaborative project on early detection of persons with harmful alcohol consumption—II. *Addiction, 88,* 791–804.

Scott, E., & Anderson, P. (1991). Randomized controlled trial of general practitioner intervention in women with excessive alcohol consumption. *Drug & Alcohol Review, 10,* 313–321.

Skutle, A., & Berg, G. (1987). Training in controlled drinking for early-stage problem drinkers. *British Journal of Addiction, 82,* 493–502.

Suokas, A. (1992). *Brief intervention of heavy drinking in primary health care: Hämeenlinna Study.* Academic Dissertation, Research & Treatment Unit for Alcohol Diseases, University of Helsinki. Helsinki: University Printing House.

Swenson, P. R., & Clay, T. R. (1980). Effects of short-term rehabilitation on alcohol consumption and drinking-related behaviors: An eight-month follow-up study of drunken drivers. *International Journal of the Addictions, 15,* 821–858.

Taylor, C., Brown, D., Duckitt, A., Edwards, G., Oppenheimer, E., & Sheehan, M. (1985). Patterns of outcome: Drinking histories over ten years among a group of alcoholics. *British Journal of Addiction, 80,* 45–50.

Thom, B. (1986). Sex differences in help-seeking for alcohol problems: 1. The barriers to help-seeking. *British Journal of Addiction, 81,* 777–788.

Trell, E., Kristenson, H., & Fex, G. (1984). Alcohol-related problems in middle-aged men with elevated serum gamma-glutamyltransferase: A preventive medical investigation. *Journal of Studies on Alcohol, 45,* 302–309.

Walker, K., & Shain, M. (1983). Employee assistance programming: In search of effective interventions for the problem-drinking employee. *British Journal of Addiction, 78,* 291–303.

Wallace, P., Cutler, S., & Haines, A. (1988). Randomised controlled trial of general practitioner intervention in patients with excessive alcohol consumption. *British Medical Journal, 297,* 663–668.

CHAPTER 7

Antidipsotropic Medications

Richard K. Fuller

OVERVIEW

Antidipsotropic medications are pharmacological agents whose purpose is to deter the alcoholic from drinking by producing an unpleasant reaction if he or she ingests alcohol. These medications are also called *alcohol-sensitizing* or *deterrent drugs.* The reaction they produce is manifested by some or all of the following symptoms: flushing, rapid or irregular heart beat, dizziness, nausea, vomiting, difficulty breathing, and headache. Other pharmacological agents (e.g., naltrexone) are being tested as pharmacotherapies for alcoholism, but the antidipsotropic drugs are the only ones currently available that are used solely for the treatment of alcoholism. However, the antidipsotropic medications are not primary treatment by themselves. They are intended to be used as part of a multimodal treatment program to help the patient avoid drinking while he or she is restructuring his or her life.

Disulfiram (Antabuse®) and carbimide (citrated calcium carbimide, Temposil®) are the two antidipsotropic medications used in clinical practice, although the latter is not available in the United States. Disulfiram and carbimide produce the drug-ethanol reaction primarily by inhibiting the liver enzyme aldehyde dehydrogenase (ALDH), which catalyzes the oxidation of

acetaldehyde (the major metabolic product of ethanol) to acetate. The resulting accumulation of acetaldehyde is responsible for most of the symptoms of the drug-ethanol reaction.

However, there are important pharmacological differences between disulfiram and carbimide. The inhibition of ALDH by disulfiram is irreversible. For this reason, the restoration of ALDH activity after disulfiram administration is stopped requires the synthesis of new enzymes, which occurs over several days. The inhibition of ALDH by calcium carbimide is of a mixed reversible-irreversible type, and 80% of ALDH activity is restored within 24 hours. This difference in ALDH inhibition has implications for the clinical use of these drugs. Patients cannot drink for four to seven days without having a reaction after stopping disulfiram, whereas they can resume drinking 24 hours after not taking calcium carbimide. The longer duration of action of disulfiram may be an advantage because it gives the patient more time to reconsider his or her decision and resume taking the drug.

Disulfiram also inhibits other enzymes, including dopamine-beta-hydroxylase (DBH) and the microsomal mixed function oxidases. Drowsiness is a frequent side effect of disulfiram, and relapse or exacerbation of depression and schizophrenia have been reported with its use. These behavioral toxic reactions may be the

123

result of altered brain catecholamine levels resulting from the inhibition of DBH by disulfiram. The mixed function oxidases are responsible for the biotransformation of many drugs, and their inhibition by disulfiram can result in toxic levels of drugs catabolized by these enzymes. Since calcium carbimide does not inhibit these enzyme systems, it has fewer side effects and fewer drug interactions than disulfiram.

Most of the discussion in the following sections will be about disulfiram because the amount of available information about disulfiram is much greater than that about calcium carbimide. Since the disulfiram-ethanol reaction can be fatal, and serious adverse reactions have been reported with the use of disulfiram, it is important that patients be evaluated to be sure that disulfiram is appropriate for them before prescribing the drug. This will be discussed more completely in the section on patient selection.

The results of a multicenter study of disulfiram suggest that disulfiram is helpful in reducing the frequency of drinking in those who have relapsed, particularly for the slightly older and more socially stable patient. A major problem with disulfiram is that patients often stop taking it; sometimes because of side effects but usually because of a conscious or subconscious decision to resume drinking. To improve compliance with the disulfiram regimen, researchers have developed strategies in which spouses or treatment staff watch the patient ingest the medication and then reinforce him or her for taking it. Controlled studies using these strategies report better outcomes than if the patient takes disulfiram at his or her discretion.

Efforts have been made to develop either a long-acting oral antidipsotropic medication or an injectable or implantable form of disulfiram, but to date these have been unsuccessful. The development of such drugs would overcome, to a large degree, the problem of compliance with disulfiram treatment. The following sections focus on how to select patients, contraindications, a protocol for using these medications, and a discussion of their effectiveness.

SELECTION OF PATIENTS

There are two aspects to the appropriate selection of patients. The first is to select those who are more likely to benefit from disulfiram treatment. The second is not to use the medication with those who are at risk for a serious adverse reaction.

Patients Most Likely to Benefit from Disulfiram Treatment

In a Department of Veterans Affairs multicenter study (Fuller et al., 1986), the addition of disulfiram to a multimodal treatment program did not result in more patients maintaining continuous abstinence for one year than was achieved without the use of disulfiram. However, a substantial subset of the men who relapsed drank significantly less frequently during the year if they had been given a conventional therapeutic 250 mg dose of disulfiram compared to those who were either given a subtherapeutic 1 mg dose or were not given disulfiram. The subset who benefited from the 250 mg dose were older and more socially stable.

In view of these findings, I do not recommend disulfiram as part of one's initial treatment. I reserve it for those who relapse. The aim of treatment is abstinence, and if an alcohol-dependent patient can achieve abstinence without disulfiram, there is no need to prescribe a medication which, like most pharmacological agents, has the risk of side effects and adverse reactions. However, because alcohol dependence is a relapsing illness (Peachey & Annis, 1984), many alcoholics will become candidates for disulfiram therapy.

Similar to the VA multicenter study, Baekeland, Lundwall, Kissin, and Shanahan (1971) found that middle-aged and/or more socially stable men are more likely to benefit from disulfiram than younger, less socially stable men. In addition to age and better social stability (defined as living with someone or being employed), they also found that the following characteristics were associated with a good outcome with disulfiram: (1) a longer history of heavy drinking, (2) a history of delirium tremens, (3) good motivation manifested by contact with Alcoholics Anonymous and/or abstinence at intake, and (4) not being treated with antidepressant medications. Others have reported that depressed men do poorly on disulfiram. It has been suggested that those with a compulsive personality style do well with disulfiram treatment. Similar data for women currently are not available. Also, as yet there are no empirically based guidelines regarding who is most likely to benefit from calcium carbimide.

In summary, the middle-aged alcohol dependent male who has relapsed, has some degree of social stability, and is not significantly depressed is the most suitable candidate for disulfiram therapy.

CONTRAINDICATIONS TO DISULFIRAM TREATMENT

Toxicity from disulfiram can occur from the disulfiram-ethanol reaction, an adverse reaction to the drug itself, or interactions with drugs other than alcohol (see Table 7.1).

Disulfiram should not be used or used cautiously in any person who is at increased risk for having a toxic reaction.

A significant drop in blood pressure can occur during the disulfiram-ethanol reaction (DER). Fatal DERs and nonfatal heart attacks and strokes have occurred. Therefore, disulfiram is contraindicated in patients with cardiovascular or cerebrovascular disease. For similar reasons, the presence of severe lung disease and chronic kidney disease is a contraindication to disulfiram administration. Because of the possibility of occult vascular disease, do not prescribe disulfiram for persons over 60 years of age. Others consider diabetes mellitus a contraindication to its use (Sellers, Naranjo, & Peachey, 1981).

Disulfiram also is contraindicated in persons with organic brain syndrome because patients who take Antabuse must fully comprehend the potentially dangerous consequences of the DER. Do not give disulfiram to individuals with a history of or who currently have symptoms of schizophrenia or a major affective illness, because exacerbation or development of serious neuropsychiatric illnesses have been reported with disulfiram. For the same reason, the

Table 7.1   Medical Contraindications to the Use of the Antidipsotropic Medications

---

Disulfiram

Cardiovascular disease
Cerebrovascular disease
Severe chronic pulmonary disease
Chronic renal failure
Neuropsychiatric disease
   Organic brain disease
   Psychosis
   Depression requiring treatment
Idiopathic seizure disorder
Neuropathy
Pregnancy
Chronic liver disease complicated by portal
   hypertension

Calcium Carbimide

Thyroid disease
Neuropathy

---

concurrent use of disulfiram and antidepressants is not recommended. However, Larson, Olincy, Rumnans, and Morse (1992) in their review of the literature found that most psychiatric complications with the use of disulfiram were reported before 1970 when dosages of 1 to 2 g/day were often used, and concluded that at a dosage of 250 mg/day, "disulfiram does not appear to increase significantly the risk of psychiatric complications." They suggest that disulfiram is a treatment option for patients with alcohol dependence and other psychiatric conditions within the context of a "structured supervised aftercare program." Banys (1988) has agreed with this but, in addition, stated that "schizophrenic or severely depressed patients may require maintenance at a lower dose (125 mg) in order to avoid side effects or an exacerbation of psychiatric symptoms."

Ten patients in the VA multicenter study had neuropsychiatric illnesses requiring hospitalization. However, the illnesses occurred equally among the 250 mg disulfiram patients and the patients in two control groups (Branchey, Davis, Lee, & Fuller, 1987). The fact that the disulfiram-treated patients did not have more serious psychiatric illnesses than the control patients is probably because patients with a history of schizophrenia or major affective disorders were excluded from the study.

Patients who have an idiopathic seizure disorder should not be prescribed disulfiram because it may lower the seizure threshold (McConchie, Panitz, Sauber, & Shapiro, 1983). If a patient only has alcohol-related seizures, I have prescribed disulfiram after the withdrawal period is finished since the risk of seizure from drinking is probably greater than from disulfiram. However, I explain the risk to the patient and follow that person more closely during the first month of treatment.

Peripheral neuropathy has been reported with the use of both disulfiram and calcium carbimide. Thus, these drugs should not be prescribed to patients with preexisting peripheral neuropathy, and patients receiving disulfiram should be periodically examined for neurological signs. If neurological symptoms or signs occur, stop the disulfiram.

One of the few absolute contraindications (Banys, 1988) is gender specific. Nora, Nora, and Blu (1977) indicated that disulfiram should not be used in pregnant women or women who are actively trying to become pregnant, because birth defects have been reported with its use.

Metronidazole (Flagyl®) can cause a DER-like reaction in individuals taking metronidazole who drink alcohol. Disulfiram is contraindicated for those taking metronidazole. This is because confusion, inappropriate behavior, delusions, and hallucinations occurred in 6 of 29 men on disulfiram who were given metronidazole, suggesting a combined disulfiram-metronidazole toxicity (Rothstein & Clancy, 1969).

Disulfiram has to be used carefully in patients taking certain drugs. Disulfiram interferes with the biotransformation of phenytoin (Dilantin®), warfarin (Coumadin®), isoniazid, rifampin, diazepam (Valium®), chlordiazepoxide (Librium®), and the antidepressants imipramine and desipramine. The concurrent administration of disulfiram may result in toxic levels of these drugs. If it is necessary to prescribe an anxiolytic drug (and the risk of abuse of these drugs usually contraindicates their use in people with alcohol dependence), consider oxazepam (Serax®). It can be used because oxazepam is metabolized by glucuronidation and disulfiram does not affect glucuronidation to a significant degree (MacLeod et al., 1978). If it is necessary to use disulfiram in patients taking the drugs listed above, serum drug levels or the prothrombin time, in the case of those taking Coumadin, should be monitored. If these tests indicate toxic levels, the dosage of these drugs should be decreased. If that does not result in resolution of toxic blood levels and/or symptoms, disulfiram should be discontinued. Stop disulfiram in those patients taking disulfiram and isoniazid concurrently if unsteady gait or changes in mental status occur.

Because drugs that impair the regulation of blood pressure (alpha- and beta-adrenergic receptor antagonists and vasodilators) might result in a severe DER, do not give disulfiram to patients taking these drugs. Sellers and colleagues (1981) have also suggested that drugs that are mediated by norepinephrine or dopamine (e.g., phenothiazines) or that inhibit the same enzyme as disulfiram (e.g., monamine oxidase inhibitors) might result in a serious DER. However, as discussed earlier, patients with neuropsychiatric illnesses severe enough to require these medications should probably not receive disulfiram.

Liver cirrhosis often is listed as a contraindication to the use of disulfiram. However, evidence for this is scanty. Disulfiram can cause a severe, occasionally fatal hepatotoxic reaction, but this is idiosyncratic, and the presence of cirrhosis does not appear to predispose to it. I have prescribed disulfiram to patients with compensated cirrhosis, pro-

vided there is no evidence of portal hypertension (ascites, splenomegaly, or esophageal varices) and have observed no adverse reactions in these patients. Avoid using disulfiram in those with portal hypertension because of the danger of vomiting during the DER and precipitating hemorrhage from esophageal varices.

Since disulfiram causes drowsiness, particularly during the first few weeks of treatment, do not prescribe it to those whose lives would be endangered if they were drowsy on the job (e.g., house painters working on ladders, window washers). For other potentially dangerous jobs (e.g., driving trucks and working with machinery), prescribe disulfiram if the patient agrees to begin the medication on a weekend, to take it at bedtime, and to stop it if he or she is still drowsy upon awakening after two or three days on the drug.

Calcium Carbimide

Calcium carbimide has not been released for use in the United States because of an antithyroid effect observed in experimental animals. Otherwise, clinically it appears to be relatively free from side effects. For those who practice in countries in which calcium carbimide is available, it is prudent not to prescribe it for patients with a history of thyroid disease.

PROTOCOL FOR USE OF THE ANTIDIPSOTROPIC MEDICATIONS

The antidipsotropic medications are not likely to be effective as the only treatment and should be used as one component of a multimodal treatment program. The steps involved in the use of these medications are (1) selection of appropriate patients, (2) description of the disulfiram-ethanol reaction, (3) a discussion of the benefits and risks, (4) a decision whether the patient will self-medicate or have others administer the medication, and (5) follow-up. Some of these steps overlap. With a patient who is desirous of taking a deterrent drug and comprehends all that is involved, the first four steps may be accomplished in one session. For others, it may take several discussions between patient and physician.

Selection of Patients

As described in the preceding section, I reserve disulfiram for the patient who has relapsed. If your patient has relapsed and you are considering disulfiram, review the medical record to see whether any of the exclusions listed in the previous section are present. If this review indicates they are not present, discuss briefly with the patient the benefits and risks of disulfiram. At this point, if the patient is interested in taking disulfiram, take a medical history, do a physical examination of the heart, abdomen, and nervous system, and order an electrocardiogram and liver function tests. If the history, physical examination, and laboratory tests indicate that the patient is a suitable candidate for disulfiram therapy, move to the next step.

Description of the Disulfiram-Ethanol Reaction

When disulfiram was first introduced, the practice was to have the patients experience the disulfiram-ethanol reaction. An electrocardiogram and sphygmomanometer were attached to the patient, and oxygen and vasopressor agents were available to treat serious hypotensive reactions. This practice has been replaced by vividly describing the disulfiram-ethanol reaction (DER). Inform the patient that if he or she starts drinking within two weeks of stopping the medication, he or she runs the risk of having a DER with all its consequences. It is unusual for a patient to have a DER if several days have elapsed since the last drink, but the manufacturer states that a DER may occur within two weeks of the last drink. It is important to emphasize that severe hypotension and arrhythmias can occur with the DER and, although rare, there have been fatal DERs. The patient must fully understand the risks of the DER, and you cannot overemphasize the severity of the reaction. Also warn the patient not to ingest liquid medications that contain alcohol (e.g., cough syrups or food cooked in wine) and to avoid other things that contain disguised alcohol (e.g., aftershave lotions, back rubs).

Discussion of Benefits and Risks

Building on the previous discussions, continue the conversation with the patient, moving it to the point of making a mutual decision to initiate treatment. If you encounter ambivalence or resistance, consider using strategies presented in Chapter 5. If a spouse is available, it is useful to have him or her at this session.

Many people have become abstinent without taking disulfiram. However, since this particular patient has relapsed, he or she may require something "extra." That something extra may be disulfiram. The simple act of taking a pill daily produces a chemical "fence" for the patient. This can be very helpful if each day is a struggle to avoid taking a drink. Knowing that one will become sick if he or she drinks provides another incentive not to drink. This frees patients from the struggle of deciding whether to take a drink or not and allows them to devote their emotional energy to restructuring their lives.

If the patient is still ambivalent about taking disulfiram, it is important to explore whether the hesitancy to take disulfiram is a subconscious reluctance to accept the concept of abstinence. Also, the patient may feel he or she is relinquishing control over an aspect of his or her life to an external agent and is relying on a "crutch." Since drinking often results in loss of control over one's life, this reluctance to take disulfiram may not be realistic. Point out that crutches are needed if someone breaks a leg, and, similarly, one may need a crutch in the early months of sobriety. Furthermore, taking disulfiram daily is an act of self-control. On the other hand, a truck driver may be realistic by expressing concerns about drowsiness being an occupational hazard. Acknowledge the possible side effects of disulfiram and the risks of the DER. However, a discussion of the toxicity of disulfiram has to be balanced against the toxicity of alcohol. To minimize somnolence, the most common side effect, advise patients to take disulfiram at bedtime.

The benefits and risks of taking disulfiram are weighed. Never insist that a patient take disulfiram, but if a person's life is being destroyed by alcohol and he or she has no contraindication to its use, this could be the step that changes that patient's life.

If, after weighing these factors, the patient decides to use disulfiram, the next step is to discuss whether the patient will take it himself or herself or have someone at the clinic or a family member administer it ("supervised" administration). Controlled studies have indicated that the directly observed, and reinforced, administration of disulfiram will achieve better results than self-administration, but this is not a settled issue (see Effectiveness section). Supervised administration has to be done sensitively (see Chapter 15 for a protocol on monitored disulfiram). If there is considerable conflict between the patient and the spouse, the spouse's administration of disulfiram can become another power struggle between the two. Therefore, I prefer to initiate disulfiram treatment by prescribing the drug for the patient to self-administer. However, Azrin (1976) has had success with the spouses giving the Antabuse. He emphasizes that treatment is a common goal and works with the patient to view the spouse as a "helper" or caring friend. It also helps to rebuild trust between the spouse and the patient.

If self-administration fails, discuss supervised disulfiram self-administration with the patient and explain that some have found that this method is more effective than self-administration. Choosing a member of the treatment staff to observe the ingestion may be preferable. A staff member often is less judgmental than a spouse, and the patient often views the staff member as a neutral person whose role is to help him or her to stop drinking. However, it is often inconvenient for the patient to return to the clinic frequently. If there is a supportive family member who can give positive reinforcement, he or she is the most appropriate person to observe the taking of the medication.

Dosage

Obviously, disulfiram should not be given until alcohol has been eliminated from the patient's body. To be safe, do not give disulfiram until 24 hours after the last drink. The usual dosage of disulfiram is 250 mg daily. However, some practitioners begin treatment with 500 mg daily for one to two weeks and then reduce the dosage to 250 mg daily. The 250 mg disulfiram dose is popular because it is sufficient to cause a DER, and there are fewer dose-related side effects (Peachey & Annis, 1984). Some researchers (Lake, Major, Ziegler, & Kopin, 1977) have reported side effects with the 500 mg dose (i.e., small but significant increases in blood pressure). Also, Major and Goyer (1978) reported increases in serum cholesterol with the 500 mg but not the 250 mg dose.

In the VA multicenter study, side effects, except for somnolence, were no more common in the 250 mg disulfiram patients than in the members of the two control groups. On the other hand, Brewer (1984) in the United Kingdom has suggested that the 250 mg dose is often not sufficient to result in a DER if a patient drinks. In his study of 63 patients, 17 needed daily doses of disulfiram in the range of 400 to 500 mg to achieve a DER, 6 required doses in the range of 600 to 700 mg, and 7 required 800 to 1,500 mg. This has not been the usual clinical experience,

however, and these results have not been replicated. Srinivasan, Babu, Appaya, and Subrahmanyam (1986) from India reported that 60 of 61 patients on 500 mg disulfiram daily had a DER when they drank. All of those who had a reaction experienced flushing, rapid heart beat, headache, nausea, and a "slight fall in blood pressure." Five patients developed hypotension of sufficient degree to require medical intervention, and one patient developed hemorrhage from a tear in the lining of the stomach because of protracted vomiting.

In summary, I recommend the 250 mg dose, recognizing that some patients may require a 500 mg dose because they only experience a mild DER when taking the 250 mg dose. Wallet-sized cards provided by the manufacturer stating that the patient is taking disulfiram should be given to the patient to carry on his or her person in the event the person has a DER.

Calcium carbimide is usually given at a dose of 50 mg twice daily.

Follow-Up

In addition to a structured treatment program, I recommend this follow-up schedule: weekly intervals for the first two weeks, biweekly intervals for the next six weeks, monthly for the next four months, and finally bimonthly for the remainder of the year, if feasible. This schedule may have to be adjusted for several reasons, including convenience for the patient, reimbursement, and so on. The purpose of follow-up visits is to monitor the response to treatment, assess the occurrence of side effects, and answer questions the patient may have. If the patient "forgets" to take the medication, this may be a prelude to drinking and should be discussed with the patient. At the end of one year, a discussion about the appropriateness of stopping the disulfiram component of the treatment is held. Most patients, in my experience, elect to stop it, but some feel it is important for their sobriety to continue taking it.

If the patient should drink and have a DER, the treatment is supportive. If the patient is hypotensive, intravenous fluids, oxygen, and a vasopressor (e.g., ephedrine sulfate) are indicated. There is no evidence that antihistamines or vitamin C is beneficial.

During the first six months, the patient should be monitored for the possibility of hepatoxicity secondary to disulfiram. Disulfiram hepatoxicity is rare, but fatal cases have been reported. This is an idiosyncratic reaction, so it is impossible to predict which person will develop it. Most patients who develop hepatoxicity do so within the first three months of treatment, and almost all have nausea, malaise, and fatigue preceding the development of jaundice (yellow coloration of eyes, inside of mouth, and skin). Many will also have fever, arthralgias, rash, or itching. These symptoms and signs should alert you to the possibility that a hepatotoxic reaction is occurring. Instruct your patients to call you if they experience such symptoms because acute disulfiram hepatitis may progress to a fulminant stage between scheduled appointments. It is important to have baseline liver tests prior to starting treatment and to repeat the tests at two-week intervals for two months and at three- to six-month intervals thereafter (Wright, Vafier, Lake, & Raymond, 1988).

A modest elevation in the serum aspartate aminotransferase (AST) may indicate the resumption of drinking rather than disulfiram hepatitis. An elevated AST, which is less than 250 IU, does not require the automatic termination of disulfiram treatment. Persons who are drinking can have AST levels up to 250 IU. Disulfiram hepatoxicity is usually associated with AST values above 250 IU. In the VA cooperative study in which liver tests were done bimonthly, an increase in the values of the liver tests usually indicated resumption of drinking (Iber, Lee, Lacoursiere, & Fuller, 1987). If the serum AST is below 250 IU, discuss these findings with your patient. That discussion often will reveal that the patient is drinking. If the patient insists he is not drinking and there is no other evidence to the contrary, discontinue the disulfiram. If the patient has symptoms or signs consistent with a hepatotoxic reaction or the serum AST is above 250 IU, stop the disulfiram.

EFFECTIVENESS

Disulfiram was introduced into clinical use in 1948. Many clinical studies initially reported excellent results with the drug. However, most of these studies were uncontrolled. None were double-blind except for a study evaluating implanted disulfiram, and few monitored compliance with the medication. Reviews of the studies evaluating the efficacy of disulfiram (Lundwall & Baekeland, 1971; Mottin, 1973) have criticized their methodological soundness. Also, pharmacokinetic and formal dose response studies of disulfiram were not done. Thus, this drug was introduced into clinical practice without much of the information that is considered standard for introduction of a new drug today. In fairness to those who did the initial studies, controlled clinical trials were in their infancy, and the methodology for studying the pharmacokinetics of disulfiram was not available at that time.

Two of the earlier studies had shown that disulfiram was not effective in the "Skid Row" type alcoholics or alcoholics without families. The studies were not blinded, but they were randomized and controlled. Gallant and colleagues (1968) studied men who were repeat legal offenders. These men had been arrested an average of 14 times during the preceding year. They were assigned to disulfiram alone, disulfiram with group counseling, group counseling alone, and routine sentencing. While attrition was high, Gallant and his colleagues achieved a remarkable follow-up rate in a group notoriously difficult to locate; they were able to locate more than 90% of the subjects at the end of six months. Unfortunately, almost all of the subjects had resumed drinking.

Gerrein, Rosenberg, and Manohar (1973) studied men, most of whom lived alone or in a sheltered environment. Again, disulfiram was not effective, except in those men who were observed ingesting the medication by the treatment staff ("monitored" or "supervised" disulfiram treatment). However, the study period was only eight weeks. Whether long-term benefit can be achieved with monitored disulfiram in this poor risk group of patients is not known.

The uncertainty about the efficacy of disulfiram treatment stimulated Harold Roth and me to design a study that we hoped would correct many of the deficiencies identified in previous studies. To that end, we designed a double-blind, controlled study. We recruited men who were married because (1) we wanted sources of information about the patients' drinking behavior in addition to self-report and (2) we wanted to study men who had the potential for family support. We employed assessors of treatment outcome who had no involvement in the treatment of the subjects and built in measures to monitor compliance with the drug regimen (Fuller & Roth, 1979).

Furthermore, we used two control groups because of the unique nature of the deterrent drugs (i.e., the basis for their effectiveness being the patient's fear of becoming sick with resumed drinking). This was aptly stated by Enoch

Gordis when he wrote, "It is probable that it is the patient's belief that he is taking disulfiram (whether or not he actually is) that is therapeutic and not the action itself . . ." (Gordis & Peterson, 1977, p. 215). Therefore, we had a control group whose members received a 1 mg dose (insufficient to cause a DER), and a second control group whose members were willing to take disulfiram but did not receive it. Those patients who received either the conventional 250 mg dose or the 1 mg dose were told they were receiving disulfiram. Thus, the patients receiving the 1 mg dose had the expectation that they would become ill if they drank. Those who were assigned to the no-disulfiram group received riboflavin and were informed that they were not getting Antabuse but were receiving a vitamin. Thus, these patients did not have the expectation of becoming sick if they drank.

However, our study had a flaw that was not apparent until it was nearly finished—that is, insufficient sample size. This occurred because we overestimated the effectiveness of disulfiram when we calculated the sample size prior to initiating the study. We enrolled 128 men and followed them for one year. After one year, 23% of the men given either dose of disulfiram had been continuously abstinent whereas only 12% of the no-disulfiram men had been totally abstinent. This difference, although twofold, is not statistically significant. Thus, we could not state that disulfiram was effective. On the other hand, if we had claimed that disulfiram was not effective, we would have had a 48% chance of being wrong (a Type II error because a sample size of 128 men is not large enough to protect against this type of false claim).

We corrected this problem in the VA multicenter study (Fuller et al., 1986). In a study whose design was similar to my study with Roth, 605 men were recruited and randomly assigned to a 250 mg disulfiram dose, a 1 mg dose, or no disulfiram. All of the patients received the benefit of a multimodal treatment program. The staff of these programs was multidisciplinary in composition, including physicians, psychologists, nurses, social workers, certified alcoholism counselors, and chaplains. The primary goal of the treatment was abstinence. Most of the patients were treated initially for two to four weeks in a hospital setting where they received education about the deleterious effects of alcohol and were counseled in preventing relapse.

After discharge from the hospital, patients were asked to return for clinic visits at least weekly for the first six months and biweekly for the next six months for counseling. Most of the counseling occurred in group sessions led by a psychologist, social worker, nurse, or a certified alcoholism counselor. The discussions in the group sessions were primarily devoted to living a life free of alcohol and coping with personal problems. Individual sessions to address specific psychological and social problems were available if requested by the patients or deemed necessary by the therapist. Attendance at Alcoholics Anonymous (AA) was not mandatory, but we encouraged the patients to attend AA meetings. The therapists and the interviewers who assessed treatment effect were blind to the drug treatment the patients were receiving.

The assessment procedures consisted of bimonthly interviews of the patients and a friend or relative with whom the patient was living. If the patient returned to the clinic for his bimonthly interview, we obtained and analyzed blood samples for ethanol and liver tests. When a patient returned for a clinic visit, a urine sample was collected and was analyzed for ethanol.

There were 202 men assigned to the 250 mg dose, 204 men to the 1 mg dose, and 199 men to the no-disulfiram group. The three treatment groups were comparable in age, race, marital status, employment status, education, income, and duration of alcohol abuse. After one year of treatment, there were no significant differences among the three groups in continuous abstinence during the year: 18.8% (38/202), 22.5% (46/204), and 16.1% (32/199) were continuously abstinent in the 250 mg disulfiram, 1 mg, and no-disulfiram groups, respectively. There were no significant differences in the median time to the first drink, which varied from 41 days in the no disulfiram group to 65 days in the 1 mg dose group. However, among those patients who drank and supplied all seven scheduled assessment interviews, those in the 250 mg disulfiram group reported significantly fewer drinking days (49 + 8.4) than the patients in the other two treatment groups (75.4 ± 11.9 and 86.5 ± 13.6 days for the 1 mg disulfiram and no disulfiram groups, respectively). These reports of significantly fewer drinking days in the 250 mg disulfiram-treated patients were corroborated by the relatives or friends of the patients. The men who relapsed but provided all interviews were slightly but significantly older and had lived longer at their current address than the other patients who had relapsed but did not provide all interviews. On the two parameters of social stability that we measured, continuous employment and remaining with relative or friend during the year, there were no significant differences among the treatment groups.

Only 20% of 577 patients who finished the study were judged compliant, and there were no significant differences among the three treatment groups in compliance with the drug regimen. Compliance with any of the three drug treatments was associated with total abstinence during the year: 43% of the compliers were continuously abstinent, whereas only 8% of the noncompliers were totally abstinent. This suggests that some patients (unfortunately, a minority) entered into the aftercare process with a high degree of motivation and thus achieved both high compliance and total abstinence. On the other hand, poor compliance with the disulfiram regimen appears to be a major reason for its limited efficacy.

The results of this large multicenter clinical trial indicate that disulfiram given to patients to take at their discretion is not effective in promoting continuous abstinence. However, there does appear to be a subset of men who will partially benefit from taking disulfiram because they drink less frequently during the year. This suggests that, while disulfiram is not a panacea, it does have a useful role in selected patients. There were no women and relatively few college graduates or professional people in the study, and the results may not be generalizable to these individuals.

Since poor compliance with the drug regimen is the Achilles' heel of conventional disulfiram treatment, researchers have developed several strategies to improve compliance. These strategies usually have used some variation of spouses or treatment staff administering the drug. Unfortunately, many of the studies evaluating these strategies have "serious flaws in research design" (Allen & Litten, 1992). However, the better controlled studies suggest that these strategies result in enhanced compliance and less drinking. A recent controlled study (Chick et al., 1992) of 126 patients found that the supervised administration of 200 mg disulfiram under the supervision of a relative, colleague, or clinic staff member reduced total six months' alcohol consumption compared to a control group whose members received supervised administration of 100 mg vitamin C. While this study was well done methodologically, it does not provide a direct answer to the question of whether supervised disulfiram administration is superior to unsupervised administration.

Monitored or supervised disulfiram treatment has been used with particular effectiveness in patients over whom the therapist has leverage. This technique has been labeled *mandatory disulfiram treatment*. Brewer and Smith (1983) reported that 9 out of 16 alcoholics who took disulfiram under supervision as a condition of probation were "entirely successful," and the average period of abstinence for all 16 patients was 30 weeks, compared with 6 weeks during the previous two years. Brewer (1987) is emphatic that this is the only way to use disulfiram. However others (Peachey & Annis, 1984; Marcos & Marcos, 1980; Miller & Hester, 1986) have questioned whether it is legal and ethical to coerce people to take disulfiram. Sereny, Sharma, Holt, and Gordis (1986) studied patients who had failed previous treatment but still wanted to be in the treatment program. These patients were offered supervised disulfiram with the condition that if they did not cooperate, they would be discharged from the program. They observed a 40% (27/68) continuous abstinence rate for one year, compared to a 15% rate for their regular outpatient treatment program.

Using supervised disulfiram treatment in patients who have failed the regular program but who wish to remain in treatment is less objectionable than coercing patients to undergo this form of treatment, but these results should be replicated in a randomized, controlled study. While conceptually supervised disulfiram should improve treatment outcome compared to unsupervised administration, Heather (1989) is correct in stating that a large, properly designed treatment trial comparing supervised with unsupervised use of disulfiram is needed.

In other efforts to improve compliance, researchers have implanted disulfiram into the subcutaneous fat of the abdominal wall of patients. Because the tablets dissolve slowly, patients frequently do not experience a DER or have a mild one if they drink. Wilson, Davidson, and Blanchard (1980) randomly assigned 40 patients to a disulfiram implant, 40 to a placebo implant, and 10 to a no-implant control group; they also followed 10 patients who refused an implant. In both implant groups, 25% were lost to follow-up, and corroboration of self-report was possible in only 15 of the original 100 patients. There was no significant difference in continuous abstinence between the two implant groups, although the disulfiram implant patients reported significantly more abstinent days (361 versus 307). None of the nonoperated patients remained totally abstinent.

A recent double-blind study (Johnsen & Mørland, 1991) found no significant differences after approximately 300 days of follow-up between disulfiram and placebo implants in number of abstinent weeks, time to first drink, or reduction in average daily ethanol consumption. None of the disulfiram patients reported having a DER. Five of the disulfiram implanted patients and one of the placebo patients developed wound infections. The lack of proven efficacy and the frequent local reactions to implantation do not justify this form of disulfiram administration except as part of a research study.

The preceding discussion has been devoted exclusively to disulfiram because few controlled studies of calcium carbimide have been done. Thus, knowledge of the effectiveness of calcium carbimide (Temposil®) is limited. An advantage to calcium carbimide is that it has relatively few side effects. However, one can drink without having a reaction 24 hours after stopping Temposil®. Since compliance is a problem with disulfiram, this shorter duration of action would appear to limit the effectiveness of calcium carbimide.

Annis and Peachey (1992) have evaluated the strategy of patients using calcium carbimide on an "as needed" basis to maintain abstinence. They studied two groups. The members of the first group were counseled by a physician and encouraged to reduce the twice daily dosage only if they felt they could remain abstinent without the deterrence of a chemical "fence." The members of the second group were taught to identify and anticipate high-risk situations for drinking (relapse prevention) and to initially use calcium carbimide when they were entering high-risk situations but progressively enter such situations without using calcium carbimide. Patients were followed and assessed at 6-, 12-, and 18-month posttreatment. There were no significant differences between the two groups on either drinking frequency or quantity, although by 18 months those who received relapse prevention training were drinking less often than those who did not. As well done as this study was, it does not directly answer the question if calcium carbimide enhances alcohol treatment and should be incorporated into practice.

In summary, disulfiram remains the model of the antidipsotropic medications. It has been studied the most extensively, and there is a large body of clinical experience with the drug. Disulfiram should always be used as part of a comprehensive treatment program. In a large, controlled, blinded, multicenter study of disulfiram, the drug did not add additional benefit to counseling in helping patients achieve continuous abstinence. However, the use of disulfiram was accompanied by significant reduction in drinking days in a subgroup of men who were slightly older and more socially stable. Because of the risk of potential toxicity, patients have to be carefully screened so that the drug is not inappropriately prescribed. The medication usually is given to the patient to self-administer, although some studies suggest its effect may be enhanced if the patient ingests it under the supervision of a staff member or significant other.

REFERENCES

Clinical Guidelines

Banys, P. (1988). The clinical use of disulfiram (Antabuse): A review. *Journal of Psychoactive Drugs, 20*, 243–647. This is an excellent review of the pharmacology and metabolism of disulfiram, the disulfiram-ethanol reaction, and the clinical use of disulfiram. Under the topic of clinical use, the author presents a thorough discussion of adverse effects, contraindications, drug interactions, selection of appropriate patients, practical information on prescribing disulfiram and working with the patient to take the medication.

Peachey, J. E. (1981). A review of the clinical use disulfiram and calcium carbimide in alcoholism treatment. *Journal of Clinical Psychopharmacology, 1*, 368–375. This is an excellent review of the clinical use of the antidipsotropic medications. The author discusses the clinical use, efficacy, factors influencing treatment outcome, treatment strategies, and toxicity. His discussion leads to a recommended treatment plan.

Peachey, J. E., & Annis, H. (1984). Pharmacologic treatment of chronic alcoholism. *Psychiatric Clinics of North America, 7*, 745–756. This is the result of a fruitful collaboration between a pharmacologist and psychologist. They begin their discussion of drug treatments for alcoholism with a section on the antidipotropic medications. It is a good companion article to Peachey (1981).

Wright IV, C., Vafier, J. A., & Lake, C. (1988). Disulfiram-induced fulminating hepatitis: Guidelines for liver-panel monitoring. *Journal of Clinical Psychiatry, 49*(11), 430–434. The authors review the literature on fulminant disulfiram hepatitis and recommend a schedule for obtaining liver function tests in order to detect hepatoxicity early and prevent a fatal outcome.

Research

Allen, J. P., & Litten, R. Z. (1992). Techniques to enhance compliance with disulfiram. *Alcoholism: Clinical and Experimental Research, 16*, 1035–1041.

Annis, H. M., & Peachey, J. E. (1992). The use of calcium carbimide in relapse prevention counseling: Results of a randomized controlled trial. *British Journal of Addiction, 87*, 63–72.

Azrin, N. H. (1976). Improvements in the community-reinforcement approach to alcoholism. *Behavioral Research and Therapy, 14*, 339–348.

Azrin, N. H., Sisson, R. W., Meyers, R., & Godley, M. (1982). Alcoholism treatment by disulfiram and community reinforcement therapy. *Journal of Behavioral Therapy and Experimental Psychiatry, 13*, 105–112.

Baekeland, F., Lundwall, L., Kissin, B., & Shanahan, T. (1971). Correlates of outcome in disulfiram treatment of alcoholism. *Journal of Nervous and Mental Diseases, 153*, 1–9.

Banys, P. (1988). The clinical use of disulfiram (Antabuse): A review. *Journal of Psychoactive Drugs, 20*, 243–260.

Barchiesi, A., & Voris, J. C. (1985). Surveying patterns of change in disulfiram use. *VA Practitioner, 2*, 76–78.

Branchey, L., Davis, W., Lee, K. K., & Fuller, R. K. (1987). Psychiatric complications following disulfiram treatment. *American Journal of Psychiatry, 144*, 1310–1312.

Brewer, C. (1984). How effective is the standard dose of disulfiram? A review of the alcohol-disulfiram reaction in practice. *British Journal of Psychiatry, 144*, 200–202.

Brewer, C. (1987). Disulfiram treatment of alcoholism. *Journal of the American Medical Association, 257*, 926.

Brewer, C., & Smith, J. (1983). Probation linked supervised disulfiram in the treatment of habitual drunken offenders: Results of a pilot study. *British Medical Journal, 287*, 1282–1283.

Chick, J., Gough, K., Falkowski, W., Kershaw, P., Hore, B., Mehta, B., Ritson, B., Popner, R., & Torley, R. (1992). Disulfiram treatment of alcoholism. *British Journal of Psychiatry, 161*, 84–89.

Fuller, R. K., & Roth, H. P. (1979). Disulfiram for the treatment of alcoholism: An evaluation in 128 men. *Annals of Internal Medicine, 90*, 901–904.

Fuller, R. K., Branchey, L., Brightwell, D. R., Derman, R. M., Emrick, C. D., Iber, F. L., James, K. E., Lacoursiere, R. B., Lee, K. K., Lowenstam, I., Maany, I., Neiderheiser, D., Nocks, J. J., & Shaw, S. (1986). Disulfiram treatment of alcoholism: A Veterans Administration cooperative study. *Journal of Nervous and Mental Diseases, 256*, 1449–1455.

Gallant, D. M., Bishop, M. P., Falkner, M. A., Simpson, L., Cooper, A., Lathrop, D., Brisolara, A. M., & Bossetta, J. B. (1968). A comparative evaluation of compulsory (group therapy and/or Antabuse and voluntary treatment of the chronic alcoholic municipal court offender. *Psychosomatics, 9*, 306–310.

Gerrein, J. R., Rosenberg, C. M., & Manohar, V. (1973). Disulfiram maintenance in outpatient treatment of alcoholism. *Archives of General Psychiatry, 28*, 798–802.

Gordis, E., & Peterson, K. (1977). Disulfiram therapy in alcoholism: Patient compliance studied with a urine detection procedure. *Alcoholism: Clinical and Experimental Research, 1*, 213–2 16.

Heather, N. (1989). Disulfiram treatment for alcoholism. *British Medical Journal, 299*, 471–472.

Iber, F., Lee, K., Lacoursiere, R., & Fuller, R. (1987). Liver toxicity encountered in the Veterans Administration trial of disulfiram in alcoholics. *Alcoholism: Clinical and Experimental Research, 11*, 301–304.

Johnsen, J., & Mørland, J. (1991). Disulfiram implant: A double-blind placebo controlled follow-up on treatment outcome. *Alcoholism: Clinical and Experimental Research, 15*, 532–536.

Johnsen, J., Stowell, A., Bache-Wiig, J. E., Stensrud, T., Ripel, A., & Mørland, J. (1987). A double-blind placebo controlled study of male alcoholics given a subcutaneous disulfiram implantation. *British Journal of Addiction, 82*, 607–613.

Lake, C. R., Major, L. F., Ziegler, M. G., & Kopin, I. J. (1977). Increased sympathetic nervous activity in alcoholic patients treated with disulfiram. *American Journal of Psychiatry, 134*, 1411–1414.

Larson, E., Olincy, A., Rummans, T. A., & Morse, R. M. (1992). Disulfiram treatment of patients with both alcohol dependence and other psychiatric disorders: A review. *Alcoholism: Clinical and Experimental Research, 16*, 125–130.

Lundwall, L., & Baekeland, F. (1971). Disulfiram treatment of alcoholism. *Journal of Nervous and Mental Diseases, 153*, 381–394.

MacLeod, S. M., Sellers, E. M., Giles, H. G., Billings, B. J., Martin, P. R., Greenblatt, D. J., & Marshman, J. A. (1978). Interaction of disulfiram with benzodiazepines. *Clinical Pharmacology and Therapeutics, 24*, 583–589.

Major, L. F., & Goyer, P. F. (1978). Effects of disulfiram and pyridoxine on serum cholesterol. *Annals of Internal Medicine, 88*, 53–56.

Marco, C. H., & Marco, J. M. (1980). Antabuse medication inexchange for limited freedom—is it legal? *American Journal of Law and Medicine, 5*(3), 295–330.

McConchie, R. D., Panitz, D. R., Sauber, S. R., & Shapiro, S. (1983). Disulfiram-induced de novo seizures in the absence of ethanol challenge. *Journal of Studies on Alcohol, 44*, 739–743.

Miller, W. R., & Hester, R. K. (1986). The effectiveness of treatment techniques: What the research reveals. In W. R. Miller and N. Heather (Eds.), *Treating addictive behaviors: Process of change* (pp. 121–174). New York: Plenum.

Mottin, J. L. (1973). Drug-induced attenuation of alcohol consumption: A review and evaluation of claimed, potential or current therapies. *Quarterly Journal of Studies on Alcohol, 34*, 444–472.

Nora, A. H., Nora, J. J., & Blu, J. (1977). Limb-reduction anomalies in infants born to disulfiram-treated alcoholic mothers. *Lancet, 2*, 664.

Peachey, J. E., & Annis, H. (1984). Pharmacologic treatment of chronic alcoholism. *Psychiatric Clinics of North America, 7*, 745–756.

Rothstein, E., & Clancy, D. D. (1969). Toxicity of disulfiram combined with metronidazole. *New England Journal of Medicine, 280*, 1006–1007.

Sellers, E. M., Naranjo, C. A., & Peachey, J. E. (1981). Drugs to decrease alcohol consumption. *New England Journal of Medicine, 305*, 1255–1262.

Sereny, G., Sharma, V., Holt, J., & Gordis, E. (1986). Mandatory supervised antabuse therapy in an outpatient alcoholism program: A pilot study. *Alcoholism: Clinical and Experimental Research, 10*, 290–292.

Srinivasan, K., Babu, R. K., Appaya, P., & Subrahmanyam, H. S. (1986). Disulfiram-ethanol reaction. *Journal of Association of Physicians of India, 34*, 505.

Wilson, A., Davidson, W. J., & Blanchard, R. (1980). Disulfiram implantation: A trial using placebo implants and two types of controls. *Journal of Studies on Alcohol, 41*, 429–436.

CHAPTER 8

Aversion Therapies

Carl T. Rimmele
Matthew O. Howard
Marian L. Hilfrink

OVERVIEW

Aversion therapies are designed to reduce or eliminate an individual's desire for alcohol. A variety of methods pairing unpleasant stimuli or images with alcohol consumption have been used to decrease urges to drink. The intended result of such treatment is to reduce or eliminate alcohol consumption by producing a conditioned negative response to the cues associated with drinking (e.g., taste, smell, sight).

The most commonly discussed types of aversion therapy are nausea, electric shock, imagery, and apnea. Nausea is the oldest and most frequently used approach. Ancient Romans placed eels, spiders, and other repellent objects in wine cups to be discovered by the drinker upon draining the vessel. In the United States, more than 35,000 patients have received nausea-based aversion treatment since 1935 (Elkins, 1991a, 1991b). Contemporary nausea induction is typically accomplished pharmacologically, although imagery and prolonged rotation of clients have also been employed. The drugs most commonly used to induce nausea are emetine hydrochloride, lithium carbonate, and apomorphine hydrochloride. In this approach, the drug is administered so that nausea and emesis occur immediately following the tasting, sipping, and swallowing of alcoholic beverage(s). This form of treatment is used widely in the former Soviet Union and is employed in some U.S. hospitals (e.g., Schick Shadel Hospital).

Modern application of aversion therapy commenced in 1929 when Kantorovich reported successful treatment of 20 "confirmed alcoholics" at Leningrad Psychiatric Hospital with electric shock. Electrical (or faradic) conditioning has been used within the context of well-established alcohol treatment centers (e.g., Schick Shadel Hospital) since 1970. This approach pairs a painful shock with alcohol consumption. A shock is usually administered to the hand or arm as the client reaches for or tastes the beverage. Some forms of this treatment include self-administered electrical stimulation.

A form of aversion therapy producing a terrifying paralysis of breathing was used experimentally approximately 25 years ago, with mixed results. During the period when breathing ceased (approximately 60 to 90 seconds), an alcohol beverage was placed on the patient's lips. Because of the severe nature of the treatment, it is no longer used.

Each of these procedures involves the use of unpleasant and sometimes painful stimuli. This is especially the case with the chemical and electrical aversion therapies. Because of the stressful nature of these physically aversive treatments, they require medical supervision and can have high dropout rates. Because of these considerations, it is unlikely that such procedures will be used in most outpatient clinics.

Imagery offers another approach to aversion therapy. It is not as painful, invasive, or costly as the preceding procedures. This approach, called *covert sensitization*, involves pairing imagined unpleasant scenes with imagery of drinking. This treatment typically uses scenes designed to produce nausea. Some treatments have augmented the imagination of nausea with an aversive odor (e.g., Maletzky, 1974). Evaluations have also appeared using scenes depicting plausible "negative consequences" of drinking (Miller & Dougher, 1984).

Covert sensitization requires no special equipment, involves minimal risk to clients, and can easily be conducted on an outpatient basis. Aside from other aversion therapies, it is one of the only known ways to directly impact the *desire* to drink. It has been effectively administered by paraprofessional personnel, given adequate training and supervision (Miller & Dougher, 1984). Because of the substantial practical advantages, we have devoted the bulk of this chapter to covert sensitization. Readers interested in chemical or electrical aversion therapy should consult Elkins (1991a, 1991b), Howard, Elkins, Rimmele, and Smith (1991), and Wilson (1987).

SPECIAL CONSIDERATIONS

Rationale

We will devote a large portion of this chapter to describing how to do covert sensitization. We find that the inconsistent effectiveness of covert sensitization seen in the literature (see Chapter 2) is due to inconsistent application of covert sensitization procedures. This is based on differing theoretical accounts of how covert sensitization works (Dougher, Crossen, & Garland, 1986). Indeed, those studies using covert sensitization procedures based on classical conditioning offer the only consistent results (Clarke & Hayes, 1984; Elkins, 1980; Miller & Dougher, 1984). The following procedures are derived from this classical conditioning model.

Client Selection

The literature has not progressed sufficiently to allow one to determine *before* treatment which clients are most likely to benefit from covert sensitization. However, Elkins (Elkins, 1980; Elkins & Murdock, 1977) demonstrated that with nausea covert sensitization, the success of the treatment could be predicted from the degree to which clients experienced conditioned nausea. If the client exhibits an aversion response during imagery of drinking alone, conditioned nausea is considered to have occurred. Elkins developed criteria that enable one to identify clients unlikely to benefit from covert sensitization treatment within two to six sessions, obviating the need to apply a full course of treatment. (We will discuss these criteria later.)

Covert sensitization procedures have been employed in clinical settings for approximately two decades with no reports of major risks, given proper screening. Consider the following criteria for exclusion, which have been used in clinical *research* settings: (1) history of or current gastrointestinal disorders, (2) history of or current heart disease, (3) current severe depression or suicidal ideation, and (4) current psychosis (Miller & Dougher, 1984). However, there is no literature that indicates that persons with these problems experience complications or have poorer outcomes than other populations.

In addition to these precautions, be sensitive to any adverse consequences emerging during the course of treatment. Prepare the client to experience nausea or fear during (and possibly for a brief period following) the sessions. However, in the unlikely event that the client reports continuing aversive consequences (e.g., nightmares), alter the nature of the scenes or consider termination of this treatment.

Settings and Materials

Covert sensitization may be carried out effectively without any unique materials or settings. However, we recommend a quiet room and a comfortable recliner chair in order to minimize any discomfort or distraction that may disrupt imagery. We also recommend conducting covert sensitization on a one-to-one basis. When administered in a group setting, it is difficult to incorporate enough detail to ensure realism sufficient to establish or enhance a conditioned response for any given individual client. The effectiveness of this treatment declines significantly when it is done in groups.

Equipment

Several devices will assist you at different points in the treatment process. If you are using covert sensitization on an outpatient basis, the client could be consuming alcohol prior to treatment. Although you can often detect the presence of high quantities of alcohol simply through observation, it is helpful to use a device for detecting lower blood alcohol levels from breath samples (e.g., Intoximeter). Since intoxication is likely to diminish the effectiveness of this intervention, use breath alcohol tests on a routine basis prior to beginning each session. If the client tests positive, cancel and reschedule the session.

Assisted nausea sensitization (see below) involves the presentation of a noxious odor to increase the sensation of nausea. This form of covert sensitization does not necessarily require any additional equipment beyond the chemical used for the noxious odor (valeric acid is commonly used). You should package the chemical in a manner that you can easily administer, such as a glass jar with a tight lid containing a small amount of cotton saturated with valeric acid. You can then open this jar near the client's nose at the appropriate time during imagery.

It is sometimes difficult to determine whether the client is experiencing a physical reaction to the scenes. This may be an important factor in the successful treatment process (e.g., Elkins, 1980). Several studies have utilized physiological monitoring equipment to aid in this process, reducing the ambiguity of the client's response (Elkins, 1980; Miller & Dougher, 1984). A variety of measures have been used, including skin conductance response, skin conductance level, heart rate, and breathing rate. Although you can use these measures in unison, it is also possible to use only one or two (e.g., skin conductance response) in conjunction with the client's overt responses to aid in determining conditioning (see below). The equipment for some of these measures can be purchased relatively inexpensively as biofeedback devices.

Common Concerns

Since you are trying to induce intense nausea responses in clients, you may be concerned that they might vomit. This is very rare in both the simple nausea and the assisted nausea scenes, but it has happened. As you become more experienced with the nausea reactions of each client, you will be able to detect extraordinarily intense responses in your client and terminate the scenes prior to actual vomiting. Since nausea is the desired response to be paired with drinking, vomiting will add little (if anything) to the effectiveness of the procedure. However, it is a good idea to keep a lined wastebasket available in the event that the client is especially sensitive and you do not terminate the sensitization scene early enough.

Another common concern is that you will become nauseous in response to the scenes yourself. This is unlikely. As a rule, therapists become desensitized to the scene content as they progress. Within a session, you are constantly monitoring the client's responses and any physiological monitoring equipment used, as well as describing and intensifying the scenes. Also, you have your eyes open, and are not reclining in a comfortable chair, both of which inhibit vivid imagination.

Some clients are concerned that the procedures are out of their control and that the therapist may "hypnotize" them. Reassure the client that the entire procedure is in *his or her* control and that it is up to him or her to imagine the scenes as vividly as possible.

STAGES OF COVERT SENSITIZATION

As mentioned earlier, covert sensitization primarily involves the pairing in imagery of drinking and unpleasant events. During initial scenes, the client imagines drinking in a familiar setting, then imagines aversive consequences, such as nausea and vomiting, or feared natural results of excessive alcohol consumption (Smith & Gregory, 1976). With repeated pairings, the unpleasant images come to be attached to alcohol itself, diminishing the client's desire for and attraction to alcohol.

Components of Covert Sensitization

The initial procedure involves pairing drinking stimuli with the vivid imagination of nausea or uncomfortable consequences of drinking. With the help of the client, construct several drinking scenes that are typical for him or her. You will subsequently describe these scenes to the client. Solicit his or her description of nausea or fear experiences to assist in describing the second (or sensitization) portion of each scene. For the purpose of this chapter, the presentation of drinking scenes followed by sensitization scenes will be described as the *pairing* phase of covert sensitization.

In addition to the pairing phase of treatment, covert sensitization also involves two other phases: escape and avoidance (See Figure 8.1). Begin the *escape* phase with imagery of

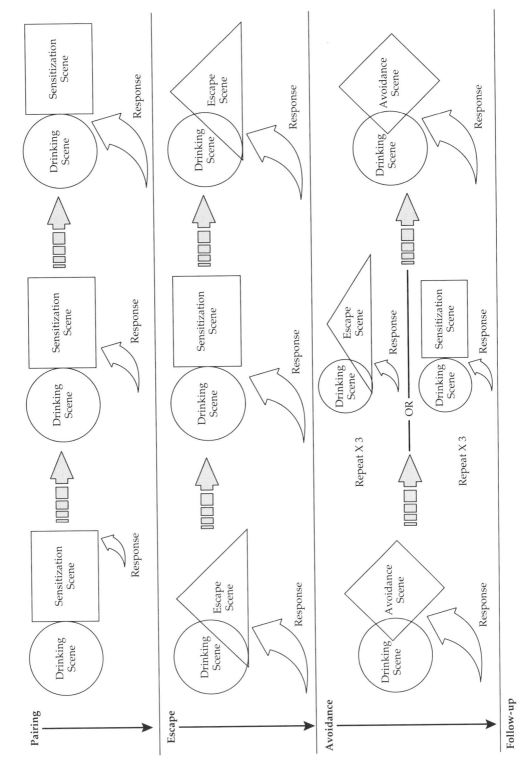

Figure 8.1 Covert Sensitization Flowchart

137

plausible drinking scenes, similar to the *pairing* phase, but when the client begins consistently experiencing discomfort, alter the scene to include nondrinking alternatives, such as pouring out the drink or leaving the drinking setting. Include suggestions of relief and positive self-regard (*aversion-relief statements*) in these scenes. Start the *avoidance* phase with the same imagery of drinking scenes. However, in these scenes, you will present nondrinking alternatives *prior* to the client experiencing any significant uncomfortable or aversive reactions. You will also include aversion-relief statements during this treatment phase.

When to Use Each Component

Begin covert sensitization with *pairing* scenes. During this phase of treatment, the client will typically begin showing a response when you describe the sensitization portion of the scene. The response at this time is called an *unconditioned response*. As you continue the presentation, he or she will begin to experience nausea or discomfort (determined by self-report, behavioral observation, and/or physiological monitoring) when imagining drinking. A response at this point is called a *conditioned response*. Continue the *pairing* phase until a conditioned response appears. Later, we will discuss in more detail the indications of conditioning and the way in which you may assess conditioning.

Once you note a consistent conditioned response, shift to presenting *escape* scenes. This allows the client to exit the drinking setting (in imagination) after beginning to experience some discomfort but before the aversive response is intensified. Alternate *pairing* scenes with *escape* scenes to ensure the conditioned response remains firmly established.

Finally, introduce *avoidance* scenes to reinforce proactive nondrinking behavior. Stop covert sensitization treatment shortly thereafter. Take care to avoid overpracticing these scenes, as this may result in the client becoming used to the aversive elements of the scenes. We will present the specific criteria to transition between treatment phases shortly.

This sequence of scene elements (pairing, escape, and avoidance) was used in two studies showing a link between conditioning and successful outcome (Elkins, 1980; Miller & Dougher, 1984). We will present examples of each type of scene element.

ASSESSMENT

Because you must individually tailor scenes to each client, it is important to do an in-depth assessment before you begin covert sensitization. During this interview, elicit information regarding the client's most recent drinking pattern, including his or her beverage preferences, typical drinking settings, and reasons for drinking. Use additional information about the client's daily habits, hobbies, and interests to build each component of the scenes. We use a structured interview designed explicitly to provide this information about alcohol consumption—the Comprehensive Drinker Profile (Marlatt & Miller, 1984). Without such detailed information, you may have difficulty structuring scenes in a realistic manner without frequently asking questions during imagery.

When using covert sensitization, it is important to evaluate its effect on both drinking behavior and urges to drink. Self-monitoring gives you this information and it helps the client to increase his or her awareness of behaviors that help maintain abstinence. For this purpose, use a simple diary card that includes spaces for the client to record the date and time, the type and amount of drink (or the strength of the urge to drink), and critical aspects of the situation, such as setting and companions (Miller & Muñoz, 1982). Print up cards small enough so that he or she can carry them at all times. Instruct the client to record *every* drink and *each* occurrence of an urge to drink at the time it occurs, rather than waiting to reconstruct the event at a later time. You may define "urges" as any craving, thought, or desire for a drink, and may be rated using a 1–5 scale for intensity. Anticipate the problems the client may have with self-monitoring, and rehearse strategies to deal with those situations.

Constructing Scenes

It is important to prepare a general outline of the scenes you will present prior to the initial sensitization session in the pairing phase. If you have conducted a detailed evaluation interview, you can prepare initial scripts for the drinking scenes from that information. Ensure that you are including relevant details that help the client to vividly imagine the scenes. You will probably make extensive modifications to the scripts in the first few sessions as you find out which elements are useful and which elements interfere with the client's imagination.

Drinking Stimulus Scenes

These scenes include details of typical drinking settings for clients, as well as many details of drinking itself. It is *essential* that you include a full range of beverages unique to the client to ensure that the effect of the sensitization will apply to each beverage. This is because it is possible to produce a conditioned aversion to the taste of one alcoholic beverage without affecting the response to others (Baker & Cannon, 1979; Quinn & Henbest, 1965). For the same reason, it is also important to include a variety of drinking settings. This will reduce the monotony of the scene presentations and assist in generalization of the aversive response. One way to do this is to present the full range of each client's beverage preferences within each of three or more drinking settings.

In presenting the scenes, emphasize details that the client would actually *experience* when drinking in each setting. Peter Lang (Lang, Kozak, Miller, Levin, & McLean, 1980) found that doing so enhanced imagery appreciably. Although details of the setting (e.g., colors, people present, sounds) are important in the initial scene elements, place major emphasis on *experiences* the client would have just before and during drinking. Examples of experiences include the feel and the temperature of the container in the client's hand, the sound of ice cubes in the glass, the smell of the beverage as it is brought close to the lips, the taste and feel of sipping and swallowing the drink, and so on.

Drinking Scene Components

Following is an example of a drinking scene. Since each client will have different drinking settings and beverage preferences, this is only an example of how one drinking scene could be constructed.

Sample Drinking Scene

It's been a long, hard day at work. You've been driving home thinking about how tired and hot you are, and how good a nice cold drink would taste. You arrive home, unlock the door, and realize you're very hot and sweaty. You wipe your forehead, and feel the moisture on the palm of your hand—you wipe your hand on your pants. Your mouth is dry, and you can feel yourself swallowing. You're thinking now about how much you would like a nice cold beer.

You go into the kitchen and head toward the refrigerator. You grasp the handle and can feel the coolness of it in your hand. You have to tug a little to break the seal, and then the door opens. Inside, in the light, you can see the six pack of beer. The cans are held together by plastic, and you can see the red and white labels. You can see the beads of moisture on the cans. You reach in, grasp hold of one can, and pry it out of the plastic. You can feel the round coldness of the beer can in your hand, and you can feel the moisture—the condensation—against your palm. With the other hand, you lift the pop top and hear the hiss as it snaps open. You can see the white bubbles from the beer and can hear the fizz as you bend the pop top back down.

You can almost taste the coolness of the beer already. You bring the can up to your mouth and feel the cool, round metal on your lips. As you tip the can back, you can feel the bubbles of beer bursting on your lips, and you let it flow into your mouth. It tastes great! You can smell the hops—that heavy good aroma of the beer. You feel the beer in your mouth—all over your tongue, that kind of sharp, cool, bitter, malty taste. You swallow and feel the coolness spread down your throat and into your stomach. You can still taste and smell the beer in your mouth. This is just what you wanted!

You bring the can up to your mouth again, and feel that cool liquid flow over your lips and into your mouth. You take a bigger swallow this time, and you can taste and smell that distinctive aroma of the beer as you swallow.

It is important that you ask your client during a scene to elaborate on details to assist in intensifying the realism of the scene. However, the questions you ask at this time should only be about the elements of the scene itself, and should not incorporate demand characteristics (i.e., do not ask, "Can you imagine the taste yet?").

Example

Therapist: You are finally home. You unlock the front door of your house. Would there be anyone else home?

Client: No, just myself.

Therapist: OK, you open the front door and walk into the house. It's cool and quiet inside. You close the door and walk into the kitchen. You're thinking of that nice, cool drink. You go over to the refrigerator. What color is it?

Client: Green.

Therapist: You can see the green refrigerator. You reach out and grasp the handle. . . .

Interactions with the client will diminish as the scenes progress, but should be encouraged, especially during the first few sessions. The interaction assists you *and* the client, since it encourages active participation in the imagination process by him or her. However, you can more effectively use interaction in the drinking stimulus portion of the scenes than in the sensitization portion.

Limit drinking scenes to approximately two to three minutes in length. The purpose of these scenes is to allow the client to vividly imagine the drinking setting and the drink itself. When drinking scenes are longer than this, too many extraneous elements are included, and it quickly becomes unclear what is to be paired with the discomfort. If scenes are much shorter than two minutes, the client may have difficulty generating the image as vividly or realistically as possible. However, the exact time for each scene will vary as a function of the scene, the individual's abilities, and his or her experience.

Consider using a recording log for tracking client responses, as well as reconstructing previous scenes (see Figure 8.2). Information that you would include on such a log would be the scene number, scene component (pairing, escape, avoidance), self-report (number of fingers raised to indicate level of nausea, and when), behavioral signs (gag, choke, flushing, squirming), and physiological changes (as shown by monitoring equipment), each of which are described below.

Sensitization Scenes

Construct sensitization scenes to produce unpleasant responses such as anxiety, horror, disgust, and revulsion. There are three general types of sensitization scenes that you may use, each corresponding to a different modality of covert sensitization. *Nausea* sensitization is the form of sensitization most commonly used. It involves the presentation of scene elements designed to produce an intense experience of nausea in the client (Elkins, 1980; Miller & Dougher, 1984). *Assisted nausea* sensitization is similar, in that the scenes can be identical to those used in nausea sensitization. However, the presentation of a noxious odor is added during the sensitization portion of the scenes (Maletzky, 1974; Miller & Dougher, 1984). The third form of sensitization, *emotive* sensitization, has been used less

Figure 8.2　Recording Log

Scene #	Scene Component	Self-Report	Behavioral Signs	Physiological Changes

frequently. This form of covert sensitization uses scenes designed to evoke strong emotions or feelings other than nausea, such as disgust, embarrassment, anxiety, or horror. In order to induce such feelings, these scenes use believable negative consequences of heavy drinking (Smith & Gregory, 1976).

Currently, it is unclear for whom each type of sensitization scene is most effective, but it appears important to apply only one modality at a time with a client. If one form of sensitization does not appear to be effective and is not producing a response, then switch to one of the other modalities. We will discuss this issue later.

When constructing both the drinking scenes and the sensitization scenes, explore with the client exactly what scene elements should be included, and use his or her own words during the scene. For nausea scenes, ask about the client's responses during the first few sessions. This will help you to tailor the scenes for each person. For emotive scenes, it may be helpful to administer the Fear Survey Schedule (Wolpe & Lang, 1969) or the Schedule of Aversive Consequences of Drinking (Miller & Olson, 1982) to help you to design initial scene scripts. In any case, unless you ask direct questions about scenes and use the information to refine scene elements, you will compromise the effectiveness of the sensitization process.

Sensitization Scene Elements

Begin covert sensitization scenes by pairing the drinking and sensitization scene elements. You will present the drinking stimulus portion of each scene exactly as described earlier, but at the point of the first taste, introduce the sensitization scene elements. From that point on, combine elements of the drinking scene, which include the taste and smell of the alcoholic beverage with the sensitization elements of the scene. Continue to mix these elements throughout the entire sensitization scene to ensure a pairing of the client's drinking experiences with discomfort.

Sensitization scene elements are designed to evoke intense responses. Thus, like the drinking stimulus scenes, you should emphasize descriptions of what the client would actually experience in each scene: feelings, sights, sounds, tastes, and smells.

The following is an example of a sensitization scene using the nausea modality.

Tailor these scenes to the individual within the second session to include elements the client provides.

Sample Nausea Sensitization Scene (Follows Drinking Scenes)
You finish the first sip of beer and you can feel the coolness spreading down to your stomach. You notice a funny feeling in your stomach—in fact, it feels a little queasy. You're not sure what is going on, and you think that maybe you're just a little hungry. Maybe another drink will help. You bring the can up to your lips and you feel the coolness against your hand. As you tip it back, you feel the beer pour over your lips and into your mouth, and you start to swallow.

But suddenly, that funny feeling in your stomach is stronger, and you feel like you need to burp. You can feel the belch coming up, and it meets the beer you just swallowed. You swallow again, trying to force it down, but it doesn't work. You can feel the gas coming up, and you can tell there is some liquid with it, some chunks of food. You swallow more, but suddenly your mouth is filled with a sour liquid that burns the back of your throat and goes up your nose.

You feel you have to cough, and you spew the liquid all over the counter and sink. You can tell that it is vomit mixed with the beer, and you can see the chunks of food and brownish vomit all over the counter and top of the beer can. You can smell the sour odor of the beer and the stench of the vomit. Your throat and nose are really burning now. As you feel the puke running down your chin, you try to wipe it off, but that pressure in your stomach is now a nauseous heaving. You feel your stomach contract, and your throat fills with more burning vomit.

You lean over the sink, and your mouth and nose fill with horrible stinging puke, mixed with the taste of beer. Your stomach heaves uncontrollably, and vomit spews out of your mouth into the sink, splashing back up into your face. You can see the chunks of food and the vomit oozing down the drain, and you notice that there are spots of blood in the vomit as well. You try to spit that sour beer and vomit taste out of your mouth, but your stomach won't quit heaving.

Now greenish bile is in your mouth and running into the sink. Your eyes are watering, and your nose and throat are burning. You can still taste the beer, and you try to spit that taste out as well. The stench from the sink is almost unbearable—the sour odor of vomit, half-digested food, and beer. That smell triggers another heave in your stomach, but there is nothing left to come up. Still, your stomach continues to churn and heave.

You may construct sensitization scenes using realistic fears of the results of excessive drinking in a similar manner. Once again, emphasize what the client would *experience*, rather than the stimulus elements of the scene. As before, present the taste and smell of the alcohol beverage throughout the scene.

Sample Emotive Sensitization Scene

You finished that first sip of beer, and now it is a little while later. You have just entered your car and are preparing to back out of the driveway, on your way to the store. With one hand on the hot steering wheel, you reach forward to insert the key in the ignition. As you feel it slide home, you swallow and notice the taste of beer in your mouth. You can smell it, as if you just swallowed a large sip. You turn the key, and the engine surges to life. As you pull the shift lever into reverse, you glance over your shoulder to make sure it is clear behind the car. You press on the accelerator and begin backing out.

Suddenly, there is a blur of motion in the corner of your vision. You jam your foot on the brake as you hear a horrible crunch from behind the car. The car gives a sickening lurch as if you ran over a small bump. The taste of beer is strong in your mouth as you open the door and look toward the back of the car. You are horrified to see a small foot sticking out from behind your rear tire. You jump from the car and run toward that small crumpled body pinned under the rear of your car. You're down on your hands and knees, and as you peer under the car, you can clearly see the blood puddling under the small child's body. There is no movement, and you cannot tell if the child is alive.

The smell of beer is strong on your breath, and the smell mixes with the warm odor of the blood on the ground. You are horrified—you cannot think straight, as you stare at the broken body. You notice that the child's arms are bent unnaturally, and you see the stark white color of bone protruding through the clothing. The sour taste of beer surges into your mouth, and burning fear and horror fills you, as you see the child's limbs give a series of twitches.

Like the drinking scenes, you should make these scenes two to three minutes in length. If you extend beyond this, the client will not be able to sustain a response for the entire period and is likely to become used to the scene, rendering it useless. Within this time constraint, clients will differ as to how quickly they will be able to experience a response, and you should adapt the scene elements accordingly. However, as a general rule, you should initiate the sensitization scene as intensely and rapidly as possible at the first taste of alcohol in the drinking position of the scene.

Record each and every scene on a scene log (as mentioned earlier). This will allow you to monitor the progress of conditioning and to aid in determining the appropriate time to switch from pairing to escape and to avoidance phases.

ADMINISTERING COVERT SENSITIZATION

Pairing Phase

Session One

In the first session, elicit the full cooperation of the client. It is important to explain clearly the goal of treatment, emphasizing that covert sensitization is designed specifically to reduce urges or desire to drink by pairing drinking with uncomfortable feelings in imagination. Also spend some time helping the client understand how imagination alters feelings, possibly through some examples (imagining biting into a lemon or eating a favorite food results in an increase in saliva).

While explaining the procedure for imagining the scenes, emphasize the client's need to *experience* the scenes for effective treatment, as well as the need for him or her to suggest changes in the scenes to enhance vividness. Emphasize that the treatment is a cooperative effort to build scenes that the client finds effective. It is important to minimize the demand characteristics of the procedures as well. To accomplish this, avoid telling the client to expect that he or she will begin to automatically experience an aversion response to the imagery of drinking. Toward these ends, it may be helpful to describe the client's aversion response simply as "discomfort" and to suggest that he or she reports it *whenever* it occurs. A useful method for signaling is the raising of a number of fingers of the dominant hand: one finger for the first indication of any discomfort, two fingers for moderate discomfort, three fingers for severe discomfort, and four fingers for very severe discomfort. Ask the client to hold the appropriate number of fingers elevated until you touch his or her hand. This ensures that you see the signal.

During the first session, gather specific information about drinking settings, preferred beverages, and other data relevant to the client's drinking behavior. If this session was preceded by a structured interview (e.g., the Comprehensive Drinker Profile), you need only fill in any gaps in the prepared script. You should also use the initial session to gather specifics for the sensitization scenes. Regardless of the type of sensitization to be used, find out which descriptors the client would actually use, rather than your interpretation of his or her feelings. Fine-tune these points in the next several sessions.

Session Two

Starting with the second session, present the pairing scenes. To prepare the client for the imagery, do a brief relaxation exercise (approximately five minutes) at the start of the session(s). This serves to decrease distractions and to focus him or her on the imagery process. Relaxation can include breathing exercises, components of progressive muscle relaxation, or both. If you use physiological monitoring equipment, you must first extinguish any response the client has to the drinking scenes alone. Do not use any aversive imagery at this time, and explain this to the client in advance. Present only the drinking scene components. Without this step, physiological equipment is useless in determining the beginning of an aversion response since a client's anticipatory responses may appear identical to aversion responses. During this process, you must present each drinking scene to be used until no response is noted on the monitoring equipment. You may also use this time to intensify the vividness and realism of the drinking scenes through inquiry. When this process is used on an outpatient basis, there is some concern in letting the client leave after vividly imagining drinking alcohol without any aversive imagery. Thus, extend this "extinction" session up to two hours, and terminate with the presentation of at least three pairing scenes.

If no physiological monitoring equipment is to be used, begin presenting both drinking and sensitization scene components. It is important in this session to introduce the client to the use of imagery, and to assist him or her in overcoming blocks to vivid and realistic imagination. When presenting the scenes, instruct the client to use *active* imagination, as if he or she were really there, seeing the scene through his or her own eyes, experiencing tastes, smells, temperature, sounds, and feelings. This means that the client should not "picture" the scene as if he or she were watching it on television but should attempt to experience the physical sensations he or she would have if the scene were real.

Present the scenes at a slow, relaxed, yet deliberate pace while the client reclines in a comfortable chair with his or her eyes closed. It is *vital* to emphasize the sensory aspects of the scenes, especially taste and swallowing when describing the actual consumption of the alcohol. Throughout each of the scenes, continue to use descriptions of what the client would experience, rather than simply descriptions of the scene itself.

Continuing the Pairing Phase

The initial goal of the pairing phase is to obtain a *response* from the client during the sensitization portion of the scenes. The presence of a response during the presentation of the sensitization scene is called an *unconditioned response*. If no unconditioned response is noted within the first four scenes, you may need to radically alter sensitization scene elements to produce the realism necessary to get a response. Should this occur, stop the presentation process and ask the client to help you modify the sensitization scenes.

Present the *entire* sensitization scene portion when in the pairing phase. Some therapists are tempted to begin terminating the sensitization portion as soon as their client exhibits a significant unconditioned response. This is likely to be counterproductive. Intensifying the client's response ensures that it will become associated with the imagery of drinking. However, with some rare clients, you must walk a fine line between sufficiently intensifying the scene and terminating prior to actual vomiting.

After presenting any scene in which the client has exhibited a response, pause for several minutes to allow the responses to diminish prior to initiating the next scene. This is especially important when using physiological monitoring, to allow the readings to stabilize or return to baseline.

What Is a Response?

Preliminary research relied primarily on the self-report of the client to determine the presence of discomfort. However, this appears inadequate and does not control for the demand characteristics of the procedures. Researchers now employ client self-report, behavioral observations, and physiological monitoring equipment. We suggest that you use the following guidelines, which have been used in research at the University of New Mexico. They allow you to determine more reliably a client's response:

- *Self-Report*: A finger signal of 2 (moderate discomfort) or more
- *Behavioral Observations:* Noticeable choking, coughing, gagging, eyes watering, grimacing, moaning, gasping, panting, swallowing or burping
- *Physiological Monitoring*:
    Skin Conductance Level: An increase of at least five microsiemens relative to baseline.

Skin Conductance Response: Two discrete phasic changes of at least 0.3 microsiemen within 10 seconds
Heart Rate: A change of at least four beats per minute relative to baseline
Respiration: A change in breaths per minute or amplitude of breath of at least 30% relative to baseline

It is not necessary for changes to occur in each of the three areas for a significant response. A useful criterion includes a change on one physiological measure and a response on either the self-report or behavioral observations. If the client appears to be responding on physiological measures or showing behavioral signs, but is not indicating discomfort through the finger signals, spend a few moments between scenes to discuss the self-report signals and ask about his or her subjective experience.

Transition to Escape Phase

Continue presenting the drinking and sensitization scenes together in order to strengthen the client's response. The ultimate goal of the pairing phase is to establish a conditioned response to drinking stimuli. When these responses begin occurring *during the drinking scene, prior to beginning the presentation of the sensitization scene*, a conditioned response has occurred. This is an important event. Thus, you should present pairing scenes until one of the following occurs:

1. Until four scenes have been presented with no (unconditioned) response at all—As mentioned above, stop the presentation procedure, inquire about vividness and realism, then modify and intensify the scenes. Then continue within the pairing phase until one of the following occurs.

1a. If no *unconditioned response* occurs within 12 scenes, even with intensification of the sensitization scene, terminate treatment within this sensitization modality with an avoidance scene. Research indicates that if an unconditioned response is to occur, it will occur within this period (Elkins, 1980). Continued presentation of the scenes within the pairing phase is unlikely to result in an unconditioned response. However, at this time you can switch to another sensitization modality. Thus, if you tried nausea, you may try assisted nausea or construct sensitization scenes based on emotive elements. Apply the same criteria for termination of pairing.

1b. If an *unconditioned response* occurs, but a *conditioned response* is never established, terminate treatment after 40 scenes or six to eight sessions (if a conditioned response is to occur, it will occur within this period). This is based on Elkins's (1980) research, confirmed in pilot work at the University of New Mexico. Make the final scene an avoidance scene (see below) to enhance the introduction of nondrinking behavior.

2. If a *conditioned response* occurs, begin alternating escape scenes and pairing scenes (see Figure 8.1).

The Escape Phase

Begin *escape* scenes in the same manner as pairing scenes. The drinking scene elements are initially identical, but at the sign of a significant response from the client, introduce *aversion relief*, and never begin the sensitization scene. The goal of the escape phase is to allow the client to remove himself or herself from the drinking setting (e.g., leaving the bar, pouring out the drink) and thus avoid intensification of the aversive response.

The aversion relief elements will not always be identical, and you will need to adjust them to fit into the scene the client is imagining. Always include statements about feelings of relief and self-confidence. Here is an example of an aversion-relief statement:

> You feel the glass in your hand—the moisture of the condensation against your palm. You can smell the tartness of the orange juice and the heavy aroma of the vodka. You can almost taste the drink in your mouth—the coolness, the sweetness. You bring the glass up to your lips, but suddenly you think: What am I doing? I don't want this drink at all—in fact, I don't even like the smell! You pour the drink into the sink, and you can see the orange juice, the vodka, and the ice cubes swirling down the drain. You feel a sense of relief, a good feeling as you rinse the glass. You're not quite sure why, but you feel happy and confident about yourself.

Introduce aversion relief elements (during the escape phase) at the occurrence of a *significant* client response. If signs of a response appear but are not significant (e.g., only a 1 finger signal or a finger signal of 2 but no physiological change), prolong the drinking stimulus portion of the scene to intensify the response. However, if a significant response does not occur, or if you inadvertently begin describing actual alcohol consumption, continue through to the sensitization portion, and present the entire sensitization scene to more firmly establish conditioned responding. In other words, if you do not get a conditioned response or begin to describe actual drinking, switch from an escape scene to a pairing scene.

Transition to Avoidance Phase

1. Once consistent conditioned responding during the escape phase is noted (conditioned responses on three consecutive pairing or escape scenes), present an avoidance scene (see Figure 8.1).
2. If, at any point, the conditioned response does not appear, return to the pairing phase, intensifying the sensitization scene. When a conditioned response is reestablished, reapply the above criteria.

Avoidance Phase

The goal in the avoidance phase is to remove the client from the imagined drinking setting *prior* to a full conditioned response. This will require you to monitor and record the point in the presentation of the scene at which the client initiates a full conditioned response within each scene. Then, just prior to that critical point, introduce the aversion-relief element. Construct the aversion-relief element in the same way as you did in the escape phase.

Occasionally, a client will not consistently exhibit a conditioned response at the same point in a drinking scene, making it difficult to predict the appropriate time for an aversion-relief element. In such a case, as soon as he or she exhibits a response that is *not* significant (a finger signal of only 1 or a finger signal of 2 without a physiological change), immediately introduce the aversion-relief element. This allows the client to remove himself or herself from the drinking scene without experiencing any significant aversive responses.

Transition to Follow-Up

1. Terminate treatment with the presentation of an avoidance scene following the second block of three consecutive conditioned responses (see Figure 8.1).
2. In any event, discontinue treatment after 50 scenes (with scene 50 being an avoidance scene). Covert sensitization is not likely to be any more effective beyond 50 scene presentations.

When doing covert sensitization, meet with the client often to ensure maintenance of the imagery skills and the conditioning. We schedule two 60-minute sessions per week and think this is the minimum effective frequency. With each scene being a maximum of 8 minutes, it is possible to include six to eight scenes per session, including time for inquiry. Thus, it is rare for treatment to extend beyond eight sessions, or four weeks. If the sessions are scheduled more frequently, treatment will be significantly shorter.

Use follow-up meetings and booster sessions to reinforce the conditioned aversion. We recommend monthly sessions for six months to maintain the effect of conditioning on suppressing urges to drink. Include problem-solving and coping strategies in the follow-up sessions to help clients generalize gains made in treatment to their daily life.

EFFECTIVENESS

The outcome literature for aversion therapies in general is encouraging. Evaluations of chemical aversion therapy have been reported for more than 50 years, with consistently high rates of abstinence (Elkins, 1991; Howard, Elkins, Rimmele, & Smith, 1991; Miller & Hester, 1980). Controlled evaluations are few, but point to higher rates of abstinence among patients receiving chemical aversion than among those in comparison groups, at least over the six months following treatment (Boland, Mellor, & Revusky, 1978; Cannon, Baker, & Wehl, 1981). Dale Cannon's research also supports a relationship between the establishment of a conditioned aversion to alcohol and successful abstinence (Cannon et al., 1981; Cannon, Baker, Gino, & Nathan, 1986).

Controlled studies of the effectiveness of covert sensitization offer mixed results. An early study reported that 40% of the clients receiving covert sensitization were abstinent at six months, whereas none of the control group were abstinent (Ashem & Donner, 1968). Similarly, Maletzky (1974) reported that clients undergoing covert sensitization fared better than those randomly assigned to a halfway house program.

Comparative evaluations of covert sensitization have offered somewhat different results. In one study, sensitization resulted in a 74% improvement rate, which was better than that resulting from electrical aversion but poorer than that for family counseling or desensitization (Hedberg & Campbell, 1974). Similarly, Olson, Ganley, Devine, and Dorsey (1981) found that when used as an adjunct to milieu therapy, covert sensitization did not result in different abstinent rates than transactional analysis, which was also provided as an adjunct to milieu therapy.

Two other studies failed to find covert sensitization to be more effective than problem-solving therapy, desensitization, or insight therapy (Fleiger & Zingle, 1973; Piorkorsky & Mann, 1975), although high dropout rates in the latter study make interpretation of the results problematic.

The methodological analysis of the alcohol treatment outcome literature presented earlier in this edition (see Chapter 2) shows a small literature with mixed results. However, positive cumulative evidence scores for both nausea-based aversion therapy as well as covert sensitization appear. Other methods of aversion therapy show less positive evidence scores (apneic, electrical/faradic aversion therapy).

As we alluded to earlier, these results are confusing. On the one hand covert sensitization appears to be responsible for 40% abstinent rates and 74% improvement, while on the other hand, it is no better than milieu therapy. One reason for these inconsistencies may be the lack of a uniform set of procedures used in "covert sensitization." Studies that have carefully defined sensitization procedures and have documented the occurrence of classical conditioning have shown the most encouraging results. Elkins (Elkins, 1980; Elkins & Murdock, 1977) was the first to demonstrate a relationship between the establishment of a conditioned aversion response and the effectiveness of covert sensitization with alcoholics. Similarly, Miller and Dougher (1984) found that conditioning appeared to play a role in outcome for those clients receiving nausea aversion, whereas conditioning did not appear to play as strong a role for clients receiving covert sensitization using plausible negative consequences of drinking.

Thus, research suggests that when the procedures for covert sensitization are well defined, this treatment can result in a significant reduction in drinking behavior at least for a period of months. However, as suggested by Nathan (1976), unidimensional treatments often do not continue to remain effective without booster sessions. It appears that covert sensitization is an effective way to modify desire for alcohol, but it may be most effective when combined with other problem-solving forms of treatment designed to provide alternative coping strategies. In fact, covert sensitization may be most appropriate as an adjunct to a multimodal approach to treatment, with the goal of covert sensitization to reduce or eliminate urges to drink (which may be strongest early in the treatment process). The literature also suggests that conditioning is a good predictor of effectiveness, at least with nausea conditioning, and should be corroborated with some form of psychophysiological assessment.

REFERENCES

Treatment Procedures

Ashem, B., & Donner, L. (1968). Covert sensitization with alcoholics: A controlled replication. *Behaviour Research and Therapy, 6,* 7–12. This is a well-controlled study describing individualized procedures for using covert sensitization with inpatient alcoholics. It also addresses such issues as forward versus backward conditioning.

Elkins, R. L. (1980). Covert sensitization and alcoholism: Contributions of successful conditioning to subsequent abstinence maintenance. *Addictive Behaviors, 5,* 67–89. This article describes in detail Elkins's procedures for conducting covert sensitization with inpatient alcoholics.

Maletzky, B. M. (1974). Assisted covert sensitization for drug abuse. *The International Journal of the Addictions, 9,* 411–429. This article briefly describes the manner in which an odor assist is integrated with covert sensitization with outpatients.

Miller, W. R., & Dougher, M. J. (1986). Covert sensitization in alcoholism treatment. Unpublished manual. This manual outlines the procedures used in applying covert sensitization in a research setting at the University of New Mexico. Copies may be obtained by writing William R. Miller, Ph.D., Department of Psychology, University of New Mexico, Albuquerque, NM 87131.

Treatment Research

Ashem, B., & Donner, L. (1968). Covert sensitization with alcoholics: A controlled replication. *Behaviour Research and Therapy, 6,* 7–12.

Baker, T. B., & Cannon, D. S. (1979). Taste aversion therapy with alcoholics: Techniques and evidence of a conditioned response. *Behaviour Research and Therapy, 17,* 299–242.

Boland, F. J., Mellor, C. S., & Revusky, S. (1978). Chemical aversion treatment of alcoholism: Lithium as the aversive agent. *Behaviour Research and Therapy, 16,* 401–409.

Cannon, D. S., Baker, T. B., Gino, A., & Nathan, P. E. (1986). Alcohol-aversion theory: Relationship between strength of aversion and abstinence. *Journal of Consulting and Clinical Psychology, 54,* 825–830.

Cannon, D. S., Baker, T. B., & Wehl, C. K. (1981). Emetic and electric shock alcohol aversion therapy: Six- and twelve-month follow-up. *Journal of Consulting and Clinical Psychology, 49,* 360–368.

Cautela, J. R. (1966). Treatment of compulsive behavior by covert sensitization. *Psychological Record, 16,* 33–41.

Cautela, J. R. (1967). Covert sensitization. *Psychological Reports, 20,* 459–468.

Cautela, J. R. (1970). The treatment of alcoholism by covert sensitization. *Psychotherapy: Theory, Research and Practice, 7,* 86–90.

Cautela, J. R., & Baron, M. G. (1977). Covert conditioning: A theoretical analysis. *Behavior Modification, 1,* 351–368.

Clarke, J. C., & Hayes, D. (1984). Covert sensitization, stimulus relevance and the equipotentiality premise. *Behavior Research and Therapy, 22,* 451–454.

Dougher, M. J., Crossen, J. R., & Garland, R. (1986). An experimental test of Cautela's operant explanation of covert conditioning procedures. *Behavioral Psychotherapy, 14,* 226–248.

Elkins, R. L. (1980). Covert sensitization and alcoholism: Contributions of successful conditioning to subsequent abstinence maintenance. *Addictive Behaviors, 5,* 67–89.

Elkins, R. L. (1991a). An appraisal of chemical aversion (emetic therapy) approaches to alcoholism treatment. *Behavior Research and Therapy, 29,* 387–413.

Elkins, R. L. (1991b). Chemical aversion treatment of alcoholism: Further comments. *Behavior Research and Therapy, 29,* 421–428.

Elkins, R. L., & Murdock, R. P. (1977). The contribution of successful conditioning to abstinence maintenance following covert sensitization (verbal aversion) treatment of alcoholism. *IRCS Medical Science: Psychology & Psychiatry: Social & Occupational Medicine, 5,* 167.

Fleiger, D. L., & Zingle, H. W. (1973). Covert sensitization treatment with alcoholics. *Canadian Counsellor, 7,* 269–277.

Hedberg, A. G., & Campbell, L. M. (1974). A comparison of four behavioral treatment approaches to alcoholism. *Journal of Behavior Therapy and Experimental Psychiatry, 5,* 251–256.

Howard, M. O., Elkins, R. L., Rimmele, C. T., & Smith, J. W. (1991). Chemical aversion treatment of alcohol dependence. *Drug and Alcohol Dependence, 29,* 101–143.

Kantorovich, N. (1929). An attempt at curing alcoholism by associated reflexes. Abstract published in *Behavioral Abstracts, 4* (4282), 1930.

Lang, P. J., Kozak, M. J., Miller, G. A., Levin, D. N., & McLean, A. (1980). Emotional imagery: Conceptual structure and pattern of somato-visceral response. *Psychophysiology, 17,* 179–192.

Little, L, M., & Curran, J. P. (1978). Covert sensitization: A clinical procedure in need of some explanations. *Psychological Bulletin, 85,* 513–531.

Maletzky, B. M. (1974). Assisted covert sensitization for drug abuse. *The International Journal of the Addictions, 9,* 411–429.

Marlatt, G., & Miller, W. R. (1984). *The Comprehensive Drinker Profile.* Odessa, FL: Psychological Assessment Resources.

Miller, W. R., Brown, J. M., Simpson, T. S., Handmaker, N. S., Bien, T. H., Luckie, L. F., Montgomery, H. A., Hester, R. K., & Tonigan, J. S. (1995). What works? A methodological analysis of the alcohol treatment outcome literature. In R. K. Hester & W. R. Miller (Eds.), *Handbook of alcoholism treatment approaches* (2nd ed.). (pp. 12–44). Boston: Allyn and Bacon.

Miller, W. R., & Dougher, M. J. (1984). Covert sensitization: Alternative treatment procedures for alcoholics. *Alcoholism: Clinical and Experimental Research, 8,* 108.

Miller, W. R., & Hester, R. K. (1986). The effectiveness of alcoholism treatment methods: What research reveals. In W. R. Miller & N. Heather (Eds.), *Treating addictive behaviors: Processes of change.* New York: Plenum.

Miller, W. R., & Muñoz, R. (1982). *How to control your drinking* (Rev. ed.). Albuquerque: University of New Mexico Press.

Miller, W. R., & Olson, J. (1982). *Schedule of aversive consequences of drinking.* Albuquerque, NM: Department of Psychology, University of New Mexico.

Nathan, P. E. (1976). In H. Leitenberg (Ed.), *Handbook of behavior modification and behavior therapy.* Englewood Cliffs, NJ: Prentice-Hall.

Nathan, P. E. (1985). Aversion therapy in the treatment of alcoholism: Success and failure. *Annals of the New York Academy of Science, 443,* 357–364.

Olson, R. P., Ganley, R., Devine, V. T., & Dorsey, G. C., Jr. (1981). Long-term effects of behavioral versus insight-oriented therapy with inpatient alcoholics. *Journal of Consulting and Clinical Psychology, 49,* 866–877.

Piorkorsky, G. K., & Mann, E. T. (1975). Issues in treatment efficacy research with alcoholics. *Perceptual and Motor Skills, 41,* 695–700.

Quinn, J. T., & Henbest, R. (1967). Partial failure of generalization in alcoholics following aversion therapy. *Quarterly Journal of Studies on Alcohol, 28,* 70–75.

Smith, R., & Gregory, P. (1976). Covert sensitization by induced anxiety in the treatment of an alcoholic. *Journal of Behavioral Therapy and Experimental Psychiatry, 7,* 31–33.

Wilson, G. T. (1987). Chemical aversion conditioning as a treatment for alcoholism: A re-analysis. *Behavior Research and Therapy, 25,* 503–576.

Wolpe, J., & Lang, P. L. (1969). *Fear survey schedule.* San Diego, CA: Educational and Industrial Testing Service.

CHAPTER 9

Behavioral Self-Control Training

Reid K. Hester

OVERVIEW

Behavioral self-control training (BSCT) is a treatment approach used to pursue either a goal of abstinence or a goal of moderate and nonproblematic drinking. It consists of behavioral techniques of goal setting, self-monitoring, managing consumption, rewarding goal attainment, functionally analyzing drinking situations, and learning alternate coping skills. It is educational in that the therapist introduces specific components, one at a time, and assigns "homework" tasks between sessions. The client maintains primary responsibility for making decisions throughout the training.

Research shows that BSCT can be either self-directed (with a self-help manual) or therapist directed. In general, controlled outcome research has not found a difference in outcome based on whether the treatment is self-directed or therapist directed. There are, however, therapist characteristics associated with better outcomes than self-directed change. (I will discuss this in the next section.) BSCT can also be conducted in group format. In our clinic, we conduct therapist-directed treatment in groups of 8 to 10, which meet weekly for 90 minutes for eight weeks. In the self-directed format, the

client works with minimal therapist consultation, using a self-help manual. Periodic follow-ups are advisable.

SPECIAL CONSIDERATIONS

Because BSCT has most often been offered with a goal of "controlled drinking," it has been a controversial procedure. In fact, the principles of BSCT may be used to pursue a goal of total abstinence (e.g., Graber & Miller, 1988; Sanchez-Craig, Annis, Bornet, & MacDonald, 1984). It is appropriate here, however, to consider briefly the treatment issue of moderation as a goal of change.

There is little question that following treatment for alcohol problems, some clients do achieve and maintain moderate and problem-free drinking outcomes (Heather & Robertson, 1983). Although treatment with a goal of moderation has been controversial, researchers have extensively studied its effectiveness. BSCT appears to yield success rates comparable to treatments with a goal of abstinence. Current data suggest that moderation is most successful with clients who, at the beginning of treatment, were experiencing less severe alcohol problems and dependence. Abstinence is a more stable outcome among more severe alcohol dependent clients.

There are several reasons for offering an intervention with a goal of moderation. First, some clients refuse to consider abstinence without at least a reasonable trial at achieving moderation. Writers, beginning with Marty Mann (1950), have often suggested that such persons should try to control their drinking as way of discovering whether abstinence is necessary for them. The "Big Book" of Alcoholics Anonymous (1976) contains a number of references to moderate drinking and suggests people try it to see whether they can achieve it. Second, if you work with a client and he or she is unsuccessful in moderating drinking, you have already developed a therapeutic relationship and may be in a better position to help him or her pursue abstinence. Third, if the client achieves moderation, you will have been successful with relatively brief treatment. Fourth, as will be discussed later, many people who moderate their drinking eventually shift to abstinence.

Another reason to consider a moderation-goal option is that you can attract and treat a broader range of drinkers with alcohol problems. Epidemiological data suggest that within the general population there are far more problem drinkers than severely dependent alcoholics (Cahalan, 1987; Moore & Gerstein, 1981). This problem drinker population has been largely ignored or at least underserved (Institute of Medicine, 1990). Less severe problem drinkers (and those who do not consider themselves alcoholics or problem drinkers) are more likely to accept services when goals other than lifelong abstinence are possible (see Chapter 5 on motivation). To offer only one alternative, total abstention, is to turn away a large population in need of services.

Data on the characteristics of clients who are most likely to benefit from BSCT are somewhat mixed (Rosenberg, 1993). The most consistent characteristics, however, are a shorter duration of problem drinking and less severe dependence and problems (Miller & Hester, 1986b). Several studies have also found women to be more successful than men in maintaining moderation following BSCT. Conversely, research has noted relatively little success in teaching moderation to severely dependent alcoholics. You may find it helpful to distinguish, in your own mind, between problem drinkers and alcoholics, viewing abstinence as the only ultimately feasible goal for the latter. This distinction, though an oversimplification, is generally consistent with the matching data.

Situations arise where an evaluation suggests that a client has a low probability of succeeding with a goal of moderation, but he or she wishes to pursue it anyway. In those cases, where we disagree with a client's desire to pursue a goal of moderation, we negotiate a contract. We agree to work with the client for six to eight weeks, providing them training in BSCT. We agree, however, that if at the end of that time the client is still having difficulty drinking moderately, he or she will consider a goal of abstinence. If a client has not been successful by the end of training, the chances of success in the future are not good. This prediction is based on data from Miller and colleagues' long-term follow-up of clients who received BSCT (Miller, Leckman, Delaney, & Tinkcom, 1992). We have yet to have a client refuse to enter into this contract or refuse to pursue a goal of abstinence if he or she is unsuccessful with BSCT.

Other contraindications to pursuing a goal of moderation include pregnancy or trying to become pregnant, medical or psychological problems that are worsened by any drinking, and strong family pressures for the client to abstain.

Another consideration is the choice of therapists to conduct BSCT. As will be discussed in the section on effectiveness, there is some evidence that empathic therapists enhance BSCT outcomes.

Before you begin BSCT, ask yourself whether the client might benefit as much from a brief intervention and self-help instructions (see Chapter 6). Providing a comprehensive assessment and personalized feedback in a motivational interviewing style may be sufficient for many clients. BSCT would then be a contingency option in the event that the brief intervention was not sufficient to affect drinking behavior and alcohol related problems. This assumes, of course, that you follow clients with whom you have done brief interventions.

Before you begin treatment, it is important to emphasize to clients that BSCT is not an effective approach for everyone. Clients need to know that alternatives do exist and that you will continue to work with them if they are not successful with this approach. If this occurs, it is best to interpret the failure as a lack of an appropriate match between the client and treatment. Explaining a failure in this way will help to maintain motivation for change in the client. Then collaborate with the client in choosing a treatment approach with a goal of abstinence.

There are a few items that make it easier to provide BSCT. At our clinic, we have a computer software program that prints out personalized blood alcohol concentration (BAC) tables (see clinical references section). We also print quantities of self-monitoring cards on card stock paper, cut them out, and distribute them to clients. An example self-monitoring card is presented in Table 9.1. Finally, we use client summary sheets to keep track of total number of drinks per week, estimated peak BACs, and the number of drinks over how many hours to achieve peak BACs for the week.

Although we prefer to conduct BSCT in groups (a more cost-effective mode), occasionally clients will ask for individual treatment. When working with individuals, we see them weekly for 45 to 50 minutes for eight weeks. We conduct monthly follow-ups for six months following the end of treatment. Clients view follow-ups as a type of caring, additional treatment. Follow-ups also give you valuable information for program evaluation and help you decide which clients may need additional interventions.

DESCRIPTION

There are various protocols for BSCT. Although we use the Miller and Muñoz (1982) manual, *How to Control Your Drinking*, there are other good manuals: Robertson and Heather's (1986) *Let's Drink to Your Health*, Sanchez-Craig's (1993) *Saying When: How to Quit Drinking or Cut Down*, and Sobell and Sobell's (1993) *Problem Drinkers: Guided Self-Change Treatment*. Sanchez-Craig's manual is the basis for a new program called Drinkwise. Drinkwise is a commercial program that markets a comprehen-sive package of screening, assessment, BSCT training, follow-up, and quality-assurance materials. Another alternative protocol under development is an interactive computer software program that trains clients in BSCT (Hester, 1994).

As we have offered it, BSCT involves eight steps that occur in the following order:

1. Setting limits on the number of drinks per day and on peak BACs
2. Self-monitoring of drinking behaviors
3. Changing the rate of drinking
4. Practicing assertiveness in refusing drinks
5. Setting up a reward system for achievement of goals
6. Learning which antecedents result in over-drinking and which in moderation
7. Learning other coping skills instead of drinking
8. Learning how to avoid relapsing back into heavy drinking

The remainder of this section explains these steps in detail.

Setting Limits

To set limits, you first have to agree on what constitutes a "drink." Our group uses the convention that defines one drink or SEC (standard ethanol content) as $1/2$ ounce of pure ethanol (Miller, Heather, & Hall, 1991). That is the amount of alcohol in each of the following:

Table 9.1 Self-Monitoring Card

	DATE	DAY	TIME	DRINK TYPE	AMOUNT	STD. DRINKS	WHERE	WITH WHOM
1								
2								
3								
4								
5								
6								
7								
8								

1 oz. of 100-proof distilled spirits

1.25 oz. of 80-proof distilled spirits

2.5 oz. of fortified wine (20% alcohol)

4 oz. of table wine (12% alcohol)

10 oz. of beer (5% alcohol)

Here is the formula for calculating the number of SECs in a drink. It is the number of ounces of beverage times the proportion of alcohol times two. For example 12 ounces of 5% beer is 1.2 SECs ($12 \times .05 \times 2 = 1.2$). The easiest way for clients to learn how to calculate SECs is by giving them sample problems and having them work through the formula. We always define a "drink" as 1 SEC.

When clients are learning how to calculate SECs, they will realize that they often do not know how much alcohol is in a particular drink. It becomes, then, their responsibility to find out how much alcohol is in a particular drink. Problem solving and role-playing are often helpful here to help the clients learn how to get this information, especially when they are drinking at a bar. We role-play a variety of situations with the therapist asking about alcohol content in drinks.

To help clients choose their limits, we provide information on the behavioral effects of different BAC levels in persons without significant tolerance to alcohol. We also give them data on the rates of consumption in the U.S. adult population (Cahalan, 1987) and the relationship between consumption levels and health risks (Klatsky, Friedman, & Giegelaub, 1981; Saunders & Aasland, 1987). With this information in mind, clients choose two sets of limits: a regular and an absolute limit. The regular limit is the number of drinks and a peak BAC the client does not want to exceed during an average day. The absolute limits are usually a little higher and are for special occasions. Both sets of limits include a maximum number of drinks per day and a maximum peak BAC. We encourage clients to set a limit on the total number of drinks per week. As a weekly goal, we recommend that males and females set it at or below 12 and 7 drinks, respectively. While acknowledging that there is no "safe" level of drinking, when drinking exceeds 3 drinks per day, negative health consequences increase dramatically (Klatsky et al., 1981; Saunders & Aasland, 1987). Finally, we encourage clients not to drink daily.

It is important to help clients set realistic goals. If a client's estimated pretreatment peak BAC for a typical week is 250 mg%, it may be un-realistic to set a BAC limit of 40 mg% as the first goal. For such clients, setting intermediate goals, increases the chance of initial success that will help to maintain their motivation. Once clients have met intermediate goals then they can shoot for lower levels of drinking.

Self-Monitoring

An important step in BSCT is the self-monitoring of drinking. Give your clients enough cards to last for several weeks, and provide additional cards as needed. Emphasize that they should fill out the information on each drink before they begin to drink it. Self-monitoring directs their attention to their drinking and reminds them that they are trying to moderate their consumption. The information includes the date, time, drink type (e.g., beer, scotch), amount of alcohol in the drink, place of drinking, and with whom they are drinking. As they write down the data on each drink, it brings to their attention how long it has been since their last drink and how many drinks they have already had that day. If clients realize they are not self-monitoring when they are drinking, we ask them to reconstruct their drinking pattern and then go on, rather than to forget the whole matter for the rest of the day. Similarly, if a client realizes that she or he has forgotten to self-monitor the previous day, it is better late than never to attempt to reconstruct the drinking behavior. In practice, however, this does not occur too often. Once clients have self-monitored for several weeks, it becomes a habit.

Besides showing clients how to fill out the self-monitoring cards, address the problems they anticipate experiencing in making this a regular habit. Some clients will anticipate embarrassment or anxiety at the idea of self-monitoring. Role-playing appropriate responses is helpful. Clients will often need a range of responses to the questions of others. Some responses may be humorous (e.g., "I'm working for the CIA and taking notes on some suspects at the end of the bar"), while others may be more direct and assertive (e.g., "It's none of your business" or "I'm trying to cut down on my drinking and am keeping track of my drinks"). You can assure them that they will become more comfortable in responding to others after they have done it for a week or two. Incidentally, we often hear from clients that their good friends are supportive of their efforts. On the other hand, some of their "drinking buddies" who are not good friends may continue to hassle them about self-monitoring. Perceptive clients will see that their "drinking buddies" feel threatened by their efforts to reduce their consumption.

Self-monitoring also often results in clients making other realizations about their drinking. While you address many of these concerns at different times during the program, it is important to acknowledge these realizations as they occur and help your clients understand how such knowledge fits into the overall pattern of their drinking. As an example, Joan might realize that she always overdrinks at the Watering Hole but rarely does so at the King's Pub. Armed with this knowledge, she might choose not to go to the Watering Hole. She might try doing different activities if she goes there, sitting in a different place, or visiting with people other than her usual companions. She might also try to strictly limit the amount of time she spends there by scheduling other activities around her drinking.

Goal setting and self-monitoring is usually covered in the first session. At the beginning of the second and subsequent sessions, we have the clients report to the group their total SECs for the previous week and their peak BACs. This allows peer pressure to come into play, and clients who are making progress often receive quite a bit of support for their efforts from other group members. Spouses can also attend the group and provide reinforcement and support for moderation.

Rate Control

Once clients have self-monitored their drinking for a week and have set limits for themselves, they are then ready to try some different strategies to control their rate of drinking. We encourage clients to try each different strategy and find out which one(s) works best for them.

The first strategy is to switch from stronger to weaker drinks. Rather than drinking hard liquor straight or on ice, switch to highballs (1 ounce of liquor with a glass of mixer). If clients drink more than 1 ounce of hard liquor in a drink, have them reduce it to that amount. (By now they should know how much alcohol is in a given drink even if it is served to them in a bar.) Warn clients about having drinks that are very tasty and sweet and/or where the amount of alcohol is masked. These kinds of drinks are usually consumed quickly. Encourage them to switch to different drinks. Clients often report that they drink some drinks more slowly than others. While they may have a really favorite drink, switching to a less favored drink that goes down more slowly will help them control their rate of drinking. This can be especially helpful for beer drinkers. Switching from their favorite beer to a different type of beer or to wine can help if they drink it more slowly.

Another tactic to reduce consumption has to do with sipping. Many heavy drinkers tend to gulp their drinks with little time between gulps. To change these behaviors, they first need to self-monitor how many sips they take of a drink and how long they wait between sips. They can then try to increase the number of sips per drink to 12. This strategy, however, should also include a spacing of sips across time, lest the clients compensate by sipping faster! A good target to shoot for is 60 seconds between sips. By timing themselves, they can get a "feel" for this rate of sipping. It is also helpful to put the glass down between sips.

Spacing drinks across time is probably the most frequently used tactic. Have your clients calculate how many drinks they can have over a four-hour period given the regular and absolute BAC limits they have set for themselves. By dividing this number of drinks into four hours, or 240 minutes, they can figure the average and minimum length of time between drinks to keep their BACs within their limits. Ways to increase the time between drinks include sipping smaller amounts with more time between sips, allowing time to pass between finishing one drink and starting another, having a nonalcoholic drink between drinks, and adding ice or additional mixer to the drink to keep it cool and make it last longer.

Drink Refusal

At some point, most clients will have to decline offers of additional drinks, either because they have reached their limit or because they are spacing their drinks out across time. For many of your clients, it is not sufficient to tell them to "just say no!" Instead, provide them with training in assertiveness skills. Illustrate the verbal and nonverbal components of assertiveness with role-playing. Put yourself in the "hot seat" and have a group of clients pressure you to drink while you assertively refuse. Then go back and point out the various components of eye contact, body language, voice tone and volume, in addition to the verbal content. Next, go around the group and have each client describe the setting in which they have had or might have the greatest difficulty refusing drinks. Then role-play that scene with others from the group. After each role-play, have group members provide feedback on what the person did well and what aspects need improvement. If a client does poorly during role-play, we ask him or her to practice during the week with friends or family. We then give that client another chance to role-play during the next session. The improvement is usually noticeable.

Researchers who have done drink refusal training with a goal of maintaining abstinence have found that the longer a client takes to respond to social pressure to drink, the more likely he or she will resume drinking after treatment. We give clients this information and encourage them to think ahead so that they can have a preplanned response. For more information on drink refusal training, see Chapter 13.

Setting Up Reward Systems for Success

As clients progress toward their goals, we encourage them to set up a reward system for achieving their goals. Congratulatory self-talk is important after even a minor victory. Assure them that they are not crazy for talking to themselves. Encourage them to give themselves a pat on the back for refusing a drink or keeping their BACs within their limits.

It is also helpful to use tangible, tailor-made rewards given as soon as possible after the achievement. *Tailor-made* means that the rewards are satisfying and pleasurable to the individual client. (Clearly, this means that the clients need to choose their own rewards.) Finally, the rewards need to be readily accessible. A trip to Hawaii next year for success this week is not a timely reward. Rewards involving time (especially for busy clients) might include an hour of doing absolutely nothing or taking the time to read a favorite book.

If a client develops a set of personal rewards, have him or her draw up a contract. This contract would specify what reasonable amount of progress deserves a reward. Write out the contract. If you are running a group, have each client tell the group the details of the contract. These latter two actions increase the probability that a client will carry through with the contract.

If, and only if, a client develops a reward system (which not all will do) then she or he can consider having penalties for not achieving his or her goals. A penalty should be something that the client genuinely dislikes but is in some way constructive. Examples might include cleaning out the garage or picking up litter in the neighborhood. Once the client chooses the penalty, he or she writes up the agreement just as she or he did with the reward system. We discourage clients from setting up a system of penalties without there also being a system of rewards.

Antecedents to Overdrinking

After clients have self-monitored for several weeks, have them review all their self-monitoring cards and look for patterns in their drinking behaviors. They may have already realized that they drink more at certain bars or with certain people, and that is a good start. Go through each of the different situational factors and have the clients describe how they are associated with overdrinking for them. The factors include day of the week, time of day, places where they drink, people with whom they drink, the presence of hunger and/or thirst, activities associated with drinking (e.g., watching TV), how much money and/or alcohol they have at their disposal, and the presence of various emotional states. Similarly, ask them to consider factors associated with moderate drinking.

Once the antecedents to their overdrinking are established, clients can begin to make systematic changes in their responses to these situational factors. Strategies might include:

1. Avoid drinking altogether in the presence of a particular antecedent (e.g., after an argument with a spouse).
2. Limit either the amount of time or money available for drinking.
3. Be aware that overdrinking is especially likely in particular situations and take precautions at these times.
4. Find alternate ways of coping with particular antecedents such as anger or frustration.

Alternate Coping Skills: The New Roads Model

People at least *perceive* that drinking results in some positive consequences; otherwise, they would not drink. For some, it may result in the achievement of positive mental states, while for others, it may help them to avoid negative emotional or physical states. If drinking alcohol is the only way clients can achieve a need, then when they want to fulfill that need, the probability that they will respond with drinking will increase. If, on the other hand, clients have other ways to satisfy that need, then the probability of drinking will decrease. This section deals with identifying the needs that drinking fulfills and developing alternate ways of satisfying those needs. It is based on the "New Roads" model of Miller and Pechacek (1987).

Clients may be surprised to hear you say that drinking alcohol has some positive consequences. If you ask them to tell you the positive and desired effects of drinking, they can usually list two or three benefits of drinking. As they list these "desired effects," it is helpful to write them down on a blackboard under this heading (see column 2 of Table 9.2). The most frequently cited effects are relaxation, getting a "buzz" on, and some type of disinhibition. After you have generated this list with your client(s), ask him or her if any of these additional effects might be appropriate: courage, avoidance, mood change, increased sociability, consciousness change, sleep, forgetting, and numbing. When you have finished this column, start a second column, to the left. Label this column "Triggers" (see the first column in Table 9.2). In this column, list the situations and emotional states when the client(s) wants these desired effects. Some examples might include feeling frustrated over work, an argument with a spouse, and celebration of a baseball game win. Last, start a final list labeled "New Roads."

Have the client(s) brainstorm other ways to achieve the "desired effects" without overdrinking. As alternatives are generated, you can also add skills such as relaxation training or self-hypnosis, assertiveness training, systematic desensitization, mood management skills, social skills training, and so on. Emphasize that the more options they have at their disposal to achieve a certain effect, the less likely they are to overdrink in those high-risk situations.

If a client asks for additional training in these various skills, you have several options. The first is to recommend appropriate self-help manuals. The second is to provide this training yourself. The third option is to refer the client to other competent professionals in your community who do such training if you do not wish or know how to train these skills.

Because many clients rank relaxation high on their list of "desired effects," we provide some exposure to relaxation training using progressive muscle relaxation techniques (Benson, 1975). We then give them exposure to guided visual imagery. We tell them that these are but two examples of relaxation techniques we have chosen from an assortment of many.

These seven strategies constitute the course of treatment. Over time, however, we have added a relapse prevention component to the end of the program. The purpose of this is to help clients deal appropriately with relapses, which do occur. The message is that a relapse is an indication that a client needs to learn to cope more effectively with some antecedent to his or her overdrinking. Follow-ups at regular intervals also focus on relapse prevention. For a thorough discussion of relapse prevention, see Chapter 11.

EFFECTIVENESS

There have now been 30 controlled clinical trials of BSCT. Using the rules for inclusion in our literature review in Chapter 2, BSCT has been tested in more controlled clinical trials than any other intervention for alcohol problems. BSCT also has the second largest number of positive studies. Researchers have evaluated BSCT in a wide range of clinical populations and compared it to other effective interventions. There have, however, been negative studies of BSCT. Close examination of these studies reveals two issues. First, BSCT with a goal of moderation is, in general, less effective than purely abstinence-

Table 9.2   The "New Roads" Exercise

TRIGGERS	DESIRED EFFECTS	NEW ROADS
Hard day at work	Relaxation	Aerobic exercise
Fight with spouse	Escape	Better communication skills

oriented approaches for more severely dependent clients (e.g., Foy, Nunn, & Rychtarik, 1984). Second, brief interventions and self-directed BSCT are often as effective as more extensive, therapist-directed BSCT.

What these latter comparisons do not reveal, however, is a client-therapist interaction. Miller and colleagues examined the contribution of therapist empathy on outcomes in a trial that compared therapist-directed and minimal therapist contact conditions (Miller, Taylor, & West, 1980). They found a positive correlation between the level of therapist empathy and therapist-directed treatment outcomes at 12-month follow-up. Therapists with lower levels of empathy had outcomes worse than the self-directed BSCT group, while those with higher levels of empathy had outcomes that exceeded the self-directed group.

Review of Specific Studies

The first evaluations of treatments aimed at a goal of moderation appeared in the early 1970s. Lovibond (1975) evaluated a complex BSCT program that included actual drinking by clients and electric shock aversion. Working with a drunk-driver population, he found their moderation training program to be superior to an untreated control condition. Brown (1980) and Coghlan (1979) similarly found that a BSCT program was significantly more effective in altering the drinking behavior of drunk-driving offenders, as compared with an alcohol education program.

Vogler and his colleagues conducted a series of studies in the mid-1970's. With 12-month follow-ups, Vogler reported rates of moderate drinking ranging from 21 to 68% (Vogler, Compton, & Weissbach, 1975; Vogler, Weissbach, & Compton, 1977; Vogler, Weissbach, Compton, & Martin, 1977). Alden (1978) reported comparable results. Other evaluations reported similar outcomes when comparing BSCT procedures with other approaches (Hedberg & Campbell, 1974; Miller, 1978; Pomerleau, Pertschuk, Adkins, & d'Aquili, 1978).

Mark and Linda Sobell conducted what was to become the most publicized evaluation of self-control training procedures (Sobell & Sobell, 1973). In a controlled evaluation with inpatient gamma alcoholics, they reported greater improvement in an experimental group receiving moderation training than in three comparison groups in abstinence-focused treatment. Pendery and colleagues questioned the success of this treatment (Pendery, Maltzman, & West, 1982), reporting an independent review of the experimental cases. The controversy surrounding this study is complex (Marlatt, Larimer, Baer, & Quigley, 1993; Sobell & Sobell, 1984). A fair conclusion is that few of the alcoholics receiving experimental treatment sustained moderate drinking over an extended period, but they fared no worse than those receiving standard abstinence-oriented treatment. This conclusion is consistent with the findings of a subsequent study with a similar inpatient population (Foy et al., 1984).

Martha Sanchez-Craig and colleagues at the Addiction Research Foundation have conducted some of the best-designed studies of BSCT procedures (Sanchez-Craig, 1980; Sanchez-Craig et al., 1984). They randomly assigned less severe problem drinkers to moderate drinking or abstinence goals, with both groups receiving outpatient BSCT. Both groups improved substantially during the two years of follow-up, with no significant differences between groups over time. A small-scale replication by Graber and Miller (1987) similarly yielded no differences between groups assigned to abstinence or moderation goals. Sanchez-Craig and colleagues have also consistently found that women have better outcomes with BSCT than do men (Sanchez-Craig, Leigh, Spivak, & Lei, 1989; Sanchez-Craig, Spi-vak, & Davila, 1991).

Nick Heather and colleagues have studied the impact of mailing self-help manuals to individuals who respond to media announcements. In two studies they found that people who received a BSCT self-help manual did better than those who received a book of general information about alcohol problems and advice (Heather, Whitton, & Robertson, 1986; Heather, Kissoon-Singh, & Fenton, 1990).

In a series of evaluations, Miller and colleagues have evaluated alternate modes for offering BSCT to problem drinkers. These controlled comparisons consistently found no significant differences in effectiveness between a self-administered mode with minimal therapist contact (Miller & Muñoz, 1982) and a therapist-directed mode of delivery, with clients in both conditions showing significant improvement at follow-ups to eight years (Buck & Miller, 1981; Miller & Baca, 1983; Miller & Taylor, 1980; Miller et al., 1980, 1992; Miller, Gribskov, & Mortell, 1981). Group and individual therapy formats for BSCT also seem to yield comparable results (Miller, Pechacek, & Hamburg, 1981; Miller et al., 1980). (There is, however, evidence of client-therapist interactions as discussed earlier.) Longer-range follow-ups at three to eight years found increasing proportions of clients becoming total abstainers, and a consistent 10 to 15% of treated outpatients sustaining moderate and problem-free drinking outcomes (Miller et al., 1992).

Other researchers have compared brief interventions, motivational interventions, self-directed BSCT, and therapist-directed BSCT of varying degrees of intensity. Baldwin and colleagues (Baldwin et al., 1991) randomly assigned 78 legal offenders to receive either BSCT or nondirective counseling following a motivational screening interview. Follow-up data on 18 of the 32 clients who completed treatment found no significant main effects but interaction effects. BSCT clients drank less per drinking episode pre- to posttreatment, whereas the control group clients drank more. Also, BSCT clients had fewer life problems and lower conviction rates pre- to posttreatment. There were no significant differences in the control group on these measures pre- to post-treatment.

Alden (1988) randomly assigned clients to receive either BSCT or developmental counseling. The latter included self-monitoring, goal setting, and discussions of drinking patterns and life problems with an empathic counselor who followed a treatment manual. The developmental counseling also appeared to have elements of motivational enhancement interventions. Although both groups significantly decreased their drinking to moderate levels in the range of other BSCT studies, there were no significant differences between groups. Harris and Miller (1990) compared self-directed and therapist-directed BSCT with two wait-list control groups, one of which self-monitored their drinking. Again, there were no differences in outcomes between the two treatment groups, both of which fared better than two control groups.

Skutle and Berg (1987) randomly assigned clients to self-directed or therapist-directed BSCT, a coping skills training group, or a combination of coping and therapist-directed BSCT. All groups showed significant declines in drinking with no significant differences between groups during 12 months of follow-up.

Carpenter, Lyons, and Miller (1985) randomly assigned American Indian High School students to receive either a comprehensive BSCT and education program, BSCT without the education classes, or self-monitoring and meetings with peer counselors. Clients in all groups significantly reduced their drinking, but there were no differences in outcomes between the groups.

Sannibale (1988) randomly assigned coerced clients from the legal system to a brief intervention, standard treatment, or alternative treatment with moderation and abstinence goals. With small sample sizes in each group,

she found no significant differences between groups.

Finally, Kivlahan and colleagues (Kivlahan, Marlatt, Fromme, Coppel, & Williams, 1990) compared BSCT to an alcohol information group (based on the Washington State DWI education program) and a self-monitoring wait-list group. Both treatment groups significantly reduced their drinking compared to pretreatment levels and the control group during follow-up, with no differences between the groups.

Gerard Connors and colleagues have examined the impact of aftercare or follow-ups with clients treated with BSCT (Connors, Tarbox, & Faillace, 1992). They randomly assigned clients to receive either group, telephone, or no aftercare following BSCT. They found no differences in outcomes between the aftercare groups and the no-aftercare control group. Their results suggest that aftercare with this population may not be necessary for maintenance of treatment gains. This is a different conclusion regarding the importance of aftercare than that for alcoholic patients (see Ito & Donovan 1986 for a review). They also found a correlation between using drinking reduction strategies and less drinking during follow-up. Finally, they used a no-treatment comparison group of individuals who were willing to come for an assessment and to be followed up but not "treated." This nonequivalent comparison group reduced their drinking as much as the groups that received treatment. This again suggests that brief interventions may be as effective with a subset of this population of early stage problem drinkers who are concerned about their drinking but not actively seeking treatment.

Many, but not all, outcome studies found that self-directed BSCT with minimal therapist contact was as effective as more intensive therapist-directed treatment. Robertson and colleagues (Robertson, Heather, Dzialdowski, Crawford, & Winton, 1986) found that clients who received a more intensive version of BSCT fared better than those who received a brief intervention. In explaining this finding that is contrary to most other studies, they noted that the dependence levels in their client population were somewhat higher. In view of this, it is sensible to offer both modes of delivery.

In summary, BSCT procedures have been extensively studied. These studies collectively show that some problem drinkers do respond favorably to this approach, sustaining moderate and nonproblematic drinking over extended periods. Other clients, following BSCT with a moderation goal, opt for total abstinence, some with and some without additional treatment. When clients are assigned at random to treatment programs with abstinence or moderation goals, long-term results are consistently comparable. Brief interventions are also often effective with this population and should be considered as a cost-effective alternative, at least for those clients not seeking treatment.

A final recommendation is to make BSCT procedures available as one option among many within a treatment program wishing to serve a broad range of problem drinkers. Moderation-oriented BSCT is most likely to be attractive and effective for less severe problem drinkers. We do not recommend the pursuit of a moderation goal with severely dependent alcoholics.

REFERENCES

Clinical Guidelines

Hester, R. K. (1994). *Behavioral self-control training*. This is an interactive computer software program under development. It will teach BSCT skills to clients with minimal therapist supervision. Anticipated release date is late 1996.

Markham, M. R., Miller, W. R., & Arciniega, L. (1993). *BACCuS 2.01*. Catalog No. A–015. This is a computer software program that generates personalized BAC tables, converts alcohol consumption data into standard drink units, and can do peak BAC estimates. You can order it by writing to W. R. Miller, Ph.D., Dept. of Psychology, University of New Mexico, Albuquerque, NM 87131–1161.

Miller, W. R., & Muñoz, R. F. (1982). *How to control your drinking* (rev. ed.). Albuquerque: University of New Mexico Press. This book describes a self-directed program of BSCT for problem drinkers. Its effectiveness has been tested in six studies, which indicate that clients working with minimal therapist supervision and using this manual fare as well on average as those receiving a therapist-directed BSCT program. Therapists can also learn the basic outline and procedures of BSCT by reviewing this manual. You can order it by writing to W. R. Miller, Ph.D., Dept. of Psychology, University of New Mexico, Albuquerque, NM 87131–1161.

Robertson, I., & Heather, N. (1986). *Let's drink to your health: A self-help guide to sensible drinking*. (Published by the British Psychological Society, St. Andrews House, 48 Princess Road East, Leicester, LEI 7DR, U.K.) This cleverly produced self-help manual combines practical information and BSCT techniques with cartoons, drawings, and fill-in boxes. Highly readable and briefer than most other manuals (127 pages + appendices), it is particularly appropriate for British audiences.

Sanchez-Craig, M. (1984). *Therapist's manual for secondary prevention of alcohol problems: Procedures for teaching moderate drinking and abstinence*. Toronto: Addiction Research Foundation. (May be purchased by writing to the Addiction Research Foundation Bookstore, 33 Russell Street, Toronto, Ontario, M58 2S1, Canada.) This therapist manual provides guidelines for conducting BSCT with either a goal of abstinence or a goal of moderation. Procedures are divided into preparatory, acquisition, and maintenance strategies. The appendices include practical forms, procedures, and additional guidelines.

Sanchez-Craig, M. (1993). *Saying when: How to quit drinking or cut down*. Toronto, Ontario: Addiction Research Foundation. This is a self-contained client manual that teaches clients self-control skills. It is also the basis for a new program called Drinkwise. Drinkwise is a commercial program that markets a comprehensive package of screening, assessment, BSCT training, follow-up, and quality-assurance materials. The business aspects of Drinkwise are in the developmental stage but eventually it will be marketed as a franchise. Contact Dr. Sanchez-Craig for further information.

Sobell, M. B., & Sobell, L. C. (1993). *Problem drinkers: Guided self-change treatment*. New York: Guilford. This is another excellent self-help manual for clients to learn self-control skills. It contains useful forms and guidelines.

Vogler, R. E., & Bartz, W. R. (1982). *The better way to drink*. New York: Simon & Schuster. (Now available from New Harbinger Publications, 2200 Adeline, Suite 305, Oakland, CA. 94607.) Another self-help manual, based on Roger Vogler's research in teaching moderation to problem drinkers.

Research References

Alcoholics Anonymous. (1976). *Alcoholics anonymous*. New York: Alcoholics Anonymous World Services.

Alden, L. (1978). Evaluation of a preventive self-management programme for problem drinkers. *Canadian Journal of Behavioural Science, 10,* 258–263.

Alden, L. E. (1988). Behavioral self-management controlled-drinking strategies in a context of secondary prevention. *Journal of Consulting and Clinical Psychology, 56,* 280–286.

Baldwin, S., Heather, N., Lawson, A., Robertson, I., Mooney, J., & Braggins, F. (1991). Comparison of effectiveness: Behavioural and talk-based alcohol education courses for court-referred young offenders. *Behavioural Psychotherapy, 19,* 157–172.

Benson, H. (1975). *The relaxation response*. New York: William Morrow & Co.

Brown, R. A. (1980). Conventional education and controlled drinking education courses with convicted drunken drivers. *Behavior Therapy, 11,* 632–642.

Buck, K. A., & Miller, W. R. (November 1981). *Why does bibliotherapy work?* Paper presented at the annual meeting of the Association for Advancement of Behavior Therapy, Toronto.

Cahalan, D. (1987). *Understanding America's drinking problem: How to combat the hazards of alcohol*. San Francisco: Jossey-Bass.

Carpenter, R. A., Lyons, C. A., & Miller, W. R. (1985). Peer-managed self-control program for prevention of alcohol abuse in American Indian high school students: A pilot evaluation study. *International Journal of the Addictions, 20,* 299–310.

Coghlan, G. R. (1979). *The investigation of behavioral self-control theory and techniques in a short-term treatment of male alcohol abusers.* Unpublished doctoral dissertation, State University of New York at Albany, University Microfilms No. 7918818.

Connors, G. J., Tarbox, A. R., & Faillace, L. A. (1992). Achieving and maintaining gains among problem drinkers: Process and outcome results. *Behavior Therapy, 23,* 449–474.

Foy, D. W., Nunn, B. L., & Rychtarik, R. G. (1984). Broad-spectrum behavioral treatment for chronic alcoholics: Effects of training controlled drinking skills. *Journal of Consulting and Clinical Psychology, 52,* 213–230.

Graber, R. A., & Miller, W. R. (1988). Abstinence and controlled drinking goals in behavioral self-control training of problem drinkers: A randomized clinical trial. *Psychology of Addictive Behaviors, 2,* 20–33.

Guydish, J. R. (1987). *Self-control bibliotherapy as a secondary prevention strategy with heavy drinking college students.* Unpublished doctoral dissertation, Washington State University.

Harris, K. B., & Miller, W. R. (1990). Behavioral self-control training for problem drinkers: Components of efficacy. *Psychology of Addictive Behaviors, 4,* 82–90.

Heather, N., Campion, P. D., Neville, R. G., & Maccabe, D. (1987). Evaluation of a controlled drinking minimal intervention for problem drinkers in general practice (the DRAMS scheme). *Journal of the Royal College of General Practitioners, 37,* 358–363.

Heather, N., Kissoon-Singh, J., & Fenton, G. W. (1990). Assisted natural recovery from alcohol problems: Effects of a self-help manual with and without supplementary telephone contact. *British Journal of Addiction, 85,* 1177–1185.

Heather, N., & Robertson, I. (1983). *Controlled drinking.* London: Methuen.

Heather, N., Whitton, B., & Robertson, I. (1986). Evaluation of a self-help manual for media-recruited problem drinkers: Six month follow-up results. *British Journal of Clinical Psychology, 25,* 19–34.

Hedberg, A. G., & Campbell, L. M. (1974). A comparison of four behavioral treatment approaches to alcoholism. *Journal of Behavioral Therapy and Experimental Psychiatry, 5,* 251–256.

Institute of Medicine (1990). *Broadening the base of treatment for alcohol problems.* Washington, D.C.: National Academy Press.

Ito, J. R., & Donovan, D. M. (1986). Aftercare in alcoholism treatment: A review. In W. R. Miller & N. Heather (Eds.), *Treating addictive behaviors: Process of change* (pp. 435–456). New York: Plenum Press.

Kivlahan, D. R., Marlatt, G. A., Fromme, K., Coppel, D. B., & Williams, E. (1990). Secondary prevention with college drinkers: Evaluation of an alcohol skills training program. *Journal of Consulting and Clinical Psychology, 58,* 805–810.

Klatsky, A. L., Friedman, G. D., & Giegelaub, A. B. (1981). Alcohol and mortality: A ten-year Kaiser-Permanente experience. *Annals of Internal Medicine, 95,* 139–145.

Lovibond, S. H. (1975). Use of behavior modification in the reduction of alcohol-related road accidents. In T. Thompson & W. S. Dockens, III (Eds.), *Applications of behavior modification* (pp. 399–406). New York: Academic Press.

Lovibond, S. H., & Caddy, G. (1970). Discriminated aversive control in the moderation of alcoholics' drinking behavior. *Behavior Therapy, 1,* 437–444.

Mann, M. (1950). *Primer on alcoholism.* New York: Rhinehart.

Marlatt, G. A., Larimer, M. E., Baer, J. S., & Quigley, L. A. (1993). Harm reduction for alcohol problems: Moving beyond the controlled drinking controversy. *Behavior Therapy, 24,* 461–504.

Miller, W. R. (1978). Behavioral treatment of problem drinkers: A comparative outcome study of three controlled drinking therapies. *Journal of Consulting and Clinical Psychology, 46,* 74–86.

Miller, W. R. (1985). Motivation for treatment: A review. *Psychological Bulletin, 98,* 84–107.

Miller, W. R., & Baca, L. M. (1983). Two-year follow-up of bibliotherapy and therapist-directed controlled drinking training for problem drinkers. *Behavior Therapy, 14,* 441–448.

Miller, W. R., Gribskov, C. J., & Mortell, R. L. (1981). Effectiveness of a self-control manual for problem drinkers with and without therapist contact. *International Journal of the Addictions, 16,* 1247–1254.

Miller, W. R., Heather, N., & Hall, W. (1991). Calculating standard drink units: International comparisons. *British Journal of Addiction, 86,* 43–47.

Miller, W. R., & Hester, R. K. (1986a). The effectiveness of treatment techniques: What the research reveals. In W. R. Miller & N. Heather (Eds.), *Treating addictive behaviors: Process of change.* (pp. 121–174). New York: Plenum Press.

Miller, W. R., & Hester, R. K. (1986b). Matching problem drinkers with optimal treatments. In W. R. Miller & N. Heather (Eds.), *Treating addictive behaviors: Processes of Change* (pp. 175–204). New York: Plenum.

Miller, W. R., Leckman, A. L., Delaney, H. D. , & Tinkcom, M. (1992). Long-term follow-up of behavioral self-control training. *Journal of Studies on Alcohol, 53,* 249–261.

Miller, W. R., & Muñoz, R. F. (1982). *How to control your drinking* (rev. ed.). Albuquerque, NM: University of New Mexico Press.

Miller, W. R., & Pechacek, T. F. (1987). New Roads: Assessing and treating psychological dependence. *Journal of Substance Abuse Treatment, 4,* 73–77.

Miller, W. R., Pechacek, T. F., & Hamburg, S. (1981). Group behavior therapy for problem drinkers. *International Journal of the Addictions, 16,* 827–837.

Miller, W. R., & Taylor, C. A. (1980). Relative effectiveness of bibliotherapy, individual and group self-control training in the treatment of problem drinkers. *Addictive Behaviors, 5,* 13–24.

Miller, W. R., Taylor, C. A., & West, J. C. (1980). Focused versus broad-spectrum behavior therapy for problem drinkers. *Journal of Consulting and Clinical Psychology, 48,* 590–601.

Moore, M. H., & Gerstein, D. R. (Eds.). (1981). *Alcohol and public policy: Beyond the shadow of prohibition.* Washington, DC: National Academy Press.

Pendery, M. L., Maltzman, I. M., & West, L. J. (1982).

Controlled drinking by alcoholics? New findings and a reevaluation of a major affirmative study. *Science, 217,* 169–175.

Pomerleau, O., Pertschuk, M., Adkins, D., & d'Aquili, E. (1978). Treatment for middle income problem drinkers. In P. E. Nathan, G. A. Marlatt, & T. Lørberg (Eds.), *Alcoholism: New directions in behavioral research and treatment.* (pp. 143–160). New York: Plenum.

Robertson, I., Heather, N., Dzialdowski, A., Crawford, J., & Winton, M. (1986). A comparison of minimal versus intensive controlled drinking treatment for problem drinkers. *British Journal of Clinical Psychology, 25,* 185–194.

Rosenberg, H. (1993). Prediction of controlled drinking by alcoholics and problem drinkers. *Psychological Bulletin, 113,* 129–139.

Sanchez-Craig, M. (1980). Random assignment to abstinence or controlled drinking in a cognitive-behavioral program: Short-term effects on drinking behavior. *Addictive Behavior, 5,* 35–39.

Sanchez-Craig, M., Annis, H. M., Bornet, A. R., & MacDonald, K. R. (1984). Random assignment to abstinence and controlled drinking: Evaluation of a cognitive-behavioural program for problem drinkers. *Journal of Consulting and Clinical Psychology, 52,* 390–403.

Sanchez-Craig, M., Leigh, G., Spivak, K., & Lei, H. (1989). Superior outcome of females over males after brief treatment for the reduction of heavy drinking. *British Journal of Addiction, 84,* 395–404.

Sanchez-Craig, M, Spivak, K., & Davila, R. (1991). Superior outcome of females over males after brief treatment for the reduction of heavy drinking: Replication and report of therapist effects. *British Journal of Addiction, 86,* 867–876.

Sannibale, C. (1988). The differential effect of a set of brief interventions on the functioning of a group of "early stage" problem drinkers. *Australian Drug and Alcohol Review, 7,* 147–155.

Saunders, J. B., & Aasland, O. G. (Eds.). (1987). *WHO collaborative project on identification and treatment of persons with harmful alcohol consumption: Report on phase I development of a screening instrument.* Geneva, Switzerland: World Health Organization.

Skutle, A., & Berg, G. (1987). Training in controlled drinking for early-stage problem drinkers. *British Journal of Addiction, 82,* 493–501.

Sobell, M. C., & Sobell, L. C. (1984). The aftermath of heresy: A response to Pendery et al.'s (1982) critique of "Individualized behavior therapy for alcoholics." *Behavior Research and Therapy, 22,* 413–440.

Sobell, M. B., & Sobell, L. C. (1973). Individualized behavior therapy for alcoholics. *Behavior Therapy, 4,* 49–72.

Vogler, R. E., Compton, J. V., & Weissbach, T. A. (1975). Integrated behavior change techniques for alcoholism. *Journal of Consulting and Clinical Psychology, 43,* 233–243.

Vogler, R. E., Weissbach, T. A., & Compton, J. V. (1977). Learning techniques for alcohol abuse. *Behaviour Research and Therapy, 15,* 31–38.

Vogler, R. E., Weissbach, T. A., Compton, J. V., & Martin, G. T. (1977). Integrated behavior change techniques for problem drinkers in the community. *Journal of Consulting and Clinical Psychology, 45,* 267–279.

CHAPTER 10

Self-Help Groups

Barbara S. McCrady
Sadi Irvine Delaney

INTRODUCTION

People with problems in their lives seek many routes to alleviate their distress. They turn inward to their own personal resources, seek the help of family or friends, seek religion, study and acquire knowledge about their problems, seek the help of professionals, or seek the help of others with similar problems. This latter approach, termed *self-help* or *mutual aid* (Robinson, 1979), has become an increasingly common source of assistance. Self-help groups have proliferated for persons with a wide array of problems, such as family members of the chronically mentally ill, parents who have lost a child, or persons with chronic medical problems such as diabetes or rheumatoid arthritis. A national center devoted to the study of self-help groups is located in Michigan (Center for Self-help Research and Knowledge Dissemination), and directories of self-help resources are published in many states (e.g., New Jersey Self-help Clearinghouse, 1993).

In the alcohol and drug field, self-help groups have proliferated for persons with substance use problems and for family members. This chapter will provide an overview of the range of self-help groups available for persons who wish to change their drinking, and will provide guidelines for practitioners about how to

select appropriate self-help groups for their clients and facilitate their clients' involvement in these groups.

The earliest of the contemporary self-help groups is Alcoholics Anonymous (AA). Founded in Akron, Ohio, in 1935, AA is the largest self-help group, reporting approximately 87,000 groups in 150 countries, and over 1.7 million members worldwide (Alcoholics Anonymous, 1990a). Closely allied with AA are self-help recovery groups for friends and family members, such as Alanon for adult family members and friends of alcoholics, and Alateen and Alatot for children with alcoholic parents. Adult Children of Alcoholics (ACOA) groups are intended to help persons who grew up with an alcoholic parent to understand the effects their childhood experience has had on their current functioning, and to facilitate change in maladaptive patterns of behavior believed to be caused by growing up in an alcoholic family.

A number of self-help groups are modeled after AA, especially groups for recovery from other psychoactive drug use, such as Narcotics Anonymous (NA) or Cocaine Anonymous (CA). Within AA, there are groups for persons with particular individual characteristics, such as groups for young people, women, nonsmokers, gays and lesbians, or persons who also have a major psychiatric disorder such as schizophrenia or manic-depressive illness. There are also special self-help groups that are either a part of AA or modeled after AA, for professionals who also have alcohol and drug problems, such as physicians, dentists, social workers, nurses, pharmacists, veterinarians, psychologists, attorneys, realtors, and the clergy.

If we focus particularly on alcohol, there are a number of other self-help groups that either complement AA or provide an alternative. Complementary self-help groups include Overcomers Outreach, a program for evangelical Christians that applies the bible to the 12 steps of AA, and the Calix Society, a program for Catholics who are recovering from alcoholism. Overcomers Outreach was started in 1985, and reports having 1,000 groups in 49 states and 10 foreign countries. The Calix Society was founded in 1947, and reports having 67 units in the United States, Canada, Scotland, and England. Both Overcomers Outreach and the Calix Society focus on spirituality and religious study in the context of recovery from alcoholism through AA.

In contrast, several self-help groups have developed that offer a very different view of recovery from alcoholism. All emphasize rationality and personal responsibility, and are intended to provide an alternative for those who are not comfortable with the approach to recovery provided by AA. Rational Recovery (RR) was begun in 1986, and now reports having close to 600 groups. The program is based on the principles of rational emotive therapy (RET; Ellis & Velten, 1992). The Secular Organizations for Sobriety/Save Our Selves (SOS) were founded in 1985, and report having 1,000 groups. The program separates religion or spirituality from sobriety, and supports a scientific approach to recovery.

Women for Sobriety was begun in 1976 as a self-help group addressed to the needs of women. The program believes that it is important for women to take charge of their own lives, develop a sense of competence, and put past behaviors behind them. Recognition of negative cognitions is also an important part of the program. Women for Sobriety reports 325 groups in the United States, Canada, England, New Zealand, Australia and Finland.

SPECIAL CONSIDERATIONS

The current practice of many clinicians is to refer most or all alcoholic clients to AA. It is not clear that this is optimal practice, since no evidence suggests that all problem drinkers benefit from what AA has to offer. AA's triennial survey of its membership suggests that the vast majority of persons who initiate involvement with AA will discontinue their involvement in less than a year (AA, 1990a). If it were possible to determine what characteristics predicted successful involvement with self-help groups, in general, or in particular, clinicians would be better able to match clients to the most appropriate program, thereby increasing clients' chances of successful resolution of their drinking problems.

We are assuming that, with a plethora of self-help groups to choose from, the practitioner treating a person with an alcohol problem would benefit from information to guide the selection of a self-help group that is most likely to be helpful to a particular client. Unfortunately, researchers have not yet conducted controlled trials in which clients are randomly assigned to different kinds of self-help groups to determine the characteristics of clients who are most successful in different groups, nor have researchers tested *a priori* assumptions about appropriate matching to self-help groups in a systematic fashion. However, there are some data available about the characteristics of persons who most successfully affiliate with AA, and characteristics of persons who have sought out alterative self-help groups such as RR.

There are a number of conceptual and methodological problems that surface when attempting to identify characteristics of successful affiliates with self-help groups. First, there is a lack of a consistent definition of what is meant by affiliation. *Affiliation* may be defined as attending a certain number of meetings; joining a group; maintaining involvement over a certain length of time; or self-defined involvement. Second, affiliation alone may not imply successful recovery, and researchers need to determine the associations between successful affiliation and successful recovery. Third, a conglomeration of personal characteristics have been studied, and most such investigations have not had a clear theoretical rationale for the selection of variables. Fourth, measures of involvement or affiliation are usually developed by each individual investigator. Reliability and validity data are lacking, and cross-study comparisons are made difficult by the lack of uniformity of measures. Fifth, it has been difficult to develop methodologies to conduct randomized clinical trials of AA in particular, even though such trials provide the most unambiguous findings. Finally, since self-help groups do not have defined beginnings and endings, and involvement may span many years, it is difficult to design studies with clear pre-post-follow-up test points that could have any uniformity across experimental groups.

Despite these methodological problems, there are some useful data about affiliation. Emrick, Tonigan, Montgomery, and Little (1993) conducted a meta-analysis of the literature on AA. As part of the meta-analysis, they reviewed a broad literature on affiliation. Based on the findings from more than one research study, they concluded that those most likely to affiliate with AA had a history of using external supports to stop drinking, were more likely to have experienced loss of control over their drinking, were more anxious about their drinking, typically drank more heavily, were obsessively-compulsively involved with their drinking, and believed that alcohol enhanced their mental functioning. Demographic variables did not distinguish AA affiliators from nonaffiliators. A number of individual studies have found support for other characteristics of AA affiliators, but the findings have not been replicated (see Emrick et al., 1993, for details).

Two research groups have begun to study the characteristics of people who become involved with RR. Galanter and Egelko (in press) obtained questionnaire data from 433 participants in RR groups. The majority (75%) had previously been involved with AA, and 80% of these felt that RR had been more helpful for them than AA. Participants were predominantly male (72%), educated, and employed. Willis (1993) analyzed 223 responses to a questionnaire in the back of *The Small Book*, the principle writing associated with RR. Demographically, respondents were similar to those in the Galanter and Egelko survey, and 89% had previously been involved with AA. Most had definite reasons for discontinuing their involvement with AA: conflict with the spiritual aspects of the program, feeling that AA could not help them, finding AA unscientific or irrational, not fitting in to AA, not liking the meetings, objecting to the concept of powerlessness, or rejecting the notion of lifelong involvement with AA.

The preceding data provide some limited information for the practitioner who wants to attempt to match individual clients with different self-help groups. Demographic characteristics do not appear to be strong defining characteristics of membership, except that all members of Women for Sobriety are women, members of the Calix Society are Catholic, and members of Overcomers Outreach are evangelical Christians. People most likely to affiliate successfully with AA have a history of using the support of others to deal with their drinking problems, but there is no evidence that that is unique to AA in contrast to other self-help groups. AA members are anxious about their drinking, have rather severe drinking histories, and experience classical loss of control drinking. Persons who seek alternative organizations, such as RR or WFS, appear to place a higher value on rationality, and may find spirituality and reliance on a higher power incompatible with their philosophy of life.

Prospective research studies are needed to facilitate prediction of clients most likely to affiliate successfully with different kinds of self-help groups. With increasing interest in matching clients to treatment, it seems that further research to identify the distinguishing characteristics of affiliates of different types of self-help groups is important.

DESCRIPTION OF SELF-HELP ORGANIZATIONS

In these next sections, we will describe the organizational structure of AA and, to a lesser extent, the other self-help groups, and then describe the underlying philosophy and program of change associated with the six self-help groups reviewed in the introduction. Finally, we will discuss how to integrate self-help groups with clinical practice, with a particular emphasis on AA.

Overview of the Organization of Self-Help Groups

All of the self-help groups have certain organizational characteristics in common. First, all were begun by an individual or individuals with drinking problems who found existing resources inadequate or incompatible with their needs. Each has grown initially through word of mouth, and each has become more organized over time. At present, each of the six self-help groups that are the focus of this chapter have a national headquarters and telephone number, a periodic publication such as a newsletter, and core literature. All are supported primarily by member contributions and the sale of literature. Calix has a membership fee.

The self-help organizations differ in the format and organization of their meetings. AA, Overcomers Outreach, and SOS meetings are peer led. Each RR group has a professional affiliated with the group who can provide guidance and information and WFS meetings are led by a trained moderator. Calix units each have an associated chaplain. With the exception of AA, each self-help organization has only one format for meetings. The format is defined by the organization, with clear guidelines for how the meetings should be conducted.

Alcoholics Anonymous (AA)

AA Organization and Principles

AA is larger and more heterogeneous than other self-help groups, and has a set of specific organizational principles that guide the practice of AA and AA members. In this section, we will describe the format and heterogeneity of AA, and the principles that guide its functioning.

There are 12 traditions in AA, which are intended to preserve the integrity of the AA program. The fourth AA tradition (see Table 10.1)

states that every AA group is autonomous; therefore a group is free to hold almost any kind of meeting it chooses. In general, there are two basic types of AA meetings, which differ according to who is permitted to attend. *Open* meetings are available to any interested person, regardless of whether or not he or she has a drinking problem. *Closed* meetings are open only to AA members or to persons who would like to do something about their drinking. Whenever two or more alcoholics meet together for the purpose of sobriety and are self-supporting and without outside affiliation, they may call themselves an AA group.

When a group is first formed, members decide whether the meeting will be open or closed, and the format of the meeting. Many open meetings choose to have speakers address the group,

Table 10.1   The 12 Traditions and 12 Steps of Alcoholics Anonymous

The 12 Traditions

Tradition 1	Our common welfare should come first—personal recovery depends upon AA unity.
Tradition 2	For our group purpose there is but one ultimate authority—a loving God as he may express Himself in our group conscience. Our leaders are but trusted servants; they do not govern.
Tradition 3	The only requirement for AA membership is a desire to stop drinking.
Tradition 4	Each group should be autonomous except in matters affecting other groups or AA as a whole.
Tradition 5	Each group has but one primary purpose—to carry its message to the alcoholic who is still suffering.
Tradition 6	An AA group ought never endorse, finance or lend the AA name to any related facility or outside enterprise, lest problems of money, property and prestige divert us from our primary purpose.
Tradition 7	Every AA group ought to be fully self-supporting, declining outside contributions.
Tradition 8	Alcoholics Anonymous should remain forever nonprofessional, but our service centers may employ special workers.
Tradition 9	AA, as such, ought never be organized; but we may create service boards or committees directly responsible to those they serve.
Tradition 10	Alcoholics Anonymous has no opinion on outside issues; hence the AA name ought never be drawn into public controversy.
Tradition 11	Our public relations policy is based on attraction rather than promotion: we need always maintain personal anonymity at the level of press, radio and films.
Tradition 12	Anonymity is the spiritual foundation of our traditions, ever reminding us to place principles before personalities.

The 12 Steps

Step 1	We admitted we were powerless over alcohol—that our lives had become unmanageable.
Step 2	Came to believe that a Power greater than ourselves could restore us to sanity.
Step 3	Made a decision to turn our will and our lives over to the care of God *as we understood him.*
Step 4	Made a searching and fearless moral inventory of ourselves.
Step 5	Admitted to God, to ourselves and to another human being the exact nature of our wrongs.
Step 6	Were entirely ready to have God remove all these defects of character.
Step 7	Humbly asked Him to remove our shortcomings.
Step 8	Made a list of all persons we had harmed, and became willing to make amends to them all.
Step 9	Made direct amends to such people wherever possible, except when to do so would injure them or others.
Step 10	Continued to take personal inventory and when we were wrong promptly admitted it.
Step 11	Sought through prayer and meditation to improve our conscious contact with God *as we understood him,* praying only for knowledge of his will for us and the power to carry that out.
Step 12	Having had a spiritual awakening as the result of these steps, we tried to carry this message to alcoholics and to practice these principles in all our affairs.

Source: The Twelve Steps and Twelve Traditions are reprinted with permission of Alcoholics Anonymous World Services, Inc. Permission to reprint and adapt this material does not mean that AA has reviewed or approved the contents of this publication, nor that AA agrees with the views expressed herein.

rather than adopting an interactive format. These AA members may be visitors from another group who are part of a speaker exchange program (called a "commitment") or may be members of the group holding the meeting. The speakers tell the audience what they were like when they were drinking, what happened to bring them to AA, and what they are like in recovery. An advantage of open speaker meetings is that the newcomer or visitor usually is not asked to speak.

Closed meetings are generally smaller, and each member is more visible to the group as a whole. These meetings are more often "discussion" meetings, which include as many members as possible in active discussion on a topic chosen either by the chairperson, or, in the case of step and tradition meetings, the topic is one of the steps or traditions. Another type of meeting combines these two formats by having the speaker lead the group in a discussion after the presentation of his or her "story."

There are certain characteristics of a typical AA meeting, even though the reader should keep in mind that details differ across meetings and geographical locations. A meeting is usually preceded by a period of social interaction when those who have arrived early greet each other and introduce any new member or visitor. When meeting time arrives, the chairperson calls the meeting to order and introduces himself or herself to the group by first name and as an alcoholic. After welcoming all members and visitors, some segments may be read from the book *Alcoholics Anonymous* (AA World Services, 1980), which is commonly known as the "Big Book."

At this point, the group's officers report any AA-relevant information, which ranges from announcements about upcoming social functions to financial reports. General announcements from the floor are invited, as well as introductions from anyone who is new or coming back to AA following a relapse. Anniversaries recognizing months or years of continual sobriety in AA are celebrated according to the custom of the group. The celebrant receives a medallion, which indicates the length of that person's abstinence from alcohol. Following a reminder about the importance of anonymity, the meeting begins with the introduction of speakers or discussion leaders. AA meetings often open with the group recitation of a prayer, and might close with all present standing, holding hands, and saying the Lord's Prayer.

An important part of the AA experience is sponsorship. The process of sponsorship involves two alcoholics, one of whom has made more progress in recovery and who shares that experience in an ongoing manner with another who is trying to achieve or maintain sobriety. Some groups offer temporary sponsors, matching a newcomer with someone until they are able to meet enough members to select their own sponsor. A sponsor should be the same gender as the person being sponsored and is contacted as often as needed. For example, if a person is having an urge to drink or is feeling lonely or sad, he or she is encouraged to call the sponsor rather than trying to "go it alone." Sponsors help with an assortment of problems—ranging from how to stay away from the first drink to what to do if a relapse occurs to how to work the 12 steps of the program. AA members are encouraged to have a network of AA members they can call on for support, rather than relying solely on the sponsor.

Most groups have officers who fulfill the roles of chairperson, secretary, treasurer, *Grapevine* representative, intergroup representative, and general service representative. Some groups select other positions, such as a special institutions representative, a steering committee, or a hospitality committee. Officers serve for a period of time established by the members of the group. Rotating officers is an important part of the AA program since it avoids the potential problem of any person or persons gaining too much power, and it offers more people the opportunity to serve.

AA is organized at a level above that of the individual group through the conference plan. This organization is consistent with the ninth tradition of AA (see Table 10.1). Each group may elect a general service representative (GSR), who links the individual group and AA as a collective entity, and a district committee member (DCM). Every two years, GSRs and DCMs convene for an area assembly to elect a delegate to represent the area at the annual conference meeting in New York. The General Service Conference supplies the means for the group conscience to be heard and to influence the execution of worldwide AA services. Decisions made at the conference include approval of AA literature, establishment of guidelines for maintaining anonymity, and approval of General Service Board nominees.

The General Service Board (GSB) is composed of alcoholic and nonalcoholic trustees who serve as the primary service tool of the conference. They may not make decisions that could affect AA as a whole, but they are involved in all matters of policy and business matters within the AA service enterprise.

The 12 Traditions

The major function of all officers is to uphold the 12 traditions. We have already referred to two of the 12 traditions in discussing the structure of AA: the fourth tradition, which asserts the autonomy of each group, and the ninth tradition, which deems that AA ought never be organized in the sense that no one has authority or can govern. The remaining traditions are important to review, since AA's success is often attributed to its adherence to these traditions.

The first tradition emphasizes that AA must put the common welfare of AA before the welfare of the individual. This first tradition views AA unity as the foundation of personal recovery. The second tradition addresses the question of who is in charge of the AA group, emphasizing that only God has authority; group leaders merely serve the group. The fifth tradition states that the primary purpose of AA is to carry its message to alcoholics. In order to ensure that AA can carry out this purpose, the sixth tradition addresses "money, power and prestige" (AA World Services, 1978, p. 155) as barriers that may prevent this "spiritual aim" from being realized. This is the reason why the sixth tradition maintains that an AA group should never affiliate with any outside organization. The seventh tradition indicates that AA should attempt to avoid disputes over money, which could also divert AA from its primary purpose. Groups are therefore self-supporting, declining contributions from any sources outside of AA.

The eighth tradition addresses how AA can interact with outside organizations without affiliating with them. An important implication of this tradition is that AA members are never to receive payment for twelfth-step work, which is helping another alcoholic within the AA context.

The ninth tradition, which stipulates that AA ought never be organized, is directed to the common practice of many other organizations to impose rules, dues, directives, and punishments on members. No one can decide that someone is not practicing the AA program correctly and should not be allowed to return, nor can any group be told how to function. The third tradition makes membership requirements minimal—a desire to stop drinking. AA's willingness to allow each member and group to follow or not follow the AA suggestions is based on the faith that the AA program works and that those

who choose not to adhere to its principles are likely to fail.

It is believed that if AA were to become involved in any outside issues, its members might begin to use AA for their own purposes rather than for purposes of AA unity. Therefore, the tenth tradition protects AA unity by sanctioning against its involvement in external affairs.

The eleventh tradition is concerned with public relations policy for AA. AA is willing to publicize its "principles and its work, but not its individual members." If an individual breaks his or her anonymity and is seen as a spokesperson for AA, the entire fellowship may be damaged by the actions of one member. AA also emphasizes that anonymity is both a public relations issue and a spiritual principle—it discourages personal ambition and self-seeking, which are viewed as deadly to the alcoholic and to AA as a whole.

The twelfth tradition considers anonymity to be a spiritual concept, perpetuated by the willingness of AA members to "give up personal desires for the common good" (AA World Services, 1978, p. 184). This is a continuing theme throughout the AA principles and steps; it is of critical importance that recovering alcoholics shift their focus from self to others.

The 12 Steps

Although the 12 steps of AA are the foundation of the program, they are often overlooked or referred to only in passing. The AA World Services (1978) publishes a book whose purpose is to provide an interpretation of the 12 steps. This book is often used at AA step meetings where a portion or the entire step is read and discussed by the group. Chapters five through seven of the AA "Big Book" (AA World Services, 1980) also provide a practical description of how to implement the steps, which are seen as necessary tools to be used by each AA member in the process of recovery. AA offers a developmental model of recovery, which allows for individual differences when each step is taken. It is suggested that new members start at the first step and proceed sequentially and at their own pace through the remaining steps. The steps have no time limit in which they must be taken, and the amount of time spent varies among individuals. Many AA members review the steps and attend step meetings throughout their recovery to avoid falling back into a cycle of self-absorption and drinking. What follows is a brief outline of the 12 steps as reflected in the AA literature. The steps are outlined in Table 10.1.

The first step is the necessary foundation for the remaining steps, as the AA member admits to complete defeat as far as alcohol is concerned. The notion that alcohol can be overcome by sheer will must be abandoned in order for recovery to begin. The second step is taken when the alcoholic acknowledges that he or she is not the center of the universe and that there is a power greater than the self. This step requires that the AA member acknowledge that life with alcohol is not sane, but wrought with mental obsessions, physical maladies, and spiritual deprivation. AA sees the alcoholics' major problem as one of selfishness and obsession with self—a condition that can only be remedied by turning outside of oneself.

The third step requires a decision by each individual. Although the term *God* is often used in AA, there is no prescription about how an individual member should conceive of his or her Higher Power. Each individual must define his or her Higher Power and be willing to place complete dependence on that Higher Power. AA members are told that if the third step is taken "honestly and humbly," the effects may be felt immediately. Reliance on a Higher Power in all aspects of daily life is an immense goal, which often begins piecemeal. Early in recovery, a new member may be willing to turn his or her drinking over to a Higher Power, but not other aspects of life.

The fourth and fifth steps involve introspective and self-evaluative processes, followed by the disclosure to another person of all that has been uncovered. AA sees alcohol as a symptom of the alcoholic's warped perception of "self." AA literature (AA World Services, 1980) states that in order for the alcoholic to be free from the compulsion to drink, these underlying "causes and conditions" must be eliminated. For example, *resentment* is defined as a spiritual malady which, if overcome, will be followed by improvement in the physical and mental realms. As a method for taking the fourth step, it is suggested that the alcoholic review his or her life and list the "people, institutions and principles" against which resentments are being held. The purpose of this inventory lies in the discovery that one is responsible for himself or herself, and that the actions of others cannot be used as excuses for resentment, wrongdoing, or drinking. The focus turns to mistakes the alcoholic made, rather than how he or she was wronged by the world.

The fifth step offers the opportunity for the AA member to reinforce the notion that the alcoholic cannot live in a vacuum. AA stresses that the alcoholic who insists on keeping the contents of the fourth step a secret will have difficulty maintaining sobriety. The *Twelve Steps and Twelve Traditions* (AA World Services, 1978) refers to the chronic physical and emotional isolation of the active alcoholic and how this can be alleviated by sharing one's worst with another human being. The fifth step is also seen as a vehicle for allowing the AA member to forgive himself or herself, in addition to the ability to forgive others that was fostered by the fourth step.

The sixth and seventh steps involve the relinquishment, not of responsibility, but of control over the "character defects" uncovered in the fourth step. The sixth step refers to the beginning of the lifelong process of spiritual growth. Being ready and open to God's intervention in the removal of the defects that have contributed to past drunkenness requires a spiritual state of willingness. The seventh step emphasizes the importance of humility in maintaining sobriety. *Humility* is defined in spiritual terms, as a reliance on God as the source of power through which shortcomings can be resolved. The seventh step broadens the perception of powerlessness over alcohol, introduced in the first step, to point out the powerlessness of the alcoholic over other problems as well.

The next two steps require that the AA member examine and take action in his or her interpersonal relationships. The eighth step calls for a retrospective examination of one's relationships to determine where one has been at fault. A list of persons and situations is constructed, and a willingness to make every effort to correct any wrongdoing is expressed.

The ninth step asks the alcoholic to make every effort to repair the damage he or she had done to others. This step is not to be interpreted as an attempt to apologize to wronged parties; it is concerned with making amends and restitution where possible. The AA literature emphasizes that the alcoholic has apologized innumerable times over the years without instituting any actual change. The eighth and ninth steps demand changes in attitudes and behavior. The AA member is cautioned against unburdening his or her own guilt over some previous action at the expense of another's well-being.

The tenth step encourages the AA member to make daily use of the new way of life established in the first nine steps. Now that measures have been taken to assess character defects and past mistakes and to make amends, it is necessary to maintain the associated gains by practicing a daily inventory of new attitudes and behaviors. The tenth step is seen as a practical means for avoiding a slip back into destructive thinking patterns and drinking.

The eleventh step is also concerned with the maintenance of sobriety. Anticipating that the recovering alcoholic might begin to neglect prayer and meditation once life begins to be more satisfying, this step is a reminder of the source of that satisfaction. It also provides guidance about the most effective way to pray, by suggesting that AA members avoid selfish requests and focus instead on understanding God's will in every situation. This step is related to the third step, which asks that the alcoholic turn his or her will and life over to the care of God. Both steps serve to counteract the alcoholic's tendency to insist that he or she needs no one, and to foster a dependence on a Higher Power.

The twelfth step states the goal of all the other eleven steps. A spiritual awakening is "the result," not an accidental by-product, of following the suggestions of the steps. A *spiritual awakening* is defined by AA as "a new consciousness and being" (AA World Services, 1978, p. 107). In this new state of awareness, the alcoholic finds meaning and purpose in life where there was none previously. This sense of purpose is given an outlet by the portion of the step that encourages the AA member to take the AA message to other alcoholics. This is seen as crucial to maintaining sobriety, and the sentiment is often heard in AA meetings that "you can't keep it unless you give it away." The final suggestion of this step is that the principles acquired by practicing the steps should be practiced in all portions of one's life, and not be limited to contact with AA.

Overcomers Outreach (OO)

OO has many similarities to AA. Designed as a complement to AA and other 12-step groups, OO makes explicit connections between the Christian Bible and the 12 steps. Unlike AA, OO is available to persons with any kind of addictive behavior problem, as well as others who consider themselves "codependent." OO is a nonprofit ministry and is financed by contributions from individuals and groups as well as Christian businesses. Specific materials are available for family members, adults who had alcoholic parents, smokers, overeaters, "sex addicts," and so on. OO groups meet "to study God's Word as it relates . . . to the 12 Steps of AA, to study relevant subjects in the light of the Scriptures, to share with one another, . . . and to pray" (Overcomers Outreach, 1985a).

Overcomers Outreach is organized around 12 traditions. These traditions will not be discussed in detail here, as they are virtually identical to those of AA (see Table 10.2). They differ

Table 10.2 Overcomers Outreach Group Traditions

---

1. Our common welfare should come first. Personal recovery depends upon God's grace and our willingness to get help.
2. For our group purpose there is but one ultimate authority—a loving god as He expresses Himself through His Son Jesus Christ and the Holy Spirit. Our leaders are but trusted servants; they do not govern.
3. The only requirement for Overcomers Outreach membership is a desire to stop addictive or compulsive behavior.
4. Each group should be autonomous except in matters affecting other groups or Overcomers Outreach as a whole.
5. The primary purpose of each group is to serve as a "bridge" between traditional 12 Step groups and the church. We carry the message of Christ's delivering power to individuals and family members both within and without the church who still suffer.
6. An Overcomers Outreach group uses The Holy Bible along with the 12 Steps of Alcoholics Anonymous for its tools of recovery. Outside enterprises are prayerfully evaluated lest problems of money, property and prestige divert us from our primary purpose.
7. Every Overcomers Outreach group ought to be fully self-supporting, declining outside contributions.
8. Overcomers Outreach groups should remain forever nonprofessional, but our Service Centers may employ special workers.
9. Overcomers Outreach, as such, ought never be organized, but group coordinators network with the Central Service Center, seeing that the group is facilitated through adherence to the Freed Book's "Meeting Format" and rotation of leadership.
10. Overcomers Outreach is, without apology, a Christ-centered recovery group; however, persons of all faiths are welcome. Discussions of doctrine should be avoided; our focus must be upon our mutual recovery.
11. Our public relations policy is based upon attraction rather than promotion; we need to always seek the Holy Spirit's discernment whenever sharing in the media, in order to maintain personal anonymity of all Overcomers Outreach group members.
12. Jesus Christ is the spiritual foundation of all our traditions, ever reminding us to place principles before personalities. We claim God's promise that His power can set us FREE!

Source: Reprinted by permission, Overcomers Outreach.

primarily in their greater emphasis on Jesus and the Bible and their discussion of the purpose of OO as a bridge between traditional 12-step groups and the church. OO does not have a set of steps different from AA, but does show the clear biblical links to each of the steps. Table 10.3 reproduces the OO cited biblical passages.

Each OO group has a designated "leader" who is responsible for keeping meetings running on schedule. Meeting format is prescribed by one of the major OO publications, *FREED* (Overcomers Outreach, 1985b). Meetings begin with leader introductions and an opening prayer. Persons new to the group are then asked to introduce themselves by first names, and group members are encouraged to greet them. Other group members then introduce themselves by first names, and indicate with what recovery program they are affiliated (AA, CA, etc.). The meeting then may continue with some songs or hymns, the reading of the Overcomers Outreach preamble, reading of the 12 steps, and a group recitation of the Serenity Prayer. The balance of the meeting is devoted to study of a particular step or topic. The meeting ends with a voluntary collection and a prayer.

Calix Society

The Calix Society was founded in 1947 to help Catholics "regain" their spiritual life. Similar to Overcomers Outreach, all those involved with Calix should also be involved with AA. Calix is organized around "units." Calix is a small organization, listing only 67 units in the United States, 3 in Canada, 10 in Scotland, and 9 in England in April of 1992. When a new unit is formed, founders must obtain the permission of the bishop of the diocese. Although Calix is a lay organization, priests are important leaders and provide "spiritual guidance" to members. Calix charges a membership fee of $24 per member, and members receive a bimonthly newsletter.

The purpose of Calix is to interest Catholics who have drinking problems in "the virtue of total abstinence" (Calix Society, undated, p. 1) and in engaging in a program of spiritual growth to go along with their abstinence. *Calix* is the Latin word for "chalice," and members see themselves as "substituting the cup that sanctifies for the cup that stupifies [sic]" (Calix Society, undated, page 2). The program is intended only for alcoholics who are already abstinent, and the focus of the program is, in essence, on the eleventh step of AA (see Table 10.1). Similar to OO, Calix members believe that their higher power is Jesus. Units meet monthly, with meetings including a mass, Holy Communion, breakfast, and a spiritual message from the local chaplain. Members are asked to pray daily, and specific prayers are provided (Calix Society, 1971).

Table 10.3 Overcomers Outreach Scriptures Related to the 12 Steps of AA

Step 1	"We felt we were doomed to die and saw how POWERLESS we were to help ourselves; but that was good, for then we put everything into the hands of God, who alone could save us." (2 Corinthians 1:9)
Step 2	"A man is a fool to trust himself! But those who use God's wisdom are safe." (Proverbs 23:26)
Step 3	"Trust in the Lord completely; don't ever trust yourself. In everything you do, put God first, and he will direct you and crown your efforts with success." (Proverbs 3:5-6)
Step 4	"Let us examine ourselves and repent and turn again to the Lord. Let us lift our hearts and our hands to him in heaven." (Lamentations 3:40-41)
Step 5	"Admit your faults to one another and pray for each other so that you may be healed." (James 5:16)
Step 6	"So give yourselves humbly to God... then, when you realize your worthlessness before the Lord, He will lift you up, encourage and help you." (James 4:7-10)
Step 7	"But if we confess our sins to Him, He can be depended on to forgive us and to cleanse us from every wrong." (1 John 1:9)
Step 8	"If you are standing before the altar... and suddenly remember that a friend has something against you, leave your sacrifice there and go and be reconciled... and then come and offer your sacrifice to God." (Matthew 5:23-24)
Step 9	"You can pray for anything, and if you believe, you have it; it's yours! But when you are praying, first forgive anyone you are holding a grudge against, so that your Father in heaven will forgive you your sins too." (Mark 11:24-25)
Step 10	"But how can I ever know what sins are lurking in my heart: Cleanse me from these hidden faults. And keep me from deliberate wrongs; help me to stop doing them. Only then can I be set free of guilt." (Psalm 19:12)
Step 11	"If you want better insight and discernment, and are searching for them as you would for lost money or hidden treasure, then wisdom will be given you, and knowledge of God himself; you will soon learn the importance of reverence for the Lord and of trusting Him." (Proverbs 2:3-5)
Step 12	"Quietly trust yourself to Christ your Lord and if anybody asks why you believe as you do, be ready to tell him, and do it in a gentle and respectful way." (1 Peter 3:15)

Source: Reprinted by permission, Overcomers Outreach.

Rational Recovery

The first three self-help groups described all are similar in their focus on spirituality and faith as central to recovery, and view recovery as a life-long process. All are grounded in a disease conception of alcohol problems. The second three groups to be described take a very different approach, placing greater emphasis on rational thought, and viewing drinking problems as, in essence, problems in living for which people need to learn particular cognitive and behavior skills.

Rational Recovery (RR) is grounded in the principles of Rational Emotive Therapy (RET; Ellis & Velten, 1992). RR views the use of psychoactive substances as an "irrational choice," and believes that persons can learn to use their rational mind, rather than spirituality, to "empower" themselves in order to choose not to drink. Trimpey (1992), the founder of RR, suggests that people "approach [their] lives and problems as ones who either have *faith* in unchanging principles or as ones who think things through and use *reason* as the light

that shows the way" (p. xxii). From his perspective, AA is based in faith; RR in reason.

RR has several key concepts. First is the concept of self-esteem. RR suggests that it is more useful to like and respect yourself than not to, and that a person should stop drinking or drugging *because* he or she has self-esteem, rather than to obtain it. A second core construct in RR is that persons should take a rational approach to change, making a decision to stop using alcohol or drugs (and following through with that decision), and developing a plan for change. The third core concept is that of "voices," RR's way of discussing irrational thinking. RR suggests that alcohol- and drug-dependent persons have a set of irrational cognitions about alcohol or drugs that leads them to use and to relapse. Trimpey calls these irrational ideas "The Beast," a metaphor to describe various ways that irrational cognitions may lead to relapse. RR provides a number of useful, rational disputations for the ideas of the "Beast." These are reproduced in Table 10.4, along with a

Table 10.4   Rational Recovery Ideas

1. I have considerable voluntary control over my extremities and facial muscles.
2. It is *because* I am worthwhile to myself that I will decide to stop drinking and build a better life.
3. Some discomfort is a necessary, inevitable, and entirely harmless part of becoming and remaining sober.
4. I feel the way I think, and so have *enormous* control over my emotions, sorrows, and disturbances.
5. I am a fallible human being. While I may feel regrets, remorse, or sadness for my alcoholic behavior, I need not conclude that I am a worthless person.
6. As time goes by drinking appears increasingly stupid because of the obvious selfish advantages of sobriety, but, if I ever stupidly relapsed by drinking, it wouldn't be awful because I would very likely recover again.
7. Because rational sobriety is self-fulfilling, and because there is so much more to life than a constant struggle to remain sober, I can gradually close the book on that sorry chapter in my life and become vitally absorbed in activities and projects outside of myself that are unrelated to my former alcoholism.

Additional Rational Recovery Ideas:
1. I am aware that I am chemically dependent, and the consequences of that dependency are unacceptable.
2. I accept that, in order to get better, I had better refrain from any use of alcohol or drugs, because any use will very likely lead to more, and then a return to my previous addiction.
3. I accept that I will likely benefit from residential care, because I have been unsuccessful in previous attempts to resist my desire to drink or use drugs.
4. Although I may have serious personal problems, I still have the capacity to learn about myself, about new ideas, and about how to achieve a satisfying, rational sobriety.
5. The idea that I must depend on something greater than myself in order to stay sober is only another dependency idea, and dependency is my original problem.
6. I am willing to reject ideas of perfection for myself and for others, and my first goal is to learn to accept myself as I am—a fallible, yet worthwhile, human being.
7. I place a high value on the principles of rationality, learning, objectivity, self-forgiveness, and on my own self-interest.
8. I recognize that, even though I am chemically dependent, I am responsible for my own emotions and behavior.
9. With the passage of time I may learn that refraining from mind-altering drugs is easier than trying to control them, and that too much is at stake to risk further use. Intoxicants have considerably less appeal to physically and mentally healthy people.
10. I will eventually complete my recovery and live a normal life.
11. There are no perfect solutions to life's problems, and that uncertainty is the spice of life, so therefore I am willing to take risks to achieve my own self-defined goals.
12. I will choose to give up ideas of guilt, blame, and worthlessness as a matter of principle, and also because those emotions are inappropriate for an adult.
13. Now certain of my own human worth, I can take the risks of loving others, for loving is far better than being loved.

set of 13 rational ideas for recovery that appear to provide an RR alternative to the 12 steps of AA.

RR suggests abstinence as the safest route to dealing with an alcohol or drug problem, but emphasizes rational decision making, and acknowledges that some members may make a rational decision to drink moderately rather than abstain.

RR groups are peer led, but all groups have a professional therapist associated with them as an advisor, and professionals may be involved in getting groups started. RR members are encouraged to attend meetings for a period of 6 to 12 months, and then to move on with their lives. RR does not present itself as a lifelong program of recovery that requires regular attendance at meetings. There are no membership fees, but monies are collected at meetings, and additional funds from the sale of books and other publications provide financial support for the program.

Secular Organizations for Sobriety—Save Our Selves

SOS was begun in 1985 as a self-help program for those uncomfortable with the "spiritual content" of 12-step programs. SOS views sobriety as separate from either religion or spirituality. It promotes the use of the scientific method to achieve sobriety and endorses a "healthy skepticism." SOS has several major principles that guide the program. First, the program is open to anyone who "sincerely seeks sobriety." In this way, the program is similar to AA. It emphasizes that it is not a "spinoff" from any religious group. SOS promotes the importance of supportive others in achieving and maintaining sobriety, and believes that abstinence, rather than moderate drinking, is a necessary goal. SOS emphasizes that individuals with drinking problems need to choose "non-destructive, non-

delusional, . . . rational approaches to living" (SOS, undated, p. 3). SOS has adopted two principles similar to those of AA: It provides no opinions on issues outside of SOS, and it encourages anonymity, although the latter is suggested to avoid embarrassment to members, and has no spiritual component.

SOS suggests that there are three major aspects of addiction—physiological need, a learned habit, and denial of the need and the habit. To achieve sobriety, SOS suggests that persons need to acknowledge their addiction, accept that they have a disease or bad habit, and make their sobriety a priority each day.

SOS provides a set of suggested guidelines for sobriety, reproduced in Table 10.5, and has several books that provide additional information to members (e.g., Christopher, 1989). The program offers various suggestions to facilitate initial sobriety—meeting attendance, having telephone numbers of other SOS members and calling them, developing a set of routines and structures in the individual's life, reading about alcoholism and recovery, consuming healthy foods and drinks, and "being gentle on yourself."

Women for Sobriety

Women for Sobriety (WFS) is designed specifically to help women recover from alcohol problems. The program was begun based on the belief that the concepts underpinning AA, such as powerlessness, turning over one's will, and the importance of keeping memories of drinking behavior fresh are countertherapeutic to the needs of women. The defined purpose of WFS is to help women recover "through the discovery of self, gained by sharing experiences, hopes, and encouragement with other women" (Women for Sobriety, 1976). WFS believes that women's drinking develops as a way to cope with negative emotional states such as loneliness or frus-

---

Table 10.5   Secular Organizations for Sobriety: Suggested Guidelines for Sobriety

1. To break the cycle of denial and achieve sobriety, we first acknowledge that we are alcoholics or addicts.
2. We reaffirm this truth daily and accept without reservation the fact that, as clean and sober individuals, we can not and do not drink or use, no matter what.
3. Since drinking or using is not an option for us, we take whatever steps are necessary to continue our Sobriety Priority lifelong.
4. A quality of life—"the good life"—can be achieved. However, life is also filled with uncertainties. Therefore, we do not drink or use regardless of feelings, circumstances, or conflicts.
5. We share in confidence with each other our thoughts and feelings as sober, clear individuals.
6. Sobriety is our Priority, and we are each responsible for our lives and our sobriety.

Source: Reprinted by permission, S.O.S. National Clearinghouse.

tration, and that the drinking eventually leads to physical addiction. The program emphasizes total abstinence from alcohol, and states the requirements of membership as a "desire to stop drinking and a sincere desire for a new life" (Women for Sobriety, 1976).

The WFS program can be contrasted to AA along several dimensions: an emphasis on personal control, an emphasis on developing a self-identity as a competent woman rather than as an alcoholic, a focus on putting the past behind, and a belief that once a woman can cope she no longer needs WFS meetings. WFS believes that women alcoholics experience humiliation and that a sense of helplessness and powerlessness is central to their lives. WFS attempts to counter these experiences through the program.

The program is organized around 13 statements (reproduced in Table 10.6) that constitute the "New Life Acceptance Program." The program has six levels: (1) acceptance of the woman's physical dependence on alcohol; (2) eliminating negative thoughts and learning more problem-solving-oriented thinking; (3) creating a new self-identity as a competent woman; (4) translating these more positive thoughts and attitudes into new behaviors; (5) improving interpersonal relationships; and (6) focusing the woman's priorities on emotional and spiritual growth and a sense of responsibility for herself.

WFS meetings are led by a "certified moderator," and in that sense are not strictly self-help groups. The moderator must have a stable recovery herself and understand the philosophy and program of WFS. Meetings have a fairly defined structure. They begin with reading the statement of purpose, and close with an affirmation statement. The core of each meeting is the discussion of a particular topic. The WFS newsletter provides suggested topics for each meeting. Donations are collected at the end of the meeting. WFS has a variety of books and other readings available to members (e.g., Kirkpatrick, 1978).

INTEGRATING SELF-HELP GROUPS WITH PROFESSIONAL PRACTICE

In the previous section, we described the principles and structure of several different self-help groups. In this section, we will consider how you, as a professional practitioner, can integrate self-help groups with your clinical practice. While some people with drinking problems seek out self-help groups as their primary source of assistance, never using the services of a clinical professional, for this book it is most important to consider how you as a professional can integrate self-help groups with your professional practice.

Practice Issues

If you are working toward an abstinence goal with a client, any of the self-help groups described in this chapter may be appropriate. If you and the client select a goal of moderation, then only RR is a clear self-help option. Self-help groups provide a readily accessible and free support system, and members of most self-help groups are available to help group members at any hour, an accessibility that most therapists cannot provide to their clients. In this section, we suggest clinical guidelines for selecting and suggesting self-help groups, and techniques for integrating these groups with professional treatment. Since there are no empirical studies that guide the methods that a therapist should use to facilitate self-help involvement, and since there are no data to support client-self-help group matching, our guidelines must be viewed as tentative.

Before referring a client to a self-help group, develop familiarity with these organizations. Attend group meetings and read some of the basic literature, such as *Alcoholics Anonymous* (often called the "Big Book") (AA World Services, 1980), *Twelve Steps and Twelve Traditions* (AA World Services, 1978), *Unhooked: Staying Sober and Drug Free* (Christopher, 1989), *Turnabout: New Help for the Woman Alcoholic* (Kirkpatrick, 1978), *The Small Book: A Revolutionary Alternative for Overcoming Alcohol and Drug*

Table 10.6 Women for Sobriety "New Life" Acceptance Program

1. I have a life-threatening problem that once had me.
2. Negative thoughts destroy only myself.
3. Happiness is a habit I will develop.
4. Problems bother me only to the degree I permit them to.
5. I am what I think.
6. Life can be ordinary or it can be great.
7. Love can change the course of my world.
8. The fundamental object of life is emotional and spiritual growth.
9. The past is gone forever.
10. All love given returns.
11. Enthusiasm is my daily exercise.
12. I am a competent woman and have much to give life.
13. I am responsible for myself and my actions.

Source: Reprinted by permission, Women for Sobriety.

Dependence (Trimpey, 1992), or *FREED* (Over-comers Outreach, 1985). Familiarize yourself with various pamphlets and newsletters published by the self-help groups. Consider maintaining a stock of introductory pamphlets in the office. Be aware of the different types of meetings, what the basic principles and beliefs are that underpin each program, and basic terminology (e.g., sponsor, higher power, beast, addictive voice).

When you introduce self-help group involvement to the client, provide a clear rationale for involvement. These groups provide a place where the client can meet others who have had similar problems and experiences, who will be supportive and helpful in sharing their own experiences. Therapy is a time-limited, place-limited proposition, and many self-help groups provide a support system that is available throughout the country and for as long as the client decides to use it. Self-help groups may also provide the sense of meaning—the friendships, closeness, and fun that many experience in groups. Finally, many individuals feel they have had tremendous success with self-help groups.

Clients often have questions or negative reactions when self-help groups are introduced. Many are familiar only with AA, and hold negative stereotypes. Clients may express concern that AA is for deteriorated, skid-row alcoholics; the belief that their drinking problem is not "that bad"; concern about the "religious" aspects of the program, feeling that they can do it on their own; a belief that many people who go to AA are hypocritical because they go to meetings and then drink; or a belief that AA is ineffective because of personal knowledge of someone who relapsed while involved with AA.

To address these concerns, discuss the various self-help group options, and educate the client about what the groups offer and how they are different. Consider the individual characteristics of the client, and provide suggestions about what group you believe would be the best fit for the client. We recommend AA to clients who value faith and intuition; RR or SOS to clients who are firmly irreligious or who place a high value on independence and logic. Clearly, this is not a precise matching criterion, as many in AA would suggest that those who have no faith or spirituality most need what AA has to offer. Calix and Overcomers Outreach are specifically for Catholics and evangelical Christians, and clients should be informed of the unique programs that they offer. Where available, we usually suggest Women for Sobriety for female clients, or suggest that women begin AA attending women-only groups, because there are some data suggesting that women have better treatment outcomes when treated in all-female treatment programs (Dahlgren & Willander, 1989). We also believe that some clients are not good candidates for any kind of self-help groups—clients who are intensely private, acutely uncomfortable in groups, or who typically are successful in resolving their problems through self-reliance.

If clients express reluctance or concerns about self-help groups, we attempt to address their concerns. We present the groups as a possible part of the client's treatment program, but we do not insist on attendance. Throughout treatment, we fully involve the client in the decision-making process, and believe that giving the client a sense of choice and involvement in all aspects of the treatment will enhance compliance (Miller & Rollnick, 1991).

Having several tools available facilitates involvement in self-help groups. Listings of meeting schedules are essential and can be obtained at meetings or ordered. Examine the schedule with the client to select a meeting for him or her to attend. Some introductory pamphlets also may help to answer the client's questions. Ideally, you might have the names of several members of different self-help groups to call on and arrange for the client and the group member to meet and go to a meeting together.

A final aspect of helping the client to get to a first meeting is to explain what to expect in the meeting. We describe a typical meeting and tell clients that they do not have to be a member to attend a meeting, and that they do not have to talk during the meeting (they can "pass" if called on). For AA, we also explain the types of meetings, including open and closed meetings, discussion and speaker meetings, step meetings, and beginners' meetings.

After the client attends a meeting, ask about his or her experiences and reactions. Discuss concerns and negative reactions and encourage the client to sample several different meetings of the same self-help group, or try a different self-help group. For some clients, negative reactions to self-help group meetings allow you to identify interpersonal anxiety or social skills deficits, or identify significant ambivalence about changing drinking. You can then work fruitfully on these areas in the therapy.

As a client continues his or her involvement in a self-help group, have the client set goals for attendance, as he or she would for other behavioral changes. Self-recording forms should include space to record self-help group attendance. To track the client's progress in becoming involved, inquire about whether the client has obtained any program literature, has begun to speak to people before or after meetings, found a group that is comfortable, joined a group, or, in the case of AA, obtained a sponsor. All are markers of the beginning of more serious group involvement. Most of the self-help group programs are progressive, and you can assess a client's progress through the steps of the program.

In addition to showing knowledgeable and unambivalent interest in the client's progress in the self-help group, you can facilitate links between therapy and self-help. For cognitive-behavior therapists, such links are easy to make with RR, SOS, and WFS, as all are closely linked to cognitive therapy techniques. For AA, you must be intimately familiar with the similarities in practice between AA and behavior therapy (see McCrady, in press, for a detailed discussion of these similarities). For example, if stimulus control procedures are introduced, AA meetings can be used as an example of an activity incompatible with drinking. Other simple AA suggestions—such as calling an AA member when tempted to drink, reading AA literature, or going to a meeting—are all examples of active behavioral alternatives to drinking. AA talks about changing "persons, places and things," clearly the essence of stimulus control.

Rehearsal of the negative consequences of drinking is another behavioral technique closely allied to AA. Writing down a list of negative consequences of drinking and reviewing it is similar to the fourth step in AA, and also similar to telling one's story in an AA meeting.

Many times, involvement with a self-help group leads clients to identify feelings or problems that cannot be dealt with effectively in the self-help group. You can provide structured behavioral, cognitive, or affective skills training to complement the assistance they receive from the self-help group.

THE EFFECTIVENESS OF SELF-HELP GROUPS

Controlled outcome research on self-help groups is limited, with a few reported studies on AA, and none on the other self-help groups described in this chapter. In this section, we will address four major sources of information about the effectiveness of AA: (1) controlled studies using randomized assignment to experimental groups; (2) quasi-experimental designs comparing AA to other forms of treatment; (3) single group studies that follow subjects after involvement with AA or treatment based on AA principles; and (4) treatment outcomes that look at the relationships between AA attendance and professional treatment.

Before addressing the relevant research, it is important to comment on some of the reasons for the paucity of research on AA and other self-help groups. Some of the self-help groups are of relatively recent origin (e.g., RR, SOS), and although they welcome research, controlled studies have just not been completed to date. For AA and other 12-step programs, the traditions of anonymity and refusal to affiliate with any other groups make it difficult to track persons involved with AA. There are, however, a number of creative research strategies that could be used to conduct research on AA (see McCrady & Miller, 1993, for a more complete discussion of this topic).

We believe that some of the barriers to studying AA are as much attitudinal as scientific. AA is a program based on experience and grounded in faith, and the usual kind of objective scrutiny of science is anathema to the values of AA. Because so many clinicians involved in treating alcoholics have themselves successfully recovered through AA, the same faith and acceptance that guided their personal recovery has guided their acceptance of the universal effectiveness of AA. As will become apparent in this section, despite the large membership of AA and the enthusiasm for AA held by so many in the alcoholism field, there is a paucity of research supporting the purported superior effectiveness of AA.

Randomized Clinical Trials

As noted in Chapter 2, only three studies have reported the results of randomized clinical trials that included AA. All three studies were conducted using coerced populations (chronic drunkenness offenders, persons convicted of DWI, employees referred to an employee assistance program). Because AA is intended to be a voluntary program open to persons with a desire to stop drinking, evaluating its effectiveness with persons who are required to attend and who do not necessarily want to stop drinking, does not provide a fair test of its effectiveness. AA as delivered in these studies also had other limitations—meeting locations were prescribed (Brandsma, Maultsby, & Welsh, 1980), or subjects were required to attend only one meeting per week (Brandsma et al., 1980; Dittman, Crawford, Forgy, Moskowitz, & MacAndrew, 1967). Overall, none of the controlled trials found AA to be more effective than alternative treatment. One study found greater attrition from the AA experimental condition (Brandsma et al., 1980) and one reported more frequent relapses and need for hospitalization among subjects assigned to attend only AA (Walsh et al., 1991).

Quasi-Experimental Studies

Smith (1985, 1986) used a quasi-experimental design to compare men and women treated in a halfway house setting to clients treated in a hospital-based detoxification center in Australia. Clients were matched on demographic variables. Treatment consisted of daily AA meetings and a work program, as well as contact with recovering alcoholic program staff. Clients were followed 14 to 19 months after treatment. Differences in self-reported rates of continuous abstinence were statistically significant and dramatic: 79% of treated women and 61.8% of treatment men reported abstinence following treatment, compared to 3% of control women and 5.1% of control men.

Smith's research represents a serious attempt to identify an appropriate comparison group, even though random assignment to groups was not used. However, although the outcomes appeared quite positive, the studies were really evaluating the effectiveness of AA in the context of a more comprehensive treatment program, rather than as a program of change by itself. The studies also had other methodological flaws that detract from their overall value.

Single-Group Evaluations of AA

A number of researchers have reported on the outcomes of treatment from programs that use many of the principles of AA. In addition, AA conducts triennial surveys of the members, which provide information about abstinence rates reported by members attending meetings. The most recent membership survey (Alcoholics Anonymous, 1990a) reports that 65% of those responding reported sobriety of one year or more, but also report that the majority of persons who begin to attend AA discontinue their attendance in the first year.

Studies of treatment programs based on AA principles have all derived from inpatient programs. These studies typically report rates of continuous abstinence around 50% for one year (e.g., Alford, 1980), although programs that follow all clients who begin treatment (rather than just treatment completers) and count as relapsers those clients unavailable to follow-up typically report lower abstinence rates (e.g., Filstead, 1990).

AA AND PROFESSIONAL TREATMENT

In their meta-analysis of research on AA, Emrick and colleagues (1993) examined the additive effects of AA and professional treatment. They reported that participation in AA prior to treatment is not correlated with the outcomes of treatment, but that there is a positive association between AA attendance during and after professional treatment and drinking outcomes. They note, however, that a number of variables may contribute to variability in that correlation, and that the overall effects, while positive, are modest.

CONCLUSIONS

The data about the effectiveness of self-help groups are limited and mixed. No controlled evaluations of self-help groups other than AA have been reported, and controlled trials of AA have not yielded positive findings. However, evaluation studies provide suggestive hints of the positive benefits of AA—large numbers of persons attend, and those who maintain their involvement are likely to abstain from the use of alcohol. Evidence suggests that combining AA and professional treatment may enhance the probability of a positive treatment outcome.

At this point in the history of alcohol treatment, clinicians are best advised to take a client-treatment matching approach to their clinical decision making. Clearly, individuals use multiple methods to successfully deal with alcohol problems, and a wide variety of self-help groups are available that are based in different perspectives on the nature of alcohol problems and the process of change. These groups should be considered as an important potential source of assistance, but, like any therapeutic technique, should be selected with the unique problems, beliefs, and life circumstances of the individual client kept firmly in mind.

REFERENCES

Clinical References

AA World Services. (1980). *Alcoholics Anonymous*. New York: Author. This volume is the basic text of AA and is often referred to as the AA "Big Book." It contains chapters describing AA's perception of alcoholism, the AA program and how it works, and how spouses and families might best cope with the alcoholic in recovery. The second portion of the book contains the personal stories of 26 alcoholics who recovered through AA.

AA World Services. (1978). *Twelve steps and twelve traditions*. New York: Author. An interpretation of the basic tenets of the program by one of its cofounders. It describes each step and tradition in a manner that can be useful both to new members and longer-term members. This book is often used at Step and Tradition meetings as a guide to the discussion.

Calix Society (undated). *Calix. What and why*. Minneapolis, MN: Author. This pamphlet provides basic information about Calix.

Calix Society. (1971). *A word for the problem drinker! and Program of prayer*. Minneapolis, MN: Author. This pamphlet provides more detailed information about Calix, and prayers for different situations and concerns.

Center for Self-help Research and Knowledge Dissemination, School of Social Work, University of Michigan, Ann Arbor, MI. This center conducts research on self-help groups and serves as a resource for the professional community.

Christopher, J. (1989). *Unhooked. Staying sober and drug free*. Prometheus Books. This is the basic book that introduces the philosophy of SOS.

Kirkpatrick, J. (1978). *Turnabout. New help for the woman alcoholic*. Garden City, NY: Doubleday. This is the basic book that introduces the philosophy of WFS.

New Jersey Self-help Clearinghouse. (1993). *The self-help group sourcebook*. Denville, NJ: Author. This sourcebook lists information about a variety of self-help group meetings in New Jersey, and information about self-help clearinghouses in other states.

Overcomers Outreach. (1985a). *Chemically dependent Christian...Get loose*. LaHabra, CA: Author. This pamphlet provides basic information about OO.

Overcomers Outreach. (1985b). *FREED (Fellowship in recovery, Reconciliation to God & His family, Education about Chemicals & addiction, Edification through faith in Christ, Dedicated service to others)*. La Habra, CA: Author. This pamphlet provides guidelines for running OO meetings as well as other program information.

Overcomers Outreach. (1988). *The 12 steps . . . with their corresponding scriptures?* LaHabra, CA: Author. This pamphlet lists the 12 steps and supporting biblical materials.

Secular Organizations for Sobriety (undated). *Secular Organizations for Sobriety/Save Our Selves. A reasonable approach to recovery*. Buffalo, NY: Author. This pamphlet provides basic information about SOS.

Trimpey, J. (1992). *The small book: A revolutionary alternative for overcoming alcohol and drug dependence* (third edition). New York: Delacorte Press. This is the basic book that introduces the philosophy and approach of RR.

Women for Sobriety. (1976). *AA and WFS*. Quakertown, PA: Author. This pamphlet provides a comparison of AA and WFS, and contains the WFS statement of purpose.

Treatment Effectiveness

Alcoholics Anonymous. (1990a). *Alcoholics Anonymous 1989 membership survey*. New York: Alcoholics Anonymous World Services.

Alford, G. S. (1980). Alcoholics Anonymous: An empirical outcome study. *Addictive Behaviors, 5*, 359–370.

Brandsma, J. M., Maultsby, M. C., & Welsh, R. J. (1980). *Outpatient treatment of alcoholism. A review and comparative study*. Baltimore, MD: University Park Press.

Dahlgren, L., & Willander, A. (1989). Are special treatment facilities for female alcoholics needed: A controlled 2-year study from a specialized female unit (EWA) versus a mixed male/female treatment facility. *Alcoholism: Clinical and Experimental Research, 13*, 499–504.

Dittman, K. S., Crawford, G. C., Forgy, E. W., Moskowitz, H., & MacAndrew, C. (1967). A controlled experiment on the use of court probation for drunk arrests. *American Journal of Psychiatry, 124*, 160–163.

Ellis, A., & Velten, E. (1992). *Rational steps to quitting alcohol*. Fort Lee, NJ: Barricade Books, Inc.

Emrick, C. D., Tonigan, S., Montgomery, H., & Little, L. (1993). Alcoholics Anonymous: What is currently known? In B. S. McCrady & W. R. Miller (Eds.), *Research on Alcoholics Anonymous: Opportunities and alternatives* (pages 41–79). New Brunswick, NJ: Alcohol Research Documentation, Inc., Rutgers University.

Filstead, W. J. (1990). *Treatment outcome: An evaluation of adult and youth treatment services*. Park Ridge, IL: Parkside Medical Services Corporation.

Galanter, M., & Egelko, S. (in press). Rational Recovery. Combined cognitive and peer-led treatment for substance abuse. *American Journal of Drug and Alcohol Abuse*.

McCrady, B. S. (in press). AA and behavior therapy: Can habit be treated as diseases? Can diseases be treated as habits? *Journal of Consulting and Clinical Psychology*.

Miller, W. R., & Rollnick, S. (1991). *Motivational interviewing*. New York: Guilford Press.

Robinson, D. (1979). *Talking out of alcoholism*. London: Croom Helm.

Smith, D. I. (1985). Evaluation of a residential AA program for women. *Alcohol and Alcoholism, 20*, 315–327.

Smith, D. I. (1986). Evaluation of a residential AA program. *International Journal of the Addictions, 21*, 33–49.

Walsh, D. C., Hingson, R. W., Merrigan, D. M., Levenson, S. M., Cupples, L. A., Heeren, T., Coffman, G. A., Becker, C. A., Barker, T. A., Hamilton, S. K., McGuire, T. G., & Kelly, C. A. (1991). A randomized trial of treatment options for alcohol-abusing workers. *New England Journal of Medicine, 325*, 775–782.

Willis, C. (1993, August). *Self-help for alcoholism: Alternative paths to recovery and self-reported reasons for rejection of Alcoholics Anonymous*. Paper presented at the Annual Meeting of the American Psychological Association, Toronto, Ontario, Canada.

CHAPTER 11

Relapse Prevention

Linda A. Dimeff
G. Alan Marlatt

OVERVIEW

The most common treatment outcome for alcoholics and addicts is relapse. In the classic review of the treatment outcome literature on studies of habitual smokers, heroin addicts, and alcoholics, relapse curves across these addictions showed a strikingly similar pattern (Hunt, Barnett, & Branch, 1971). Approximately 66% of all research participants relapsed by the 90-day follow-up assessment, with the majority of these relapses occurring within the initial month following termination of treatment. Early approaches to treatment focused exclusively on making initial changes in behavior, and not on maintaining these changes over time. This approach often resulted in a "revolving door" approach to treatment where relapse offenders returned to treatment following each relapse. For the past 15 years, relapse prevention (RP) has offered alternative strategies to the "revolving door" phenomenon through an integration of behavioral skills training and cognitive intervention strategies aimed at maintaining the behavioral goal.

Marlatt and Gordon (1985) defined RP as a cognitive-behavioral self-management program (Craighead, Craighead, Kazdin, & Mahoney, 1994) that combines behavioral skills training procedures with cognitive techniques to help individuals maintain their desired behavioral change. Integrating principles from social-cognitive theory (Bandura, 1986), health psychology, and psychoeducational therapeutic approaches, RP focuses on strategy building in three distinct areas: (1) anticipating and preventing relapses from occurring, (2) coping humanely and effectively with a relapse to minimize its negative consequences and outcome and maximize learning from the experience, and (3) reducing global health risks and replacing lifestyle imbalance with balance and moderation. With skills training as the cornerstone of the RP approach, RP teaches clients how to anticipate, identify, and manage high-risk situations while also making security preparations for their future by striving for broader lifestyle balance. RP operates at two levels in tandem: enhancing effectiveness in managing specific high-risk situations and balancing one's lifestyle through more global behavioral modifications or changes. RP is easily tailored for use across a wide range of addictive habits in a heterogeneous population of clients seeking professional help.

Relapse prevention is based on four assumptions: First, different processes govern the cessation and maintenance stages of behavior change (Bandura, 1977; Marlatt & Gordon, 1985;

Brownell, Marlatt, Lichtenstein, & Wilson, 1986). Second, RP is most successful when the client confidently acts as his or her own therapist following treatment. Instead of relying on "willpower," RP views the client as his or her own "maintenance person," facile and fully equipped with the necessary behavioral "tools" to use when signs of trouble appear (Marlatt, 1982). Third, relapse risks are complex and involve individual, situational, physiological and sociocultural factors. Finally, relapse and the process of recovery is an ongoing process, and not an endpoint or terminal episode to be equated with treatment failure.

Alan Marlatt and colleagues initially developed RP for use in the treatment of addictive behaviors, with abstinence as the most common behavioral goal (Marlatt, 1978; Marlatt & Gordon, 1985). Originally, RP was intended to augment treatment aimed at cessation of behavior. While intended as a maintenance program, clinicians have used RP as a "solo" treatment for the cessation and maintenance phases. In recent years, both the application and goal of this original model have expanded considerably. Since its formation, clinicians and researchers have applied RP principles to the treatment of other addictive behaviors, such as eating and dieting, sexual compulsions, and gambling (Laws, 1989; Daley, 1988). RP has also been used to treat other impulsive and problematic behaviors with clear, identifiable antecedents such as domestic violence (Wilson, 1992; Laws, in press).

More recently, Marlatt and colleagues have applied RP to the secondary prevention of alcohol problems among college heavy drinkers. Within this RP application, the "bottom" is raised for less problematic drinkers by teaching students specific ways to moderate and reduce their consumption. The aim of this approach is to reduce health risks and negative consequences associated with heavy alcohol use in college students (Dimeff, Baer, & Marlatt, 1991; Baer, Kivlahan, Fromme, & Marlatt, 1988).

The specific strategies of relapse prevention described in this chapter are flexible and easily tailored to the needs and motivational interests of the client. Depending on the needs of the client, RP can occur in conjunction with Alcoholics Anonymous (AA), individual psychotherapy, or hospital-based treatment (Gorski & Miller, 1982). As a centerpiece of treatment, RP is well suited for groups (Wanigaratne, Wallace, Pullin, Keaney, & Farmer, 1990).

SPECIAL CONSIDERATIONS

The clinician's and client's beliefs, expectations, and attitudes regarding addictive behaviors can and usually do impact the treatment approach and its overall effectiveness. For clients who have had "unsuccessful" attempts to modify their problem behavior, "failings" are often understood as personal shortcomings, deficiencies of determination, or indicative of deep-seated psychological conflicts or a pathologic self-defeating style. Similarly, family members, friends, and therapists may also end up frustrated with the client for his or her inability to "follow through" on the path of behavior change in response to the seemingly endless ebb and flow of the recovery process. We instead recommend viewing the process of change from a perspective that facilitates greater understanding and compassion. Rather than blaming a client for difficulties that arise during the course of treatment, emphasis is placed instead on the specific context and related situational factors in which the slip or relapse occurs.

In their two-factor attributional analysis of helping and coping, Brickman and colleagues (1982) examined four principle models based on determinants of etiology and determinants of behavior change. As applied to addictions, the model posed two central questions: (1) Is the addict/alcoholic responsible for the development of the problem (etiology) and (2) is the addict/alcoholic responsible for changing the problem? When placed in a 2×2 matrix, the four specific models created provide a general framework for understanding addictions problems and a jumping off point for considering approaches to treatment and relapse. The four models include the moral model, the disease model, the spiritual (12-step) model, and the compensatory model (see Figure 11.1).

The moral model assumes the individual is responsible both for the development of the addiction and for changing or failing to change the addictive behavior. Failure to change, or relapse, is believed to be caused by a lack of willpower. Implicit in this model is the belief that addicted persons have the capacity to overcome their plight if only they were interested in doing so or possessed sufficient moral fiber. Unfortunately, this perspective often results in a "blaming the victim" mentality.

In contrast, the disease model posits that the addictive behavior is a manifestation of an underlying disease process rooted in the individual's

Figure 11.1   An Attribution Model of Addiction and Relapse

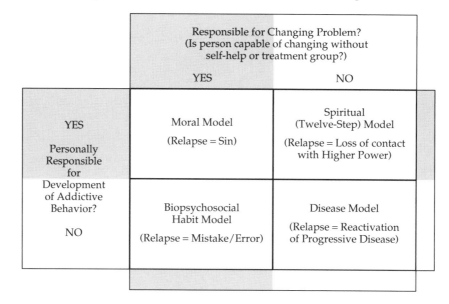

genetic or physiological make-up. The addict is often told that there is no cure for the disease, that his or her affliction is progressive in nature. Like the diabetic who must resist the craving to eat sugar lest she or he experience a seizure or death, the addict must resist all use of the substance. While blame is alleviated, the addict forever fears the resurgence of the uncontrollable disease. From this perspective, relapse is a reactivation of the disease process.

The spiritual or "enlightenment" model considers the addict as personally responsible to some extent for the emergence of the addiction. It also requires that the individual give up personal control in order to change. Exemplified by the 12-step tradition, the addict is viewed as a self-centered individual who has often placed his or her own selfish needs first, often resulting in the hurt feelings of others. Recovery is achieved by making amends to those harmed by selfish aims and greed, and by turning one's life (including personal control) over to a higher power. From this perspective, relapse derives from an alienation from one's higher power or group.

The compensatory model believes that the individual "compensates" for a problem not of her or his own making by assuming active responsibility and self-mastery in the change process. Relapse is viewed as a mistake or error in the new learning. Closely linked to the biopsychosocial habit model, this approach recognizes the influence of multiple factors on the etiology

of addictions (Marlatt, 1992). This model recognizes the client's power and influence in the process of change. The RP approach to understanding and treating addictive behaviors favors the compensatory model. It recognizes the multiple determinants of etiology while viewing the client as the rightful change agent. We have found that this particular combination works to build self-efficacy.

A second consideration of RP involves the client's degree of motivation to change behavior. Because RP equips the client with the necessary skills to act as his or her own future therapist, client motivation is a necessary ingredient to its success. Motivation-enhancing strategies are often aimed at the initial phase of treatment. RP encourages clients to regularly reexamine their reasons for maintaining their goal as a means of sustaining motivation.

Finally, we believe it is essential to consider the role of ethnicity, culture, gender, and social class when providing RP training to clients (Collier-Phillips & Marlatt, in press). A central question that emerges when considering the influence of marginalization and lack of basic resources (e.g., employment, adequate housing and food, child care, etc.) is this: How do the internalized effects of race, class, and/or gender prejudice and discrimination interact with efforts to establish and maintain self-efficacy? While the goal is to heighten the client's sense of competence in order to achieve a particular goal, could learned helplessness (Maier & Seligman, 1976) and real socioeconomic disadvantages undermine this aim? In a society in which women, ethnic minorities, and working class individuals are often portrayed negatively via societal images and stereotypes, and are categorized as "low achievers" (Wallace, 1991), minority clients may be vulnerable to perpetuating self-fulfilling prophecies of underachievement. Motivation to maintain treatment gains may diminish, in addition to one's belief in her or his competence as a result.

DESCRIPTION

Introducing Clients to Relapse Prevention

We typically begin relapse prevention by exploring with the client his or her own subjective associations to the word *relapse*. Responses often convey a sense of failure to attain a desired goal, or as recurrence of symptoms of a disease after a period of remission. For many clients, it is difficult to view relapse in anything but dichotomous terms (e.g., "Either I am clean and sober, or I've failed," "You're either on the wagon or off the wagon," etc.). This may be particularly true of clients who ascribe to a disease model or 12-step perspective. Viewed in this light, relapse, or the recurrence of a disease state, is diametrically opposed to doing well, or abstaining. From this all-or-nothing outlook, relapse is an end-state, or a dead end where the client is either a treatment success (e.g., abstaining) or failure (e.g., any violation of the abstinence).

There are several problems with the traditional view of relapse. First, this dichotomy creates an expectation or "mind-set" about what will occur in the event of a relapse. Addicts and alcoholics often believe that a relapse will result in a full loss of control. From this perspective, the client is either in full control, perhaps a master of restraint, or out of control, unable or unwilling to muster up even the slightest modicum of restraint over his or her indulgent and possibly destructive behavior. As one addict commented, "Either I'm controlling it, or it's controlling me." This view could result in a self-fulfilling prophecy in the event of a relapse.

Second, this dichotomous view sets the client up as a passive victim by faulting internal factors (e.g., irresistible physiological urges) as causing the relapse. Just as there is little a client can do to heal a broken bone or break a fever, one can neither prevent nor gain control over a relapse. Aside from passively waiting for the fever to abate or bone to heal, there is little the client can do to directly expedite the healing process.

We reframe relapse as a transitional process, one in which an initial slip or lapse may or may not result in a full return to pretreatment levels of use. From this perspective, a single occurrence of the problem behavior, or a lapse, is distinguished from a full-blown relapse. Lapses and relapses are instead viewed as mistakes and, more importantly, opportunities for additional learning. In this sense, the alcoholic can possibly benefit from a lapse. Just as a child who is learning to ride a bicycle sometimes benefits from a slip or fall by learning that the brakes need to be applied slowly in rounding a corner, so an individual who is attempting to change a habit may sometimes find that a lapse provides important information about the factors that led up to the event and how to make corrections in the future. From this perspective, it may be more appropriate to reframe this outcome as a "prolapse," since the overall beneficial outcome moves the individual ahead (Marlatt & Gordon, 1985). For example, following a lapse, the problem drinker decides to no longer spend time with former user-friends, recognizing that the temptation to use crack is too great when in their company.

In preparing our clients for the work that lies ahead, we use metaphors as a way to describe the course of habit change (Marlatt & Fromme, 1987). The process of change is described as a journey comprised of three important stages: preparation, departure, and the trip itself. We liken the goal of treatment to an expedition involving planning and a degree of determinism, such as backpacking in the Olympic Mountains in the Pacific Northwest. One must prepare for this journey by selecting a destination goal (moderation or abstinence), obtaining a suitable backpack, sleeping bag and other necessary equipment (the method of change, whether self-initiated or in consultation with a therapist; the type of treatment; etc.), locating maps, obtaining mountain survival skills, and so on. The novice hiker may see such preparation as overwhelming at times and the summit insurmountable. Such feelings can result in postponement of the departure ("I'll quit tomorrow") and ambivalence about one's initial decision ("Maybe I don't really need to change my behavior"). In our experience, these conflicts are best dealt with during the preparation stage. Premature departures (i.e., a sudden decision to quit) often lead to early setbacks that can diminish motivation. The goal of treatment in RP is to prepare in advance for as many specific potential threats to maintaining the behavioral goal as possible.

While preparation and a solid departure are essential components in the path of behavior change, RP emphasizes the importance of staying the course of change despite obstacles that may occur. To further extend the journey metaphor, we tell clients that relapse rates are particularly high during the first three months after quitting. We emphasize that many people take up to several years before they ultimately reach their goal to their satisfaction. Many proceed at a slow pace, some travel in a zigzag during the journey, moving back and forth, in and out of their target behavior. In the area of smoking and weight loss, for example, it is not uncommon for a person to require between two to five attempts before he or she is able to successfully maintain the target goal over time (Schachter, 1982).

Mistakes can and do happen. By allowing people to make mistakes, we interrupt the perceived state of control/out-of-control dichotomy we described earlier. Instead, we emphasize problem solving, learning from the experience, and action steps over moral condemnation or purely insight-oriented discussions. Although preparations made in advance of our departure usually pay off handsomely during the trip, it is impossible to totally predict and prepare for all the possible situations that might arise and pose a threat to our success or undermine our goal. Contrary to the weather forecast, a storm could blow in; the zipper in our sleeping bag could jam; we might miscalculate our stamina and overdo it on the first leg of our journey, resulting in weariness and muscle fatigue the following day. Because life is unpredictable (and it is impossible to predict when life will be unpredictable), a necessary goal of the maintenance phase is to focus on the development of global strategies for coping and living that can enhance the client's ability to respond to these unpredictable situations.

Rather than imaging oneself on the edge of a cliff, RP attempts to prepare the client for the possibility of a lapse or relapse. We do this without giving the client "permission" to drink or conveying an expectation that the client will lapse or relapse during the journey. We have found the use of metaphor (e.g., comparing RP to the need for fire or earthquake drills) effective in conveying the essence of relapse prevention philosophy.

Consider the following example: Before taking off in an airplane, flight attendants routinely instruct passengers in how to properly buckle up their seatbelts, locate their emergency exit, make use of the oxygen mask that will fall from their overhead compartment in the event of problems with the cabin pressure, and convert their seat to a life preserver in the "unlikely" event of a water landing. No one expects the airplane to crash; no one expects to need the emergency safety instructions. Nonetheless, many of us "tune in" and take note. As one pilot recently announced in preparing for flight, "It is better to know it and not need it than to need it and not know it." This is a slogan that corresponds well with the RP philosophy.

The Relapse Prevention Model

For our purposes, *relapse* is defined as any violation of a self-imposed rule regarding a particular behavior. According to the model, individuals experience a sense of perceived control over this behavior while maintaining the target goal. This sense of self-efficacy or perceived control strengthens over time so long as the undesirable behavior does not recur. It will continue until the individual encounters a high-risk situation. Defined broadly, a *high-risk situation* is one in which the individual's sense of perceived control is threatened. High-risk situations can include an environmental occurrence, an interpersonal interaction, or an affective, cognitive, or physiological internal state that serves as a trigger or cue for engaging in the behavior. If the person copes effectively in the high-risk situation, RP hypothesizes that the individual will experience an increase in self-efficacy, a belief that he or she will be able to continue to successfully respond to similar high-risk situations in the future and maintain the goal. Such an experience should thereby decrease the probability of a future relapse. Similarly, with each hurdle successfully leaped by a runner, the more confident she or he becomes in mastering future hurdles.

What about individuals who are unable to cope effectively? It may be that the individual does not have the necessary coping skills. He or she may have known what to do but did not out of fear or anxiety (e.g., feeling cognitively "blocked" or embarrassed, etc.). Perhaps the person does not recognize the presence of risk until it is too late, once the relapse has occurred. If the person does not cope effectively, he or she may experience a decrease in self-efficacy and an increase in passivity, feeling helpless and out of control as shown in Figure 11.2. As one's expectations for successful coping diminish, positive expectancies about the perceived benefit of engaging in the prohibited behavior may increase. Individuals may believe that the old habitual response will increase their sense of power ("I'll be much better prepared to handle this after I have a drink"), diminish their stress ("Only a drink can help me relax now"), or aid in their celebration ("I deserve this drink!"). These outcome expectancies, if fulfilled by the initial pharmacological effects of the substance, are reinforced and increase the probability of a lapse.

The first step in constructing an effective RP plan is to identify the client's high-risk situations and the relapse "chain" or process. Once identified, the therapist can then turn to problem-solving and skill-building activities directed at these high-risk areas. In an early analysis of 311 initial lapses obtained retrospectively from clients with a variety of problem behaviors (e.g., problem drinking, smoking, heroin addiction, compulsive gambling, and overeating), three primary high-risk situational factors were associated with approximately 75% of the cases (Cummings et al., 1980; Marlatt & Gordon,

1985): negative emotional states, interpersonal conflict, and social pressure.

Approximately 35% of all relapses in the sample occurred in situations where the individual reported experiencing negative or unpleasant emotions, such as frustration, anger, depression, anxiety, and boredom, prior to or during the first lapse. In 16% of the relapses, clients described involvement in an ongoing or relatively recent interpersonal conflict with a partner, family member, friend, employer, or employee. In 20% of relapses, peer pressure exerted by a single individual or group of individuals was identified as the primary precipitant. Social pressure to drink can be either direct (e.g., through the use of verbal persuasion) or indirect (e.g., being in the presence of others who are drinking, even though no verbal pressure is involved). Other high-risk situational factors identified included negative physical states (3%), testing personal control (5%), and responsivity to substance cues, such as urges and cravings (9%). These findings suggest that a common set of relapse triggers underlie most relapse episodes.

The client's cognitive-affective response to a slip can further increase the probability of a full-blown relapse. Clients who view relapse in

Figure 11.2   Relapse Prevention: Specific Intervention Strategies

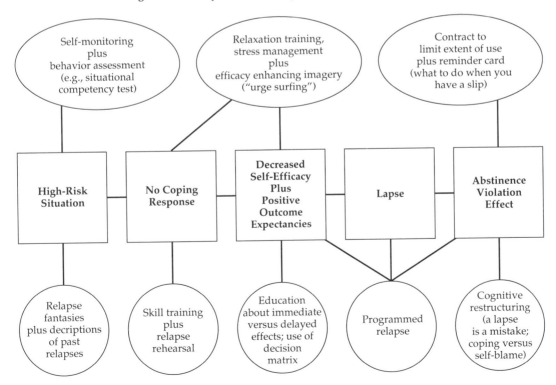

dichotomous terms, in particular, may believe that there is no going back once the line has been crossed: Once committed, the deed is done. To account for this transgression, the abstinence violation effect, or AVE (Curry et al., 1987; Marlatt & Gordon, 1985; Collins, 1993), was postulated. AVE has two key cognitive-affective elements: cognitive dissonance (Festinger, 1964) and self-attribution (Harvey, Ickes, & Kidd, 1964).

According to cognitive dissonance theory, a cognitive conflict develops from the disparity between the individual's beliefs about himself or herself (e.g., "I'm an abstainer") and the occurrence of the forbidden behavior. To the extent that the individual has used the behaviors to cope with guilt and conflict in the past, she or he is likely to continue engaging in the behavior. The individual might try to reduce the conflict by altering her or his self-image to bring it in line with the behavior (e.g., "Just goes to show you I really am a drunk."). Cognitive dissonance can also provide rationalization for abandoning the goal or rule and discontinuing attempts to regain control. This often leaves the person feeling guilty, discouraged, depressed, and at risk for dropping out of treatment. Instead of viewing relapse as arising out of a particularly difficult and complex situation for which they were ill prepared, the individual may instead view herself or himself as personally weak or a failure.

Four hypothesized conditions are necessary but not essential for the AVE and may predict the magnitude of AVE a client might respond to in a relapse. First, how committed was the client to the particular goal? Second, how much effort did the client exert toward the goal? Third, how long had the client maintained the goal? Fourth, how much value did the individual place in the progress made thus far to maintain the goal? In addition, external factors, such as the response of one's social support network may also affect the AVE.

While identifying high-risk situations and developing cognitive and behavioral strategies to reduce these risks and the probability of relapse, a problem still remains: The unsuspecting individual may be caught off guard in a situation that is rapidly escalating in the absence of an adequate coping response. In most relapse episodes, the high-risk situation may be the last link in a chain of events that precede the first lapse. Consider the case of the compulsive gambler who came to see the second author for help in controlling his habit (Marlatt & Gordon, 1985). Before beginning treatment, the gambler had managed to abstain from all gambling activ-

ities for approximately six months, followed by a relapse and inability to regain control. When asked to initially describe his last relapse, he stated, "There's nothing much to talk about. I was in Reno and I started gambling."

At first, it appeared that he was simply a victim of circumstance, caught at the wrong place at the wrong time. A closer examination of the events preceding the relapse, however, revealed a clear chain of events, or choice points (forks in the road). The client made a series of mini-decisions that brought him closer and closer to the actual relapse. Instead of proceeding through Placerville on their way home to Seattle from San Francisco, the gambler decided at the last minute to take a more scenic route home through Lake Tahoe, just a few miles from Reno. One thing led to another and soon the gambler found himself in Reno placing a dollar into a slot machine—an event that triggered a weekend-long binge of costly gambling. These mini-decisions that bring the individual closer and closer to the brink of relapse have been described as seemingly irrelevant decisions (SIDS) (previously known as apparently irrelevant decisions, or AIDS).

Why would an individual voluntarily get into a situation so tempting to begin with? Cognitive distortions seem to play a key role in accounting for the SIDS that ultimately lead to a destructive relapse. By making use of such cognitive distortions as denial and rationalization, the individual may have minimized the perceived costs of taking such action and maximized the perceived benefit. In doing so, the individual can then deny both the intent to relapse and the importance of the long-range negative consequences.

Perhaps the most tempting of potential rationalizations is the belief that the yielding to the temptation is justified. The degree of lifestyle balance seems to have a significant impact on the individual's desire for indulgence or immediate gratification (Marlatt & Gordon, 1985). Within this context, *balance* is defined as the degree of equilibrium that exists in one's daily life between perceived external demands ("shoulds") and perceived desires ("wants"). We have found that a lifestyle encumbered by a preponderance of perceived shoulds may result in increasing feelings of perceived self-deprivation and a corresponding desire for indulgence and gratification (e.g., "I earned this drink!"). The desire for indulgence is often expressed in the form of urges and cravings, which are mediated by the positive outcome expectancies from engaging in the prohibited behavior. For our purposes here, an *urge* is defined

Figure 11.3   Relapse Prevention: Global Self-Control Strategies

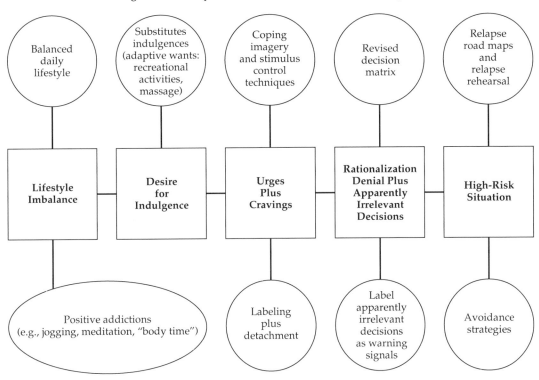

as an impulse to engage in an act, whereas a *craving* is the subjective desire to experience the effects or consequences of that act (Marlatt, 1982).

Global intervention procedures, as illustrated in Figure 11.3, comprise the final aspect of the RP self-management program. Lifestyle imbalance increases the risk of relapse by heightening cognitive and affective processes that justify indulgence and fuel SIDS. Consequently, we believe it is insufficient just to teach patients mechanistic skills for handling high-risk situations without attending to the client's maladaptive lifestyle. For this reason, a comprehensive RP self-management program should also try to balance the client's overall lifestyle by increasing his or her capacity to cope effectively with more pervasive stress factors that are antecedents to the occurrence of high-risk situations.

Overview of Specific and Global Intervention Procedures

As previously noted, relapse prevention is designed to be effective, short term, and intensive. RP can be provided to a client individually, in groups, or as an adjunct to marital and family thearpy (O'Farrell, 1993). Most RP treatment programs consist of approximately eight sessions and several additional follow-up sessions. In an effort to traverse theoretical abstractions to clinical application, the following section provides a "generic" user's guide to RP organized by session. We wish to caution readers against viewing it as a blueprint treatment plan or map; instead, it should be seen as an example. Like many prevention and treatment programs, RP is most effective when client-treatment matching procedures are used, and when the program is tailored to the needs of the client.

The first two sessions are usually devoted to establishing a working therapeutic relationship, presenting the rationale for RP, enhancing motivation, and assessing the history of problem behavior and current pattern of use. In addition, we communicate our basic philosophy: With appropriate information and skills, clients can learn to exert more influence over their responses to high-risk situations instead of responding reactively or passively. The subsequent six or so sessions focus on training in coping with immediate problematic situations, learning to identify and cope with specific high-risk situations, and modifying (e.g., balancing) the client's lifestyle. Clients are typically assigned homework to complete between sessions. These assignments typically build on material covered during the session. Homework is reviewed at the beginning of the subsequent session.

Session 1

As part of the treatment overview, we provide the client with information about our general approach to treating addictive behaviors and our primary aim: to provide the client with tools to use in the maintenance of the desired behavior and in the event of slips. Evoking the journey of fire-drill metaphors, we emphasize that learning new behaviors is a process that takes patience and practice. It is useful also to assess which Brickman model fits best with the client's self-understanding.

Gather a thorough history of the problem behavior during this session. Pertinent information usually includes onset, duration, attempts and success of these attempts to stop or gain control, consequences resulting from the addictive habit, and the effect of the habit on the client's primary relationships, family, work, and physical, and psychological well-being. We also recommend obtaining information about the client's family history of substance abuse. The Brief Drinker Profile (Marlatt & Miller, 1987) and the Comprehensive Drinker Profile (Miller & Marlatt, 1984) are examples of two structured interview protocols we have found useful for this purpose.

We recommend assessing the client's motivation early on in the treatment, preferably during this initial session. Given the obvious difficulty of assessing an individual's inward state of motivational readiness, we recommend performing a functional analysis by examining various functions served by the drinking behavior. Additionally, we gather information regarding the perceived positive and negative consequences of this behavior currently experienced, and the anticipated positive and negative consequences and effects of drinking following modification of the behavior.

Clients often hold multiple, competing motivations. The therapist can help clients systematically sort through these motivations by using a decision matrix, as illustrated in Figure 11.4. This eight-cell matrix requires the client to consider and compare the short term and long term costs and benefits of enduring behavioral change or maintaining the old habit. To illustrate the relative strengths of reasons provided, the client can assign a numerical rating to each of the positive and negative outcomes listed. Because these consequences are likely to change over

time, encourage the client to reconsider these motivational currents throughout and beyond the course of therapy by updating the matrix whenever necessary for the duration of therapy.

Homework Assignment for Session 1

- *Self-Monitoring.* Learning to recognize one's high-risk situations is among the first exercises assigned to the client. One effective strategy to increase the client's awareness of these situations is self-monitoring. Using wallet-sized cards as illustrated in Figure 11.5, we ask our clients to begin monitoring their drinking on a daily basis and throughout the duration of treatment. As little as 10 days of self-monitoring data can often highlight situational influences and skills deficits that underlie an addictive behavior pattern. We ask the client to record pertinent information for each drink, including the time a particular drink was consumed, the type of drink consumed, the amount, the location of drinking (e.g., a bar, home, a sporting event, a restaurant, "outdoors," etc.), persons present at the time (e.g., male and/or female friends, large or small group, etc.), and his or her mood or feeling (e.g., happy, sad, bored, celebrating, etc.). If the client is already abstinent, monitoring urges and cravings can provide similar information (see discussion below). We also encourage keeping track of abstinent days using the monitoring cards.

  The task of self-monitoring proves useful as both an assessment procedure and intervention strategy. Information obtained from self-monitoring can increase the client's awareness of a behavior or set of behaviors that may have become routine and habitual, and aid in determining the antecedents of the behavior. This latter purpose can later help the client to anticipate and prepare for future high-risk situations. In order to minimize cognitive and affective processes that may compromise compliance with this exercise (e.g., guilt, denial, concern about being judged or labeled an alcoholic, etc.) and bolster motivation to record these behaviors, we explain the reasons for self-monitoring to the client.

- *Autobiographical Sketch.* We encourage our clients to write out a brief autobiographical depiction of any experiences, images, and feelings related to the current pattern of drinking that are personally meaningful. The client may want to consider how and why she or he began drinking, her or his

Figure 11.4 Decision Matrix for Resumption of Alcohol Use

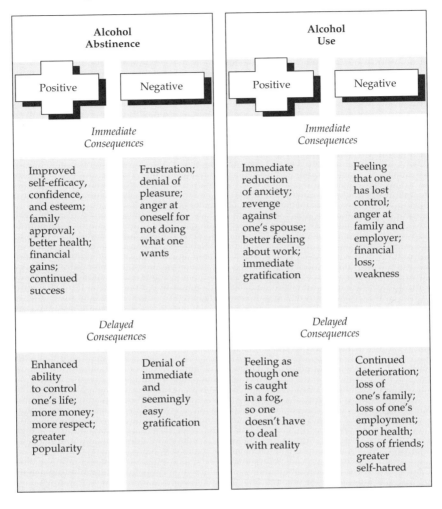

Alcohol Abstinence		Alcohol Use	
Positive	Negative	Positive	Negative
Immediate Consequences		*Immediate Consequences*	
Improved self-efficacy, confidence, and esteem; family approval; better health; financial gains; continued success	Frustration; denial of pleasure; anger at oneself for not doing what one wants	Immediate reduction of anxiety; revenge against one's spouse; better feeling about work; immediate gratification	Feeling that one has lost control; anger at family and employer; financial loss; weakness
Delayed Consequences		*Delayed Consequences*	
Enhanced ability to control one's life; more money; more respect; greater popularity	Denial of immediate and seemingly easy gratification	Feeling as though one is caught in a fog, so one doesn't have to deal with reality	Continued deterioration; loss of one's family; loss of one's employment; poor health; loss of friends; greater self-hatred

understanding of why the drinking pattern changed, descriptions of important people she or he associates with drinking, and so on. The purpose of this exercise is to capture the client's self-image as a drinker, one that includes both positive and negative associations. The writing can be as loose and unchronological as the client might like. We then ask the client to write a second brief description of his or her life as an abstainer (or moderate drinker), as she or he anticipates it might be. We recommend that clients first imagine that they have already achieved the goal and are writing the description "after the fact." From this vantage point, the client can comment on how different aspects of his or her lifestyle look (e.g., personal relationships, work, exercise, diet, etc.), on difficult situations encountered on the way to

success, and on helpful ways the client eased the transition of change.

Session 2

An important objective for this session is to continue examining high-risk situations and the client's repertoire of effective coping responses and skills deficits. Having already established a general history of drinking, we often use this session as an opportunity to gather the client's personal psychosocial background. The session typically begins by examining the homework from the previous week, including the monitoring cards. While examining these cards, take care to note the situational determinants of heavy drinking, then review the autobiographical statements. Discuss and compare them to the motivational factors listed in the prior session on the decisional matrix.

Figure 11.5 Monitor Card for Recording Drinking Behavior

Date	Time	a.m. p.m.	Drink Type	Amount (ozs.)	Where (code)	W/whom (code)	Mood (code)	Comments

Subject #:

House #:

Card #:

Use drink scale on back (below) for **Amount** category.
Use codes on back (below) for **Where, With Whom** and **Mood** categories.

Codes for MOOD STATES

1 Happy
2 Outgoing
3 Romantic/sexy
4 Relaxed
5 Desire to celebrate
6 Sad/depressed
7 Frustrated
8 Shy/self-conscious
9 Angry
10 Anxious/stressed
11 Restless/bored
12 Other (specify)

Codes for WITH WHOM

1 Alone
2 Relatives including family
3 Male friend(s)
4 Female friend(s)
5 Friends of both sexes
6 Strangers or people you've met after beginning to drink
7 Other (specify)

Codes for WHERE

1 Tavern/bar
2 Restaurant (with meal)
3 Own residence
4 Other's residence
5 Work/school
6 Private club, fraternity, sorority
7 Social event (wedding, party, sports event)
8 In a car
9 Out-of-doors
10 Other (specify)

For ALL questions, one drink equals:

12 ozs. beer

1 cocktail, or 1 shot

4 ozs. wine, or 1 cooler

Record additional factors not initially captured on the matrix in the appropriate cell. By the end of this session, you should have a well-developed understanding of the client's motivation for changing his or her drinking behavior and potential barriers he or she might come up against during the course of therapy.

Homework Assignment for Session 2

- *Continued self-monitoring.*
- *Completion of the Inventory of Drinking Situations (IDS–100)* (Annis, 1982; Annis, Graham, & Davis, 1987). This 100-item self-report questionnaire provides an eight-category profile of situations in which the client drank heavily over the past year. These categories are the same as the high-risk situations described in this text. They include unpleasant emotions, physical discomfort, pleasant emotions, testing control over alcohol, urges and temptations to drink, conflict with others, pressure from others to drink, and pleasant times with others. Develop a hierarchy of high-risk drinking situations from this assessment.

Session 3

Determining the adequacy of preexisting coping abilities is an important RP assessment component. Continuing from the prior week's discussion, assess coping strategies and high-risk situations using one of several structured assessment instruments. The therapist-administered Situational Confidence Questionnaire (SCQ–39) (Annis, 1988; Annis & Davis, 1989) assesses gains in the client's self-efficacy during the course of treatment. The SCQ–39 asks clients to describe how they would respond to a number of high-risk situations ("What would you do if you found yourself at a wedding reception where everyone had been drinking?"). Following their response, they are asked to rate how confident they would feel executing the described response using a self-efficacy rating index. Ratings across a wide range of situations enable the individual to identify both problematic situations and skills deficits in need of remedial training. Results from these types of assessments can later dictate the focus of skills training procedures. Such ratings of efficacy in specific situations are predictive of actual relapse episodes (Condiotte & Lichtenstein, 1981).

Other exercises used to examine high-risk situations include careful examination of *past relapses* and analysis of *relapse fantasies*. To the ex-

tent that the best predictor of future behavior is past behavior, past slips or relapses can serve as a rich source of information. In addition to gleaning high-risk situational determinants that led up to the drink, discussion of past slips provides an opportunity to examine the client's cognitive and affective response to the goal violation.

A micro-analysis of relapse fantasies can also lend additional information regarding potential high-risk factors, specific vulnerabilities, coping skills, the client's self-image, and the role alcohol plays in that self-image. To assess relapse fantasies, ask the client to sit back, close his or her eyes, and imagine an actual relapse episode. You might begin by saying, "Although we hope that a relapse will not occur in your case, it still would be helpful in our work together if you would pretend that you are having difficulty refraining from drinking sometime in the future. What kind of situation or event would it take for you to go back to drinking? Try to imagine this scene as clearly as you can and give me a description of the situation and your feelings." Frequently, clients who have stopped using alcohol will report dreams in which a relapse occurred. A description of the dream can also serve as a useful starting point for the guided relapse fantasy.

Include alternative strategies to enhance the client's coping repertoire in high-risk situations during this assessment. While you are likely to return to this area throughout subsequent sessions as additional high-risk situations are identified, we have found it useful to introduce some "standard" RP strategies aimed at bolstering the client's confidence and hope. Such strategies include the following: substituting nonalcoholic drinks; avoiding drinking cues, such as certain places and people; traveling a different daily route in order to avoid these cues; engaging in distracting activities, such as hobbies, exercise, or social events where alcohol is not available; and refusing drinks and invitations to occasions where drinking may occur.

Many clients report having cravings for years following the cessation of drinking, although with lessening intensity and frequency. These sensations can range from a fleeting moment to feeling overwhelmed by a drive to drink. For the newly sober client, these experiences are often disconcerting and frightening. For this reason, it is important to put cravings and urges into perspective early on in the therapy by explaining that these sensations and thoughts usually diminish over time, and by teaching clients how to effectively manage them.

The most important point to emphasize is that urges and cravings will arise and subside on their own. "Giving in" to these internal experiences will only serve to increase the strength of the craving and ensure its continued existence. On the other hand, if the individual can wait out the waxing and waning current without engaging in the old habit, the internal pressure to respond will eventually fade out through the process of extinction.

Using labeling and detachment, clients learn to make a healthy separation from them. Instead of identifying with the urge (e.g., "I really want a drink right now!"), train the client to monitor the urge or desire from the perspective of a detached observer (e.g., "I am now experiencing an urge to have a drink"). By externalizing the craving/urge and "watching" it come and go, the tendency to identify with it and feel overwhelmed by it steadily decreases. Like an ocean surfer riding a wave, the task of the client is to "urge surf" by observing and predicting the ebb and flow of the wave as it rises, crests, and falls, and to learn to ride out the urge wave while maintaining balance so as not to "wipe out" (George, 1989).

In addition, coping imagery can aid the client in externalizing the urge and to cope with it with greater mastery and self-efficacy. For example, ask the client to imagine that he or she is a samurai warrior who has assumed guard duty against enemy attack (urges and cravings). The samurai's assignment is a simple one—to recognize an urge when it first appears and to wield the "sword of awareness" to slay the urge.

Homework Assignment for Session 3
- *Continued self-monitoring.*
- *Craving Diary.* Another approach to managing urges and craving is to find out what triggers them, thereby allowing the client either to avoid or to prepare for them. The most reliable way to detect triggers is to monitor the actual urges and cravings for a long enough time that patterns begin to emerge. Using the Diary Monitoring Card illustrated in Figure 11.5, we ask the client to track every craving or urge, taking note of the severity of feeling and its duration, in addition to the other specified situational factors listed on the card.

Session 4

Up to this point, therapy has focused on identifying high-risk situations and the client's coping resources. Around this point in treatment, attention shifts to developing more effective coping strategies. This will remain an ongoing theme throughout the course of therapy. Define coping for the client as a form of action or response to reduce a danger and/or achieve a goal (Wanigaratne, Wallace, Pullin, Keaney, & Farmer, 1990). Make distinctions between specific coping strategies (e.g., skills training, cognitive reframing, etc.) and global lifestyle coping strategies (e.g., balancing one's lifestyle), with the latter serving as the focus of subsequent sessions.

Review and discuss homework from the previous week, emphasizing new information about additional information regarding high-risk situations and effective and ineffective coping strategies. Take note of the client's confidence in his or her ability to make use of the new coping skills repertoire. Focus on strong urge situations and on modeling and rehearsing appropriate responses where necessary. Emphasize the client's gains, however small they may seem, and resist the temptation to focus exclusively on the client's failures, fears, and deficits. Encourage the client to incorporate his or her success into a set of expectations of continuing adaptive responding, with each new success broadening and increasing sense of personal mastery.

Around this point in therapy, we discuss the abstinence violation effect (AVE) and the second broad goal of RP: ways to minimize the negative effects of a slip or relapse should one occur. If the client reports a slip earlier on in treatment, it is naturally advised to discuss the AVE at that time in an effort to "normalize" what is often a demoralizing and shameful experience and to prevent further lapses. If abstinence is successfully maintained, ask the client to describe what he or she might experience in such a situation, or what he or she has observed in others. We then describe the difference between a lapse and a relapse, how the AVE operates to increase the chance of relapse, and associated cognitive-behavioral strategies for coping with the AVE.

In discussing lapses, emphasize four points: (1) a lapse is a specific, unique event in time and space; (2) the lapse can be reattributed to external specific and controllable factors that can be handled by effective coping strategies; (3) a lapse can be turned into a prolapse instead of a relapse; and (4) abstinence or control is always only a moment away. Provide information about drug effects, including how the pharmacologic action of the substance used may enhance the erroneous belief that the person is empowered by the drug.

With this second goal of RP in mind, ask the client to develop a proactive plan to carry out in the event of a lapse. Recognizing that the most dangerous, and hence most important, period for decisive action is the time immediately following the lapse, what emergency procedures might the client make use of? We review six important steps: stop, look and listen; keep calm; renew your commitment; review the situations that led up to the lapse; make an immediate plan for your recovery; and ask for help. The client is given a two-sided wallet-sized card to carry at all times that summarizes these points on one side and specifies the client's personalized plan on the other.

Homework Assignment for Session 4

• *Continue monitoring drinking/abstinent days and cravings to drink.*
• *Write coping instructions on an index or wallet-sized card for use in case of a slip.*

Session 5

Following up the prior week's discussion of coping, this session centers on understanding and coping with various cognitive and affective states. Because a vital element of RP is acquiring and using information to enhance coping, it is necessary to increase the client's awareness of thoughts and feelings. The next step is to help the client see the relationship between cognitions, affect, physiological responses, and behavior. We have found it useful to center this discussion around anxiety because clients often report feeling anxious during the initial phases of maintenance and while experiencing urges and cravings. The client often thinks that heightened anxiety is a sign that she or he is losing her or his footing or personal control. For many, the experience of anxiety has signaled the need to manage their mood or situation by obtaining a "quick fix"; hence, anxiety serves as a strong cue for drinking. We explain to our clients that these negative thoughts or feelings can lead them into a downward spiral and affect how they behave.

We typically differentiate among three separate components, or factors, of anxiety: (1) cognitive factors (e.g., distortions, overgeneralizing, depersonalization, detachment, negative or catastrophic thinking, errors in thinking or perception, dichotomous thinking, assuming excessive responsibility, selective abstraction, etc.); (2) physical factors (e.g., palpitations, dizziness, nausea, muscle tension, stomach pain, headaches, sweating); and (3) behavioral factors

(e.g., avoidance, fighting, using drugs). Once the client understands these various components, you can then consider ways to effectively counter each.

Cognitive coping strategies might include, for example, identifying negative or erroneous thoughts and replacing them with a positive reframe through self talk, or distracting oneself from the thought by "overriding" his or her cognition with other mental stimulation (e.g., reading a book, engaging in a conversation, etc.). Similarly, the client might identify physiologic responses to anxiety, then receive instruction in stress management or relaxation training techniques to reduce these physical indicators. Behavioral coping strategies for negative emotional states might include assertiveness training or practice via role-playing.

Homework Assignment for Session 5

• *Have the client keep a daily record of his or her negative thoughts and negative feelings (e.g., anxiety, anger or depression) for a period of two weeks.*

Session 6

During approximately the sixth session, therapeutic interventions broaden from managing specific day-to-day high-risk situations to addressing more global lifestyle management. The client learns how an unbalanced lifestyle or a persistent disequilibrium between shoulds and wants can pave the way to relapse. Lifestyle imbalance can produce a chronic sense of deprivation which can then ignite urges, cravings, and cognitive distortions that lead clients "unintentionally" closer to the brink of relapse. First, ask the client to describe "stress" and then describe the difference between life events and day-to-day upsets as they relate to stress. Next, use the "shoulds-wants ratio" concept (Marlatt & Gordon, 1980) to make the point that excessive indulgence in any consummatory behavior is often an attempt to compensate for a sense of deprivation; feeling "deprived" is often caused by an excess of obligation (shoulds) and a dearth of reward (wants)—a condition that often results in stress and can lead to SIDS.

A number of treatment strategies short-circuit the covert antecedents to relapse and promote mental and physical wellness. One way is to have clients assess their own "shoulds-wants" ratio by exploring their perceptions of their lifestyle within the session. To encourage clients to seek a restoration of balance, the client is asked to generate several ideas regarding healthy indulgences she or he might consider. Some examples include engaging in daily healthy lifestyle habits or positive addictions (e.g., running, exercising, meditating, etc.) (Glasser, 1976). The advantage of this shift from negative (e.g., excessive drinking) to positive addiction lies in the latter's capacity to contribute toward the client's long-term health and well-being while also providing an adaptive coping response for life stressors and relapse situations. Concomitantly, as long-range health benefits accrue, self-confidence and self-efficacy are further heightened. Meditation and other relaxation techniques, as well as aerobic exercise, are easily learned and readily available methods for achieving a constructive "high" experience.

The client can also see a program of lifestyle change as a journey of exploration and trial. The aim is to eventually arrive at a program that is suitable to and individualized for the client (Wanigaratne, Wallace, Pullin, Keaney, & Farmer, 1990). Such positive life changes often involve overcoming significant psychological hurdles, including boredom, physical discomfort, resistance, and fear. Just as quitting drinking often involves benevolently coaching through the Stages of Change, clients often need special assistance in learning how to balance their lifestyle, meditate and manage stress.

Homework for Session 6

- *Monitor all activities for at least two normal week days and one typical weekend.* For each activity, the client should record the event and a numerical value using a nine-point scale to indicate the extent to which the activity constituted a "want" or a "should" (e.g., 1 represents pure "should," 5 represents an equal proportion of "should" and "want," and 9 represents pure "want"). At the day's end, the client can calculate his or her daily score by adding up the daily total and dividing that score by the number of events.
- *Set aside at least one half hour per day for "self-time."* We recommend that the client consider Glasser's (1976) requirements for positive addiction when choosing an activity: engaging in a solitary, noncompetitive activity of value to the individual that is not subject to self or other evaluation or criticism; an activity that does not require a great deal of mental effort to do it well, and is possible for the individual to do with ease. Such examples could include meditat-

ing, physical exercise, a hobby, or listening to music. We have found this technique most helpful when the client blocks out the time beforehand, just as he or she would with any another appointment.
- *Continued monitoring of abstinent days, and urges and cravings.*

Session 7

Discuss homework from the previous week. This session covers more troubleshooting, practice in adaptive responses to problematic situations, a review of the client's progress (including positive addictions), and problem solving, should a slip occur.

Homework for Session 7

- *Continued monitoring of abstinent days, and urges and cravings.*
- *Instruct the client to draw a "road map" to illustrate his or her individualized plan for relapse prevention.* This map can be as straightforward or creative a task as the client desires. The goal of this homework assignment is for the client to include all major high-risk situations she or he is aware of, based on the work the client has done up to that point. Once this first step is completed, the client notes one or more coping responses he or she would use at each high-risk junction.

Session 8

Review the homework from the previous week and act as a consultant on the client's road map. We recommend that the client visually "rehearse" for a relapse under direct supervision. Before commencing with this in-session exercise, reiterate the purpose of such practice (e.g., equipping oneself for such an emergency, much as one preparing for a fire during a fire-drill exercise). In no way should you predict that the client will inevitably relapse or encourage that the client do so to "test their limits."

The client first selects a particularly troubling high-risk situation and describes it in detail to you. Using stress-reduction relaxation techniques, have the client become comfortable and relaxed. Once the client is relaxed, describe the aforementioned high risk situation in vivid detail, just as the client had previously described. In your depiction, indicate that the client has just experienced a slip. Then ask the client to imagine as vividly as possible all the thoughts and feelings that arise in reaction to the slip. Finally, ask the client to imagine coping successfully with the AVE by stopping the behavior and reinstating the desired responses. You may wish to conduct some of this session in vivo or with the forbidden substance in the room.

Continued Sessions and Fading Out

The next few sessions focus on continued strengthening of coping responses via modeling and role-plays, preparing for additional high-risk situations, and continuing management of lifestyle balance and health. Several additional sessions may be required for purposes of "putting it all together." After this is accomplished, sessions should be faded out. During this "fading out" phase, make arrangements for the client to report in by phone or mail during the intervals between sessions. Plan and prearrange as many of the details as possible for these future contacts. Construct the fading out plan to allow for the client to gradually experience an increase in her or his sense of control without your active support.

EFFECTIVENESS

In a discussion of the utilization and effectiveness of relapse prevention, Wilson (1992) observed that in light of its widespread use within and beyond the field of addictive behaviors, it is surprising that the general RP model and its separate components have not been subjected to more empirical scrutiny through controlled outcome studies. As a point of fact, few controlled trials of RP's efficacy have been conducted. Others have argued that proof of its effectiveness rests in its popular usage, particularly within the addictions treatment industry. We begin this section by reviewing the research literature on the efficacy of RP and conclude with an examination of specific challenges to RP research.

Chaney, O'Leary, and Marlatt conducted the first controlled outcome study of RP in 1978. Forty male subjects participating in inpatient treatment for alcohol dependence were randomly assigned to one of three conditions: skills training (RP), insight-oriented discussion group (DG), and a no additional treatment-control group. The RP group rehearsed adequate coping skills in high-risk situations using modeling, role-playing, and instructional procedures. General problem solving and assertiveness training were also taught. The DG participants were encouraged to verbally explore feelings and motivations that may interfere with the utilization of

skills they were assumed to possess. All participants also received the standard inpatient treatment course.

Results consistently favored RP. Drinking rates in the RP group were significantly lower compared to the other two conditions. Additionally, the RP condition showed gradual improvement over time, presumably because the skills became sharpened with experience. While overall abstinence rates did not significantly differ at the 12-month posttreatment follow-up assessment, the RP group experienced less severe lapses for shorter periods compared to the other conditions. If a relapse did occur, the RP group stopped drinking sooner than the other conditions (an average of 5 days compared to an aggregate average of 45 days, respectively). Furthermore, the RP group drank less, experienced fewer days of intoxication and demonstrated more "controlled drinking" compared to the other groups.

Since this seminal empirical investigation of RP, several additional studies have provided further support for the efficacy of RP. In a recent controlled study of Finnish inpatient alcohol abusers, Koski-Jannes (1992) compared RP to three common treatment modalities: psychodynamic, systems theory, and social learning theory. Treatment adherence and satisfaction was greater in the RP condition. Results at one-year revealed significant reductions in drinking rates in all groups, but more specific outcome measures favored RP (e.g., reduced lengths of inpatient stay and fewer alcohol related arrests).

Ito, Donovan, and Hall (1988) compared RP to interpersonal process therapy (IP) in hospitalized male alcoholics. The IP group focused on developing insight related to underlying conflicts that might lead to maladaptive behaviors. Six-month follow-up data found that in the RP and IP groups, 50% and 42% of the subjects, respectively, had abstained continuously. Results favored the RP on various measures: The RP group drank on fewer days and completed more aftercare than the IP group (80% vs. 58%, respectively). Average daily ethanol consumption diminished from 5 ounces in both groups to .21 ounce in RP and to .43 ounce in the IP group. The differences were not, however, statistically significant most likely due to the insufficient sample size ($n = 39$) and resulting inadequate statistical power.

Utilizing random assignment, Allsop and Saunders (1989) compared a performance-based RP with a verbally mediated RP discussion group and a treatment-as-usual group. Results favored the performance condition to the verbally mediated RP. By the six-month follow-up, subjects in the discussion and control groups reported twice as many heavy-drinking days as participants in the active RP condition. Posttreatment self-efficacy was the best predictor of outcome in this study.

In a similar study utilizing RP techniques, Annis and Davis (1988) focused on assisting subjects to identify and anticipate high-risk situations and self-monitoring behaviors within the context of combined group and individual therapy over eight sessions. At the three-month assessment, average drinking rates among subjects were reduced from 45 drinks weekly to fewer than 2 drinks, and fewer than 6 drinks at six months. Importantly, as drinking rates reduced, self-efficacy rating increased. In one of the few studies conducted at outpatient clinics and that allowed clients to select their own treatment goal, Sandahl and Ronnberg (1990) found similar overall reductions in drinking at 12 months. Successful outcome was related to enhancement of self-efficacy throughout treatment and the client's degree of readiness to change his or her behavior at the outset of treatment.

In a replication and extension of the Chaney and colleagues (1978) study, Jones, Kanfer, and Lanyon (1982) compared treatment effects across the original three conditions (RP, discussion group, and a no-treatment control) in a group of male *and female* alcoholics of higher socioeconomic status (SES) receiving treatment from a private inpatient program. Unfortunately, results from this study were significantly compromised by poor subject participation during the 12-month follow-up, with fewer than half of the original sample ($n = 31$; 45.6%) completing the posttreatment assessment. Available follow-up data revealed no statistically significant difference between the RP and discussion group; both conditions demonstrated significant gains, however, over the no-treatment control group. This finding led the investigators to cautiously conclude that verbal transmission of RP was as effective as skills training in higher SES persons.

An analysis of the reviewed data suggests that RP may be most efficacious when applied to clients in a high state of distress or for persons with moderate to severe alcohol dependence and a significant history of problematic drinking. A recent study that incorporates RP with behavioral marital therapy (BMT) in couples where one spouse member is receiving treat-

ment for alcohol problems provide further support for this hypothesis. O'Farrell (1993) randomly assigned couples receiving treatment for alcohol problems to one of two conditions: BMT or BMT in combination with RP. Abstinence rates were highest for low-distress couples with BMT only. However, high-distress couples obtained their highest abstinence rates when receiving BMT in combination with RP.

In a Norwegian study by Skuttle and Berg (1987), minimal behavioral self-control training (BSCT) bibliotherapy was found as effective as more intensive coping skills training (CST) fashioned after RP in a group of early-stage outpatient problem drinkers pursuing moderation drinking goals. BSCT consisted of self-monitoring, goal setting, controlling drinking rate, self-reinforcement strategies, and identifying antecedents of overdrinking and high risk situations. In addition to identifying high-risk situations, CST clients learned specific coping skills using role-playing, relaxation, and instructional techniques. No differences were found among groups at the 3-, 6-, and 12-month follow-ups. All four conditions resulted in a significant reduction of drinking and life problems. Consistent with research on the efficacy of brief interventions, as described in Chapter 6 of this text, Skuttle and Berg concluded that "more (treatment) is not better" when treating early-stage problem drinkers.

Examination of the RP outcome research literature raises a number of important issues. First, what constitutes an appropriate comparison group in which to evaluate RP? If conceptualized as a maintenance program (and not a treatment aimed at the cessation of drinking), as it was originally described, studies of RP should compare it to other programs that aim to sustain change once it has been initiated, such as AA or Rational Recovery. As the previous review makes clear, many studies on RP have instead used RP as the single treatment intervention for cessation of drinking.

Second, what constitutes the best measures of treatment outcome? While traditional outcome studies measure treatment efficacy on the degree to which the clinical results "stick" or wear off over time, RP is rooted in a prevention framework and thus requires a different "standard" in which to evaluate its success. Specifically, outcome studies utilizing RP should focus on change over time, as characterized by gradual improvement over the duration of the follow-up period.

Third, RP is designed to be highly ideographic and hypothesized to work best when tailored to the individual (Somers & Marlatt,

1992). Given this, it is likely that important information about who benefits the most from RP under what conditions becomes obscured through the use of group designs that aggregate data.

REFERENCES

Clinical Guidelines

Daley, D. C. (1991). *Kicking addictive habits once and for all.* Lexington, MA: Lexington Books. This book is intended as a self-help RP guide. In addition to providing a practical and easy-to-comprehend theoretical overview of addictions and relapse, it provides numerous illustrations and RP exercises drawn from the cognitive-behavioral RP literature. Approached from the spiritual-model perspective, this self-help manual may be best suited for persons involved in 12-step programs or comfortable with this model.

Marlatt, G. A., & Gordan, G. R. (1985). *Relapse prevention: Maintenance strategies in the treatment of addictive behaviors.* New York: Guilford. This comprehensive text provides a thorough theoretical overview of the cognitive-behavioral relapse prevention model with numerous clinical illustrations for practical application. In addition to its focus on problem drinking, RP is applied to other addictive behaviors, including smoking and obesity.

Wanigaratne, S., Wallace, W., Pullin, J., Keaney, F., & Farmer, R. (1990). *Relapse prevention for addictive behaviours: A manual for therapists.* London: Blackwell Scientific Publications. This manual provides an excellent overview of RP theory and application. Nicely organized and simply written, the manual guides the practitioner through the steps to implement an RP group, from recruitment and orientation strategies to specific learning objectives and techniques for each session.

Wilson, P. H. (Ed.). (1992). *Principles and practice of relapse prevention.* New York: Guilford. This book reviews the diverse and "cutting edge" literature of RP that spans various clinical disorders, including eating disorders, sexual deviance, depression, anxiety, obsessive-compulsive disorder, marital dissatisfaction, and chronic pain. Examining prediction, prevention, and relapse processes across these varied clinical domains, each chapter includes a review of relevant theoretical and empirical considerations and summaries of clinical outcome studies.

Research References

Annis, H. M. (1982). *Inventory of drinking situations (IDS–100).* Toronto, Canada: Addiction Research Foundation of Ontario.

Annis, H. M., & Davis, C. S. (1989). Relapse prevention. In R. K. Hester & W. R. Miller (Eds.), *Handbook of alcoholism treatment approaches: Effective alternatives* (pp. 170–182). New York: Pergamon.

Annis, H. M., & Graham, J. M. (1988). *Situational confidence questionnaire (SCQ) user's guide.* Toronto, Canada: Addiction Research Foundation of Ontario.

Annis, H. M., Graham, J. M., & Davis, C. S. (1987). *Inventory of drinking situations (IDS) user's guide.* Toronto, Canada: Addiction Research Foundation of Ontario.

Bandura, A. (1977). Self-efficacy: Toward a unifying theory of behavioral change. *Psychological Review, 84,* 191–215.

Bandura, A. (1986). *Social foundations of thought and action.* Englewood Cliffs, NJ: Prentice Hall.

Brickman, P., Rabinowitz, V. C., Karuza, J., Coates, D., Cohn, E., & Kidder, L. (1982). Models of helping and coping. *American Psychologist, 37,* 368–384.

Brownell, K. D., Marlatt, G. A., Lichtenstein, E., & Wilson, G. T. (1986). Understanding and preventing relapse. *American Psychologist, 41,* 765–782.

Chaney, E. R., O'Leary, M. R., & Marlatt, G. A. (1978). Skill training with alcoholics. *Journal of Consulting and Clinical Psychology, 46,* 1092–1104.

Collier-Phillips, W. C., & Marlatt, G. A. (in press). Relapse prevention. In A. J. Goreczny (Ed.), *Handbook of recent advances in behavioral medicine.* New York: Plenum Press.

Collins, R. L. (1993). Drinking restraint and risk for alcohol abuse. *Experimental and Clinical Psychopharmacology, 1,* 44–54.

Condiotte, M. M., & Lichtenstein, E. (1981). Self efficacy and relapse in smoking cessation programs. *Journal of Consulting and Clinical Psychology, 49,* 648–658.

Craighead, L. W., Craighead, W. E., Kazdin, A. E., & Mahoney, M. J. (1994). *Cognitive and behavioral interventions: An empirical approach to mental health problems.* Boston: Allyn and Bacon.

Cummings, C., Gordon, J. R., & Marlatt, G. A. (1980). Relapse: Strategies of prevention and prediction. In W. R. Miller (Ed.), *The Addictive Behaviors* (pp. 291–321). Oxford, England: Pergamon.

Curry, S. J., Marlatt, G. A., & Gordon, J. R. (1987). Abstinence violation effect: Validation of an attributional construct with smoking cessation. *Journal of Consulting and Clinical Psychology, 55,* 145–149.

Daley, D. C. (1988). *Relapse: Conceptual, research and clinical perspectives.* New York: Haworth Press.

Dimeff, L. A., Baer, J. S., & Marlatt, G. A. (1991). Alcohol skills training: An application of cognitive-behavioral relapse prevention strategies to alcohol abuse. *The Counselor, 9,* 22–25.

Festinger, L. (1964). *Conflict, decision and dissonance.* Stanford, CA: Stanford University Press.

George, W. H. (1989). Marlatt & Gordon's relapse prevention model: A cognitive-behavioral approach to understanding and preventing relapse. *Journal of Chemical Dependency Treatment, 2,* 125–152.

Glasser, W. (1976). *Positive addiction.* New York: Harper & Row.

Gordon, J. R., & Marlatt, G. A. (1981). Addictive behaviors. In J. L. Shelton & R. L. Levy (Eds.), *Behavioral assignments and treatment compliance: A handbook of clinical strategies* (pp. 167–186). Champaign, IL: Research Press.

Gorski, T. T., & Miller, M. (1982). *Counseling for relapse prevention.* Independence, MO: House-Independence Press.

Hunt, W. A., Barnett, L. W., & Branch, L. G. (1971). Relapse rates in addiction programs. *Journal of Clinical Psychology, 27,* 455–456.

Ito, J. R., & Donovan, D. M. (1990). Predicting drinking outcome: demography, chronicity, coping, and aftercare. *Addictive Behaviors, 15,* 553–559.

Ito, J. R., Donovan, D. M., & Hall, J. J. (1988). Relapse prevention and alcohol aftercare: Effects on drinking outcome, change process, and aftercare attendance. *British Journal of Addiction, 83,* 171–181.

Jones, S. L., Kanfer, R., & Lanyon, R. I. (1982). Skills training with alcoholics: A clinical extension. *Addictive Behaviors, 7,* 285–290.

Kivlahan, D. R., Marlatt, G. A., Fromme, K., Coppel, D. B., & Williams, E. (1990). Secondary prevention with college drinkers: Evaluation of an alcohol skills training program. *Journal of Consulting and Clinical Psychology, 58,* 805–810.

Koski-Jannes, A. (1992). *Alcohol addiction and self-regulation: A controlled trial of relapse prevention program for Finnish inpatient alcoholics.* Finland: The Finnish Foundation for Alcohol Studies.

Laws, D. R. (in press). A theory of relapse prevention. In W. O'Donohue & L. Krasner (Eds.), *Theories in behavior therapy.* Washington, DC: American Psychological Association.

Laws, D. R. (1989). *Relapse prevention with sex offenders.* New York: Guilford.

Maier, S. F., & Seligman, M. E. (1976). Learned helplessness: Theory and evidence. *Journal of Experimental Psychology: General, 105,* 3–46.

Marlatt, G. A. (1978). Craving for alcohol, loss of control and relapse: A cognitive-behavioral analysis. In P. E. Nathan, G. A. Marlatt, & T. Loberg (Eds.), *Alcoholism: New directions in behavioral research and treatment* (pp. 271–314). New York: Plenum.

Marlatt, G. A. (1982). Relapse prevention: A self-control program for the treatment of addictive behaviors. In R. B. Stuart (Ed.), *Adherence, compliance, and generalization in behavioral medicine* (pp. 329–378). New York: Brunner/Mazel.

Marlatt, G. A. (1992). Substance abuse: Implications of a biopsychosocial model for prevention, treatment and relapse prevention. In J. Grabowski & G. R. VanderBos (Eds.), *Psychopharmacology: Basic mechanisms and applied intervention.* Washington, DC: American Psychological Association.

Marlatt, G. A., & Barrett, K. (in press). Relapse prevention in the treatment of substance abuse. In M. Galanter & H. D. Kleber (Eds.), *The treatment of substance abuse.* New York: American Psychiatric Press.

Marlatt, G. A., & Fromme, K. (1987). Metaphors for addiction. *Journal of Drug Issues, 17,* 9–28.

Marlatt, G. A., & George, W. H. (1984). Relapse prevention: Introduction and overview of the model. *British Journal of Addiction, 79,* 261–273.

Marlatt, G. A., & George, W. H. (1990). Relapse prevention and the maintenance of optimal health. In S. Shumaker, E. Schron, & J. K. Ockene (Eds.), *The handbook of health behavior change* (pp. 44–63). New York: Springer.

Marlatt, G. A., & Gordon, J. R. (1985). *Relapse prevention.* New York: Guilford.

Marlatt, G. A., & Gordon, J. R. (1980). Determinants of relapse: Implications for the maintenance of behavior change. In P. O. Davidson & S. M. Davidson (Eds.), *Behavioral medicine: Changing health lifestyles* (pp. 410–452). New York: Brunner/Mazel.

Marlatt, G. A., & Gordon, J. R. (1989). Relapse prevention: Future directions. In M. Gossop (Ed.), *Relapse and addictive behavior.* London: Tavistock/Routledge.

Marlatt, G. A., & Miller, W. R. (1984). *Comprehensive Drinker Profile.* Odessa, FL: Psychological Assessment Resources.

Miller, W. R., & Marlatt, G. A. (1987). *The Brief Drinker Profile.* Odessa, FL: Psychological Assessment Resources.

O'Farrell, T. J. (1993). Couples relapse prevention sessions after a behavioral marital therapy couples group program. In T. J. O'Farrell (Ed.), *Treating alcohol problems: Marital and family interventions* (pp. 305–326). New York: Guilford.

Rosenberg, H., & Brian, T. (1986). Cognitive-behavioral group therapy for multiple-DUI offenders. *Alcoholism Treatment Quarterly, 3,* 47–65.

Sandahl, C., & Ronnberg, S. (1990). Brief group psychotherapy in relapse prevention for alcohol dependent patients. *International Journal of Group Psychotherapy, 40,* 453–476.

Schachter, S. (1982). Recidivism and self-cure of smoking and obesity. *American Psychologist, 37,* 436–444.

Skuttle, A., & Berg, G. (1987). Training in controlled drinking for early-stage problem drinkers. *British Journal of Addiction, 82,* 493–501.

Somers, J. M., & Marlatt, G. A. (1992). Alcohol problems. In P. H. Wilson (Ed.), *Principles and practice of relapse prevention* (pp. 23–42). New York: Guilford.

Wallace, B. C. (1991). *Crack cocaine: A practical treatment approach for the chemically dependent.* New York: Brunner/Mazel.

Wanigaratne, S., Wallace, W., Pullin, J., Keaney, F., & Farmer, R. (1990). *Relapse prevention for addictive behaviors: A manual for therapists.* London: Blackwell Scientific Publications.

Wilson, P. H. (Ed.). (1992). *Principles and practice of relapse prevention.* New York: Guilford.

ACKNOWLEDGMENTS

We would like to gratefully thank Jewel Brien for the design of the graphics contained in this manuscript.

CHAPTER 12

Marital and Family Therapy

Timothy J. O'Farrell

OVERVIEW

Marital and family treatment (MFT) approaches have been called "the most notable current advance in the area of psychotherapy of alcoholism" (Keller, 1974, p. 116), and enthusiasm derives from several sources. Many alcoholics have extensive marital and family problems (e.g., O'Farrell & Birchler, 1987), and positive marital and family adjustment is associated with better alcoholism treatment outcomes at follow-up (e.g., Moos, Finney, & Cronkite, 1990). Further, there exists growing clinical and research evidence of reciprocal relationships between marital-family interactions and abusive drinking.

It is widely known that abusive drinking leads to marital and family discord, among the more serious of which are separation/divorce and child and spouse abuse. At the same time, the role played by marital and family factors in the development and maintenance of alcohol problems is considerable. Individuals reared with an alcohol-abusing parent are at risk for developing alcohol problems due both to genetic factors and to faulty role modeling. Marital and

family problems may stimulate excessive drinking, and family interactions often help to maintain alcohol problems once they have developed. Excessive drinking may provide more subtle adaptive consequences for the couple or family, such as facilitating the expression of emotion and affection or regulating the amount of distance and closeness between family members. Finally, even when recovery from the alcohol problem has begun, marital and family conflicts may often precipitate renewed drinking by abstinent alcoholics (Maisto, O'Farrell, Connors, McKay, & Pelcovits, 1988).

This chapter presents MFT interventions for use with alcohol abusers and alcoholics during three broadly defined stages of recovery (Prochaska & DiClemente, 1983): (1) initial commitment to change—recognizing that a problem exists and deciding to do something about it, (2) the change itself—stopping abusive drinking and stabilizing this change for at least a few months, and (3) the long-term maintenance of change. The focus is primarily on marital or spouse-involved therapy methods, drawn from a behavioral orientation because these methods, having been used and studied more extensively than others, have greatest empirical support. This also is the area of the author's primary expertise. Applications of these methods to family therapy will be noted.

Note: The National Institute on Alcohol Abuse and Alcoholism grant R01 AA08637 and the Department of Veterans Affairs provided support for preparation of this chapter.

SPECIAL CONSIDERATIONS

Clients Most and Least Likely to Benefit

Unfortunately, studies examining predictors of response to MFT with alcoholics are not yet available. However, clinical experience and studies of factors that predict alcoholics' acceptance and completion of MFT (Noel, McCrady, Stout, & Nelson, 1987; O'Farrell, Kleinke, & Cutter, 1986; Zweben, Pearlman, & Li, 1983) provide some information on clients most likely to benefit from such treatment since the clients must accept and stay in therapy to benefit. Clients most likely to accept and complete MFT have the following characteristics: (1) have a high school education or better; (2) are employed full time if able and desirous of working; (3) live together or, if separated, are willing to reconcile for the duration of the therapy; (4) are older; (5) have more serious alcohol problems of longer duration; (6) enter therapy after a crisis, especially one that threatens the stability of the marriage; (7) spouse and other family members not alcoholic; (8) alcoholic, spouse, and other family members without serious psychopathology or drug abuse; and (9) absence of family violence that has caused serious injury or is potentially life threatening.

Further, evidence that the alcoholic is motivated to change and to take an active role in a psychologically oriented treatment approach also suggests potential for benefiting from MFT. Such evidence includes contact with the treatment program personally initiated by the alcoholic and a history of successful participation in other outpatient counseling or self-help programs (as opposed to those only admitted to detoxification for relief of physical distress due to heavy drinking, without further active ongoing treatment participation). Compliance with the initial month of outpatient treatment—including abstinence, keeping scheduled appointments, and completing any required assignments—are process measures that seem to predict likely benefit on a clinical basis.

These characteristics may sound like those of model clients who are likely to benefit from nearly any treatment method. However, clients do not have to fit these criteria for therapists to use MFT methods described in this chapter. Rather, the MFT methods have to be adapted for some of the more difficult cases—generally by going slower, individualizing the approach to a greater degree, and dealing with more varied and more frequent obstacles and resistances. Strategies for dealing with some of the more difficult cases (e.g., the separated alcoholic, the family with more than one alcohol-abusing member) have been presented elsewhere (O'Farrell, 1986).

Therapist Attributes and Behaviors Needed

Our clinical experience suggests that certain therapist attributes and behaviors are important for successful MFT with alcoholics. From the outset, the therapist must structure treatment so that control of the alcohol abuse is the first priority, before attempting to help the couple or family with other problems. Many of our clients have had previous unsuccessful experiences with therapists who saw the couple in MFT without dealing with the alcohol abuse. The hope that reduction in marital or family distress will lead to improvement in the drinking problem rarely is fulfilled. More typically, recurrent alcohol-related incidents and interactions undermine whatever gains have been made in marital and family relationships.

Therapists must be able to tolerate and deal effectively with strong anger in early sessions and at later times of crisis. The therapist can use empathic listening to help each family member feel he or she has been heard and insist that only one person speaks at a time. Helping the couple or family defuse their intense anger is very important, since failure to do so often leads to a poor outcome (Gurman & Kniskern, 1978).

Therapists need to structure and control treatment sessions, especially during the early assessment and therapy phase and at later times of crisis (e.g., episodes of drinking or intense family conflict). Highly structured therapy sessions with a directive, active therapist are more effective for alcoholic families than is a less structured mode of therapy. Many therapists' errors involve difficulty establishing and maintaining control of the sessions and responding to the myriad forms of resistance and noncompliance presented by couples and families. Therapists must steer a middle course between lack of structure and being overly controlling and punitive in response to noncompliance. Therapists need to clearly establish and enforce the rules of treatment and also acknowledge approximation to desired behavior despite significant shortcomings.

Finally, therapists need to take a long-term view of the course of change—both the alcoholism problem and associated marital and family distress may be helped substantially only by repeated efforts, including some failed attempts. Such a long-term view may help the therapist encounter relapse without becoming overly discouraged or engaging in blaming and recriminations with the alcoholic and family. The therapist also should maintain contact with the family long after the problems apparently have stabilized. Leaving such contacts to the family usually means no follow-up contacts occur until the family is back in a major crisis again.

DESCRIPTION

Initiating Change and Helping the Family When the Alcohol Abuser Resists Treatment

Four MFT approaches address the difficult and all-too-common case of the alcoholic who is not yet willing to stop drinking. Three of the approaches try to help the spouse and family members to motivate the uncooperative, denying alcoholic to change his or her drinking. Community reinforcement training for families is a program (see Chapter 15) for teaching the nonalcoholic family member (usually the wife of a male problem drinker) (1) how to reduce physical abuse to herself, (2) how to encourage sobriety, (3) how to encourage seeking professional treatment, and (4) how to assist in that treatment (Sisson & Azrin, 1986, 1993).

The Johnson Institute "intervention" procedure involves three to four educational and rehearsal sessions to prepare family members. During the intervention session itself, family members confront the alcoholic about his or her drinking and strongly encourage the alcohol abuser to enter an alcoholism treatment program (Johnson, 1973; Liepman, 1993).

The unilateral family therapy (UFT) approach assists the nonalcoholic spouse to strengthen his or her coping capabilities, to enhance family functioning, and to facilitate greater sobriety on the part of the alcohol abuser (Thomas & Ager, 1993). UFT provides a series of graded steps the spouse can use prior to confrontation. These steps may be successful in their own right or at least pave the way for a positive outcome to a UFT "programmed confrontation" experience, which is similar to the Johnson approach and adapted for use with an individual spouse.

A fourth and final approach is a group program for wives of treatment-resistant alcoholics

(Dittrich, 1993). This program tries to help alcoholics' wives cope with their emotional distress and concentrate on their own motivations for change rather than trying to motivate the alcoholic to change. This approach borrows many concepts from Al-Anon, by far the most widely used source of support for family members troubled by a loved one's alcoholism. Al-Anon advocates that family members detach themselves from the alcoholic's drinking in a loving way, accept that they are powerless to control the alcoholic, and seek support from other members of the Al-Anon program (Al-Anon Family Groups, 1981).

Goals and Preparations for MFT

Goals

Once the alcoholic has decided to change his or her drinking, MFT has two basic objectives in order to stabilize short-term change in the alcohol problem and in the alcoholic's marriage and family relationships. The first goal is to reduce or eliminate abusive drinking and support the alcoholic's efforts to change. To this end, a high priority is changing alcohol-related interactional patterns (e.g., nagging about past drinking but ignoring current sober behavior). One can get abstinent alcoholics and their spouses to engage in behaviors more pleasing to each other, but if they continue talking about and focusing on past or "possible" future drinking, frequently such arguments lead to renewed drinking (Maisto et al., 1988). They then feel more discouraged about their relationship and the drinking than before, and are less likely to try pleasing each other again.

The second goal involves altering general marital and family patterns to provide an atmosphere that is more conducive to sobriety. This involves helping the couple repair the often extensive relationship damage incurred during many years of conflict over alcohol, as well as helping them find solutions to relationship difficulties that may not be directly related to the alcoholism. Finally, the couple must learn to confront and resolve relationship conflicts without the alcoholic's resorting to drinking.

After the change in the alcohol problem has been stable for three to six months, the goals of marital therapy in contributing to long-term maintenance of change are to (1) help the couple prevent relapse to abusive drinking and (2) deal with marital issues frequently encountered during long-term recovery. Methods that therapists can use to reach each of these goals will be presented in detail after we consider the initial assessment and crisis intervention sessions that are so important if therapeutic goals are to be accomplished.

Assessment and Crisis Intervention

In the initital interview, the therapist needs to: (1) determine at what stage the alcoholic is in the process of changing his or her alcohol abuse, (2) assess whether there is a need for crisis intervention prior to a careful assessment, and (3) orient the couple to the assessment procedures. If the alcoholic already has initiated changes in the drinking, or at least clearly recognizes that a problem exists and may want to change it, then proceeding with the assessment makes sense. If the alcoholic has not yet made a firm decision to change the drinking, then facilitating this decision becomes one of the goals of the assessment.

It is very important to give priority to the alcoholic's drinking in the initial sessions. We generally attempt to establish at least a temporary contract of abstinence during the two to four assessment sessions. A minimal requirement is abstinence on the days of assessment sessions, and clients are informed that an alcohol breathalyzer test is a standard feature of all assessment sessions we conduct. An inquiry about the extent of drinking and urges to drink between sessions is a routine part of each assessment session. We also ask the couple to commit themselves, for the time period needed to complete the assessment, to stay living together, not to threaten separation or divorce, and to refrain from bringing up the past in anger at home.

The therapist evaluates whether any serious negative consequences are likely to occur if two to four assessment sessions are conducted before taking action on the presenting complaints. For example, crisis intervention is necessary for cases in which violence or divorce seems a likely result of delayed action or for cases in which the drinker is ready to stop drinking but needs immediate hospitalization for detoxification and starting alcoholism treatment. Often, the usual assessment can be conducted after the crisis has been resolved. Other issues that also may present obstacles to assessment and require intervention are discussed in more detail below after considering assessment methods.

Assessment Targets and Procedures

A series of assessment issues or targets are investigated in progressively greater depth as the assessment progresses. In the initial session, the therapist's clinical interview should gather information about: (1) the alcoholic's drinking—especially recent quantity and frequency of drinking, whether the extent of physical dependence on alcohol requires detoxification to obtain abstinence during the assessment, what led to seeking help at this time and prior help-seeking efforts, and whether the alcoholic's and spouse's goal is to reduce the drinking or to abstain either temporarily or permanently; (2) drug use other than alcohol; (3) the stability of the marriage in terms of current planned or actual separation as well as any past separations; (4) recent violence and any fears of recurrence; (5) suicidal ideation or behavior for either the client or the spouse; and (6) the existence of alcohol-related or other crises that require immediate attention. Allowing 75 to 90 minutes for the initial session and including 5 to 10 minutes separately with each spouse alone provides sufficient time to gather the needed information and to learn of important material (e.g., plans for separation, fears of violence) that either spouse may be reluctant to share during the conjoint portion of the interview.

Our own practice makes use of a number of structured assessment instruments and procedures after the initial interview session to explore in greater detail the issues covered in the initital session (see O'Farrell, 1993a, for more details). The marital relationship also is explored in depth in these subsequent assessment sessions with special attention being given to the overall level of satisfaction experienced in the relationship, specific changes desired in the relationship, sexual adjustment, and level of communication skills especially when talking about conflicts and problems. The goal of this additional assessment is to determine (1) what changes are needed in marital and family life as well as other day-to-day activities in order to achieve and maintain the goal for the alcoholic's drinking and (2) what marital changes are desired to increase marital satisfaction, if one assumes that the drinking goal will be achieved.

After the assessment information has been gathered, the couple and therapist meet for a feedback session in which the therapist shares impressions of the nature and severity of the drinking and marital problems and invites the couple to respond to these impressions. This session allows therapists the opportunity to increase motivation for treatment by reviewing in a nonjudgmental, matter-of-fact manner the negative consequences of the excessive drinking. A second goal of the feedback session is to decide whether or not the couple will begin short-term MFT and prepare them for the MFT if that is the decision.

Assuming the decision is to start MFT, the therapist usually emphasizes the value of MFT in achieving sobriety and a more satisfying relationship and tries to promote favorable therapeutic expectations. The therapist asks the husband and the wife to promise that they will live together for at least the initial course of therapy, not threaten divorce or separation during this period, and do their best to focus on the future and the present (but not the past) in the therapy sessions and at home. The therapist also asks the couple to agree to do weekly homework assignments as part of the therapy. Finally, the therapist gives an overview of the course of therapy and tells the couple in more detail about the content of the first few sessions.

Obstacles Frequently Encountered During Initial Sessions

Alcohol-Related Crises. Despite their seeming suitability for MFT, many alcoholics and their spouses will present the therapist with substantial obstacles. Common problems encountered during assessment are pressing alcohol-related crises (e.g., actual, impending, or threatened loss of job or home, or major legal or financial problems) that preclude a serious and sustained MFT focus. The therapist can help the couple devise plans to deal with the crisis or refer them elsewhere for such help, often after estabishing a behavioral contract about drinking and alcohol-related interactions (see below). Other assessment and therapy procedures can be started when the crisis has been resolved.

Potential for Violence. Many couples whose negative interactions escalate quickly have difficulty containing conflict between sessions and pose a potential for violence in some instances. Responses to initial interviews with the couple (and with the spouses separately) and further inquiry during subsequent sessions help identify many such violence-prone couples during the pretherapy assessment. Once identified, these couples have conflict containment as an explicit goal of their therapy from the outset. For couples with a history of interspousal violence, it is important to determine whether the violence was limited to occasions when the alcoholic had been drinking. If so, then methods to deal with the alcohol abuse may relieve much of the couple's concern about violence.

Nonetheless, an additional procedure described by Shapiro (1984) can be very useful in cases where violence still seems likely. This involves a written agreement that spouses are not to hit or threaten to hit each other, and that if they do, one of the spouses (named in the agreement) will leave the home and go to a designated place for 48 to 72 hours. A "time-out" agreement is another useful procedure for containing conflict. In this procedure if either party gets uncomfortable that a discussion may be escalating, he or she says, "I'm getting uncomfortable. I want a five-minute time-out." Spouses go to separate rooms and use slow deep breathing to calm themselves. Afterward, the couple may restart the discussion if both desire it. If either partner requests a second time-out, then the couple definitely must stop the discussion.

The Blaming Spouse. It usually is not helpful to interpret the nonalcoholic spouse's frequent conversations about past or possible future drinking as an attempt to punish the alcoholic or sabotage the alcoholic's recovery. Overtly disapproving of the spouse's blaming behavior also does not help. The therapist can empathize with the spouse by sympathetically reframing the spouse's behavior as trying to protect the couple from further problems due to alcohol. From this perspective, the spouse's talk about drinking is intended to be sure the alcoholic (1) knows fully the negative impact of the past drinking (and this is plausible since often the drinker does not remember much of what happened); (2) is aware of the full extent of the problem so his or her motivation toward sobriety will be fortified; and (3) is prepared for situations that may lead to a relapse or lapse in motivation. Once the spouse feels understood, he or she becomes more receptive to the therapist's suggestion that the spouse has been "doing the wrong thing for the right reason" and to suggestions about more constructive methods to achieve the same goal.

Typical Structure and Sequence of Therapy Sessions

Once assessment is complete and initial obstacles have been overcome, MFT to help stabilize short-term change in the alcoholism and associated marital discord usually consists of 10 to 20 therapy sessions each of which last 60 to 75 minutes. Sessions tend to be highly structured, with the therapist setting the agenda at the outset of each meeting.

A typical session begins with an inquiry about any drinking or urges to drink that have occurred since the last session including compliance with any sobriety contract (see below) that has been negotiated. It moves from a review of the homework assignment from the previous session to considering important events of the past week. Then the session considers new material, such as instruction in and rehearsal of skills to be practiced at home during the week. It ends with the assignment of homework and answering questions. Generally, the first few sessions focus on decreasing alcohol-related feelings and interactions and increasing positive exchanges. This decreases tension about alcohol (and the risk of abusive drinking) and builds goodwill. Both are necessary for dealing with marital problems and desired relationship changes in later sessions using communication and problem-solving skills training and behavior change agreements. The following section describes typical interventions used.

Once the alcohol problem has been under control for three to six months, the structure and content of marital therapy sessions often change as the emphasis of the therapy becomes maintaining gains and preventing relapse. This phase of therapy is described later in the chapter.

Producing Short-Term Drinking and Relationship Changes

Alcohol-Focused Interventions

General Goals and Issues. After the alcohol abuser has decided to change his or her drinking, the spouse and other family members can be included in treatment designed to support the alcoholic in adhering to this difficult and stressful decision. The first purpose of such treatment is to estabish a clear and specific agreement between the alcohol abuser and family member(s) about the goal for the alcoholic's drinking and the role of each family member in achieving that goal. Behavioral contracting can be very useful for this purpose and is described further below.

Specifying other behavioral changes needed in the alcoholic or the family requires a careful review of individual situations and conditions. Possible exposure to alcoholic beverages and alcohol-related situations should be discussed. The spouse and family should decide if they will drink alcoholic beverages in the alcoholic's presence whether alcoholic beverages

will be kept and served at home, if the couple will attend social gatherings involving alcohol, and how to deal with these situations. Particular persons, gatherings, or circumstances that are likely to be stressful should be identified. Couple and family interactions related to alcohol also need to be addressed, because arguments, tensions, and negative feelings can precipitate more abusive drinking. Therapists need to discuss these patterns with the family and suggest specific procedures to be used in difficult situations. The remainder of this section describes specific methods and examples of how to achieve the general goals just described.

Behavioral Contracting. Written behavioral contracts, although different in many specific aspects of the agreements, have a number of common elements that make them useful. The drinking behavior goal is made explicit. Specific behaviors that each spouse can do to help achieve this goal are als detailed. The contract provides alternative behaviors to negative interactions about drinking. Finally, and quite importantly, the agreement decreases the nonalcoholic spouse's anxiety and need to control the alcoholic and his or her drinking.

Structuring the spouse's and the alcoholic's role in the recovery process. Daniel Kivlahan and Elizabeth Shapiro (personal communication, May 18, 1984) have alcoholics and their spouses engage in what they call a *sobriety trust contract*. Each day, at a specified time, the alcoholic initiates a brief discussion and reiterates his or her desire not to drink that day. Then the alcoholic asks if the spouse has any questions or fears about possible drinking that day. The alcoholic answers the questions and attempts to reassure the spouse. The spouse is not to mention past drinking or any future possible drinking beyond that day. The couple agrees to refrain from discussing drinking at any other time, to keep the daily trust discussion very brief, and to end it with a positive statement to each other.

Two examples illustrate other types of contracts we have used with alcoholic couples. In the first case, a male alcoholic, who recognized he had an alcohol problem and had abstained for three months in the past year, was trying to engage in "social drinking." Periodically he would drink heavily for a period of three to five days, and three serious binges had occurred in the past six weeks. Each binge ended after an intense fight in which the husband became verbally abusive and the wife threatened to terminate their relationship. At a conjoint session with the wife, the following agreement was negotiated: (1) the husband's goal was at least six months' abstinence from alcohol; (2) if he drank before then, he would start daily Antabuse and continue it at least to the end of the six-month period; (3) if the wife thought he had been drinking, she would remind the husband of their agreement and ask him to start the Antabuse; (4) if the husband refused, the wife would refrain from arguing or threats and leave their home until the husband had stopped drinking and started the Antabuse. Two weeks later, the husband drank and then voluntarily started the Antabuse. Both husband and wife were pleased that their customary intense argument was not necessary to terminate the drinking.

In the second case, a chronic alcoholic with serious liver cirrhosis reported good progress in outpatient sessions but complained that his wife was unfairly accusing him of drinking and they were arguing about financial and other problems. At about the same time, liver function tests showed elevated liver enzymes, most likely indicating recent drinking. Couple sessions were begun and the following agreement was established: (1) each evening the husband would take an alcohol breath test using a Mobile Breath Alcohol Tester ("Mobat"; Sobell & Sobell, 1975) to verify he had not been drinking; (2) the wife would refrain from accusations about current drinking or complaints about past drinking; (3) the daily Mobat review would continue until normal liver test results and no evidence of drinking were achieved for two consecutive months; (4) the couple would continue in conjoint sessions about their other relationship problems. Only two isolated instances occurred in which the Mobat indicated the husband had been drinking that day and the couple's conflicts were resolved satisfactorily in later sessions.

Participation in AA and Al-Anon self-help groups is often part of the behavioral contracts we negotiate with couples. As with any other behavior that is part of a "sobriety contract," as we call the various forms of behavior contracts we use, attendance at AA and Al-Anon meetings is reviewed at each therapy session.

Antabuse contracts to promote abstinence.

Antabuse (Disulfiram), a drug that produces extreme nausea and sickness when the person taking the drug ingests alcohol, is widely used in treatment for persons with a goal of abstinence (see Chapter 8). Antabuse therapy often is not effective because the alcoholic discontinues the drug prematurely. The Antabuse contract, or Disulfiram assurance plan, is a procedure that has been used by a number of investigators (e.g., Azrin, Sisson, Meyers, & Godley, 1982; O'Farrell, Cutter, & Floyd, 1985). It is designed to maintain Antabuse ingestion and abstinence from alcohol and to decrease alcohol-related arguments and interactions between the alcoholic and his or her spouse. Before negotiating such a contract, the therapist should be sure that the alcoholic is willing and medically cleared to take Antabuse and that both alcoholic and spouse have been fully informed and educated about the effects of the drug.

In the Antabuse contract, the alcoholic agrees to take Antabuse each day while the spouse observes. The spouse, in turn, agrees to positively reinforce the drinker for taking the Antabuse, to record the observation on a calendar provided by the therapist, and not to mention past drinking or any fears about future drinking. Each spouse should view the agreement as a cooperative method for rebuilding lost trust and not as a coercive checking-up operation. Other articles (e.g., O'Farrell & Bayog, 1986) present more details on how to implement the Antabuse contract and how to deal with common resistances to this procedure (see also Chapter 15).

Reducing hazardous drinking.

Peter Miller (1972) used contingency contracting with an excessive drinker and his wife to produce reduced consumption and fewer arguments about drinking. The couple signed a contract that required the husband to limit his drinking to between one and three drinks a day (in the presence of his wife before the evening meal) and the wife to refrain from negative verbal or nonverbal responses to her husband's drinking. Each partner agreed to pay the other $20 if he or she broke the agreement. Each spouse received a few fines during the first few weeks of the contract, but the infractions rapidly diminished when each partner learned that the contract would, in fact, be enforced.

The alcohol abuser treated by Miller was employed, showed no medical damage from his excessive drinking, and the negative impact of his drinking was confined to the marital relationship. These factors suggested an attempt to reduce rather than eliminate the drinking. Therapists need to choose carefully in each individual case whether the goal of treatment should be moderation or total abstinence. Therapists should use available guidelines (Heather & Robertson, 1981, pp. 215–240; Miller & Caddy, 1977) prior to implementing such a behavioral contracting procedure.

Decreasing Family Members' Behaviors that Trigger or Enable Drinking.

Noel and Mc-Crady (1993) implemented procedures to decrease spouse behaviors that trigger or enable abusive drinking with a female alcohol abuser, Charlotte, and her husband, Tom. The couple identified behaviors by Tom that triggered drinking by Charlotte (e.g., drinking together after work, trying to stop her from drinking, arguing with her about drinking). Charlotte reacted by criticizing Tom until he left her alone and drinking still more. Moreover, Tom unwittingly reinforced Charlotte's drinking by protecting her from the consequences of her drinking (e.g., by helping her to bed when she was drunk, cleaning up after her when she drank). Noel and McCrady helped the couple find mutually comfortable and agreeable methods to reverse Tom's behavior that inadvertently had promoted Charlotte's drinking. Tom decided to give up drinking. He worked hard to change his feelings that he must protect Charlotte from the negative consequences of her drinking. The therapists also taught Tom to provide positive reinforcers (such as verbal acknowledgment, going to movies and other events together) only when Charlotte had not been drinking.

Dealing with Drinking during Treatment.

Drinking episodes often occur during MFT with alcoholics. MFT works best if the therapist intervenes before the drinking goes on for too long a period. Having the alcoholic keep a daily record of urges to drink (and any drinking that occurs) and reviewing this record each session can help alert the therapist to the possible risk of a relapse. Between-session phone calls to prompt completion of homework assignments can also alert the therapist to precursors of a drinking episode or to drinking already in progress. Once drinking has occurred, the therapist should try to get the drinking stopped and to see the couple as soon as possible to use the relapse as a learning experience.

At the couple session, the therapist must be extremely active in defusing hostile or depressive reactions to the drinking. The therapist should stress that drinking does not constitute total failure, and that inconsistent progress is the rule rather than the exception. The therapist should help the couple decide what they need to do to feel sure that the drinking is over and will not continue in the coming week (e.g., restarting Antabuse, going to AA and Al-Anon together, reinstituting a sobriety trust contract, entering a detoxification ward). Finally, the therapist also should try to help the couple identify what couple conflict (or other antecedent) led up to the relapse and generate alternative solutions other than drinking for similar future situations.

Repeated drinking episodes can present a particularly difficult challenge. As indicated, each drinking episode should be used as a learning experience, and depending on what is discovered, different strategies may be helpful. Sometimes a careful analysis will show that the drinking is being precipitated by factors outside the marital relationship, such as work pressures or job-related drinking situations (see Chapter 4). Individual sessions with the alcoholic to devise methods to deal with the nonmarital precipitants often can be useful in such cases. Another nonmarital factor that can lead to repeated drinking episodes is the alcoholic's ambivalence about whether to stop drinking or attempt to drink "socially." Often, an individual session with the alcoholic helps the therapist establish the alcoholic's ambivalence as the basis for the repeated drinking and matter of factly lay out the choices facing the alcoholic about his or her drinking behavior (see Chapter 5).

At times, repeated drinking episodes are related, at least in part, to marital relationship issues. When the drinking has adaptive consequences for the relationship (e.g., facilitates sexual interaction or emotional communication for one or both spouses), the main strategy is to strengthen controls against drinking while working intensively with the couple to attain the same adaptive relationship consequences without the aid of alcohol. For other couples, repeated drinking episodes are a response to recurring, intense marital conflicts. The best approach for these couples is to (1) devise specific methods tailored to their idiosyncratic needs that they can use to contain conflict and that the alcoholic can use to avoid drinking; (2) strengthen nonmarital alcohol coping mechanisms (e.g., AA, Antabuse); and (3) learn alternative communication and problem-solving skills.

Interventions to Improve the Marital and Family Relationship

Once the alcohol abuser has decided to change his or her drinking and has begun successfully to control or abstain from drinking, the therapist can focus on the alcoholic's marital and family relationships. Family members often experience resentment about past abusive drinking and fear and distrust about the possible return of abusive drinking in the future. The alcoholic often experiences guilt and a desire for recognition of current improved drinking behavior. These feelings experienced by the alcoholic and the family often lead to an atmosphere of tension and unhappiness in marital and family relationships.

There are problems caused by drinking (e.g., bills, legal charges, embarrassing incidents) that still need to be resolved. There is often a backlog of other unresolved marital and family problems that the drinking obscured. These longstanding problems may seem to increase as drinking declines, when actually the problems are simply being recognized for the first time, now that alcohol cannot be used to excuse them. The family frequently lacks the communication skills and mutual positive feelings needed to resolve these problems. As a result, many marriages and families are dissolved during the first one or two years of the alcohol abuser's recovery. In other cases, marital and family conflicts trigger relapse and a return to abusive drinking by the alcoholic. Even in cases where the alcoholic has a basically sound marriage and family life when he or she is not drinking, the initiation of sobriety can produce temporary tension and role readjustment and provide the opportunity for stabilizing and enriching the marriage and family. For these reasons, many alcoholics can benefit from assistance to improve their marital and family relationships once changes in drinking have begun.

Two major goals of interventions focused on the alcoholic's marital/family relationship are (1) to increase positive feeling, goodwill, and commitment to the relationship; and (2) to resolve conflicts, problems, and desires for change. Procedures useful in achieving these two goals will be covered separately even though they often overlap in the course of actual therapy sessions. More detailed descriptions of the procedures are available elsewhere (O'Farrell, 1993a). The general sequence in teaching couples and families skills to increase positive interchanges and resolve conflicts and problems is (1) therapist instruction and modeling, (2) the couple practicing under therapist supervision, (3) assignment for homework, and (4) review of homework with further practice.

Increasing Positive Interchanges. Increasing positive feelings and activities can build relationship satisfaction and family cohesion. This produces a more positive family environment and reduces the risk of relapse. Methods used include increasing pleasing behaviors, planning recreational activities, and enacting core symbols of couple and family meaning.

Increasing pleasing behaviors. A series of procedures can increase a couple's awareness of benefits from the relationship and the frequency with which spouses notice, acknowledge, and initiate pleasing or caring behaviors on a daily basis. The therapist tells the couple that *caring behaviors* are "behaviors showing that you care for the other person," and assigns homework called "Catch Your Partner Doing Something Nice" to assist couples in *noticing* the daily caring behaviors in the marriage. This requires each spouse to record one caring behavior performed by the partner each day on sheets provided by the therapist (see Figure 12.1).

Figure 12.1 Sample Record Sheet of Daily Caring Behaviors

"CATCH YOUR PARTNER DOING SOMETHING NICE"

Name: Mike   Name of Partner: Nancy

Day	Date	Pleasing Behavior
Mon.	4/6	Waited to have dinner with me because I had to stay late to work. Made me feel good.
Tues.	4/7	Told me she loved me.
Wed.	4/8	Cooked a delicious Italian dinner and afterwards we had a very romantic evening.
Thur.	4/9	Was patient with me as I came home tired and moody from work.
Fri.	4/10	Enjoyed a walk together around the neighborhood.
Sat.	4/11	Woke me gently and rubbed my back.
Sun.	4/12	Was the perfect hostess for an afternoon party with some friends of ours.

The couple reads the caring behaviors recorded during the previous week at the subsequent session. Then the therapist models *acknowledging* caring behaviors ("I liked it when you _____. It made me feel _____.") and notes the importance of eye contact, a smile, a sincere and pleasant tone of voice, and only positive feelings. Each spouse then practices acknowledging caring behaviors from his or her daily list for the previous week. After the couple practices the new behavior in the therapy session, the therapist assigns for homework a two- to five-minute daily communication session at home in which each partner acknowledges one pleasing behavior noticed that day. As couples begin to notice and acknowledge daily caring behaviors, each partner beings *initiating* more caring behaviors. Often the weekly reports of daily caring behaviors show that one or both spouses are fulfilling requests for desired change voiced before the therapy. In addition, many couples report that the two- to five-minute communication sessions serve to initiate more extensive conversations.

A final assignment is that each partner give the other a "caring day" during the coming week by performing special acts to show caring for the spouse. The therapist should encourage each partner to take risks and to act lovingly toward the spouse rather than wait for the other to make the first move. Finally, the therapist can remind spouses that at the start of therapy they agreed to act differently (e.g., more lovingly) and then assess changes in feelings, rather than wait to feel more positively toward their partner before instituting changes in their own behavior.

Planning shared recreational and leisure activities. Many alcohol abusers' families have discontinued or decreased shared leisure activities because in the past the drinker frequently sought enjoyment only in situations involving alcohol and embarrassed the family by drinking too much. Reversing this trend is important because participation by the couple and family in social and recreational activities is associated with positive alcoholism treatment outcome (Moos et al., 1990). Planning and engaging in shared rewarding activities (SRA) can be initiated by simply having each spouse make a separate list of possible activities. Each activity must involve both spouses, either by themselves or with their children or other adults, and can be at or away from home. Before giving the couple a homework assignment of planning an SRA, the therapist should model an SRA planning session illustrating solutions to common pitfalls (e.g., waiting until the last minute so that necessary preparations cannot be made, getting sidetracked on trivial practical arrangements). Finally, the therapist should instruct the couple to refrain from discussing problems or conflicts during their planned SRAs.

Core symbols. Core symbols, or symbols of special meaning, offer another means to enhance positive feelings and interactions in a relationship. A *core symbol* is any event, place, or object that carries special meaning for the relationship to both marital partners (Liberman, Wheeler, deVisser, Kuehnel, & Kuehnel, 1980). A special song, the honeymoon, the place where the couple met, pictures, eating by candlelight, and wedding rings are examples. Rituals and activities (e.g., going out for breakfast on Sunday morning), which go beyond recreational activities because of their special meaning to the couple, also can become a core symbol and represent an intimate shared time set aside for closeness.

Therapists should introduce core symbols only after tension over drinking has decreased and the partners are beginning to experience some goodwill and positive feeling for each other. After each partner gives one example of such a symbol, each spouse lists as many core symbols as possible for a homework assignment. In subsequent sessions, the couple chooses one or more core symbols to reexperience or reestablish in their day-to-day lives together. In relationships where the search for core symbols not poisoned by alcohol proves fruitless, therapists should help the couple develop and enact new core symbols. Identifying and participating in such core symbols can help couples foster positive feelings that have been buried for years under many layers of hostility and disappointment. For some couples, a reestablishment of spiritual and religious practices is an important consideration here.

Applications to family therapy. Core symbols, planning recreational and leisure activities, and increasing positive behaviors can be applied to family therapy that includes children and their parent(s). Family therapy sessions are particularly useful and indicated when an adolescent has an alcohol problem (e.g., Trepper, Piercy, Lewis, Volk, & Sprenkle, 1993) or when the alcohol-abusing parent and his or her spouse have made some progress and the therapist wishes then to include the children in the therapy. Using core symbols in family therapy sessions can be very powerful because special activities and rituals forge strong family ties and traditions. Similarly, planning recreational and leisure activities for the whole family or selected members (e.g., father and son) can be quite rewarding, and the preceding procedures for couples are directly applicable. The procedures directed to increasing pleasing behavior often can lead to dramatic changes in the emotional tone of the family, especially when the therapist can get the entire family to participate.

Resolving Conflicts and Problems. Inadequate communication is a major problem for alcohol abusers and their spouses (O'Farrell & Birchler, 1987). Inability to resolve conflicts and problems can cause abusive drinking and severe marital and family tension to recur (Maisto et al., 1988). Teaching couples and families how to resolve conflicts and problems can reduce family stress and decrease the risk of relapse.

Training in communication skills. We generally begin our work on training in communication skills by defining *effective communication* as "message intended (by speaker) equals message received (by listener)." The chart presented in Figure 12.2 helps explain this definition further, including factors (e.g., "filters") in each person that can impede communication and the need to learn both "listening" and "speaking" skills. Therapists can use instructions, modeling, prompting, behavioral rehearsal, and feedback to teach couples and families how to communicate more effectively. Learning communication skills of listening and speaking and how to use planned communication sessions are essential prerequisites for problem solving and negotiating desired behavior changes. The training starts with nonproblem areas that are positive or neutral and moves to problem areas and charged issues only after each skill has been practiced on less problematic topics.

Communication sessions are planned, structured discussions in which spouses talk privately, face-to-face, without distractions, and with each spouse taking turns expressing his or her point of view without interruptions. Communication sessions can be introduced for two to five minutes daily when couples first practice acknowledging caring behaviors, and in 10- to 15-minute sessions three to four times a week in later sessions when the concern is to practice a particular skill. The therapist discusses with the couple the time and place that they plan to have their assigned communication practice sessions. The success of this plan is assessed at the next session, and any needed changes are suggested. Just establishing a communication session as a method for discussing feelings, events, and problems can be very helpful for many couples. The therapist encourages couples to ask each other for a communication session when they want to discuss an issue or problem and to keep in mind the ground rules of behavior that characterize such a session.

Listening skills help each spouse to feel understood and supported and slow down couple interactions to prevent quick escalation of aversive exchanges. The therapist instructs spouses to repeat both the words and the feelings of the speaker's message and to check to see if the message they received was the message intended by their partner ("What I heard you say was . . . . Is that right?"). When the listener has understood the speaker's message, roles change and the first listener then speaks. Teaching a partner in an alcoholic marriage to communicate support and understanding by summarizing the spouse's message and checking the accuracy of

Figure 12.2   Illustration of Communication Used at Start of Training in Communication Skills

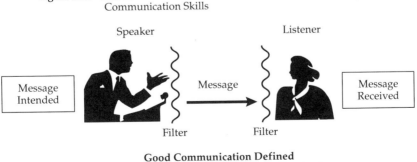

Speaker   Listener

Message Intended   Message   Message Received

Filter   Filter

Good Communication Defined
Message Intended Equals Message Received

Source: From *A Couple's Guide to Communication* (p. 1) by J. Gottman, C. Notarius, J. Gonso, & H. Markman, 1976, Champaign, IL: Research Press. Copyright 1978 by Research Press. Adapted by permission.

the received message before stating his or her own position is often a major accomplishment that has to be achieved gradually. A partner's failure to separate understanding the spouse's position from agreement with it often is an obstacle that must be overcome.

Speaking skills—expressing both positive and negative feelings directly—can be taught as an alternative to the blaming, hostile, and indirect responsibility-avoiding communication behaviors that characterize many alcholic marriages. The therapist instructs that when the speaker expresses feelings directly, there is a greater chance that he or she will be heard because the speaker says these are his or her feelings, his or her point of view, and not some objective fact about the other person. The speaker takes responsibility for his or her own feelings and does not blame the other person for how he or she feels. This reduces listener defensiveness and makes it easier for the listener to receive the intended message.

The therapist presents examples of differences between direct expressions of feelings and indirect and ineffective or hurtful expressions. The use of statements beginning with "I" rather than "You" is emphasized. After rationale and instructions have been presented, the therapist models correct and incorrect ways of expressing feelings and elicits the couple's reactions to these modeled scenes. Then the couple role-plays a communication session in which spouses take turns being speaker and listener, with the speaker expressing feelings directly and the listener using the listening response. During this role-playing, the therapist coaches the couple as they practice reflecting the direct expressions of feelings. Similar communication sessions, 10 to 15 minutes each three to four times weekly, are assigned for homework. Subsequent therapy sessions involve more practice with role-playing, both during the sessions and for homework. The topics on which the couple practices increase in difficulty each week.

Problem-solving skills training. After the couple has first learned basic communication skills, they can next learn skills to solve problems stemming from both external stressors (e.g., job, extended family) and relationship conflicts. In solving a problem, the couple should first list a number of possible solutions. Then, while withholding judgment regarding the preferred solution, the couple considers both positive and negative, and short-term and long-term consequences of each solution. Finally,

the spouses rank the solutions from most to least preferred and agree to implement one or more of the solutions. Use of problem-solving procedures can help spouses avoid polarizing on one solution or another. It also avoids the "yes, but . . . " trap of one partner pointing out the negative consequences to the other partner's solution.

Behavior change agreements. Many alcohol abusers and their spouses need to learn positive methods to change their partner's behavior to replace the coercive strategies previously used. Many changes that spouses desire from their partners can be achieved through the aforementioned caring behaviors, rewarding activities, and communication and problem-solving skills. However, deeper, emotion-laden conflicts that have caused considerable hostility and coercive interaction for years are more resistant to change. Learning to make positive specific requests (PSR) and to negotiate and compromise can lead to sound behavior-change agreements to resolve such issues.

Positive specific requests are an alternative to the all-too-frequent practice of couples complaining in vague and unclear terms and trying to coerce, browbeat, and force the other partner to change. The couple is told that "each partner has to learn to state his or her desires in the form of: (1) *positive*—what you want, not what you don't want; (2) *specific*—what, where, and when; and (3) *requests*—not demands that use force and threats, but rather requests that show possibility for negotiation and compromise." The therapist gives sample requests that do and do not meet these requirements. For homework, each partner lists at least five PSRs.

Negotiation and compromise comes next. Spouses share their lists of requests, starting with the most specific and positive items. The therapist gives feedback on the requests presented and helps rewrite items as needed. Then the therapist explains that negotiating and compromising can help couples reach an agreement in which each partner will do one thing requested by the other. After giving instructions and examples, the therapist coaches a couple while they have a communication session in which requests are made in a positive, specific form, heard by each partner, and translated into a mutually satisfactory, realistic agreement for the upcoming week. Finally, the agreement is recorded on a homework sheet that the couple knows will be reviewed during the next session.

Agreements can be a major focus of a number of therapy sessions. Couples negotiate written behavior-change agreements for the forthcoming week, often with very good effects on their relationship. Figure 12.3 shows a typical example of a couple agreement. During the sessions, the therapist reviews unkept agreements briefly, provides feedback about what went wrong, and suggests changes needed in the coming week. After completing agreements under therapist supervision, the couple uses a communication session at home to negotiate an agreement on their own and to bring it to the following session for review. A series of such assignments can provide a couple with the opportunity to develop skills in behavior change that they can use after the therapy ends. We encourage good-faith agreements in which each partner agrees to make his or her change independent of whether or not the spouse keeps the agreement and without monetary or other rewards or punishments. This approach stresses the need for each spouse freely and unilaterally to make the changes needed to improve the marital relationship.

Applications to family therapy. Communication, problem-solving, and behavior-change skills also apply to family therapy sessions involving an alcoholic and his or her children and spouse, or an adolescent alcohol abuser and his or her parent(s). We relabel the communication sessions as family council meetings or family meetings. We emphasize very strongly some additional ground rules that characterize such a meeting: one person speaks at a time, no interrupting is permitted, and a consensus must be

Figure 12.3 Sample Couple Agreement

COUPLE CONTRACT/FULFILLMENT RECORD

Name: Mike & Nancy Jones   **Week Beginning:** 4/8 (Fri.)

Mike's Responsibilities (Mike checks when performed)

	Fri.	Sat.	Sun.	Mon.	Tues.	Wed.	Thurs.
1. Install kitchen appliance on Thursday night.							✓
2. Take Nancy and kids for a ride and visit to her parents on Sunday.			✓				
3.							

Nancy's Responsibilities (Nancy checks when performed)

	Fri.	Sat.	Sun.	Mon.	Tues.	Wed.	Thurs.
1. Have a special dinner for the two of us on Wed. night.						✓	
2. Make an effort to have some time alone each day to talk and check in with one another.	✓		✓	✓	✓		
3.							

reached to enact a decision. The latter guards against parents (or other subgroups) forcing their will on weaker family members.

Behavioral family therapy with adolescents and parents, (e.g., Robin & Foster, 1989) can be extremely useful for families with alcohol problems because many adult alcoholics have severe problems with their adolescent offspring. The growing number of adolescent alcohol abusers frequently have quite troubled relationships with their parents (Trepper et al., 1993). Behavior-change agreements are also quite useful with children and their parents, but the behavior changes of the children may be more numerous than those of the parents. Often reward-punishment contingencies are useful because (unlike a marriage) the parent-child relationship is not one of equal partners.

Maintaining Drinking and Relationship Changes

Preventing Relapse

Methods to ensure long-term maintenance of the changes in alcohol problems made through MFT are beginning to receive attention (McCrady, 1993; O'Farrell, 1993b). We use three general methods during the maintenance phase of treatment, defined somewhat arbitrarily as the phase that begins after at least six consecutive months of abstinence or consistent nonproblem drinking have been achieved. First, the therapist must plan maintenance prior to the termination of the active treatment phase. We review the previous MFT sessions with the clients to determine which therapeutic interventions or behavior changes (e.g., Antabuse contract, communication sessions) have been most helpful. Then we plan how the family can continue to engage in the desired new behaviors when needed (e.g., rehearsing how to cope with situations likely to interfere with the new behavior, rereading handouts from the therapy periodically, agreeing to periodic monitoring by the therapist).

A second method is to anticipate what high-risk situations for relapse to abusive drinking may be likely to occur after treatment. Discuss and rehearse possible coping strategies that the alcoholic and other family members can use to prevent relapse when confronted with such situations.

A third method is to discuss and rehearse how to cope with a relapse when it occurs. Here, the techniques suggested by Marlatt and Gordon (1985) can be useful. Allow a delay after the first drink. Call the therapist. Engage in realistic and rational thinking about the slip. A specific couple-family relapse-episode plan, written

and reheased prior to ending active treatment, can be particularly useful. Early intervention at the beginning of a relapse episode is essential and must be stressed with the couple-family. Often, spouses and family members wait until the drinking has reached dangerous levels again before acting. By then, much additional damage has been done to the marital and family relationship and to other aspects of the drinker's life.

We suggest continued contact with the couple/family via planned in-person and telephone follow-up sessions, at regular and then gradually increasing intervals, for three to five years after a stable pattern of recovery has been achieved. The therapist uses this ongoing contact to monitor progress, to assess compliance with planned maintenance procedures, and to evaluate the need for additional therapy sessions. The therapist must take responsibility for scheduling and reminding the family of follow-up sessions and for placing agreed-upon phone calls so that continued contact can be maintained sucessfully. The therapist tells couples and families the reason for continued contact is that alcohol abuse is a chronic health problem that requires active, aggressive, ongoing monitoring to prevent or to quickly treat relapses for at least five years after an initial stable pattern of recovery has been established. The follow-up contact also provides the opportunity to deal with marital and family issues that appear after a period of recovery.

Marital and Family Issues in Long-Term Recovery

Many alcohol abusers continue to experience significant marital and family difficulties after a period of stable recovery has been established. Although a wide variety of issues can present difficulties during long-term recovery, a number of concerns and life patterns predominate. These problem areas include: (1) role readjustment when the the alcoholic tries to regain important family roles lost through drinking; (2) sex and intimacy; and (3) parent-child relationships, especially communication and behavior management with adolescents. Finally, families during the recovery process seem particularly vulnerable to stresses created by critical transitions in the family life cycle (e.g., children leaving home), external life change events (e.g., job loss), and/or developmental changes in any of the family members (e.g., midlife crisis).

These marital and family issues are by no means unique to alcohol abusing families. However, the therapist has two additional responsibilities when such issues are presented by alcoholic families during long-term recovery. First, the therapist must determine if a relapse is imminent so that necessary preventive interventions can be instituted immediately. Second, the therapist must (1) determine each family member's view of the relationship between the former alcohol problem and the current marital/family difficulties and (2) carefully assess whether or not he or she shares the family member's view. The latter is important because family members often continue to attribute difficulties in their relationships to the previous alcohol problem, rather than to their current life situation.

A final problem encountered all too frequently is that even though the alcohol problem is under control, the marriage is no longer viable. We label this "successful sobriety and the bankrupt marriage" to the couples we work with and consider "breaking up without breaking out" a major accomplishment. Spouses may have grown apart, or one may be unwilling to set aside the past hurts. Whatever the reason, facing the emptiness and inevitable dissolution of the marriage often precipitates a dangerous crisis. If there has been a strong tendency to blame the alcoholic for relationship problems, there is a strong push to want the alcoholic to drink again to provide the reason for the marital breakup. The therapist can try to help the couple confront separation and divorce without requiring the alcoholic to fail again and be the scapegoat for the breakup. If the couple can separate without the alcoholic drinking, the alcoholic's future relationship with his or her children may be preserved, and both spouses may be able to obtain a realistic assessment of the basis for their divorce. Unfortunately, many couples cannot do this.

EFFECTIVENESS

The present review of outcome research on MFT with alcoholics covers studies that included a comparison group of some type and at least some follow-up data. This review is organized according to the stage of the alcoholics' change to which the MFT in each study was directed.

Studies of MFT to Initiate Change in the Alcoholic and Help the Family When the Alchol Abuser Resists Treatment

In an early report, Cohen and Krause (1971) evaluated a family service agency program for wives who presented the husband's drinking as a major problem at intake. They randomly assigned 292 wives to caseworkers specially trained in alcoholism (experimental group) or to caseworkers working as usual (control group). Experimental group cases, when compared with control group cases, were more likely to continue treatment after the initial contact, attended more treatment sessions, and had more of their alcohol-abusing husbands eventually seen in treatment. Further, the husbands' antisocial behavior improved in more experimental than control cases.

Unilateral family therapy (UFT) with the spouses of alcoholics has been evaluated in two studies. An initial pilot study (Thomas, Santa, Bronson, & Oyserman, 1987) randomly assigned 15 spouses of alcoholics to receive either immediate or delayed UFT and studied 10 other nonrandom comparison cases who dropped out after little or no treatment. From 13 (of 15) UFT treated cases with usable data, 8 drinkers (62%) had entered treatment and/or reduced drinking, whereas none of the 10 untreated cases with available data had done so ($p = .02$ by Fisher's Exact Test). Results also showed a decrease in spouses' emotional distress and increases in marital satisfaction after UFT. A second study (Thomas, Yoshioka, Ager, & Adams, 1993) randomly assigned spouses to either an immediate ($n = 27$) or delayed ($n = 28$) UFT treatment. An additional nonrandom, untreated comparison group consisted of 14 spouses. Results showed reductions after UFT in certain spouse behaviors, including enabling, attempts to control the alcoholics' drinking, psychopathology and life distress, and improvements in marital adjustment and satisfaction. Treatment entry of the alcohol abuser was significantly higher immediately following spouse treatment than at comparable time periods for the delayed and untreated cases. The preliminary reports of these two studies (Thomas et al. 1987, 1993) present favorable outcomes for UFT. We need a more complete report of the findings of these studies to evaluate the effectiveness of UFT more fully.

In their study of community reinforcement training (CRT) for families, Sisson and Azrin (1986) randomly assigned 12 family members to either the CRT program or to a "traditional disease model program" of alcohol education, individual supportive counseling, and referral to Al-Anon. Six of seven alcoholics entered treatment after relatives had received CRT for a mean of 58.2 days and an average of 7.2 sessions. During the five months after their relative started CRT, the alcoholics showed more than a

50% reduction in average consumption prior to treatment entry and nearly total abstinence in the three months after entering treatment. None of the 5 drinkers whose relatives received the traditional program (mean of 3.5 sessions) entered treatment, and their drinking was not reduced during the three months for which outcome data were available. The impressive results, the small sample size, and the differential credibility and intensity of the CRT and comparison treatments argue strongly for the need to replicate the results.

Research support for the Johnson Institute intervention approach comes from a demonstration project (Liepman, Nirenberg, & Begin, 1989) in which less than 30% (7 out of 24) of families given the intervention training completed the confrontation. Of the seven alcoholics who were confronted by their families and social networks, six (86%) entered treatment as compared with 17% of those not confronted. The confronted alcoholics had longer periods of abstinence on average (11 months versus 3 months) than those not confronted. Given the self-selected rather than random assignment to confronted and non-confronted groups, this study provides only very modest support for the Johnson intervention. The low rate of performing the confrontation was unexpected. Only further study can determine the extent of this problem and the efficacy of the Johnson approach.

Dittrich and Trapold (1984) randomly assigned 23 wives of treatment-resistant alcoholics to an 8-week group therapy program with a primarily disease concept focus ($n = 10$) or a waiting-list control condition ($n = 13$). Results showed significant improvements in enabling behaviors, anxiety, and self-concept at the end of treatment for the experimental group relative to the waiting-list control; similar improvement occurred for those on the waiting list once they had completed treatment. Improvements were maintained at the 2- and 4-month follow-up. Outcomes during the 12 months after intake showed that 48% of the husbands had entered some form of treatment for their alcoholism and 39% of the wives had either separated from or divorced their husband.

Al-Anon is by far the most widely used source of support for family members troubled by a loved one's alcoholism. Although no controlled research is available concerning the effectiveness of Al-Anon, a small number of correlational studies have been done. Among wives of alcoholics, Al-Anon membership is associated

with (1) fewer ineffective ways (e.g., covering up for the alcoholic, nagging, trying to control the drinking) of coping with their husbands' drinking (Gorman & Rooney, 1979; Rychtarik, Carstensen, Alford, Schlundt, & Scott, 1988) and (2) better abstinence rates for alcoholics whose wives are receiving outpatient counseling (Wright & Scott, 1978).

Studies of MFT to Stabilize Changes When the Alcohol Abuser Seeks Help

Separate Concurrent Treatment of the Alcoholic and the Family

Smith (1969) offered wives of hospitalized alcoholics attendance in a weekly therapy group that focused on increasing wives' understanding of alcoholism and the role of the marital relationship in the husband's alcoholism. He found that significantly more husbands of wives who chose to attend the therapy group were abstinent or improved at 16-month follow-up than were alcoholics whose wives refused to attend the therapy group. The self-selected rather than randomized comparison group weakens the Smith study.

Separate concurrent treatment for the alcohol abuser and family remains quite popular in clinical practice in the United States. The Hazelden 3- to 5-day residential psychoeducational program for spouses and family members of alcoholics is a well-known example. Based on the 12-step Al-Anon program, the Hazelden family program advocates that family members should detach from the alcoholic and focus on themselves in order to help reduce their own emotional distress and improve their own coping. Although program evaluation reports have shown participants' satisfaction with various program elements, attitude changes targeted by the program, and Al-Anon involvement by about half (e.g., Laundergan & Williams, 1979, 1993), controlled studies are needed to provide support for the effectiveness of the Hazelden family program. This is important because many treatment agencies use such a psychoeducational disease model program as their "family program" component. In contrast with clinical practitioners, outcome researchers have paid little attention to separate and concurrent treatment for the alcoholic and family. MFT research of the last 20 years has concentrated on methods that involve the alcohol abuser and family member together in treatment.

Nonbehavioral Conjoint Treatment
of the Alcoholic and the Family

A number of early MFT studies examined non-behavioral couples group therapy. Burton and Kaplan (1968) reported client satisfaction data for 179 alcoholics and their spouses. Overall, 76% of couples treated in multiple couple groups reported that counseling had been a positive experience, while only 57% of couples in which the alcoholic and/or spouse had been treated in individual counseling felt similarly.

Corder, Corder, and Laidlaw (1972) added a four-day intensive residential marital couples group workshop to a standard three-week inpatient alcohol rehabilitation program. In contrast to a control group that was treated with the standard individual inpatient rehabilitation program only, at six-month follow-up the experimental groups showed significantly better outcomes of higher sobriety rates (11/19 = 58% vs. 3/20 = 15%), better aftercare participation (9/19 = 47% vs. 3/20 = 15%), more recreational activities together, and fewer unemployed alcoholics (1/19 = 5% vs. 10/20 = 50%).

Cadogan (1973) studied 40 inpatient alcoholics and their spouses who were willing to participate in outpatient marital group interactive therapy after the alcoholics' hospital discharge. At six months after hospital discharge, the 20 alcoholics who received the couples therapy differed significantly from the 20 control subjects who did not: 9 subjects of the couples' treatment group remained abstinent, 4 subjects reported some drinking, and 7 subjects had relapsed; whereas in the control condition, only 2 subjects remained abstinent, 5 subjects reported some drinking, and 13 subjects had relapsed.

Building on earlier studies, McCrady, Paolino, Longabough, and Rossi (1979) evaluated the relative effectiveness of adding joint hospitalization and couples therapy to individual treatment for alcoholics. Subjects were randomly assigned to (1) individual involvement in which only the alcoholic attended group therapy; (2) couples involvement in which the alcoholic and spouse participated in an outpatient interactional couples therapy group in addition to concurrent individual treatment groups for each spouse; or (3) joint admission in which both partners were initially hospitalized and then participated in both the couples group therapy and individual therapy groups following discharge. At six-month follow-up, findings indicated significant decreases in alcohol intake for both the couples involvement and joint admission treatment groups but not for the individual treatment group. All groups showed significant decreases in marital problems.

Zweben and colleagues (Zweben, Pearlman, & Li, 1988) conducted the only controlled outcome study to date of a family systems approach to treating alcohol problems. The study randomly assigned 116 alcohol abusers to either (1) eight sessions of conjoint therapy based on a communication-interactional approach in which the presenting problem (alcohol abuse) was viewed from a systemic perspective as having adaptive or functional consequences for the couple (Berenson, 1976; Steinglass, 1979) or (2) a single session of advice counseling which also involved the spouse. Results over an 18-month follow-up period indicated that couples in both advice counseling and conjoint therapy showed significant improvement on all marital adjustment and drinking-related outcome measures, but there were no significant between-group differences on any of the outcome measures. Thus, a single session of advice counseling was as effective as eight sessions of systems based conjoint therapy. Zweben and colleagues noted that their subjects had only a moderate degree of alcohol-related difficulties and relatively nondistressed marital relationships, and suggested that their findings may be limited to this specific client population.

Behavioral Conjoint Treatment
of the Alcoholic and the Family

Behavioral Contracting to Maintain Antabuse (Disulfiram) Ingestion. Azrin and colleagues (1982) randomly assigned alcohol-abusing outpatients to one of three treatment groups: (1) traditional, self-initiated Disulfiram treatment; (2) Disulfiram assurance with a significant other, usually the spouse, observing and reinforcing the ingestion of the medication; and (3) Disulfiram assurance plus a multifaceted behavior therapy program. At six-month followup, the behavior therapy plus Disulfiram assurance group was almost fully abstinent, drinking on the average 0.4 day a month. The traditional group, in contrast, had stopped Disulfiram and was drinking on the average 16.4 days a month. Although follow-up measures for the Disulfiram assurance group as a whole were intermediate between the other two groups, for married alcoholics, Disulfiram assurance alone was sufficient to produce almost total abstinence.

Keane, Foy, Nunn, and Rychtarik (1984) randomly assigned male alcoholics being discharged from a four-week behaviorally oriented inpatient alcoholism treatment program to: (1) Disulfiram prescription and contract with significant other, usually the wife, plus instructions for the wife to use positive reinforcement for contract compliance; (2) Disulfiram prescription and contract with significant other; or (3) Disulfiram prescription without contract. At three-month follow-up, 84% of all subjects were still abstinent and taking Disulfiram daily by collateral report, with no significant differences among treatment groups. A greater proportion of subjects in the contract groups had filled all three monthly prescriptions of Disulfiram, but this difference did not significantly distinguish the groups.

The Azrin (1982) and Keane (1984) studies of spouse behavioral contracting to maintain Disulfiram ingestion reach opposite conclusions about the usefulness of such procedures. A number of differences in the studies may explain the differing results. The Azrin study was with applicants for outpatient treatment who received five weekly outpatient sessions, the spouse was not involved in the prescription only condition, and data were gathered for six-month follow-up. In the Keane study, subjects started Disulfiram after at least four weeks of inpatient treatment; the spouse and patient together received a videotape on the use of Disulfiram and its effects in all conditions, including the prescription-only group, and only three-month follow-up data were gathered. Given these differing results and the evidence from other studies showing that patients who stay on Disulfiram have better alcoholism treatment outcomes (Allen & Litten, 1992; O'Farrell Choquette, Cutter, Brown, & McCourt, 1993), further research is needed.

Multifaceted Behavioral MFT. Hedberg and Campbell (1974) compared behavioral family counseling with various individually oriented behavioral treatments. Subjects were randomly assigned to (1) systematic desensitization, (2) covert sensitization, (3) electric shock avoidance conditioning, or (4) behavioral family counseling (BFC) in communication skills and learning principles with use of behavioral contracts with each family member. At six-month follow-up, BFC was the most effective treatment for all patients regardless of whether the patients' goal was abstinence or controlled drinking; and BFC was particularly effective for patients with abstinence goals. Specifically, 80% (8/10) of BFC clients

achieved their goal of abstinence for the six-month follow-up period, as compared to 42% (11/26) of alcohol abusers in the three other individual behavioral treatments. Further, when clients with both abstinence and controlled drinking goals were considered, there was a trend for better BFC outcomes in that 73% (11/15) of BFC clients, as compared to 47% (16/34) of those in the other treatments, achieved their goal.

The program for alcoholic couples treatment (PACT) study compared three types of behavioral spouse-involved treatment. McCrady and colleagues (McCrady et al., 1986) randomly assigned alcohol abusers and spouses to one of three outpatient behavioral treatments: (1) minimal spouse involvement (MSI) in which the spouse simply observed the alcohol abuser's individual therapy; (2) alcohol-focused spouse involvement (AFSI), which included teaching the spouse specific skills to deal with alcohol-related situations plus the MSI interventions; and (3) alcohol behavioral marital therapy (ABMT) in which all skills taught in the MSI and AFSI conditions were included as well as BMT. Results at six-month follow-up indicated that all subjects had decreased drinking and reported increased life satisfaction and suggested ABMT led to better treatment outcomes than the other spouse-involved therapies. Specifically, ABMT couples (1) maintained their marital satisfaction after treatment better and tended to have more stable marriages than the other two groups and (2) were more compliant with homework assignments, decreased the alcoholics' number of drinking days during treatment, and their posttreatment drinking increased more slowly than AFSI couples.

In an initial counseling for alcoholics' marriages (CALM) project study, we (O'Farrell & Cutter, 1982; O'Farrell, Cutter, & Floyd, 1985) investigated the effect of adding behavioral marital therapy (BMT) couples group treatment to individually oriented outpatient treatment of married male alcohol abusers. A total of 36 couples, in which the husband had recently begun individual alcoholism counseling that included an Antabuse prescription, were randomly assigned to a no-marital-treatment control group or to 10 weekly sessions of either a BMT (Antabuse contract plus behavioral rehearsal of communication skills and marital agreements) or an interactional (largely verbal interaction and sharing of feelings and Antabuse without spouse involvement) couples group. Assessment of marital and drinking adjustment provided comparison data pre- and posttreatment and at two- and six-month follow-up. Results for marital adjustment showed the BMT couples (1) improved from pre to post on a variety of measures and remained significantly improved at follow-ups; (2) did better than control couples who did not improve on any measures; and (3) did better than interactional couples whose improvement from pre to post on two measures was not sustained at follow-up. On drinking adjustment, alcoholics in all three treatments showed significant improvements that were sustained at follow-ups and BMT subjects did better than interactional subjects at post and at two month follow-up. O'Farrell and colleagues concluded that adding a BMT couples group to outpatient alcoholism counseling showed clear advantages for the alcoholics' marital relationships but no additional gains in drinking adjustment. The less positive results for the interactional couples group suggested that just talking about relationship problems without making specific changes may lead to conflict and drinking and that the Antabuse contract protected the BMT couples while they learned new skills to confront their problems without alcohol.

In another study of couples group therapy, Bowers and Al-Rehda (1990) randomly assigned 16 alcohol abusers to standard outpatient individual counseling or to short-term couples group therapy. The couples group had considerable attention devoted to rehearsal of communication skills as well as specification of desired individual and relationship changes. Assessments were conducted before and after treatment and at 6- and 12-month follow-up. Results at the end of therapy showed significant and similar reductions in drinking for both treatments, but the conjointly treated alcohol abusers had significantly lower alcohol consumption at 6-month follow-up and a trend toward lower consumption at 12-month follow-up. These results were due to a marked deterioration in many standardly treated alcohol abusers that did not occur in the couples therapy cases. There also was a trend for the conjointly treated to have better marital adjustment scores at 6-month follow-up. Bower notes the couples therapy appeared to facilitate greater maintenance of improvement. He also acknowledged that despite random assignment, the conjointly treated alcohol abusers had happier marriages before treatment and received more treatment (18.5 vs. 11.15 hours). The former is a potentially serious problem since more positive pretreatment marital adjustment is associated with less drinking after alcohol treatment (Moos et al., 1990). The latter confound may have occurred because alcohol abusers treated with their spouses were less likely to discontinue treatment prematurely.

Monti and colleagues (Monti et al., 1990) randomly assigned 69 male alcohol abusers receiving a 28-day inpatient alcohol treatment program to one of three additional treatments. These were a communication skills training group (CST), a communication skills training group with family participation (CST-FAM), or a cognitive behavioral mood management training group (CBMMT). Subjects who received CST or CST-FAM drank significantly less alcohol per drinking day during the six months after treatment than those in CBMMT. Groups did not differ in abstinence rates or latency to relapse. Although all groups improved in alcohol-specific coping skills, those in CST improved most in skill in alcohol-specific high risk role plays. The researchers suggested that the failure to find an advantage for adding family members to CST may have occurred for two reasons. First, family members were involved in the standard inpatient program that was based on a family systems model and required family members (or a close friend) to be involved in family therapy, education, and Al-Anon/Al-Ateen. Second, including family members in CST approximately doubled the therapy group size and this may have reduced the opportunities for clients to practice the new skills in the CST-FAM sessions.

Longabaugh and colleagues (Longabaugh, Beattie, Noel, Stout, & Malloy, 1993) conducted a study of patient treatment matching to determine which clients have better drinking outcomes in individual versus MFT treatment methods. Alcohol abusers were randomly assigned to one of two 20-session group (preferred) or individual (the fall-back option) outpatient treatments: individually focused cognitive behavioral therapy or relationship-enhanced cognitive behavioral therapy. The former method precluded participation of significant others from the patient's social environment. The latter method involved 4 to 8 sessions devoted to MFT where people named as important by the patient were included in the treatment sessions. Half of those assigned to relationship-enhanced therapy received 8 MFT sessions and half received 4 MFT sessions (with 4 sessions devoted to clients' occupation).

The MFT sessions taught techniques to help the relationship reinforce abstinence and deal with slips, to enhance reinforcements in the relationship, and to increase problem-solving skills. In addition, two didactic sessions on contingency management were offered to all significant others. The sample consisted of 107 alcohol abusers (from a sample of 229) who provided complete data on variables of interest.

Results on percent days abstinent during the 12 months after treatment showed individual and relationship enhanced treatment did not differ for the sample as a whole. A significant interaction was noted for posttreatment social support of abstinence and treatment focus. For alcohol abusers with a high level of support for abstinence, the two treatments did not differ in extent of abstinence. For alcohol abusers with low social support of abstinence, individually focused therapy produced more abstinence than relationship-enhanced therapy. The Longabaugh results are the first to find superior outcomes for individual as compared with behavioral MFT. However, key features of the study must be considered. The nature of the MFT intervention is one issue. Compared with other studies, the MFT intervention in the Longabaugh study was less intense (20 to 40% of a total of 20 sessions, most of which were conducted in groups). It also varied in the number of sessions and the nature of significant other (spouse vs. friend) involved in the MFT. The sample consisted of 45% (107/229) of those assigned to study treatments who complied with all data collection. Outcome assessments were limited to days abstinent. Therefore, considerable caution must be exercised in interpreting these results.

McKay and colleagues (McKay, Longabaugh, Beattie, Maisto, & Noel, 1993), using a subsample of participants in the Longabaugh (1993) study just described, examined functioning in the families of alcohol abusers undergoing outpatient treatment. Alcohol abusers were randomly assigned to two 20-session social learning-based alcoholism treatments, one of which had only individual therapy ($n = 26$) and one of which contained a conjoint therapy component ($n = 25$). Subjects were selected for this study from the larger Longabaugh (1993) investigation if they were both living with immediate family members (e.g., spouse, parents, or children) and had an identified adult "significant other" (e.g., spouse, relative, or friend) who was living in the same household and willing to participate in treatment and provide ratings of family functioning. In addition, patients in the conjoint condition were included only if they were being treated with a spouse or other immediate family member. This was done to screen out patients who were living with family members but were treated with a nonfamily member such as a friend living in their household. Only 51 of the 87 patients who met these criteria provided follow-up data on family functioning and were included in the study. Patients (Pts) and significant others (SOs) provided ratings of family functioning before treatment and at a six-month follow-up.

Results showed that according to the perceptions of both Pts and SOs, there were significant improvements in family functioning in a number of areas at six-month follow-up when the entire sample ($n = 51$) was considered. Contrary to what was expected, however, the improvements generally were not greater in the conjoint condition. Although conjoint treatment brought greater improvement than individual treatment on Pts' scores on one subscale of the family assessment device (FAD; Epstein, Baldwin, & Bishop, 1983), treatments did not differ for SOs on any of the six FAD subscales. The usefulness of alcoholics' level of autonomy as a matching variable also was explored. According to the perceptions of both Pts and SOs, posttreatment family functioning was better when low-autonomy alcoholics were treated without other family members. There also was evidence that conjoint treatment was more effective with high-autonomy alcoholics and their families.

The McKay study results should be considered cautiously. In addition to concerns about the intensity of the MFT noted with the Longabaugh (1993) study, McKay and colleagues reported a number of important significant prestudy differences between the subjects in the two treatments and between the subjects who did and did not provide family functioning data.

Studies of MFT and Long-Term Maintenance

Research on the effects of MFT during long-term recovery are of two types. The first consist of data from long-term follow-up outcomes of recent studies, the intermediate term outcomes of which have just been reviewed. The second involves specific use of MFT to maintain treatment gains and prevent relapse. Each will be considered in turn.

Long-Term Results of MFT Studies

Four-year follow-up data from the McCrady (1979) joint hospitalization and couples therapy outcome study showed there were no longer any significant differences among the different treatment groups in the study on either marital or drinking adjustment (McCrady, Moreau, Paolino, & Longabaugh, 1982). The results of this study also showed a commonly observed pattern of decay in outcomes over time with more than 75% of the subjects showing improvement at six-month follow-up but less than one-third functioning consistently well over the four years.

Follow-up data through 18 months from the PACT study (McCrady, Stout, Noel, Abrams, & Nelson, 1991) showed that patients who received marital therapy (i.e., ABMT group) had fewer marital separations and more improvement in marital satisfaction and subjective well-being than those who received individual alcohol-focused therapy only (MSI group) or individual plus spouse focus to change drinking (AFSI group). Furthermore, ABMT had better drinking outcomes at 18-month follow-up than MSI or AFSI.

Two-year follow-up data from the initial Project CALM study (O'Farrell, Cutter, Choquette, Floyd, & Bayog, 1992), known as CALM–1, showed that alcohol abusers and their wives who received BMT in addition to individual counseling remained significantly improved on marital and drinking adjustment throughout the two years. Although BMT remained superior to individual counseling alone on marital adjustment throughout much of the two-year follow-up, the strength and the consistency of findings favoring BMT diminished as time after treatment increased. Similarly, the superiority of BMT over the interactional group on marital outcomes faded as a function of time after treatment. On drinking, BMT remained superior to interactional for part of the first year after treatment, but by 24 months follow-up, there were no differences between groups all of which remained significantly improved from pretreatment levels. Finally, alcohol abusers with the most severe marital and drinking problems prior to treatment had the worst outcomes in the two years after treatment.

Thus, CALM–1 study results showed that the addition of BMT to individual counseling produced (1) marital (but not drinking) outcomes that were markedly superior to individual counseling alone during and in the six months after treatment that had faded in strength and consistency by the end of the two year follow-up; and (2) marital and drinking outcomes modestly superior to the interactional couples therapy through six-month follow-up that diminished rather quickly thereafter. These results suggested that a logical next step in research on BMT would involve an outcome study of treatment methods to maintain the gains produced by BMT, especially for drinking and related behaviors.

MFT Specifically for Maintenance and Relapse Prevention

Couples Relapse Prevention Sessions. The CALM–1 results just described led to a CALM–2 study to evaluate the usefulness of couples relapse prevention (RP) sessions for maintaining changes in marital and drinking adjustment produced by short-term BMT couples groups. A couples-based maintenance intervention was used because, in earlier BMT research, events in the marriage and factors involving the spouse were the reasons most frequently cited by the alcoholics as the cause of relapse and as reasons for ending a relapse episode (Maisto et al., 1988). In this study, 59 couples with an alcohol-abusing husband, after participating weekly for 5 months in a BMT couples group program, were assigned randomly to receive or not receive 15 additional couples RP sessions over the next 12 months. Outcome measures were collected before and after BMT and at quarterly intervals for the 2 1/2 years after BMT. The CALM–2 study (O'Farrell, Choquette, Cutter, Brown, & McCourt, 1993; Cutter, O'Farrell, Choquette, Brown & McCourt, 1993) produced two major findings.

First, results for the entire sample showed the additional RP sessions produced better outcomes during and for the 6 to 12 months after the end of RP. Specifically, alcohol abusers who received RP after BMT had more days abstinent and used the Antabuse contract more than those who received BMT alone with the superior RP drinking outcomes lasting through 18 months follow-up (i.e., 6 months after the end of RP). Couples who received the additional RP also maintained their improved marriages longer (through 24-month follow-up) than did their counterparts who received BMT only (through 12-month follow-up).

Second, for alcohol abusers with more severe marital and drinking problems, RP produced better marital and drinking outcomes throughout the 30-month follow-up period. Specifically, alcoholics with more severe marital problems at study entry had better marital adjustment and more abstinent days and maintained relatively stable levels of abstinence if they received the additional RP. Their counterparts who did not receive RP had poorer marital adjustment and fewer abstinent days and showed a steep decline in abstinent days in the 30 months after BMT. Further, alcohol abusers with more severe alcohol problems at study entry used the Antabuse contract more and showed a less steep decline in use of the Antabuse contract in the 30 months after BMT if they received the additional RP than if they did not.

Thus, the CALM–2 study indicated that adding couples RP sessions in the year after BMT produced better marital and drinking outcomes than BMT alone. These better RP outcomes persisted through 18 to 24 months after BMT for the entire sample and throughout the entire 30-month follow-up after BMT for those with more severe marital and drinking problems. The better results cannot be attributed with certainty to the couples RP sessions since this CALM–2 study did not include control groups that received aftercare sessions without the spouse involved and without a specific RP focus.

The CALM–2 study also examined the mechanisms whereby BMT and RP produce change. We assume that BMT produces better outcomes because BMT increases marital relationship factors that are conducive to sobriety. These factors include social support for abstinence, relationship cohesion, and effective communication. BMT attempts to provide social support for abstinence so that the spouse reinforces behaviors leading toward abstinence (e.g., Antabuse) and refrains from punishing attempts at sobriety (e.g., by nagging about past or feared future drinking). Building relationship cohesion and positive activities together provides a less stressful family environment which reduces the risk of relapse. Teaching the couple effective communication and problem-solving skills provides coping skills for dealing with marital and environmental stressors. In the CALM–2 study (O'Farrell et al., 1993), we found that the additional RP produced greater continued use of behaviors targeted by BMT (e.g., the Antabuse contract, shared recreational activities, constructive communication) than did BMT alone. Further, greater use of BMT-targeted behaviors was associated with better marital and drinking outcomes after BMT irrespective of the amount of aftercare received.

Aftercare Contracts. Ossip-Klein and Rychtarik (1993) studied behavioral contracts between alcoholics and family members to improve aftercare participation and maintain sobriety after inpatient alcoholism treatment. They randomly assigned 50 male alcohol abusers who had just completed a four-week VA inpatient alcoholism program to receive a calendar prompt and behavioral contract with a family member to reinforce aftercare attendance or standard aftercare arrangements. During the 6 months after hospital discharge, while the contracts were in effect, results showed significant aftercare attendance differences between groups, with nearly twice as many contract subjects as standard control subjects attending aftercare sessions (Ossip-Klein, VanLandingham, Prue, & Rychtarik, 1984). Of the 50 subjects, 36 (18 subjects per condition and 72% of total sample) were contacted 12 months after hospital discharge and the aftercare conditions were compared on outcomes during the year after discharge.

Results showed that subjects in the contract condition, when compared with the standard aftercare control group, had significantly more months abstinent and were more likely to be employed and classified as a treatment success (abstinent or nonproblem drinking for at least 90% of the year) (Ahles, Schlundt, Prue, & Rychtarik, 1983). These results are impressive given the simple, cost-effective, and rather limited nature of the aftercare contract intervention and the clear pattern of results favoring this method. Confidence is much stronger in the results for the aftercare attendance findings based on the entire sample than it is for drinking and related outcome results based on an incomplete sample. Thus, only future research can determine whether aftercare contracts lead to better drinking outcomes once the contract is no longer in force.

CONCLUSIONS AND FUTURE DIRECTIONS IN MFT OUTCOME RESEARCH

Six studies show that MFT can be used effectively to motivate an initial commitment to change in the alcoholic (Liepman et al., 1989; Thomas et al., 1987, 1993; Sisson & Azrin, 1986) and help the spouse when the drinker is unwilling to seek help (Cohen & Krause, 1971; Dittrich & Trapold, 1984). Further, correlational research shows an association between spouse involvement in Al-Anon and more sobriety for the alcoholic and better coping for the spouse (e.g., Rychtarik et al., 1988; Wright & Scott, 1978).

Two conclusions can be drawn from this work on MFT to initiate change and help the family when the alcohol abuser resists treatment. First, these studies require replication since they generally have relatively small samples and present a variety of methodolical concerns. Second, the most popular and frequently used methods—the Johnson Institute intervention and Al-Anon—have little or no controlled research supporting their effectiveness. Conversely, methods that have at least some controlled research support for their effectiveness—community reinforcement training, unilateral family therapy, Dittrich's groups therapy for spouses—are used infrequently, if at all.

Evidence continues to accumulate that MFT helps stabilize marital and family relationships and supports improvements in alcoholics' drinking during the 6- to 12-month period following treatment for alcohol problems. MFT produces better results during this time period than methods that do not involve the spouse or other family members. We reviewed 15 MFT studies here that included a comparison groups and some follow-up data. A variety of pragmatic and eclectic methods were used by 5 early MFT studies, all of which showed better results for MFT than for the comparison group(s) (Burton & Kaplan, 1968; Cagogan, 1973; Corder et al., 1972; McCrady et al., 1979; Smith, 1969). Of 9 behavioral MFT studies, 6 showed better outcomes for MFT than for the comparison group(s) (Azrin, 1982; Bowers, 1990; Hedberg & Campbell, 1974; McCrady et al., 1986; Monti et al., 1990; O'Farrell et al., 1982, 1985). For the remaining 3 studies of behavioral MFT versus other treatments, 1 showed overall weak superiority of MFT with clearly better outcomes for a subset of clients (McKay et al., 1993); 1 showed no difference (Keane et al., 1984); and 1 showed no difference overall with worse outcomes for a subset of clients (Longabaugh et al., 1993). The study that examined a systems approach to MFT did not find better results for an eight-session systems MFT than for a single session of advice (Zweben et al., 1988). No comparative studies examined a family disease model MFT approach (e.g., Laundergan & Williams, 1993).

Two conclusions can be drawn from this work on MFT to stabilize changes in drinking and relationships for the alcohol abuser who seeks help. First, the most promising MFT method is a behavioral approach that combines both a focus on the drinking and drinking-related interactions plus work on more general marital relationship issues. Second, reminiscent of concerns about MFT to initiate change, the most popular, most influential, and most frequently used methods—family systems and family disease models—have little or no research support for their effectiveness. Conversely, methods that have the strongest research support for their effectiveness—various behavioral MFT methods—enjoy little popularity and are used infrequently, if at all.

Studies of MFT to promote long-term recovery are relatively recent and consist solely of behavioral methods. Two studies suggest that BMT with both an alcohol and relationship focus may reduce marital and/or drinking deterioration during long-term recovery better than individually focused methods (McCrady et al., 1991; O'Farrell et al., 1992). Two additional studies support the effectiveness of behavioral MFT methods to promote continued aftercare (Ossip-Klein & Rychtarik, 1993) and prevent relapse (O'Farrell et al., 1993). Despite these recent positive beginnings, more research is needed to understand the potential of MFT in maintaining gains and preventing relapse.

Future directions for MFT outcome research follow from the current review of MFT to initiate, stabilize, and maintain changes in drinking and relationships among alcohol abusers and their families. First, narrowing the gap between research and practice is an important future direction for work on MFT. To narrow this gap, future work should replicate promising approaches, evaluate popular but untested methods, and apply research tested methods to clinical practice. Second, MFT research must expand its focus. To test the generalizability of current MFT research findings, we need studies with broader target populations that include women and minorities and a wide range of clients from poorer prognosis cases with comorbid psychopathology and drug problems to those with mild to moderate alcohol problems. Expanded research questions will move beyond issues of effectiveness to questions about patient treatment matching and the mechanisms whereby MFT produces change. Finally, MFT outcome domains will go beyond statistical significance of comparisons between groups on measures of drinking and relationship adjustment. Future MFT studies should evaluate the clinical and societal significance of changes observed and the functioning of spouses and children.

This chapter shows that MFT, particularly behavioral methods, is an effective treatment for alcohol problems. Future work will narrow the gap between research and practice and expand the focus of MFT research to consider family systems and 12-step family disease approaches. This future work, much of which is now in progress, will aid our efforts to help alcohol abusers and their families.

REFERENCES

Clinical Guidelines

Al-Anon Family Groups. (1981). *This is Al-Anon.* New York: Al-Anon Family Groups. Describes 12-step program for alcoholics' families.

Johnson, V. A. (1973). *I'll quit tomorrow.* New York: Harper & Row. Detailed account of alcoholism treatment approach at the Johnson Institute in Minneapolis where the "intervention" method is used with significant others to motivate the alcoholic to seek treatment.

Miller, P. M. (1972). The use of behavioral contracting in the treatment of alcoholism: A case report. *Behavior Therapy, 3,* 593–596. Presents case in which a behavioral contract between an alcohol abuser and his wife is used to reduce problem drinking to an acceptable level.

O'Farrell, T. J. (1986). Marital therapy in the treatment of alcoholism. In N. S. Jacobson & A. S. Gurman (Eds.), *Clinical handbook of marital therapy* (pp. 513–535). New York: Guilford. Provides a detailed consideration of marital therapy for alcoholics using a behavioral approach. Case illustrations and considerable procedural detail are included.

O'Farrell, T. J. (Ed.). (1993). *Treating alcohol problems: Marital and family interventions.* New York: Guilford. Chapters by leading clinician-researchers present practical "how to" information on research tested marital and family therapy methods for use at different stages of the alcoholism recovery process. Each method included has a detailed description of practical guidelines for implementing the approach, an extended case study, and a summary of outcome research for the method. Most of the methods described in the present chapter are included.

O'Farrell T. J., & Bayog, R. D. (1986). Antabuse contracts for married alcoholics and their spouses: A method to insure Antabuse taking and decrease conflict about alcohol. *Substance Abuse Treatment, 3,* 1–8. Presents step-by-step instructions on how to implement an Antabuse contract with alcoholic couples and how to deal with common resistances to this procedure.

Shapiro, R. J. (1984). Therapy with violent families. In S. Saunders, A. Anderson, C. Hart, & G. Rubenstein (Eds.), *Violent individuals and families: A handbook for practitioners* (pp. 112–136). Springfield, IL: Charles C. Thomas. Describes methods for use with marital and family violence many of which are applicable to alcoholics.

Research

Ahles, T. A., Schlundt, D. C., Prue, D. M., & Rychtarik, R. C. (1983). Impact of aftercare arrangements on the maintenance of treatment success in abusive drinkers. *Addictive Behaviors, 8,* 53–58.

Allen, J. P., & Litten, R. Z. (1992). Techniques to enhance compliance with disulfiram. *Alcoholism: Clinical and Experimental Research, 16,* 1035–1041.

Azrin, N. H., Sisson, R. W., Meyers, R., & Godley, M. (1982). Alcoholism treatment by Disulfiram and community reinforcement therapy. *Journal of Behavior Therapy and Experimental Psychiatry, 13,* 105–112.

Berenson, D. (1976). Alcohol and the family system. In P. J. Guerin (Ed.). *Family therapy: Theory and practice* (pp. 284–296). New York: Gardner Press.

Bowers, T. G., & Al-Rehda, M. R. (1990). A comparison of outcome with group/marital and standard/individual therapies with alcoholics. *Journal of Studies on Alcohol, 51,* 301–309.

Burton, G., & Kaplan, H. M. (1968). Group counseling in conflicted marriages where alcoholism is present: Client's evaluation of effectiveness. *Journal of Marriage and the Family, 30,* 74–79.

Cadogan, D. A. (1973). Marital group therapy in the treatment of alcoholism. *Quarterly Journal of Studies on Alcohol, 34,* 1187–1194.

Cohen, D. C., & Krause, M. S. (1971). *Casework with the wives of alcoholics.* New York: Family Service Association of America.

Corder, B. F. , Corder, R. F. , & Laidlaw, N. D. (1972). An intensive treatment program for alcoholics and their wives. *Quarterly Journal of Studies on Alcohol, 33,* 1144–1146.

Cutter, H. S. G., O'Farrell, T. J., Choquette, K. A., Brown, E. D., McCourt, W. F. (1993, November). Couples relapse prevention sessions after behavioral marital therapy for alcoholics and their wives: Outcomes during three years after starting treatment. In T. J. O'Farrell (Chair) *State of the art: Marital and family therapy in alcoholism treatment.* Symposium conducted at the Annual Convention of the Association for the Advancement of Behavior Therapy, Atlanta.

Dittrich, J. E. (1993). A group program for wives of treatment resistant alcoholics. In T. J. O'Farrell (Ed.), *Treating alcohol problems: Marital and family interventions.* (pp. 78–114). New York: Guilford.

Dittrich, J. E., & Trapold, M. A. (1984). Wives of alcoholics: A treatment program and outcome study. *Bulletin of the Society of Psychologists in Addictive Behaviors, 3,* 91–102.

Epstein, N. B., Baldwin, L. M., & Bishop, D. S. (1983). The McMaster family assessment device. *Journal of Marital and Family Therapy, 9,* 171–180.

Gorman, J. M., & Rooney, J. F. (1979). The influence of Al-Anon on the coping behavior of wives of alcoholics. *Journal of Studies on Alcohol, 40,* 1030–1038.

Gurman, A. S., & Kniskern, D. P. (1978). Deterioration in marital and family therapy: Empirical, clinical and conceptual issues. *Family Process, 17,* 3–20.

Heather, N., & Robertson, I. (1981). *Controlled drinking.* London: Methuen.

Hedberg, A. G., & Campbell, L. (1974). A comparison of four behavioral treatments of alcoholism.

Journal of Behavior Therapy and Experimental Psychiatry, 5, 251–256.

Keane, T. M., Foy, D. W., Nunn, B., & Rychtarik, R. G. (1984). Spouse contracting to increase Antabuse compliance in alcoholic veterans. *Journal of Clinical Psychology, 40,* 340–344.

Keller, M. (Ed.). (1974). Trends in treatment of alcoholism. In *Second special report to the U.S. Congress on alcohol and health* (pp. 145–167). Washington, DC: Department of Health, Education, and Welfare.

Laundergan, J. C. & Williams, T. (1979). Hazelden: Evaluation of a residential family program. *Alcohol Health and Research World, 13,* 13–19.

Liberman, R. P., Wheeler, E. G., de Visser, L. A., Kuehnel, J., & Kuehnel, T. (1980). *Handbook of marital therapy: A positive approach to helping troubled relationships.* New York: Plenum Press.

Liepman, M. R. (1993). Using family member influence to motivate alcoholics to enter treatment: The Johnson Institute Intervention approach. In T. J. O'Farrell (Ed.), *Treating alcohol problems: Marital and family interventions* (pp. 54–77). New York: Guilford.

Liepman, M. R., Nirenberg, T. D., & Begin, A. M. (1989). Evaluation of a program designed to help family and significant others to motivate resistant alcoholics into recovery. *American Journal of Drug and Alcohol Abuse, 15,* 209–221.

Longabaugh, R., Beattie, M., Noel, N., Stout, R., & Malloy, P. (1993). The effect of social investment on treatment outcome. *Journal of Studies on Alcohol, 54,* 465–478.

Maisto, S. A., O'Farrell, T. J., Connors, G. J., McKay, J., & Pelcovits, M. A. (1988). Alcoholics' attributions of factors affecting their relapse to drinking and reasons for terminating relapse events. *Addictive Behaviors, 13,* 79–82.

Marlatt, G. A., & Gordon, J. (1985). *Relapse prevention: Maintenance strategies in the treatment of addictive behaviors.* New York: Guilford.

McCrady, B. S., Moreau, J., Paolino, T. J., Jr., & Longabaugh, R. (1982). Joint hospitalization and couples therapy for alcoholism: A four-year follow-up. *Journal of Studies on Alcohol, 43,* 1244–1250.

McCrady, B. S., Noel N. E., Abrams, D. B., Stout, R. L., Nelson, H. F., & Hay, W. N. (1986). Comparative effectiveness of three types of spouse involvement in outpatient behavioral alcoholism treatment. *Journal of Studies on Alcohol, 47,* 459–467.

McCrady, B. S., Paolino, T. J., Jr., Longabaugh, R., & Rossi, J. (1979). Effects of joint hospital admission and couples treatment for hospitalized alcoholics: A pilot study. *Addictive Behaviors, 4,* 155–165 .

McCrady, B., Stout, R., Noel, N., Abrams, D., & Nelson, H. (1991). Comparative effectiveness of three types of spouse involved alcohol treatment: Outcomes 18 months after treatment. *British Journal of Addiction, 86,* 1415–1424.

McKay, J. R., Maisto, S. A., Beattie, M. C., Longabaugh, R., & Noel, N. E. (1993). Does adding conjoint therapy to individually focused alcoholism treatment lead to better family functioning? *Journal of Substance Abuse, 5,* 45–59.

Miller, W. R., & Caddy, G. R. (1977). Abstinence and controlled drinking in the treatment of problem drinkers. *Journal of Studies on Alcohol, 38,* 986–1003.

Monti, P. M., Abrams, D. B., Binkoff, J. A., Zwick, W. R., Liepman, M. R., Nirenberg, T. D., & Rohsenow, D. J. (1990). Communication skills training, communication skills training with family and cognitive behavioral mood management training for alcoholics. *Journal of Studies on Alcohol, 51,* 263–270.

Moos, R. H., Finney, J. W., & Cronkite, R. C. (1990). *Alcoholism treatment: Context, process, and outcome.* New York: Oxford University Press.

Noel, N. E., McCrady, B. S., Stout, R. L., & Nelson, H. F. (1987). Predictors of attrition from an outpatient alcoholism treatment program for alcoholic couples . *Journal of Studies on Alcohol, 48,* 229–235 .

O'Farrell, T. J. (1993a). A behavioral marital therapy couples group program for alcoholics and their spouses. In T. J. O'Farrell (Ed.), *Treating alcohol problems: Marital and family interventions* (pp. 170–209). New York: Guilford.

O'Farrell, T. J. (1993b). Couples relapse prevention sessions after a behavioral marital therapy couples group program. In T. J. O'Farrell (Ed.), *Treating alcohol problems: Marital and family interventions* (pp. 305–326). New York: Guilford.

O'Farrell, T. J., & Birchler, G. R. (1987). Marital relationships of alcoholic, conflicted, and nonconflicted couples. *Journal of Marital and Family Therapy, 13,* 259–274.

O'Farrell, T. J., Choquette, K. A., Cutter, H. S. G., Brown, E. D., & McCourt, W. F. (1993). Behavioral marital therapy with and without additional relapse prevention sessions for alcoholics and their wives. *Journal of Studies on Alcohol, 54,* 652–668.

O'Farrell, T. J., & Cutter, H. S. G. (1982, November). Effect of adding a behavioral or an interactional couples group to individual outpatient alcoholism counseling. In T. J. O'Farrell (Chair), *Spouse-involved treatment for alcohol abuse.* Symposium conducted at the Sixteenth Annual Convention of the Association for the Advancement of Behavior Therapy, Los Angeles.

O'Farrell, T. J., Cutter, H. S. G., Choquette, K. A., Floyd, F. J., & Bayog, R. D. (1992). Behavioral marital therapy for male alcoholics: Marital and drinking adjustment during the two years after treatment. *Behavior Therapy, 23,* 529–549.

O'Farrell, T. J., Cutter, H. S. G. , & Floyd, F. J. (1985). Evaluating behavioral marital therapy for male alcoholics: Effects on marital adjustment and communication from before to after therapy. *Behavior Therapy, 16,* 147–167.

O'Farrell, T. J., Kleinke, C., & Cutter, H. S. G. (1986). Differences between alcoholic couples accepting and rejecting an offer of outpatient marital therapy. *The American Journal of Drug and Alcohol Abuse, 12,* 301–310.

Ossip-Klein, D. J., & Rychtarik, R. G. (1993). Behavioral contracts between alcoholics and family members to improve aftercare participation and maintain sobriety after inpatient alcohol treatment. In T. J. O'Farrell (Ed.), *Treating alcohol problems: Marital and family interventions* (pp. 281–304). New York: Guilford.

Ossip-Klein, D. J., VanLandingham, W., Prue, D. M., & Rychtarik, R. G. (1984). Increasing attendance at alcohol aftercare using calendar prompts and home based contracting. *Addictive Behaviors, 9,* 85–89.

Prochaska, J. O., & DiClemente, C. C. (1983). Stages and processes of self change of smoking: Toward an integrative model of change. *Journal of Consulting and Clinical Psychology, 51*, 390–395.

Rychtarik, R. G., Carstensen, L. L., Alford, G. S., Schlundt, D. G., & Scott, W. O. (1988). Situational assessment of alcohol-related coping skills in wives of alcoholics. *Psychology of Addictive Behavior, 2*, 66–73.

Sisson, R. W., & Azrin, N. H. (1993). Community Reinforcement Training for families: A method to get alcoholics into treatment. In T. J. O'Farrell (Ed.), *Treating alcohol problems: Marital and family interventions* (pp. 34–53). New York: Guilford.

Sisson, R. W., & Azrin, H. H. (1986). Family-member involvement to initiate and promote treatment of problem drinking. *Journal of Behavior Therapy and Experimental Psychiatry, 17*, 15–21.

Smith, C. G. (1969). Alcoholics: Their treatment and their wives. *British Journal of Psychiatry, 115*, 1039–1042.

Steinglass, P. (1979). Family therapy with alcoholics: A review. In E. Kaufman & P. Kaufmann (Eds.), *Family therapy of drug and alcohol abuse* (pp. 147–186). New York: Gardner Press.

Thomas, E. J., Santa, C. A., Bronson, D., Oyserman, D. (1987). Unilateral family therapy with spouses of alcoholics. *Journal of Social Service Research, 10*, 145–162.

Thomas, E. J., Yoshioka, M., Ager, R. D., & Adams, K. B. (1993). Experimental outcomes of spouse intervention to reach the uncooperative alcohol abuser: Preliminary report. Unpublished manuscript.

Wright, K. D., & Scott, T. B. (1978). The relationship of wives' treatment to the drinking status of alcoholics. *Journal of Studies on Alcohol, 39*, 1577–1581.

Zweben, A., Pearlman, S., & Li, S. (1983). Reducing attrition from conjoint therapy with alcoholic couples. *Drug and Alcohol Dependence, 11*, 321–331.

Zweben, A., Pearlman, S., & Li, S. (1988). A comparison of brief advice and conjoint therapy in the treatment of alcohol abuse: The results of the Marital Systems study. *British Journal of Addiction, 83*, 899–916.

CHAPTER 13

Coping and Social Skills Training

Peter M. Monti
Damaris J. Rohsenow
Suzanne M. Colby
David B. Abrams

OVERVIEW

Coping/social skills training (CSST) has evolved over two decades from a social cognitive learning theoretical orientation to specific programs for the treatment and prevention of addictive behaviors (Abrams & Niaura, 1987; Marlatt & Gordon, 1985). The research evidence for the efficacy of the core elements in CSST is strong (see Chapter 2). The core elements are used in a range of interventions from early intervention/prevention such as those used in schools and the "Drinker's Check-Up" (Miller & Sovereign, 1989) to more broad spectrum treatments, including social skills, cue exposure, community reinforcement, marital/family, behavioral self-control training, relapse prevention, and other cognitive-behavioral approaches (Chapter 2; Monti et al., 1990; Monti, Abrams, Kadden, & Cooney, 1989; Monti et al., 1993c).

Since the essential core elements in CSST have a strong theoretical base as well as solid empirical support from research treatment outcome studies, they should be an integral part of any state-of-the-art intervention for clients with addictive behaviors in general, and of alcohol prevention and treatment in particular. Indeed, clients increasingly abuse more than one substance, and the evidence is mounting that treatment programs need to be more comprehensive. Since empirical evidence supports CSST approaches across several substances, including comorbid tobacco dependence (e.g., Abrams et al., 1992; Sobell, Kozlowski, & Toneatto, 1990; Calfas et al., 1993) and cocaine abuse (Rohsenow, Monti, & Abrams, in press), CSST may be particularly appropriate with mixed substance abusers.

A CSST approach provides a common set of techniques to address the underlying conceptualization that the client lacks important coping skills for daily living. These deficits can include lack of adequate skills to regulate positive and negative mood states and to cope with social-interpersonal situations, including work, parenting, or marital relationships. Moreover, coping difficulties can be the result of person-environment interactions, such as biological predisposing factors and/or precipitating stressful environment demands.

Environmental stressors can include chronic life stress (e.g., death of a loved one) or the buildup of small daily hassles on the job or in a relationship (Abrams & Niaura, 1987; Monti et al., 1989; Wills & Shiffman, 1985). The ability to exercise healthy alternative coping skills seems to be especially difficult when the environmental context also includes peer pressure and substance-use cues such as the sight and smell of one's favorite alcoholic beverage. Many cues and substances can trigger anticipatory cognitive and neurochemical reactions that undermine a client's confidence and ability to resist temptation. Since avoidance of substance-use cues is not always possible, coping skills treatment within the context of exposure to substance-use cues has become one of the new core elements in CSST interventions (Niaura et al., 1988; Monti et al., 1989).

This brief conceptual overview of the sources of coping skills difficulties suggests the major themes or domains for CSST: (1) interpersonal skills for building better relationships (2) cognitive-emotional coping for mood regulation (3) coping skills for improving daily living and dealing with stressful life events and (4) coping in the context of substance-use cues. The interactions of these skills deficits with other vulnerabilities such as underlying biological, neurochemical, and psychophysiological reactions needs to be considered in a comprehensive treatment program. Cognitive coping includes strategies to cope with the client's psychophysiological or cognitive reactions that lead to strong urges or cravings to drink, as well as their sense of self-confidence or self-efficacy that they can resist the temptation to drink in a specific situation. Interpersonal skills include a wide variety of strategies to increase positive and decrease negative social interactions with people ranging from strangers to spouses.

As therapists, we must investigate the underlying sources of individual client vulnerability that can interact with environmental demands to precipitate problem drinking due to lack of alternative coping skills. A common issue is the existence of biological factors, including comorbid psychiatric conditions such as depression, schizophrenia, or sociopathy; neurological

or medical illnesses that can impede coping through cognitive impairment; and other relevant conditions or characterological difficulties. If such conditions exist, then we must ensure that the client obtains appropriate pharmacological, rehabilitative or other treatments.

Following referral, we can use CSST as part of the follow-through on the client's adherence to the medical recommendations. Part of coping with daily living may be to take needed medications and obtain timely professional care for oneself. The need for us to work collaboratively with the client and an interdisciplinary team of relevant health professionals is often overlooked or underestimated in many treatment approaches. As a CSST therapist, you can see the issue of adherence as simply another important aspect to be addressed when providing coping skills for a life without alcohol and other substances. Underlying biological factors and commonalities across substances of abuse can play an important role in whether CSST is optimally successful.

The process of developing a treatment plan for CSST begins with assessment. You should evaluate the client's strengths and weaknesses in the biological, cognitive-behavioral, and environmental domains related to coping difficulties that have led to past alcohol abuse (see Chapter 4). Assess high-risk situations in at least three areas: (1) intrapersonal factors such as mood regulation, especially anger, depression, positive stimulation, and stress; (2) interpersonal skills, including general social skills, communication in intimate relations, drink refusal, and other specific needs; and (3) coping in the presence of the acute stress of substance-use cues themselves, either in imagery or in vivo. Evaluate priorities among the client's strengths and weaknesses, along with the need for any outside referral for biological or medical treatments. You can match a set of diverse CSST modules to the client's profile.

In general, the process of self-control training consists of self-monitoring, goal setting, coping/social skills training, and self-evaluation and self-correction until the client has acquired the necessary skills and uses them with relative ease across many different situational contexts. The goals of treatment are developed and negotiated with the client. Together, you and the client set goals, practice skills (using role plays and corrective feedback), and evaluate progress against the goals. To assure rapid skill acquisition and robust generalization across persons and situations, encourage assignments to be done between CSST treatment sessions.

Although you can deliver CSST treatments in inpatient, outpatient, and other community settings for populations ranging from youth to the elderly, we will focus on inpatient and outpatient adult treatment. Treatment modules are flexible provided the core essential elements of the CSST theoretical model are retained. Thus, you can adapt or develop treatment modules for specific subgroups or underserved populations.

The CSST modules developed from the conceptual approach described here have been empirically evaluated in both laboratory studies of more basic mechanisms such as reactivity to cues (Abrams et al., 1991; Monti et al., 1987; Rohsenow et al., 1993) and treatment outcome studies of CSST (e.g., Monti et al., 1990; Monti et al., 1993c). In this chapter, we will present our empirically validated model of CSST, including many details of the assessment and treatment. Finally, we will present evidence of the effectiveness of this and similar approaches.

SPECIAL CONSIDERATIONS

Our skills training program has been used effectively with a variety of substance abuse and psychiatric disorders. Our experiences with clients who use alcohol (Monti et al., 1989) or cocaine (Rohsenow, Monti, & Abrams, in press) are most pertinent to this chapter with a much stronger emphasis on individuals with a primary alcohol problem. In this section, we shall consider client characteristics and setting variables that have emerged as significant factors in our treatment and/or clinical research experience. Some of these factors have been usefully discussed from other theoretical perspectives (e.g., Vannicelli, 1982) as well as by our group in somewhat more detail elsewhere (Monti et al., 1989).

Client Characteristics

Severely dependent clients are more likely to experience psychopathology or cognitive impairment. While we routinely screen out of our groups clients who are either floridly psychotic or suicidal, we see a fair amount of cognitive impairment secondary to either detoxification or chronic alcohol abuse. As impairment due to detoxification usually clears with the passage of time, we structure our inpatient skills program such that more cognitively complex sessions come later in the treatment. Indeed, with shorter

lengths of inpatient stays we have found it necessary to begin clients in our groups within three to five days after detoxification begins. The results of skills training are likely to vary, depending on whether the training is administered to still-drinking individuals, those who are early in treatment, or those abstinent for at least two to three weeks (Becker & Jaffe, 1984). However, necessity has become the mother of invention when treating inpatient clients in the current health-care environment.

Though organic impairment that is secondary to chronic alcohol abuse is a more difficult problem, our training program may be more appropriate than other forms of therapy since the core elements of our program were originally derived from our work with impaired psychiatric populations (e.g., Monti et al., 1982; Monti & Kolko, 1985). Benefits of our program for the impaired client include the use of concrete examples and props (e.g., the individual's customary alcoholic beverage), small learning units, role-plays, review sessions, homework assignments, and immediate reinforcement for specific behavior change. Furthermore, we have found that with some clients, special work outside of the group can be helpful such as periodically testing recall of material and providing written outline notes.

Dealing with severe depression that may or may not be related to alcohol and/or cocaine abuse and withdrawal is commonplace on inpatient treatment units. Although most depression improves over the course of inpatient treatment (Brown & Schuckit, 1988), shorter lengths of stay may necessitate beginning skills treatment while there is still significant depression. Though motivating the depressed client may present a special challenge, a motivational intervention (see Chapter 5) may be helpful in this regard. Nevertheless, depressed clients can and do benefit from skills training (Bellack, Hersen, & Himmelhoch, 1981) and substance-abusing clients are no exception.

Another group of clients that has routinely challenged our cotherapists are those who exhibit severe personality disorders. While such individuals may be difficult to treat, recent findings of a study that used our skills treatment program (Kadden et al., 1989) showed that it is more effective than interactional group therapy for clients with significant sociopathy or psychopathology. As this is one of the few studies in the alcohol literature that demonstrates a matching effect, it has received a great deal of attention from those clinical researchers interested in patient/treatment matching (see Chapter 17).

Some pointers may be of help when treating the personality-disordered client. We have found that such individuals tend to question our therapists, are manipulative, and are often disruptive in groups. For example, they tend to be especially critical of and resistant to the idea of role-playing. We have found firm limit setting to be helpful, but for those who insist on sabotaging their treatment, discharge may be a realistic option. This may be especially indicated if the individual client is disruptive to the treatment of others as well. Gauging how much time to spend on particularly impaired clients without boring or otherwise jeopardizing the treatment of other group members is another important issue that we have discussed in detail elsewhere (Monti et al., 1989).

One other matching issue can be considered. Clients are more likely to benefit from the mood management part of coping skills training if they have more education and less anxiety. However, they are equally likely to benefit from the social skills training regardless of education or anxiety level (Rohsenow et al., 1991).

We have found two client characteristics useful to consider when conducting the cue-exposure component of our treatment program. These are "denial" and cue reactivity per se. Let us consider denial first. The value of exposing alcoholic clients to their preferred alcoholic beverage became apparent to us in some of our early cue-reactivity assessment work (Monti et al., 1987). In these early studies, we encountered many individuals, who, when they were approached for informed consent, let us know that picking up and sniffing their favorite drink would be "no big deal." After all, they were now beyond that stage of their problem and quite committed to abstinence. The reaction of these individuals during and after our assessment sessions were quite informative to both these clients and ourselves as well. Many found our assessment exposure sessions to be quite an "eye opener." They were surprised at the extent of their reaction to their favorite drink. Indeed, for many of these individuals, this experience became a turning point in their treatment.

Another client characteristic worthy of consideration is the distinction between who is a reactor and who is not (see Cue Reactivity Assessment section). While we have discussed this reactor/nonreactor issue in a recent theoretical paper (Rohsenow et al., 1992), suffice it to say

here that reactors seem to be more responsive to alcohol cues and more likely to benefit from our cue reactivity component than nonreactors. This makes a good deal of common clinical sense and has also been supported in a recent clinical trial conducted in our laboratory (Monti et al., 1993c). While we are not quite at the stage in our research where cue reactivity is validated as a marker for relapse risk, we have begun to make progress toward such a conceptualization (Abrams et al., 1991; Monti et al., 1993b; Rohsenow et al., 1992; 1994).

Setting Considerations

Typically we deliver skills training in groups, but on two occasions we have studied individual approaches. The first involves coping skills training in the presence of alcohol. We have used an individual approach here for two reasons. The first was our relative lack of experience with this treatment technique. A second reason was our individualized approach to incorporating each client's highest risk for relapse cues in the treatment protocol. The other occasion on which we used individual coping skills training was a study with primary cocaine abusers (Rohsenow et al., in press). Early in our work with this population we discovered that when cocaine abusers were treated in a standard inpatient (largely alcohol-oriented) treatment program, many were reluctant to share their high risk for relapse situations in a group context. Thus, we tailored our standard coping skills package to be delivered in a one-on-one basis. While we have no data to back up our preference for individual approaches in these two situations, they are simply what we know the most about.

For the most part, our skills training program has been conducted in groups. We recommend using two cotherapists—one therapist to guide the group through the content of any given session and the other to attend to process issues (Monti et al., 1989). Our program has been used and tested on both inpatient (Monti et al., 1990; Monti et al., 1993c) and outpatient (Kadden et al., 1989) treatment settings. The remainder of this section shall consider issues that are pertinent to each.

As our inpatient skills training program has been designed to complement other aspects of the inpatient treatment context, it is important to consider these aspects. Since most traditional inpatient treatment components, such as involvement in AA, occupational therapy, ongoing family groups, and so on, are derived from quite different theoretical orientations, it is important to inform clients of the rationale for skills training and cue-exposure treatment. We have found it helpful to stress the complementary nature of skills training, rather than to digress into philosophical discussion about the nature of different treatment approaches.

A related issue that usually needs to be addressed is clarification as to how skills training groups will differ from other groups. Since many clients assume that all group experiences deal with the exploration of feelings, skills training therapists can be challenged by having to deal with this mindset on the part of clients and at the same time having to "keep up the pace" in a given content area. We have found it essential to develop a balance between supportive therapy and our structured, manual-guided behavioral procedures. Anything short of this delicate clinical balance is sure to result in a failed therapeutic attempt.

This issue may be especially important with outpatients who may not be engaged in any other form of active treatment. Some therapeutic time may be required to deal with crises that might not get addressed otherwise. For example, if a client announces at the beginning of group that he just separated from his wife for the first time, this issue should be addressed. If it is not, it is likely that the client will not return to group again.

Although there are pros and cons to both inpatient and outpatient treatment settings, the current health-care climate has made the traditional inpatient treatment programs a bit of a dinosaur. Thus, outpatient treatment seems to be the likely treatment setting of the nineties. This should pose a particular challenge for skills training and cue-exposure treatment. The opportunities for in vivo exposure and structured homework assignments are limited only by the imagination of our therapists and skill levels of our clients. As long as the building blocks are in place and the pace is tailored to the needs of each individual, outpatient treatment should pose no insurmountable problems for skills training approaches.

DESCRIPTION

Assessment

We have conducted several specialized forms of assessment in conjunction with the skills training or cue-exposure treatment approaches as an adjunct to more usual clinical assessments. These include assessments of (1) ability cope with simulated high-risk situations, (2) cue reactivity, and (3) individual-specific drinking triggers.

Coping Skills Assessment

Reactions to simulated situations that pose a high risk for relapse can be assessed before and after treatment with one of several role-play assessment instruments. A number of such instruments exist (Monti et al., 1993a) but three have shown utility in predicting treatment outcome for clients: the Situational Competency Test (Chaney et al., 1978), the Adaptive Skills Battery (Jones & Lanyon, 1981), and the Alcohol Specific Role Play Test (Abrams et al., 1991; Monti et al., 1993a).

The Situational Competency Test provides audiotaped presentations of 16 situations based on the four largest relapse categories found by Alan Marlatt (1978). Responses to the prompt asking clients what they would do or say are audiotaped and scored for response latency, response duration, compliance versus assertive control (dichotomous score) and specificity of problem-solving behavior (dichotomous score). In a prospective study, only response latency was predictive of treatment outcome (Chaney et al., 1978).

The Adaptive Skills Battery uses audiotape to present 30 hypothesized antecedents of drinking that a group of alcohol-dependent clients had rated as difficult and frequently occurring, and respondents report their "usual" response to 15 and their "best" response to the other 15 situations. Judges rate responses for competency on a trichotomous scale. A retrospective study found that clients whose responses to the Adaptive Skills Battery were more skillful had better outcome one year after treatment.

The Alcohol Specific Role Play Test presents 10 audiotaped situations (5 intrapersonal and 5 interpersonal) that pose a high risk for alcohol-involved clients. The instrument along with its development and psychometric properties is described in detail in Monti, Rohsenow, Abrams, and colleagues (1993a). At the end of each situation, a prompt asks clients what they would do if they were actually in the situation and trying not to drink. Trained judges rate the videotaped responses for social or coping skill (the probability of solving the problem or the emotional goal of the situation) and anxiety. After each scene, the clients complete 11-point ratings of their urge to drink, how difficult it would be for them to deal with this situation in real life, and how nervous or anxious they felt. We time the latency to response for each scene. Quantity and/or frequency of drinking after treatment was lower in clients with more skill, lower urge to drink, and faster response latency (Monti et al., 1990).

None of these measures in their full forms is practical for use in busy clinical settings. However, you could have a technician audiotape and transcribe the client's responses to any of the three measures and study the responses for strengths and weaknesses to address in group. Furthermore, you could have a technician easily administer the self-report measures with the Alcohol Specific Role Play Test and time the latency to response with a stopwatch. As described in the Patient Treatment Matching section below, you could use these self-report measures to screen clients likely to benefit from CBMMT. Also, you could use latency and urge to drink after a trial of skills training to determine who is at risk for relapse and needs additional treatment (Monti et al., 1990).

Cue-Reactivity Assessment

Prior to conducting cue-exposure treatment (CET), we measure clients' degree of reactivity to their customary alcoholic beverages (Monti et al., 1987; Monti et al., 1993b). In cue-reactivity assessment, we measure the client's urge to drink and salivation in response to the sight and smell of his or her customary alcoholic beverage. Then we compare these to the client's responses to the sight and smell of a neutral beverage. We can use this information in treatment sessions. For example, a client who salivates more but does not have increased urge to drink to alcohol cues may think he or she is not at risk. However, a client who salivates more to the alcohol cues is actually at risk of increased drinking after treatment (Rohsenow et al., 1994). You may need to make this client aware of the risk and help him or her to recognize his or her somatic reactions to drinking-related stimuli. If this is done, he or she may more readily mobilize coping resources in high risk situations.

Our cue-reactivity assessment procedure assesses various self-report measures (e.g., urge to drink, anxiety, attention to the stimulus) and psychophysiological measures (e.g., salivation, heart rate, blood pressure) in response to beverage alcohol cues. These responses are compared

to the same measures assessed in response to water cues. We assess clients after lunch so that hunger will not affect response to beverages. After the client brushes his or her teeth, we seat him or her at a table in an interview room. We hide each beverage under an inverted opaque container and place a vial containing the cotton rolls in front of the containers. We have a glass of cold water and a commercially labeled bottle of spring water under one container. We put a glass of the client's most frequently consumed alcoholic beverage prepared in the way he or she normally drinks it and its commercial container under the other container. The assessor sits out of sight behind a one-way mirror during the actual beverage exposure.

We explain the procedures and forms to the client in detail. The client practices holding and sniffing the glass in response to tones. These tones occur five seconds per sniff 13 times during each three-minute beverage trial. The client also practices inserting and removing the cotton rolls we use to collect salivation. We explain that no drinking is allowed, and that he or she can end the assessment at any time.

We present the assessment itself on audiotape. The client first relaxes for three minutes, then inserts the cotton rolls. The client next uncovers and sniffs the glass of water when signaled for three minutes, then covers the beverage, replaces the cotton rolls into the vial, and completes a self-report rating form. The client relaxes for another three minutes, inserts new cotton rolls, and repeats the beverage exposure procedures with the alcohol. We weigh the cotton rolls before and after the session to measure *salivation*. Salivation is the psychophysiological response with the best validity (Niaura et al., 1988; Rohsenow et al., 1990–1991; Rohsenow et al., 1994). Clients complete *self-report measures* immediately after each beverage exposure trial. They rate urge to drink alcohol and anxiety on 11-point anchored Likert scales. (For other measures we have used, see Monti et al., 1993b, Niaura et al., 1988; and Rohsenow et al., 1994). After the assessment, we interview the client for reactions and deal with the reactions therapeutically.

Drinking Triggers Interview

In CET, we expose clients to a wide variety of drinking cues by having them imagine being in their own highest-risk situations. Therefore, first collect information about the situations that present the highest risk for relapse for the individual client. We collect this information by means of the Drinking Triggers Interview (Monti et al., 1993c).

In this structured interview, ask clients to describe all situations or events that were frequently associated with their heavy drinking, with strong urges to drink, or with trouble resisting drinking in the past. If they report few triggers, prompt by asking whether drinking heavily was associated with any specific places, with feeling bad, with feeling good, with problems or tension with other people, with being around drinkers, with the sight of alcoholic stimuli, or with feeling sick or tired.

After you write down the list of trigger situations, have the client rank order the triggers for the *frequency* with which they occurred. Second, assess *self-efficacy* by asking, "If you were in this situation today and not in the treatment center, how confident are you that you would not drink?" Ask the client to answer by using a 0 (not at all confident) to 10 (completely confident) rating scale. Third, assess *urge to drink* by asking, "If you were in this situation today and not in the treatment center, how much would you want to have a drink?" Ask the client to answer using a 0 (no urge at all) to 10 (strongest possible urge) scale. Form a hierarchy of the triggers on the basis of urge to drink, and break ties by frequency of occurrence. Rank triggers with greater urge and frequency higher. Use this list of triggers with its ratings in the treatment sessions.

Treatment Procedures

Coping/Social Skills Training

Different research groups have investigated various forms of CSST with clients. We will describe only the approaches presented in detail by Peter Monti and our colleagues (1989, 1993c) but the procedures are similar in various programs. We can conceptually divide coping skills into interpersonal/social skills, designed to ease interactions with important people in the client's environment, and intrapersonal skills, designed to help the client deal with urges and emotional states that may increase the probability or severity of drinking. For convenience, we will first describe *communication skills training,* designed to teach interpersonal/social skills. Then we will summarize *cognitive-behavioral mood management training,* designed to teach intrapersonal skills. Finally, we will describe *cue exposure with urge*

coping skills, designed to teach intrapersonal skills to cope with urges resulting from exposure to both internal and environmental drinking cues. Researchers have studied these various approaches in combination and separately.

Communication Skills Training

Overview. Within each session, start by discussing the *rationale and goals for the session.* We present *skill guidelines* next. It is helpful if we write the points in the skills guidelines on a large board, either before the group starts or as each point is made, so that clients need not rely only on auditory memory during the behavior rehearsals. Present the skill guidelines as suggestions rather than as inflexible rules to follow. The clients will learn not just specific responses to specific situations but instead will develop a flexible problem-solving approach to coping with their own high-risk situations. The strategies any one client develops should be consistent with the individual's own personal goals, values, and life situation.

Next, *model* an ineffective and an effective response to a sample situation. We have often used standard vignettes to illustrate the skill guidelines. State the goals of the situation. Then model a response that violates the guidelines and encourage feedback from the group about how the ineffective response is likely to affect the listener and the ways in which it violates the guidelines. Afterwards, role-play the situation while modeling a response that follows the guidelines. Group members then discuss how the new response affects the listener and the probability of attaining the goal of the situation. Some groups of higher-functioning clients benefit less from these standard vignettes and more from proceeding directly to role-plays of individualized situations.

Finally, conduct *behavior rehearsal role-plays* with group members. Ask a member to describe a relevant personal situation and role-play the situation with the help of another group member. Group members provide feedback and suggestions about improved responses. Then, have the same clients model more effective responses and elicit group members' reactions to the alternative responses. Behavior rehearsal has a central role in CST and is the principal strategy by which group members acquire new skills. The chance to practice new skills in a safe environment, with self-observation and both reinforcing and corrective feedback from others, is vital to this approach.

Although some group discussion is useful, avoid lengthy discussion about problem situations, as this will interfere with allowing enough time for the actual behavior rehearsals.

At first, some group members are uncomfortable or embarrassed and unwilling to engage in role-plays. Acknowledge that this is a normal reaction and that role-plays become easier after a few experiences with it. After bolder members have engaged in role plays, more timid members are often willing to participate. Clients should initially describe personally relevant scenes that are of only moderate difficulty so that they are more likely to experience success in learning to handle the scenes. As the clients demonstrate the ability to handle these situations effectively, they can rehearse more difficult scenes. To generate scenes, ask clients to recall a situation in the recent past, have them describe a difficult situation that they anticipate, or you can suggest a situation based on your knowledge of the client.

After a client role-plays a problematic situation, you and the group members identify specific problem areas and reinforce and shape successive approximations to the targeted communication skills.

1. Always start by positively reinforcing both participants through praise and recognition of positive aspects of the role-play. Provide constructive criticism after the praise.
2. Ask the participants in the role-play about their own reactions to the performance.
3. Ask other group members for comments, ensuring members focus on relevant issues in a constructive fashion. First ask what was good about the way the situation was handled, then ask what might work better.
4. Therapists can offer their own comments on the role-play. Include both supportive comments and constructive criticism. Be specific and focus on only one or two deficiencies at a time.

The partners should then repeat the scene to practice new skills that incorporate the feedback.

Role reversal can be useful if a client is having difficulty with thinking of an effective response or is discouraged about the effectiveness of a suggested approach. In role reversal, you or a skillful group member plays the part of the targeted client while the targeted client plays the role of the other person (e.g., spouse or boss). This gives the client the chance to experience the effects of the suggested communication approach.

Introduction and Rationale Session. In a closed group, devote the first session to providing clients with an orientation. In an open group, provide this introduction individually before the client's first group session. Also give a brief orientation to the approach within the group whenever a new client joins. In the introduction session, cover the following: (1) ground rules, such as attendance, promptness, abstinence policy, handling slips and relapses, confidentiality, eating and smoking in group; (2) introductions, any group-building exercises; (3) rationale for the approach and goals of the group; and (4) client's own problem situations and how they could lead to relapse.

In the rationale for the approach, you could include the following points: Much problem drinking occurs when people are in high-risk situations, such as when they are having conflicts with other people or are feeling bad. Some examples are when feeling frustrated, angry at someone, sad, lonely, being offered a drink, and wanting a reward or a good time. What kinds of high-risk situations can you think of from your own life/lives? An important goal of this group is to teach you skills you can use to help cope with your own high-risk situations. This group will focus on ways to handle difficult interpersonal situations more effectively and comfortably so that both you and the person you are interacting with will be less likely to have negative reactions that could set the stage for relapse.

Overview of Specific Session Modules. We developed 13 different topics into modules designed to address specific high-risk situations or types of communication skills. However, not all programs allow the opportunity to address all modules, particularly in the current health-care climate. We selected 8 that seem to be of higher priority, which we will discuss first, followed by another 5 that may be covered if time permits. Select modules based on the level of functioning of the particular client sample or based on a specific issues that clients need to address on a particular day. When working with recently detoxified clients, present less complex modules first.

The eight higher-priority modules are: (1) Drink Refusal Skills, (2) Giving Positive Feedback, (3) Giving Criticism, (4) Receiving Criticism about Drinking/Drug Use, (5) Listening Skills, (6) Conversation Skills, (7) Developing Sober Supports, and (8) Conflict Resolution Skills. Additional modules include: (9) Nonverbal Communication, (10) Expressing Feelings, (11) Introduction to Assertiveness, (12) Refusing

Requests, and (13) Receiving Criticism in General. The first eight modules include the elements of appropriate assertiveness, expressing feelings, ways to receive criticism, and nonverbal communication, but it is useful to be able to focus specifically on these topics when time permits. We describe the modules, role-play situations, and practice exercises in detail in our book (Monti et al., 1989), so we will describe only the essential elements of the rationale and skills guidelines here.

Module: Drink Refusal Skills. Rationale: (1) Being offered or pressured to drink is a common high-risk situation. (2) Turning down a drink requires more than will power; it requires specific skills. (3) Alcohol is so widespread that even the person determined to avoid drinking settings will be unable to avoid all situations involving alcohol. Skills guidelines: (1) Say "No" in a clear, firm, unhesitating voice. (2) Suggest an alternative. (3) Change the subject to avoid debate. (4) Request the person to stop persisting if the person persists in the offer. (5) Avoid using excuses or vague answers that imply you might accept a drink some other time. (6) Make eye contact.

Module: Giving Positive Feedback. Rationale: (1) Satisfaction in relationships depends as much on sharing positive things with them as on solving problems. (2) Positive feedback is important with many different people. (3) People fail to give positive feedback for many reasons. (4) Relationship problems often accompany alcohol problems and the positives get overlooked. Letting people know you appreciate their support increases the likelihood of their continuing support. Skills guidelines: (1) State your own feelings rather than just facts. (2) Be sincere. (3) Be specific. (4) Choose a time when they are not busy.

Module: Giving Criticism. Rationale: (1) We need to be able to tell people what we wish they would do differently without hurting their feelings unduly or provoking needless fights and arguments. (2) Our reluctance to give criticism is usually the result of our experience with destructive, not constructive, criticism. (3) By not giving feedback when it is needed, you feel stressed, then angry or resentful, and these feelings will probably come out with that person. These irritations may build up until you explode at that person or get drunk. Giving criticism gently when the issue is still small increases your chance

of responding calmly and effectively and can reduce the likelihood of drinking. Skills guidelines: (1) State how you feel about the behavior, rather than facts or absolutes. (2) Criticize the behavior, not the person. (3) Request a specific behavior change. (4) Stick to one point. (5) Be willing to compromise. (6) Start and finish on a positive note. (7) Use a clear, firm, but not angry tone of voice. (8) Criticize in a way intended to help, not intended to hurt.

Module: Receiving Criticism about Drinking/Drug Use. Rationale: (1) It is very difficult to learn to receive criticism gracefully. (2) Criticism allows us to learn about ourselves and how we affect others and to improve ourselves. (3) Receiving criticism gracefully avoids unnecessary arguments. (4) Failure to respond to criticism effectively can lead to serious interpersonal conflicts, a high-risk situation. (5) The history of problem drinking makes a recovering person more susceptible to criticism. Define: Constructive versus destructive criticism, accurate versus unfounded accusations of slips, criticism about past versus here-and-now events. Skills guidelines: (1) Don't get defensive, debate, or counterattack. (2) Agree with something in the criticism, restate the criticism in a more direct fashion, and clarify it with sincere questions. (3) Compromise by proposing some behavioral change.

Module: Listening Skills. Rationale: (1) Listening attentively helps us to get to know someone, feel close, and resolve differences. (2) When intoxicated it is difficult to be a good listener, and listening skills may have become rusty with disuse. (3) Many people drink when lonely or become more lonely because of drinking. Listening skills help decrease loneliness by building new friendships and repairing relationships. Skills guidelines: (1) Listening is more than passively waiting for your turn; you actively attend to and try to understand the other person. (2) Use nonverbal behavior to show interest. (3) Think about what others' nonverbal behavior might mean. (4) Ask questions, paraphrase, and add comments. (5) You may share similar experiences or feelings after the person has completed their train of thought.

Module: Conversation Skills. Rationale: (1) Friendships are important in everyone's life. (2) Conversation is an important first step in building relationships. (3) Some people drink to feel comfortable with socializing, so it is important to become comfortable with conversing without a drink. (4) Some people avoid socializing because of difficulty making conversation, which leads to loneliness and boredom—common drinking triggers. (5) Recovering people need to make new sober friends to reduce the temptation to return to drinking settings. Skills guidelines: (1) Listen and watch to pick up clues about a good topic of conversation and to pick a time when there is a lull in the other person's activity or conversation. (2) Small talk is OK to get to know others. (3) Conversation is two-way. Let the person respond. (4) It is OK to talk about yourself. (5) Use open-ended questions. (6) Watch the other person's reaction. If they seem to have had enough, finish up. (7) End the conversation gracefully.

Module: Developing Sober Supports. Rationale: (1) Social supports are people who help you cope with stress. (2) People undergoing stress do much better if they have support. (3) People are often reluctant to seek support for various reasons. (4) Your old support networks may still be drinking and are not useful to you now. Building sober supports will help reduce the temptation to return to drinking buddies during stress. Skills guidelines: (1) Consider what type of support you would like: understanding and encouragement, or help with problem solving, information, resources, tasks or emergencies. (2) Consider who will be helpful to your sobriety. (3) Consider how you can get the help you need: Ask for what you need, be specific, give feedback, give your support in return. (4) Add new sober supports.

Module: Conflict Resolution Skills. Rationale: (1) It is more difficult to handle problems in close relationships than with strangers or acquaintances. (2) Effective communication in close relationships helps you and your partner feel closer, promotes better understanding, and decreases the likelihood that resentment will build up and set the stage for a relapse. The relationship is more of a sober support when difficulties have been resolved. Skills guidelines: (1) Don't expect your partner or yourself to be a mind-reader. (2) Express positive feelings about the other person: Failing to express positive feelings makes it more difficult to productively resolve problems. (3) Don't let things build up before you talk about them. (4) Stick to one point.

Module: Nonverbal Communication. Rationale: (1) Nonverbal communication (gestures, movements, eye contact, tone of voice) can convey a message different from one's words.

(2) Body language can help or hinder communication, especially if discrepant with your words. (3) Effective nonverbal behavior can help people respond positively to you and help you feel better about yourself. Skills guidelines: (1) A relaxed posture is important. (2) Personal space is important and varies among people. (3) Eye contact shows interest, but too much can make the person anxious or threatened. (4) Head nods show attention or understanding. (5) Your facial expression should agree with your words. (6) A pleasant expression can help others enjoy conversing with you. (7) Nervous movements and gestures show you are distracted or uncomfortable. (8) Tone of voice can affect how our words are interpreted.

Module: Expressing Feelings. Rationale: (1) All people have feelings in common. Sharing feelings, opinions and attitudes can form common bonds. (2) Many people have difficulty expressing feelings, but this improves with practice. (3) There are many benefits to sharing feelings. Skills guidelines: (1) It is OK to talk about your feelings. (2) Share both positive and negative feelings. (3) The goal is not to share all your feelings with everybody, but use appropriate disclosure. (4) Sharing feelings is a two-way street: Give the other person a chance to disclose too and use good listening skills.

Module: Introduction to Assertiveness. Rationale: (1) Assertiveness means recognizing your rights to make your own decisions, and respecting the rights of others. (2) These rights include the right to tell others your opinions or feelings, as long as it is not done in a hurtful way, the right to ask others to change their behavior if it affects you directly, and the right to accept or reject anything others say or request from you. (3) Passive people tend to give up their rights and not express their feelings. Aggressive people protect their own rights but run over other people's rights. Passive-aggressive people hurt others in an indirect way. Assertive people decide what they want, and find an appropriate way to get it while respecting the rights of others. Their behavior is adapted to best fit the situation. They feel satisfied with themselves and are generally well regarded by others. Skills guidelines: (1) Think before you speak and question your assumptions about what the person meant. (2) Be specific and direct. (3) Use statements not intended to hurt. (4) Be aware of your body language and tone of voice. (5) Compromise. (6) You may need to restate your concern or request.

Module: Refusing Requests. Rationale: (1) When people make requests or demands, you need to decide whether to go along. (2) You have a right to refuse requests without feeling selfish or guilty. (3) If you are unable to say "no," you lose control of your life, you get distracted from your priorities, resentment builds up, you eventually over-react, and it leads to poor communication and misunderstandings. (4) The consequences of not refusing requests are worse than the discomfort the refusal causes you. (5) People passively go along with requests for many reasons. (6) Inability to refuse may lead to resentment, loss of self-respect, and distance from others that build up and can set the stage for relapse. Skills guidelines: (1) Evaluate your reason for wanting to refuse. (2) Acknowledge the other person's feelings. (3) Be firm. (4) If you give a reason, state it in terms of your own priorities, needs, or wishes, and be brief. (5) Sometimes it is useful to compromise. (6) Make your body language consistent with what you are saying. (7) If the requester persists, pleads, or gets angry, calmly repeat your refusal.

Module: Receiving Criticism in General. Use the module on Receiving Criticism about Drinking/Drug Use, but focus the discussion on more general issues.

Cognitive Behavioral Mood Management Training

Rationale. The rationale for an intrapersonal coping skills approach includes the following points: The "final common pathway" to the decision to drink or not to drink is within the individual. That is, the cognitive-physiological-emotional *reactions* to high-risk cues act as *internal triggers*, centrally processed by a variety of mediating mechanisms. This process results in an enhanced sense of self-confidence (self-efficacy) in resisting temptations or in the undermining of self-confidence and resultant return to drinking. (For details, see Monti et al., 1989; Abrams & Niaura 1987.) Among the mediating mechanisms that play a strong role in the motivation/decision-making process are:

- Decisional balance of the pros and cons (the client's perceived positive or negative consequences of drinking at that moment)
- Physiological reactions, such as discomfort produced by withdrawal symptoms, stress, or anxiety
- Strong emotional states, especially depression/loneliness, anger/frustration and pleasure/stimulation

- Beliefs and expectations regarding what alcohol can do for the individual that are perceived as something that cannot be achieved any other way at that moment
- Self-talk: what the clients say to themselves or think
- The strength of cravings or urges to use
- Abstinence violation effect: the rationalization that once a small violation has occurred, one may as well give up trying to resist drinking and lose control completely

Information processing mechanisms such as selective attention, disassociation of important information, denial, rationalization, and intellectualization can play a crucial role in determining the perceived importance of the positive or negative consequences of drinking. The "final common pathway" appears to be self-efficacy expectations—the client's confidence that he or she can actually get through a challenging, high-risk situation without having to drink, that he or she has the tools (coping skills) to make it—no matter how uncomfortable it feels inside his or her body, mind and emotions (Abrams et al., 1986).

The goals of intrapersonal skills training are to "slow down the action" between the high-risk situations and the behavioral response (drinking). Help clients analyze the *critical paths* and chains of mediating thoughts, feelings and physical reactions that lead either to the decision to drink, or to enhanced confidence in the ability to resist temptation. Teach clients to become aware of and then to challenge their denial and rationalization. Teach alternative cognitive strategies to counteract negative thinking, rationalizations, and self-talk ("stinkin thinkin" in AA jargon). Explore with clients other ways to cope with emotions and physiological discomfort, in the form of either underarousal (boredom, fatigue, lethargy, depression) or overarousal (thrill seeking, risk taking, agitation, anxiety, anger/rage).

Overview. We describe a total of 13 different intrapersonal coping skills training modules in detail in our book (Monti et al., 1989). We have briefly listed them here and described several in more detail for illustrative purposes. Not all programs have the time to fit in all of the treatment modules. The modules presented here are roughly in the order of importance rather than in a logical sequence where each session builds on the previous session's work. The first eight sessions are considered essential but we described a more logical sequence for them in our book (Monti et al., 1989).

You can administer sessions in a group format with everyone challenged to identify their own (sometimes highly idiosyncratic) thinking and feeling patterns. The group members can brainstorm alternative ways to think or to cope with feelings or physiological discomfort. However, some thoughts and feelings are extremely private with the potential for shame, guilt, or embarrassment. An example is thoughts and feelings of worthlessness or poor self-image that could have originated in childhood through sexual, physical, or emotional abuse. You should be alert to subtle signs that might indicate the need for private one-on-one counseling rather than or in addition to group treatment.

The modules, in order of importance, are: (1) Managing Thoughts about Alcohol; (2) Awareness of Negative Thinking; (3) Managing Negative Thinking; (4) Awareness of Anger; (5) Managing Anger; (6) Seemingly Irrelevant Decisions; (7) Planning for Emergencies; and (8) Coping with Persistent Problems. Other modules include: (9) Relaxation Training I: Deep Muscle and Imagery Techniques; (10) Relaxation Training II: Letting Go; (11) Relaxation Training III: Relaxing in Stressful Situations; (12) Problem Solving; and (13) Increasing Pleasant Activities.

An introduction and rationale for cognitive treatment is crucial to obtain the client's engagement in the process and improve participation and adherence. You need to help clients understand the reasoning behind a cognitive coping approach and ensure that it makes sense to them. Draw out and discuss their doubts and skepticism to reduce resistance and nonadherence and to encourage independent use of the skills between sessions and after termination. Hold a wrap-up session to deal with issues of termination and the maintenance and generalization of the skills to everyday life.

Module: Managing Thoughts about Drinking and Coping with Craving. Rationale: (1) People commonly crave alcohol, sometimes for weeks, months, or years after quitting drinking. (2) Cravings are triggered by things that remind you of drinking. These can include people, places, feelings, and thoughts. (3) Cravings can be controlled. They are time limited. They increase in intensity and then go away like a huge ocean wave. (4) With practice, it gets easier to cope. Skill guidelines: (1) Learn to recognize the earliest signs of your own trigger situations.

(2) Use a self-monitoring diary to collect an inventory of triggers. (3) Make a list of craving triggers and plan to cope with them. (4) Try to avoid the strongest triggers, especially early in treatment. (5) When you cannot avoid triggers, try several ways to cope. If they don't work, leave the situation. (6) Use some distracting activity. (7) Talk it through with yourself or friends. (8) Urge Surf: Imagine you can ride on top of the urges as a surfer stays on a wave until it crests, breaks, and turns into a foamy harmless wave as it gets to shore. (9) Challenge and change your thoughts using self-talk. (10) Practice your skills.

Module: Managing Negative Thinking. Rationale: (1) The chain of events consists of a trigger, the thoughts and feelings, and the behavioral response. (2) You can interrupt negative thoughts and feelings about trigger events and substitute more positive healthy thoughts. Skill guidelines: (1) Become aware of negative thoughts such as "I can't do anything right." (2) Become aware of the negative feelings that result from the thoughts, such as anger or depression. (3) Develop challenging, positive alternative thoughts such as: "Sometimes I make mistakes but most times I can do OK or even very well, like the time when I . . . ." (4) Focus on the positive feelings that slowly emerge from repeating positive thoughts and challenging overly extreme negativism or "catastrophizing." (5) Develop more realistic expectations of yourself such as "No one is perfect, everyone makes mistakes sometimes, doing something bad or silly does not make someone a bad or stupid person." Blame the behavior, not the person. (6) Practice thought-stopping techniques (see Monti et al., 1989, pp. 111–117).

Module: Seemingly Irrelevant Decisions. Rationale: (1) Many ordinary choices that seem innocent at the time can lead you down the path toward exposure to a high-risk trigger or drinking later on. (2) Through a series of "minor" decisions that seem irrelevant to the risk of drinking, you can gradually get closer to a trigger that would be impossible to resist. (3) You may then see yourself as the helpless victim of events. You need to see that you made choices and "seemingly irrelevant decisions" that led you to drink. Skill guidelines: (1) Analyze all chains of events that lead up to trigger situations. (2) Become aware of the seemingly irrelevant decisions. (3) Think ahead the next time and try to catch the small decisions as early in the chain of events as possible. (4) Develop coping skills to break the chain of events as early as possible. (5) Develop a plan to protect yourself if you choose to expose yourself to a high-risk situation (such as taking along a sober friend).

This brief sample of typical cognitive coping skills sessions gives therapists an idea about how to proceed. The degree of abstract thinking and problem-solving skills involved in these sessions may be demanding for some clients. This is especially true of those with cognitive impairment due to organic brain damage or due to the early phases of recovery. Also, individuals with lower education/socioeconomic status, fewer resources to cope with basic needs, and those who have difficulty with imagery techniques ("concrete thinkers") will need special work (see Special Considerations section). The modules can be adapted with examples drawn from the everyday life of the individuals. With experience, you will become very facile at adapting the ideas to the specific needs of your clients.

Cue Exposure with Urge Coping Skills

Researchers have conducted various forms of cue-exposure treatment (CET) with alcohol-dependent clients (e.g., Blakey & Baker, 1980; Monti et al., 1993c). The earlier investigations with alcohol-dependent clients used in vivo exposure to antecedents of use without allowing drinking (e.g., Blakey & Baker, 1980). However, these researchers often provided some skills training as well. This skills training included advice about changing the high-risk situations, discussion of alternative activities, and role-playing of strategies for handling high-risk situations (Blakey & Baker, 1980).

A more recent approach involves 10 40-minute sessions of the client holding and smelling their favorite, most frequently consumed, alcoholic beverage (Drummond & Glautier, 1994). Most studies of CET with alcoholics have not evaluated the approach in controlled trials. The method described next is one that we have empirically evaluated in a controlled treatment outcome trial with alcohol-dependent clients (Monti et al., 1993c). This approach is quite similar to an approach being used by Cooney and colleagues. (1993).

Overview. We individually administer CET in 6 to 10 sessions. This form of CET has three basic goals: (1) The client learns to identify high-risk situations that result in increased urge to drink (drinking triggers). (2) The client is exposed to these triggers during treatment until his or her urge to drink has decreased. (3) The client learns specific cognitive and behavioral coping strategies to deal with urges to drink in these high-risk situations.

We start each session of exposure with a trial or two of intensive exposure to the alcoholic beverage. Then we leave the beverage uncovered on the table in plain view while conducting imaginal exposure to other drinking triggers. Clients often look at and handle the beverage while imagining other triggers. The Drinking Triggers Interview is the source of scenes for imaginal scene exposure. The client learns a new coping skill each session. The client then repeats the imaginal exposure while trying out the new skill. At the end of the session, we cover the beverage and discuss the clients' reactions to the session, defusing any negative feelings or residual urge to drink.

Introduction and Rationale. Incorporate the following points into the rationale: "Many clients react to triggers associated with drinking with a greater urge to drink. While in the hospital, many stop craving because they are not around these triggers. But after leaving the hospital and first seeing drinking triggers again, you may have a strong urge to drink with no one to help you through it. Although you plan to avoid drinking settings, no one can avoid all drinking triggers. We want to help you learn to handle your reactions to these cues. This program is designed to help you build your coping skills so you can resist temptation more easily. We will do this by asking you to experience your drinking triggers until you feel the urge decreasing. You will also learn ways to make it easier to handle urges. Do not practice exposing yourself to drinking triggers on your own."

Define urges. Explain to the client that you will have him or her report urges repeatedly on a 0 to 10 scale so you will have a better idea what he or she is experiencing. Some people will resist having an urge to drink; emphasize that this approach can help them only if they are willing to allow themselves to experience an urge in the safety of the office.

Beverage Exposure. The primary beverage you use in treatment should be the client's customary alcoholic beverage(s), prepared in the way he or she usually drinks it. Have the client pour and mix the drink (not quite full) while reporting his or her changes in urge to drink.

Ask whether the glass (or bottle or can) would give them more of an urge and have them hold that. (Many clients never drank from a glass; we provide the glass to increase the smell in the room.) Some people have more of an urge while only looking at the glass than while sniffing it; use whichever sensory route gives greater urge. Ask clients to focus on whatever aspect of the drink gives them a greater urge.

Imaginal Scene Exposure. Bring the Drinking Trigger Interview answer sheet to the sessions and add triggers as the client thinks of them. Start with the highest-ranked trigger so the most practice over sessions will occur with the most difficult trigger. Be sure to cover all triggers over the sessions to maximize generalization. Before presenting a trigger scene, ask clients to provide more details about the aspects of the scene that would increase their urge. Then ask them to imagine the scene vividly and to focus on the elements that lead to the greatest urge to drink. Clients report their urge to drink every time it changes. Clients are generally more effective in generating the scene themselves than in responding to your narration, but an occasional client will need you to narrate. If urge fails to increase or keeps going up after coping skills are applied, ask clients to describe what they were thinking and give corrective feedback.

When the trigger is a fight or other emotional interaction, the highest risk time for drinking is just after the interaction. Have the clients imagine sitting in their car with the engine off just after the fight, for example, so they have a chance to cope. Some have difficulty having any urge at first. If avoidance is the issue, stress the importance of letting themselves experience the urge in safety. If their ability to use imagery is the issue, use guided imagery.

Integrating Urge Coping Skills. When the urge has gone as high as you and the client think it will go, ask him or her to practice one of the coping strategies he or she learned while imagining still being in the scene. The scene will be terminated when the urge is as low as you think it will go, but no higher than a 2 on a 0 to 10 scale. Usually it takes between 1 second and 2 minutes for the urge to reach a maximum, and between 15 seconds and 10 minutes for the urge to decrease to a minimum.

When teaching each new coping method, first describe the method, then have clients imagine using the method while in one of their high-risk situations. After the third or fourth session, instead of telling clients which strategy to use in each scene, sometimes tell them to use any method or combination of methods to push that urge down. This encourages generalization by allowing them to practice recalling and using strategies freely. Ask clients to practice coping with any urges between sessions using these skills and to report how it went. Anticipate situations that might cause an urge before the next session. Different strategies will be more or less effective in different scenes. During the last session, review all the strategies, summarize which worked best for the clients in which situations, and remind clients of the importance of practicing these skills after treatment.

Urge Coping Strategies. The only strategies we ask clients not to practice is *escape or avoidance*, as we want to maximize exposure. Therefore, if a client uses escape or avoidance, we acknowledge that it is a good method but that we want to help them learn what to do if they can't easily leave a situation or their urge. Tell clients that it is important to have many "tools" in their "toolbox" and that they need to try out all the tools and see which work best for them. We teach the following strategies:

1. *Passive delay and delay as a cognitive strategy.* During the first session, have the clients simply wait out the urge without using any active strategy, to see how long it takes to come down. Most clients (and therapists at first) are convinced it will never come down by itself and are surprised when it does, almost always within 15 minutes. You need enough rapport that the clients will trust you during this time. Afterwards, point out that urges always decrease if they wait long enough, but that most people never have waited out a strong urge. When they have an urge, they can tell themselves that they can wait it out until it goes down. This active cognitive strategy, called the Wait It Out Tool, is most useful after treatment when combined with other tools.

2. *Negative consequences of drinking.* Have clients "think about all the bad things that could happen if you took that drink." Have them generate a list of more immediate negative consequences, then evaluate each consequence for the personal importance to them. Have them practice imagining being in a high-risk situation while thinking about either a specific consequence or any consequences they want to think of.

3. *Positive consequences of sobriety.* Have the client generate a list of "all the good things that would happen if you stayed sober." Focus on more immediate consequences. Clients have a harder time focusing on positive consequences, so make sure they are not just adding "not" to a negative consequence. When they practice this approach, make sure they are not just using a negative consequence again (e.g., "I was thinking how my wife would leave me again"). These two consequence strategies were most strongly related to reduced drinking after treatment (Monti et al., 1993c).

4. *Urge reduction imagery.* Based on Marlatt and Gordon (1985), we ask the client to mentally convert the urge into a physical object that can be overcome. Active images include stamping on the urge or slashing it with a knife. Passive images involve seeing the urge as a giant wave building up and cresting under the person, then going away. Let the clients choose their own preferred images.

5. *Alternative food or drink.* Have the clients imagine eating or drinking something else. List their preferred substitutes.

6. *Alternative behaviors.* Have the clients imagine doing some activity that could distract them. Most clients have an easy time with the alternatives strategies.

7. *Cognitive mastery statement.* Teach the clients to mentally rehearse mastery self-statements like "I can do it," "I'm strong enough to wait this urge out."

8. *Cognitive distraction.* Teach the clients to think of a pleasant imaginary environment and to practice imagining being in that environment while in a high-risk situation.

EFFECTIVENESS

Coping/Social Skills Treatment Relative to Other Treatment Modalities

Compared with all other alcoholism treatment modalities reviewed in this book, coping/social skills treatment (CSST) is one of the most effective. Using the "bottom line" summary information in Table 2.4 of Chapter 2, CSST is second only to Brief Interventions in terms of the Weighted Evidence Index, as well as the Cumulative Evidence Score. Moreover, CSST has been found to be effective with a more severely alcohol-dependent population than brief interventions, which are typically employed with less severely dependent clients. Indeed, CSST has emerged as a promising treatment approach.

Methodological Considerations

Bill Miller and colleagues (Chapter 2) have provided an excellent overview of desirable methodological elements of treatment outcome research. Their detailed methodological ratings of the outcome literature highlight current strengths and limitations of the field. Strengths include widespread use of random assignment to treatment groups, acceptable statistical methodology, in-person follow-up interviews, and accounting for treatment dropouts. Researchers in this area have also been moderately successful at standardizing treatment delivery and following up treatment participants for extended periods of time (6 to 12 months or more) at fairly high rates. Areas that indicated a need for improvement were the use of collateral interviews for corroborating self-report of drinking data, and the use of follow-up interviewers who are blind to treatment conditions. As Figure 2.1 of Chapter 2 shows, we have reason to be encouraged, however, since the methodological quality of studies is steadily improving.

In this review of CSST outcome, we have used standards parallel to those in Chapter 2: The study (1) includes at least one CSST approach intended to affect problematic alcohol consumption, (2) contrasts CSST with a control condition or any alternative treatment, (3) uses a proper treatment assignment procedure to equate groups prior to treatment, and (4) includes at least one outcome measure of drinking and/or alcohol-related problems. In rare instances, we included studies that do not meet all four criteria—if they are particularly illustrative of an important point.

Studies of Communication Skills or Cognitive-Behavioral Training

An early comparison of behavioral treatments for problem drinking randomly assigned 49 outpatient clients to one of four alcoholism treatments: behavioral family counseling, systematic desensitization, covert sensitization, or aversion therapy (Hedberg & Campbell, 1974). Behavioral family counseling, which emphasized rehearsal of communication and assertiveness skills, was the most effective of the four treatments in reducing alcohol intake at six-month follow-up.

A study of assertiveness training contrasted that treatment with human relations training (Ferrell & Galassi, 1981). The study added both treatments to standard inpatient treatment for skill-deficient chronic alcoholics. The assertiveness training included modeling, behavior rehearsal, video feedback, counselor and peer coaching, and homework assignments. In addition to assertiveness, sessions focused on refusal skills and on expressing warmth and anger. The human relations training emphasized development of self-awareness and the perceptions of others as well as enhancing clients' ability to express feelings. At six weeks follow-up, the assertiveness group showed greater interpersonal skills than the human relationships group. Results from a two-year follow-up indicated that the assertiveness group also maintained sobriety significantly longer.

Assertiveness training was not found to improve outcome when compared with other treatments for problem drinkers in another study (Miller, Taylor, & West, 1980). This study randomly assigned 56 problem drinkers to one of four treatments designed to teach moderation in alcohol consumption: bibliotherapy; 6 sessions of behavioral self-control training; 6 sessions of self-control training plus 12 sessions of relaxation, communication, and assertiveness training; and 6 sessions of self-control training plus 12 sessions of individualized broad spectrum modules. A total of 41 clients completed therapy. All did equally well, except the bibliotherapy clients; they spent the most hours per week intoxicated. The lack of differences between the other groups may be due to the small size of the groups. However, it may also be that skills training is more appropriate for severe alcoholics as they may be more likely to have skills deficits.

Ed Chaney and colleagues (1978) compared the effectiveness of skills training with a discussion control and a no additional treatment control. All clients received standard inpatient alcoholism treatment. The skills training emphasized analysis of problematic situations and production of adaptive responses in a standard set of training situations. The situations were based on Alan Marlatt's (1978) categorization of high-risk situations. In the Situational Competency Test at the conclusion of treatment, the skills training group improved in skill level in two areas (duration and specification of new behavior) but not in two other areas (latency to response and noncompliance). The groups no longer showed measurable differences in skill

level at a three-month follow-up. Still, at a one-year follow-up, clients who had received skills training experienced significantly briefer and less severe relapse episodes than clients in the other two groups.

A study by Jones, Kanfer, and Lanyon (1982) attempted to replicate the Chaney (1978) study with a group of 78 alcoholics who were of higher socioeconomic status than those originally studied. They used same CSST, and again compared it to a discussion and a no additional treatment control group. Clients in the CSST or discussion group did significantly better than clients who received no additional treatment. Unlike the Chaney (1978) results, however, the CSST and discussion groups did not differ from each other at outcome. This discrepancy in findings may be accounted for by the differences between the two discussion control groups. Chaney's discussion group emphasized how clients felt in high-risk situations, while Jones and colleagues (1982) added a component that described possible barriers to handling the situations better. Furthermore, group members frequently attempted to discuss concrete solutions to the problem situations in Jones's discussion group, whereas no such discussion was allowed in Chaney's discussion group. This increased focus on problem solving may have made Jones's discussion group more similar to CSST.

In another study of clients receiving inpatient alcoholism treatment, Greenwald and colleagues (1980) compared the effects of two types of CSST with a no additional treatment control group. Again, all clients received the standard background treatment. One of the types of CSST focused on drink refusal situations. The other focused on frustrating interpersonal situations. Both CSSTs consisted of only two sessions. Skill level was assessed pre- and posttreatment in five different categories: positive assertive responses in frustrating interpersonal situations, drink refusal skill, general refusal skills, emotional expression, and responses to others' emotional expression. Three of the five categories were not part of the CSST and presented an opportunity to assess generalization of specific skills to novel social situations. Oddly, differences on the trained situations were not statistically significant between groups, but both skills groups showed significantly greater gains than the control group in two of the remaining three skill categories. The researchers reported no follow-up data. Despite this study's obvious shortcomings, it was useful in its emphasis on the distinction between general and alcohol-specific skills in measurement and treatment.

A study by Nathan Azrin and colleagues (1982) targeted skills training to specific issues. This study randomly assigned alcoholic clients attending an outpatient clinic to one of three treatment conditions. The first was a Disulfiram group, in which therapists gave clients standard educational material about alcoholism and a prescription for Disulfiram. Clients in the second group, a "Disulfiram assurance" group, received the traditional Disulfiram program plus communication skills training specific to taking the Disulfiram (see Chapter 15). Therapists did role-plays with the clients' close relative or friend who had agreed to assure that the client was taking the medication. Role-plays focused on situations that might lead to cessation of disulfiram use. A third group of clients received all aspects of treatment discussed thus far plus behavioral therapy, which included (among other components) drink refusal skills and other social skills. All treatments consisted of five weekly sessions.

At six-month follow-up, the third group had the highest sobriety rates, while the traditional Disulfiram clients were off medication and drinking on most days. The Disulfiram assurance group was only effective for married clients. This study provides a good example of specific skills training and supports the efficacy of CSST. However, groups differed in so many elements of treatment that it is difficult to determine specific contributors to successful outcome.

Oei and Jackson conducted two studies of social skills training (1980, 1982). The first study compared social skills training to traditional supportive therapy, delivering each form of treatment in group versus individual formats. They randomly assigned 32 alcoholics to one of the four treatment conditions. Compared with supportive therapy, both group and individual skills training led to greater improvements in social skill and larger reductions in drinking over a 12-month follow-up period. Additionally, group skills training led to faster gains in social skills than did individual training, with equivalent reductions in drinking.

In the second study, Oei and Jackson (1982) randomly assigned 32 hospitalized alcoholics with mild to severe assertiveness deficits to one of four treatment combinations: social skills training, cognitive restructuring, both of those treatments combined, and traditional supportive therapy. The social skills training used didactics,

modeling, role-playing, videotaping, feedback, and homework assignments to teach a variety of social skills. Cognitive restructuring treatment did not teach specific problem-solving skills. Instead, therapists discussed effective and noneffective behaviors and attitudes, encouraged "healthy self-talk," and attempted to modify irrational beliefs by using rational persuasion.

At follow-up, clients from the traditional supportive therapy group had significantly poorer social skills and drinking outcomes than clients in the other three groups. Social skills training led to greater immediate improvements, whereas cognitive restructuring treatment was associated with better maintenance of treatment gains at later follow-up intervals. The results of this study suggest that social skills training, cognitive restructuring, and their combination all appear to provide effective treatments for clients with assertiveness deficits.

When interpreting the results of the latter study and similar studies that compare alternate forms of treatments, however, it is important to explore other differences that may exist between the treatments, aside from the therapeutic focus. For example, in this study, it is possible that the therapists could avoid talking about cognitive restructuring in the CSST groups more easily than they could prevent discussion of social skills in the cognitive restructuring groups. Additionally, clients asked more questions and therapists self-disclosed more often in the cognitive restructuring group. These factors could have affected treatment outcome by enhancing group process.

Alcoholic clients who had received social skills training in another study had significantly better drinking outcome at one-year follow-up than did discussion group members (Eriksen, Björnstad, & Götestam, 1986). Both treatments consisted of eight weekly 90-minute sessions. The CSST clients drank less, had twice as many sober and working days, and had a longer period of continuous abstinence than those who were in the discussion group. These results were particularly encouraging since they established the prospect of long-term treatment effectiveness of CSST.

A recently completed treatment outcome study involved skills training with clients in a standard inpatient alcoholism treatment program (Monti et al., 1990). This study randomly assigned 69 males to one of three treatment conditions: communication skills training, communication skills training with family member participation, or cognitive-behavioral mood management training. All treatment conditions had an equal amount of time spent in manual-guided group treatment. Both communications skills groups included both general skills training (e.g., assertiveness, conversation and listening skills) and alcohol-specific skills training (e.g., drink refusal training, receiving criticism about drinking, enhancing nonalcoholic support networks). We assessed skill level at pre- and posttreatment, using the role-play tests of both alcohol-specific and general skill (see Assessment section above).

All three groups exhibited increases in skill level at posttest, but the communication skills group without family participation demonstrated the most skill in alcohol-specific role-plays. At a six-month follow-up assessment, clients who had received any communication skills treatment reported fewer drinks per day on average than clients in the mood management training group. Family participation in the communication skills treatment was not found to significantly improve outcome, but the background treatment program included family therapy.

Patient-Treatment Matching Studies

As we mentioned at the beginning of this chapter, several researchers have explored patient-treatment matching hypotheses with CSST. This is done in an attempt to identify variables that reliably predict who will benefit most from a particular type of treatment.

Damaris Rohsenow and colleagues (1991) reported that alcoholics had worse treatment outcomes following cognitive-behavioral mood management training if they had less education or greater initial anxiety or urge to drink in high-risk role-play situations. In contrast, communication skills training was equally effective for clients irrespective of these variables, initial skill, level of alcohol dependence, and marital status.

Ron Kadden and colleagues (1989) randomly assigned clients from an inpatient alcoholism treatment facility to one of two types of aftercare treatment: skills training (both communication and cognitive behavioral) or interactional treatment. The aftercare involved 26 90-minute group sessions. Although groups did not differ in drinking outcome, CSST was more effective than interactional therapy for clients scoring higher on sociopathy or psychopathology scales. Interactional therapy was more effective for clients who scored lower on a sociopathy scale. These matching effects persisted over a two-year follow-up (Cooney et al., 1991). Additionally, clients with cognitive impairment had better two-year outcomes in interactional treatment, while those without impairment did better in CSST.

These studies are important first steps in determining a means for matching clients to optimal alcoholism treatments. Project MATCH, initiated by the National Institute on Alcohol Abuse and Alcoholism, is a multisite treatment outcome study investigating patient-treatment matching hypotheses (Project MATCH Research Group, 1993). Clients in Project MATCH received either an enhanced version of our CSST, a 12-step facilitation, or motivational enhancement therapy. Clients were also assessed on a broad array of individual difference variables to identify the best personal indicators for matching clients to treatment type. Outcome results are expected by 1995 or 1996.

Studies of Cue-Exposure Treatment

Treatment outcome studies investigating CET are not nearly as extensive as those for other types of CSST. However, early evidence suggests that these approaches have met with some success in reducing drinking after treatment. A controlled trial by Drummond and Glautier (1994) found CET to be superior to a relaxation control therapy in reducing alcohol dependence. The study sequentially assigned 35 severely alcohol-dependent male clients to either CET (400 minutes of exposure to sight and smell of preferred drinks) or relaxation therapy. The researchers administered both treatments over the course of 10 days in addition to standard inpatient treatment. During the six-month follow-up, CET clients consumed significantly less alcohol and had longer latency to relapse to heavy drinking.

A preliminary study we conducted at a Veterans Affairs Medical Center randomly assigned 34 male clients in standard inpatient alcoholism treatment to receive either CET or no additional treatment (Monti et al., 1993c). This CET consisted of six one-hour sessions that combined exposure to clients' habitual alcoholic beverages with cognitive and behavioral urge coping skills training as described earlier. Clients who had received CET had higher abstinence rates than those who had received standard care alone at follow-up three and six months after the conclusion of treatment.

Based on the promising results of this study, we are conducting a much larger-scale controlled trial (Monti, 1993). Although this trial is still ongoing in 1994, preliminary results with more than half the sample completed lend additional support to the efficacy of combining CET with skills training. This trial randomly assigned male and female clients in a residential private facility for alcoholism treatment to one of four conditions: CET plus communication skills training, CET plus general alcohol education, relaxation training plus communication skills training, or relaxation training plus general alcohol education. At six months postdischarge from treatment, fewer clients who had received CET plus communication skills training had relapsed to alcohol. Also, clients in this group were less likely to return to heavy drinking than those in the three other groups.

Pead and colleagues (1993) are currently conducting a controlled trial of cognitive-behavioral CSST alone versus in combination with CET in an outpatient setting. A major contribution of this trial is the attempt to extend the generalizability of cue-exposure scenes. For example, they have found that sustained group-based exposure provides a more realistic simulation of real-life alcohol exposure than brief individual exposures. This trial includes nine weeks of aftercare, including outings with treatment providers to potential high-risk situations (e.g., bars, restaurants). The treatment outcome findings in this trial will provide an excellent test of the additive effects of intensive CET and CSST.

CONCLUSIONS

The preceding studies provide encouraging results for the utility of CSST as a significant component of treatment for alcohol problems and dependence. CSST can contribute to clients' social effectiveness and help to reduce drinking. It is important to recognize that CSSTs vary across important dimensions such as treatment modality (group vs. individual) and content (interpersonal vs. intrapersonal vs. cue situations, standardized vs. individually tailored). Specific elements of some CSST packages (e.g., drink refusal skills) are not included in others. No one has as yet determined empirically the optimal treatment parameters for CSST. Questions remain regarding which specific treatment components are most important and what duration and number of sessions is required. Future research

should examine the relative contributions of various treatment components. Research could do this in the context of a meta-analysis, using treatment component variables to predict study effect sizes.

Finally, CET is an innovative addition to CSST that shows promise. Several well-designed controlled clinical trials are currently in progress. Their results will likely determine whether CET becomes a more standard element of skills training packages.

REFERENCES

Clinical Guidelines

Chaney, E. F., O'Leary, M. R., & Marlatt, G. A. (1978). Skill training with alcoholics. *Journal of Consulting and Clinical Psychology, 46,* 1092–1104. This publication describes the skills training procedures and the Situational Competency Test used in this landmark study.

Hodgson, R. J., & Rankin, H. J. (1982). Cue exposure and relapse prevention. In W. M. Hay & P. E. Nathan (Eds.), *Clinical case studies in the behavioral treatment of alcoholism* (pp. 207–226). New York: Plenum. This chapter describes individual applications of the earlier approaches to cue exposure treatment.

Jones, S. L., & Lanyon, R. I. (1981). Relationship between adaptive skills and outcome of alcoholism treatment. *Journal of Studies on Alcohol, 42,* 521–525. This study includes a description of the Adaptive Skills Battery.

Kadden, R. M., Carroll, K., Donovan, D., Cooney, N. L., Monti, P. M., Abrams, D., Litt, M. D., & Hester, R. (Eds.). (1992). *Cognitive-behavioral coping skills therapy manual.* Project MATCH Monograph Series (Vol. 3). Rockville, MD: National Institute on Alcohol Abuse and Alcoholism. This treatment manual describes in detail an approach to social and coping skills training, based on the material in this present chapter and Monti and colleagues (1989) plus additional modules.

Marlatt, G. A. (1985). Cognitive assessment and intervention procedures for relapse prevention. In G. A. Marlatt & J. R. Gordon (Eds.), *Relapse prevention* (pp. 201–279). New York: Guilford. This chapter describes a conceptual approach and clinical strategies for social and coping skills treatment, using the metaphor of a journey. Marlatt describes a variety of cognitive and behavioral strategies, including enhancing self-efficacy and coping with urges.

Marlatt, G. A., & Gordon, J. R. (Eds.). (1985). *Relapse prevention: Maintenance strategies in the treatment of addictive behaviors.* New York: Guilford. This book includes conceptual underpinnings, research reviews, and clinical approaches to conducting cognitive-behavioral treatment for problem drinking, obesity, and smoking.

McCrady, B. S., Dean, L., Dubreuil, E., & Swanson, S. (1985). The problem drinkers' project: A programmatic application of social-learning-based treatment. In G. A. Marlatt & J. R.Gordon (Eds.). *Relapse prevention: Maintenance strategies in the treatment of addictive behaviors* (pp. 417–471). New York: Guilford. This detailed treatment manual describes a functional-analysis based set of cognitive-behavioral strategies for dealing with high risk situations.

Monti, P. M., Abrams, D. B., Kadden, R. M., & Cooney, N. L. (1989). *Treating alcohol dependence: A coping skills training guide.* New York: Guilford. This treatment manual describes in detail the clinical methods for conducting CST and CBMMT described briefly in the present chapter.

Monti, P. M., Rohsenow, D. J., Abrams, D. B., Zwick, W. R., Binkoff, J. A., Munroe, S. M., Fingeret, A. L., Nirenberg, T. D., Liepman, M. R., Pedraza, M., Kadden, R. M., & Cooney, N. L. (1993). Development of a behavior analytically derived alcohol-specific role-play assessment instrument. *Journal of Studies on Alcohol 54,* 710–721. This article describes the materials for and administration of the Alcohol Specific Role Play Test.

Rohsenow, D. J., Niaura, R. S., Childress, A. R., Abrams, D. B., & Monti, P. M. (1990–91). Cue reactivity in addictive behaviors: Theoretical and treatment implications. *International Journal of the Addictions, 25,* 957–993. The latter part of this theoretical review paper describes clinical pointers about the conduct of cue-exposure treatment.

Research

Abrams, D. B., Binkoff, J. A., Zwick, W. R., Liepman, M. R., Nirenberg, T. D., Munroe, S. M., & Monti, P. M. (1991). Alcohol abusers' and social drinkers' responses to alcohol-relevant and general situations. *Journal of Studies on Alcohol, 52,* 409–414.

Abrams, D. B., & Niaura, R. S. (1987). Social learning theory. In H. T. Blane & K. E. Leonard (Eds.), *Psychological theories of drinking and alcoholism* (pp. 131–178). New York: Guilford.

Abrams, D. B., Niaura, R. S., Carey, K., Monti, P. M., & Binkoff, J. A. (1986). Understanding relapse and recovery. *Annals of Behavioral Medicine, 8,* 27–32.

Abrams, D. B., Rohsenow, D. J., Niaura, R. S., Pedraza, M., Longabaugh, R., Beattie, M., Noel, N., & Monti, P. M. (1992). Smoking and treatment outcome for alcoholics: Effects on coping skills, urge to drink, and drinking rates. *Behavior Therapy, 23,* 283–297.

Azrin, N. H., Sisson, R. W., Meyers, R., & Godley, M. (1982). Alcoholism treatment by disulfiram and community reinforcement therapy. *Journal of Behavior Therapy and Experimental Psychiatry, 13,* 105–112.

Becker, J. T., & Jaffe, J. H. (1984). Impaired memory for treatment-relevant information in inpatient men alcoholics. *Journal of Studies on Alcohol, 45,* 339–343.

Bellack, A. S., Hersen, M., & Himmelhoch, J. (1981). Social skills training compared with pharmacotherapy and psychotherapy in the treatment of unipolar depression. *American Journal of Psychiatry, 138,* 1562–1567.

Blakey, R., & Baker, R. (1980). An exposure approach to alcohol abuse. *Behaviour Research and Therapy, 18,* 319–325.

Brown, S. A., & Schuckit, M. A. (1988). Changes in depression among abstinent alcoholics. *Journal of Studies on Alcohol, 49,* 412–417.

Calfas, K. J., Martin, J. E., Polarek, M. S., Hofstetter, R., Noto, J., Beach, D., Patten, C., & Barett, L. K. (1993, November). Treatment of nicotine addiction among recovering alcoholic persons: Six month outcome data. In P. M. Monti & D. B. Abrams (Chairs), *Alcohol and nicotine dependence: Mechanisms, treatment, and policy implications.* Symposium conducted at the Annual Meeting of the Association for Advancement of Behavior Therapy, Atlanta, GA.

Chaney, E. F. (1989). Social skills training. In R. K. Hester & W. R. Miller (Eds.), *Handbook of alcoholism treatment approaches: Effective alternatives.* New York: Pergamon.

Cooney, N. L., Bastone, E. C., Schmidt, P. M., Litt, M. D., Bauer, L. O., & Kadden, R. (1993, January). Cue-exposure treatment for alcohol dependence: Process and outcome results. In P. M. Monti (Chair), *Cue-exposure and alcohol treatment: Where do we stand?* Symposium conducted at the Sixth International Conference on Treatment of Addictive Behaviors, Santa Fe, NM.

Cooney, N. L., Kadden, R. M., Litt, M. D., & Gerter, H. (1991). Matching alcoholics to coping skills or interactional therapies: Two-year follow-up results. *Journal of Consulting and Clinical Psychology, 59,* 598–601.

Drummond, D. C., & Glautier, S. P. (1994). A controlled trial of cue exposure treatment in alcohol dependence. *Journal of Consulting and Clinical Psychology, 62,* 809–817.

Eriksen, L., Björnstad, S., & Götestam, K. G. (1986). Social skills training in groups for alcoholics: One year treatment outcome for groups and individuals. *Addictive Behaviors, 11,* 309–329.

Ferrell, W. L., & Galassi, J. P. (1981). Assertion training and human relations training in the treatment of chronic alcoholics. *The International Journal of Addictions, 16,* 959–968.

Greenwald, M. A., Kloss, J. P., Kovaleski, M. E., Greenwald, D. P., Twentyman, G. T., & Zibung-Hoffman, P. (1980). Drink refusal and social skills training with hospitalized alcoholics. *Addictive Behaviors, 5,* 227–228.

Hedberg, A. G., & Campbell, L. (1974). A comparison of four behavioural treatments of alcoholism. *Journal of Behaviour Therapy and Experimental Psychiatry, 5,* 251–256.

Jones, S. L., Kanfer, R., & Lanyon, R. I. (1982). Skill training with alcoholics: A clinical extension. *Addictive Behaviors, 7,* 285–290.

Kadden, P. M., Cooney, N. L., Getter, H., & Litt, M. D. (1989). Matching alcoholics to coping skills or interactional therapies: Post-treatment results. *Journal of Consulting and Clinical Psychology, 57,* 698–704.

Marlatt, G. A. (1978). Craving for alcohol, loss of control, and relapse: A cognitive-behavioral analysis. In P. E. Nathan, G. A. Marlatt, & T. Loberg (Eds.), *Alcoholism: New directions in behavioral research and treatment.* New York: Plenum Press.

Miller, W. R., & Sovereign, R. G. (1989). The check-up: A model for early intervention in addictive behaviors. In T. Loberg, W. R. Miller, P. E. Nathan &

G. A. Marlatt (Eds.), *Addictive behaviors, prevention and early intervention* (pp. 219–231). Amsterdam/Lisse: Swets & Zeitlinger B.V.

Miller, W. R., Taylor, C. A., & West, J. C. (1980). Focused versus broad-spectrum behavior therapy for problem drinkers. *Journal of Consulting and Clinical Psychology, 48*, 590–601.

Monti, P. M. (1993, May). *Craving for relapse*. Paper presented to the American Society of Addiction Medicine Annual Meeting, Los Angeles, CA.

Monti, P. M., Abrams, D. B., Binkoff, J. A., Zwick, W. R., Liepman, M. R., Nirenberg, T. D., & Rohsenow, D. J. (1990). Communication skills training, communication skills training with family and cognitive behavioral mood management training for alcoholics. *Journal of Studies on Alcohol, 51*, 263–270.

Monti, P. M., Binkoff, J. A., Abrams, D. B., Zwick, W. R., Nirenberg, T. D., & Liepman, M. R. (1987). Reactivity of alcoholics and nonalcoholics to drinking cues. *Journal of Abnormal Psychology, 96*, 122–126.

Monti, P. M., Corriveau, D. P., & Curran, J. P. (1982). Social skills training for psychiatric patients: Treatment and outcome. In J. P. Curran & P. M. Monti (Eds.), *Social skills training: A practical handbook for assessment and treatment* (pp. 185–223). New York: Guilford.

Monti, P. M., & Kolko, D. (1985). A review and programmatic model of group social skills training for psychiatric patients. In D. Upper & S. M. Ross (Eds.), *Handbook of behavioral group therapy* (pp. 25–62). New York: Plenum Press.

Monti, P. M., Rohsenow, D. J., Rubonis, A. V., Niaura, R. S., Sirota, A. D., Colby, S. M., & Abrams, D. B. (1993b). Alcohol cue reactivity: Effects of detoxification and extended exposure. *Journal of Studies on Alcohol, 54*, 235–245.

Monti, P. M., Rohsenow, D. R., Rubonis, A. V., Niaura, R. S., Sirota, A. D., Colby, S. M., Goddard, P., & Abrams, D. B. (1993c). Cue exposure with coping skills treatment for male alcoholics: A preliminary investigation. *Journal of Consulting and Clinical Psychology, 61*, 1011–1019.

Niaura, R. S., Rohsenow, D. J., Binkoff, J. A., Monti, P. M., Pedraza, M., & Abrams, D. B. (1988). The relevance of cue reactivity to understanding alcohol and smoking relapse. *Journal of Abnormal Psychology, 97*, 133–152.

Oei, T. P. S., & Jackson, P. R. (1980). Long term effects of social skills training with alcoholics. *Addictive Behaviors, 5*, 129–136.

Oei, T. P. S., & Jackson, P. R. (1982). Social and cognitive behavioural approaches to the treatment of problem drinking. *Journal of Studies on Alcohol, 43*, 532–546.

Pead, J., Greeley, J., Ritter, A., Murray, T., Felstead, B., Mattick, R., & Heather, N. (1993, June). *A clinical trial of cue exposure combined with cognitive-behavioral treatment for alcohol dependence*. Presented at the 55th Meeting of the College on Problems of Drug Dependence, Toronto.

Project MATCH Research Group. (1993). Project MATCH: Rationale and methods for a multisite clinical trial matching alcohol patients to treatment. *Alcoholism: Clinical and Experimental Research, 17*, 1130–1145.

Rohsenow, D. J., Monti, P. M., & Abrams, D. B. (in press). Psychosocial assessment and coping skills treatment for cocaine abuse: Preliminary results. In F. M. Tims, J. D. Blaine, L. S. Onken, & B. Tai (Eds.), *Treatment of cocaine abuse: Outcome research*. Monograph, National Institute on Drug Abuse.

Rohsenow, D. J., Monti, P. M., Abrams, D. B., Rubonis, A. V., Niaura, R. S., Sirota, A. D., & Colby, S. M. (1992). Cue elicited urge to drink and salivation in alcoholics: Relationship to individual differences. *Advances in Behaviour Research and Therapy, 14*, 195–210.

Rohsenow, D. J., Monti, P. M., Binkoff, J. A., Liepman, M. R., & Nirenberg, T. D. (1991). Patient-treatment matching for alcoholic men in communication skills versus cognitive-behavioral mood management training. *Addictive Behaviors, 16*, 63–69.

Rohsenow, D. J., Monti, P. M., Rubonis, A. V., Sirota, A. D., Niaura, R. S., Colby, S. M., Wunschel, S. M., & Abrams, D. B. (1994). Cue reactivity as a predictor of drinking among male alcoholics. *Journal of Consulting and Clinical Psychology, 62*, 620–626.

Sobell, L. C., Sobell, M. B., Kozlowski, L. T., & Toneatto, T. (1990). Alcohol or tobacco research versus alcohol and tobacco research. *British Journal of Addiction, 85*, 263–269.

Vannicelli, M. (1982). Group psychotherapy with alcoholics. *Journal of Studies on Alcohol, 43*, 17–39.

Wills, T. A., & Shiffman, S. (1985). Coping and substance use: A conceptual framework. In S. Shiffman & T. A. Wills (Eds.), *Coping and substance use* (pp. 3–24). New York: Academic Press.

CHAPTER 14

Anxiety and Stress Management

Tim Stockwell

OVERVIEW

Drinking in order to reduce anxiety and cope with stressful situations is one of the most common reasons given by heavy social drinkers and problem drinkers for their behavior. Agoraphobia, social phobias, panic disorders, and generalized anxiety are all more commonly reported by heavy drinkers than in the general population. Research in this area has shown that for many people, alcohol can be a powerful anxiolytic, although paradoxically, if taken in large quantities for a prolonged period, it may actually *elevate* anxiety levels. This simple concept of opposing short-term and long-term consequences of alcohol consumption is central to the following account of assessment and treatment of the anxious problem drinker.

The terms *anxiety* and *stress* are frequently used loosely in everyday language. For present purposes, we will employ the term *stress* when referring to an entire process of interaction between external "stressors" (e.g., work commitments, criticism, unrealistic demands) and an individual's reactions to these, or "stress responses." Anxiety, fear, anger, and depression are all examples of stress responses. Anxiety-

and stress-management approaches attempt to enable individuals to gain control of their reactions to stress in the following ways: (1) by altering their perception of the degree of threat posed by the stressor, (2) by altering their lifestyle to reduce both the frequency and severity of external stressors, and (3) by enabling them to use active coping strategies that inhibit or replace disabling stress responses such as extreme anxiety or fear.

Other chapters in this book deal with methods for helping a person to modify a tendency toward depressed mood states and for reducing social anxiety by training assertiveness and other social skills (see Chapter 13). While this chapter will focus more specifically on lifestyle modification and anxiety-management techniques, bear in mind that a flexible, individualized treatment will always draw upon ideas and methods from many other sources.

The seemingly paradoxical two-way relationship between the experience of anxiety and the consumption of alcohol is well illustrated when a heavy drinker stops drinking. The extent to which this "withdrawal" period will be characterized by raised anxiety levels, or even panic attacks, will be determined by many factors: the extent of uninterrupted prior drinking, preexisting anxiety levels, current stresses, and degree of learned dependence on alcohol. While only a small minority of drinkers experience severe withdrawal or "rebound anxiety" when stopping drinking for a period, many such individuals who seek help at clinics will do so. Thus, anxiety and stress management procedures may be needed both to enable and maintain a reduction in drinking.

SPECIAL CONSIDERATIONS

There are many instances when treating anxiety in a problem drinker will be ineffective or even counterproductive. Many hours of therapy have been wasted by not observing certain basic ground rules with this client group. In many instances, this will be due to the therapist being *unaware* of their client's drinking habits. There is persuasive evidence that only a small minority of problem drinkers are identified as such, but continue to be heavy users of physical and mental health care resources which are directed at correcting the *consequences* of excessive drinking. Thus, the first ground rule must be that any treatment—whether pharmacological, psychotherapeutic, or behavioral—aimed at anxiety or stress reduction should not be delivered without a prior assessment of the recipient's drinking *and* drug use.

Numerous simple and nonthreatening assessment methods have been designed for this purpose (see Chapter 3). One such is the Health Questionnaire (Wallace & Haynes, 1985), which inquires about a variety of health-related behaviors, including alcohol consumption. To continue to treat anxiety levels that are being continuously fueled by heavy alcohol consumption is almost invariably futile, and, in the case of drug treatments, potentially dangerous. Try to explain these issues to your colleagues in general medicine and adult mental health. In a year, they may see many more cases in which alcohol use is a factor than you or they realize.

The following ground rules assume that the client or patient has both been asked and is open about her or his alcohol and drug intake.

Client's Motivational Status

As with all addictive or dependency problems, an assessment of the clients' perception of the relative balance of the benefits and drawbacks of their alcohol or drug use is an early treatment priority (see Chapter 4). I recommend the Readiness to Change Questionnaire (Rollnick, Heather, Gold, & Hall, 1992) for assessment of drinkers' motivational status and their "Stage of Change" (DiClemente & Hughes, 1990). If the client is unwilling to reduce or stop excessive drinking as a condition of treatment, it is either necessary to dedicate time toward persuading the client further or to firmly refuse treatment. If need be, the client can be invited to attempt to reduce his or her intake as an "experiment" to discover the subsequent effect upon his or her anxiety before making any long-term commitment.

Client's Drinking and Drug Use Status

Many clients who drink heavily or abuse other anxiolytic drugs will experience substantial or complete recovery from extreme anxiety following successful detoxification. It is prudent to focus initially on achieving an alcohol- and drug-free state of at least two weeks' duration before assessing the need for offering intensive anxiety-management treatment. Heavy alcohol use over a prolonged period of time stimulates the autonomic nervous system, often causing symptoms of severe anxiety. Such overstimulation gradually subsides and may disappear altogether after a two-week "rest" from drinking (often termed "alcohol withdrawal").

Further research is needed to discover the exact levels and patterns of consumption that worsen rather than alleviate anxiety. We recommend the following guidelines based on our clinical experience:

1. Advise clients to avoid entirely using alcohol and drugs in order to help cope with anxiety.
2. Otherwise, advise clients to reduce their consumption to below five standard drinks per day for men and four standard drinks for women—or *less* than five days per week in each case. (One "standard drink" in the UK contains 10cc of alcohol.)
3. Avoid the use of other anxiolytic medication unless prescribed for a specific and time-limited therapeutic purpose (e.g., detoxification or *occasional* facilitation of sleep).

Cognitive Impairment

Many heavy and problem drinkers suffer from a degree of cognitive impairment ranging in severity from forgetfulness ("the morning after the night before") to the permanent loss of ability to remember new information, as displayed in full-blown Korsakoff's Psychosis. Rapid recovery of learning and problem-solving abilities are the norm following reduced intake or abstinence. However, assess the level at which any individual client is performing and take this into account when designing the treatment program. I also recommend a special emphasis on simple instructions plus readily understood written and audio or visual materials.

Screening Out Specific Clinical Conditions

Anxiety-related symptoms are perhaps the most common across the whole range of mental health problems. As a consequence, when an individual complains of high levels of anxiety, it may be related to an underlying psychiatric condition. Panic attacks may be a feature of an "agitated" depression; neurological impairment and psychotic illness can also be the underlying cause of clinically severe anxiety. A thorough psychiatric and psychological assessment is necessary in order to exclude these possible underlying causes.

In summary, there are several special considerations to bear in mind before including a problem drinker in an anxiety- and stress-management program:

1. Certain types of cause for the anxiety need to be excluded.
2. It is essential that the client is sufficiently motivated to tackle his or her drinking problem.
3. Drug and alcohol use should be under control before anxiety-focused work need begin.

DESCRIPTION

It is not possible to describe a precise set of procedures or a "recipe" for the treatment of every case where an anxiety-related problem is responsible for an individual's excessive drinking. Rather, I will outline a set of principles and describe a range of alternative procedures that may or may not be applicable for a particular client.

As indicated, anxiety- and stress-management procedures are indicated for problem drinkers to aid short-term drinking reduction or "withdrawal" and to minimize the possibility of future relapse. Accordingly, I have subdivided this section and ex-

amined assessment and management issues separately in each case.

Anxiety Management during Alcohol Withdrawal

It is traditional practice to provide anxiety-reducing medication on a reducing schedule to ensure a smooth withdrawal from alcohol (see Chapter 16). In Australia and the United Kingdom, chlordiazepoxide or chlormethiazole tend to be preferred and are reduced over a period of up to seven days according to severity of withdrawal symptoms. There are considerable risks of overdose with the latter drug if prescribed to outpatients with minimal supervision. Alternative, drug-free methods, such as electro-acupuncture and intensive social and emotional support, are increasingly being employed. The risks of a drug-free withdrawal include grand mal seizures and the bizarre behavior associated with delerium tremens. However, the dangers of these conditions should not be exaggerated, as nonmedical detoxification centers have successfully treated several thousand problem drinkers with extremely few serious complications (Pederson, 1986).

A useful assessment tool for predicting severity of withdrawal symptomatology is the Severity of Alcohol Dependence Questionnaire-Form C, or SADQ-C (Stockwell, Sitharthan, McGrath, & Lang, 1994). This 20-item questionnaire assesses degree of alcohol dependence on a 0 to 60 scale for the client's last three months of drinking. Higher scores predict more severe withdrawal. Remember that alcohol withdrawal symptoms consist mainly of the psychophysiological signs of extreme anxiety—trembling, sweating, racing pulse, subjective experience of anxiety, and even panic. During the withdrawal phase, an excellent instrument for monitoring symptoms is the Selected Symptom Checklist (Murphy, Shaw, & Clarke, 1983). This easily administered scale assesses both objective and subjective signs of withdrawal and also provides an overall measure of withdrawal severity.

Since someone undergoing alcohol withdrawal has to cope with uncomfortable levels of anxiety, even on the best medication regimen, it is important to give psychological assistance as well. It is possible to apply psychological principles so as to ensure that anxiety is minimized and chances of success are maximized.

Removal of Alcohol and Alcohol-Related Cues

Do not use procedures to help the recovering drinker cope actively with available alcohol at this stage. Normally, it is necessary for alcohol to be removed from the drinker's house and for steps to be taken to reduce the likelihood of family members or friends bringing in new supplies or inviting the individual out for a drink. When the home carries too many associations with drinking or when access to alcohol is too easy, then the client may need to be admitted to a hospital or a detoxification unit. In most cases this will be unnecessary and withdrawal can be supervised in the client's home (Stockwell et al., 1990).

Reduction of Social and Environmental Stress

It is important to give careful attention to the setting for alcohol withdrawal. A busy general or psychiatric hospital ward is often too noisy, frightening, impersonal, and unsupportive. Continuing to work may either provide vital distraction or create intolerable stress. Staying at home may be counterproductive if there are severe tensions in the marriage or family. In general, a quiet environment without social stress or demands, low lighting, warmth, and company available if needed constitute ideal conditions for minimizing stress.

Reducing Conflict about Whether to Drink Alcohol

The experience of conflict between two competing and quite incompatible courses of action is notoriously stressful. The problem drinker is well used to such stress in relation to his or her drinking. Again, the importance of establishing the individual's commitment or motivation cannot be overemphasized; the stronger the commitment, the less the decisional conflict that will be experienced. Having the individual client elect for alcohol and alcohol-related cues to be absent will also minimize the experience of such conflict. Some may even find talking or thinking about alcohol produces such conflicts. One advantage of an institutional setting can be the existence of a firm "no drinking" rule (i.e., instant discharge if it is broken), which can also minimize such conflict. In noninstitutional settings, a good technique for increasing commitment, and hence reducing decisional conflict, is to formalize a therapeutic agreement by means of a signed contract that specifies the roles and responsibilities of all parties.

Provision of Accurate Information to Prevent Faulty Attributions

The individual needs to be able to discuss the symptoms he or she is experiencing—to have these explained if need be, but to ideally have been well prepared for these from the outset. There is often a tendency to wrongly attribute anxiety symptoms either to an external cause or to an enduring feature of the experience of abstinence. I stress once more the importance of simplicity, clarity, and repetition of such information, as cognitive impairment will be maximal at this point.

Avoiding Stimulants

Many people cope with alcohol withdrawal by consuming large quantities of nonalcoholic drinks. Unfortunately, this often leads to taking great amounts of caffeine, which may both intensify the experience of anxiety and render sleeping very difficult. Remember that many soft drinks—not just tea and coffee—contain caffeine. The great majority of heavy drinkers also smoke cigarettes, and will greatly increase their smoking during alcohol withdrawal. While it is not generally advisable to press for these to be given up at the same time as alcohol, I advise that smoking be limited, as nicotine is also a powerful stimulant. It is an intriguing possibility that much anxiety associated with alcohol withdrawal is caused by clients substituting these stimulant drugs for alcohol.

Simple Relaxation Methods

Cognitive coping strategies, other than the very simplest, may be impractical at this stage. However, practicing simple relaxation techniques and deep breathing exercises may be invaluable. These will be discussed shortly.

Anxiety Management and Relapse Prevention

One of the most common causes of relapse into heavy drinking is known to be the experience of negative emotions—often those caused by interpersonal stress (see Chapter 11). Many people can successfully "dry out" or temporarily reduce their consumption to safe levels. However, it can be far harder to sustain reduced consumption in the face of life's inevitable stresses and anxieties.

For many drinkers, the experience of extreme anxiety is only a feature of a heavy drinking period or of withdrawal. Subsequently, they may need only to practice coping with normal levels of anxiety in the absence of alcohol a few times for their discomfort and urge to drink to dissipate.

It is usually possible to predict the extent of recovery from anxiety following reduced alcohol intake and, hence, to judge the subsequent need for the input of anxiety-management training. The best approach is to take a detailed history that explores relative changes in drinking, alcohol dependence, and anxiety, giving the most weight to recent experiences. The retrospective use of the SADQ and the Fear Questionnaire (Marks & Mathews, 1979) are valuable assessment tools for this. The latter instrument is particularly useful, as it picks up not only a wide range of fears and anxieties but also the extent of avoidance provoked by each and an overall rating of different mood states. The extent to which heavy drinking developed as an attempt to obtain relief from anxiety symptoms and to which the anxiety symptoms were created or "fueled" by heavy drinking will usually become apparent. In general, clients with severe degrees of alcohol dependence will experience the greatest reduction in fear and anxiety by simply stopping drinking.

Such an assessment helps you to make an important clinical decision—how soon to recommend active coping strategies, as opposed to avoidance strategies, for dealing with anxiety-provoking situations. In this context, *active* coping strategies involve confronting and experiencing those situations that most tempt the client to take a drink (e.g., social drinking situations). The rule of thumb is to plan avoidance strategies during the initial recovery phase but then to gradually introduce active coping strategies at a pace that is comfortable for the individual drinker (see Chapter 11).

At a more practical level, also assess whether there are pressing external worries concerning court cases, family problems, work, or financial problems. Often, simple, short-term actions will reduce worry and uncertainty, and hence the stressfulness of such difficulties.

A formal assessment of the anxious problem drinker will itself frequently raise anxiety levels, as this may generate a long list of concerns. It is vital to be aware of this and to help the client to order and place priorities on what might otherwise feel a totally overwhelming set of problems. As discussed in Chapter 5, if you can help

the client to feel valued and optimistic, then raising such anxieties can *increase* his or her motivation to find alternative coping methods to drinking alcohol.

Some basic anxiety-management procedures will now be outlined. More detailed discussions of these can be found in the clinical guidelines of the references.

Exercises to Induce a State of Relaxation

There are many relaxation, breathing, yoga, and meditation techniques that are widely practiced and written about. Different methods will appeal to different individuals, and offering a wide range of choices is recommended. Methods that can be practiced in real-life anxiety-provoking situations are the most effective. They provide an active coping response and lower anxiety by inducing a sense of control.

A classic example of this is learning to control one's breathing to cope with panic attacks. A frequently experienced aspect of panic is for breathing to become fast, shallow, and erratic. Such breathing (or hyperventilation) may even *cause* a panic attack by lowering levels of carbon dioxide. A simple remedy is to breathe into a paper bag to restore carbon dioxide levels. Learning to recognize incorrect breathing patterns also helps. One method is to place your hands on your abdomen and breathe in to a slow count of 10. If correctly done, you will feel your abdomen expand. Hold the breath for a further count of 10 and release it slowly, also to a count of 10. You will feel your abdomen contracting as you do this.

Most relaxation exercises are more difficult to use in real anxiety-provoking situations. For example, a classic exercise involves tensing and then relaxing muscle groups in the body one by one so as to gradually induce a state of relaxation. On occasion, it is possible to find a quiet place to practice a speeded up version of what normally takes 15 minutes. Using the same breathing pattern outlined above, however, you can simultaneously tense *all* your muscles while breathing in, then hold the tension and gradually release it while breathing out. Repeating this process several times can often counteract quite high levels of anxiety.

Another effective technique that can be applied whenever a client experiences a stress response is called *Autogenic Training*. It is more akin to self-hypnosis or autosuggestion. It involves concentrating on different parts of the body (arms, legs, abdomen, chest, neck, head) in turn and making suggestions to oneself of sensations being experienced there: mainly sensations of warmth and heaviness. Involving no active effort or movement, repeated practice can create a powerful relaxation response in association with such simple suggestions as "My whole body feels calm and relaxed" or "My arms feel warm and heavy." Another advantage of this method is that clients find it requires less effort and are more likely to practice it regularly. Clients also appreciate using an audiotape to learn the basic technique.

People vary widely in their response to different relaxation techniques. An alternative method known as *progressive muscle relaxation (PMR)* is sometimes preferred. It is a flexible technique in that the basic principle is to tense and then relax individual muscle groups. Many clients discover they have particular areas of muscle tension that cause them difficulties (e.g., the hands and arms for those with writer's cramp, or the neck and head for those with tension headaches). They may find it sufficient to work only on these muscle groups or to give them extra attention while practicing a full PMR procedure.

Here is the usual routine for training yourself in PMR:

1. Lie down or sit in a comfortable chair in a quiet room, free from distractions. Do not cross your arms or legs.
2. To the count of 10, gradually tense the following muscle groups, hold that tension for a further 10 seconds, and then relax gradually, also for a count of 10 seconds. Do this for your:
   - hands (clench them into your fists)
   - arms (raise your hands to your shoulders)
   - shoulders (hunch them)
   - neck (press your head backwards against the bed or chair)
   - face (screw up all facial muscles and close your eyes)
   - chest (take in a deep breath)
   - abdomen (pull it in tightly)
   - buttocks (clench them tightly)
   - thighs (clench)
   - calves (point feet upwards, bending from ankle)
   - feet (clench toes together).
3. Make positive suggestions about "letting go of tension" as you relax each muscle group. Try to concentrate on the exercise and shut out other thoughts and worries.

4. Repeating these exercises twice should be sufficient to attain a deep state of relaxation. Some anxious clients may need to make several attempts before they benefit from this exercise. Some find it very hard to let go of their exaggerated self-control. Such clients often report upsetting thoughts and images entering their mind as soon as they begin to relax successfully. Help clients verbalize these thoughts and to deal with them. Point out that learning PMR is like learning to play a piano—the more you practice, the better you get.

Behavioral Strategies

A behavioral program may be needed to help clients cope with situations that are intensely fear-arousing. In this context, avoidance should not merely be construed as physical avoidance; using alcohol or anxiety-reducing drugs to feel courageous are other methods of avoiding the *experience* of fear and anxiety. Indeed, one of the more common anxiety-related disorders associated with problem drinking, agoraphobia, is now known to constitute a "fear of fear," and the associated avoidance behaviors are an attempt to avoid experiencing fearfulness.

A powerful therapeutic principle here is to help the client remain in fear-arousing situations long enough for the fearfulness to subside. Short exposures may actually *worsen* a phobia, whereas exposures in excess of 30 minutes—and often of several hours—represent an ideal target. A closely related therapeutic principle involves overcoming craving for alcohol in such situations. Researchers have found that *long* exposures to craving are needed for this to occur (see Chapter 13). In such cases, a behavioral approach must involve graded and prolonged exposures to cues for drinking while preventing *any* avoidance response, be it physical avoidance or use of anxiety-reducing substances.

The exact procedures used closely mirror those described elsewhere for the treatment of phobic anxiety states and obsessional disorders. However, a few novel considerations apply when alcohol or drug use needs to be prevented for treatment to be successful. First, as noted earlier, there is usually no point in encouraging such exposure and response prevention approaches until the full benefits of reducing alcohol intake have been appreciated (i.e., rebound anxiety has returned to "normal" levels). By contrast, avoidance strategies should be actively recommended during this initial phase to give such recovery processes the best chance of occurring.

Second, when embarking on an active exposure program, consider the extent of *craving* a particular task will generate as well as the level of fear of anxiety. For example, walking into a bar may arouse only moderate anxiety but very high levels of craving for alcohol. Tasks need to be graded, therefore, in terms of both these considerations, then approached and mastered, starting with the least challenging. You can use a number of strategies to reduce the likelihood of drinking occurring: Involve family, friends, or volunteer helpers to accompany the client and/or use an alcohol-sensitizing agent (e.g., Disulfiram). Some client services in the United Kingdom have even made use of an alcohol-free "pub" to enable anxious clients to adjust to socializing without being tempted to drink alcohol (see Chapter 15).

Another technique that aims to help clients cope with situations graded in order of difficulty is known as "systematic desensitization." This involves clients *imagining* fear-arousing situations after having attained a deep state of relaxation. As soon as any fear begins to interfere with the relaxed state, the client must stop thinking about the situation. While there is some evidence that this method is effective, it is more time consuming than both real-life exposure techniques and also imaginal techniques requiring prolonged exposure to fear-inducing images. I recommend that practitioners familiarize themselves with each of these alternatives and use them flexibly. Wherever possible, use long exposure times and real-life situations. Some feared situations, or those which induce craving for alcohol, occur rarely or are hard to replicate for therapeutic purposes and so imaginal methods are required. Some clients will only accept the "gently" approach of systematic desensitization.

Again, the client's rehearsal of assertive responses, coping and social skills before entering situations alcohol and drug free will often be very valuable. Often clients do not lack skills—but confidence in their ability to use their existing skills without alcohol. Thus, I strongly recommend guided practice with plenty of support and positive feedback. Having clients attend group therapy based on problem-solving and behavioral principles is another method of enabling them to learn to communicate in a sober state.

Cognitive Strategies

For some years clinicians have realized that many negative mood states result from a tendency to misconstrue events and communications. In response, they have developed cognitive therapies that focus on identifying distorted and negative patterns of perception and then teaching methods of correcting these patterns. Thought patterns that lead to excess anxiety are characterized by an exaggerated perception of the likelihood of negative consequences or eventualities (e.g., having a panic attack, being criticized, or failing in the eyes of important other people).

There are excellent manuals that explain these new and sophisticated cognitive therapies in detail (e.g., Beck & Emery, 1979). Such therapy proceeds by explaining the rationale carefully, using examples drawn from the client's experience. Next, the therapist helps the client to be aware of negative automatic thoughts or images associated with acute anxiety. Access to these may often be difficult, and the use of diaries, guided fantasies, and role play may be needed. (One of our clients discovered she always had a fleeting image of her stepmother scolding her when she felt anxious—even though she hadn't lived with her for 20 years. She developed a strategy of mentally shouting at her to "leave me alone!")

The next step is to train clients to step back from their negative thoughts, to devise alternative constructions, and to challenge their negative thinking. A simple example is to learn that social anxiety normally declines after an initial high, even if one does not drink alcohol. Often anxiety reduction is incorrectly attributed to alcohol when alcohol may merely, by an act of faith or placebo effect, enable a person to remain long enough in a situation for anxiety to naturally subside.

Bibliotherapy

Many readable self-help guides have been written and are widely available. Some of these (e.g., *Living with Fear* by Isaac Marks) are based on cognitive and behavioral principles similar to those outlined above.

Lifestyle Management

Many aspects of lifestyle contribute to the experience of stress. Most common are those involving the acceptance of unrealistic workloads and responsibility, whether at work or at home. These are, of course, avoidable. Help the client to be aware of this and encourage him or her to assertively resist pressure.

There are many "naturally" occurring, positive therapeutic processes that serve to prevent or reduce anxiety: satisfying social and sexual relationships, regular physical exercise, and regular sleep. A great many activities and interests are intrinsically relaxing, but very often anxious individuals fail to plan sufficient time for these. A full assessment of all these factors—as well as of the use of psychotropic substances—will invariably point to several effective methods for rapidly reducing anxiety and stress.

EFFECTIVENESS

Given the variety of therapeutic principles and procedures outlined here, it is not surprising that no single controlled study can be cited to support the overall approach. Rohsenow, Smith, and Johnson (1985) and McLellan, Woody, and Luborsky (1983) conducted the two studies that come closest to this ideal. Rohsenow and colleagues tested a comprehensive cognitive-affective stress-management package for heavy social drinking male college students. The training combined deep muscle relaxation, meditation, cognitive restructuring, and the rehearsal of coping skills while experiencing anxiety. Significant short-term changes in subjects' drinking behavior occurred, despite their not being explicitly motivated toward this end. Only modest longer-term changes occurred, however. This once more underlines the need for first working on clients' motivation to reduce drinking if durable treatment effects are to be obtained.

McLellan and colleagues (1983) evaluated a sophisticated cognitive-behavioral package designed for drug and alcohol abusers and compared it to supportive psychotherapy and counseling from volunteers. Although this treatment focused on anxiety and stress management as but *one* major problem area, the rigor of the research design, including screening for high motivation and random assignment to groups, provided an exacting test of the overall approach. They found that both cognitive-behavioral therapy and supportive psychotherapy were significantly superior to counseling.

Oei and Jackson (1982) have also produced encouraging evidence for the efficacy of a cognitive-behavioral approach for treating social anxieties in problem drinkers. Positive and sustained outcomes were obtained for the treatment

group in comparison with an untreated control group. However, anxiety-management techniques were only part of the overall package, which also included training in social skills.

The treatments described here do not fall neatly into any one of the categories used in Chapter 2 but span a range of these. Some of the skills training described are a subset of social skills training that ranks highly on overall effectiveness. Others, such as relaxation techniques, rank low. The latter result is sometimes due to these techniques being provided to unselected groups of problem drinkers, some of whom will have no need of them. Giving every client you treat some relaxation training is not an efficient use of your time. As stated throughout this book, you need to select and match clients to treatments and not just give everyone everything.

An abundance of research evidence exists to support some of the therapeutic principles described in the previous section. The evidence that prolonged alcohol consumption raises anxiety levels while abstinence reliably reduces them has been reviewed elsewhere (Stockwell & Bolderston, 1987). Ashton (1987) recently reviewed an extensive literature on the health consequences of caffeine intake, including studies linking caffeine to sleep disorders. Litman, Stapleton, Oppenheim, Peleg, and Jackson (1984) found that "survivors" (as opposed to "relapsers") of alcoholism treatment were characterized by an early phase of reliance on avoidance strategies, and then, between 6 weeks and 4 months, by an increase in the use of active coping strategies (e.g., refusing drinks at parties instead of avoiding parties). Stern and Marks (1973) and Rankin, Hodgson, and Stockwell (1983) have demonstrated the value of long exposures to cues triggering fear and craving, respectively. There is also much basic research linking certain cognitive coping styles with the experience of fear and anxiety (e.g., Clark, 1986).

There is clearly a need for further, well-designed treatment studies. These would need to control for the various drinking, drug use, and motivational variables described earlier, and ensure that all subjects still experienced a significant level of anxiety prior to treatment. While there are always further research questions to pursue, I confidently assert that assessing and treating anxiety should be an integral part of any comprehensive alcohol treatment program.

REFERENCES

Clinical Guidelines

Self-Help and Treatment Manuals

Annis, H. (1983). *A relapse prevention model for the treatment of alcoholics.* Addiction Research Foundation, 33 Russell St., Toronto, Ontario, Canada. A clear account of a cognitive-behavioral approach to help problem drinkers cope in a variety of high-risk situations.

Beck, A. T., & Emery, G. (1979). *Cognitive therapy of anxiety and phobic disorders.* Philadelphia, PA: Center for Cognitive Therapy. Everything one needs to know about cognitive therapy in relation to anxiety.

Marks, I. (1978). *Living with fear.* New York: McGraw-Hill. A clear self-help guide written by an expert in the field.

Miller, W. R., & Muñoz, R. F. (1982). *How to control your drinking* (rev. ed.). Albuquerque, NM; University of New Mexico Press. See their section on Relaxation Training.

Rosa, K. (1976). *You and A.T.: Autogenic training.* New York: Dutton. A straightforward account of this useful relaxation technique.

Assessment Questionnaires

Marks, I., & Mathews, A. (1979). Brief standard self-rating for phobic patients. *Behavior Research and Therapy, 17,* 263–267. The "Fear Questionnaire" described in this chapter.

Murphy, D., Shaw, C., & Clarke, I. (1983). Tiapride and chlormethiazole in alcohol withdrawal: A double-blind trial. *Alcohol & Alcoholism, 18,* 227–237. An easy to use and well-researched assessment of alcohol withdrawal severity.

Rollnick, S., Heather, N., Gold, R., & Hall, W. (1992) Development and validation of short "readiness to change" questionnaire for use in brief, opportunistic interventions among excessive drinkers. *British Journal of Addiction, 87,* 5, 743–754.

Stockwell, T., Sitharthan, T., McGrath, D., & Lang, E. (1994) The measurement of alcohol dependence and impaired control in community samples. *Addiction, 89,* 2. Useful for predicting severity of

alcohol withdrawal (especially anxiety components) and longer-term recovery from alcohol induced fear and anxiety.

Wallace, P., & Haines, A. (1985). Use of a questionnaire in general practice to increase the recognition of problem drinkers. *British Medical Journal, 290,* 1949–1953.

Research

Ashton, C. H. (1987). Caffeine and health. *British Medical Journal, 195,* 1293–1294.

Clark, D. M. (1986). A cognitive approach to panic. *Behavior Research and Therapy, 24,* 4, 461–470.

DiClemente, C., & Hughes, S. O. (1990) Stages of change profiles in outpatient alcoholism treatment. *Journal of Substance Abuse, 2,* 217–235.

Litman, G. L., Stapleton, J., Oppenheim, A., Peleg, M., & Jackson, P. (1984). The relationship between coping behaviors, their effectiveness and alcoholism relapse and survival. *British Journal of Addiction, 79,* 3, 283–292.

Oei, T. P. S., & Jackson, P. R. (1984). Some effective therapeutic factors in group cognitive-behavioral therapy with problem drinkers. *Journal of Studies on Alcohol, 45,* 119–123.

Pederson, C. (1986) Hospital admissions from a non-medical alcohol detoxification unit. *Alcohol and Drug Review, 5,* 133–137.

Rankin, H., Hodgson, R., & Stockwell, T. (1983) Cue exposure and response prevention with alcoholics: A controlled trial. *Behavior Research and Therapy, 21,* 435–446.

Rohsenow, D. J., Smith, R. E., & Johnson, S. (1985). Stress management training as a prevention program for heavy social drinkers: Cognitive affect, drinking and individual differences. *Addictive Behaviors, 10,* 45–54.

Stern, R., & Marks, I. (1973) Brief and prolonged flooding. *Archives of General Psychiatry, 28,* 270–276.

Stockwell, T., & Bolderston, H. (1987). Alcohol and phobias. *British Journal of Addiction, 82,* 9, 971–981.

Stockwell, T., Bolt, L., Milner, I., Pugh, P., & Young, I. (1990). Home detoxification for problem drinkers: Acceptability to clients, relatives, general practitioners and outcome after 60 days. *British Journal of Addiction, 85,* 61–70.

CHAPTER 15

The Community Reinforcement Approach

Jane Ellen Smith
Robert J. Meyers

OVERVIEW

The Community Reinforcement Approach (CRA) is a broad spectrum behavioral treatment approach for substance-abuse problems. It was developed to utilize social, recreational, familial, and vocational reinforcers to aid clients in the recovery process. CRA acknowledges the powerful role of environmental contingencies in encouraging or discouraging drinking, and attempts to rearrange these contingencies such that sober behavior is more rewarding than drinking behavior.

CRA emphasizes motivational techniques and uses positive reinforcement rather than confrontation whenever possible. For example, instead of routinely presenting the message "You're an alcoholic and you should never drink again," the CRA therapist begins by asking questions about *why* an individual is drinking, and by identifying the client's reinforcement systems. One basic tool used in CRA to gather this information is the functional analysis. Once the parameters of typical drinking episodes are outlined via functional analysis, a technique called *Sobriety Sampling* is used to initiate the process of behavior change.

An optional part of CRA is a Disulfiram (Antabuse®) compliance program. This combines Disulfiram treatment with a supportive monitor (Azrin, Sisson, Meyers, & Godley, 1982). The procedure ensures that the drinker actually takes the Disulfiram and is reinforced for doing so.

A smooth transition from CRA's assessment component into the formal therapy phase is facilitated by CRA's own set of procedures and forms. These were designed both to assist in the development of a positive and comprehensive treatment plan initially, and to monitor progress throughout the course of therapy.

CRA aspires to replace a client's old maladaptive drinking behaviors with new, appropriate coping strategies. To accomplish this, skills training is an essential ingredient of the package. This training focuses on diverse areas, such as communicating effectively and learning how to find and keep a job. Other important components of the CRA program include helping the client develop satisfying social and recreational activities that compete with alcohol use and support sobriety, relationship counseling, and relapse prevention strategies.

SPECIAL CONSIDERATIONS

One of the unique aspects about CRA is its compatibility with many other approaches to substance abuse treatment. Perhaps this is most evident in the domain of goals. CRA is appropriate for individuals who are striving for either lifelong abstinence or moderation. In addition, CRA's positive, motivational approach has much to offer in your struggle to gain full cooperation from clients. Also, CRA can be tailored to fit each client's special needs. The complete CRA package contains a variety of procedures that can be used or not used, depending on the situation. For example, CRA has a valuable job-training component for the unemployed, and a Social Club for single, socially isolated individuals.

CRA has demonstrated its effectiveness in both inpatient (Hunt & Azrin, 1973; Azrin, 1976) and outpatient settings (Azrin et al., 1982) and with individuals and couples (Azrin et al., 1982). Furthermore, there are CRA procedures for the spouses of unmotivated problem drinkers. Not only do the nondrinking spouses learn skills for coping with difficulties at home but the drinkers eventually seek therapy themselves (Sisson & Azrin, 1986). CRA's effectiveness also has been proven across a broad array of alcohol problems, ranging from mild to severe. And finally, CRA's efficacy has been documented in treatment formats varying from 50 hours of therapy (Hunt & Azrin, 1973) to as little as 5 hours (Azrin et al., 1982).

The first three CRA studies were conducted in rural settings (Hunt & Azrin, 1973; Azrin, 1976; Azrin et al, 1982). Consequently, we are anxiously awaiting the results of several ongoing urban trials. However, one of the advantages of starting in rural settings was that the counselors and clients learned how to fully explore and exploit the limited community resources. We have incorporated what we learned from the early studies into the current version of the CRA package. Knowing how to maximize community resources is an integral part of the Community Reinforcement Approach.

A number of questions remain regarding CRA's generalizability and the duration of treatment effects. Fortunately, most are being addressed in current research projects funded by the National Institute on Alcohol Abuse and Alcoholism (NIAAA). These programs have diverse ethnic representation, larger samples of women, and extended follow-up periods. In addition, the studies were designed to answer such important questions as the contribution of the motivational component of disulfiram use.

PROGRAM DESCRIPTION

CRA Functional Analysis

A traditional functional analysis is a structured interview that examines the antecedents and consequences of a specific behavior, such as drinking. It begins with an outline of the chain of events that leads an individual to drink, and continues with the immediate and long-term consequences of the behavior.

The CRA functional analysis is unique, as it carefully examines both drinking *and* nondrinking behaviors. We typically chart several representative examples of each. As with traditional functional analyses, start with an exploration of antecedents, or "triggers," to drinking. These are thoughts, feelings, and behaviors that precede a drinking episode, and that are instrumental in leading the individual to drink. The CRA Functional Analysis for Drinking Behavior (Initial Assessment) form is useful here (see Meyers & Smith, in press). Figure 15.1 is the nondrinking behavior version of this form. A description of the procedure follows.

Many CRA therapists have found it helpful to rely on a set of questions that looks first at the external and then the internal triggers. Specific questions asked about *external* triggers include: (1) "Who are you usually with when you drink?" Certain friends or relatives may be common antecedents to drinking episodes. (2) "Where do you usually drink?" Conceivably, the client may say, "Well, I went to a bar with a friend, but I meant to drink only a soda." (This is your opportunity to start pointing out high-risk environments.) (3) "When do you usually drink? Are there certain days? Times of the day?"Next, ask specific questions about *internal* triggers for drinking: (1) "What are you usually thinking about right before you drink?" Encourage the client to report as many thoughts as he or she can remember. (2) "What are you usually feeling physically right before you drink?" With some prompting, clients can focus in on bodily sensations that may suggest various states of arousal. (3) "What are you usually feeling emotionally right before you drink?" Clients often are unaware of this at first, and need to be trained to recognize and then label their feelings (e.g., sadness or anger).

At this point, move directly from triggers for drinking to the drinking behavior itself. This impresses on the client the crucial connection between triggers, such as thoughts and feelings, and drinking. It also is a good time to gather explicit details on the drinking pattern. The final part of the CRA Functional Analysis for Drinking Behavior is an exploration of the consequences. Upon first drinking alcohol, most clients experience some short-term positive effects. It is important to acknowledge these positive effects and point out that these benefits are always short-lived. Then review the negative consequences of excessive alcohol consumption. Since it is fairly common for clients to minimize these negative consequences, it is imperative to have a clear and complete profile of the client's history. Most of this information should be contained in the assessment material.

The second phase of the functional analysis, the CRA Functional Analysis for Nondrinking Behavior, is one of CRA's most important contributions to the field (see Figure 15.1). It also begins with an exploration of triggers, but this time the focus is on *nondrinking* behaviors. One purpose of this analysis is to show the client that he or she already enjoys certain activities that do not involve alcohol, and that a number of positive benefits are associated with these activities. Later, you would encourage the client to add more of these nondrinking activities, or new ones, to his or her daily schedule.

In the process of completing this second functional analysis, it becomes clear that many interesting and enjoyable activities frequently have an unpleasant component as well. Often, this negative side of the activity (e.g., the "cost" to the client in terms of time, money, or energy) is more immediate than the positive aspects. Although the negative effects typically are brief in duration, nevertheless, at times they may deter the client from engaging in the nondrinking activity altogether. In the course of discussing this with the client, move directly to the final part of the form, in which the long-term positive consequences of the particular nondrinking behavior are outlined. Devote considerable time to this section, as it will motivate the client to engage in these nondrinking behaviors more often in the future.

The completed functional analysis charts are referred to at various times during treatment. They are useful for reminding the client of both high-risk and low-risk drinking situations, and for monitoring changes in alcohol consumption over time. Later we will show you how to use a modified version of the functional analysis chart to address a relapse.

Sobriety Sampling

Many traditional alcohol programs in the United States use abstinence as their only drinking goal; consequently, clients are informed from the start that they can *never* drink again. The idea of remaining abstinent for the rest of one's life is a concept that many people have great difficulty accepting—especially those who remain unconvinced that they have a drinking problem. Ultimately, a significant number of these individuals either drop out of treatment prematurely or decide not to begin in the first place. CRA's Sobriety Sampling procedure can play an important role with these clients. It operates on the assumption that you can be more successful in engaging clients in treatment by not overwhelming them with rigid rules and frightening expectations. In Sobriety Sampling, you negotiate to get the client to commit to abstinence for a mutually agreed-upon, limited period of time. We use it with all clients, regardless of whether their final drinking goal is abstinence or moderation.

Once an individual has made a commitment to enter a program that only initially requires a limited period of sobriety, the many other advantages of this "time-out" from drinking technique become apparent:

1. It affords you the opportunity to build rapport with the client while helping him or her recognize the severity of the drinking problem.
2. It enables you and the client to set a goal together that the client feels is appropriate and obtainable. It does not frighten the client into deeper resistance.
3. It allows the client to experience the sensation of being sober. Frequently, this automatically focuses attention on positive changes in physical, cognitive, and emotional symptoms.
4. It actively disrupts old habits and drinking patterns, giving the client the opportunity to replace these behaviors with new coping skills.
5. Through the experience of setting and reaching goals of short-term sobriety, a client learns self-efficacy and self-control.
6. The feeling of success that comes with achieving short-term goals boosts self-confidence and enhances motivation.

Figure 15.1   CRA Functional Analysis for Nondrinking Behavior (_____)
                                                                behavior/activity

- TRIGGERS -

EXTERNAL	INTERNAL	BEHAVIOR
1. <u>Who</u> are you usually with when you _____ ? (behavior/activity)	1. What are you usually <u>thinking</u> about right before you _____ ? (behavior/activity)	1. <u>What</u> is the nondrinking behavior/activity?
2. <u>Where</u> do you usually _____ ?	2. What are you usually <u>feeling physically</u> right before you _____ ?	2. <u>How often</u> do you usually _____ ?
3. <u>When</u> do you usually _____ ?	3. What are you usually <u>feeling emotionally</u> right before you _____ ?	3. <u>How long</u> does _____ usually last?

7. Sobriety Sampling demonstrates the client's commitment to change, which in turn elicits the much-needed trust and support of family members.
8. Difficulties experienced within a monitored sampling period illustrate that additional assistance is required.
9. Sobriety Sampling paves the way for the introduction of Disulfiram (Antabuse®) in some cases.

How to Introduce Sobriety Sampling

Once you and the client agree that time-limited sobriety is a treatment goal, together you must decide on a reasonable period of time over which to sample sobriety. We usually begin by asking the client to specify the longest period of time he or she was able to remain sober in the past when not institutionalized. Regardless of the response given, CRA therapists often first suggest a 90-day sampling period. Most clients will express despair at the notion of being able to

achieve such an extended period of sobriety. If your encouragement does not convince them, adjust the sampling period downward to a goal of 60 days. In some cases, this process may need to continue moving toward a much shorter sampling period, such as 2 weeks or even 2 days. But by selecting a 90-day period at the onset, you provide yourself with ample room to bargain (see Meyers & Smith, in press).

Once you have negotiated the time period, then the task is to determine *how* to achieve it. Make it clear that despite the client's good intentions, without a solid plan it will be nearly impossible to honor one's commitment to abstain. Now you face the dilemma of having to provide the client with some strategies before he or she has learned the various CRA skills needed to maintain sobriety. We recommend several steps. First, schedule the next few sessions to take place quickly. Second, use the already completed functional analysis to remind the client of his or her specific drinking triggers. Third, help the

SHORT-TERM NEGATIVE CONSEQUENCES	LONG-TERM POSITIVE CONSEQUENCES
1. What do you dislike about _____ with _____ ? (behavior/activity) (who)	1. What were the positive results of _____ in each of these areas: (behavior/activity)
	a) Interpersonal:
2. What do you dislike about _____ _____ ? (behavior/activity) (where)	b) Physical:
3. What do you dislike about _____ _____ ? (behavior/activity) (when)	c) Emotional:
	d) Legal:
4. What are some of the unpleasant <u>thoughts</u> you usually have while you are _____ ?	e) Job:
5. What are some of the unpleasant <u>physical feelings</u> you usually have while you are _____ ?	f) Financial:
6. What are some of the unpleasant <u>emotional feelings</u> you usually have while you are _____ ?	g) Other:

client identify behaviors that compete with drinking in those high-risk situations. Finally, provide some basic instruction in problem-solving.

Sobriety Sampling is another example of CRA's preference for motivational procedures and positive reinforcement over confrontation. It can be used throughout treatment, regardless of whether a client relapses along the way. Goals for periods of sobriety can be renegotiated at any time.

Disulfiram

A behavioral compliance program with Disulfiram is another option to help a client successfully achieve a period of sobriety. Disulfiram is a medication that causes illness if an individual drinks alcohol while taking it. It serves as a deterrent to impulsive drinking. Present Disulfiram as an adjunct to treatment and list its many benefits. The individual taking Disulfiram often sees:

1. A reduction in family worry about future drinking episodes
2. An increase in family trust, since taking Disulfiram demonstrates a commitment to stop drinking
3. A reduction in "slips" that result from impulsive drinking
4. An increase in productive use of therapy time, since he or she can now deal objectively and constructively with other current life problems
5. A necessary increase in the reliance on new coping skills, since drinking is no longer an option
6. A reduction in complicated, agonizing daily decisions about drinking, because there now is only one decision to make each day: whether or not to take the pill
7. An increase in opportunities for positive reinforcement, since at the very least he or she will be praised daily by the Concerned Other who is monitoring the Disulfiram

The following dialogue shows a therapist introducing Disulfiram in an effort to help the client attain his goal of 90 days of abstinence.

> *THERAPIST:* Now that you've decided to stay sober for the next 90 days, let's talk about how you are going to accomplish this goal. Do you have some kind of plan in mind?
>
> *CLIENT:* I just won't drink. I can do it if I just make my mind up not to drink. I just never really wanted to stop before.
>
> *THERAPIST:* Have you ever told your wife and family that you were going to stop drinking before? How many times were you successful?
>
> *CLIENT:* Well, this time is different. I really want to quit.
>
> *THERAPIST:* That's great. I really believe you. And my job is to try to help. But I think we need to be realistic. It's not going to be easy without some kind of plan. Now you say that this time is different—that you *really* want to quit. I bet you'll do whatever it takes to reach your goal.
>
> *CLIENT:* That's right. I told you I really want to stop drinking.
>
> *THERAPIST:* What if I told you that I have a tool that would help you reach your goal, and if used correctly it would greatly improve your chances of achieving sobriety?
>
> *CLIENT:* OK. What's the catch?
>
> *THERAPIST:* No catch. There is a medication that deters people from using alcohol, because alcohol and this drug together cause a negative reaction; it will make you very sick. Now I certainly don't want to see you sick, but I do want to help you stay sober for the 90 days. This drug, Antabuse, is called a deterrent since it deters people from starting to drink. As long as you don't drink any alcohol, you will not have the negative reaction.
>
> *CLIENT:* I've heard of that stuff. A friend of mine got really sick using it. No thanks!
>
> *THERAPIST:* But the important thing to remember is that you only get sick if you drink. And you've just convinced me that you have no intention of doing that.
>
> *CLIENT:* I know, but . . .
>
> *THERAPIST:* Let me tell you about all the benefits of being on Antabuse.

The therapist would then review the seven main advantages to taking Disulfiram (described above). Each reason is personalized and applied to the client's particular situation, while keeping a positive tone and perspective throughout.

If the client still refuses to start on Disulfiram, allow him or her to attempt to stop drinking according to the client's own plan for a limited period of time. However, it is important to have the client sign a contract whereby he or she agrees to take Disulfiram in the event that sobriety becomes impossible to achieve or maintain.

If the client agrees to try Disulfiram, he or she must be medically cleared first (see Chapter 7). It is useful to have a relationship established with a physician who is knowledgeable about Disulfiram use and who is willing to prescribe it when indicated. The client's primary care physician may also be willing to serve in this role once the client's treatment plan is explained.

The Disulfiram Monitor

An important component of successful Disulfiram treatment is having a monitor (Azrin et al., 1982). Although the monitor typically is a spouse or a close friend, it can be any concerned person who is willing to spend the time and energy to help the client. Both the client and the monitor must understand that the monitor's role is not a punitive one but a supportive one.

CRA offers a specific Disulfiram compliance procedure. In a session with both the client and monitor, first have them identify a time that they usually spend together every day. Ideally, the Disulfiram should be taken the same time and place each day, for consistency is the key to establishing a successful routine. Next, train the monitor to give the Disulfiram in a positive way that will help promote sobriety. This also is an opportunity to teach both the client and the monitor basic, positive communication skills (described below) using the Disulfiram procedure as the forum.

The actual training of the monitor begins with a physical description of the Disulfiram pill and a demonstration of how to prepare it. Place the pill in a clear glass and pour in water until the glass is half full. Allow the pill to dissolve for a minute and crush the remainder with a spoon. Hand the glass to the client and watch him or her drink it. Praise the individual for taking it and for all that he or she has achieved since deciding to stop drinking. Encourage the monitor to use statements that express understanding, show acceptance of partial responsibility, and offer to help. Role-play numerous possible scenarios until both participants are comfortable with the procedures. The monitor will then administer the Disulfiram in the session. This allows you to support and praise the couple for their hard work and to troubleshoot any problems.

CRA Treatment Plan

The next step is to take the information collected thus far and to incorporate it into CRA's formal treatment plan. The foundation of this comprehensive working plan is based on two instruments: the Happiness Scale and the Goals of Counseling form.

The first step in developing the treatment plan is to have the client complete the Happiness Scale (Figure 15.2). This scale has 10 life categories: drinking/sobriety, job or educational progress, money management, social life, personal habits, marriage/family relationships, legal issues, emotional life, communication, and general happiness. The client indicates how happy or satisfied he or she currently is with an area by rating each category on a scale of 1 (completely unhappy) to 10 (completely happy).

The Happiness Scale serves several purposes: (1) it provides a precounseling baseline that indicates which areas of the client's life are in most need of immediate attention, (2) it motivates the client by pinpointing specific problem areas, (3) it evaluates ongoing progress in therapy, and (4) it helps the client discriminate problem areas from nonproblem areas. Information from the initial Happiness Scale is used in goal setting during the second phase of developing the treatment plan. You can also monitor progress by having the client complete a new Happiness Scale at the start of each session.

The next step in formulating a CRA treatment plan is completing the Goals of Counseling form with the client (a sample page is shown in Figure 15.3). The 10 life areas on the Happiness Scale are found on this second form as well. The Goals of Counseling form helps you set specific goals for each of the client's major problem areas. You also use it to list the strategies the client will employ to reduce or eliminate the problems. Put the desired changes in quantifiable terms whenever possible. This makes it easier to measure progress.

One of the advantages of using the Goals of Counseling form is that it highlights the fact that the problem drinking is only one of the life areas needing attention. Many clients already are cognizant of these other problem areas and drink excessively to cope with them. The ultimate goal of CRA is to foster happiness in all aspects of the client's life, thereby reducing the chance that he or she will risk losing this happiness by returning to drinking.

The guidelines for completing the form are in line with CRA's overall positive approach. Teach clients to adhere to three basic rules:

1. Keep statements brief.
2. Always state goals in a positive way.
3. Use only observable and measurable behaviors.

Figure 15.2　Happiness Scale

This scale is intended to estimate your *current* happiness with your life on each of the 10 areas listed. You are to circle one of the numbers (1–10) beside each area. Numbers toward the left end of the 10-unit scale indicate various degrees of unhappiness, whereas numbers toward the right end of the scale reflect increasing levels of happiness. Ask yourself this question as you rate each life area: "How happy am I *with this area of my life?*" In other words, state according to the numerical scale (1–10) exactly how you feel today. Try to exclude all feelings of yesterday and concentrate only on the feelings of today in each of the life areas. Also try *not* to allow one category to influence the results of the other categories.

	COMPLETELY UNHAPPY								COMPLETELY HAPPY
1. Drinking/Sobriety	1	2	3	4	5	6	7	8	9	10
2. Job or Educational Progress	1	2	3	4	5	6	7	8	9	10
3. Money Management	1	2	3	4	5	6	7	8	9	10
4. Social Life	1	2	3	4	5	6	7	8	9	10
5. Personal Habits	1	2	3	4	5	6	7	8	9	10
6. Marriage/Family Relationships	1	2	3	4	5	6	7	8	9	10
7. Legal Issues	1	2	3	4	5	6	7	8	9	10
8. Emotional Life	1	2	3	4	5	6	7	8	9	10
9. Communication	1	2	3	4	5	6	7	8	9	10
10. General Happiness	1	2	3	4	5	6	7	8	9	10

Name _____

Date _____

Figure 15.3 Goals of Counseling

Name: _____   Date: _____

PROBLEM AREAS/GOALS	INTERVENTION	TIME FRAME
1) In the area of drinking/sobriety, I would like:		
2) In the area of job/educational progress, I would like:		
3) In the area of money management, I would like:		

258

You can use behavioral rehearsal and modeling to shape the client's behavior when filling out these forms. Rather than beginning with a client's most difficult problem areas, start with a category from the Happiness Scale that the client has noted as having at least a fair amount of satisfaction. This enables the client to practice setting goals and devising interventions for more manageable problems first.

Basic Skills Training

Skills training is an essential ingredient in the CRA package. We have modified skills training techniques over the years to incorporate parts of other effective behavioral training programs. In this chapter, we will present three examples of skills training: communication skills training, problem-solving training, and drink refusal training.

Communication Skills Training

CRA recognizes that communication skills are an integral part of one's basic repertoire of skills. Our goal in teaching these skills is to increase positive interchanges. In its most simplified version, CRA's three major components of communication skills training are (1) giving an understanding statement, (2) taking partial responsibility, and (3) offering to help. We begin with giving an understanding statement. This introduces feelings into the discussion, particularly empathy. We view a partial responsibility statement as an indication that the speaker is willing to accept his or her role in creating and solving a specific problem. Yet another way to help solve a problem through positive communication is by offering to help. In this training, your client role-plays each type of communication response during the session, to ensure that he or she fully comprehends the meaning of each statement. This also allows you to shape the client's behaviors. More complex versions of communication skills training are available in the marital therapy section of this chapter.

Problem-Solving Training

The main purpose of the problem-solving procedure is to teach a client new and more appropriate strategies for coping with his or her stressful environment without resorting to alcohol use. We use a modified version of D'Zurilla and Goldfried's (1971) problem-solving approach. The following steps may be applied in an individual or group format:

1. *Defining the Problem*
   a. Help your client define the problem as specifically as possible.
   b. Show your client how to separate out any secondary or related problems.
2. *Generating Alternatives*
   a. Assure your client that brainstorming is welcomed when generating potential solutions.
   b. Inform your client that criticism of suggestions is inappropriate.
   c. Encourage your client to go for quantity; the more potential solutions, the better!
   d. Remind your client to stay within the problem area.
   e. Have your client state solutions in specific terms.
   f. Demonstrate for your client how combinations of solutions can be considered.
3. *Deciding on a Solution*
   a. Have your client eliminate any solutions that he or she would not feel comfortable attempting. No explanations are needed.
   b. Prompt your client to identify the probable consequences for each remaining alternative while evaluating its worth.
   c. Ask your client to decide on one solution and have him or her describe exactly how it will be carried out.
   d. Encourage your client to consider possible obstacles to enacting the solution.
   e. Assist your client in generating "back-up" plans to circumvent these obstacles.
   f. Have your client commit to trying the selected solution an agreed-upon number of times before the next session.
4. *Evaluating the Outcome*
   a. Review with your client the outcome at the next session and have your client rate his or her satisfaction with it.
   b. Determine with your client whether the solution needs to be modified, and assist in the process if necessary.
   c. If an entire new solution is required, have your client repeat the problem-solving procedure.

Problem-solving training plays an important role in teaching a client to become independent. You can illustrate the importance of this skill by relying on a problem-solving approach during sessions. Also, it is useful to give frequent homework assignments to the client, so that he or she can practice on current problems. When you give take-home tasks, be sure to review the results at the next session, offering feedback and reinforcement as indicated.

Drink Refusal Training

Typically, we set the stage for drink refusal training by asking the client to inform family members and close friends about his or her decision to stop drinking and to enlist their support. Next, we review the client's CRA Functional Analysis for Drinking Behavior chart. This reminds the client of his or her high-risk drinking situations, as well as the specific triggers. From here, we introduce drink refusal training, a type of assertiveness skills training. Essentially, we teach a client several ways to refuse a drink. Our procedure draws heavily from the work of Monti and colleagues (1989; see also Chapter 13).

Although many clients feel equipped to attempt sobriety with this degree of drink refusal training, others feel less confident. For the less confident, add a form of cognitive restructuring that uses the internal trigger section of the functional analysis. First, have the client review the types of thoughts and feelings that lead to drinking episodes. Then teach him or her how to substitute new thoughts for the negative or irrational ones. Sometimes the double-column technique is useful here. The client records the self-defeating trigger statement in one column and a positive counterstatement in the second. Help the client to generate this second column by challenging the rationality of the drinking trigger statements and offering alternative coping responses. As the client practices this thought substitution, have him or her try to imagine the new feelings that would automatically follow these new thoughts. Then ask the client to agree to using this cognitive restructuring procedure during the upcoming week on a trial basis. Review the results in the next session.

Job Club

Having a satisfying job encourages sobriety and provides many valuable positive reinforcers. Often we work with clients who do not need vocational training but who instead lack the skills necessary to *find* and *keep* gainful employment. The CRA approach to job-training utilizes behavioral principles in a step-by-step approach. There are five major job-finding areas: (1) developing a resume, (2) completing job applications, (3) generating job leads, (4) telephone skills training, and (5) interview rehearsal. Techniques

for keeping a job are addressed primarily in a problem-solving manner. There are full descriptions of job club procedures in the Meyers and Smith (in press) CRA book and in Azrin and Besalel's (1980) manual.

Social/Recreational Counseling

Most often, by the time a client enters into treatment, he or she is totally enmeshed in a "drinking culture" in which friendships and recreational activities center around drinking. Continued contact with such an environment can serve as a trigger for future relapse. But changing peer reference groups and developing healthier alcohol-free social outlets are not simple processes, and consequently require training during the early phase of CRA counseling.

It may be necessary to illustrate clearly the relationship between the client's drinking and his or her social activities. Ask the client first to identify friends and activities that always have been associated with the use of alcohol, and then do the same for nondrinking periods. Once this relationship becomes apparent, encourage the client to make a commitment to establish new friendships and to "try out" alternative social activities supportive of sobriety. Then help the client identify appealing recreational activities that he or she is willing to try. Frequently, it is worthwhile to discuss accessible local events in which alcohol is not a major element, and where clients can meet new nondrinking friends.

Identifying areas of interest is only the first step. Many clients are reluctant to follow through and actually participate in a novel activity, especially when they are sober. The process of "trying out" or experimenting with alternative activities is called *Reinforcer Sampling*. A client needs to sample activities in order to determine if there is any potential for enjoyment. If indicated, explore the basis for a client's reluctance to become involved in a new social network and problem-solve solutions.

Another technique for assisting a well-meaning client to reach a new social event is called *Systematic Encouragement* (Sisson & Mallams, 1981). It entails three major components: (1) Never assume that a client will make the first contact on his or her own. Once the client agrees to try a new function, a role-play of the initial phone call to the organization is conducted in the counseling session. After sufficient feedback and rehearsal, the client makes the phone call in the session. (2) Whenever possible, a contact person for the organization should be located on your community resource list. Make arrangements with this person either to escort the client to the event or to meet him or her at the door. (3) Review the experience with your client in the next session to determine the activity's reinforcement value. In other words, does the client want to attend again? Use problem-solving techniques to help the client overcome any obstacles to future attendance.

Another way to give clients an opportunity to develop and practice new social skills in a nonthreatening alcohol-free environment is to establish a *Social Club* similar to the one outlined by Hunt and Azrin (1973) and Mallams, Godley, Hall, and Meyers (1982). Typically, this is a weekly alcohol-free social event that is attended by clients in the recovery process. It offers several advantages over the available programs in most communities: (1) Many clients are more inclined to attend Social Club rather than church or AA functions, because they are not required to prescribe to any specific religious or recovery belief system. (2) Single, socially-isolated clients can receive social support and develop nondrinking friendships. (3) All club functions are typically free-of-charge or very low in cost. (4) Through *Reinforcer Sampling* the club allows clients and their Concerned Others to experience a wide variety of social interactions. Informed decisions can then be made regarding which ones are most satisfying. (5) The club serves as a stepping-stone back into the larger society by providing the problem drinker with a "safe" place to work on sobriety.

CRA's Marital Therapy

If the marital situations of most clients do not improve significantly, you can anticipate that any changes in the client's drinking problem will be temporary. CRA's relationship counseling focuses on teaching skills that can be applied to present day problems. It views most marital conflicts as arising from unrealistic expectations, inadequate communication and problem-solving skills, and poor attempts to control the partner's behavior through aversive means.

Marriage Happiness Scale

Begin the marital session by explaining the importance of working on the couple's relationship and by setting positive expectations for change. The second step differs, depending on whether the client is on Disulfiram. If he or she is, re-

hearse the Disulfiram compliance procedure. Then give each individual a Marriage Happiness Scale to complete independently. The scale is modeled after the Happiness Scale but is adapted for couples work. The problem categories include household responsibilities, raising the children, social activities, money management, communication, sex and affection, job or school, emotional support, and partner's independence. The tenth category, general happiness, provides a summary of the couples' current situation. Instruct the couple to indicate how satisfied they presently feel *with their partner* in these 10 life areas.

Perfect Marriage Form

Once they each have completed a Marriage Happiness Scale, review the results with them. Then begin specifying the behaviors that need to be changed to enhance the couple's relationship in the designated problem areas. The Perfect Marriage form (a sample page is shown in Figure 15.4) facilitates this process. Both partners independently identify behaviors that they would like to see their spouse change. Begin with a category that both partners rated highly on their Marriage Happiness Scale. Instruct the client and partner to fill in the blanks by being brief, positive, and stating in a measurable way what they would like to see their partner do. Most couples need help with this. Depending on the couple's abilities, you may decide to rehearse several examples of requests within one category before assigning homework to continue.

Daily Reminder to Be Nice

Next, ask the couple if they remember the types of "little things" they used to do for each other that they do not routinely bother with now. Then move them toward reestablishing a relationship that favors pleasant interactions by introducing a Daily Reminder to Be Nice form. This chart lists seven general categories of "pleasing" behaviors that happy couples often engage in and distressed couples rarely do: expressing appreciation for something the partner does, offering compliments, giving a pleasant surprise, visibly expressing affection, devoting complete attention to a pleasant conversation, initiating pleasant conversation, and offering to help. Ask the couple to think of several behaviors in each group that they would like to see their partner do. Then have them take turns giving specific examples to each other. Once the couple agrees

Figure 15.4   Perfect Marriage

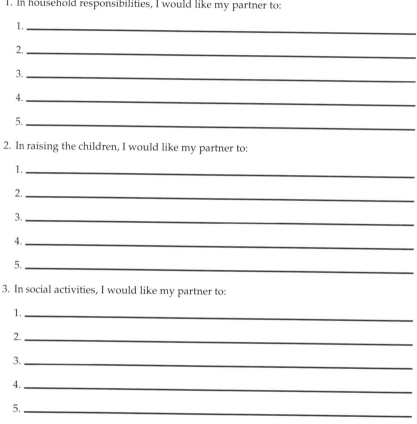

Under each area listed below, write down what activities would occur in what would be for *you* an ideal marriage. Be brief, be positive, and state in a specific and measurable way what you would like to occur.

1. In household responsibilities, I would like my partner to:

    1. _____

    2. _____

    3. _____

    4. _____

    5. _____

2. In raising the children, I would like my partner to:

    1. _____

    2. _____

    3. _____

    4. _____

    5. _____

3. In social activities, I would like my partner to:

    1. _____

    2. _____

    3. _____

    4. _____

    5. _____

to use the form, stress the importance of making a commitment to carry out specific caring behaviors *regardless* of whether their partner follows through with his or her part. This usually ends the first marital session.

Subsequent marital therapy sessions often begin by focusing on specific tasks:

1. Performing the Disulfiram compliance procedure (if applicable)
2. Completing new Marriage Happiness Scales
3. Reviewing the Daily Reminder to Be Nice forms
4. Reminding the couple of new skills that were taught the previous week (e.g., problemsolving) and asking them to demonstrate the skills in a relevant role-play

Communication Skills Training

Much of the remainder of subsequent sessions is devoted to teaching communication skills. The simplified version we presented earlier typically is added to the guidelines used when completing the Perfect Marriage forms. Give the couple a copy of the communication rules listed below. Explain that the first three should look familiar because they were introduced along with the Perfect Marriage form. The last three were taught earlier as part of the individual client's training in communication skills. The communication rules for a couple are:

1. Be *brief* and present *one* issue at a time.
2. Be *positive* and *avoid* all *blaming* statements.

3. Define the issue clearly and in *measurable* terms.
4. Try to view the issue from your partner's perspective, and offer an *understanding statement* to that effect.
5. Accept *partial responsibility* for any problem raised.
6. *Offer* to *help*.

Start the role-plays by referring to the couple's Perfect Marriage forms where they have specified brief, positive, and measurable requests. Have the client and the spouse take turns making a request of each other, while following all the steps of good communication skills. Be prepared to provide plenty of guidance and support. After requests have been presented and polished, be sure to discuss with each individual what it felt like to converse with their partner in this new manner.

The following dialogue is a couple's first attempt at making verbal requests based on their Perfect Marriage forms. The therapist helps to incorporate all of the basic communication skills.

> *THERAPIST:* I'm really impressed with the work you both put into completing your Perfect Marriage forms this week. Now it's time to practice making those requests out loud to your partner. Let's begin by reviewing the rules you followed for making requests. Start with only one brief request, state it in positive terms, and make sure it's measurable. If you check back with your entries on your Perfect Marriage forms, you'll notice that your requests already follow these three rules. So let's pick a category from the form that you rated fairly high to begin with, and practice adding the next three parts of a good conversation: Making an understanding statement, accepting partial responsibility for the problem, and offering to help. What category would you like to try?
>
> *BUD:* How about "social activities"? We each rated that an 8 on the Marriage Happiness Scale. What do you say, Glo?
>
> *GLORIA:* Sounds OK to me.
>
> *THERAPIST:* Good. Bud, why don't you start us off. Look at what you wrote, and present the basic request to Gloria. We'll help you polish it up in a minute.
>
> *BUD:* I'm just going to jump right in. Glo, I'd like you to come bowling with me on Tuesday nights.
>
> *THERAPIST:* Good job, Bud. You followed the three basic rules. But don't respond yet, Gloria. We're not done! Bud, I take it that your wife has not been going bowling with you on Tuesdays?
>
> *BUD:* No. She says she's too busy.
>
> *THERAPIST:* Then it's a perfect opportunity for you to add the next three parts of a good conversation. Can you first make an understanding statement and then accept partial responsibility?
>
> *BUD:* Sure. Gloria, I know you *are* really busy all of the time, especially in the middle of the week. And I

> know I don't make it easy, because I hardly ever help with the dishes. Maybe you'd have time to join me if I made a point of doing the dishes on Tuesday nights.
>
> *THERAPIST:* Bud, Bud, you're way ahead of me! That was great! Not only did you make an understanding statement and accept partial responsibility but you offered to help too. So let's see what Gloria thought of it. Now remember, you're not allowed to say "no" outright. You could offer an alternative instead.
>
> *GLORIA:* I'd be happy to go bowling with you on Tuesday nights Bud, as long as you're not drinking. And it *would* really help if you did the dishes those nights.
>
> *THERAPIST:* Excellent. This appears to be straightforward, but let's summarize and make sure you both have agreed to the same thing. Gloria, you've agreed to go bowling with Bud on Tuesday nights if he does the dishes and as long as he's sober.
>
> *GLORIA:* That's right.
>
> *THERAPIST:* Bud, do you agree to this?
>
> *BUD:* Of course; it was my idea. And I don't intend to drink at the bowling alley or any place else.
>
> *THERAPIST:* Great job. You seem to have a good understanding of the process. Gloria, now it's your turn to request something in the area of "social activities." Why don't you take a look at your Perfect Marriage form for that category.
>
> *GLORIA:* Bud, I would really enjoy it if you took me out to dinner once a week—not at a really expensive restaurant, but not at a fast-food place either. I'd prefer Friday or Saturday night.
>
> *THERAPIST:* That's a good start. You were brief and you put it in measurable terms. I bet you could make it sound a little more positive though, if you told him exactly what type of restaurant you *did* want, as opposed to those you didn't.
>
> *GLORIA:* Oh, I see what you mean. Sure. I'd like to go to a medium-range restaurant in terms of price, like Chili Heaven or the American Burger Palace.
>
> *THERAPIST:* Excellent. Now, how about adding the last three parts: an understanding statement, a partial responsibility statement, and an offer to help.
>
> *GLORIA:* Bud, I know you're worried about our financial situation. I've even watched you lose sleep over it. I probably could save some money each week if I watched the newspaper for sales more. And then I could put part of this money I'd saved toward a meal out.
>
> *THERAPIST:* Sounds reasonable to me! And you included all three parts. Terrific! But Bud's opinion is what really counts.
>
> *BUD:* OK. I don't have a problem with that.
>
> *THERAPIST:* Good job. To make the agreement more concrete, I might suggest that you identify an amount of money that is affordable. You may also want to come up with a list of restaurants that fit your needs.

It is important to reinforce the couple for their efforts, and to guide them in their struggle to follow what may seem to be a long list of guidelines. You would next have the couple agree to granting their partner's revised request in the upcoming week. Again, be sure to check on the status of the assignment in the subsequent session, and help them modify the requests if necessary.

Relapse Prevention

CRA offers several approaches to relapse prevention. Actually the process begins with the identification of triggers during the completion of the initial functional analysis. But CRA later goes beyond this and offers a plan of action in the event that these triggers surface. The Early Warning System is a self-monitoring procedure designed to track a client's behaviors that are his or her antecedents to drinking. The system is most successful when a Concerned Other is trained in the procedure along with the client. Both individuals agree that if either one detects the return of old high-risk behaviors, they immediately will discuss in a prearranged fashion the next step to take in order to prevent a relapse. This could mean notifying the therapist, but problem-solving might suggest other possibilities.

CRA also offers a relapse prevention strategy that can be introduced after a relapse has occurred. It is based on the functional analysis principle but it uses a separate functional analysis form for a single relapse episode. The form enables you to break down the relapse into minute details to determine what precipitated it and how to prevent it in the future.

Begin the procedure in the same manner as the initial functional analysis, identifying external and internal triggers. Follow with a complete description of the drinking episode. Next, gather information about the short-term positive consequences of drinking in that situation. You may then either continue with the chart and outline the long-term negative consequences of the drinking, or instead inquire about alternative behaviors that also could have given the client those positive short-term consequences. Problem solving is productive here. Take this opportunity to show how the alternative behaviors could have provided the short-term positive consequences without the drinking-related long-term negative consequences. Once completed, use the relapse chart to review the triggers that led to the client's series of costly decisions. Then introduce clinical procedures such as cognitive restructuring and problem solving to train appropriate ways to cope in the future.

EFFECTIVENESS

The Earliest CRA Trials

Azrin and colleagues demonstrated in three well-designed alcohol studies that CRA was superior to standard treatment procedures. In the original matched control study with 16 alcoholic inpatients (Hunt & Azrin, 1973), one member of each pair was randomly assigned to receive CRA counseling. Subjects in the control group received the "standard treatment," which was the hospital's traditional Alcoholics Anonymous (AA) program.

Posttreatment results showed that subjects who received CRA counseling spent significantly less time drinking and in institutions than did standard treatment subjects, and significantly more time working and being with their families. More specifically, the six-month follow-up results found that CRA group members were drinking 14% of the follow-up days in contrast to the standard treatment group's report of 79% of the days. Striking results were noted in the other areas as well.

A second CRA trial showed similar results (Azrin, 1976). This study introduced four new procedures: a prescription of Disulfiram, the Disulfiram compliance program and the early warning monitoring components discussed earlier, and a buddy system as a source of continued social support. The control group received the hospital's standard disease model services. The study was conducted with nine pairs of inpatients using a matched control design.

The CRA group showed superior outcomes relative to their control counterparts at the six-month follow-up. The percent of follow-up time spent drinking averaged 2% for the CRA group and 55% for the control group. Also, 20% of the CRA group was unemployed compared to 56% of the control group. Significant differences also were found for the number of nights spent away from one's family and for institutionalized days. Results were still impressive at the time of the two year follow-up; the abstention rate for the CRA group was 90%.

Application of CRA to Outpatients

The third CRA study was the first one to treat outpatients (Azrin et al., 1982). It examined the contribution of the Disulfiram compliance program by contrasting it with the traditional procedure for dispensing Disulfiram (Antabuse).

Eligible subjects were randomly assigned to one of three treatment conditions. The traditional group ($n = 14$) consisted of 12-step counseling plus a Disulfiram prescription. The second group, Antabuse Assurance ($n = 15$), received this same program, but were also instructed in the Disulfiram compliance procedure discussed earlier. The third group, CRA Plus Antabuse Assurance ($n = 14$), received the CRA procedures introduced in the earlier studies and several new ones: sobriety sampling, Disulfiram administration during the first session, drink refusal training, and relaxation training.

The two groups that included the Antabuse Assurance component reported the highest abstinence rates overall. While all three groups achieved almost complete abstinence during the first month of treatment, differences emerged throughout the remainder of the six-month follow-up. In the final month of follow-up, the abstinence rates for the Antabuse Assurance, CRA Plus Antabuse Assurance, and traditional treatment were 74%, 97%, and 45%, respectively. The couples in the Antabuse Assurance group performed better than the single subjects, to the point of matching the CRA Plus Antabuse Assurance group's success on several variables. Noteworthy differences in unemployment rates also were found between the traditional group and the CRA Plus Antabuse Assurance subjects.

Examination of the Social Club Component of CRA

Another study examined the Social Club component of CRA (Mallams et al., 1982). The Social Club was created primarily to provide an alcohol-free recreational environment that would be available during high-risk drinking times. The control group, Minimum Awareness ($n = 16$), was informed about the Social Club and given directions on how to locate it. The experimental group, Encouragement ($n = 19$), received additional interventions: repeated contacts by a counselor to encourage the subject to attend, flyers describing upcoming club events, transportation to and from the club, membership cards, and problem-solving assistance from a counselor if obstacles interfered with attendance.

The Encouragement group attended the Social Club more often than the Minimum Awareness group. More importantly, the members of the Encouragement group reported an average daily alcohol consumption of 0.8 ounce, which was significantly less than that of the Minimum Awareness group's average of 3.3 ounces.

CRA with Significant Others

Sisson and Azrin (1986) evaluated the viability of using CRA procedures for working with a problem drinker's Significant Other. In this trial, a concerned nondrinking family member was taught how to decrease the likelihood of further physical abuse, how to increase an uninterested problem drinker's motivation for change and treatment, and how to later assist in that treatment.

Subjects were randomly assigned to either the traditional program ($n = 5$) that centered around a group education, disease concept approach to alcoholism, or the CRA program ($n = 7$). The latter included training in awareness of alcohol problems, discussions of the positive consequences for not drinking, the scheduling of activities that competed with drinking, the introduction of outside activities for the nondrinker, training in how to respond when the problem drinker was drinking, learning how to allow the drinker to accept responsibility for the consequences of drinking episodes, instruction in how to handle dangerous situations, and increasing awareness of optimal moments for suggesting treatment to the drinker.

Six of the seven drinkers whose Significant Others were involved in the CRA group initiated treatment. None of the control group drinkers sought treatment. Drinkers associated with Significant Others in the CRA group decreased their average number of drinking days by more than half during the time that only the nondrinker was in treatment. This dropped significantly lower when the drinker entered treatment. This was not the pattern noted for drinkers whose Significant Other was involved in the traditional program. Three months into treatment, these individuals were still drinking nearly the same number of days per month as they had been during the baseline.

The Megatable Review

An innovative review of controlled alcohol treatment programs, including CRA, was conducted recently by Miller and colleagues. It considered the methodological quality of the studies and the strength of the support for treatment efficacy. CRA was ranked fourth out of 43 treatment modalities in terms of the Cumulative Evidence Score (see Chapter 2).

Ongoing Controlled CRA Trials

We currently have two ongoing controlled CRA trials that target alcohol abusing or dependent individuals. The first is a replication and extension of the original CRA outpatient trial (Azrin et al., 1982), and the second is an application of

CRA to a homeless population. Results should be ready for presentation in 1995.

CRA for Other Substance Abuse Problems

In recent years CRA has been combined with a contingency management program and used with cocaine dependent individuals. Promising results have been found in three separate studies (Budney, Higgins, Delaney, Kent & Bickel, 1991; Higgins et al., 1991; 1993). A trial of CRA with a heroin abusing population also is in progress.

REFERENCES

Clinical Guidelines

Azrin, N. H., and Besalel, V. A. (1980). *Job club counselor's manual.* Baltimore: University Park Press. The authors present a step-by-step explanation of how to find a suitable job. It includes items such as developing a resume, preparing for job interviews, and following-up on phone calls. Forms and charts are provided.

Meyers, R. J., and Smith, J. E. (in press). *Treating alcohol abuse: The Community Reinforcement Approach.* New York: Guilford. This manual provides a theoretical framework for CRA, and a detailed description of each procedure. Examples of therapist and client dialogues are included.

Research References

Azrin, N. H. (1976). Improvements in the community reinforcement approach to alcoholism. *Behaviour Research and Therapy, 14,* 339–348.

Azrin, N. H., Naster, B. J., and Jones, R. (1973). Reciprocity counseling: A rapid learning-based procedure for marital counseling. *Behaviour Research and Therapy, 11,* 365–382.

Azrin, N. H., Sisson, W., Meyers, R., and Godley, M. (1982). Alcoholism treatment by Disulfiram and community reinforcement therapy. *Journal of Behavior Therapy & Experimental Psychiatry, 13,* 105–112.

Budney, A. J., Higgins, S. T., Delaney, D. D., Kent, L., and Bickel, W. K. (1991). Contingent reinforcement of abstinence with individuals abusing cocaine and marijuana. *Journal of Applied Behavior Analysis, 24,* 657–665.

D'Zurilla, T. J., and Goldfried, M. R. (1971). Problem solving and behavior modification. *Journal of Abnormal Psychology, 78,* 107–126.

Higgins, S. T., Budney, A. J., Bickel, W. K., Hughes, J. R., Foerg, F., and Badger, G. (1993). Achieving cocaine abstinence with a behavioral approach. *American Journal of Psychiatry, 150,* 763–769.

Higgins, S. T., Delaney, D. D., Budney, A. J., Bickel, W. K., Hughes, J. R., Foerg, F., and Fenwick, J. W. (1991). A behavioral approach to achieving initial cocaine abstinence. *American Journal of Psychiatry, 148,* 1218–1224.

Hunt, G. M., and Azrin, N. H. (1973). A community-reinforcement approach to alcoholism. *Behaviour Research and Therapy, 11,* 91–104.

Mallams, J. H., Godley, M. D., Hall, G. M., and Meyers, R. J. (1982). A social-systems approach to resocializing alcoholics in the community. *Journal of Studies on Alcohol, 43,* 1115–1123.

Monti. P. M., Abrams, D. B., Kadden, R. M., and Cooney, N. L. (1989). *Treating alcohol dependence* (pp. 20–76). New York: Guilford.

Sisson, R. W., and Azrin, N. H. (1986). Family-member involvement to initiate and promote treatment of problem drinkers. *Behavior Therapy and Experimental Psychiatry, 17,* 15–21.

Sisson, R. W., and Mallams, J. H. (1981). The use of systematic encouragement and community access procedures to increase attendance at Alcoholics Anonymous and Al-Anon meetings. *American Journal of Drug and Alcohol Abuse, 8,* 371–376.

CHAPTER 16

Psychotropic Medications

Lisa A. Rone
Sheldon I. Miller
Richard J. Frances

OVERVIEW

Clinicians have long used psychotropic medications in the treatment of alcohol dependence for several reasons (for reviews, see Charnoff, Kissin, & Reed, 1963; Ditman, 1967; Kissin, 1975; Kissin & Gross, 1968; Miller & Hester, 1986; Peachey & Naranjo, 1984). First, there is the need for medications to ameliorate the symptoms of withdrawal during alcohol detoxification. Second, some authors have noted that often there is a close association between alcohol dependence and other psychiatric problems, such as depression and anxiety, for which psychotropics are clearly a useful form of treatment (Anthenelli & Schuckit, 1993). Last, there is a continuing interest in medications, including psychotropics, which may have the potential to reduce alcohol consumption or to attenuate its effects, even in the absence of other psychopathology (Volpicelli, Alterman, Hayashida, & O'Brien, 1992; Extein & Gold, 1993).

The efficacy of psychotropics, particularly benzodiazepines, is well established in the treatment of alcohol withdrawal symptoms (for reviews, see Favazza, 1982; Schuckit, 1984; Thompson, 1978; Zimberg, 1982). Although

some authors promote new possibilities for the use of opioid antagonists (Volpicelli et al., 1992; O'Malley et al., 1992; Volicelli, Davis, & Olgin, 1986), we do not think there is sufficient evidence that any psychotropic has been proven useful as a *primary* therapeutic tool for alcohol dependence. At present, psychotropic medications are adjuncts to behavioral and psychosocial therapies.

In this chapter, we will outline procedures for using psychotropics during detoxification and rehabilitation. Since the use of the antidipsotropic drugs, including Disulfiram (Antabuse®), is covered in Chapter 8, we will not discuss them here.

SPECIAL CONSIDERATIONS

There are certain side effects and risks associated with the use of medications of any kind. However, the use of psychotropic medication requires some special considerations when treating patients with alcohol dependence. Sedative-hypnotic medications require particular consideration since they are cross-reactive with alcohol. When used in detoxification or when treating patients with other psychiatric illnesses in addition to alcohol dependence, you should prescribe drugs from the benzodiazepine class conservatively and closely monitor patients to prevent abuse or the development of cross-dependency. Such careful monitoring is particularly important for alcohol-dependent patients who also abuse other substances. These patients represent an increasingly large proportion of the clinical population of alcohol-dependent patients (Schuckit, 1984; Zimberg, 1982). As Peachey and Naranjo (1984) have discussed, the primary criterion for any successful therapy in the treatment of alcohol dependency is the facilitation of continued abstinence, not the creation of new dependencies.

Although psychotropics have no place in the rehabilitative treatment of the "uncomplicated" alcohol-dependent patient after detoxification, alcohol dependency is seldom a single disorder. We recommend that you distinguish between primary and secondary dependency. *Primary alcohol dependency* (although not incorporated in the *DSM-IV* criteria for diagnosis due to its etiological implication) is generally conceptualized as an entity that is unaccompanied by a prior history of other psychiatric illnesses (Allen & Frances, 1985; Goodwin & Guze, 1977; Schuckit, 1973, 1983, 1984, 1986; Solomon, 1982; Zimberg, 1982). In some studies, approximately 70% of alcohol-dependent patients are in this category (Cadoret & Winokur, 1974; Schuckit & Winokur, 1972; Sedlacek & Miller, 1982). Although primary alcohol-dependent patients may present with other symptoms suggestive of concomitant psychopathology, successful cessation of drinking will often result in improvement in other problem areas, including general life problems (Miller, Hedrick, & Taylor, 1983).

Secondary alcohol dependence accompanies a preexisting psychiatric disorder. Most patients in this category may have an underlying primary affective illness but it can also be accompanied by schizophrenia, anxiety disorders, attention deficit disorder, and a wide range of personality disorders that present as alcohol dependence (for a review, see Allen & Frances, 1985). Some studies suggest that 25 to 70% of patients seeking alcohol- or substance-abuse treatment have coexisting psychiatric disorders (Drake & Wallach, 1989; Ross, Glaser, & Germanson, 1988). The term *secondary alcohol dependence* does not imply a less severe or less important form of alcohol abuse. It may be difficult, in many cases, to get a clear picture retrospectively of which illness developed first—the primary psychiatric disorder or the alcohol dependence. There are two clues that help sort out this picture: a history of psychiatric symptoms that continue during alcohol-free intervals and a family history of psychiatric disorders.

However, even if the alcohol dependence is secondary to another disorder, treating the underlying pathology may not result in abstinence from alcohol. Although alcohol may have been used initially to self-medicate these underlying psychiatric problems, alcohol abuse often becomes a self-perpetuating disorder (Sedlacek & Miller, 1982; Woodruff, Guze, Clayton, & Carr, 1973).

Depression, either primary or secondary, is commonly associated with alcohol dependence (Allen & Frances, 1985; Keeler, Taylor, & Miller, 1979; Weissmen & Myers, 1980). Hence, the dangers of overdose and abuse are important factors to consider when prescribing medications. In alcohol-dependent patients who suffer from affective disorders, suicidal ideation or psychotic symptoms are common. The actual incidence of suicide in alcohol-dependent patients is as high as 15% (Frances, Franklin, & Flavin, 1987) and the majority of successful suicides overall were either alcohol-dependent, depressed, or both (Barraclough, Bunch, Nelson, & Sainbury, 1974; Dorpat & Ripley, 1960; Robins, Murphy, Wilkinson, Gassner, & Kayes, 1959).

Careful monitoring of patients' medical and psychiatric status during treatment is essential. Specifically, you need to monitor (1) compliance with therapy in general; (2) reported use of alcohol or other substances by the patient or significant others during treatment; (3) status of social and family relations; (4) financial and employment status; and (5) and any adverse effects of medication or the development of other medical or psychiatric problems.

CLINICAL APPLICATION

Psychotropics in Detoxification

The first phase of treatment of an acutely intoxicated patient involves evaluating the blood alcohol level, doing a drug screen, and conducting a physical examination. Psychotropics, particularly the benzodiazepines, are frequently indicated to treat or prevent the symptoms of withdrawal, including agitation, anxiety, irritability, sleeplessness, tremors, autonomic instability, and, in severe cases, hallucinations or frank seizures (Favazza, 1982; Schuckit, 1984; Sellers & Kalant, 1978). Such symptoms usually become pronounced within 12 to 60 hours after the cessation of drinking.

Although barbiturates (particularly pheno-barbital) have a history of use in the treatment of withdrawal symptoms, they may have a lower margin of safety, carrying a more serious risk of overdose and respiratory depression than the benzodiazepines. You may choose to use them in special cases of withdrawal (e.g., pregnant patients), but they carry a high cross-addiction potential.

Coadminister vitamin replacement therapy, particularly with thiamine, to treat the neurological or cognitive impairments such as disorientation or sixth nerve palsies, more suggestive of a Wernicke-Korsakoff syndrome (Frances & Franklin, 1987). Rapid administration during detoxification may prevent irreversible neurological sequelae. Give thiamine at 100 mg IM or PO for the first few days, accompanied by oral preparations of B- and C-complex vitamins.

Nonpharmacological inpatient "social setting" detoxification is effective for uncomplicated cases of mild withdrawal, as described by Femino & Lewis (1982). This approach involves managing patients in withdrawal in a quiet, secure hospital setting for two to seven days. During this time, staff monitor and help the patients to achieve nonpharmacological control.

If other supportive therapy fails within the first few hours, you should administer benzodiazepines. Using benzodiazepines for withdrawal symptoms is particularly desirable because they are pharmacologically similar to alcohol, have longer half-lives, have low liver toxicity, and have a generally low risk of respiratory depression or overdose. They help (1) reduce anxiety, including that associated with depression or other affective illnesses; (2) as hypnotics; (3) reduce autonomic hyperactivity and tremulousness; and (4) prevent seizures.

Vegetative symptoms of withdrawal indicating a need for medication include tachycardia, fever, systolic hypertension, gastrointestinal distress, tremor, and diaphoresis (Favazza, 1982; Greenblatt, Divoll, Abernethy, Ochs, & Shader, 1984; Peachey & Naranjo, 1984). You should assess the overall mental status of the patient, including any impairment in orientation, and decide whether to continue medications based on the patient's response and clinical condition. Although benzodiazepines are relatively safe,

overdose or cross-reactivity between them and abused substances can result in respiratory depression, ataxia, and an overall clinical decline. They also have a great potential for addiction themselves. To avoid the development of new substance dependencies, you should prescribe them for as short a period as possible during the initial phase of detoxification.

Some studies have demonstrated that carbamazepine (Tegretol) may be beneficial in reducing alcohol withdrawal symptoms in the initial stages of detoxification (Bjorkqvist, Isohanni, Makela, & Malinen, 1976; Malcom, Ballenger, Sturgis, & Anton, 1989). This method may be particularly useful if the alcohol-dependent patient is also already benzodiazepine dependent prior to the detoxification phase. There is some evidence that in addition to decreasing withdrawal symptoms from alcohol, carbamazepine may also decrease the severity of withdrawal from benzodiazepines (Schweizer, Rickels, Case, & Greenblatt, 1991).

After making a complete medical and psychiatric assessment of the patient, you may treat mild withdrawal symptoms on an outpatient basis in highly motivated patients with oral benzodiazepines (such as 100–200 mg of chlordiazepoxide daily in divided doses). Outpatient detoxification requires daily follow-up and a strong support system. In cases where continued alcohol use is likely, or where there are complicating medical problems, including concomitant psychiatric illnesses, inpatient or social setting detoxification is indicated. Patients with withdrawal syndromes severe enough to require hospitalization may be given oral or intravenous diazepam (2.5 mg/min) or oral chlordiazepoxide (25–50 mg every four to eight hours).

Most patients tolerate oral medications well, but choose the intravenous route when there is nausea and vomiting or the patient is at risk of developing delirium tremens and requires rapid treatment. If the patient is already combative and disoriented, administer intramuscular lorazepam (1–2 mg every three to four hours) for adequate and rapid control of the patient's behavior and withdrawal symptoms. Reduce the dosage gradually by about 20% daily over the next several days. For patients cross-addicted to other substances or benzodiazepines themselves, reduce the dosage more gradually (e.g., 10%).

Although the benzodiazepines are similar in their anxiolytic, sedative/hypnotic, and anticonvulsant properties, their pharmakokinetic profiles differ substantially (Greenblatt et al., 1984; Peachey & Naranjo, 1984). Diazepam, for example, has a long half-life and has particular value as a muscle relaxant and anticonvulsant. However, administer it carefully in patients with possible liver damage. Lorazepam (Ativan) does not utilize the hepatic mixed oxidase system for metabolism as much as the longer acting benzodiazepines. As such, it may be a safer choice for patients with hepatic or respiratory problems or in geriatric patients who may be on other medications affecting benzodiazepine metabolism. With the exception of lorazepam, do not give the benzodiazepines intramuscularly since absorption may be quite erratic by this route.

If a patient in severe withdrawal has a seizure disorder, a history of withdrawal seizures, or is at risk for developing seizures, coadminister anticonvulsant medication. We recommend IV diazepam over IV phenytoin since it has multiple therapeutic uses. However, you may want to follow this regimen by both oral benzodiazepines and oral phenytoin (100mg TID) for one to two weeks for seizure prevention. Magnesium sulfate is also effective for seizure prevention and may be administered intramuscularly for the first two or three days of detoxification.

If primarily associated with alcohol withdrawal, the risk of seizures should subside as detoxification continues. Seizures that persist after the patient's withdrawal symptoms are stabilized suggest the need for further neurological investigation.

Although benzodiazepines are the primary psychotropic tool in treating withdrawal and produce the fewest complications, clinicians frequently use a variety of other medications, including antipsychotics. However, we urge you to avoid the use of neuroleptics in the treatment of uncomplicated withdrawal. In addition to the risk of developing tardive dyskinesia, some neuroleptics, particularly the phenothiazines, decrease the seizure threshold. Carefully evaluate the symptoms of agitation or combativeness for which you might use neuroleptics and consider whether you can treat them with more appropriate agents, as discussed earlier.

However, if psychotic symptoms are prominent, distinguishing between a primary psychosis and hallucinosis and delusions accompanying severe withdrawal may be difficult (Peachey & Naranjo, 1984; Schuckit, 1982; Zimberg, 1982). Although alcoholic hallucinosis and paranoia may in some cases be symptomatic of an organic psychosis, less than 10% (no greater than in the general population) of alcohol-dependent patients are schizophrenic (Goodwin & Guze, 1977; Peachey & Naranjo, 1984; Schuckit, 1984). Symptoms of alcoholic psychosis generally subside as detoxification proceeds.

Many practitioners use a variety of other agents. In some cases, their efficacy has not been firmly established and associated risks and side effects may outweigh their potential benefits. However, many deserve mention.

Clonidine (Catapres), an alpha-agonist antihypertensive medication, can aid in treating opiate withdrawal symptoms (Charney et al., 1982; Charney et al., 1981; Franz, Hare, & McCloskey, 1982; Gold, Pottash, & Kleber, 1981). Some studies suggest it may have some efficacy in treating alcohol withdrawal (Peachey & Naranjo, 1984). Propanolol, a beta-blocker, can be used in small doses (0.1–0.5mg IV) in detoxification to control some of the autonomic hyperactivity associated with alcohol withdrawal and peripheral symptoms of tremor (Carlsson, 1971; Carlsson & Johansson, 1971; Gallant, 1982; Zilm, Sellers, McLeod, & Degani, 1975). Although propanolol may be useful in certain instances during detoxification, we do not recommend you use it routinely.

Historically, clinicians have used paraldehyde as a hypnotic agent during detoxification (Gallant, 1982; Schuckit, 1984). Like barbiturates, however, it is far more addicting and dangerous than the benzodiazepines. Others often recommend the use of antihistamines as hypnotics as an alternative to other psychoactive medications (Gallant, 1982). With some patients, the anticholinergic side effects of these medications may become problematic (Favazza, 1982).

There is some evidence that lithium can suppress withdrawal symptoms (Ho & Tsai, 1976; McMillan, 1981; Sellers, Cooper, Zilm, & Shankes, 1976). If you administer lithium, you must include regular monitoring of blood levels to prevent toxicity. Toxicity can be a serious problem in severe cases of withdrawal, since alcohol-dependent patients may acutely present with fluid and electrolyte imbalances. Currently, we do not recommend lithium for withdrawal.

Psychotropics in Rehabilitation

Although intoxication makes accurate psychiatric diagnoses more difficult, rehabilitation can start during detoxification for the patient with a clear mental status. A complete psychiatric assessment at this time should include a life history of alcohol use and any other substance abuse or psychiatric problems.

Some studies indicate a possible role for the opioid antagonists such as naloxone or naltrexone, as an adjunctive therapy during rehabilitation (Volpicelli et al., 1992; O'Malley et al., 1992; Volpicelli, Davis, & Olgin, 1986). These studies found a significantly lower relapse rate in alcohol-dependent patients when treated with these agents during the first three months of rehabilitation. Some researchers have suggested that the use of opioid antagonists may block opiate receptors that seem to be enhanced by alcohol and may contribute to increased alcohol craving (Volpicelli et al., 1986). However, at this time, no treatment regimen with the use of these agents has been firmly established in alcohol rehabilitation.

If indicated, you should begin and continue treatment of other psychiatric disorders with psychotropic medication in conjunction with behavioral and psychosocial rehabilitative therapies. For example, a patient with a clear history of bipolar disorder and a good response to lithium should be maintained on it. Similarly, a patient with schizophrenia or schizoaffective disorder will need maintenance on neuroleptics. Treatment for other patients may involve the use of tricyclics or the serotonin-reuptake inhibitors (such as fluoxetine, sertraline or paroxetine) for dysthymic patients or those with panic disorder. Serotonergic agents may additionally decrease alcohol use (as in rat studies: Alvarado, Contreras, Segovia-Riquelme, & Mardones, 1990; Volpicelli et al., 1992). A patient may require continuation of anticonvulsants for a coexisting seizure disorder, tricyclic agents or serotonin-reuptake inhibitors for a major depression, and a wide-range of concomitant treatments.

Depression is the most common psychiatric disorder among alcohol-dependent patients, and can be an impediment to rehabilitation. Antidepressants should be reserved for treatment of a concurrent major depression or dysthymia after a two- to four-week detoxification period. This assumes there are no medical or psychosocial contraindications or that the patient's psychiatric condition (such as severe depression or acute suicidal state) does not require earlier intervention. Depression generally remits in two to four weeks, when secondary to direct effects of alcohol are seen; therefore, this conservative approach is indicated.

Monoamine-oxidase inhibitors were once used more widely. Today, with safer medications, their utility is limited and should be used with particular caution in the alcohol-dependent population given the lethal consequences of noncompliance with a tyramine-free diet. However, take care when prescribing psychotropic medication to avoid abuse, cross-tolerance, or dangerous side effects that may develop from administering them to patients with alcohol or polysubstance abuse histories. Because the complex effects of alcohol on the liver may lead to either increased or decreased metabolism, it is important to closely monitor blood levels of medications, when possible, and the patient's clinical response.)

EFFECTIVENESS

Detoxification

The effectiveness of psychotropics, particularly the benzodiazepines, for relieving symptoms of withdrawal is well established (Favazza, 1982; Schuckit, 1984; Thompson, 1978; Zimberg, 1982).

Research continues to explore the usefulness of opiate antagonists in counteracting alcohol intoxication. A growing number of studies have shown that you can reduce or reverse the adverse effects of acute alcohol intoxication, including coma, with Naloxone (Cholewa, Pach, & Macheta, 1983; Ducodu, 1984; Guerin & Friedberg, 1982; Jeffreys, Flanagan, & Volans, 1980; Lyon & Anthony, 1982). Other studies, however, have refuted these findings (Mackenzie, 1983; Nuotto, Palva, & Lahdenranta, 1983). These agents are not routinely administered in alcohol or opiate detoxification.

Rehabilitation

There are a number of problems associated with evaluating the efficacy of psychotropic medications in alcohol rehabilitation. These problems include (1) differences in subject populations (e.g., dually diagnosed patients vs. primary alcohol-dependent patients); (2) inadequate or no control populations; (3) high dropout and noncompliance rates; (4) inconsistencies in outcome measures; (5) inadequate follow-up periods in which to evaluate outcomes; and (6) possible interactions between pharmacological and psychosocial therapies when combined in the same study. It is also difficult to control for the variability in socioeconomic factors among subjects.

You need to be aware of these potentially confounding factors when evaluating the data concerning the efficacy of psychotropics in alcohol rehabilitation.

Lithium

Some researchers suggest that giving lithium during rehabilitation can prevent the deficits of cognitive and motor performance produced by alcohol (Judd et al., 1977; Judd & Huey, 1984; Linnoila, Saario, & Maki, 1974). It may also possibly alter the subjective experience of intoxication and facilitate abstinence (Fawcett et al., 1987). Since lithium is an effective mood stabilizer for bipolar illness or schizoaffective disorder (Baastrup, Poulsen, Schou, Thomsen, & Amdisen, 1970; Coppen et al., 1971, 1973; Coppen, Montgomery, Gupta, & Bailey, 1976), it is not surprising that it is useful in treating a portion of alcohol-dependent patients (for reviews, see McMillan, 1981; Miller & Hester, 1986; Pond et al., 1981; Schou, 1978).

Controlled studies indicate that lithium is more helpful than placebo in reducing drinking in *depressed* alcohol-dependent patients (Fawcett et al., 1984; Kline, Wren, Cooper, Varga, & Canal, 1974; Merry, Reynolds, Bailey, & Coppen, 1976; Pond et al., 1981). Differences among studies with respect to psychiatric diagnoses of subjects, outcome measures, and high noncompliance and dropout rates make comparisons of experimental data difficult. However, we do not think that lithium is effective in the rehabilitation of alcohol-dependent patients *without* affective disorder.

Lithium has been shown to reduce alcohol consumption in laboratory animals (Ho & Tsai, 1976; Truitt & Vaughen, 1976). Some researchers suggest it may be a useful antidipsotropic for humans (Revusky, 1973; Revusky, Parker, Coombes, & Coombes, 1976; Revusky & Taukulis, 1975; Fawcett et al., 1987). However, at this juncture, it is not a well-established practice to prescribe lithium for alcohol-dependent patients without underlying primary affective disorders. There are several reasons for not using lithium in this group. First, lithium is a potentially dangerous medication. Therapeutic doses for bipolar illness can approach toxic levels, particularly in patients with other sources of fluid and electrolyte imbalances. Second, the aversive effects of lithium in maintaining sobriety are equivocal since toxic blood levels may also produce nausea and gastrointestinal distress unrelated to relapse (McMillan, 1981; Schou, 1978).

Third, blood levels must be carefully monitored in patients receiving lithium therapy. Until unequivocal evidence establishes its usefulness in treatment of primary alcohol dependence, the potential risks of using lithium in alcohol rehabilitation outweigh any clear benefit.

Carbamazepine

Some have suggested that carbamazepine therapy may be useful in treating alcohol withdrawal symptoms and in facilitating abstinence during the rehabilitative period (Bjorkqvist, Isohanni, Makela, & Malinen, 1976; Malcom, Ballenger, Sturgis, & Anton, 1989). However, as with lithium treatment, it is difficult to determine how much the medication may be stabilizing mood for those with an underlying mood disorder or the mood lability associated with some personality disorders during rehabilitation. There are many side effects associated with carbamazepine therapy such as hepatic dysfunction and leukopenia, and such risks make routine treatment of alcohol dependence with cabamazepine implausible.

Antidepressants

There is some evidence that antidepressants, as well as lithium, may be helpful in the rehabilitation of some alcohol-dependent patients (for reviews, see Baekeland, 1977; Miller & Hester, 1986; Alvarado, Contreras, Segovia-Riquelme, & Mardones, 1990; Fawcett et al., 1987). However, the current wisdom is that they primarily alter mood or general appetitive behavior rather than consistently alter drinking behavior per se. Comparison of results of the relatively few controlled studies of antidepressants is difficult because of a lack of consistency in (1) study design, (2) subject populations, (3) outcome measurements (such as reduction of drinking rates vs. amelioration of anxiety or depression, and (4) adequacy and length of follow-up.

Moreover, the problem of effective dosage and that of possible drug interactions in some studies combining antidepressants with other psychotropics (usually neuroleptics or benzodiazepines) has not always been adequately addressed (Baekeland, 1977). This issue is particularly difficult with agents for which there are no measurable therapeutic blood levels, as with the serotonin-reuptake inhibitors.

Borg (1983) found that zimelidine, a serotonin-reuptake inhibitor (not marketed in the United States) can reduce drinking in alcohol-dependent patients. Others have found the tricyclic antidepressant imipramine (Tofranil) to be more effective than placebo in preventing recurrence of drinking, either when administered separately (Baekeland & Lundwall, 1975; Butterworth, 1971; Shaw, Donley, Morgan, & Robinson, 1975; Wilson, Alltop, & Riley, 1970) or in combination with chlordiazepoxide (Librium) (Kissin & Gross, 1968; Kissin, Platz, & Su, 1979). Outcome measures in these studies all varied from reduction in alcohol consumption to relief in anxiety and depressive symptoms to other unspecified "improvement" measurements (Butterworth, 1971).

Butterworth and Watts (1971) found doxepin (Sinequan), another tricyclic, was more effective than chlordiazepoxide in reducing anxiety and depression in alcohol-dependent male patients. This finding was consistent with that of Overall, Brown, Williams, & Neil (1973), who found that chlordiazepoxide was less effective than either mesoridazine or amitriptyline (Elavil). Although some have postulated that serotonin-reuptake inhibitors may reduce drinking (Alvarado, Con-treras, Segovia-Riquelme, & Mardones, 1990), few studies support the notion. Additionally, there are no data supporting that antidepressants are more effective in controlling alcohol use than psychosocial therapies. In fact, Kissin and colleagues (Kissin et al., 1970) found that the combination of imipramine and chlordiazepoxide was less effective than psychotherapy. Until more unequivocal data are available, we recommend that you use antidepressants only for treatment of affective disorders that persist after sobriety has been achieved.

Tranquilizers

As we discussed earlier, you should limit the use of sedative-hypnotic and anxiolytic agents (barbiturates or benzodiazepines) to detoxification only. These medications present great potential for producing cross-dependence, synergism with alcohol, and the danger of overdose (Zimberg, 1982). Hoff (1961) initially found a higher proportion (72%) of patients with reduced alcohol consumption after being treated with chlordiazepoxide relative to matched controls (52% reduction in drinking scores). Subsequent studies, however, have failed to show significant differences between chlordiazepoxide-treated subjects and controls on measures of either drinking behavior or psychosocial functioning (Bartholomew & Guile, 1961; Charnoff et al., 1963; Mooney, Dittman, & Cohen, 1961; Rosenberg, 1974; Shaffer et al., 1964). There are no com-

pelling studies supporting the efficacy of benzodiazepines in treatment of alcohol dependence after detoxification.

Antipsychotics

All classes of neuroleptics are generally contraindicated in the rehabilitation of primary, uncomplicated alcohol dependence. Experimental data have not established their effectiveness and they have a relatively high risk of side effects, including the development of long-term difficulty with tardive dyskinesia. Small doses (25–50 mg) of Mellaril, a sedating neuroleptic, may be used as a hypnotic (Zimberg, 1982) on a short-term basis during detoxification. You may also need to use antipsychotic medications or increased doses of benzodiazepines for psychotic patients during detoxification and rehabilitation. Although early reports were hopeful (e.g., Fox & Smith, 1959), there is no evidence that any antipsychotic has a clear utility in treating nonpsychotic alcohol-dependent patients.

Opiate Antagonists and Other Psychotropics

Recent studies have demonstrated that opiate antagonists may show promise for facilitating abstinence during the rehabilitation phase for alcohol-dependent patients (Volpicelli, Alterman, Hayashida, & O'Brien, 1992; O'Malley et al., 1992; Volpicelli et al., 1986). Some researchers hypothesize that alcohol and dopamine condensations produce compounds called tetraisoquinolines that can directly stimulate opiate receptors. Additionally, endorphin binding may be enhanced by alcohol. Both of these mechanisms are blocked by opiate antagonists. Although they are still experimental models, they may explain why agents such as naloxone or naltrexone may reduce drinking and facilitate rehabilitation (Altshuler, Phillips, & Feinhandler, 1980; Ross, Hartmann, & Geller, 1976). Moreover, these agents block the psychomotor impairments in human subjects (Jeffcoate, Cullen, Herbert, Hastings, & Walder, 1979). However, some of these findings are still controversial (see Bird, Chester, Perl, & Starmer, 1982; Catley et al., 1981; Mattila, Nuotto, & Seppala, 1981; Whalley, Freedmen, & Hunter, 1981).

There is some evidence that bromocriptine, an ergot derivative that acts as a dopamine agonist, reduces alcohol consumption in heavy social drinkers (Naranjo et al., 1983). It may, however, simply produce an aversion to alcohol unrelated to specific neuropharmacological effects.

Investigators are continuing to search for new pharmacological therapies for alcohol dependence. However, research has not yet established the efficacy of continued treatment of uncomplicated dependence with psychotropic medications. Our position remains that, until their safety and efficacy has been proven, psychotropics are contraindicated for uncomplicated recovering patients with alcohol dependence.

REFERENCES

Clinical Guidelines

Anthenelli, R. M., & Schuckit, M. A. (1993). Affective & anxiety disorders and alcohol and drug dependence: diagnosis and treatment. *Journal of Addictive Diseases, 12*, 73–87.

Favazza, A. R. (1982). The alcohol withdrawal syndrome and medical detoxification. In E. M. Pattison & E. Kaufman (Eds.), *Encyclopedic handbook of alcoholism* (pp. 1068–1075). New York: Gardner Press. Provides guidelines for identifying patients in need of detoxification and for medical management of alcohol withdrawal, particularly the administration of benzodiazepine tranquilizers.

Forest, J. L., Frances, R. J., & Mooney, III, A. J. (1987). Alcoholism Rx: How you can help. *Patient Care*, Jan, 92–97. Provides detailed sample inpatient detoxification protocol, including dosages for magnesium sulfate and vitamins.

Frances, R. J., & Franklin, J. E. (1987). Alcohol-induced organic mental disorders. In R. E. Hales & S. C. Yodofsky (Eds.), *Textbook of neuropsychiatry* (pp. 410–431). Washington, DC: APP Press. Gives criteria for distinguishing between patients in need of inpatient versus outpatient treatment for withdrawal and detailed descriptions of withdrawal syndromes. Also provides background necessary for diagnosing specific alcohol-related organic mental illnesses and detailed regimes—both inpatient and outpatient—for the management of withdrawal.

Zimberg, S. (1982). *The clinical management of alcoholism*. New York: Brunner/Mazel. A thorough guide to the diagnosis and treatment of alcoholism in general, including detoxification, management of psychiatric-neurological complications, and various alternative approaches to rehabilitation.

Research

Allen, M. H., and Frances, R. J. (1985). Varieties of psychopathology found in patients with addictive disorders: A review. In R. Meyer (Ed.), *Psychopathology of addiction* (pp. 17–38). New York: Guilford.

Altschuler, H. L., Phillips, P. E., & Feinhandler, D. A. (1980). Alteration of ethanol self-administration by Naltrexone. *Life Sciences, 26*, 679–688.

Alvarado, R., Contreras, S., Segovia-Riguelme, N., & Mardones, J. (1990). Effects of serotonin uptake blockers and of 5-hydroxytryptophan on the voluntary consumption of ethanol, water and solid food by UChA and UChB rats. *Alcohol, 7*, 315–319.

Baastrup, P. C., Poulson, J. C., Schou, M., Thomsen, K., & Amdisen, A. (1970). Prophylactic lithium: Double blind discontinuation in manic-depressive and recurrent-depressive disorders. *Lancet, 2*, 326.

Baekeland, F. (1977). Evaluation of treatment methods in chronic alcoholism. In B. Kissin & H. Begleiter (Eds.), *The biology of alcoholism Vol. 5. Treatment and rehabilitation of the chronic alcoholic* (pp. 385–440). New York: Plenum.

Baekeland, F., & Lundwall, L. K. (1975). Effects of discontinuity of medication on the results of a double-blind drug study in outpatient alcoholics. *Journal of Studies on Alcohol, 36*, 1268–1272.

Barraclough, J., Bunch, J., Nelson, D., & Sainsbury, P. (1974). 100 cases of suicide: Clinical aspects. *British Journal of Psychiatry, 125*, 355–373.

Bartholomew, A. A., & Guile, L. A. (1961). A controlled evaluation of "Librium" in the treatment of alcoholics." *Medical Journal of Australia, 2*, 578–581.

Bird, K. D., Chester, G. B., Perl, J., & Starmer, G. A. (1982). Naloxone has no effect on ethanol-induced impairment of psychomotor performance in man. *Psychopharmacology, 76*, 193–197.

Bjorkquist, S. E., Isohanni, M., Mkela, R., & Malinen, L. (1976). Ambulant treatment of alcohol withdrawal symptoms with carbamazepine: A formal multicenter double-blind comparison with placebo. *Acta Psychiatrica Scand, 53*, 333–342.

Borg, A. (1983). Bromocriptine in the prevention of alcohol abuse. *Acta Psychiatrica, 68*, 100–110.

Butterworth, A. T. (1971). Depression associated with alcohol withdrawal: Imipramine therapy combined with placebo. *Quarterly Journal of Studies on Alcohol, 32*, 343–348.

Butterworth, A. T., & Watts, R. D. (1971). Treatment of hospitalized alcoholics with doxepin and diazepam: a controlled study. *Quarterly Journal of Studies on Alcohol, 32*, 78–81.

Cadoret, R., & Winokur, G. (1974). Depression in alcoholism. *Annals of the New York Academy of Science, 233*, 34–39.

Carlsson, C. (1971). Haemodynamic effects of adrenergic beta-receptor blockade in the withdrawal phase of alcoholism. *International Journal of Clinical Pharmacology, Supplement No. 3*, 61–63.

Carlsson, C., & Johansson, T. (1971). The psychological effects of propranolol in the abstinence phase of chronic alcoholics. *British Journal of Psychiatry, 119*, 605–606.

Catley, D. H., Jordan, C., Frith, C. D., Lehane, J. R., Rhodes, A. M., & Jones, J. G. (1981). Alcohol induced discoordination is not reversed by naloxone. *Psychopharmacology, 75*, 65–68.

Charney, D. S., Riordan, C. E., Kleber, H. D., Murburg, M., Braverman, P., Sternberg, D. E., Heninger, G. R., & Redmond, D. E. (1982). A safe, effective, and rapid treatment of abrupt withdrawal from methadone therapy. *Archives of General Psychiatry, 39*, 1327–1332.

Charney, D. S., Sternberg, D. E., Kleber, H. D., Heninger, G. R., & Redmond, D. E. (1981). The clinical use of clonidine in abrupt withdrawal from methadone. *Archives of General Psychiatry, 38,* 1273–1277.

Charnoff, S. M., Kissin, B., & Reed, J. I. (1963). An evaluation of various psychotherapeutic agents in the long-term treatment of chronic alcoholism. *American Journal of Medical Sciences, 246,* 172–179.

Cholewa, L., Pach, J., & Macheta, A. (1983). Effects of naloxone on ethanol-induced coma. *Human Toxicology, 2,* 217–219.

Coppen, A., Montgomery, S. A., Gupta, R. K., & Bailey, J. E. (1976). A double-blind comparison of lithium carbonate and maprotiline in the prophylaxis of affective disorders. *British Journal of Psychiatry, 128,* 479.

Coppen, A., Noguera, R., Bailey, J., Burns, B., Swani, M., Hare, E., & Gardner, R. (1971). Prophylactic lithium in affective disorders. *Lancet, 2,* 275.

Coppen, A., Peet, M., Bailey, J., Nogura, R., Burns, B., Swani, M. S., Maggs, R., & Gardner, R. (1973). Double-blind and open prospective studies of lithium prophylaxis in affective disorders. *Psychiatria, Neurologia, Neurochirugia, 76,* 501.

Ditman, K. S. (1967). Review and evaluation of current drug therapies in alcoholism. *International Journal of Psychiatry, 3,* 248–258.

Dorpat, T. L., & Ripley, H. S. (1960). A study of suicide in the Seattle area. *Comprehensive Psychiatry, 1,* 349–359.

Drake, R. E., & Wallach, M. A. (1989). Substance abuse among the chronically mentally ill. *Hospital & Community Psychiatry, 40,* 1041–1046.

Ducobu, J. (1984). Naloxone and alcohol intoxication. *Annals of Internal Medicine, 100,* 617–618.

Extein, I. L., & Gold, M. S. (1993). Hypothesized neurochemical models for psychiatric syndromes in alcohol and drug dependence. *Journal of Addictive Diseases, 12,* 29–43.

Favazza, A. (1982). The alcohol withdrawal syndrome and medical detoxification. In E. M. Pattison & E. Kaufman (Eds.), *Encyclopedic handbook of alcoholism* (pp. 1068–1075). New York: Gardner Press.

Fawcett, J., Clark, D. C., Aagesen, C. A., Pisani, V. D., Tilkin, J. M., Sellers, D., McGuire, M., & Gibbons, R. D. (1987). A double-blind, placebo-controlled trial of lithium carbonate therapy for alcoholism. *Archives of General Psychiatry, 44,* 248–256.

Fawcett, J., Clark, D. C., Gibbons, R. D., Aagesen, C. A., Pisani, V. D., Tilkin, J. M., Sellers, D., & Stutzman, D. (1984). Evaluation of lithium therapy for alcoholism. *Journal of Clinical Psychiatry, 45,* 494–499.

Femino, J., & Lewis, D. C. (1982). *Clinical pharmacology and therapeutics of the alcohol withdrawal syndrome* (Report No. 0372). Rockville, MD: National Institute on Alcohol Abuse and Alcoholism.

Fox, V., & Smith, M. A. (1959). Evaluation of a chemopsychotherapeutic program for the rehabilitation of alcoholics: Observations over a two-year period. *Quarterly Journal of Studies on Alcohol, 20,* 767–780.

Frances, R. J., & Franklin, J. E. (1987). Alcohol-induced organic mental disorders. In R. E. Hales & S. C. Yudofsky (Eds.), *Textbook of neuropsychiatry* (pp. 410–431). Washington, DC: APP Press.

Frances, R. J., Franklin, J., & Flavin, D. K. Suicide and alcoholism. *American Journal of Alcohol and Drug Abuse, 13,* 327–341.

Franz, D. N., Hare, B. D., & McCloskey, K. L. (1982). Spinal sympathetic neurons: Possible sites of opiate-withdrawal suppression by clonidine. *Science, 215,* 1643–1645.

Gallant, D. M. (1982). Psychiatric aspects of alcohol intoxication, withdrawal, and organic brain syndromes. In J. Solomon (Ed.), *Alcoholism and clinical psychiatry* (pp. 141–162). New York: Plenum.

Gold, M. S., Pottash, A. C., & Kleber, H. D. (1981). Outpatient clonidine detoxification. *Lancet, 1,* 621.

Goodwin, D. W., & Guze, S. B. (1977). *Psychiatric diagnosis* (2nd ed.). New York: Oxford University Press.

Gorski, T. T. (1977). *Neurologically-based alcoholism diagnostic systems* (NADS). Harvey, IL: Ingalls Memorial Hospital.

Greenblatt, D. J., Divoll, M., Abernethy, D. R., Ochs, H. R., & Shader, R. I. (1984). Benzodiazepine pharmokinetics: An overview. In G. D. Burrows, T. R. Norman, & B. Davies (Eds.), *Antianxiety agents* (pp. 79–92). Amsterdam: Elsevier.

Guerin, J. M., & Friedberg, G. (1982). Naloxone and ethanol intoxication. *Annals of Internal Medicine, 97,* 932.

Ho, A. K. S., & Tsai, C. S. (1976). Effects of lithium on alcohol preference and withdrawal. *Annals of the New York Academy of Science, 273,* 371–377.

Hoff, E. C. (1961). The use of pharmacological adjuncts in the psychotherapy of alcoholics. *Quarterly Journal of Studies on Alcohol,* Suppl. No. 1, 138–150.

Jeffcoate, W. J., Cullen, M. A., Herbert, M., Hastings, A. G., & Walder, C. P. (1979). Prevention of effects of alcohol intoxication by Naloxone. *Lancet, 1,* 1157–1159.

Jeffreys, D. B., Flanagan, R. F., & Volans, G. W. (1980). Reversal of ethanol induced coma with naloxone. *Lancet, 1,* 308–309.

Jeffreys, D. B., & Volans, G. W. (1983). An investigation of the role of the specific opioid antagonist naloxone in clinical toxicology. *Human Toxicology, 2,* 227–231.

Judd, L. L., Hubbard, R. B., Huey, L. Y., Attewell, P. A., Janowsky, D. S., & Takahashi, K. I. (1977). Lithium carbonate and ethanol induced "highs" in normal subjects. *Archives of General Psychiatry, 34,* 463–467.

Judd, L. L., & Huey, L. Y. (1964). Lithium antagonizes ethanol intoxication in alcoholics. *American Journal of Psychiatry, 141,* 1517–1521.

Keeler, M. H., Taylor, C. I., & Miller, W. R. (1979). Are all recently detoxified alcoholics depressed? *American Journal of Psychiatry, 1136,* 586–588.

Kielholz, P. (1970). Alcohol and depression. *British Journal of Addiction, 65,* 187–193.

Kissin, G. (1975). The use of psychoactive drugs in the long-term treatment of chronic alcoholics. *Annals of the New York Academy of Science, 252,* 385–395.

Kissin, B., & Gross, M. M. (1968). Drug therapy in alcoholism. *American Journal of Psychiatry, 125,* 31–41.

Kissin, B., Platz, & Su, W. H. (1970). Social and psychological factors in the treatment of chronic alcoholism. *Journal of Psychiatric Research, 8,* 13–27.

Kline, N. S., Wren, J. C., Cooper, T. B., Varga, E., & Canal, O. (1974). Evaluation of lithium therapy in chronic alcoholism. *American Journal of the Medical Sciences, 268,* 15–22.

Klotz, U., Ziegler, G., Rosenkranz, B., & Mikus, G. (1986) Does the benzodiazepine antagonist RO 15–1788 antagonize the action of ethanol? *British Journal of Pharmacology, 22,* 513–520.

Linnoila, M., Saario, I., & Maki, M. (1974). Effect of treatment with diazepam or lithium and alcohol on psychomotor skills related to driving. *European Journal of Clinical Pharmacology, 7,* 337–342.

Lyon, L. J., & Anthony, J. (1982). Reversal of alcoholic coma by naloxone. *Annals of Internal Medicine, 96,* 464–465.

Mackenzie, A. I. (1979). Naloxone in alcohol intoxication. *Lancet, 1,* 733–734.

Mackenzie, A. I. (1983). Naloxone for ethanol intoxication? *Lancet, 2,* 145–146.

Malcom, R., Ballenger, J. C., Sturgis, E. T., & Anton, R. (1989). Double-blind controlled trial comparing carbamazepine to oxazepam treatment of alcohol withdrawal. *American Journal of Psychiatry, 146,* 167–621.

Mattila, M. J., Nuotto, E., & Seppala, T. (1981). Naloxone is not an effective antagonist of ethanol. *Lancet, 1,* 775–776.

McMillan, T. M. (1981) Lithium and the treatment of alcoholism: A critical review. *British Journal of Addiction, 76,* 245–258.

Merry, J., Reynolds, C. M., Bailey, J., & Coppen, A. (1976). Prophylactic treatment of alcoholism by lithium carbonate: a controlled study. *Lancet, 2,* 481–482.

Miller, W. R., Hedrick, K. E., & Taylor, C. A. (1983). Addictive behaviors and life problems before and after treatment of problem drinkers. *Addictive Behaviors, 8,* 403–412.

Miller, W. R., & Hester, R. K. (1986). The effectiveness of alcoholism treatment: What research reveals. In W. R. Miller & N. Heather (Eds.), *Treating addictive behaviors: Processes of change* (pp. 121–174). New York: Plenum.

Mooney, H. B., Ditman, K. S., & Cohen, S. (1961). Chlordiazepoxide in the treatment of alcoholics. *Diseases of the Nervous System, 22* (Supplement), 44–51.

Moss, L. M. (1973). Naloxone reversal of non-narcotic induced apnea. *Journal of the American College of Emergency Physicians, 2,* 46–48.

Naranjo, C. A., Lawrin, M., Addison, D., Roach, C. A., Harrison, M., Sanchez-Craig, M., & Sellers, E. M. (1983). Zimelidine decreases alcohol consumption in non-depressed heavy drinkers. *Clinical Pharmacology and Therapeutics, 33,* 241.

Nuotto, E., Palva, E. S., & Lahdenranta, U. (1983). Naloxone fails to counteract heavy alcohol intoxication. *Lancet, 2,* 167.

O'Malley, S. S., Jaffe, A. J., Chang, G., Schottenfeld, R. S., Meyer, R. E., Rounsaville, B. (1992). Natrexone and coping skills therapy for alcohol dependence. *Archives of General Psychiatry, 49,* 881–887.

Overall, J. E., Brown, D., Williams, J. D., & Neill, L. T. (1973). Drug treatment of anxiety and depression in detoxified alcoholic patients. *Archives of General Psychiatry, 29,* 218–221.

Peachey, J. E., & Naranjo, C. A. (1984). The role of drugs in the treatment of alcoholism. *Drugs, 27*(2) 171–182.

Pond, S. M., Becker, C. E., Vandervoort, R., Phillips, M., Bowler, R., & Peck, C. C. (1981). An evaluation of the effects of lithium in the treatment of chronic alcoholism. I. Clinical results. *Alcoholism: Clinical and Experimental Research, 5,* 247–251.

Revusky, S. (1973). Some laboratory paradigms for chemical aversion treatment of alcoholism. *Journal of Behavioural Therapy and Experimental Psychiatry, 14,* 15.

Revusky, S., Parker, J. A., Coombes, J., & Coombes, S. (1976). Rat data which suggest alcoholic beverages should be swallowed during chemical aversion therapy, not just tasted. *Behavioural Research and Therapy, 14,* 189.

Revusky, S., & Taukalis, H. (1975). Effects of alcohol and lithium habituation on the development of alcohol aversions through contingent lithium injection. *Behaviour Research and Therapy, 13,* 163.

Robins, E., Murphy, G. E., Wilkinson, R. H., Jr., Gasner, S., & Kayes, J. (1959). Some clinical consideration in the prevention of suicide based on a study of 134 successful suicides. *American Journal of Public Health, 49,* 888–889.

Rosenberg, C. M. (1974). Drug maintenance in the outpatient treatment of chronic alcoholism. *Archives of General Psychiatry, 30,* 373–377.

Ross, D., Hartmann, R. J., & Geller, I. (1976). I. Ethanol preference in the hamster: effects of morphine sulfate and Naltrexone, a long-acting morphine antagonist. *Proceedings of the Western Pharmacological Society, 19,* 326–330.

Ross, H. E., Glaser, F. B., & Germanson, T. (1988). The prevalence of psychiatric disorders in patients with alcohol and other drug problems. *Archives of General Psychiatry, 45,* 1023–1032.

Schenk, G. K., Engelmeier, M. P., Maltz, D., & Pach, J. (July, 1978). High dosage Naloxone treatment in acute alcohol intoxication. *Proceedings of the CINP (Collegium Internationale Neuropsychopharmacologicum) Congress,* Vienna, p. 386 (Abstract).

Schou, M. (1978). The range of clinical uses of lithium. In F. N. Johnson & S. Johnson (Eds.), *Lithium in medical practice* (pp. 21–40). Baltimore: University Park Press.

Schuckit, M. A. (1973). Alcoholism and sociopathy: Diagnostic confusion. *Quarterly Journal of Studies on Alcohol, 34,* 157–164.

Schuckit, M. A. (1983). A study of alcoholics with secondary depression. *American Journal of Psychiatry, 140,* 711–714.

Schuckit, M. A. (1984). *Drug and alcohol abuse: A clinical guide to diagnosis and treatment.* New York: Plenum.

Schuckit, M. A. (1986). Genetic and clinical implications of alcoholism and affective disorder. *American Journal of Psychiatry, 143*(1), 140–147.

Schuckit, M. A., & Winokur, G. (1972). A short-term follow-up of women alcoholics. *Diseases of the Nervous System, 33,* 672–678.

Schweizer, E., Rickels, K., Case, W. G., and Greenblatt, D. J. (1991). Carbamazepine treatment in patients discontinuing long-term benzodiazepine therapy. *Archives of General Psychiatry, 48,* 448–452.

Sedlacek, D., & Miller, S. I. (1982). A framework for relating alcoholism and depression. *Journal of Family Practice, 14*(1), 41–44.

Seller, E. M., Cooper, S. D., Sen, A. K., & Zilm, D. H. (1974). Lithium treatment of alcohol withdrawal. *Clinical Pharmacology and Therapeutics, 15,* 218 (Abstract).

Sellers, E. M., Cooper, S. D., Zilm, D. H., & Shanks, C. (1976). Lithium treatment during alcohol withdrawal. *Clinical Pharmacology and Therapeutics, 20*, 199.

Sellers, E. M., & Kalant, H. (1978). Pharmacology of acute and chronic alcoholism and alcohol withdrawal syndrome. In A. J. Clark & J. del Guidice (Eds.), *Principles of pharmacology* (2nd ed.) (pp. 721–740). New York: Academic Press.

Sellers, E. M., Naranjo, C. A., & Peachey, J. E. (1981). Drugs to decrease alcohol consumption. *New England Journal of Medicine, 305*, 1255–1262.

Shaw, J. A., Donley, P., Morgan, D. W., & Robinson, J. A. (1975). Treatment of depression in alcoholics. *American Journal of Psychiatry, 132*, 641–644.

Shaw, J. M., Kolesar, G. S., Sellers, E. M., Kaplan, H. I., & Sandor, P. (1981). Development of optimal treatment tactics for alcohol withdrawal. I. Assessment and effectiveness of supportive care. *Journal of Clinical Pharmacology, 1*, 382–389.

Solomon, J. (1982). Alcoholism and affective disorders: Methodological considerations. In J. Solomon (Ed.), *Alcoholism and clinical psychiatry* (pp. 81–95). New York: Plenum.

Sorenson, S. C., & Mattison, K. W. (1978). Naloxone as an antagonist of severe alcohol intoxication. *Lancet, 2*, 688–689.

Thompson, W. L. (1978). Management of alcohol withdrawal syndromes. *Archives of Internal Medicine, 138*, 278–283.

Truitt, E. B., & Vaughen, C. M. (1976). Effects of lithium on chronic ethanol consumption and behavior. *Federal Proceedings, 35*, 814 (Abstract).

Volpicelli, J. R., Alterman, A. I., Hayashida, M., & O'Brien, C. P. (1992). Naltrexone in the treatment of alcohol dependence. *Archives of General Psychiatry, 49*, 876–880.

Volpicelli, J. R., Davis, M. A., & Olgin, J. E. (1986). Naltrexone blocks the post-shock increase of alcohol consumption. *Life Sciences, 38*, 841–847.

Weissman, M. M., & Myers, J. K. (1980). Clinical depression in alcoholism. *American Journal of Psychiatry, 137*, 372–373.

Whalley, L. J., Freedman, C. P., & Hunter, J. (1981). Role of endogenous opioids in alcoholic intoxication. *Lancet, 2*, 89.

Wilson, I. C., Alltop, L. B., & Riley, L. (1970). Tofranil in the treatment of post alcoholic depressions. *Psychosomatics, 11*, 488–494.

Woodruff, R. A., Jr., Guze, S. B., Clayton, P. J., & Carr, D. (1973). Alcoholism and depression. *Archives of General Psychiatry, 28*, 97–100.

Wren, J. C., Kline, N. S., Cooper, T. B., Varga, E., & Canal, O. (1974). Evaluation of lithium therapy in chronic alcoholism. *Clinical Medicine, 81*, 33–36.

Young, L. D., & Keeler, M. M. (1977). Sobering data on lithium in alcoholics. *Lancet, 1*, 144.

Zilm, D. H., Sellers, F. M., MacLeod, S. M., & Degani, N. C. (1975). Propranolol effect on tremor in alcoholic withdrawal. *Annals of Internal Medicine, 83*, 234–236.

Zimberg, S. (1982). *The clinical management of alcoholism.* New York: Brunner/Mazel.

Matching Clients to Alcohol Treatments

John P. Allen
Ron M. Kadden

Treating clients for alcohol problems is complex. At least three critical activities are involved: choosing "generally effective" interventions, such as those discussed in Chapters 6 through 16 of this text; assigning individuals to treatments found especially effective for clients of particular types; and providing specialized interventions to resolve unique needs of individual clients.

As Chapter 2 indicates, research has now shown several types of treatment to be effective in resolving drinking problems. Few studies, however, have directly contrasted these "generally effective" interventions with each other. Therefore, treatment programs that want to develop maximally helpful programs may find it difficult to choose which particular strategies to implement. Fortunately, to the extent that several of these approaches are similar, or at least compatible, a program could likely institute them together.

The second consideration in treatment planning, assigning clients to interventions shown particularly effective with clients of their subtype, is usually termed *treatment matching* in the substance-abuse literature and *aptitude-treatment*

interaction (Snow, 1991) in the psychotherapy literature. The Institute of Medicine (1990) has compellingly and succinctly summarized the rationale for alcoholism treatment matching:

> There is no single treatment approach that is effective for all persons with alcohol problems. A number of different treatment methods show promise in particular groups. Reason for optimism in the treatment of alcohol problems lies in the range of promising alternatives that are available, each of which may be optimal for different types of individuals. (p. 147)

Although this chapter focuses on the value of treatment matching, it is important to bear in mind that implementing matching strategies is not at odds with a program's emphasis on employing generally effective treatment approaches. For one thing, we often do not know or have at hand specific treatments optimal for all types of clients. Second, even when optimal client-treatment matching assignments are known and available, they can usually be provided in a program built around a core of effective interventions. Third, it seems reasonable to assume that treatments found effective for clients in general may prove of even greater benefit for certain types of clients. In fact, research on matching has typically studied treatments that have a solid track record of general effectiveness.

The third consideration in treatment planning involves designing treatments to address specific client needs. For example, individuals who suffer unusual cognitive, psychiatric, or physical disabilities, who have a spouse or significant other who also has a serious alcohol problem, or who abuse drugs and alcohol together in an atypical pattern require special management. It is unlikely that at any one time a program would have enough clients with these problems to establish groups for whom appropriate interventions could be delivered. Little research has been done on the crucial topic of fully individualizing alcoholism treatment and, due to the myriad of possible client needs, such research will probably not be forthcoming.

NATURE OF MATCHING RESEARCH

In his previous review, Miller (1989) noted that programs could match clients to treatment in at least four ways. They could assign clients to alternative treatment *goals*, such as abstinence or moderation. They might also assign clients to treatments varying in *intensity* from brief intervention to long-term residential treatment. They could also use interventions differing in *content*, such as a disease-oriented approach or a skill-based method. Finally, clients could be offered various options for *maintaining* their gains after treatment. This would involve, for example, setting up alternative aftercare arrangements.

Table 17.1, a synopsis of a table originally included in Mattson and colleagues (1994), summarizes studies demonstrating positive effects on the three latter ways of matching. Client characteristics that have shown matching effects fall into three broad classes: demographic, alcohol-related, and personality/psychological variables. Table 17.1 is organized according to this schema. (A small number of studies simultaneously considered variables from more than one domain. We have classified these by what appears to be the major focus of the project.)

To be included in Table 17.1 the investigation had to discover a client-treatment interaction in at least one of the groups studied. Second, the effect had to be statistically tested and found significant at an alpha level of at least .05. Third, the outcome variable had to be either related to posttreatment drinking or to some other important concern of a treatment program such as reduced client dropout. Finally, the client variable serving as the basis for matching had to be measured at the beginning of treatment.

As is evident from reading down the first column of Table 17.1, studies on matching effects are becoming increasingly popular. In fact, over half of the investigations have been conducted in the past five years. These recent studies differ from earlier projects in several important respects. Most notably, they tend to be much more rigorously controlled in terms of satisfying the experimental design criteria specified in Chapter 2. The tighter design of these trials allows researchers and clinicians to have considerably more confidence in their results.

Researchers now also seem to pay far more attention to measurement of client variables, the exact nature of the treatments, and a variety of outcome effects. Earlier studies sometimes evaluated client variables simply by observation, typically did not describe the treatments in detail, and often measured outcome in imprecise terms such as "improved" rather than determining specifically how much matching actually ameliorated drinking status over either just assigning all the clients to one of the treatments or assigning them to the mismatched intervention.

Also in recent studies, the reasons for the matching effect are usually more intuitively reasonable. In the older studies, matching effects often seem to have been found by serendipity and secondary data analysis. Researchers today are more likely to hypothesize matching effects in advance and to design the study to specifically evaluate the predicted matching effects.

Recent studies also tend to be superior to earlier projects in that the client's drinking is looked at at several follow-up points. Analysis of these data allows the researcher to assure that the matching effect is robust and consistent and that the choice of treatment would not vary depending on how long after treatment one looked at drinking behaviors.

Finally, researchers now seem more likely to explore the matching potential of client variables directly related to drinking rather than to personality or demographic characteristics.

MATCHING EFFECTS

Most of the matching effects demonstrated so far are of a "qualitative" nature (Longabaugh et al., 1994). Here, the client-matching characteristic

Table 17.1   Summary of Positive Findings in Client-Treatment Matching Research Literature

Personality/Psychological Variables

REFERENCE	CLIENT VARIABLE	TREATMENTS	MATCHING EFFECTS
Kissen et al., 1970	Social stability Verbal I.Q. Performance I.Q. Field dependence	Psychotherapy vs. inpatient rehabilitation	Socially & psychologically stable did best with psychotherapy; less psych. sophisticated did best with drugs; soc. unstable but intellectually intact did best with inpatient rehabilitation.
McLachlan,[1] 1974	Conceptual level	Conceptual level of therapist	Clients matched with therapists on conceptual level improved more in treatment than those mismatched.
McLachlan,[1] 1974	Conceptual level	Structured vs. unstructured psychotherapy	Inpatients matched with therapists on conceptual level were more likely to be rated as improved than those mismatched. Further improvement resulted when high conceptual level clients were assigned to less structured aftercare services.
Merry et al.,[2] 1976	Depression	Lithium vs. placebo	Lithium reduced days dkg. intoxicated for depressed but not for non-depressed.
Welte et al., 1981	Social stability	Longer vs. shorter inpatient stay	Ss low in social stability did better with lengths of stay beyond 30 days but extending inpatient care did not further benefit higher social stability Ss.
McLellan et al.,[3] 1983a	Legal severity Family severity	Diverse VA programs	Among clients with middle range psychiatric severity, matches with a variety of VA treatment programs occurred as a function of age, legal, family, or employment status.
McLellan et al.,[3] 1983b	Psych. severity Emp. severity	Diverse VA programs	Male alc. veterans matched to varying tx. progs. did better in tx. motivation discharge status and scores on majority of ASI scales than did unmatched clients.
Spoth, 1983	Locus of Control	Low structure vs. high structure in anxiety control tx.	Anxiety was reduced more for internals by less structured anxiety control tx. For externals, anxiety was reduced more with more structured anxiety control tx.
Hartman et al., 1988	Locus of Control	Intensive coping skills tx vs. brief unstructured session	Externals did better than internals on all outcomes with structured, more intensive (coping skills) counselling than with a brief (5 min) unstructured session. The addition of relaxation strategies to the structured module improved outcome in externals.

Source: Mattson, M. E., Allen, J. P., et al. (in press). A chronological review of empirical studies matching alcoholic clients to treatment. In D. Donovan & M. Matson (Eds.), *Alcoholism treatment research: Client treatment matching in the context of multisite clinical trials. Journal of Alcoholic Studies Monograph.* Reprinted by permission.

[1]McLachlan, 1972 same sample as McLachlan, 1974.
[2]In a larger study (n=457) by Dorus et al. (1989), lithium treatment was not shown to influence the course of alcoholism in either depressed or non depressed subjects.
[3]McLellan, 1983a same sample as McLellan, 1983b.

Table 17.1 (continued)

Personality/Psychological Variables (continued)

REFERENCE	CLIENT VARIABLE	TREATMENTS	MATCHING EFFECTS
Kadden et al.,[4] 1989; Cooney et al.,[4] 1991	Sociopathy Global psychopathology Cognitive	Interactional therapy vs. coping skills therapy	(1) Ss high in psych. sev. were more likely to relapse and had more days drinking with interactional therapy than Ss low in psych. sev. Probability of relapse was inversely related to psych. sev. in coping skills tx. (2) Sociopathy was related directly to relapse and time to relapse in interactional therapy but inversely so in coping skills tx. (3) Ss high in neuropsych. impairment experienced longer periods until relapse if assigned to interactional therapy than to coping skills tx.
Rohsenow et et al., 1991	Anxiety Urge to drink Education	Communication skills vs. mood management	Those with less education, higher urge to drink and higher anxiety benefitted more from beh. oriented communication skills tx. than from cog. beh. mood management. Those with opposite characteristics did equally well in both tx.
McKay et al. (in press)	Autonomy	Conjoint vs. non-conjoint coping skills	Ss low in autonomy did better with non-conjoint coping skills tx. Conjoint coping skills tx. appeared more helpful for those high in autonomy.
Pettinati et al. (in press)	Psych. severity Social support	Inpatient vs. outpatient treatment	Inpatients with high psych. severity or low social support were less likely to be early treatment failures than outpatients with these characteristics.
Longabaugh et al. (in press)	Diagnosis of anti-social personality disorder	Cognitive behavioral vs. relationship enhancement	ASP clients treated with extended cognitive behavior therapy did better at 12-month follow-up than those treated in relationship enhancement therapy. The trend continued at extended follow-up, although the effect was not significant. Non ASP clients did equally well in either tx.

Demographic Variables

REFERENCE	CLIENT VARIABLE	TREATMENTS	MATCHING EFFECTS
Sokolow et al., 1980	Gender	Peer/gender orientation	Females did better in low peer orientation programs than in high; males did better in high peer orientations.
Azrin et al., 1982	Marital status	Traditional disulfiram (TD) vs. supervised disulfiram (DA) vs. community reinforcement approach (CRA)	Married clients did better in both disulfiram assurance (DA) alone, or DA combined with CRA, with both superior to traditional disulfiram (TD). Single clients, however, did much better with DA & CRA than in either DA alone or TD.

[4]Kadden, et al., 1989; Cooney, et al., 1991; Litt, et al., 1992 and Kadden, et al., 1992 all used the same population.

Table 17.1   (continued)

Demographic Variables (continued)

REFERENCE	CLIENT VARIABLE	TREATMENTS	MATCHING EFFECTS
Cronkite & Moos, 1984	Gender	Educational programs vs. group therapy	For males, participation in group therapy sessions was related to lower consumption, and participation in lectures and films to higher consumption. For females, lectures and films were associated with less severe dkg. pattern, less dkg. impairment and lower consumption and group therapy sessions to higher consumption and worse dkg. pattern.
Anderson & Scott, 1992; Scott & Anderson, 1990	Gender	Brief intervention vs. simple assessment only	Brief intervention was more effective than simple assessment of dkg. for male heavy dkg. Ss. Female Ss showed comparable benefits for both conditions.
Rice et al. (in press)	Age	Cognitive behavioral vs. relationship/ vocational	Older Ss did better with cog. beh. tx. than with relationship and vocational enhancement tx. No tx. differences in younger Ss.

Alcohol-Related Variables

Orford & Openheimer, 1976	Gamma vs. non-gamma alcoholics	Brief counseling vs. intensive tx	Non-gamma alcoholics did better with brief counseling. Gammas did better with intensive treatment.
Lyons et al., 1982	Behaviorally impaired drinkers vs. alcoholics	Medical/rehab. focus vs. peer group focus	Males with fewer behavioral symptoms of alcoholism had higher rates of abstinence if treated in programs with high rehabilitation orientation or high medical orientation than in progs. with high peer group focus.
Annis & Davis, 1989	Differentiation of high-risk drinking situations	Traditional counseling vs. coping skills tx.	Ss with differentiated profiles did better with training in coping with high risk stimuli than with traditional counseling. No difference in tx. effectiveness for Ss with generalized profiles.
Babor & Grant, 1992	Recent alc-rel. prob. Gender	Simple advice vs. brief counseling vs. control condition	(1) For males, simple advice and brief counselling improved drinking outcome equally as compared to control condition. Females showed reductions than males. (2) Simple advice was most effective for males drinkers with recent alc.-related problem. Brief counseling was most effective for those without recent alc.-related problem.
Kadden et al.,[4] 1992	Role-play skill Anxiety Urge to drink	Interactional vs. coping skills	Clients with more skill in role play situations, less anxiety or lower urge to drink had better outcomes in interactional therapy than in coping skills tx. Those with less skill, more anxiety or greater urge to drink did better in coping skills tx.

Table 17.1   (continued)

Alcohol-Related Variables (continued)

REFERENCE	CLIENT VARIABLE	TREATMENTS	MATCHING EFFECTS
Litt et al.,[4] 1992	Alc. typology (Type A vs. Type B)	Interactional therapy vs. coping skills	Type B clients had fewer heavy drinking days with coping skills therapy and Type A's with interactional tx. Mismatched clients relapsed sooner.
Gerra et al., 1992	Family history of alcoholism	Fluoxetine vs. Ca-acetyl homotaurinate	Fluoxetine significantly reduced avg. daily dkg for Ss with family history of alcoholism. No effect for family history negative Ss. Conversely, Ca-acetyl homotaurinate significantly decreased daily alcohol intake for non-familial clients but had no effect on those with a positive family history for alcoholism.
Heather et al., 1993	Motivation to change drinking	Skill based counseling vs. motivational interviewing	A single session of skill-based counseling or motivational interviewing were equally effective in reducing alc. consumption among heavy drinkers. For those low in initial motivation to change, however, motivational interviewing was more effective than skill-based counseling.
Miller et al. (in press)	Client's view of alcoholism	Confrontive vs. empathetic therapist	Ss seeing alcoholism as a "bad habit" did better with empathetic than with confrontive therapist. No difference for those seeing alcoholism as a disease.

involves either a variable having only a small number of possible values, such as gender, or a continuous variable that has been artificially dichotomized, usually at the midpoint. The practice of dividing the continuous variable into simply upper and lower halves is probably due to the research need for a small enough number of groups to allow statistical analyses to be performed. On the down side, failing to consider the actual levels of the client variable makes it difficult to estimate the range over which the variable has implications for treatment matching. Furthermore, separation at the median almost always results in assigning a large number of cases with scores differing only slightly to opposing groups, thereby diminishing the observed interaction between the client variable and treatment. With larger samples it would be possible to test out different cut-points on the client variable to discover where optimal matches with treatment occur.

Most of the matching effects discovered to date are also of an "ordinal" or weak "disordinal" (Longabaugh et al., 1994) nature. The observed matching effect occurs with only one of the treatments and then only for individuals at either high or low levels of the client characteristic.

While various studies often report results on different outcomes, it is encouraging that the findings are not contradictory. Similarly, in studies that have measured multiple types of outcome at the same time, we found no real contradictions, although the matching effect might not have occurred on all the outcome dimensions. Neither did we find any instances in which the project suggested that one of the treatments would be chosen for a subtype of clients to maximize success on one outcome measure but that the other treatment would be chosen to maximize success on some other outcome dimension. Finally, no reverse "sleeper effects" have been reported suggesting that one treatment would be preferable for achieving a positive outcome at an early follow-up point but that another intervention would be better if the goal were to optimize outcome at long term follow-up.

The situation described by Miller (1989) in his previous review that "research data are currently insufficient to recommend particular approaches based on client traits" (p. 269) seems to have appreciably improved over the past five years. Although few studies are true replications of each other, nevertheless, we believe that at least two tentative general conclusions on matching strategies are warranted.

First, clients suffering more severe problems—such as severity of dependence, severity of collateral psychopathology, lack of social support, and so on—seem to do better with more intense treatments. Those with less severe problems often do at least as well with less intensive interventions. We would slightly temper this conclusion by noting that oftentimes the alternative interventions studied differed not only in intensity but also somewhat in content.

Second, two well-controlled, independent studies now argue that clients high in sociopathy should probably be treated with interventions based on training in coping skills. Those low in sociopathy will likely do as well or better in relationship enhancement treatment. While more research is needed, we believe that treatment programs might consider implementing this matching strategy now. Later in this chapter, we will describe procedures for the relationship enhancement intervention, and in the final section of this chapter, we will review the research literature on matching to coping skills versus relationship enhancement therapy.

Although research on client-treatment matching continues to grow in popularity, there are many questions related to treatment that have not yet been studied. We need to know, for example, whether some clients would do better with traditional "Minnesota Model" programs (Cook, 1988) than with newer treatment approaches; whether some clients would profit more from treatments that emphasize overall health and well-being rather than from interventions that focus almost entirely on drinking; whether some clients would gain more from programs that give them more choices rather than in programs totally prescribed by treatment staff; and which type of counselors work best with which type of clients. Well-controlled research is badly needed to provide treatment staff answers to fundamental, applied questions such as these.

Practical Concerns in Matching

Although clients are more likely to benefit from treatments demonstrated as effective with individuals of a similar type, matching may not be helpful for everyone. McLellan and colleagues

(1983a), for example, noted that some alcoholic clients suffer such profound collateral psychiatric problems that none of the currently available interventions are probably adequate to assist them. On the other hand, highly motivated clients with low levels of alcohol dependence and ample personal and social supports for sobriety generally do quite well regardless of the program to which they are assigned.

Of course, it also is possible that a given client would have some combination of characteristics that would lead to conflicting recommendations regarding optimal treatment. The current research literature suggests that clients matched to interventions tend to do better than those unmatched or mismatched. Still, all clients with the characteristic do not profit equally from matching. No doubt, some actually gain less from the intervention typically more effective for their subtype than they would have from the "mismatched" treatment. Further research should more carefully identify factors that strengthen or reduce the matching potential of client characteristics.

Extraneous circumstances may render matching impractical or impossible for certain clients. Some lack financial resources sufficient to cover the cost of the preferred treatment. Externally imposed barriers, such as utilization review standards of a third-party payer or court mandate for a particular type of treatment, might also preclude optimal treatment matching. Educating outside agencies on client-treatment matching effects should reduce such constraints.

Adoption of a matching strategy would, of course, also place additional, but manageable, demands on treatment facilities. Program staff with skills in a wider range of interventions would be required, and additional costs in training staff would likely be incurred. In order to accurately identify client needs, more comprehensive assessment would probably be necessary. On the positive side, however, research suggests that clients particularly value assessment and also that dropout rates may be lower in programs that do a more thorough job of client assessment. More time would also be demanded to design treatment plans and to make sure that interventions are being properly conducted.

Perhaps most difficult would be programmatic decisions as to the types of clients a particular facility can best treat. As Miller (1989) has observed, providers may be reluctant to refer paying clients to other programs for whom they are better suited. Facilities truly able to offer treatments tailored to a broad variety of individuals would likely have to be quite large and well endowed with resources. They would also have to be committed to genuine matching of treatments to client needs.

Matching would also impose new challenges on treatment staff. More training would need to be devoted to master new treatments. Fortunately, a variety of manuals are now available describing specific types of treatments. Likely somewhat more difficult would be the necessity of consistently following the prescribed treatment protocol. Periodic audio- or videotaping of sessions with feedback provided to counselors should enhance treatment integrity. Adhering closely to a treatment manual rather than improvising and integrating treatments might seem constraining to counselors valuing independence and personal discretion in treating clients. Changes in counselor attitudes would need to occur. Although matching clearly does not diminish the need for sound clinical judgment, it redirects clinical discretion primarily to responding to idiosyncratic client needs. Freed from having to make intuitive, basic decisions on treatment, counselors would be better able to focus on the unique needs of individual clients.

TREATMENT PROCEDURES FOR INTERACTIONAL THERAPY

As noted earlier, a growing body of evidence suggests that individuals with alcohol problems who have higher degrees of sociopathy do better with training in coping skills. Other alcohol clients seem to do at least equally well with treatment designed to enrich social relationships. Since these are the most specific client-treatment matches to have received empirical support, we will focus primary attention on them. Coping skills training (Monti, Abrams, Kadden, & Cooney, 1989) fosters acquisition of skills to manage urges to drink, negative moods, and interpersonal deficiencies. Additional skills include problem solving and ability to identify and handle situations involving high risk for relapse. Skills training methods include didactic instruction, behavioral rehearsal, and homework practice exercises. Since Chapter 13 reviews coping skills training in considerable depth, we will limit our discussion here to interactional therapy.

The treatment approach designed for Kadden and colleagues' (1989) matching study, characterized as "Short Term Interactional Group Therapy" (Getter, 1984), followed Yalom's (1974) general recommendations for the treatment of individuals suffering alcohol problems (Brown & Yalom, 1977). The treatment manual by Getter served as the basis for therapist training and supervision, conducting therapy, and evaluating the distinctiveness of the interventions employed in the study (Getter, Litt, Kadden, & Cooney, 1992).

The premise of this therapy is that maladaptive behavior patterns, including compulsive drinking, arise from dysfunctional or unfulfilling interpersonal relationships. The goal of the treatment is to employ group process techniques so that the group itself becomes the therapeutic agent. Members work through personal problems by dealing with conflicts and other relationship issues as they arise within the group (Yalom, 1975). The primary emphasis of interactional therapy is interpersonal pathology and conflicts rather than abstinence per se.

The Inner Circle Exercise and Life History Technique of Lazarus (1971) were utilized in the first three sessions to quickly establish a therapeutic climate and self-disclosure. Group members were encouraged to begin interacting spontaneously and openly with one another, rather than addressing the group leaders.

As the groups developed, attention shifted to "here and now" issues identifying the meaning of experiences as they actually occurred in the group and fostering a climate of honest emotional expression. The therapeutic approach was now targeted toward four goals: (1) developing awareness of one's personal style and how it affects others; (2) increasing acceptance of self and others through cognitive restructuring to correct irrational thoughts and overgeneralizations; (3) using self-disclosure in a supportive group environment to reduce tension; and (4) learning to relate more effectively through enhanced listening, self-expression, self-disclosure, and management of interpersonal conflict.

Clients were encouraged to adopt a self-reflective approach; to explore each other's ways of relating, defenses, and emotional reactions; to accept differences with other members; and to develop effective ways of managing conflicts. Each group began to develop its own set of behavioral norms and expectations and a commitment to honesty and trust within the group.

Over the course of the group's further development, participants discovered more satisfying ways of relating to others and accepted mutual responsibility. They thereby achieved a more profound sense of intimacy and greater willingness to explore close relationships.

The two therapists in the group facilitated member-to-member interactions and encouraged expression of immediate feelings. They attempted to help the group reflect on itself. For example, the therapists monitored clients' fears, anxiety, and resistance, exploring them with group members and assessing their impact on the group's progress. Very importantly, they also encouraged transference of interpersonal learning that occurred within the group to outside relationships. As the group's final session approached, emotional issues surrounding termination were identified and explored. After each meeting, the therapists also wrote a summary of the session and sent it to all participants for to review. The summary further developed a sense of group process, building cohesiveness, and controlling anxiety (Yalom, Brown, & Bloch, 1975).

Group management issues, especially relating to use of alcohol, were generally managed according to recommendations by Vannicelli (1982). A written "group members' contract" specified norms regarding attendance, confidentiality, importance of openness in the group sessions, and agreement to work toward abstinence. Intoxicated clients were denied admission to group sessions. Group members discussed lapses to drinking and recommended a course of remedial action. The therapists also had guidelines for managing other problems common in groups of alcoholic clients such as dependency issues, guilt, anger, depression, defensiveness, resistance, and sexual concerns.

Alcoholics Anonymous (AA) was viewed as complementary to the treatment strategy. Clients were encouraged to discuss in group any outside contacts they had had with fellow group members, whether at AA meetings or elsewhere. Therapists rarely provided private consultations. Instead, they invited clients to explore their concerns in the group.

EFFECTIVENESS OF MATCHING TO COPING SKILLS: INTERACTIONAL THERAPY

We now move to a somewhat detailed review of studies of the effectiveness of matching clients based on degree of sociopathy with either coping skills treatment or treatment geared to enhancing the quality of personal interactions.

In the first of these investigations, Kadden and colleagues (1989) randomly assigned alcohol-dependent clients who had completed a 21-day inpatient treatment program to either coping skills or interactional aftercare therapy. Treatment was provided in a group format with up to 12 clients per group in 26 weekly 90-minute treatment sessions.

At six-month follow-up, clients higher in general psychopathology, as measured by the Psychiatric Severity subscale of the Addiction Severity Index, and those higher in sociopathy, as assessed by the Socialization subscale of the California Psychological Inventory, were more likely to be abstinent and less likely to suffer alcohol-related problems following coping skills treatment. On the other hand, those lower in sociopathy had more favorable outcomes on both variables if they had received interactional therapy.

Clients high in psychopathology assigned to interactional therapy also reported more days of heavy (exceeding 6 drinks) consumption than did those given coping skills training or those low in psychopathology who had been given interactional treatment. Conversely, neuropsychologically impaired individuals had better alcohol-related outcomes if they were treated with interactional therapy.

The researchers reported three other thought-provoking findings. First, the client variables were independent of each other in terms of their relationship with matching. Second, therapists, who did not know the hypotheses under consideration, were unable to predict at above a chance level which treatment strategy would prove more effective for their clients. Finally, the matching effect was statistically significant only if sociopathy was measured using the Socialization subscale of the California Psychological Inventory, a continuous variable. The effect was not demonstrated if sociopathy was defined by a *DSM-III* diagnosis of antisocial personality disorder. (The difference in the usefulness of these two variables for matching purposes might have been due to either content variability or differences in statistical power between a continuous and an inherently dichotomous variable.)

Cooney and colleagues (1991) reported 12- and 24-month follow-up results to evaluate longer-term resiliency of the matching effects. As before, at long-term follow-up, the two treatments were of approximately equal overall effectiveness. Using survival analysis, with the event of interest being the first day on which the client consumed more than 6 drinks, the researchers largely reconfirmed the initial matching hypotheses. Clients higher in psychopathology treated with coping skills therapy and those lower in psychopathology treated with interactional therapy maintained abstinence or moderated consumption longer than their mismatched peers. This was in contrast to the six-month follow-up study that had demonstrated a matching effect for clients high in psychopathology but not for those with low levels of psychopathology.

The treatment-matching effect for sociopathy endured through follow-up, producing a dramatic difference—45% nonrelapse to heavy drinking by matched clients versus only 25% for mismatched ones. Cognitively impaired clients continued to profit more from interactional group therapy than from coping skills treatment. Cognitively more intact clients did equally well regardless of which intervention they had received.

Secondary analyses of results from male participants in this study were performed by Litt and colleagues (1992). Matching effects were examined as a function of client subtype using a classification system quite similar to that described by Babor and colleagues (1992). "Type A" subjects reported later onset of problematic drinking, were less likely to have first-degree relatives who were themselves alcoholic, evidenced fewer problems related to drinking, and suffered less psychopathology—including depression, anxiety, and sociopathy—than "Type B" subjects.

Although the two types of treatment were in general equally effective over 18 months of posttreatment follow-up, important client-treatment interactions were identified. Type B clients drank heavily on fewer follow-up days if they had received coping skills treatment rather than interactional therapy. The matching effect was statistically significant and clinically quite important. Notably, Type B clients who had received coping skills therapy were, on average, drinking heavily on fewer than half as many days as Type Bs treated with interactionally focused treatment. Matched- and mismatched-to-therapy groups also differed substantially in time to first drink following treatment. With coping skills treatment, Type B clients, in fact, avoided relapse as long as the less impaired Type As.

Visual inspection of the plot of proportion of heavy drinking days suggests that matching was particularly important for Type B clients, who appeared to enjoy substantially better outcomes with coping skills treatment. Although Type A clients assigned to coping skills generally did about as well as those assigned to interactional treatment, Type A clients assigned to interactional therapy maintained total abstinence longer than did those assigned to coping skills treatment.

Longabaugh and colleagues (in press) recently performed a highly informative study evaluating effectiveness of matching clients to coping skills therapy versus relationship enhancement treatment. Unlike the preceding study, therapy involved outpatients rather than aftercare clients and was done on a one-to-one basis rather than in groups. Individually Focused Extended Cognitive Behavioral Therapy consisted of sessions dealing with identification of antecedents and consequences of drinking, weakening the association of cues to drinking responses, developing alternatives to drinking, assertion training, and constructively dealing with slips or relapses. Relationship Enhanced Cognitive Behavior Therapy included sessions to increase the reinforcement value of relationships with significant others and to reshape these interpersonal relationships to better sustain abstinence. Significant others attended from 4 to 8 of the treatment sessions. Both treatment approaches included 6 sessions of functional analysis of drinking behavior. Also, both approaches consisted of 20 sessions, 18 of which were conducted within a four- to six-month period. A booster session was given three months after completion of treatment and a second one at a year after treatment entry.

The matching variable was presence or absence of formal diagnosis of antisocial personality disorder. Neither type of treatment proved superior to the other nor was there a significant matching effect when average drinks per day served as the outcome variable. However, during the 12-month follow-up, clients with antisocial personality disorder who had participated in coping skills treatment drank less on the days when they did drink than did similarly diagnosed ones assigned to relationship enhancement treatment. This finding was similar to results of the study cited above. Non-antisocial clients seemed to do equally well with either treatment.

Three other investigations have also demonstrated matching effects for coping skills treatment versus an alternative intervention. Beyond the major matching effect they found, Kadden and colleagues (1989) also discovered relationships between alcohol-related clients variables, as measured by standardized role-play exercises, and choice of treatment (Kadden et al., 1992). Clients who reported less "urge to drink" at intake or who exhibited lower anxiety related to drinking stimuli in the role-plays avoided relapse to heavy drinking longer during the two-year follow-up period if given the inter-actional-based intervention rather than coping skills treatment. Coping skills treatment, how-ever, was more effective for clients higher in urge to drink or anxiety in role-play drinking sit-uations. The matching effect for urge to drink was independent of the matching effect for de-gree of sociopathy.

Researchers have found that other client characteristics may be associated with better prognosis in coping skills treatment. In a study of employed alcoholics recently completing a three-week inpatient treatment program, Annis and Davis (1989) discovered that the degree to which clients clearly differentiated stimuli for their drinking interacted with the type of after-care treatment.

The coping skills intervention consisted of eight individually tailored treatment sessions over three months. Typical "homework" assign-ments included monitoring high-risk drinking situations and thoughts, anticipating problem situations, rehearsing appropriate nondrinking responses to the situations, establishing new be-haviors, and developing a stronger sense of self-efficacy in coping with drinking stimuli. Subjects with clearly defined profiles on the Inventory of Drinking Situations who received coping skills training reported lower levels of daily alcohol consumption than did similar clients assigned to standard aftercare counseling. For clients who did not distinguish particular types of stimuli as having more frequently prompted them to drink in the past, the two interventions produced equivalent outcomes. While the authors did not report the size of the matching effect in terms of drinking reduction, they noted that the effect ac-counted for over 30% of the variance in outcome.

Hartman and colleagues (1988) investiga-ted whether locus of control predicted response to a three-session intervention of either (1) dir-ective advice, development of treatment goals, and increased awareness of alcohol problems; or (2) this core plus a coping skills-based inter-vention with or without additional relaxation

training modules. The results were striking. "Externals," as identified by Rotter's Locus of Control Scale, benefited far more from coping skills training in terms of days abstinent and number of drinks per occasion than did "inter-nals." Interestingly, among externals, adding a re-laxation module seemed to even further increase the effectiveness of the coping skills approach.

Testing of Matching Effects in Treatment Programs

Although conducting formal research on client-treatment matching interactions is often com-plex, treatment programs themselves might want to explore how the different types of clients they serve respond to different options in treatment.

To do so, clients would need to be carefully assessed on the variable that is believed to have implications for treatment matching. Counselors and program staff would be kept "blind" to this information. Clients would then be randomly assigned to the treatment options. Finally, the outcomes of interest to the treatment program would need to be carefully and objectively mea-sured. Statistical analyses would be performed to answer three questions:

1. Based on their initial score on the matching variable, did clients actually do better if they were assigned to what was assumed to be the more appropriate treatment than if they were given the alternative treatment?
2. Did clients with the opposite characteristic do better with the other treatment or did they do about the same regardless of which of the treatments they were given?
3. Did clients, in general, regardless of their initial scores on the assumed matching vari-able, do better or worse in one of the alter-native treatments.

Answers to these questions would allow pro-gram staff to determine if matching effects exist, and if so, what type of matching, and also if one treatment is generally more effective than an al-ternate treatment. Treatment planning for future clients could then incorporate information de-rived from the research.

While many treatment programs may not be able or willing to randomly assign clients to radically different treatment alternatives, such as inpatient versus outpatient treatment or mod-erated drinking goals versus abstinence, it may be feasible for them to test less extreme treatment options. These might include randomly assigning clients to different counselors, giving clients coping skills training versus relationship enhancement therapy, using group versus individual aftercare, and so on.

CONCLUSION

Although research on matching has yielded findings that are particularly intriguing and promising, this line of alcoholism treatment research is still in an early stage. Most of the investigations up to now have included fairly small numbers of subjects, have considered different outcome variables, and have yet to be replicated in more varied samples of clients with alcohol problems. Only a small number of client variables have been considered and only a few treatment options evaluated.

Nevertheless, some clinically relevant patterns have begun to emerge. Most importantly, two rigorously controlled studies have replicated the finding that sociopathic alcoholics do better with coping skills therapies than with therapies that focus on the quality of interpersonal interactions. Additional studies have found that coping skills interventions are advantageous for clients with other types of characteristics.

The potential value of assigning clients with alcohol problems to interventions particularly appropriate for them has prompted the National Institute on Alcohol Abuse and Alcoholism to establish a multisite clinical trial to more fully explore client-treatment matching possibilities. This effort, Project MATCH, is the largest and likely most complex investigation of effectiveness ever undertaken in the field of alcoholism treatment (Project MATCH Research Group, 1993). Project MATCH includes over 1,700 subjects recruited from very diverse settings across the United States. It assesses an extensive range of client and therapist variables, includes three different treatment interventions, and collects information on a comprehensive set of outcome variables reflecting drinking behavior, adjustment status, subsequent health-care costs, and so on.

Analyses of the rich and detailed database being created by Project MATCH should significantly advance understanding of how differing types of clients respond to alternative alcoholism interventions and may also suggest possibilities for further tests of matching. Results from Project MATCH should begin to appear by the middle of 1995. These findings should also lead to exciting new hypotheses to be evaluated

further by alcoholism treatment research. Most importantly, results from Project MATCH should substantially assist treatment programs in more appropriately assigning clients with alcohol problems to various types of interventions, thus improving outcome.

REFERENCES

Clinical Guidelines

Brown, S. & Yalom, I. D. (1977). Interactional group therapy with alcoholics. *Journal of Studies on Alcohol, 38*, 426–456. Describes the various phases of group psychotherapy with alcoholic clients.

Getter, H. (1984). *Aftercare for alcoholism: Short term interactional group therapy manual.* Unpublished manuscript. A comprehensive manual for conducting time-limited interactional group therapy with alcoholic clients. The Manual for Short-Term Interactional Group Therapy with Alcoholics may be obtained from Professor Herbert Getter, Department of Psychology, University of Connecticut, Box U–20, 406 Babbidge Road, Storrs, CT 06269–1020.

Lazarus, A. A. (1971). *Behavior therapy and beyond.* New York: McGraw-Hill. Contains materials to introduce clients to group therapy and to enhance their openness and involvement with one another.

Monti, P. M., Abrams, D. B., Kadden, R. M., & Cooney, N. L. (1989). *Treating alcohol dependence: A coping skills training guide.* New York: Guilford. Provides detailed session-by-session guidelines for conducting cognitive-behavioral therapy in group or individual format with alcoholic clients.

Vannicelli, M. (1982). Group psychotherapy with alcoholics: Special techniques. *Journal of Studies on Alcohol, 43*, 17–37. Discusses problems likely to arise in conducting group therapy with alcoholics and suggests techniques for dealing with them.

Yalom, I. D. (1974). Group therapy and alcoholism. *Annals New York Academy of Sciences, 233*, 85–103. Describes strategies and tactics for conducting interactional group therapy with alcoholics.

Yalom, I. D. (1975). *The theory and practice of group psychotherapy* (2nd ed.). New York: Basic Books. Comprehensive description of interactional group therapy, with detailed guidelines for therapists. Not specifically tailored for alcoholic clients.

Yalom, I., Brown, S., & Bloch, S. (1975). The written summary as a group psychotherapy technique. *Archives of General Psychiatry, 32*, 605–613. Describes use of written summaries of group sessions that are mailed to participants and their advantages for both clients and therapists.

Research References

Anderson, P., & Scott, E. (1992). The effect of general practitioner's advice to heavy drinking men. *British Journal of Addiction, 87*, 891–900.

Annis, H. M., & Davis, C. S. (1989). Relapse prevention. In R. K. Hester & W. R. Miller (Eds.), *Handbook of alcoholism treatment approaches* (pp. 170–182). New York: Pergamon Press.

Azrin, N. H., Sisson, R. W., Meyers, R., & Godley, N. (1982). Alcoholism treatment by disulfiram and community reinforcement therapy. *Journal of Behavioral Therapy and Experimental Psychiatry*, 13(2), 105–112.

Babor, T. & Grant, M. (Eds.) (1992). *Project on identification and management of alcohol-related problems.* Geneva: World Health Organization, pp. 265.

Babor, T. F., Hofmann, M., DelBoca, F. K., Hesselbrock, V., Meyer, R. E., Dolinsky, Z. S., & Rounsaville, B. (1992). Types of alcoholics: I. Evidence for an empirically-derived typology based on indicators of vulnerability and severity. *Archives of General Psychiatry*, 49, 614–619.

Cook, C. C. H. (1988). The Minnesota Model in the management of drug and alcohol dependency: Miracle, method or myth? Part 1. The philosophy and the programme. *British Journal of Addiction*, 83, 625–634.

Cooney, N. L., Kadden, R. M., Litt, M. D., & Getter, H. (1991). Matching alcoholics to coping skills or interactional therapies: Two year follow-up results. *Journal of Consulting and Clinical Psychology*, 59, 598–601.

Cronkite, R. C. & Moos, R. H. (1984). Sex and marital status in relation to the treatment and outcome of alcoholic patients. *Sex Roles*, 11(1/2), 93–112.

Dorus, W., Ostrow, D., Anton, R., Cushman, P., Collins, J. F., Schaffer, M., Charles, H. L., DeSai, P., Hayashida, M., Malkerneker, V., Willenbring, M., Fiscella, R., & Satger, M. R. (1989). Lithium treatment of depressed and nondepressed alcoholics. *Journal of the American Medical Association*, 262(12), 1646–1652.

Gerra, G., Caccavari, R., Delsignore, Bocci R., Fertonani, G., & Passeri, M. (1992). Effects of fluoxetine and ca-acetyl-homotaurinate on alcohol intake in familial and nonfamilial alcoholic patients. *Current Therapeutic Research*, 52(2), 291–295.

Getter, H., Litt, M. D., Kadden, R. M. & Cooney, N. L. (1992). Measuring treatment process in coping skills and interactional group therapies for alcoholism. *International Journal of Group Psychotherapy*, 42, 419–430.

Hartman, L., Krywonis, M., & Morrison, E. (1988). Psychological factors and health-related behavior change: Preliminary findings from a controlled study. *Canadian Family Physician*, 34, 1045–1050.

Heather, N., Rollnick, S., Bell, A., & Richmond, R. (1993). *Effects of brief counselling among male heavy drinkers identified on general hospital wards.* International Conference on Treatment of Addictive Behaviors. Sante Fe, NM.

Institute of Medicine. (1990). *Broadening the base of treatment for alcohol problems.* Washington, DC: National Academy Press.

Kadden, R. M., Cooney, N. L., Getter, H., & Litt, M. D. (1989). Matching alcoholics to coping skills or interactional therapies: Post treatment results. *Journal of Consulting and Clinical Psychology*, 57, 698–704.

Kadden, R., Litt, M., Cooney, N., & Busher, D. (1992). Relationship between role-play measures of coping skills and alcoholism treatment outcome. *Addictive Behaviors*, 17, 425–437.

Kissen, B., Platz, A., & Su, W. H. (1970). Social and psychological factors in the treatment of chronic alcoholism. *Journal of Psychiatric Research*, 8, 13–27.

Litt, M. D., Babor, T. F., DelBoca, F. K., Kadden, R. M., & Cooney, N. (1992). Types of alcoholics: II. Application of an empirically-derived topology to treatment matching. *Archives of General Psychiatry*, 49, 609–614.

Longabaugh, R., Malloy, P., Rubin, A., Beattie, M., Clifford, P., & Noel, N. (in press). Drinking outcomes of alcohol abusers diagnosed as antisocial personality disorder. *Alcoholism: Clinical and experimental research.*

Longabaugh, R., Wirtz, P., DiClemente, C., & Litt, M. (1994). *Issues in the development of patient-treatment matching hypotheses.* Manuscript submitted for publication.

Lyons, J. P., Welte, J., Brown, J., Sokolow, L., & Hynes, G. (1982). Variation in alcoholism treatment orientation: Differential impact upon specific subpopulations. *Alcoholism: Clinical and Experimental Research*, 6, 333–343.

Mattson, M. E., Allen, J. P., Longabaugh, R., Nickless, C. J., Connors, G., & Kadden, R. M. (1994). *Historical perspectives on matching alcoholic patients to treatment.* Manuscript submitted for publication.

McKay, J. R., Longabaugh, R., Beattie, M., Maisto, S., & Noe, N. (in press). Does adding co-joint therapy to individually focused alcoholism treatment lead to better family functioning? *Journal of Substance Abuse.*

McLachlan, J. F. C. (1972). Benefit from group therapy as a function of patient-therapist match on conceptual level. *Psychotherapy: Theory, Research and Practice*, 9, 317–323.

McLachlan, J. F. C. (1974). Therapy strategies, personality orientation and recovery from alcoholism. *Canadian Psychiatric Association*, 19, 25–30.

McLellan, A. T., Luborsky, G. E., O'Brien, C. P., Woody, G. E., & Druley, K. A. (1983a). Predicting response to alcohol and drug abuse treatments: Role of psychiatric severity. *Archives of General Psychiatry*, 40, 620–625.

McLellan, A. T., Woody, G. E., Luborsky, L., O'Brien, C. P., & Druley K. A. (1983b). Increased effectiveness of substance-abuse treatment. *Journal of Nervous and Mental Diseases*, 171(10), 597–605.

Merry, J., Reynolds, C. M., Bailey, J., & Coppen, A. (1976). A prophylactic treatment of alcoholism by lithium carbonate: A controlled study. *The Lancet*, 2, 481–487.

Miller, W. R. (1989). Matching individuals with interventions. In R. K. Hester & W. R. Miller, (Eds.), *Handbook of alcoholism treatment approaches: Effective alternatives.* New York: Pergamon Press, pp. 261–271.

Miller, W. R., Benefield, R. G., & Tonigan, J. S. (in press). Enhancing motivation for change in problem drinking: A controlled comparison of two therapist styles. *Journal of Consulting and Clinical Psychology.*

Monti, P. M., Abrams, D. B., Kadden, R. M., & Cooney, N. L. (1989). *Treating alcohol dependence. A coping skills training guide.* New York: Guilford Press.

Orford, J. E., Openheimer, E., & Edwards, G. (1976). Abstinence or control: The outcome for excessive drinkers two years after consultation. *Behavioral Research Therapy, 14,* 409–418.

Pettinati, H. M., Meyers, K., Jenson, J. M., Kaplan, F., & Evans, B. D. (in press). Inpatient versus outpatient treatment for substance dependence revisited. *Psychiatric Quarterly.*

Project MATCH Research Group. (1993). Project MATCH: Rationale and methods for a multisite clinical trial matching patients to alcoholism treatment. *Alcoholism: Clinical and Experimental Research, 17*(6), 1130–1145.

Rice, C., Longabaugh, R., Beattie, M., & Noel, N. (in press). Age group differences in response to treatment for problematic alcohol use. *British Journal of Addiction.*

Rohsenow, D. J., Monti, P. M., Binkoff, J. A., Leipman, M. R., & Nirenberg, T. D. (1991). Patient-treatment matching for alcoholic men in communication skills versus cognitive-behavioral mood management training. *Addictive Behaviors, 16,* 63–69.

Scott, E. & Anderson, P. (1990). Randomized controlled trial of general practitioner intervention in women with excessive alcohol consumption. *Drug and Alcohol Review, 10,* 313–321.

Snow, R. E. (1991). Aptitude-treatment interaction as a framework for research on individual differences in psychotherapy. *Journal of Consulting and Clinical Psychology, 59,* 205–216.

Spoth, R. (1983). Differential stress reduction: Preliminary applications to alcohol-abusing population. *The International Journal of the Addictions, 18*(6), 835–849.

Sokolow, L., Welte, J., Hynes, G., & Lyons, J. (1980). Treatment-related differences between female and male alcoholics. Focus on Women: *Journal of Addictions and Health, 1,* 43–56.

Welte, J., Hynes, G., Sokolow, L., & Lyons, J. P. (1981). Effects of length of stay in inpatient alcoholism treatment on outcome. *Journal of Studies on Alcohol, 42*(5), 483–491.

Name Index

Subject Index